Miller Revenue Recognition Guide

by Ashwinpaul C. Sondhi and Scott Taub

Miller Revenue Recognition Guide is a comprehensive reference manual covering key concepts and issues that arise in determining when and how to recognize revenue. It covers the litany of existing authoritative literature related to revenue recognition and clarifies those revenue recognition concepts that are vague. The *Guide* also provides examples of key points, includes excerpts from the financial statements of public companies to illustrate key concepts and judgments, and discusses revenue recognition projects on the agendas of the various accounting standard-setters.

Highlights

2006 Edition

This edition covers several new revenue-related accounting standards, issued in response to specific revenue recognition problems or other prevalent accounting issues:

- FSP EITF 85-24-1, "Application of EITF Issue No. 85-24, 'Distribution Fees by Distributors of Mutual Funds That Do Not Have a Front-End Sales Charge,' When Cash for the Right to Future Distribution Fees for Shares Previously Sold is Received from Third Parties."

- SOP 04-2, *Accounting for Real Estate Time-Sharing Transactions.*

The 2006 edition also provides discussion on revenue-related projects currently on the standard-setters' agendas. In-depth coverage is provided for the most significant of these projects, the FASB's Revenue Recognition project. The discussion on this project includes examples illustrating the significant changes that are being considered by the FASB. Various other revenue-related, or revenue-affecting, projects are also discussed.

CCH Learning Center

CCH's goal is to provide you with the clearest, most concise, and up-to-date accounting and auditing information to help further your professional development, as well as a convenient method to help you satisfy your continuing professional education requirements. The CCH Learning Center* offers a complete line of self-study courses covering complex and constantly evolving accounting and auditing issues. We are continually adding new courses to the library to help you stay current on all the latest developments. The CCH Learning Center courses are available 24 hours a day, seven days a week. You'll get immediate exam results and certification. To view our complete accounting and auditing course catalog, go to: **http:// cch.learningcenter.com**.

Accounting Research Manager™

Accounting Research Manager is the most comprehensive, up-to-date, and objective online database of financial reporting literature. It includes all authoritative and proposed accounting, auditing, and SEC literature, plus independent, expert-written interpretive guidance.

---

* CCH is registered with the National Association of State Boards of Accountancy (NASBA) as a sponsor of continuing professional education on the National Registry of CPE Sponsors. State boards of accountancy have final authority on the acceptance of individual courses for CPE credit. Complaints regarding registered sponsors may be addressed to the National Registry of CPE Sponsors, 150 Fourth Avenue North, Nashville, TN 37219-2417. Telephone: 615-880-4200.

* CCH is registered with the National Association of State Boards of Accountancy as a Quality Assurance Service (QAS) sponsor of continuing professional education. Participating state boards of accountancy have final authority on the acceptance of individual courses for CPE credit. Complaints regarding QAS program sponsors may be addressed to NASBA, 150 Fourth Avenue North, Suite 700, Nashville, TN 37219-2417. Telephone: 615-880-4200.

Our Weekly Summary e-mail newsletter highlights the key developments of the week, giving you the assurance that you have the most current information. It provides links to new FASB, AICPA, SEC, PCAOB, EITF, and IASB authoritative and proposal-stage literature, plus insightful guidance from financial reporting experts.

Our outstanding team of content experts takes pride in updating the system on a daily basis, so you stay as current as possible. You'll learn of newly released literature and deliberations of current financial reporting projects as soon they occur! Plus, you benefit from their easy-to-understand technical translations.

With **Accounting Research Manager**, you maximize the efficiency of your research time while enhancing your results. Learn more about our content, our experts, and how you can request a FREE trial by visiting us at **http://www.accountingresearchmanager.com.**

12/05

2006

MILLER
Revenue Recognition
Guide

Ashwinpaul C. Sondhi

and

Scott Taub

CCH INCORPORATED
Chicago
A WoltersKluwer Company

This publication is designed to provide accurate and authoritative information in regard to the subject matter covered. It is sold with the understanding
that the publisher is not engaged in rendering legal, accounting, or other professional services. If legal advice or other professional assistance is
required, the services of a competent professional person should be sought.

—From a *Declaration of Principles* jointly adopted by
a Committee of the American Bar Association and a
Committee of Publishers and Associations

ISBN 0-8080-8999-4

No claim is made to original government works; however, within this Product or
Publication, the following are subject to CCH's copyright: (1) the gathering, compila-
tion, and arrangement of such government materials; (2) the magnetic translation
and digital conversion of data, if applicable; (3) the historical, statutory and other
notes and references; and (4) the commentary and other materials.
Portions of this work were published in a previous edition.

Printed in the United States of America

Contents

Preface

Revenue recognition . . . The mere mention of the topic elicits thoughts of complex accounting and difficult judgments fraught with the potential for unfavorable high-profile financial statement restatements. Revenue is the top line in the income statement, and one of the most important indices of financial health to both preparers and users of financial statements. Reporting the correct amount of revenue on a timely basis is also one of most difficult tasks in financial reporting.

Despite the importance of revenue recognition to the financial statements of virtually all companies, the accounting literature addressing revenue recognition is not as well-developed as the literature addressing many other areas of financial reporting. Although many accounting pronouncements directly or indirectly address revenue recognition, most of the guidance is extremely narrow in scope and addresses a particular issue or narrowly defined transaction. This lack of authoritative literature addressing certain issues and industries has resulted in the development of revenue recognition for some transactions on the basis of industry practice.

The lack of comprehensive guidance combined with the variety and complexity of revenue transactions has resulted in a large number of issues in revenue recognition, including many financial statement restatements and SEC enforcement cases. In fact, two reports issued by the SEC staff in 2003 illustrate that revenue recognition is an area prone to problems: (1) Report pursuant to Section 704 of the Sarbanes-Oxley Act of 2002 (the Section 704 Report) and (2) Summary by the Division of Corporate Finance of Significant Issues Addressed in the Review of the Periodic Reports of the Fortune 500 Companies (the Fortune 500 Report). The Section 704 Report showed that improper revenue recognition was the area where the SEC brought the greatest number of enforcement actions during the report period and the Fortune 500 report found that accounting policy disclosures related to revenue recognition was an area frequently questioned by the SEC's Division of Corporate Finance. These reports confirmed the findings from several other studies conducted in recent years.

In response to the growing number of problems in the area of revenue recognition, the SEC Staff issued Staff Accounting Bulletin No. 101 (SAB 101), *Revenue Recognition in Financial Statements*, in late 1999. SAB 101 summarized the existing revenue recognition guidance and the SEC Staff's views on the application of that guidance. In addition to causing a number of companies to change their revenue recognition policies, SAB 101 also helped to focus the attention of nearly every public company as well as analysts and other financial statement users on revenue recognition.

As a result of these developments, many accounting standard-setters around the world have begun a number of new projects on revenue recognition. Although many of these projects are limited in scope and address very specific revenue recognition issues, the ultimate goal of one project (the FASB's Revenue recognition project) is to address revenue recognition on a comprehensive basis. However, until that project is completed, available revenue recognition guidance will remain incomplete and scattered throughout the accounting literature.

The principal objective of *Miller Revenue Recognition Guide* is to fill this void. This book addresses the key issues faced in revenue recognition, identifies the appropriate accounting literature, explains both the required accounting and explains the reasons for that guidance, and often illustrates the application through recourse to disclosures and excerpts from the financial statements of publicly traded companies. For issues not addressed in the accounting literature, this book suggests accounting treatments that are consistent with general revenue recognition concepts and principles. This book also highlights the problem areas noted in the Section 704 and the Fortune 500 Reports.

The 2006 edition of the *Miller Revenue Recognition Guide* is current through October 24, 2005. As such, it includes discussion related to the following recently issued authoritative pronouncements:

- FSP EITF 85–24–1, "Application of EITF Issue No. 85–24, 'Distribution Fees by Distributors of Mutual Funds That Do Not Have a Front-End Sales Charge,' When Cash for the Right to Future Distribution Fees for Shares Previously Sold is Received from Third Parties."
- SOP 04–2, *Accounting for Real Estate Time-Sharing Transactions.*

In addition, Chapter 13, "Revenue Recognition: The Future," includes a discussion of revenue-related projects on the standard-setters' agendas. A comprehensive discussion is provided of the most significant of these projects, the FASB's Revenue Recognition project. This discussion includes examples illustrating the significant changes that are being considered by the FASB. Various other revenue-related, or revenue-affecting, projects (for example, IFRIC pronouncements and projects) are also discussed.

How This Book Is Organized

Miller Revenue Recognition Guide contains the following 13 chapters:

1. Introduction
2. A Brief Survey of Revenue-Related Literature
3. General Principles

4. Multiple-Element Arrangements

5. Product Deliverables

6. Service Deliverables

7. Intellectual Property Deliverables

8. Miscellaneous Issues

9. Contract Accounting

10. Software—A Complete Model

11. Presentation

12. Disclosures

13. Future Expectations and Projects

Within these chapters, a number of Observations, Practice Pointers, and Practice Alerts highlight key consequences of the accounting guidance and identify issues to watch for when dealing with certain revenue transactions. SEC Registrant Alerts highlight issues that the SEC is particularly focused on, as well as additional guidance provided by the SEC beyond the guidance typically followed by non-public companies.

The book also includes a topical index as well as a cross-reference to the authoritative literature that indicates the chapters where specific pieces of authoritative literature are discussed. In addition, the text includes references to the paragraphs of the authoritative literature that address key points.

Abbreviations

The following abbreviations are used throughout the text to represent the various sources of authoritative literature discussed in this book:

AAG	AICPA Audit and Accounting Guide
AcSEC	AICPA Accounting Standards Executive Committee
AICPA	American Institute of Certified Public Accountants
APB	Accounting Principles Board Opinion
ARB	Accounting Research Bulletin
CIRP	SEC Current Issues and Rulemaking Projects
CON	FASB Statement of Financial Accounting Concepts
EITF	Emerging Issues Task Force

FAS	FASB Statement of Financial Accounting Standards
FASB	Financial Accounting Standards Board
FSP	FASB Staff Position
FTB	FASB Technical Bulletin
IAS	IASB International Accounting Standard
IASB	International Accounting Standards Board
IFRIC	International Financial Reporting Interpretations Committee
REG S-X	SEC Regulation S-X
SAB	SEC Staff Accounting Bulletin
SEC	Securities and Exchange Commission
SOP	AICPA Statement of Position
TPA	AICPA Technical Practice Aid

Acknowledgments

Ashwinpaul Sondhi thanks his wife, Jean, for her support and Raj Malhotra for his assistance during the writing of this book. Scott Taub thanks all of the members of the Professional Standards Group at Arthur Andersen for their guidance, counsel, and friendship. A better group of people will never be found. Most important, Scott thanks his wife, Lynn, for her endless patience during the writing of this book and her support of Scott in every one of his career decisions.

About the Authors

Ashwinpaul (Tony) C. Sondhi is the Founder and President of A. C. Sondhi & Associates, LLC, a Financial Advisory Services firm located in New Jersey. He is currently a member of the Emerging Issues Task Force (EITF) of the Financial Accounting Standards Board (FASB). From September 2001 to September 2003, he was a member of the Planning Subcommittee of the Accounting Standards Executive Committee (AcSEC) of the American Institute of Certified Public Accountants (AICPA). He has also been a member of the Global Financial Reporting Advocacy Committee and Chairman of the Financial Accounting Policy Committee of the CFA Institute.

Mr. Sondhi served on the FASB Task Force on Accounting for Impairments of Long-lived Assets and on the Steering Committee for the Statement of Cash Flows of the International Accounting Standards Committee. He has taught at New York University, Columbia University, and at Georgetown University. He has been a Visiting Professor at Stockholm University, Sweden, and Copenhagen Business School, Denmark.

Mr. Sondhi received his Ph.D. in Accounting and Economics/ Management Science in 1985 from New York University. His research has been published in several accounting and finance journals. He is a co-author of *The Analysis and Use of Financial Statements, Third Edition, 2003.* Mr. Sondhi has also edited *Credit Analysis of Nontraditional Debt Securities,* co-authored *Impairments and Write-offs of Long-Lived Assets,* and co-edited *CFA Readings in Financial Statement Analysis* and *Off-Balance Sheet Financing Techniques.*

Mr. Sondhi serves on the Board of Directors of an investment advisory services firm and one charitable foundation and is an advisor to several U.S. and foreign companies. His consulting activities include revenue recognition, valuation, and comparative analyses of financing and capital structure alternatives, creation and operation of finance, securitization, intellectual property, and investment subsidiaries, analyses of covenants, and the development of debt agreements.

Scott A. Taub is an accounting and auditing expert. Until July 2002, he was a partner in Arthur Andersen's Professional Standards Group, where he worked with clients on matters of accounting and auditing, developed Arthur Andersen's accounting policies, and represented the firm before the Financial Accounting Standards Board, the Emerging Issues Task Force (EITF), the U.S. Securities and Exchange Commission (SEC), the American Institute of Certified Public Accountants (AICPA), and the International Accounting Standards Board.

Mr. Taub rejoined the Professional Standards Group in 2001 after spending two years on the staff of the Office of the Chief Accountant of the SEC. While there, he worked with registrants on many accounting and reporting issues, including the implementation of Staff Accounting Bulletin No. 101 on revenue recognition, and served as the SEC Observer on several working groups of the EITF. Mr. Taub began his career with Arthur Andersen in 1990, and spent seven years in the audit practice before originally joining the Professional Standards Group in 1997.

Subsequent to writing this book, Mr. Taub rejoined the SEC staff as a Deputy Chief Accountant in the Office of the Chief Accountant. In that role, he is responsible for resolution of accounting and auditing practice issues, rulemaking projects, and oversight of private sector standard-setting efforts and regulation of auditors. He also chairs the accounting, audit and disclosure standing committee of the International Organization of Securities Commissions.

Mr. Taub has spoken to numerous audiences, including Financial Executives International, the AICPA, the Institute of Management Accountants, and various industry groups. He was a contributing author of several Arthur Andersen publications, including the highly respected *Accounting for Business Combinations.* Mr. Taub attended the University of Michigan in Ann Arbor, where he received an undergraduate degree in economics and accounting in 1990.

CHAPTER 1
INTRODUCTION

CONTENTS

OVERVIEW

Revenue is one of the most important indicators of a successful business. It receives more attention than many other statistics or barometers of the financial health of a company. The source, amount, and timing of reported revenue is relevant to all parties interested in financial data: company management, regulators, auditors, and users of financial statements alike. Determining when and how much revenue to recognize are key questions that accountants and industry professionals have wrestled with for many years and revenue remains one of the most difficult numbers to accurately report in the financial statements.

This is where the *Miller Revenue Recognition Guide* comes in. The *Guide* has been written to comprehensively address the key issues faced in revenue reporting. It describes the appropriate accounting for each issue, and explains the reason for that accounting. The *Guide* also provides practice examples and financial statement disclosures from public companies that illustrate the application of key concepts and judgments.

WHY A BOOK ON REVENUE RECOGNITION

Revenue Recognition Is Important to Financial Statement Users

Revenue-generating transactions are varied and can be extremely complicated. Because revenue reporting has a significant effect on a company's results of operations, a thorough understanding of how revenue is recognized is essential to understanding the financial statements of a company.

The importance of revenue recognition to analyzing a company's performance has been very much in the forefront of the business world in the last several years. In fact, during the late 1990s, revenue was often looked at as the main driver of value of many companies, especially those that were Internet-based. Small changes in revenue could often lead to huge changes in the market value of those companies. The steep stock price declines of so many publicly traded Internet companies were attributed, in part, to the fact that their revenue numbers were not sustainable, and, in some cases, misleading.

The Authoritative Literature Does Not Address All of the Issues

Despite the importance of revenue recognition to the financial statements of virtually all companies, the accounting literature addressing revenue recognition is not comprehensive or easy to follow. The literature is often criticized for being incomplete and for being overly complex, depending upon the transaction. Over 100 pieces of accounting literature address revenue recognition in one way or another, however, most of the guidance is in scope very narrow, and addresses only a particular issue or type of transaction. Due to the lack of authoritative literature addressing certain issues and industries, revenue recognition for some transactions has developed based on industry practices.

Revenue Recognition Is a Leading Cause of Financial Reporting Errors

The lack of comprehensive guidance, in combination with the variety and complexity of revenue transactions, has resulted in a large number of financial reporting errors in the area of revenue recognition. In fact, the SEC staff issued two reports in early 2003 that highlighted revenue recognition as an area prone to problems: (1) Report Pursuant to Section 704 of the Sarbanes-Oxley Act of 2002 (the Section 704 Report) and (2) Summary by the Division of Corporation Finance of Significant Issues Addressed in the Review of the Periodic Reports of the Fortune 500 Companies (the Fortune 500 Report).

In compiling the information in the Section 704 Report, the SEC staff studied enforcement actions filed during the period July 31, 1997, through July 30, 2002. Improper revenue recognition was the area where the SEC brought the greatest number of enforcement actions during this period. The nature of the improprieties ranged from the improper timing of revenue recognition (e.g., improper recognition of revenue related to bill-and-hold sales and consignment sales, etc.) to fictitious revenue (e.g., falsification of sales documents, failure to consider side letter agreements, etc.) to improper valuation of revenue (e.g., failure to appropriately consider rights of return). Other revenue-related areas where the SEC brought a significant number of actions were nondisclosure of related party transactions and the accounting for nonmonetary and round-trip transactions.

The Fortune 500 Report resulted from the SEC's Division of Corporation Finance's (Corp Fin) review of all annual reports filed by Fortune 500 companies. This report provides insight into areas commonly questioned by Corp Fin during their reviews of annual reports. Revenue recognition accounting policy disclosures was an area frequently questioned by Corp Fin. In many cases, Corp Fin requested that companies significantly expand their revenue recognition accounting policy disclosures. Industries where these requests were common included computer software, computer services, computer hardware, communications equipment, capital goods, semiconductor, electronic instruments and controls, energy, pharmaceutical, and retail. The revenue-related topics involved in these requests included accounting for software, multiple-element arrangements, rights of return, price protection features, requirements for installation of equipment, customer acceptance provisions, and various types of sales incentive programs.

In addition, several other studies have shown that revenue recognition is the most common accounting issue that causes financial statement restatements. Several high-profile revenue restatements in the past several years have reinforced the focus of regulators and the investing public on revenue recognition policy and disclosure.

The Authoritative Literature Is Changing

Largely in response to these problems, the SEC staff issued Staff Accounting Bulletin No. 101 (SAB 101) in late 1999. SAB 101 summarized the SEC staff's views on the application of the existing revenue recognition guidance. In addition to requiring a number of companies to change their revenue recognition policies, SAB 101 also served to focus the attention of most every public company on revenue recognition policies and procedures. Even companies whose revenue recognition policies did not change as a result of the issuance of SAB 101 generally have paid more attention to their revenue recognition policies and procedures since it was issued.

This recent attention to revenue recognition has also resulted in a number of new projects being taken on by various accounting standard-setters, including projects addressing the accounting and reporting for discounts and rebates, transactions with multiple elements, and whether or not certain items should be reported as revenues. Various standard-setters are working on still more guidance, and, for the first time, the FASB has added a project to its agenda intended to provide comprehensive guidance on revenue recognition. This project could produce wholesale changes in revenue recognition and is discussed in detail in Chapter 13, "Future Expectations and Projects."

Tying the Literature Together

As noted above, the accounting literature that addresses revenue recognition is incomplete and spread across many different pronouncements. This makes it very difficult for companies to identify the appropriate literature that either applies to, or provides analogous guidance for, a transaction. This book makes it easier to identify the appropriate literature to follow, or analogize to, by addressing the issues in a topical manner, and providing references to the authoritative literature where appropriate.

Seeing the Big Picture

The discussion above points out several good reasons to write a book on revenue recognition. Indeed, all of them were considered when the decision was reached to write this book. But one other reason to write a book addressing revenue recognition on a comprehensive basis is that looking at revenue recognition on the whole, instead of issue-by-issue or transaction-by-transaction, makes it easier to understand the fundamental principles of revenue recognition. Given the number of pieces of accounting literature that have been published, it is surprising to realize that, for the most part, each follows the same underlying concepts and principles. Looking at the body of revenue recognition guidance all at once, it is easier to see the common threads that run through the literature. Focusing on the underlying principles also can reveal the underlying logic that causes seemingly inconsistent guidance. Although the same principles may be used to account for two or more revenue transactions, the facts and circumstances related to each transaction will have a significant effect on the judgments related to applying those principles, and, ultimately, the accounting for those transactions.

HOW THIS BOOK IS ORGANIZED

Introduction and Framework of Revenue Recognition

After the introduction and brief survey of the authoritative accounting literature, this book frames the discussion of revenue recognition in Chapter 3, "General Principles," by discussing in detail the conceptual guidance on revenue recognition provided by the FASB, and then focusing on the conditions for revenue recognition that commonly appear in the revenue recognition literature. This chapter explains how those conditions are consistent with the conceptual framework and provides guidance as to how to evaluate compliance with those conditions.

Applying the Literature to Specific Transactions

The framework discussed in Chapter 3, "General Principles," is enhanced in Chapters 4–8, which discuss the application of the general principles and conditions to specific types of transactions and issues. Chapter 4, "Multiple-Element Arrangements," addresses multiple-element considerations, explaining when and how to separate deliverables in the same arrangement for accounting purposes. Chapters 5–7 then discuss product, service, and intellectual property deliverables, explaining how the general principles and conditions should be applied to those types of transactions. Chapter 8, "Miscellaneous Issues," addresses a number of issues that can affect revenue recognition in certain types of transactions. All of these chapters discuss the issues they address in the context of the conceptual framework.

Detailed Models in the Accounting Literature

Chapters 9, "Contract Accounting," and 10, "Software—A Complete Model," discuss two revenue recognition models that are comprehensively addressed in the accounting literature. Each of these models applies to a narrow group of transactions—Chapter 9 addresses the accounting for certain long-term contracts, while Chapter 10 addresses software revenue recognition. Whereas the discussion of other issues in this book relies, to a large extent, on analogy to certain principles and concepts that are common in revenue accounting, the guidance on contract accounting and software revenue recognition comes directly from the accounting literature that was created to address those transactions. Therefore, the recognition guidance in Chapters 5–8 generally does not apply to them.

Financial Reporting

The next two chapters deal with issues that directly affect the financial statements. Chapter 11, "Presentation," focuses on an issue that is perhaps just as important as revenue recognition—the determination of what amounts should be reported on the revenue line of the financial statements as opposed to some other line. Chapter 12, "Disclosures," then discusses revenue recognition disclosures that are either required or desirable in the financial statements.

A Look Toward the Future

The book closes with a discussion of projects on the agendas of the various accounting standard-setters that have not yet been completed. Given the ever-changing nature of the accounting literature on revenue recognition and the broad implications that certain projects-in-progress will have on revenue recognition, these projects should be closely monitored to keep on top of the latest developments.

CHAPTER 2
A BRIEF SURVEY OF REVENUE-RELATED LITERATURE

CONTENTS

BACKGROUND

Revenue recognition generally receives just as much, or more, attention as any other accounting topic. Normally, this attention would merit a separate authoritative pronouncement. Unfortunately, this is not yet the case with revenue recognition. The topic of revenue recognition has historically been dealt with by the standard-setters on a fragmented basis. This means that there are many pieces of literature from many different standard-setters that deal with many different topic- or industry-specific issues.

☞ **PRACTICE ALERT:** In response to the level of attention paid to revenue recognition and the state of the authoritative literature dealing with revenue recognition, the FASB has undertaken a project to comprehensively address this subject. The tentative conclusions reached to date by the FASB would result in a significant departure from current practice. Chapter 13, "Future Expectations and Projects," discusses the status of this project, the key preliminary decisions reached by the FASB, and differences between these decisions and current practice.

Given the multitude of ways companies can earn revenue, it is hardly surprising that separate standards were developed for specific types of transactions. Selling real estate is certainly different than selling software. Leasing a product is certainly different from charging loan origination fees. Accordingly, different models were developed by standard-setters to address revenue recognition in these situations and others. All this makes navigating your way through the revenue recognition literature quite difficult.

OVERVIEW

To help navigate the variety of literature that exists, this chapter provides a high-level overview of the revenue recognition literature in existence today. The literature is broken down into three sections. The first section is literature that provides general guidance broadly applicable to all (or most) revenue transactions. As noted above, there is not very much of this literature. The second section includes literature that addresses specific transactions or types of revenue, and the third includes literature that addresses specific issues in revenue recognition that may arise in various types of transactions.

The transaction- and issue-specific literature is categorized by topic. To the extent certain literature provides the overall accounting framework for a specific topic, that literature is referred to as the Base Literature. Other literature that provides incremental guidance for that revenue topic is listed as Supplemental Literature. In some cases, there is no literature that provides a unique, overall accounting framework for a specific revenue topic (i.e., no Base Literature). However, there is Supplemental Literature that discusses applying general revenue recognition concepts to that specific revenue topic. In those cases, only the Supplemental Literature is listed.

> ☞ **PRACTICE ALERT:** This chapter only identifies literature that has been finalized and is therefore authoritative at this time. Several projects in process will have significant effects on revenue recognition. These projects are discussed in Chapter 13, "Future Expectations and Projects."

Many of the topics for which the literature is identified in this chapter are not addressed in the balance of this publication because the topic is too narrow or too complicated to tackle in a book intended to broadly address revenue recognition. Consult the "Cross-Reference to Original Pronouncements" (CR.01) at the end of this book for a listing of accounting literature discussed further in this book and the chapters in which that literature is discussed. Literature not listed in that cross-reference is not discussed further in this book.

GAAP HIERARCHY

Before launching into an overview of the revenue recognition literature, a brief discussion of the GAAP hierarchy is called for. The GAAP hierarchy was developed because there are so many sources of generally accepted accounting principles. The hierarchy defines which sources take precedence over others. To the extent a particular issue is addressed in two pieces of literature, the literature that falls higher on the GAAP hierarchy is the literature that should be applied. The various pieces of literature that exist to address revenue recognition fall within all categories of the GAAP hierarchy.

In addition, even though there are numerous pieces of literature addressing various revenue recognition topics, a company may find itself in a position where there is no literature that is directly on-point to the transaction or issue it is dealing with. In these situations, the company may need to analogize to another piece of literature that deals with a similar, but not identical, transaction, to determine the appropriate accounting. To the extent there are two pieces of literature that the company might be able to analogize to, stronger consideration should be given to the piece of literature that falls higher in the GAAP hierarchy.

The GAAP hierarchy is presented below.

EXHIBIT 2-1
THE GAAP HIERARCHY

Category	Established Accounting Principles
A	FASB Statements and Interpretations, APB Opinions, AICPA Accounting Research Bulletins, and, for SEC registrants, the Rules and interpretive releases of the SEC
B	FASB Technical Bulletins, AICPA Industry Audit and Accounting Guides cleared by the FASB, and AICPA Statements of Position cleared by the FASB
C	Consensus positions of the FASB Emerging Issues Task Force and AICPA AcSEC Practice Bulletins cleared by the FASB
D	AICPA Accounting Interpretations, FASB Implementation Guides (Q&As), and widely recognized and prevalent industry practices
Other	Other accounting literature, including FASB Concepts Statements, APB Statements, AICPA Issues Papers, International Accounting Standards, GASB literature (Statements, Interpretations, and Technical Bulletins), pronouncements of other professional associations or regulatory agencies, AICPA Technical Practice Aids, and other accounting publications (textbooks, handbooks, articles, etc.)

Sources: Paragraph 25 of FAS-111, *Rescission of FASB Statement No. 32 and Technical Corrections,* and SEC Accounting Disclosure Rules and Practices, Topic Four.II.C.3.c.7.

NOTE: In early 2003, the FASB staff introduced FASB Staff Positions (FSPs) as the primary method of communicating implementation guidance. FSPs are expected to replace other means of providing FASB staff views and may replace Technical Bulletins for narrow and limited revisions to existing standards. FSPs are subject to certain due process procedures that include exposure for comment and review by the FASB. In addition, certain FSPs have been issued by the staff at the Board's direction.

In general, FSPs are in Category C of the GAAP hierarchy; however, Board-directed FSPs are considered to be in Category B. In April 2005, the FASB issued an Exposure Draft, "The Hierarchy of Generally Accepted Accounting Principles," proposing modifications to the GAAP hierarchy. In addition to addressing FAS-133 implementation issues, the Exposure Draft proposes treating FSPs as sources of Category A GAAP.

Chapter 13, "Future Expectations and Projects," contains a discussion of the April 2005 Exposure Draft, "The Hierarchy of Generally Accepted Accounting Principles."

In August 2003, the SEC staff issued the Study Pursuant to Section 108(d) of the Sarbanes-Oxley Act of 2002 on the Adoption by the United States Financial Reporting System of a Principles-Based Accounting System (the Section 108(d) Study). The objective of the Section 108(d) Study was to assess the merits of establishing accounting principles (a) on a principles-only basis or (b) using a rules-based approach. The SEC staff ultimately recommended "that those involved in the standard-setting process more consistently develop standards on a principles-based or objectives-oriented basis." The SEC staff identified a number of implementation steps necessary to adopt this approach. One of those steps involves a reconfiguration of the GAAP hierarchy. The SEC staff made key observations in this regard, including:

- Responsibility for the GAAP hierarchy should rest with the appropriate standard-setting bodies. Currently, responsibility for the GAAP hierarchy rests with the AICPA. The SEC staff suggests that it should rest with the PCAOB and FASB.

- The GAAP hierarchy should only include two levels. The SEC staff suggests that the GAAP hierarchy should include only an authoritative level and a non-authoritative level. Within the authoritative level would be FASB conceptual framework documents, FASB Statements, FASB Interpretations, APB

Opinions, ARBs, EITF Consensuses, and FSPs. Within the non-authoritative level would be industry group positions and positions of knowledgeable professional organizations or entities. Presumably, there would not be any conflicts between the literature within each of these levels in order for a two-tier approach to be effective.

The SEC staff acknowledges that before these changes can occur, the FASB needs to finish its project on improving its conceptual framework. In addition, before these or other changes to the GAAP hierarchy are introduced, a significant amount of communication and training will need to take place within the financial reporting community. As such, it is likely to be some time before changes are made to the GAAP hierarchy. Given the significance such changes could have on financial reporting, however, interested parties should monitor discussions by the standard-setters on this issue.

SEC Staff Accounting Bulletins

Periodically, the SEC staff issues a Staff Accounting Bulletin (SAB) to describe the SEC staff's interpretations of existing accounting literature. For SEC registrants, SABs are considered Category A GAAP. Because SABs are not intended to contradict or supersede existing accounting literature, however, the guidance in a SAB should not be followed if it contradicts accounting literature in Categories A through D of the GAAP hierarchy.

In December 1999, the SEC staff issued a significant SAB related to revenue recognition: SAB 101, *Revenue Recognition in Financial Statements.* SAB 101 was codified in SAB Topic 8A, *Retail Companies— Sales of Leased or Licensed Departments,* and SAB Topic 13, *Revenue Recognition.* Since the issuance of SAB 101, the SEC staff has updated and revised the guidance in SAB Topic 13 to conform it to current accounting literature. The SEC staff used SAB 103, *Update of Codification of Staff Accounting Bulletins,* and SAB 104, *Revenue Recognition,* to make the following types of changes to various SAB Topics, including SAB Topic 13: (a) deletion of obsolete guidance, (b) revisions to guidance based on outdated literature, and (c) replacement of superseded references with current references.

For SEC registrants, SAB Topics 8A and 13 are Category A GAAP. The interaction of these SAB Topics with other authoritative literature is clearly described in SAB Topic 13A1. In summary, if other authoritative literature exists that is applicable to the situation, that literature should be followed. If no other authoritative literature is applicable to the situation, however, the guidance in the SAB Topics should be followed in lieu of analogizing to other authoritative literature.

While SAB Topics 8A and 13 do not affect the conclusions reached in accounting literature in levels A through D of the GAAP hierachy, there are cases in which SAB Topics 8A and 13 address an issue that other literature is silent on. In those cases, the registrant should follow the guidance of SAB Topics 8A and 13, even if they do not follow other parts of SAB Topics 8A and 13 due to the existence of other accounting literature. For example, SAB Topic 13 provides specific guidance regarding FOB terms and bill-and-hold transactions (see Chapter 5, "Product Deliverables"). That guidance must be applied by public software companies, because there is no corresponding or conflicting guidance in SOP 97-2, *Software Revenue Recognition*.

GENERAL REVENUE RECOGNITION LITERATURE

While no single piece of literature comprehensively addresses revenue recognition, two of the FASB Concepts Statements do provide some overall guidance. FASB Statement of Financial Accounting Concepts No. 5, *Recognition and Measurement in Financial Statements of Business Enterprises* (CON-5), provides broad recognition guidance and, FASB Statement of Financial Accounting Concepts No. 6, *Elements of Financial Statements* (CON-6), provides broad presentation guidance. In addition, SAB Topic 13 provides a general framework for recognizing revenue.

Aside from those three pieces of literature, the remaining literature addresses revenue recognition for either a specific type of revenue or a specific revenue recognition issue.

SPECIFIC TYPES OF REVENUE

Product Sales Not Addressed Elsewhere

Base Literature: SAB Topic 13, Revenue Recognition

Supplemental Literature
- FAS-48, Revenue Recognition When Right of Return Exists
- FAS-49, Accounting for Product Financing Arrangements
- EITF 95-1, Revenue Recognition on Sales with a Guaranteed Minimum Resale Value
- EITF 95-4, Revenue Recognition on Equipment Sold and Subsequently Repurchased Subject to an Operating Lease
- EITF 01-8, Determining Whether an Arrangement Contains a Lease
- EITF 03-12, Impact of FASB Interpretation No. 45 on Issue No. 95-1

Real Estate

Base Literature: FAS-66, Accounting for Sales of Real Estate

Supplemental Literature

- FAS-67, Accounting for Costs and Initial Rental Operations of Real Estate Projects
- FAS-98, Accounting for Leases, an amendment of FASB Statements No. 13, 66, and 91 and a rescission of FASB Statement No. 26 and Technical Bulletin 79-11
- FAS-152, Accounting for Real Estate Time-Sharing Transactions—An Amendment of FAS-66 and FAS-67
- FIN-43, Real Estate Sales, an interpretation of FASB Statement No. 66
- SOP 92-1, Accounting for Real Estate Syndication Income
- SOP 04-2, Accounting for Real Estate Time-Sharing Transactions
- Audit and Accounting Guide for Common Interest Realty Associations
- EITF 84-17, Profit Recognition on Sales of Real Estate with Graduated Payment Mortgages or Insured Mortgages
- EITF 86-6, Antispeculation Clauses in Real Estate Sales Contracts
- EITF 86-7, Recognition by Homebuilders of Profit from Sales of Land and Related Construction Contracts
- EITF 87-9, Profit Recognition on Sales of Real Estate with Insured Mortgages or Surety Bonds
- EITF 88-12, Transfer of Ownership Interest As Part of Down Payment under FASB Statement No. 66
- EITF 88-14, Settlement of Fees with Extra Units to a General Partner in a Master Limited Partnership
- EITF 88-21, Accounting for the Sale of Property Subject to the Seller's Preexisting Lease
- EITF 88-24, Effect of Various Forms of Financing under FASB Statement No. 66

Construction Contracts

Base Literature: ARB-45, Long-Term Construction-Type Contracts

SOP 81-1, Accounting for Performance of Construction-Type and Certain Production-Type Contracts

Supplemental Literature
- Audit and Accounting Guide for Construction Contractors

Federal Government Contractors

Base Literature: ARB-43, Restatement and Revision of Accounting Research Bulletins, Chapter 11, Government Contracts

Supplemental Literature
- Audit and Accounting Guide for Audits of Federal Government Contractors

Agriculture

Base Literature: SOP 85-3, Accounting by Agricultural Producers and Agricultural Cooperatives

Supplemental Literature
- Audit and Accounting Guide for Audits of Agricultural Producers and Agricultural Cooperatives

Oil and Gas

Base Literature: FAS-19, Financial Accounting and Reporting by Oil and Gas Producing Companies

SAB Topic 12, Oil and Gas Producing Activities

Supplemental Literature
- FAS-25, Suspension of Certain Accounting Requirements for Oil and Gas Producing Companies, an amendment of FASB Statement No. 19
- FAS-69, Disclosures about Oil and Gas Producing Activities, an amendment of FASB Statements 19, 25, 33, and 39
- Audit and Accounting Guide for Audits of Entities with Oil and Gas Producing Activities

Service Transactions Not Addressed Elsewhere

Base Literature: SAB Topic 13, Revenue Recognition

Supplemental Literature

- EITF 01-8, Determining Whether an Arrangement Contains a Lease

- EITF Topic D-96, Accounting for Management Fees Based on a Formula
- FASB Invitation to Comment: Accounting for Certain Service Transactions

Cable Television Fees

Base Literature: FAS-51, Financial Reporting by Cable Television Companies

Insurance

Base Literature: FAS-60, Accounting and Reporting by Insurance Enterprises

Supplemental Literature

- FAS-97, Accounting and Reporting by Insurance Enterprises for Certain Long-Duration Contracts and for Realized Gains and Losses from the Sale of Investments
- FAS-113, Accounting and Reporting for Reinsurance of Short-Duration and Long-Duration Contracts
- SOP 01-6, Accounting by Certain Entities (Including Entities with Trade Receivables) That Lend to or Finance Activities of Others
- SOP 03-1, Accounting and Reporting by Insurance Enterprises for Certain Nontraditional Long-Duration Contracts and for Separate Accounts
- Audit and Accounting Guide for Audits of Property and Liability Insurance Companies
- Audit and Accounting Guide for Life and Health Insurance Entities
- FTB 90-1, Accounting for Separately Priced Extended Warranty and Product Maintenance Contracts
- FSP FAS 97-1, Situations in Which Paragraphs 17(b) and 20 of FASB Statement No. 97, "Accounting and Reporting by Insurance Enterprises for Certain Long-Duration Contracts and for Realized Gains and Losses from the Sale of Investments," Permit or Require Accrual of an Unearned Revenue Liability

Research and Development Arrangements

Base Literature: FAS-68, Research and Development Arrangements

Supplemental Literature

- REG S-X, Rule 5-03, Income Statements
- SAB Topic 13, Revenue Recognition

Utilities

Base Literature: FAS-71, Accounting for the Effects of Certain Types of Regulation

Supplemental Literature

- EITF 91-6, Revenue Recognition of Long-Term Power Sales Contracts
- EITF 92-7, Accounting by Rate-Regulated Utilities for the Effects of Certain Alternative Revenue Programs
- EITF 96-17, Revenue Recognition under Long-Term Power Sales Contracts That Contain both Fixed and Variable Pricing Terms

Financial Services

Base Literature: FAS-91, Accounting for Nonrefundable Fees and Costs Associated with Originating or Acquiring Loans and Initial Direct Costs of Leases, an amendment of FASB Statements No. 13, 60, and 65 and a rescission of FASB Statement No. 17

FAS-140, Accounting for Transfers and Servicing of Financial Assets and Extinguishments of Liabilities, a replacement of FASB Statement No. 125

Supplemental Literature
- SAB Topic 5DD, Miscellaneous Accounting—Loan Commitments Accounted for as Derivative Instruments
- FIN-45, Guarantor's Accounting and Disclosure Requirements for Guarantees, Including Indirect Guarantees of Indebtedness of Others, an interpretation of FASB Statements No. 5, 57, and 107, and rescission of FASB Interpretation No. 34
- SOP 01-6, Accounting by Certain Entities (Including Entities with Trade Receivables) That Lend to or Finance the Activities of Others

- SOP 03-3, Accounting for Certain Loans or Debt Securities Acquired in a Transfer
- Audit and Accounting Guide for Depository and Lending Institutions: Banks and Savings Institutions, Credit Unions, Finance Companies and Mortgage Companies
- Audit and Accounting Guide for Audits of Investment Companies
- Audit and Accounting Guide for Brokers and Dealers in Securities
- EITF 84-5, Sale of Marketable Securities with a Put Option
- EITF 84-15, Grantor Trusts Consolidation
- EITF 84-20, GNMA Dollar Rolls
- EITF 85-13, Sale of Mortgage Service Rights on Mortgages Owned by Others
- EITF 85-20, Recognition of Fees for Guaranteeing a Loan
- EITF 85-24, Distribution Fees by Distributors of Mutual Funds That Do Not Have a Front-End Sales Charge
- EITF 86-8, Sale of Bad-Debt Recovery Rights
- EITF 88-22, Securitization of Credit Card and Other Receivable Portfolios
- EITF 90-18, Effect of a "Removal of Accounts" Provision on the Accounting for a Credit Card Securitization
- EITF 95-5, Determination of What Risks and Rewards, If Any, Can Be Retained and Whether Any Unresolved Contingencies May Exist in a Sale of Mortgage Loan Servicing Rights
- EITF 97-3, Accounting for Fees and Costs Associated with Loan Syndications and Loan Participations after the Issuance of FASB Statement No. 125
- FSP FIN 45-2, Whether FASB Interpretation No. 45, Guarantor's Accounting and Disclosure Requirements for Guarantees, Including Indirect Guarantees of Indebtedness of Others, Provides Support for Subsequently Accounting for a Guarantor's Liability at Fair Value
- FASB Staff Implementation Guidance, A Guide to Implementation of Statement 91 on Accounting for Nonrefundable Fees and Costs Associated with Originating or Acquiring Loans and Initial Direct Costs of Leases: Questions and Answers

Contributions Received

Base Literature: FAS-116, Accounting for Contributions Received and Contributions Made

Supplemental Literature
- Audit and Accounting Guide for Not-for-Profit Organizations

Health Care

Base Literature: Audit and Accounting Guide for Health Care Organizations

Freight

Base Literature: EITF 91-9, Revenue and Expense Recognition for Freight Services in Process

Airlines

Supplemental Literature
- Industry Audit Guide for Audits of Airlines

Casinos

Supplemental Literature
- Audit and Accounting Guide for Audits of Casinos

Employee Benefit Plans

Supplemental Literature
- SOP 92-6, Accounting and Reporting by Health and Welfare Benefit Plans
- Audit and Accounting Guide for Audits of Employee Benefit Plans

Leases

Base Literature: FAS-13, Accounting for Leases

Supplemental Literature
- FAS-29, Determining Contingent Rentals, an amendment of FASB Statement No. 13
- FAS-91, Accounting for Nonrefundable Fees and Costs Associated with Originating or Acquiring Loans and Initial Direct Costs of Leases, an amendment of FASB Statements No. 13, 60, and 65 and a rescission of FASB Statement No. 17
- FAS-98, Accounting for Leases, an amendment of FASB Statements No. 13, 66, and 91 and a rescission of FASB Statement No. 26 and Technical Bulletin No. 79-11

- FAS-145, Rescission of FASB Statements No. 4, 44, and 64, Amendment of FASB Statement No. 13, and Technical Corrections
- SAB Topic 13, Revenue Recognition
- FTB 85-3, Accounting for Operating Leases with Scheduled Rent Increases
- FTB 88-1, Issues Relating to Accounting for Leases
- EITF 84-37, Sale-Leaseback Transaction with Repurchase Option
- EITF 85-27, Recognition of Receipts from Made-Up Rental Shortfalls
- EITF 86-17, Deferred Profit on Sale-Leaseback Transaction with Lessee Guarantee of Residual Value
- EITF 87-7, Sale of an Asset Subject to a Lease and Nonrecourse Financing: "Wrap Lease Transactions"
- EITF 95-1, Revenue Recognition on Sales with a Guaranteed Minimum Resale Value
- EITF 95-4, Revenue Recognition on Equipment Sold and Subsequently Repurchased Subject to an Operating Lease
- EITF 98-9, Accounting for Contingent Rent
- EITF 01-8, Determining Whether an Arrangement Contains a Lease
- EITF 01-12, The Impact of the Requirements of FASB Statement No. 133 on Residual Value Guarantees in Connection with a Lease
- EITF 03-12, Impact of FASB Interpretation No. 45 on Issue No. 95-1
- EITF Topic D-107, Lessor Consideration of Third-Party Residual Value Guarantees
- FASB Staff Implementation Guidance, A Guide to Implementation of Statement 91 on Accounting for Nonrefundable Fees and Costs Associated with Originating or Acquiring Loans and Initial Direct Costs of Leases: Questions and Answers

Licenses of Intellectual Property Not Addressed Elsewhere

Supplemental Literature
- SAB Topic 13, Revenue Recognition

Software

Base Literature: SOP 97-2, Software Revenue Recognition

Supplemental Literature

- SOP 98-9, Modification of SOP 97-2, Software Revenue Recognition, With Respect to Certain Transactions
- EITF 00-3, Application of AICPA Statement of Position 97-2 to Arrangements That Include the Right to Use Software Stored on Another Entity's Hardware
- EITF 03-5, Applicability of AICPA Statement of Position 97-2 to Non-Software Deliverables in an Arrangement Containing More-Than-Incidental Software
- FSP FIN 45-1, Accounting for Intellectual Property Infringement Indemnifications under FASB Interpretation No. 45, Guarantor's Accounting and Disclosure Requirements for Guarantees, Including Indirect Guarantees of Indebtedness of Others
- Various AICPA Technical Practice Aids (Section 5100)

Motion Pictures

Base Literature: SOP 00-2, Accounting by Producers or Distributors of Films

Franchises

Base Literature: FAS-45, Accounting for Franchise Fee Revenue

Records and Music

Base Literature: FAS-50, Financial Reporting in the Record and Music Industry

Broadcasting

Base Literature: FAS-63, Financial Reporting by Broadcasters

SPECIFIC REVENUE RECOGNITION ISSUES

Nonmonetary Transactions

Base Literature: APB-29, Accounting for Nonmonetary Transactions

Supplemental Literature

- EITF 87-10, Revenue Recognition by Television "Barter" Syndicators

- EITF 93-11, Accounting for Barter Transactions Involving Barter Credits
- EITF 99-17, Accounting for Advertising Barter Transactions
- EITF 01-2, Interpretations of APB Opinion No. 29

Equity Received as Compensation in Revenue Transaction

Base Literature: EITF 00-8, Accounting by a Grantee for an Equity Instrument to Be Received in Conjunction with Providing Goods or Services

Multiple-Element Arrangements

Base Literature: EITF 00-21, Revenue Arrangements with Multiple Deliverables

Supplemental Literature

- SAB Topic 13, Revenue Recognition
- EITF 01-8, Determining Whether an Arrangement Contains a Lease
- EITF 03-5, Applicability of AICPA Statement of Position 97-2 to Non-Software Deliverables in an Arrangement Containing More-Than-Incidental Software

Rights of Return or Cancellation

Base Literature: FAS-48, Revenue Recognition When Right of Return Exists

SAB Topic 13, Revenue Recognition

Warranties

Base Literature: FAS-5, Accounting for Contingencies

FTB 90-1, Accounting for Separately Priced Extended Warranty and Product Maintenance Contracts

Supplemental Literature

- FIN-14, Reasonable Estimation of the Amount of a Loss, an interpretation of FASB Statement No. 5
- FIN-45, Guarantor's Accounting and Disclosure Requirements for Guarantees, Including Indirect Guarantees of Indebtedness of Others, an interpretation of FASB Statements No. 5, 57, and 107, and rescission of FASB Interpretation No. 34

Customer Acceptance Provisions

Base Literature: SAB Topic 13, Revenue Recognition

Supplemental Literature

- FAS-5, Accounting for Contingencies

Guarantees and Indemnifications

Base Literature: FAS-5, Accounting for Contingencies

FIN-45, Guarantor's Accounting and Disclosure Requirements for Guarantees, Including Indirect Guarantees of Indebtedness of Others, an interpretation of FASB Statements No. 5, 57, and 107, and rescission of FASB Interpretation No. 34

Supplemental Literature

- EITF 03-12, Impact of FASB Interpretation No. 45 on Issue No. 95-1
- FSP FIN 45-1, Accounting for Intellectual Property Infringement Indemnifications under FASB Interpretation No. 45, Guarantor's Accounting and Disclosure Requirements for Guarantees, Including Indirect Guarantees of Indebtedness of Others
- FSP FIN 45-2, Whether FASB Interpretation No. 45, Guarantor's Accounting and Disclosure Requirements for Guarantees, Including Indirect Guarantees of Indebtedness of Others, Provides Support for Subsequently Accounting for a Guarantor's Liability at Fair Value

Sales of Future Revenues

Base Literature: EITF 88-18, Sales of Future Revenues

Sales Incentives

Base Literature: EITF 01-9, Accounting for Consideration Given by a Vendor to a Customer (Including a Reseller of the Vendor's Products)

Supplemental Literature

- EITF 02-16, Accounting by a Customer (Including a Reseller) for Certain Consideration Received from a Vendor
- EITF 03-10, Application of Issue No. 02-16 by Resellers to Sales Incentives Offered to Consumers by Manufacturers

Installment Method of Accounting

Base Literature: APB-10, Omnibus Opinion—1966, Installment Method of Accounting

Preexisting Sales/Purchase Agreement between Parties to a Business Combination

Base Literature: EITF 04-1, Accounting for Preexisting Relationships between the Parties to a Business Combination

Presentation

Base Literature: REG S-X, Rule 5-03, Income Statements

Supplemental Literature

- SAB Topic 8, Retail Companies
- SAB Topic 13, Revenue Recognitioin
- EITF 99-19, Reporting Revenue Gross as a Principal versus Net as an Agent
- EITF 00-10, Accounting for Shipping and Handling Fees and Costs
- EITF 01-9, Accounting for Consideration Given by a Vendor to a Customer (Including a Reseller of the Vendor's Products)
- EITF 01-14, Income Statement Characterization of Reimbursements Received for "Out-of-Pocket" Expenses Incurred
- EITF 02-3, Issues Involved in Accounting for Derivative Contracts Held for Trading Purposes and Contracts Involved in Energy Trading and Risk Management Activities
- EITF 02-16, Accounting by a Customer (Including a Reseller) for Certain Consideration Received from a Vendor
- EITF 03-10, Application of Issue No. 02-16 by Resellers to Sales Incentives Offered to Consumers by Manufacturers
- EITF 03-11, Reporting Realized Gains and Losses on Derivative Instruments That Are Subject to FASB Statement No. 133 and Not "Held for Trading Purposes" as Defined in Issue No. 02-3

REVENUE RECOGNITION UNDER INTERNATIONAL FINANCIAL REPORTING STANDARDS

IAS Literature

Another source of revenue recognition literature is international accounting literature. This literature comprises Statements of International Accounting Standards (IASs) and International Financial Reporting Standards (IFRSs) promulgated by the International Accounting Standards Board (IASB) and Interpretations from the International Financial Reporting Interpretations Committee (IFRIC), which replaced the Standing Interpretations Committee (SIC). The IAS Statements and IFRSs are roughly the equivalent of the FASB Standards in the U.S. GAAP literature; the Interpretations are roughly the equivalent of the EITF Issues in the U.S. GAAP literature.

IAS Framework

The IASB's framework defines income as "increases in economic benefits during the accounting period in the form of inflows or enhancements of assets and decreases of liabilities that result in increases in equity, other than those relating to contributions from equity participants." The framework goes on to distinguish between the two main components of income, revenue and gains. Revenue arises "in the course of the ordinary activities of an entity." Gains are contrasted as "other items that meet the definition of income and *may or may not* [emphasis added] arise in the course of the ordinary activities of an entity." The framework goes on to explain that because gains are not different in nature from revenues, they are not regarded as a separate element.

Applicable Standards

The IASB's IAS 18, *Revenue,* is a comprehensive statement which addresses revenue recognition for three significant types of revenue: product sales, service transactions, and rights to use assets. IAS 18 defines revenue as the "gross inflow of economic benefits during the period arising from the course of the ordinary activities of the entity when those inflows result in an increase in equity, other than increases resulting from contributions by equity participants." The Standard notes that such inflows must be on the entity's own account; revenue does not include amounts collected on behalf of a third party. Three additional IASB standards comprehensively address other significant types of revenue: IAS 11 (construction contracts), IAS 17 (leases), and IAS 41 (agriculture). Limited revenue recognition guidance for the insurance industry also is provided in IFRS 4, *Insurance Contracts.*

To the extent that a topic or issue is covered by both U.S. and international GAAP literature, a U.S. company must follow the guidance in U.S. literature. To the extent a topic or issue is not covered in U.S. literature but is covered in IASB literature, however, a U.S. company can refer to IASB literature for accounting guidance and policies that are likely to be acceptable in the U.S. GAAP framework. Referring to IASB literature provides the perspective of a standard-setter that has specifically focused on and addressed an accounting topic or issue. This perspective can be helpful to the U.S. company in determining how to account for a particular topic or issue not covered in U.S. GAAP.

Presentation and Other Issues

Presentation of revenue on the income statement is addressed in IAS 1, *Presentation of Financial Statements.* IAS 1 gives preparers of financial statements considerable flexibility on the introduction of additional revenue line items, sub-totaling, and ordering.

IAS 14, *Segment Reporting,* defines "segment result" as "segment revenues less segment expenses" and has definitions of both segment revenues and expenses with specific items to be included or excluded from those amounts. For example, segment revenue includes "an entity's share of profits and losses of associates, joint ventures, or other investments accounted for under the equity method if those items are included in consolidated or total entity revenue" and segment expenses specifically excludes these amounts. This is relevant regarding where such profit and losses should appear on the consolidated statement of income.

IFRIC is currently working on a more comprehensive interpretation for Service Concessions. An exposure draft has been issued and comments received.

Base Literature: IAS 18, *Revenue*

Supplemental Literature

- Interpretations Referenced in IAS 18: SIC 27, *Evaluating the Substance of Transactions in the Legal Form of a Lease;* SIC 31, *Revenue—Barter Transactions involving Advertising Services*

- Other Interpretations Referencing IAS 18: SIC 13, *Jointly Controlled Entities—Non-Monetary Contributions by Ventures* (See Basis for Conclusions)

- Other Interpretations Addressing Revenue Recognition Issues not Addressed Elsewhere: SIC 29: *Disclosure—Service Concessions*

Standards and Relevant Interpretations Governing Items Excluded from the Scope of IAS 18

- IAS 11, *Construction Contracts* [IAS 18, par. 4]
- IAS 17, *Leases* (lease agreements) [IAS 18, par. 6]
- SIC 15, *Operating Leases—Incentives* [IAS 18, par. 6]
- SIC 27, *Evaluating the Substance of Transactions in the Legal Form of a Lease* [IAS 18, par. 6]
- IFRIC 4, *Determining Whether an Arrangement Contains a Lease* [IAS 18, par. 6]
- IAS 28, *Investment in Associates* (dividends from investments) [IAS 18, par. 6]
- IAS 39, *Financial Instruments: Recognition and Measurement* (change in fair value of financial assets and liabilities, interest revenue) [IAS 18, par. 6]
- IAS 41, *Agriculture* (initial recognition and changes in fair value of biological assets related to agricultural activity and initial recognition of agricultural produce) [IAS 18, par. 6]
- IFRS 4, *Insurance Contracts* (insurance contracts within scope) [IAS 18, par. 6]

CHAPTER 3
GENERAL PRINCIPLES

CONTENTS

BACKGROUND

Revenue is the top line in the income statement, and one of the most important figures to both preparers and users of financial statements. The way in which revenue is recognized can have a significant effect on the way a company's results of operations will look. Additionally, the vast array of revenue-generating transactions that companies enter into ensures that this area of accounting will continue to generate new questions and issues.

To address these questions and issues as they arise, financial statement preparers, auditors, and accounting standard-setters refer to the general principles and concepts on which accounting for revenue is based. As in other areas of accounting, these principles and concepts are set out in the FASB concept statements. For revenue recognition, the underlying concepts indicate that revenue should be recognized when it is both earned and either realized or realizable (CON-5, par. 83).

In many cases, applying the "earned and realizable" concepts is fairly straightforward and no additional guidance is necessary for determining the appropriate point at which to recognize revenue. For example:

- A restaurant's revenue generally is earned and realizable at the end of the meal, when it has been eaten and paid for by the diner.
- A retail store's revenue generally is earned and realizable when the customer pays for the merchandise at the cash register.
- A manufacturer's revenue generally is earned and realizable upon delivery for COD orders.
- Plumbers, lawn care providers, and many other service providers generally earn their revenue as they perform the related services, and get paid upon completion of those services.

The above examples are all situations in which revenue is earned and realized at the same, or almost the same, time. There are many other common and fairly simple transactions, however, in which the two events occur at different times. In some cases, revenue is realized before it is earned. For example:

- Magazine subscriptions are often paid in advance. In this situation, the publisher realizes the revenue before any magazines are delivered. However, the delivery of the magazines is when the revenue is earned.
- Airlines generally require payment immediately upon the purchase of a ticket, thus realizing the revenue at that time. However, the revenue is not earned until transportation is provided.

In other cases, revenue is earned before it becomes realizable. For example:

- A manufacturer may sell products on credit. The revenue in that situation is earned when the products are delivered. However it may not be immediately realizable if the customer's ability to pay is in question.
- Certain retailers provide products to customers on a trial basis, wherein the customer has no commitment to pay for the goods unless he or she keeps them for a particular period

of time. Although the earnings process may arguably be complete when the product is delivered, the revenue does not become realizable until the trial period lapses.

The common transactions discussed above are all examples in which the "earned and realizable" concepts are fairly easy to apply, without any additional guidance or interpretation. Because the guidance can be easy to apply in many situations, the FASB and other accounting standard-setters have not provided additional guidance on applying these concepts to most transactions. Instead, guidance has been provided on how to apply the basic concepts to certain transactions in which applying those concepts is difficult, and other guidance has been provided on how certain common issues affect the application of the basic concepts. Thus, as discussed in Chapter 2, "A Brief Survey of Revenue-Related Literature," the applicability of most of the revenue recognition guidance that exists is limited to a small portion of transactions. Unfortunately, it has recently become clear that there are far more transactions for which these concepts are difficult to apply than the standard-setters have addressed.

SURVEY OF ACCOUNTING LITERATURE

The general principles to be met before revenue is recognized under U.S. GAAP are set forth in the FASB's Conceptual Framework. The purpose of the conceptual framework is to establish fundamental principles on which authoritative accounting literature will be based. The concept statements therefore are not intended to provide sufficient guidance to allow preparers to determine the proper accounting for a particular transaction. Rather, the concept statements are meant to provide a basis upon which the FASB, AICPA, and other accounting standard-setters can develop necessary guidance. The concept statements provide the goals that the more detailed standards are designed to achieve.

With respect to revenue recognition, those goals, as set forth in CON-5, paragraph 83, are that "recognition involves consideration of two factors, (a) being realized or realizable and (b) being earned, with sometimes one and sometimes the other being the more important consideration." This conceptual guidance has been unchanged since it was first issued by the FASB in 1984.

In many areas of accounting, the conceptual guidance is augmented by more specific guidance in the form of one or more Statements on Financial Accounting Standards that provide more detailed guidance on applying the concepts. Although many pieces of literature deal with applying the basic concepts for revenue recognition to specific industries or transactions, the only general guidance on applying the basic concepts to transactions in general comes from SAB Topic 13.

LISTING OF APPLICABLE LITERATURE

CON-5	Recognition and Measurement in Financial Statements of Business Enterprises
FAS-5	Accounting for Contingencies
FAS-13	Accounting for Leases
FAS-48	Revenue Recognition When Right of Return Exists
FAS-66	Accounting for Sales of Real Estate
FAS-71	Accounting for the Effects of Certain Types of Regulation
FAS-133	Accounting for Derivative Instruments and Hedging Activities
FAS-140	Accounting for Transfers and Servicing of Financial Assets and Extinguishments of Liabilities
ARB-45	Long-Term Construction-Type Contracts
APB-10	Omnibus Opinion—1966, Installment Method of Accounting
SOP 81-1	Accounting for Performance of Construction-Type and Certain Production-Type Contracts
SOP 97-2	Software Revenue Recognition
SOP 00-2	Accounting by Producers or Distributors of Films
EITF D-96	Accounting for Management Fees Based on a Formula
EITF 01-8	Determining Whether an Arrangement Contains a Lease
EITF 01-9	Accounting for Consideration Given by a Vendor to a Customer (Including a Reseller of the Vendor's Products)
SAB Topic 13	Revenue Recognition

OVERVIEW

The two concepts—earned and realized or realizable—are meant to ensure that (1) the company does not recognize revenue unless and until it has performed under the terms of the arrangement, thereby giving it the right to receive and retain payment as documented in the arrangement, and (2) the company will indeed receive and retain payment in a form that has value to it.

Earned

As stated in CON-5, "revenues are considered to have been earned when the entity has substantially accomplished what it must do to be entitled to the benefits represented by the revenues." This may be delivering goods, performing services, providing information, or any other activity for which one entity would pay another entity. The acts the seller performs to fulfill the earned criteria are termed the "earnings process."

Thus, to meet the earned criteria, the earnings process must already have been completed, at least in part. In substance, revenue is earned when the seller has fulfilled its end of the bargain. This requirement is basically common sense. Until the company has performed a service, it should not recognize revenue related to amounts it will be paid in return for that performance. In most cases, the point at which revenue is earned is fairly clear from the terms of the transaction. For example:

- A lawn care service's revenue is earned when it mows the lawn.

- A restaurant's revenue is earned when the customer eats his or her meal.

- An automobile part manufacturer's revenue is earned when it delivers parts to its customers pursuant to orders.

- A car rental agency's revenue is earned via the passage of time as it allows a customer to use one of its cars.

- A grocery store's revenue is earned when the customer proceeds through the checkout line with groceries.

In many other transactions, however, it is unclear when revenue has been earned. For example, an executive recruiter performs many activities as part of a search, including contacting potential candidates, setting up interviews, assisting in salary negotiations, etc. However, it is not until somebody has been hired that the customer sees the benefits of all of these activities. Similarly, a sales agent performs many activities to line up purchasers of its customer's products. However, it is not until products are purchased that its customer sees the benefits of these activities. In these situations, it is not immediately clear whether revenue is earned over time (e.g., the period over which the search for candidates or purchasers is performed), or only upon successful completion of all necessary activities (e.g., acceptance by a candidate or orders placed by a purchaser).

It is important to note that the completion of the earnings process may have nothing to do with the timing of the payments under the contract. For example, the receipt of a deposit or up-front fee in an arrangement does not indicate that revenue has been earned, even if the deposit or fee is non-refundable. On the other hand, the fact that payment in an arrangement is not due for some period of time does not necessarily indicate that the revenue has not yet been earned.

Realized or Realizable

Revenue is considered to be realized or realizable when the seller receives cash from the customer or receives an asset, such as a note receivable, that is readily convertible into cash. In addition, the receipt of nonmonetary assets that are not readily convertible into cash also meets the realizability criterion as long as the fair values of such assets are readily determinable (see further discussion in Chapter 8, "Miscellaneous Issues").

Much like the earned criterion, the requirement that revenue be realizable before it is recognized also seems to be common sense. If the company has not received a benefit from the arrangement, it would seem illogical to recognize the revenue. Also similar to the earned criterion, it is often easy to determine whether the realizable criterion has been met. In general, this occurs when either a cash payment is received or the customer becomes legally obligated to make such a payment because the seller has fulfilled its responsibilities under the contract.

However, many provisions can exist in arrangements that raise questions about the realizability of revenue. For example, when payment is received but the customer has a right of return, the right of return may raise realizability questions. The fee in other arrangements may be variable based on the outcome of one or more events whose outcome will not be known until after delivery or even until after initial payment. Again, this raises questions about the realizability of the arrangement fee.

Four Conditions for Recognition

The accounting literature that has been developed since the conceptual framework guidance was introduced has attempted to provide additional conditions for determining when revenue has been earned and is realizable. As previously mentioned, some of that literature is transaction-specific (e.g., SOP 00-2 on the licensing of motion pictures), and some of it is issue-specific (e.g., FAS-49, *Accounting for Product Financing Arrangements,* on product financing arrangements). In contrast, SAB Topic 13 is more general in nature.

Although different pieces of literature use different terms to get their ideas across, all of the literature generally indicates that revenue is both earned and realizable when each of the following four conditions is met (SAB Topic 13A1; SOP 97-2, par. 8; SOP 00-2, par. 7):

1. Persuasive evidence of an arrangement exists.

2. The arrangement fee is fixed or determinable.

3. Delivery or performance has occurred.

4. Collectibility is reasonably assured.

The intent of these four conditions is to provide conditions that can be consistently evaluated in determining when revenue is both earned and realizable. There is a fair amount of guidance useful in evaluating these conditions in a variety of transactions. Although that guidance is often narrowly scoped, the guidance in each piece of literature follows concepts that are similar enough that general guidance can be developed related to those concepts, which can then be applied to almost all types of transactions.

> **OBSERVATION:** It is important to note that each of the four conditions above must be met by the end of the accounting period during which it is proposed that revenue be recognized. Meeting the conditions after the end of the period, even if earnings have not yet been reported, is not sufficient to recognize revenue in the period in question. Instead, these situations should result in revenue recognition during the period in which the final condition is met. [1]

This chapter provides discussion of each of the four criteria. The analysis of whether collectibility is reasonably assured and whether persuasive evidence of an arrangement exists generally does not change significantly based on the type of transaction involved. Thus, the discussion of those conditions in this chapter applies to all transactions, and there is no further significant discussion of these conditions in Chapters 4–7 and 9–10, which address certain issues and transaction types.

In contrast, the analysis of the condition regarding the need for a fixed or determinable fee and, especially, the condition regarding delivery or performance, can differ significantly based on the type of transaction involved. This chapter has a significant amount of guidance on these conditions. However, additional guidance is included in Chapters 4–10, based on the type of transaction involved. Therefore, the guidance in both this chapter and the chapter(s) covering the transaction being accounted for should be consulted with respect to these two conditions.

PERSUASIVE EVIDENCE OF AN ARRANGEMENT

To determine whether the "earned" criterion has been met—in other words, to assess whether the seller has substantially completed

---

[1] Meeting the revenue recognition conditions after the end of the period is a "Type II" subsequent event, as discussed in paragraph 5 of the AICPA Codification of Auditing Standards, AU Section 560, *Subsequent Events*. Type II subsequent events include " . . . those events that provide evidence with respect to conditions that did not exist at the date of the balance sheet being reported on but arose subsequent to that date. These events should not result in adjustment of the financial statements. [footnote omitted]"

what it has agreed to do—it is necessary to be able to identify what obligations that seller has undertaken. For this reason, revenue cannot be recognized until there is persuasive evidence of an arrangement. The existence of persuasive evidence of an arrangement ensures that the seller's obligations are identified. This, in turn, ensures an accurate analysis of whether the seller has fulfilled those obligations and earned the related revenue.

Persuasive evidence of an arrangement also helps to ensure that the realizability criterion is met, as it provides the legal basis on which the seller can demand payment from the customer. If no arrangement exists under which the buyer has agreed to pay the seller for performing under the contract, any revenue the seller believes he or she is owed may very well not be realizable, as the seller may not have a right to payment under the law.

What Constitutes "Persuasive Evidence"

The persuasive evidence of an arrangement condition does not require that any specific form of evidence exist. Rather, the evidence that should exist before revenue is recognized is whatever evidence the company would normally use to document a sales transaction.

Many companies routinely document sales arrangements by written contracts. For those companies, persuasive evidence of an arrangement generally would not be considered to exist until both parties sign the final contract. Thus, despite the fact that the seller may have delivered the products or services required and billed the customer, no revenue should be recognized if the final contract is still pending.

ILLUSTRATION: PERSUASIVE EVIDENCE OF AN ARRANGEMENT

(Adapted from SAB Topic 13A2, ques. 1)

Facts: Company A has product available to ship to customers prior to the end of its current fiscal quarter. Customer Beta places an order for the product, and Company A delivers the product prior to the end of its current fiscal quarter. Company A's normal and customary business practice for this class of customer is to enter into a written sales agreement that requires the signatures of the authorized representatives of the Company and its customer to be binding. Company A prepares a written sales agreement, and its authorized representative signs the agreement before the end of the quarter. However, Customer Beta does not sign the agreement because Customer Beta is awaiting the requisite approval by its legal department. Customer Beta's purchasing department has orally agreed to the sale and stated that the contract will be formally approved the first week of Company A's next fiscal quarter. Company A expects that payment will be made on normal credit terms.

Discussion: In view of Company A's business practice of requiring a written sales agreement for this class of customer, persuasive evidence of an arrangement would require a final agreement that has been executed by the properly authorized personnel of the customer. Customer Beta's execution of the sales agreement after the end of the quarter causes the transaction to be considered a transaction of the subsequent period.

EXAMPLE: PERSUASIVE EVIDENCE OF AN ARRANGEMENT

Ascential Software Form 10-K—Fiscal Year Ended December 31, 2004

Persuasive evidence of an arrangement exists: It is our customary practice to have a written contract, which is signed by both the customer and us, or a purchase order from those customers that have previously negotiated a standard end-user license arrangement or a purchase order with negotiated governing terms or volume purchase agreement, prior to recognizing revenue on an arrangement. Sales to resellers are evidenced by purchase orders submitted to us under a master agreement governing the terms of the relationship. Certain reseller arrangements are structured as royalty agreements in which royalties as a percent of either list price or net sales price are due to us upon product shipment to the end-user customer. Evidence of arrangement in these circumstances consists of request for shipment, or notification of shipment for resellers who ship duplicates directly to end-user customers from a master copy.

Other companies may use different methods of documenting sales transactions. If a company does not have a standard or customary business practice of using written contracts to document a sales arrangement, there would usually be other forms of written or electronic evidence to document the transaction. Such evidence might be as simple as a restaurant check, a cash register receipt, or a click on the "submit order" button on an Internet site (SAB Topic 13A2, ques. 1).

The methods used to document sales transactions may vary from location to location within a company, or may vary based on the type of customer (e.g., corporate vs. individual) or transaction (e.g., product vs. service). If so, each transaction should be evaluated based upon the documentation that would be expected to exist for that type of transaction.

EXAMPLE: DIFFERENT EVIDENCE OF ARRANGEMENT FOR DIFFERENT TRANSACTIONS

8X8, Inc. Form 10-K—Fiscal Year Ended March 31, 2005

For all sales, except those completed via the Internet, we use either a binding purchase order or other signed agreement as evidence of an arrangement. For sales over the Internet, we use a credit card authorization as evidence of an arrangement, and recognize revenue upon settlement of the transaction if there are no customer acceptance conditions. We do not settle credit card transactions until equipment related to the transaction, if any, is shipped to a customer.

In some instances, a company may enter into a transaction whose documentation is not consistent with the company's standard documentation for one reason or another. In these cases, judgment must be applied in assessing whether persuasive evidence of an arrangement exists. For example, if a company that normally uses written contracts to document its arrangements delivers its product to a customer, receives payment from the customer, and receives notification of customer acceptance of the product, then persuasive evidence of an arrangement may very well exist, even if the formal contract was never signed due to the customer's desire for quick delivery.

DELIVERY

To ensure that the earned criterion is met, delivery or performance must occur before revenue is recognized. This requirement goes to assessing whether the obligations undertaken by the vendor in an arrangement have been completed. Each obligation is generically referred to as an element or a deliverable. The assessment of whether the delivery or performance requirement is met is done individually for each deliverable in an arrangement. However, when multiple deliverables exist, certain issues must be considered in allocating the arrangement fee to the individual deliverables. These issues are discussed in Chapter 4, "Multiple-Element Arrangements."

Basic Models

Delivery of an element is considered to have occurred when the seller has fulfilled its obligations related to that element and the customer has realized the value of the element. Delivery of certain elements occurs all at once, while delivery of others occurs over a period of time. In fact, although an infinite variety of deliverables can be included in a revenue arrangement, delivery or performance is generally considered to occur for accounting purposes based on one of two models. The decision of which model to use is based on whether the vendor obligations are completed and value is transferred to the customer all at once or over a period of time. The first model, which is referred to in this book as the Completed Performance model, is used when a single point in time can be identified as the point in time that the vendor performs its obligation. The second model, which is referred to as the Proportional Performance model, is used when the seller completes the performance obligation and the customer receives value over a period of time.

> ☞ **PRACTICE POINTER:** No matter which model is used, the delivery condition is not met until the vendor's obligation to the customer is fulfilled. Therefore, if the vendor hires a third party to fulfill the obligation, revenue cannot be recognized until the third party actually fulfills the obligation. Merely hiring an outside party to provide a deliverable to the customer does not constitute delivery, because hiring a third party does not provide value to the customer. That value is not provided unless and until the customer actually receives the deliverable.

Choosing a Model

The choice of which of the two models to use in determining when delivery has occurred is a key step in recognizing revenue. In some cases, the identification of an appropriate model is an easy one, because the performance pattern is clear. Other situations require significant judgment. Although some generalizations can be made about what kind of deliverables should be evaluated under each model, it is important that the substance of each deliverable be reviewed in determining when delivery occurs for that deliverable.

The discussion below focuses on individual deliverables, since it is necessary to separately assess the delivery requirement for each deliverable in an arrangement. However, it is important to note that when an arrangement includes multiple deliverables, delivery of a particular item is generally not considered to have occurred if that deliverable does not have value to the customer on a standalone basis. This is further discussed in Chapter 4, "Multiple-Element Arrangements."

Products

Delivery of products is generally evaluated using the Completed Performance model, because the customer realizes all of the value at once—when the product is physically delivered to the customer. At that time, the vendor completes its entire obligation with respect to the deliverable. In fact, the Completed Performance model is sometimes referred to as the product model.

Although a manufacturer may take a number of actions related to an arrangement before delivery of the product, these actions generally do not provide value to the customer unless and until delivery occurs. Therefore, it is not usually appropriate to recognize revenue on a product sale under the Proportional Performance model as the product is manufactured. Delivery of a product is only evaluated under the Proportional Performance model when the arrangement qualifies for percentage-of-completion accounting. This method of accounting is discussed in Chapter 9, "Contract Accounting." Products may also be evaluated under the Proportional Performance model when the arrangement involves a subscription fulfilled over time.

See Chapter 5, "Product Deliverables," for further discussion on delivery of products.

> **PRACTICE ALERT:**   Situations may arise where arrangements that purport to cover only the sale of products actually contain a lease. EITF 01-8 provides guidance to assist in determining whether an arrangement contains a lease. When an arrangement does contain a lease, the portion of the arrangement that represents a lease must be accounted for as such. This is the case even though the arrangement is not formally characterized as a lease. Given the differences between the models used to account for product sales and leases, determining that an arrangement that on its face is a sale of products but, in fact, contains a lease will likely have significant effects on the timing of revenue recognition. The provisions of EITF 01-8 are discussed under "Leases" later in this chapter.

Services

In many situations delivery of a service is generally evaluated using the Proportional Performance model, since the vendor fulfills a portion of its obligations and the customer receives value as each part of the service is performed. As such, revenue is earned as each part of the service is performed as well. For example, a home health service that agrees to visit a patient once a week for a year should recognize a portion of the revenue with each visit (provided the other conditions for revenue recognition have been met). In other situations, when service is provided over a period of time, delivery may be considered to occur ratably throughout that time period. For example, the fee in an arrangement to provide high-speed Internet access for one year would be recognized ratably over the year (provided the other conditions for revenue recognition have been met).

The correct model to use for some service transactions, however, is not so clear. For example, in certain service transactions, although the service is performed over a period of time, the customer realizes value only if and when the final act of the service is performed. This may be true in the case of installation services, as the customer may not realize any value from the installation until it is completed. Similarly, a sales agent would generally not be considered to have delivered services until the customer makes a purchase from the supplier. These types of services may be best evaluated under the Completed Performance model.

See Chapter 6, "Service Deliverables," for additional discussion on the delivery of services.

> **PRACTICE ALERT:** Situations may arise where arrangements that purport to cover only the sale of services actually contain a lease. EITF 01-8 provides guidance to assist in determining whether an arrangement contains a lease. When an arrangement does contain a lease, the portion of the arrangement that represents a lease must be accounted for as such. This is the case even though the arrangement is not formally characterized as a lease. Given the differences between the models used to account for service transactions and leases, determining that an arrangement that on its face is a sale of services but, in fact, contains a lease will likely have significant effects on the timing of revenue recognition. The provisions of EITF 01-8 are discussed under "Leases" later in this chapter.

Intellectual Property

Determining when to recognize revenue in licenses of intellectual property is often a matter of determining when delivery has occurred, and, in many cases, whether delivery occurs at a point in time (the Completed Performance model) or over a period of time (the Proportional Performance model). For example, in a transaction involving the right to use copyrighted material for a two-year period, some would say that delivery occurs as soon as the license to the material begins and the customer has a copy of the material it can use, while others would suggest that delivery occurs ratably over the two-year period that the right to use the material is provided. For certain types of intellectual property transactions, industry- or transaction-specific accounting literature provides guidance on which model to use for assessing delivery. However, little literature addresses the issue for many types of intellectual property licenses. Detailed discussion of this topic can be found in Chapter 7, "Intellectual Property Deliverables." In addition, delivery of software is discussed in Chapter 10, "Software—A Complete Model."

Leases

For certain transactions, the determination of which model to use for the evaluation of delivery is addressed in the accounting literature. One major category of transaction for which significant guidance exists is lease transactions. Lease transactions are primarily addressed in FAS-13, which specifies that the lessor should treat certain leases as operating leases, and others as sales-type leases.[2] Essentially, an operating lease is evaluated under the Proportional Performance model, with revenue generally being recognized ratably over the lease term. Conversely, delivery in a sales-type lease is determined under the Completed Performance model, with performance deemed to be completed upon the physical delivery of the item being leased.

An issue that has received attention recently is the definition of a lease contained in FAS-13. This issue arises when an arrangement that purports to be only a sale of products or services in effect contains a lease. Given the differences between the models used to account for product sales or service transactions and leases, determining that an arrangement that on its face is a sale of products or services, in fact, contains a lease will likely have significant effects on the timing of revenue recognition. To bring some clarity to the definition of a lease and, in turn, to assist in determining whether an arrangement contains a lease, the EITF provided guidance in EITF 01-8. This guidance builds on the principal concepts in the definition of a lease contained in FAS-13 and requires the consideration of the following characteristics in determining whether an arrangement contains a lease:

- Only property, plant, or equipment (which includes only land and/or depreciable assets) can be the subject of a lease and a lease only exists if fulfillment of the arrangement is dependent on the use of specific property, plant, or equipment (the property, plant, or equipment can be either explicitly or implicitly identified) (EITF 01-8, pars. 9–11).

- A right to use property, plant, or equipment has been conveyed, and therefore a lease exists, if the purchaser/lessee has the right to control use of the underlying property, plant, or equipment. The right to control the use of the property, plant, or equipment exists if either of the following conditions exist:

  — The purchaser/lessee (a) has the right to operate the subject assets (either itself or through directing others) in a manner it determines, or (b) has the ability or right to control physical access to the subject assets, while obtaining or controlling more than a minor amount of the output or other utility of the subject assets; or

  — It is remote that another party or other parties will take more than a minor amount of the output or other utility

---

[2] Lease accounting is not addressed in this book. The *Miller GAAP Guide Level A* and other sources should be consulted for guidance on sales-type vs. operating lease classification.

of the property, plant, or equipment during the arrangement, and the price the purchaser will pay for the output is neither contractually fixed per unit nor equal to the current market price per unit as of the time of delivery of the output (EITF 01-8, par. 12).

EITF 01-8 also indicates that executory costs should be considered an element that falls within the scope of FAS-13, not as services that fall outside the scope of FAS-13.

If it is determined that an arrangement does contain a lease, the portion of the arrangement that represents a lease must be accounted for as such. This is the case even though the arrangement is not formally characterized as a lease. Separation of the lease element (or elements) from the other elements in the arrangement is discussed in Chapter 4, "Multiple-Element Arrangements."

Construction and Other Long-Term Contracts

Another type of transaction for which GAAP provides specific guidance on revenue recognition is construction and other long-term contracts. This guidance is included in ARB-45 and SOP 81-1. For arrangements that qualify for long-term contract accounting based upon the guidance in ARB-45 and SOP 81-1, the decision whether to use the Completed Performance or Proportional Performance model should be based on the factors set forth in those documents. For long-term contracts, the two models are referred to as the Completed Contract and Percentage-of-Completion methods, respectively. Discussion of the scope and application of long-term contract accounting is included in Chapter 9, "Contract Accounting."

ILLUSTRATION: CHOOSING THE APPROPRIATE MODEL FOR ASSESSING DELIVERY OF PRODUCTS AND SERVICES

The following examples illustrate the typical factors that must be taken into account when choosing which model to use.

EXAMPLE 1

Facts: Company A manufactures and sells furniture. It has a standard product line and customers may choose various colors, fabrics, and finishes from Company A's product catalog. Company A manufactures the furniture only after a customer places an order.

Discussion: Company A performs several activities in fulfilling a customer order, including manufacturing the furniture and physically delivering it to the customer. However, the customer only receives value upon the actual delivery of the furniture. Therefore, delivery or performance is not considered to occur during the manufacturing of the furniture. Company A should evaluate delivery under the Completed Performance model.

EXAMPLE 2

Facts: Company B charges users a fee for non-exclusive access to its web site containing proprietary databases. The fee allows access to the web site for a one-year period. After the customer is provided a user ID, there are no specific actions Company B must perform related to an individual customer. Rather, Company B must only continue to allow the customer access to the databases.

Discussion: The only specific action Company B performs with respect to a customer is providing the customer a user ID. However, the customer receives value over the course of the year that access to the databases is provided. Therefore, Company B should evaluate delivery under the Proportional Performance model.

EXAMPLE 3

Facts: Company C provides telecommunications services and enters into an arrangement to sell its business customer a number of generic telephones and to provide basic telephone service for one year.

Discussion: The customer receives some value from the arrangement when the telephones are delivered, and also receives additional value over the year that service will be provided. Company C should therefore evaluate delivery of the telephones under the Completed Performance model, and should evaluate delivery of the telephone service under the Proportional Performance model. Chapter 4, "Multiple-Element Arrangements," should be consulted for purposes of determining whether the telephones and basic telephone service should be treated as separate elements for accounting purposes.

EXAMPLE 4

Facts: Company D provides training to corporate boards of directors on carrying out their responsibilities. When Company D gets a new client, it spends time learning about the company, its industry, and its management personnel, and then customizes the training course for that company's board of directors. Company D then delivers the training to the board during a day-long session.

Discussion: Company D performs several activities in the course of fulfilling its responsibilities, some of which involve the design of customer-specific content. However, the customer receives value only when the final act, the delivery of the training, occurs. Therefore, Company D should use the Completed Performance model to evaluate delivery for its transactions.

EXAMPLE 5

Facts: Company E publishes guidance on accounting for various transactions. Company E updates its materials once per year, and prints a hardcopy book after each update. Customers may either purchase the most recent hard-copy version of the materials, or may purchase online access to the information for one year.

Discussion: Customers who buy the hard-copy book receive value from the transaction when the book is delivered, and Company E has no further obligations once the book is delivered. However, online subscribers receive value throughout the year that access is provided, and Company E fulfills a portion of its obligation each day of the year. Therefore, the Completed Performance model is appropriate for sales of books, and the Proportional Performance model is appropriate for sales of online subscriptions.

Applying the Completed Performance Model

As noted above, the Completed Performance model is used when a single point in time can be identified at which the vendor completes its obligation. This should coincide with the point in time at which the customer has realized value by obtaining an asset, the results of a service, or other benefits. In this model, the delivery criterion with respect to the element is met, in total, at that particular point in time. The Completed Performance model is therefore used when performance takes place all at once, or when it takes place over a period of time, but value is not transferred to the customer until the final act is completed. When the Completed Performance model is used, the point in time at which performance is completed must be identified. Because all revenue is recognized at that time, large differences in revenue for a financial reporting period can occur based on whether delivery occurs just before or just after period-end.

In a product sale, performance is generally completed when the product is delivered to the customer. Determining exactly when that occurs is not always straightforward, however. For example, when a product is shipped through the mail or by a third-party carrier, delivery may be considered to occur when the product leaves the seller's premises, or when it arrives at the buyer's location, depending on the shipping terms. In other situations, although the product is physically delivered, a seller may retain certain risks and rewards that indicate that performance has not actually been completed, despite physical delivery. The resolution of these types of issues and uncertainties is required to appropriately apply the Completed Performance model to a product sale.

When the Completed Performance model is applied to a service transaction, it is generally because the final act of the service is the act that allows the customer to realize the benefits of the service. Therefore, determining that the Completed Performance model is appropriate for a service also results in identifying the point at which delivery is deemed to occur (i.e., completion of the final act).

In other transactions where the completed performance model is applied, the issues that are likely to be key to determining when to recognize revenue are similar to those in a product sale. The application of the Completed Performance model to various transactions is more fully discussed in Chapters 5–10.

Applying the Proportional Performance Model

In the Proportional Performance model, revenue is recognized as performance occurs, based on the relative value of the performance that has occurred to that point in time. This model is therefore useful when the vendor fulfills its obligation over a period of time and the customer receives value throughout the performance period.

In applying the Proportional Performance model to a service transaction, the key issue is generally the pattern of performance. For example, if a service transaction involves a specified number of similar acts, such as mowing a lawn once a week for an entire summer, an equal amount of revenue should be recognized for each act. When the acts are not similar, however, revenue should be allocated based on their relative values. In other situations, value may be transferred to a customer ratably over a period of time, such as when the service is insurance coverage or access to a health club. The application of the Proportional Performance model to various transactions is discussed more fully in Chapters 5–10.

EXAMPLE: APPLYING THE PROPORTIONAL PERFORMANCE MODEL

Bally's Total Fitness Holding Corp. Annual Report—Fiscal Year Ended December 31, 2003

Other Revenue Recognition Issues

Revenues for membership initiation fees that are paid in full when sold continue to be deferred and recognized over the life of the contract, generally 36 months, on a straight-line method. Prepayments of non-obligatory monthly dues continue to be deferred and recognized ratably over the applicable prepayment period. Revenue from the sales of multiple session personal training contracts continue to be deferred and recognized as personal training sessions are performed.

FIXED OR DETERMINABLE FEE

The requirement that the fee be fixed or determinable before revenue is recognized directly addresses the realizability criterion. For example, if the fee is dependent upon future events, it is not clear that it will indeed be paid. Therefore, there is a question as to whether the fee is realizable. However, a fee that is not fixed or determinable may also indicate that the revenue has not yet been earned, if the reason the fee is not fixed or determinable is that the seller is still required to perform in some manner.

Meaning of Fixed or Determinable

Although several pieces of accounting literature, including SOP 97-2, SOP 00-2, and SAB Topic 13, refer to the need for the fee to be fixed or determinable before revenue is recognized, none of them provide a clear definition of what it means for a fee to be fixed or determinable. Instead, they use examples to illustrate certain concepts relevant to determining whether a fee is fixed or determinable.

Many arrangement terms raise questions about whether the fee is fixed or determinable. For example, customer rights of return or cancellation introduce uncertainty into the arrangement. Similarly, fees subject to change based upon the future success or failure of the work performed may indicate that a fee is not fixed or determinable. In addition, arrangements may have penalty or bonus clauses that introduce potential variability into the arrangements.

It is important to note that the answer as to whether a fee is fixed or determinable is not always an "all or nothing" answer. In many arrangements, a portion of the fee is not subject to change for any reason, but another portion of the fee varies based on one or more factors. In these instances, the portion of the fee that is not subject to change should be considered fixed or determinable, even if the rest of the fee is not.

> **OBSERVATION:** The requirement that a fee be fixed or determinable refers to whether or not the fee can vary based upon future events. In certain situations, although a fee cannot change based upon future events, it cannot be calculated until certain information related to past events is collated and evaluated. For example, consider an arrangement in which a company provides transaction processing services and prices those services based on the number of transactions processed for a particular customer each month. At month-end, the fee cannot change based on future events, but the company may not yet have calculated the fee owed by every customer, because it may need to review monthly activity reports from its various locations to make such calculations.

In other cases, a vendor may base revenue estimates on historical transactions or use information provided by licensees or resellers of its intellectual property in order to estimate royalty or fee revenue. However, changing market and technological conditions as well as a lack of adequate information from new users may not allow the vendor to develop reasonable estimates. Under these conditions, revenue cannot be recognized until the vendor receives actual use or resale information from licensees or resellers.

In these situations, the fact that information about past events must be gathered and analyzed does not preclude a conclusion that the fee is fixed or determinable. Instead, the company should record its best estimate of the revenue at period-end, and adjust that estimate when information is completely analyzed, allowing a precise determination of the fee. If this analysis is completed before the financial statements are released, its results should be incorporated into those financial statements.[3]

EXAMPLE: FIXED AND DETERMINABLE FEE

Qualcomm Inc. Form 10-K—Fiscal Year Ended September 26, 2004

The Company licenses rights to use portions of its intellectual property portfolio, which includes certain patent rights essential to and/or useful in the manufacture and sale of CDMA (including, without limitation, cdmaOne, CDMA2000, 1X/1xEV-DO/1xEV-DV, TD-SCDMA and WCDMA) products. Licensees typically pay a nonrefundable license fee in one or more installments and ongoing royalties based on their sales of products incorporating or using the Company's licensed intellectual property. License fees are recognized over the estimated period of future benefit to the average licensee, typically five to seven years. The Company earns royalties on such licensed CDMA products sold worldwide by its licensees at the time that the licensees' sales occur. The Company's licensees, however, do not report and pay royalties owed for sales in any given quarter until after the conclusion of that quarter, and, in some instances, although royalties are reported quarterly, payment is on a semi-annual basis. During the periods preceding the fourth quarter of fiscal 2004, the Company estimated and recorded the royalty revenues earned for sales by certain licensees (the Estimated Licensees) in the quarter in which such sales occurred, but only when

---

[3] The analysis of information about events that occurred before the end of the accounting period is a "Type I" subsequent event, as discussed in paragraph 3 of the AICPA Codification of Auditing Standards, AU Section 560, *Subsequent Events.* Type I subsequent events include ". . . those events that provide additional evidence with respect to conditions that existed at the date of the balance sheet and affect the estimates inherent in the process of preparing financial statements. . . . The financial statements should be adjusted for any changes in estimates resulting from the use of such evidence."

reasonable estimates of such amounts could be made. Not all royalties earned were estimated.

Royalties for licensees for which the Company had minimal reporting history and certain licensees that did not incorporate the Company's integrated circuit products into their own products were recorded one quarter in arrears, i.e. in the quarter in which the royalties were reported to the Company by those licensees. Estimates of royalty revenues for the Estimated Licensees were based on analyses of the Company's sales of integrated circuits to Estimated Licensees, historical royalty data for Estimated Licensees, an estimate of time between the Company's sales of integrated circuits to Estimated Licensees and Estimated Licensees' sales of CDMA products, average sales price forecasts, estimates of inventory levels and current market and economic trends. Once royalty reports were received from the Estimated Licensees, the variance between such reports and the estimate was recorded as royalty revenue in the quarter in which the reports were received, i.e., in most cases, the quarter subsequent to the quarter in which the estimated royalties were recorded as revenue.

Starting in the fourth quarter of fiscal 2004, the Company determined that, due to recent escalating business trends, the Company no longer has the ability to reliably estimate royalty revenues from certain licensees. These escalating trends include the commercial launches and global expansion of WCDMA networks, changes in market share among licensees due to increased global competition and increased variability in the integrated circuit and finished product inventories of licensees. Accordingly, the Company did not estimate royalty revenues earned in the fourth quarter of fiscal 2004. Starting in the fourth quarter of fiscal 2004, the Company began recognizing revenues solely based on royalties reported by licensees during the quarter. The change in the timing of recognizing royalty revenue was made prospectively and had the initial one-time effect of reducing royalty revenues recorded in the fourth quarter of fiscal 2004.

Evaluating Terms That Allow for Variable Fees

Any term in an arrangement that could result in a change in an arrangement fee should be analyzed to determine whether it should result in a conclusion that a fee (in whole or in part) is not fixed or determinable. The accounting literature provides little guidance on making such an analysis. However, by extrapolating from the guidance that does exist and applying some concepts that are prevalent in the accounting for various related issues, it is possible to develop general provisions regarding the accounting consequences of various factors that might cause a fee to be variable. To put some framework around this discussion, these factors can be grouped into the following categories:

1. *Factors in the customer's control* These include factors such as general return rights and incentive fees based on the customer's usage of a product.

2. *Factors in the seller's control*   These include factors such as certain forms of price protection and bonuses relating to cumulative performance over the term of a contract.

3. *Factors in control of a specified third party*   For example, an agent's fee might be partially refundable based on whether the end customer exercises a right of return; or, a lease agreement may require additional lease payments if the lessee exceeds certain sales levels (in this situation the additional lease payments are in control of the lessee's customers).

4. *Factors based on an index or other underlying*   These include fees based on investment return as compared to an index, fees that change with changes in the CPI or the inflation rate, and contingencies based on the weather.

Factors in the Customer's Control

General Rule

If an arrangement fee can be increased by future customer actions, the increase is not fixed or determinable until the customer takes such action. This would be the case if a vendor could receive a bonus based on the usage of a delivered product, or if a licensor of intellectual property were due a fee for each sale of a product incorporating the licensed technology. Thus, even if most customers do use the product or incorporate the licensed technology in the manner specified, revenue could not be recognized until that usage or incorporation occurs.

> **OBSERVATION:** Arrangements involving factors in the customer's control may be specified in various ways to achieve the same result. For example, an arrangement could entitle the seller to a $20,000 bonus if the customer uses the product more than 20 times in the first year after sale. Alternatively, the same economics could be created if the arrangement started with a $20,000 higher fee, and specified that a penalty of $20,000 would occur if the customer did not use the product more than 20 times in the first year after sale. Either of these arrangements should be accounted for as if the $20,000 at risk is not fixed or determinable unless and until the customer uses the product 20 times.

There are other situations in which a customer may be able to take actions or exercise rights that would reduce the amount of revenue that will ultimately be realized by the seller. Volume or other rebates and rights of return are some examples. When a customer can take an action that would reduce an arrangement fee, the portion of the fee at risk should generally not be considered fixed or determinable. In other words, revenue in this type of situation should generally be recognized as if the customer will exercise the right or take the action that would reduce the arrangement fee. However, once the customer's right to take the action that would reduce the arrangement fee has expired, then the additional revenue should be considered fixed or determinable.

Exception—Ability to Estimate Breakage

Although the general rule is that fees subject to change based on customer actions are not fixed or determinable, the fact is that there are many situations in which customers' actions with respect to certain rights can be predicted. In many cases, customers do not take advantage of the rights they have in an arrangement. This is called "breakage." FAS-48, which addresses rights to return products, established that, in certain circumstances, it is appropriate to record revenue based on estimated breakage, as long as that estimate of breakage is a reasonable and reliable one. Using FAS-48 as an analogy, accounting standard-setters have expanded the ability to recognize revenue based on breakage estimates to other types of rights as well. Importantly, this exception applies only when the customer's future action would reduce the fee. That is, recognition of revenue based on anticipated breakage is only appropriate when the customer must affirmatively take some action to reduce the fee, and the fee will be higher if the customer takes no action.

Rights of return   When a customer holds the right to receive a full refund by returning a product, a fixed or determinable fee would appear to be lacking. Indeed, some might also suggest that there is no persuasive evidence of an arrangement when the customer retains such optionality. Nevertheless, despite the existence of such rights, revenue can often be recognized before the right of return expires. These rights have been specifically addressed in FAS-48, which concludes that revenue may be recognized upon delivery in a sale with a right of return as long as a reliable estimate of returns can be made and certain other conditions are met. In general, if a company enters into a large number of homogeneous transactions, it will be capable of making such an estimate based on its historical experience. In that situation, the only revenue that must be deferred is the amount expected to be refunded. Further information about the accounting for rights of return, including a discussion of factors that may indicate a reliable estimate of returns cannot be made, is included in Chapter 5, "Product Deliverables."

Rights to cancel service transactions   In some service transactions, a customer has a right similar to a product return right—that being the right to cancel the remainder of the service and receive a full refund (i.e., not just a refund based on the remaining service to be performed). This is common in the sale of certain memberships (such as warehouse club memberships), and may exist for a limited time in the sales of insurance policies, warranties, and similar items. Cancellation rights in service transactions are not covered in FAS-48, which is limited to product returns. However, the application of similar concepts to those in FAS-48 may allow a company to make reliable estimates of refunds or cancellations. If this is true, recognition of revenue with deferral of the amount expected to be refunded is acceptable, although not required.

> **SEC REGISTRANT ALERT:** In question 1 of SAB Topic 13A4a, the SEC staff expressed its views that, while recognition of revenue based on a reliable estimate of breakage may be acceptable, deferral of all revenue until the refund period ends is preferable in these situations.

Other service transactions may include a right to cancel the remainder of the service for a pro-rata refund, i.e., a refund of only a portion of the fee, based on the proportion of the service remaining to be provided. In these situations, the fee becomes fixed or determinable ratably throughout the service period, as the amount of the refund the customer could receive decreases. Because the service is also generally considered to be delivered on a proportional basis throughout the period, these types of cancellation rights generally do not cause further delays in revenue recognition.

Further information about the accounting for service cancellation rights, including a discussion of factors that may indicate a reliable estimate of refunds cannot be made, is included in Chapter 6, "Service Deliverables."

Coupons and rebates   Certain revenue arrangements give the customer the ability to send in a form or other documentation of their purchase to obtain a full or partial rebate of the purchase price (for example, a $20 mail-in rebate found in the box of a computer printer). In other arrangements, a vendor may sell products to a retailer and also issue coupons (for example, a newspaper coupon for 50 cents off a box of cereal) to the retailers' customers. In both of these instances, a portion of the fee from the sale can change after the seller has performed under the arrangement. In general, the existence of a coupon or rebate indicates that the portion of the purchase price subject to potential rebate or refund is not fixed or determinable.

Of course, redemption rates on coupons and rebates are much lower than 100%. In fact, newspaper coupon redemption rates rarely, if ever, exceed single-digit percentages. Therefore, in EITF 01-9, the EITF concluded that revenue potentially subject to rebate or refund may be recognized as long as a reliable estimate of breakage can be made. The following factors may impair a company's ability to make a reasonable estimate of coupon or rebate redemptions (EITF 01-9, par. 23):

1. The offer period is long.
2. The absence of relevant historical experience.
3. The absence of a large volume of relatively homogeneous transactions.

Other sales incentives involve an offer to rebate or refund a specified amount of cash only if the customer completes a specified cumulative level of purchases or remains a customer for a specified time period. Similar to rebates that are exercisable based on a single purchase, revenue potentially subject to rebate may be recognized based upon estimates of breakage, if reliable estimates can be made.

In the case of either rebates available based on a single purchase and volume rebates, if a reliable estimate cannot be made, none of the revenue that is potentially subject to rebate is considered fixed or determinable, and thus such revenue cannot be recognized until the rebate right lapses.

Further information about the accounting for rebate rights, including a more detailed discussion of factors that may indicate a reliable estimate of rebates cannot be made, is included in Chapter 8, "Miscellaneous Issues."

EXAMPLE: ESTIMATE OF REBATE LIABILITY

Symantec, Inc. Form 10-K—Fiscal Year Ended April 1, 2005

Reserves for Rebates:

We estimate and record reserves as an offset to revenue for channel and end-user rebates, primarily related to products within our Consumer Products, Enterprise Security, and Enterprise Administration segments. Our estimated reserves for channel volume incentive rebates are based on distributors' and resellers' actual performance against the terms and conditions of volume incentive rebate programs, which are typically entered into quarterly. Our reserves for end-user rebates are estimated on the terms and conditions of the promotional programs, actual sales during the promotion, amount of actual redemptions received, historical redemption trends by product and by type of promotional program, and the value of the rebate. We also consider current market conditions and economic trends when estimating our reserves for rebates. If we made different estimates, material differences may result in the amount and timing of our net revenues for any period presented.

Other situations The concept of reliably estimating breakage in order to overcome a situation that initially causes a fee to appear to not be fixed or determinable has only been addressed in the specific situations discussed above. Analogy to FAS-48, question 1 of SAB Topic 13A4a, or EITF 01-9 may be appropriate in certain other limited situations.

However, no amount of evidence is sufficient to allow the recognition of revenue that will not be received unless customers take actions in the future. For example, if a fee in a license arrangement is $100 for a three-month license, and the customer has an option to extend the license to one year for an additional $50, the $50 extension fee cannot be considered fixed or determinable until the option is exercised, no matter how strong the seller's evidence is that such extension will be exercised. In these situations, any additional revenue should not be considered fixed or determinable until the customer takes the specified actions.

Factors in the Seller's Control

In some cases, the fee in an arrangement may be variable based upon the seller's performance. For example, the fee in an arrangement to deliver a large amount of equipment may have fixed fees for the equipment, plus a bonus payment if the seller completes all deliveries (or a penalty if the seller does not complete all deliveries) within a particular period of time. In other situations, a seller may offer price protection to the buyer, agreeing to rebate a portion of the arrangement fee in the event that it subsequently sells the same product or service to another customer at a lower price.

General Rule

Much like factors in the customer's control, the fact that an arrangement fee is subject to change based on the seller's future actions often results in a conclusion that the fee is not fixed or determinable. For example, if a seller can earn a bonus by completing a service ahead of schedule, that bonus should typically not be recognized until the service is completed ahead of schedule and the bonus is earned.

> **OBSERVATION:** Arrangements like this may be specified in various ways to achieve the same result. For example, an arrangement could entitle the seller to a $20,000 bonus if the service is completed by a particular date. Alternatively, the same economics could be created if the arrangement started with a $20,000 higher fee, and specified that the seller would be penalized $20,000 if it did not finish by the same date.

> Either of these arrangements should be accounted for as if the $20,000 at risk is not fixed or determinable unless and until the project is completed by the specified date.

Exception—Ability to Predict or Control Actions

Because FAS-48 and the other literature discussed above provide exceptions that allow revenue to be recognized even though it is at risk due to future customer actions, it stands to reason that similar exceptions might exist for actions in the seller's control. In fact, it should generally require a lower threshold of evidence for a seller to conclude it can predict the results of its own actions, as opposed to those of its customers. Thus, if a vendor can reliably predict the results of its actions, it should recognize revenue based on those predictions. However, if a reliable estimate cannot be made—for example, because the arrangement in question is unique or contains different performance criteria then are typically included in the vendor's arrangements—revenue should be recognized assuming that the vendor's future actions will result in only the minimum potential revenue. The accounting literature provides specific guidance on this topic in certain situations.

Conditional rights of return   Revenue attributable to delivered items in an arrangement may be potentially refundable based upon whether or not the seller delivers all of the other items in the arrangement. In these cases, the customer right of return is conditional, and will only exist if the seller fails to perform. As such, whether the customer obtains a right of return is in the seller's control. Further information about the accounting for conditional rights of return present in a multiple-element arrangement is included in Chapter 4, "Multiple-Element Arrangements."

Price protection based solely on seller's prices   A seller may agree to refund a portion of the purchase price to its customers in the event of a decrease in the seller's standard selling prices. In these situations, the seller may be able to estimate the effects of that agreement, as it is in control of whether those prices are lowered. If that is the case, the vendor may conclude that the fee is fixed in whole or in part, due to its ability to determine whether prices will be reduced and a refund triggered. However, if the vendor has shown an inability to predict price decreases or an inability to keep its prices at preferred levels, perhaps due to aggressive competition, then the fee should not be considered fixed or determinable (SOP 97-2, par. 30).

Exception—Recognition Based on Current Measurements

In some cases, a service provider may agree to a fee calculated based upon a formula applied to a particular period of time. For example, a hotel manager may agree to a fee based partially on the operating income of the hotel for a calendar year, or a sales agent may be entitled to a bonus if he or she increases sales by a certain percentage compared to the prior year. In these situations, a question arises as to whether any portion of the incentive fee is fixed or determinable before the end of the measurement period. The SEC staff commented on this situation in EITF D-96, noting that it would accept a conclusion that such fees are determinable at any point in time based on the formula and contract terms as they would be calculated at that date, whether the vendor can predict the results of its future actions or not. However, the SEC staff also indicated that it preferred a conclusion that none of the incentive fee is fixed or determinable until the end of the measurement period.

> **OBSERVATION:** In an arrangement in which a bonus or additional fee is earned if and only if a particular threshold is met, no part of the bonus or additional fee is fixed or determinable until the threshold is met, even if the progress to date indicates that the threshold will be met. Recognition at interim dates would be acceptable only if termination provisions exist calling for a final measurement based on progress to date (SAB Topic 13A4c).

> **DISCLOSURE ALERT:** See Chapter 12, "Disclosures," for information about required disclosures.

ILLUSTRATION: ACCOUNTING FOR FEES BASED ON A FORMULA

Facts: Investment Advisor A manages Fund B and is paid a flat fee per month, plus 20% of Fund B's returns in excess of 12% annually. The contract is terminable by either party with reasonable notice at the end of each quarter. In the event of a termination, the amount due for the incentive fee will be calculated at the termination date based on the fund returns to date compared to a 12% annual return pro-rated for the portion of the year that has passed.

Assume that Fund B's returns exceed 3% (1/4 of the 12% annual target) by $120,000 in the first quarter, $60,000 in the second quarter, and $50,000 in the fourth quarter, and that the return on the fund is $80,000 less than the 3% target in the third quarter. Thus, the total return of Fund B for the year exceeds the 12% target return by $150,000. Advisor A's share of the $150,000 is $30,000.

Discussion: Advisor A may choose from two accounting policies. The first would be to recognize no incentive fee revenue until the end of the one-year measurement period, under the theory that none of the incentive fee is fixed or determinable until then, as future poor performance in a subsequent interim period could cause the loss of incentive fee revenue earned in a prior interim period. This method, which is preferred by the SEC staff, would result in the recognition of $30,000 in incentive fee income on the last day of the year.

The second method would record as incentive fee revenue the amount that would be due under the formula at any point in time as if the contract was terminated at that date. Accordingly, Advisor A would record $24,000 of incentive fee revenue in the first quarter and $12,000 in the second quarter. In the third quarter, however, $16,000 of the previously recognized revenue would be reversed. Finally, $10,000 of incentive fee revenue would be recognized in the fourth quarter.

Factors in Control of a Third Party

Certain contracts have clauses that provide for a variable fee based on actions of a party other than the buyer or seller. Agency arrangements often include these clauses. For example, a sales agent may agree to refund its commission if the end customer returns the product. Alternatively, the agent may receive a bonus if a customer the agent introduces to the supplier makes additional purchases from the supplier or renews his or her subscription. Another common situation in which third-party actions may affect a company's revenue arises in leases that have contingent rentals based on the lessee's sales. Other arrangements, particularly if they are long-term in nature, may contain pricing terms that change if there are changes in tax law or industry regulations.

General Rule

Third-party actions are likely to be even more difficult to predict than customer actions. As such, it is not appropriate to assume that third parties will take actions resulting in additional payments from the customer to the vendor in an arrangement. Furthermore, if a third party can take an action that reduces a company's revenue, it is generally appropriate to assume the third party will take such action.

For example, the lessor in an operating lease that includes additional rent if sales exceed a certain level should not recognize that additional rent until the specified level of sales is reached, even if sales trends indicate that such level will be reached. Similarly, an agent whose fee is at risk if the end customer cancels its arrangement with the seller should generally not recognize the fee as revenue until the end customer's cancellation right lapses.

Exception—Ability to Estimate Breakage

Cancellation and return rights   As much as it is often possible to estimate breakage with respect to customer rights, it may be possible to estimate breakage with respect to certain third-party return or cancellation rights. And, much like the accounting when breakage with respect to customer return and cancellation rights can be reliably estimated, it is acceptable to recognize revenue despite the existence of third-party cancellation and return rights, as long as the amount of refunds can be reliably estimated. The characteristics that make reliable estimates in these situations possible are the same characteristics that would make estimating breakage with respect to potential cancellations of other service transactions possible, including the existence of a large pool of homogeneous transactions. Further discussion on estimating breakage in these situations is included in Chapter 6, "Service Deliverables."

Price-matching   Certain retailers, such as electronic stores, routinely offer a form of price protection based on their competitors' prices. These stores may offer to refund the difference between the price paid by a customer and a lower price on the same product offered by a competitor within the next 30 days. Unlike price protection based only on the particular vendor's future prices, estimating the effects of a price-matching offer is likely to be very difficult. However, if a sufficient history exists, and the competitive environment is stable, it may be possible to estimate the effects of a price-matching policy. If reliable estimates can be made, revenue may be recognized net of expected price-matching payments. If a reliable estimate cannot be made, as is likely to be the case, no revenue should be recognized until the price-matching period ends.

ILLUSTRATION: THIRD-PARTY ACTIONS AND FIXED OR DETERMINABLE FEES

(Adapted from SAB Topic 13A4a, ques. 2)

EXAMPLE 1:   A leasing broker's commission from the lessor upon a commercial tenant's signing of a lease agreement is refundable under lessor cancellation privileges if the tenant fails to move into the leased premises by a specified date.

EXAMPLE 2:   A talent agent's fee receivable from its principal (a celebrity) for arranging an endorsement for a five-year term is cancelable by the celebrity if the customer breaches the endorsement contract with the celebrity.

EXAMPLE 3:   An insurance agent's commission received from the insurer upon selling an insurance policy is entirely refundable for the 30-day period required by state law and then refundable on a declining pro rata basis until the consumer has made six monthly payments.

Discussion: In all of these cases, there is the potential for the arrangement fee to vary based upon the actions of a third party named in the contract. Thus, absent a large volume of homogeneous transactions sufficient to allow a reliable estimate of the effects of these rights to be made, the fee in question should only be recognized as the third party takes actions or as its right to take actions that affect the arrangement fee lapses.

In Examples 1 and 2, because of the unique nature of the transactions, it is highly unlikely that such a large volume of homogeneous transactions would exist to allow a reliable estimate of cancellations.

However, in Example 3, it may be possible that such a history exists. The company should therefore evaluate whether it has sufficient evidence to make a reliable estimate of cancellations, thereby allowing the recognition of revenue net of expected cancellations. If sufficient history does not exist, no revenue should be recognized until the 30-day full refund period has lapsed. The revenue would then become fixed or determinable on a ratable basis until the customer has made six payments.

Exception—Regulators' Approval of Rate Increases

In some cases, a regulated company, such as a utility, is permitted to bill requested rate increases before the regulator has ruled on the request. The fact that the regulator has the power to deny the request raises a question about whether the increased rates are fixed or determinable. The FASB addressed this question in the context of regulated businesses that are within the scope of FAS-71. The FASB concluded that, in these situations, contingent refundability should be treated as a collectibility issue, rather than a fixed or determinable issue. Thus, the criteria in paragraph 8 of FAS-5 would determine whether a provision for estimated refunds should be recognized (see "Collectibility" in this chapter).

Exception—Fees at Risk Due to Changes in Law or Regulation

When the third-party action that could change the arrangement fee is a change in a law or regulation, it is generally appropriate to predict no such changes. Thus, revenue would be recognized as if the current laws and regulations would continue. For example, FAS-109, *Accounting for Income Taxes,* in providing guidance on the effects of potential changes in tax law on income tax calculations, specifically prohibits the assumption of any changes until those changes are enacted into law. Similar analysis would generally be appropriate with respect to other changes in laws or regulations. However, if changes that would result in a reduced fee are considered probable, a reserve for refunds might be required under FAS-5.

Other Exceptions

Other exceptions to the general conclusion that the portion of a fee subject to change based on third-party actions is not fixed or determinable would be very rare. However, if the unique circumstances of the arrangement make it remote that the portion of the fee at risk will actually be lost, it may be possible to conclude that the fee is fixed or determinable, despite the existence of the contingency. Each situation should be addressed individually to determine whether this is the case.

ILLUSTRATION: FEE MAY VARY BASED ON THIRD-PARTY ACTIONS

Facts: Company X acts as a sales representative for Company Y. Company X's commission is earned on a sliding scale such that its commission on the first 10,000 units of Company Y's products sold in a year is $5 per unit, and the commission for each unit beyond that is $7 per unit. Company X has been selling Company Y's products for several years and has always sold at least 20,000 units. At the end of the first quarter, Company X has sold 5,000 units of Company Y's product, and collected $25,000 from Company Y. Company X believes that it will sell approximately 5,000 units per quarter for the rest of the year.

Discussion: Company X believes that it will eventually realize $120,000 in commissions during the year (10,000 units at $5, plus another 10,000 units at $7), an average of $6 per unit, and has historical experience that supports this estimate. Therefore, Company X may believe that it should record a receivable of $5,000 at the end of the first quarter, in addition to the revenue it has already collected. However, whether Company X meets its estimated sales is at least partially in control of third parties, that is, the customers who purchase Company Y's product. As such, the additional revenue is not fixed or determinable. Company X should therefore recognize only the $25,000 it has collected as revenue in the first quarter. Revenue attributable to additional sales should be recorded only when those sales occur.

Factors Based on an Index

Many leases have rent escalation clauses tied to the inflation rate or consumer price index. Certain arrangements to deliver commodities include fees that are based on the market price of the commodity at some particular point in time. These are just two examples of factors that may cause an arrangement fee to be variable that are not related to particular actions. In general, these factors are characterized by being out of any party's direct control.

> **PRACTICE ALERT:** These types of arrangements should be evaluated to determine whether a derivative is embedded in the sales arrangement. Some arrangements that are not derivatives in their entirety are embedded with features that have all three defining characteristics of a derivative. Depending on their nature and their relationship to the economics of the remainder of the arrangement, such embedded features may have to be accounted for separately, similar to a freestanding derivative. If that circumstance exists in a sales arrangement, the separated derivative is subject to all of the accounting requirements for a freestanding derivative, and the remaining host arrangement is accounted for based on the applicable revenue recognition principles. To the extent a sales arrangement contains fees that are affected by factors based on an index, FAS-133 should be consulted to determine whether the arrangement contains an embedded derivative and, if so, how that derivative should be accounted for.

Much like fees that vary based upon future actions of the vendor, the customer, or a third party, fees that vary based upon future changes in an index or other underlying may not be fixed or determinable, because it is not appropriate to recognize revenue based on predictions of future events. As discussed previously, there are cases in which it is permissible to recognize revenue based on predictions of future customer, seller, or third-party actions if a sufficient body of evidence exists such that reliable estimates can be made. It is generally not possible to have such evidence related to future changes in an index or other underlying. Therefore, revenue should be recognized in these situations based on the then-current measurement, assuming no future increases or decreases. The effects of changes in the index or underlying should be recognized as soon as such changes occur (FAS-13, par. 5n).

Fees Affected by Multiple Factors

Many arrangements have fees that can vary based on multiple factors, each of which may be in control of a different party or tied to a different index. In general, each factor should be evaluated separately, with revenue being recognized only if it is concluded that none of the factors preclude the fee from being considered fixed or determinable.

COLLECTIBILITY

The final condition that must be met before revenue is recognized is that collection of the fee must be reasonably assured. This condition gets to the heart of whether the fee in the arrangement is indeed

EXHIBIT 3-1
FIXED OR DETERMINABLE FEES

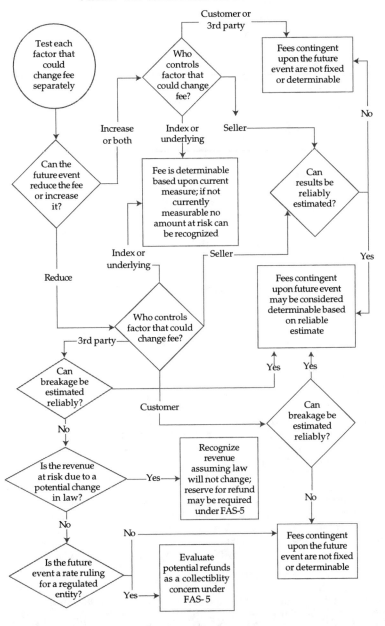

realizable. Clearly, if a fee is not collectible, no revenue should be recognized, as the company does not actually expect to benefit from the arrangement.

The accounting literature does not specify any particular criteria that should be used in evaluating whether collection is reasonably assured. However, the same factors that are evaluated when recording a bad debt reserve on accounts receivable should be useful in determining whether collection of an arrangement fee is reasonably assured. This evaluation should be performed when the other three conditions for revenue recognition are met.

Accounting If Collectibility Is Not Reasonably Assured

If collectibility is not reasonably assured at the time the other three revenue recognition conditions are met, revenue should not be recognized until collection becomes reasonably assured or occurs. In general, the direct costs of the transaction should be expensed as if revenue had been recognized. Because collection has been deemed less than reasonably assured, such costs generally would not meet the definition of an asset, and therefore should not be capitalized or remain on the balance sheet.[4]

EXAMPLE: COLLECTIBILITY NOT REASONABLY ASSURED

Covad Communications Form 10-K—Fiscal Year Ended December 31, 2004

Revenue Recognition

Revenues from recurring service are recognized when (i) persuasive evidence of an arrangement between the Company and the customer exists, (ii) service has been provided to the customer, (iii) the price to the customer is fixed or determinable, and (iv) collectibility of the sales prices is reasonably assured. If a customer is (i) experiencing financial difficulties, and (ii) is not current in making payments for the Company's services, or (iii) is essentially current in making payments but, subsequent to the end of the reporting period, the financial condition of such customer deteriorates significantly or such customer files for bankruptcy protection, then, based on this information, the Company may determine that the collectibility of revenues from this customer is not reasonably assured or its ability to retain some or all of the payments received from a customer that has filed for bankruptcy protection is not reasonably assured. Accordingly, the Company classifies this

---

[4]In rare circumstances, recognition of revenue and costs under the installment or cost recovery methods may be appropriate (APB-10, par. 12)—for example, if recovery of the value of the goods sold in a product sale is reasonably assured even though collectibility of the arrangement fee is not. However, the use of these methods is usually limited to sales of real estate (FAS-66, par. 22).

group of customers as "financially distressed" for revenue recognition purposes. Revenues from financially distressed customers are recognized when cash for the services to those customers is collected, assuming all other criteria for revenue recognition have been met, but only after the collection of all previous outstanding accounts receivable balances. Payments received from financially distressed customers during a defined period prior to their filing of petitions for bankruptcy protection are recorded in the consolidated balance sheets caption "Unearned revenues" if the Company's ability to retain these payments is not reasonably assured.

The Company has billing disputes with some of its customers. These disputes arise in the ordinary course of business in the telecommunications industry and their impact on the Company's accounts receivable and revenues can be reasonably estimated based on historical experience. In addition, certain revenues are subject to refund if the end-user terminates service within 30 days of service activation. Accordingly, the Company maintains allowances, through charges to revenues, based on the Company's estimates of (i) the ultimate resolution of the disputes and (ii) future service cancellations. The allowance for service credits and bad debts is calculated generally as a percentage, based on historical trends, of balances that meet certain criteria plus specific reserves for known disputes. As stated above, revenues from financially distressed customers are recognized when cash for the services to those customers is collected but only after the collection of all previous outstanding accounts receivable balances. Upon determining that a customer is financially distressed, the Company establishes an allowance, through a charge to bad debt expense, based on the outstanding balance of such customer.

Accounts receivable consisted of the following:

	December 31,	
	2004	2003
Gross accounts receivable	$31,607	$33,402
Allowance for service credits	(1,405)	(2,124)
Allowance for bad debts	(161)	(2,750)
Accounts receivable, net	$30,041	$28,528

The Company's accounts receivable valuation accounts were as follows:

	December 31,		
	2004	2003	2002
Allowance for service credits:			
Balance at beginning of period	$2,124	$2,077	$5,648
Provision	4,914	2,886	2,322

Write-offs	(5,136)	(1,557)	(3,748)
Recoveries	(497)	(1,282)	(2,145)
Balance at end of period	$1,405	$2,124	$2,077

Allowance for bad debts:

Balance at beginning of period	$2,750	$3,311	$2,835
Provision	487	275	3,812
Write-offs	(1,051)	(462)	(2,652)
Recoveries	(2,025)	(374)	(684)
Balance at end of period	$ 161	$2,750	$3,311

Wholesaler Financial Difficulties

During the years ended December 31, 2004, 2003 and 2002, the Company issued billings to its financially distressed customers aggregating $3,517, $5,139 and $42,881, respectively, that were not recognized as revenues or accounts receivable in the accompanying consolidated financial statements at the time of such billings. However, in accordance with the revenue recognition policy described above, the Company recognized revenues from certain of these customers when cash was collected aggregating $2,823, $4,367 and $47,609 during the years ended December 31, 2004, 2003 and 2002, respectively. Revenues from customers that filed for bankruptcy accounted for approximately 0.3%, 1.3% and 5.6% of the Company's total net revenues for the years ended December 31, 2004, 2003 and 2002, respectively. The Company had contractual receivables from its financially distressed customers totaling $1,317 and $1,093 as of December 31, 2004 and 2003, respectively, which are not reflected in the accompanying consolidated balance sheet as of such date. Although MCI filed for bankruptcy protection on July 21, 2002, the Company continued to recognize revenues from MCI on an accrual basis during 2002, 2003 and 2004 (MCI emerged from bankruptcy in April 2004) based on its specific facts and circumstances in relation to the revenue recognition criteria described above. Consequently, the amounts in this paragraph related to financially distressed customers exclude amounts pertaining to MCI.

The Company has obtained persuasive evidence indicating that the financial condition of one of its customers, which was designated as financially distressed in 2000, improved significantly during the year ended December 31, 2002, principally as a result of a capital infusion during this period. Consequently, the Company concluded that collection of its billings to this customer was now reasonably assured. Therefore, the Company resumed the recognition of revenues from this customer on an accrual basis during 2002, which resulted in the recognition of revenues in the amount of approximately $1,542 that relate to services rendered in periods ended prior to January 1, 2002. Similarly, the Company resumed the recognition of revenue on an accrual basis for another wholesale customer in 2002. The Company did not, however, recognize additional revenue from services rendered in prior periods because this customer was current in its payments. No similar amounts were recognized during the other periods reported in the accompanying consolidated financial statements.

The Company has identified certain of its customers who were essentially current in their payments for the Company's services prior to December 31, 2004, or have subsequently paid all or significant portions of the respective amounts that the Company recorded as accounts receivable as of December 31, 2004, that the Company believes may be at risk of becoming financially distressed. Revenues from these customers accounted for approximately 7.7%, 11.6% and 34.6% of the Company's total net revenues for the years ended December 31, 2004, 2003 and 2002, respectively. As of December 31, 2004, receivables from these customers comprised 8.8% of the Company's gross accounts receivable balance. If these customers are unable to demonstrate their ability to pay for the company's services in a timely manner in periods ending subsequent to 2004, revenue from such customers will only be recognized when cash is collected, as described above.

Uncollectible Amounts and Bad Debts

It is important that collectibility be evaluated before revenue is initially recognized so that collectibility problems existing before revenue recognition can be separated from similar problems that arise later. If collection is reasonably assured initially, allowing revenue to be recognized, and later events create the need for an accounts receivable reserve or write-off, the related expense should be reported as bad debt expense, which may be classified in various places in the income statement (see Chapter 11, "Presentation").

EVALUATING THE REVENUE RECOGNITION CONDITIONS

Arrangement-by-Arrangement Analysis

In evaluating whether the four conditions discussed in this chapter are met, it is important that all aspects of the arrangement be considered. To do this properly, the contracts underlying the arrangement should be reviewed in full to ensure that all contractual terms are properly considered. For most companies, this review should begin with the company's standard sales contracts. However, any modifications to the standard contract must also be evaluated for their effects on revenue recognition. Modifications from the standard contract could very well require a company to recognize revenue differently for different contracts. For example, if a company sells products with different FOB terms, revenue on those shipped FOB Shipping Point may generally be recognized upon shipment, while revenue on those shipped FOB Destination may not be recognized until the customer receives the products. Similarly, different customer acceptance provisions or cancellation rights in various contracts may cause otherwise similar contracts to be accounted for differently.

> ☞ **PRACTICE POINTER:**   Many provisions can affect the timing of revenue recognition. Companies should therefore have controls in place to limit the types of provisions that sales personnel agree to add to the standard contract. In addition, controls should be in place to ensure that all sales contracts are reviewed by accounting personnel who can appropriately evaluate whether any non-standard terms in the contract should affect revenue recognition.

All Contractual Terms Must Be Considered

Some companies may use contracts that contain terms generally ignored in practice, despite their inclusion in the contract. For example, a contract may provide a customer with the right to have an equipment vendor's engineering staff on-site for a limited period of time after installation of the equipment. However, as long as installation goes smoothly, customers typically may not take advantage of this right. In other situations, an arrangement may provide the customer with the right to a certain amount of service, but history may show that customers, on average, do not use the maximum amount of service to which they are entitled. This is the case in wireless telephone plans that include a basket of monthly minutes.

In most situations, delivery should be evaluated under the assumption that the vendor will have to fulfill all of its obligations under the arrangement, including those that are only to be performed if requested by the customer. However, if the company has significant historical experience with a large volume of homogeneous contracts that include similar terms, and that experience allows the company to reliably estimate breakage, it is acceptable to recognize revenue assuming that such breakage will occur. It is important to note that there must be significant objective evidence available to support a conclusion that obligations will not have to be fulfilled. It is rare that a company will have such evidence.

> **SEC REGISTRANT ALERT:**   In a December 2002 speech, the SEC staff discussed the issue of breakage as it arises in situations where customers prepay, on a nonrefundable basis, for services or goods that they ultimately do not demand. The SEC

staff observed that FAS-140 requires either performance or legal release to extinguish a liability. The prepayment for future delivery of services or goods creates a liability. Following a FAS-140 approach would result in no recognition of income for products or services paid for, but not demanded by the customer, until the end (or expiration) of the performance period. Alternatively, the SEC staff indicated that they will not object to revenue recognition prior to the expiration of the performance period provided both the following conditions exist:

1. Management can demonstrate that the demand for future performance is remote based on a large population of homogeneous transactions; and

2. There is objective reliable historical evidence supporting the estimate of breakage.

The SEC staff also indicated that (a) it would be skeptical of an accounting model that results in immediate income for breakage and (b) whether breakage represents revenue or a gain (i.e., other income) depends on the facts and circumstances.

Even if sufficient evidence exists to estimate breakage, it should be an extremely rare occurrence where consideration of breakage results in immediate income recognition. Instead, the arrangement fee should be recognized based on the products or services expected to be delivered to the customer over the performance period. For example, consider a situation in which a customer prepays $10,000 for 100 hours of professional services to be provided over the course of one year, but the professional services provider has sufficient history and experience demonstrating that the customer will ultimately demand only 80 hours of professional services over the performance period. In this situation, the professional services provider may adopt an accounting policy that would result in recognizing the $10,000 of revenue over the 80 hours of services expected to be provided as they are rendered—$125 per hour of service rendered. Alternatively, the professional services provider may adopt an accounting policy that would result in recognizing $8,000 of revenue over the 80 hours of services expected to be provided as they are rendered and recognizing $2,000 of breakage income upon expiration of the arrangement. However, the professional services provider may not adopt an accounting policy that would result in recognizing $2,000 of breakage income upon initiation of the arrangement and $8,000 of revenue over the 80 hours of services expected to be provided as they are rendered. To do so would be to recognize revenue before performance has occurred.

EXAMPLE: RELIABLE ESTIMATE OF BREAKAGE

Learning Tree International, Inc. Form 10-K—Fiscal Year Ended September 30, 2004

The Company offers its customers a multiple-course sales discount referred to as a "Training Passport." A Training Passport allows an individual passport holder to attend up to a specified number of the Company's courses over a one-year period for a fixed price. For a Training Passport, the amount of revenue recognized for each attendance in one of the Company's courses is based upon the selling price of the Training Passport, the list price of the course taken and the estimated average number of courses passport holders will actually attend. Upon expiration of a Training Passport, the Company records the difference, if any, between the revenues previously recognized and the Training Passport selling price. The estimated attendance rate is based upon the historical experience of the average actual number of course events that Training Passport holders have been attending. The average actual attendance rate for all expired Training Passports has closely approximated the estimated rate utilized by the Company. If the Training Passport attendance rates change, the revenue recognition rate for all active Training Passports and for all Training Passports sold thereafter is adjusted. The Company believes it is appropriate to recognize revenues on this basis in order to most closely match revenue and related costs, as the substantial majority of its Passport holders do not attend the maximum number of course events permitted under their Training Passport. The Company believes that the use of historical data is reasonable and appropriate because of the relative stability of the average actual number of course events attended by the tens of thousands of Passport holders since the inception of the program in fiscal 1993. Although the Company has seen no material changes in the historical rates as the number of course titles has changed, it monitors such potential effects. In general, determining the estimated average number of course events that will be attended by a Training Passport holder is based on historical trends that may not continue in the future. These estimates could differ in the near term from amounts used in arriving at the reported revenue.

Multiple Contracts and Side Letters

Most of the time, the boundaries of an arrangement are clear, and are defined by the contract between the parties. However, to ensure that all appropriate terms are considered in recognition of revenue for an arrangement or deliverable, it may be necessary to consider multiple contracts as part of a single arrangement. For example, a contract for the sale of products may not lay out any rights of return. However, a master supply agreement with the same customer may grant that customer significant return rights on all purchases.

In other situations, a company may enter into a side letter with the customer that effectively amends the contract between the parties by granting the customer additional rights, requiring the seller to provide additional products or services, or altering the payment terms. Obviously, any revenue accounting that does not consider such a side letter would likely reflect incorrect conclusions.

> **SEC REGISTRANT ALERT:**   In early 2003, the SEC staff issued the Report Pursuant to Section 704 of the Sarbanes-Oxley Act of 2002 (the Section 704 Report). In compiling the information in the Section 704 Report, the SEC staff studied enforcement actions filed during the period July 31, 1997, through July 30, 2002. The greatest number of enforcement actions brought by the SEC related to improper revenue recognition. A common theme in these enforcement actions related to the existence of side letters that were not considered, or inappropriately considered, in recognizing revenue. This is a strong indication that more attention should be given to uncovering the existence and understanding the terms of side agreements and the effects they have on revenue recognition.

Further guidance on combining contracts for revenue recognition purposes, including factors that should be considered in deciding whether to combine contracts, is included in Chapter 4, "Multiple-Element Arrangements."

Non-Contractual Terms

Although all of the rights and obligations of both parties to a revenue arrangement are often contractually documented, there are other situations in which rights and obligations are established by common business practice, local law, or custom. For example, rights of return are often not specifically documented in a sales arrangement, but are often accepted for a limited time if the customer is not satisfied. Similarly, even products that are not covered by a written warranty will often be replaced or repaired by the seller if they do not function properly. All such rights and obligations should be considered in the recognition of revenue.

CHAPTER 4
MULTIPLE-ELEMENT ARRANGEMENTS

CONTENTS

BACKGROUND

Many sales arrangements involve the seller taking on multiple obligations. These obligations could include any combination of obligations to deliver products, perform services, grant licenses or other rights, or take (or refrain from taking) certain actions. Arrangements involving multiple seller obligations or deliverables are generally referred to as "multiple-element arrangements." The term refers to arrangements as simple as the sale of a shirt and pants (two product deliverables) to complex arrangements such as an arrangement to design and install a computer network, which might involve the delivery of hardware, software, and electronic products, or the performance of design and installation services, or the granting of licenses to use software and patented processes.

Accounting for multiple-element arrangements presents accounting issues incremental to the issues that exist in a single-element arrangement. Key among these issues is whether, and if so, how, to allocate the arrangement consideration among the various deliverables.

SURVEY OF ACCOUNTING LITERATURE

Various pieces of industry- and transaction-specific literature include guidance on accounting for multiple-element arrangements that fall within the scope of that literature. In addition, the EITF provided more broadly applicable multiple-element arrangement guidance in EITF 00-21 that was effective during 2003. All of these pieces of literature rely on similar underlying principles for determining whether deliverables in a multiple-element arrangement should be treated separately for accounting purposes. The interaction of EITF 00-21 with higher-level authoritative literature that provides multiple-element arrangement guidance is discussed later in this chapter.

LISTING OF APPLICABLE LITERATURE

CON-5	Recognition and Measurement in Financial Statements of Business Enterprises
CON-6	Elements of Financial Statements
FAS-5	Accounting for Contingencies
FAS-13	Accounting for Leases
FAS-45	Accounting for Franchise Fee Revenue
FAS-48	Revenue Recognition When Right of Return Exists
FAS-66	Accounting for Sales of Real Estate
FAS-133	Accounting for Derivative Instruments and Hedging Activities
FIN-45	Guarantor's Accounting and Disclosure Requirements for Guarantees, Including Indirect Guarantees of Indebtedness of Others, an interpretation of FASB Statements No. 5, 57, and 107 and rescission of FASB Interpretation No. 34
FSP FIN 45-1	Accounting for Intellectual Property Infringement Indemnifications under FASB Interpretation No. 45, *Guarantor's Accounting and Disclosure Requirements for Guarantees, Including Indirect Guarantees of Indebtedness of Others*

FSP FIN 45-2	Whether FASB Interpretation No. 45, *Guarantor's Accounting and Disclosure Requirements for Guarantees, Including Indirect Guarantees of Indebtedness of Others*, Provides Support for Subsequently Accounting for a Guarantor's Liability at Fair Value
FAS-133 Guide	Guide to Implementation of Statement 133 on Accounting for Derivative Instruments and Hedging Activities
SOP 81-1	Accounting for Performance of Construction-Type and Certain Production-Type Contracts
SOP 97-2	Software Revenue Recognition
SOP 00-2	Accounting by Producers or Distributors of Films
EITF 85-20	Recognition of Fees for Guaranteeing a Loan
EITF 00-21	Revenue Arrangements with Multiple Deliverables
EITF 01-8	Determining Whether an Arrangement Contains a Lease
EITF 03-5	Applicability of AICPA Statement of Position 97-2 to Non-Software Deliverables in an Arrangement Containing More-Than-Incidental Software
SAB Topic 13	Revenue Recognition
TPA 5100.39	Software Revenue Recognition for Multiple-Element Arrangements

OVERVIEW

CON-5 sets forth the guidance that revenue should be recognized when it is both realized or realizable and earned. In discussing the "earned" criterion, CON-5 goes on to say, ". . . revenues are considered to have been earned when the entity has substantially accomplished what it must do to be entitled to the benefits represented by the revenues" (CON-5, par. 83b). When an arrangement includes multiple elements, applying this concept is not easy. One theory might be that all revenue from the entire multiple-element arrangement should be recognized when the company has substantially completed all of its obligations. Under that theory, revenue recognition for a multiple-element arrangement would be an "all-or-nothing" proposition, and would not take into account completion of one or more elements until substantially all of them were completed.

The accounting literature regarding multiple-element arrangements does not take such a narrow approach. Rather, the accounting literature recognizes that each element of a multiple-element arrangement may represent a separate earnings process, such that delivery of that item provides the customer with value, even if there are other items still to be delivered as part of the same arrangement. If an individual element represents a separate earnings process, it should generally be accounted for separately, provided that the arrangement consideration can be allocated to the individual elements. The accounting literature provides specific conditions that must be met to account for an individual element separately, including a condition related to allocation of arrangement consideration. These conditions are discussed at length later in this chapter.

This chapter focuses on determining whether a multiple-element arrangement should be separated for accounting purposes and, if so, how the arrangement consideration should be allocated to the delivered elements.

DEFINING THE ARRANGEMENT

To appropriately apply the concepts related to accounting for multiple-element arrangements, it is first necessary to define the arrangement. Most of the time, the boundaries of an arrangement are clear, and are defined by the contract between the parties. However, to ap-propriately allocate revenue between various elements and to evaluate the interactions that elements may have with each other, it is sometimes necessary to combine contracts into a single arrangement. That is particularly important because there are times in which the inclusion or exclusion of a certain element within an arrangement can significantly affect the accounting for the other elements of the arrangement (for example, one undelivered element for which objective evidence of fair value does not exist prohibits recognition of revenue upon delivery of other elements). Thus, it is important to properly identify the entire arrangement that should be analyzed as a multiple-element arrangement.

Like most things in accounting, the substance of an arrangement is more important than its form. Putting different elements of an arrangement into multiple contracts rather than one should not change the accounting for the arrangement. Therefore, if different elements are documented in multiple contracts that are part of the same arrangement, the combination of all of the contracts must be evaluated as one multiple-element arrangement. When determining whether multiple contracts should be accounted for as a single arrangement, judgment is required. Generally, separate contracts with the same entity or related parties that are entered into at or near the same time are presumed to have been negotiated as a package and should therefore be evaluated as a single arrangement (EITF 00-21, par. 2).

The accounting literature provides guidance related to when it is appropriate to combine certain types of contracts. For example, in the FAS-133 Guide, Question K1 deals with determining when separate contracts must be combined for purposes of applying the derivatives literature. In addition, the AICPA has issued TPA 5100.39 regarding combining revenue-generating contracts for purposes of applying the multiple-element guidance in the software revenue recognition literature (see Chapter 10, "Software—A Complete Model"). Combining the guidance from each of these sources provides a good listing of indicators that should be considered in determining whether separate contracts should be combined and evaluated as one multiple-element arrangement:

1. The contracts or agreements were negotiated or executed within a short time frame of each other or in contemplation of each other (TPA 5100.39; and FAS-133 Guide, Question K-1).

2. The contracts are with the same customer (or affiliates of each other) (FAS-133 Guide, Question K-1).

3. The contracts relate to the same elements, or what is, in essence, the same project (TPA 5100.39; and FAS-133 Guide, Question K-1).

4. The different elements are closely interrelated or interdependent in terms of design, technology, or function (TPA 5100.39).

5. The fee for one or more contracts or agreements is subject to refund or forfeiture or other concession if another contract is not satisfactorily completed (TPA 5100.39).

6. One or more elements in one contract or agreement are essential to the functionality of an element in another contract (TPA 5100.39).

7. Payment terms under one contract or agreement coincide with performance criteria of another contract or agreement (TPA 5100.39).

The point of this exercise is to determine if multiple contracts with various elements should be combined and evaluated as one multiple-element arrangement. The next section of this chapter discusses the conditions that must be met to treat individual deliverables within a multiple-element arrangement as separate deliverables for accounting purposes (regardless of whether those individual deliverables are all contained within one contract or spread among multiple contracts that were combined in accordance with the guidance above).

ILLUSTRATION: EVALUATING MULTIPLE CONTRACTS

EXAMPLE 1

Facts: Company G manufactures and sells computer printers. These printers use a proprietary ink cartridge design, such that the cartridges cannot be provided by any other manufacturer. The printers are sold by retailers for $100 each and the ink cartridges sell for $40 each. When a printer is sold, it includes one cartridge. Company G's printers and ink cartridges are readily available from retail distributors of Company G's products. Company G enters into a contract to supply a customer with 100 printers for $80 each. Six months later, Company G signs a contract with the same customer to provide ink cartridges for the printers on an as-needed basis for $30 each for two years.

Discussion: A review of the indicators described above shows that indicators 2, 3, 4, and 6 suggest that the contracts should be combined. However, indicators 5 and 7 do not exist, and it is not clear whether indicator 1 exists. Additional factors that Company G should consider include the fact that ink cartridges can be purchased by the customer from parties other than Company G, and the fact that Company G routinely sells printers and ink cartridges separate from each other. In this situation, Company G would likely conclude that the arrangement for the sale of printers and the arrangement for the sale of ink cartridges should not be combined. However, a slight change in the facts (for example, if the arrangements were signed less than 1 month apart) might change that conclusion.

EXAMPLE 2

Facts: Company R owns the rights to a proprietary chemical compound used to make various products. It licenses the right to use the compound in a particular product line to a customer for three years, which is the remaining life of the patent on the compound. However, Company R does not provide the customer with a license to manufacture the proprietary compound or have it manufactured—Company R maintains those rights exclusively until the patent expires. The customer will be responsible for developing the product and marketing it. An initial payment under the license is due at signing, with further payments due ratably over the term of the license. In a separate contract, contemplated at the time of the license, but negotiated and signed three months later, Company R agrees to supply the chemical compound to this customer at market prices for three years.

Discussion: A review of the indicators described above shows that indicators 1, 2, 3, 4, 6, and 7 suggest that the contracts should be combined, and indicator 5 does not exist. In this case, Company R would likely conclude that the two contracts should be combined and evaluated as one arrangement for revenue recognition purposes.

DELIVERABLES

Once the scope of the arrangement has been determined, the vendor must identify all of the deliverables in the arrangement. This step is necessary because each deliverable must be evaluated to determine whether it should be treated separately or combined with other deliverables for purposes of revenue recognition. After this determination has been made, a deliverable will qualify for separate revenue recognition treatment only if specific criteria indicate that the deliverable represents a separable earnings process.

What makes this analysis difficult is that the accounting literature does not define "deliverable"; however, the term generally has been interpreted as any performance obligation on the part of the seller. Therefore, obligations to perform services, grant licenses, provide products, etc., are all considered deliverables.

The absence of a definition means that considerable judgment is required to identify a deliverable and, in effect, separate it from other deliverables in the arrangement. For example, in an arrangement involving the sale of a specialized product, the vendor may promise not to sell a similar product to any of the customer's competitors. It is not clear whether the exclusivity provision is a separate deliverable apart from the product deliverable. Similarly, a company licensing its technology may explicitly agree to assist the customer in patent infringement allegations from third parties. In this case, it is not clear that the obligation to assist a customer in legal defense should be considered a deliverable independent of the licensing deliverable.

In addition to the problem of drawing a distinction between deliverables, the lack of a definition also suggests that two vendors may differ in their identification of deliverables in an arrangement. The conditions that must be met to treat deliverables separately for revenue recognition purposes, however, should minimize the effects of potentially different conclusions about the number of deliverables in an arrangement.

Once each deliverable is identified, the appropriate recognition principles (as discussed in other chapters of this book) should be used to determine when revenue would be recognized related to that deliverable **if** it were the only deliverable in the arrangement. At the point in time that revenue on a deliverable would be recognized **if** it were the only deliverable in the arrangement, the company must determine whether the existence of the undelivered items in the arrangement precludes recognition of that revenue. In other words, each of the deliverables in the arrangement must be evaluated to determine whether it should be treated as a separate deliverable for accounting purposes or bundled together with other deliverables in the multiple-element arrangement for accounting purposes at the inception of the arrangement and as each item in the arrangement is delivered (EITF 00-21, par. 8).

SEPARATING MULTIPLE-ELEMENT ARRANGEMENTS

Determining the Model to Apply

The goal of EITF 00-21 is to provide a model that can be applied broadly to multiple-element arrangements for the purpose of dividing those arrangements into individual units of accounting.

However, other pieces of authoritative literature that address specific transactions provide models for separating those transactions into units of accounting. Many of these pieces of authoritative literature are in a higher category of the GAAP hierarchy (see Exhibit 2-1 in Chapter 2, "A Brief Survey of Revenue-Related Literature") than EITF 00-21, and therefore must be followed to the extent they apply. For example, SOP 97-2, SOP 81-1, and FAS-13 all provide guidance related to separating multiple-element arrangements that fall within their scope. Each of these pieces of literature is higher-level GAAP than EITF 00-21. Thus, if an entire multiple-element arrangement falls within the scope of one of these pieces of such higher-level literature, the guidance in that literature related to separating multiple-element arrangements should be applied to that arrangement. The real question arises, however, when some elements in a multiple-element arrangement fall within the scope of higher-level literature that provides guidance on separating multiple-element arrangements and other elements in the arrangement do not fall within the scope of higher-level literature. The model that should be used in these situations depends on the nature of the elements involved, the related higher-level literature, and whether that literature is silent on separating multiple-element arrangements where one or more, but not all, of the elements fall within its scope.

> **PRACTICE ALERT:** Separation guidance in higher-level literature applies only when there are elements in the arrangement that fall within the scope of that literature—in other words, such literature cannot be applied by analogy in place of following the guidance in EITF 00-21. In addition, certain pieces of literature include separation guidance that applies to the separation of multiple elements that are each within the scope of that literature, but does not apply to the separation of elements within the scope of that literature and elements that are outside the scope of that literature. For these reasons, it is important to analyze whether elements fall within the scope of a particular piece of higher-level literature. In some cases, the scope of the higher-level literature is clear; in other cases, it is not. The EITF has provided guidance on the scope of two pieces of the higher-level literature that contain separation guidance. Specifically, the scope of SOP 97-2 is discussed in EITF 03-5 (see Chapter 10, "Software—A Complete Model") and the scope of FAS-13 is discussed in EITF 01-8 (see Chapter 3, "General Principles").

Higher-Level Literature Provides Separation Guidance That Applies to Entire Arrangement

If the higher-level literature includes guidance on separating multiple-element arrangements where one or more, but not all, of the elements in the arrangement fall within its scope, then the separation guidance in that higher-level literature should be applied to the entire multiple-element arrangement. In some cases, the higher-level literature provides guidance on both when to separate and how to allocate consideration among the elements in the arrangement. In these situations, the higher-level literature should be applied to determine whether the elements inside and outside its scope should be separated and, if so, how the arrangement consideration should be allocated (EITF 00-21, par. 4(a)(i)). This results in EITF 00-21's guidance not being applied to the arrangement at all.

In other cases, the higher-level literature provides guidance on when to separate elements but does not provide arrangement consideration allocation guidance. In these situations, the higher-level literature should be applied to determine whether the elements inside and outside its scope should be separated. If the elements should be separated, for purposes of allocating arrangement consideration, the relative fair value method must be used. Fair values for the elements in these situations must be determined and should be determined based on the best estimate of fair value available (EITF 00-21, par. 4(a)(ii)). In other words, the residual method should not be used based on an unavailability of sufficient fair value evidence (as is the case in certain circumstances under EITF 00-21 as discussed later in this chapter).

An example of higher-level literature that provides both separation and allocation guidance is FIN-45. FIN-45 requires that if a guarantee or indemnification that falls within the scope of its initial recognition and measurement provisions is part of a multiple-element arrangement that includes elements outside its scope, then the guarantee or indemnification should be treated as a separate element and measured initially at its fair value (for additional discussion related to FIN-45, see "Guarantees and Indemnifications in Multiple-Element Arrangements" later in this chapter). In this situation, FIN-45 requires (a) separation of the guarantee or indemnification and (b) allocation of a defined amount (i.e., fair value) to the guarantee or indemnification.

> **OBSERVATION:** A question may arise regarding the interaction of the initial recognition and measurement guidance in FIN-45 and the allocation guidance in EITF 00-21. See the Observation in the "Noncontingent Liability" section of this chapter for additional information.

An example of higher-level literature that provides separation, but not allocation, guidance is FAS-13. FAS-13 requires that if elements that fall within its scope (e.g., lease, maintenance of leased equipment) are part of a multiple-element arrangement that includes elements outside its scope, then the FAS-13 elements must be separated from the non-FAS-13 elements. However, FAS-13 does not specify how the arrangement consideration should be allocated to the FAS-13 and non-FAS-13 elements. In this situation, the arrangement consideration should be allocated between the FAS-13 elements and the non-FAS-13 elements using the relative fair value method.

EXAMPLE: FAS-13 AND NON-FAS-13 DELIVERABLES

Excerpts from the Xerox Corporation Annual Report—Fiscal Year Ended December 31, 2004

Revenue Recognition under Bundled Arrangements: We sell most of our products and services under bundled lease arrangements, which typically include equipment, service, supplies, and financing components for which the customer pays a single negotiated fixed minimum monthly payment for all elements over the contractual lease term.

Revenues under bundled arrangements are allocated considering the relative fair values of the lease and non-lease deliverables included in the bundled arrangement based upon the estimated relative fair values of each element. Lease deliverables include maintenance and executory costs, equipment and financing, while non-lease deliverables generally consist of the supplies and non-maintenance services.

Once the elements that fall within the scope of the higher-level literature have been separated from the elements that do not fall within the scope of the higher-level literature:

- Further separation of the elements within the scope of the higher-level literature is governed by the multiple-element arrangement model within that literature; and

- Further separation of the elements not within the scope of the higher-level literature is governed by EITF 00-21.

Higher-Level Literature Does Not Provide Separation Guidance That Applies to Elements Outside Its Scope

If the higher-level literature is silent on whether elements in a multiple-element arrangement that fall within its scope and elements in the multiple-element arrangement that fall outside its scope should be separated, the guidance in EITF 00-21 should be followed for purposes of separating the elements into those that fall within the scope of the higher-level literature and those that do not fall within the scope of the higher-level literature (EITF 00-21, par. 4(a)(iii)). For example, SOP 97-2 provides guidance related to separating multiple-element arrangements that fall within its scope (i.e., arrangements that include software and software-related elements). However, SOP 97-2 does not provide guidance related to separating multiple-element arrangements that contain elements that fall outside its scope (e.g., hardware where the software is not essential to the hardware's functionality). In this situation, the guidance in EITF 00-21 should be used to separate the elements into the SOP 97-2 elements and the non-SOP 97-2 elements. This approach should be followed in other situations where the higher-level authoritative literature is silent on whether and/or how the elements that fall within its scope and those that fall outside its scope should be separated (e.g., arrangements where one or more elements fall within the scope of SOP 81-1 and one or more elements fall outside the scope of SOP 81-1).

> **PRACTICE ALERT:** The multiple-element arrangement model that should be used in determining whether a multiple-element arrangement including software should be separated for accounting purposes depends on (a) whether the software involves significant production, modification, or customization and (b) whether some or all of the other elements in the arrangement are software-related. Depending on the nature of the elements in the arrangement, it may be appropriate to initially apply either the EITF 00-21 multiple-element arrangement model, the SOP 97-2 multiple-element arrangement model, or the SOP 81-1 multiple-element arrangement model. Given the differences in these models, care should be exercised in determining the appropriate model to apply. See Chapter 10, "Software-A Complete Model," for a detailed discussion of this subject.

If the elements that fall within the scope of the higher-level literature should be separated from the elements that do not fall within the scope of the higher-level literature based on applying the guidance in EITF 00-21:

- Further separation of the elements within the scope of the higher level literature is governed by the multiple-element arrangement model within that literature; and

- Further separation of the elements outside the scope of the higher-level literature is governed by the multiple-element arrangement model in EITF 00-21.

Continuing with the SOP 97-2 example from above, further separation of the SOP 97-2 elements should be based on the multiple-element arrangement guidance in SOP 97-2 and further separation of the non-SOP 97-2 elements should be based on the guidance in EITF 00-21.

If the elements that fall within the scope of the higher-level literature should not be separated from the elements that do not fall within the scope of the higher-level literature based on applying the guidance in EITF 00-21, then the elements should not be separated and the appropriate recognition of revenue would be based on the bundled group of deliverables (EITF 00-21, par. 10).

Other EITF 00-21 Scope Considerations

Other EITF 00-21 scope considerations relate to certain offers made by vendors to their customers. Specifically, the following types of vendor offers are excluded from the scope of EITF 00-21:

- Those involving free or discounted products or services to be delivered at a future date, or a rebate or refund of a determinable cash amount, if the customer reaches a predefined threshold of cumulative revenue transactions with the vendor or continues to be a customer of the vendor for a predefined period of time.

- Those related to point and loyalty programs (regardless of whether the vendor is the program operator) (EITF 00-21, 4(b)).

The scope exclusion for these types of vendor offers means that companies are not required to follow the provisions of EITF 00-21. However, as discussed in Chapter 8, "Miscellaneous Issues," a company is not precluded from adopting the provisions of EITF 00-21 as its accounting policy for these types of offers.

Basic Model

Two basic concerns are raised by the existence of multiple deliverables in an arrangement. The first is that the customer might not receive value from the delivery of a particular item because the delivered item works together with one of the other items in the arrangement not yet delivered. The second is that, because the arrangement fee was negotiated based on the entire package of deliverables in the contract, rather than deliverable-by-deliverable, it may not be clear how much revenue to allocate to a particular deliverable. Of course, both of these concerns are rendered moot once all deliverables included in the arrangement have been delivered. Therefore, the allocation of revenue to the various deliverables in an arrangement is only important if some of the items will be delivered before others.

Because the added concerns in a multiple-element arrangement relate to the relationship between the delivered and undelivered items, the accounting analysis focuses on that relationship. Specifically, the analysis is designed to determine whether the interrelationship between the delivered and undelivered items prevents either (1) the customer from having full use of the delivered item or (2) the vendor from properly allocating the arrangement fee to the delivered items. In order to appropriately address those concerns, a delivered item(s) should be considered a separate deliverable for accounting purposes only if all of the following conditions are met (EITF 00-21, par. 9):

1. The delivered item(s) has value to the customer on a standalone basis. That item(s) has value on a standalone basis if it is sold separately by any vendor or the customer could resell the delivered item on a standalone basis. The satisfaction of this condition is not dependent on there being an observable market for the deliverable being analyzed.

2. There is objective and reliable evidence of the fair value of the undelivered item(s).

3. If the arrangement includes a general right of return related to the delivered item, delivery or performance of the undelivered item(s) is considered probable and substantially in the control of the vendor.

The first condition applies only to delivered items whereas the second and third conditions apply only to undelivered items. Consider an arrangement in which both the delivered and undelivered elements have standalone value and delivery of the undelivered element is in the control of the vendor (i.e., the third condition of EITF 00-21, par. 9, also is met). Furthermore, assume that there is objective and reliable evidence of fair value (OREFV) for all the elements in the arrangement. In such an arrangement, the elements must be separated for accounting purposes.

Alternatively, assume that the vendor does not have OREFV for the delivered item. This does not hinder its separation from the undelivered element(s) for which there is OREFV. If the order of delivery were reversed in this arrangement, however, the elements could not be separated because there would be no OREFV of the undelivered element. Note that the vendor does not have the option of bundling deliverables for accounting purposes if those deliverables meet all of the separation conditions of EITF 00-21, par. 9.

EXAMPLE: BASIC MODEL

Affymetrix Inc. Form 10-K—Fiscal Year Ended December 31, 2004

The Company derives the majority of its revenue from product sales of GeneChip® probe arrays, reagents, and related instrumentation that may be sold individually or combined with any of the product or product related revenue items listed below. When a sale combines multiple elements, the Company accounts for multiple element arrangements under Emerging Issues Task Force Issue No. 00-21 ("EITF 00-21"), "Revenue Arrangements with Multiple Deliverables."

EITF 00-21 provides guidance on accounting for arrangements that involve the delivery or performance of multiple products, services and/or rights to use assets. In accordance with EITF 00-21, the Company allocates revenue for transactions or collaborations that include multiple elements to each unit of accounting based on its relative fair value, and recognizes revenue for each unit of accounting when the revenue recognition criteria have been met. The price charged when the element is sold separately generally determines fair value. In the absence of fair value of a delivered element, the Company allocates revenue first to the fair value of the undelivered elements and the residual revenue to the delivered elements. The Company recognizes revenue for delivered elements when the delivered elements have standalone value and the Company has objective and reliable evidence of fair value for each undelivered element. If the fair value of any undelivered element included in a multiple element arrangement cannot be objectively determined, revenue is deferred until all elements are delivered and services have been performed, or until fair value can objectively be determined for any remaining undelivered elements.

Product Related Revenue

Product related revenue includes subscription fees earned under GeneChip® array access programs; license fees; milestones and royalties earned from collaborative product development and supply agreements; equipment service revenue; product related scientific services revenue; and revenue from custom probe array design fees.

The identification of the deliverables in an arrangement should be initially performed at the inception of the arrangement. At that time, an initial analysis of the deliverables can be completed to determine whether each of the conditions of the model will be met when certain items are delivered. However, the final determination of whether a deliverable may be treated separately for accounting purposes should be made at the time revenue on that item would otherwise be recognizable, aside from the concerns raised by the existence of the undelivered items. Thus, as each item is delivered, the vendor in a multiple-element arrangement should review the conditions based on the status of the arrangement at that time (EITF 00-21, par. 8).

> **DISCLOSURE ALERT:** See Chapter 12, "Disclosures," for information about required disclosures.

> **SEC REGISTRANT ALERT:** In early 2003, the SEC staff issued the Report Pursuant to Section 704 of the Sarbanes-Oxley Act of 2002 (the Section 704 Report). In compiling the information in the Section 704 Report, the SEC staff studied enforcement actions filed during the period July 31, 1997, through July 30, 2002. The greatest number of enforcement actions brought by the SEC related to improper revenue recognition. One of the common revenue recognition issues highlighted in the Section 704 Report related to improper recognition of revenue from multiple-element arrangements or bundled contracts. One of the two actions discussed in the Section 704 Report in this regard involved improper allocation of arrangement consideration, and the other involved improper separation of interdependent elements. This finding is a strong indication that more

attention should be given to accounting for multiple-element arrangements.

In addition, in early 2003, the SEC staff issued the Summary by the Division of Corporation Finance of Significant Issues Addressed in the Review of the Periodic Reports of the Fortune 500 Companies (the Fortune 500 Report). This report resulted from the SEC's Division of Corporation Finance's (Corp Fin) review of all annual reports filed by Fortune 500 companies. The report provides insight into areas commonly questioned by Corp Fin during its reviews of annual reports. One area specifically mentioned in the Fortune 500 Report relates to accounting for multiple-element arrangements. Corp Fin specifically indicated that companies in the computer software, computer services, computer hardware, and communications equipment industries could improve their disclosures by expanding the discussion related to multiple-element arrangements.

Standalone Value to the Customer

In some arrangements, some or all of the deliverables do not have value to the customer on a standalone basis. To account for a delivered item as a separate deliverable, that delivered item must have value to the customer on a standalone basis (EITF 00-21, par. 9a). An item has value to the customer on a standalone basis if it is sold separately by any vendor or the customer could resell the deliverable on a standalone basis (EITF 00-21, par. 9a).

Significant judgment is necessary in evaluating whether delivered elements have value to the customer on a standalone basis and, more specifically, in evaluating whether the item being sold by a company is sold separately by any vendor or whether that item could be resold by the customer on a standalone basis. To conclude that a delivered item has standalone value to the customer because the item is sold separately by another vendor, the item sold by that other vendor should provide the same quality and value to the customer as the item sold by the company. Factors to consider in determining whether the item sold separately by the other vendor is comparable in quality and value to the item sold by the company include (but are not limited to): pricing, functionality, quality grades/assessments, ease of installation and delivery, warranty and acceptance provisions, and availability of post-sale support. To conclude that the customer could resell the deliverable on a standalone basis, the company must consider the nature of the market in which the customer can resell the item and whether the customer reselling it on a standalone basis affects the quality or value of the item. The examples below and those included in an appendix to EITF 00-21 illustrate how the "stand alone value to the customer" concept should be applied in various situations.

ILLUSTRATION: STANDALONE VALUE TO THE CUSTOMER

The following represent arrangements where the delivered item does not have value to the customer on a standalone basis:

Example 1: The arrangement involves Vendor B selling a satellite television receiver and one year of service. The receiver operates on a proprietary network and therefore can only be used with the service provided by the vendor in the arrangement. In addition, there is no secondary market for separate sales of the satellite television receiver since each receiver is uniquely identified to a particular customer and that customer's service contract. As such, the receiver does not have value to the customer on a standalone basis (i.e., absent the on-going satellite television service).

Example 2: The arrangement involves Vendor C selling a piece of equipment and installation of that equipment. The equipment is highly specialized and will not operate until certain adjustments are made during installation. Because of the unique nature and specialization of the equipment, nobody other than Vendor C manufactures or installs the equipment. This effectively prohibits the customer from reselling the equipment on a standalone basis. As such, the equipment does not have value to the customer on a standalone basis (i.e., absent the installation service).

In contrast, the following represent arrangements where the delivered item does have value to the customer on a standalone basis:

Example 3: The arrangement involves Vendor D selling office equipment and a contract to provide maintenance on that office equipment. Vendor D, as well as other vendors, sell the office equipment without the maintenance contract. As such, the office equipment has value to the customer on a standalone basis (i.e., absent the maintenance contract).

Example 4: The arrangement involves Vendor E selling two pieces of manufacturing equipment. Both pieces of equipment are needed to manufacture the intended product. Vendor E only sells the two pieces of equipment together. However, other vendors sell separately equipment that is comparable to, and compatible with, Vendor E's equipment. This also effectively results in the customer being able to resell Vendor E's equipment on a standalone basis if it chose to do so. As such, each piece of equipment has value to the customer on a standalone basis (i.e., absent the delivery of the other piece of equipment).

EXAMPLE: STANDALONE VALUE TO THE CUSTOMER

Xerox Corporation sells equipment, service, supplies, and financing under bundled lease arrangements for which customers pay a single negotiated fixed minimum periodic payment. These bundled arrangements contain both

FAS-13 and non-FAS-13 deliverables. The total arrangement consideration is allocated to the FAS-13 and non-FAS-13 deliverables on the basis of their relative fair values. Revenue is further allocated among the FAS-13 deliverables because these deliverables have standalone value. For example, equipment has standalone value since Xerox sells or leases this product separately from the bundled arrangements.

Fair Value Evidence

In every instance where the accounting literature discusses multiple-element arrangements, the goal is to allocate the arrangement consideration to the individual elements based on their fair values.[1] The EITF reinforced this approach in EITF 00-21. As a result, the allocation of arrangement consideration among the deliverables in a multiple-element arrangement must be based on the fair values of the deliverables. Allocation of arrangement consideration in a multiple-element arrangement may not be based on the cost of those deliverables, the prices stated in the arrangement for those deliverables, the time or effort that went into providing the deliverables, or any other non-fair value measure. Using these amounts to allocate arrangement consideration is not appropriate since those amounts or measures may not represent the amount at which an individual element would be sold on a standalone basis (i.e., the fair value of the individual element).

To ensure the allocation of revenue to individual elements is as objective as possible, the second criterion of the multiple-element model does not allow an allocation to be made unless it can be done based on "objective and reliable" evidence (EITF 00-21, par. 9b). Such evidence often consists of vendor-specific objective evidence (VSOE) of fair value, as discussed in the literature on software revenue recognition (see Chapter 10, "Software—A Complete Model"). VSOE of fair value is limited to (SOP 97-2, par. 10):

1. The price charged when the same element is sold separately.
2. For an element not yet being sold separately, the price established by management, if it is probable that the price, once established, will not change before the separate introduction of the element into the marketplace.

Although VSOE is required to allocate revenue to individual elements in a software arrangement, it is not required in non-software arrangements. To the extent available, however, VSOE is always considered the best evidence of fair value and is always considered sufficiently objective and reliable to meet the second condition of

---

1 For example, fair value allocation is discussed in FAS-13, FAS-45, FAS-66, FIN-45, SOP 81-1, SOP 97-2, and SOP 00-2.

the multiple-element model (EITF 00-21, par. 16). For example, if a company separately sells an element for $100, it should use $100 as the element's fair value in the allocation of arrangement consideration even if its competitors sell that item for $120 or $80.

In the event VSOE of fair value is not available, a company should look to all other available evidence including third-party sales of the same item and its own sales of similar items (EITF 00-21, par. 16). For many deliverables, such evidence may not be available. For example, objective and reliable evidence of fair value generally would not be available if (1) the vendor does not sell the product or service separately, (2) the product or service is unique to the vendor thereby eliminating the availability of third party evidence, and (3) the vendor does not sell a similar product or service on a stand-alone basis.

In evaluating whether sufficient evidence of fair value exists, a company should not refer to measures that are not objective or reliable. For example, third-party sales prices may not be reliable measures of fair value if the items sold by the third parties are not exactly the same product, since differences in quality, brand, or other factors could indicate that the items sold by the third parties have different fair values. Also, a measurement based on cost plus a "normal" gross margin is not an acceptable estimate of fair value since (1) different deliverables would be expected to have different gross margins and (2) costs incurred are rarely a good measure of the fair value of an item. Similarly, in the vast majority of instances, separate prices stated in a contract are not sufficient evidence of fair value since the contract is negotiated as a whole and the parties most likely did not separately bargain for each item. However, in the rare circumstance where the elements of the contract were each separately bid, and the customer could have accepted or rejected the companies bid for each element without affecting the other element, such prices may be objective evidence of fair value (SOP 81-1, par. 40).

EXAMPLE: FAIR VALUE EVIDENCE

Excerpt from the Xerox Corporation Annual Report—Fiscal Year Ended December 31, 2004

[*Note*: This excerpt should be read in conjunction with the Xerox Corporation example found on page 4.11.]

Revenue Recognition under Bundled Arrangements: Our revenue allocation for the lease deliverables begins by allocating revenues to the maintenance and executory costs plus profit thereon. The remaining amounts are allocated to the equipment and financing elements. We perform extensive analyses of available verifiable objective evidence of equipment fair value based on cash selling prices during the applicable period. The cash selling prices are compared to the range of values included in our lease accounting systems. The range of cash selling prices must be reasonably consistent with the lease selling prices, taking into account residual values that accrue to our benefit, in order for us to determine that such lease prices are indicative of fair value. Our pricing interest rates, which are used to determine customer lease payments, are developed based upon a variety of factors including local prevailing rates in the marketplace and the customer's credit history, industry and credit class. Effective in 2004, our pricing rates are reassessed quarterly based on changes in local prevailing rates in the marketplace and are adjusted to the extent such rates vary by twenty-five basis points or more, cumulatively, from the last rate in effect. The pricing interest rates generally equal the implicit rates within the leases, as corroborated by our comparisons of cash to lease selling prices.

Allocation of Arrangement Consideration

Two methods exist for purposes of allocating arrangement consideration to deliverables that should be treated separately for accounting purposes—the relative fair value method and the residual method. Use of one method versus the other is dictated by the facts and circumstances.

In determining the amount of total arrangement consideration to be allocated, a vendor should assume that customer actions will not result in any incremental consideration. In addition, specific refund rights and customer cancellation provisions must be considered in determining the amount of arrangement consideration ultimately attributable to a delivered item, while performance bonuses should not be considered until the performance criteria have been met (EITF 00-21, par. 11).

Relative Fair Value Method

If sufficient evidence of fair value, as discussed above, exists for all elements (deliverables), the arrangement consideration should be allocated to the individual elements based on their relative fair values (EITF 00-21, par. 12). The result of this process is that, when a multiple-element arrangement has a total fee that is less than the fee that would be determined by adding up the fair values of each of the individual elements, the discount is allocated pro rata across each of the elements. However, if generally accepted accounting principles require one of the elements to be initially recognized at its fair value and subsequently marked-to-market for accounting purposes, the amount allocated to that element should be its fair value. The remaining unallocated arrangement consideration is then allocated to the remaining elements in the arrangement using either the relative fair value or residual method, as appropriate (EITF 00-21, par. 13).

OBSERVATION: A question may arise regarding the interaction of the initial recognition and measurement guidance in FIN-45 and the allocation guidance in EITF 00-21. See the Observation in the "Noncontingent Liability" section of this chapter for additional information.

ILLUSTRATION: ALLOCATION OF ARRANGEMENT CONSIDERATION—RELATIVE FAIR VALUE METHOD

General Facts: Company W manufactures equipment that is used to make widgets. The widget-making process involves two pieces of equipment, both of which Company W manufactures. In an arrangement with a new customer, Company W sells both pieces of equipment, along with 10 days of training for the customer's employees, for a total fee of $900,000. Title transfers to each machine upon shipment. Company W does not grant general or specific refund rights to its customers.

VARIATION 1

Additional Facts: Company W sells each piece of equipment separately. In addition, competitors manufacture machines that perform the same functions as Machine 1 and 2, and machines from different manufacturers are interchangeable. Company W sells Machine 1 separately for $400,000, and Machine 2 separately for $550,000.

Company W sells training services separately to customers who already have equipment installed and want additional training for new employees. Company W charges $5,000 per day for training. However, not all customers purchase training, as Company W includes operating manuals with its equipment.

Company W delivers Machine 1 first, then Machine 2, then the training, using the installed machines to demonstrate the machines' functionality. Payment terms are $400,000 upon delivery of Machine 1, $475,000 upon delivery of Machine 2, and $25,000 upon providing the training.

Discussion: Since Company W and other vendors sell each of the machines separately and since the customer can learn how to operate the machines without buying training from Company W, Machine 1 has value to the customer on a standalone basis (i.e., absent Machine 2 and the training), and Machine 2 has value to the customer on a standalone basis (i.e., absent the training).

Evidence of fair value exists for all three deliverables in the arrangement, because Company W sells each one separately. As such, the relative fair value method should be used to allocate the arrangement consideration.

The allocation of the consideration to the three elements is as follows:

Fair Value of Machine 1	$ 400,000
Fair Value of Machine 2	550,000
Fair Value of Training	50,000
Total Fair Value	1,000,000
Less: Arrangement Fee	900,000
Discount in the Arrangement	$ 100,000
Discount as a Percentage of Fair Value	10%
Allocation to Machine 1 = $400,000 – 10%	$ 360,000
Allocation to Machine 2 = $550,000 – 10%	495,000
Allocation to Training = $50,000 – 10%	45,000
Total Arrangement Fee	$ 900,000

In addition, the allocation of arrangement consideration is not affected by payment terms or specific refund rights since the amount otherwise allocable to delivered items is not contingent upon the delivery of subsequent items.

Company W should recognize the arrangement consideration allocated to each item when the recognition criteria discussed in other chapters of this book (i.e., Chapter 5, "Product Deliverables," for Machines 1 and 2; and Chapter 6, "Service Deliverables," for the training) have been satisfied.

VARIATION 2

Additional Facts: The customer needs the machines to operate in a unique environment. As such, Machines 1 and 2 are manufactured to unique customer specifications. Company W does not sell Machine 1 and Machine 2 separately. Company W's competitors do not manufacture similar machines. Due to the unique customer specifications, there is not a secondary market in which the customer could resell the machines individually. Company W sells Machine 1 and Machine 2 together for $950,000.

Company W sells training services separately to customers who already have equipment installed and want additional training for new employees. Company W charges $5,000 per day for training. However, not all customers purchase training, as Company W includes operating manuals with its equipment. The unique customer specifications related to Machines 1 and 2 do not alter the manner in which training would take place.

Company W delivers Machine 1 first, then Machine 2, then the training, using the installed machines to demonstrate the machines' functionality. Payment terms are $400,000 upon delivery of Machine 1, $475,000 upon delivery of Machine 2, and $25,000 upon providing the training.

Discussion: Machine 1 does not have value absent Machine 2 since (a) machines from different suppliers do not work with each other, (b) Company W does not sell the machines separately, and (c) the customer cannot resell Machine 1 on a standalone basis. Because the customer can learn to operate the machines without buying training from Company W, the combination of Machines 1 and 2 has value to the customer absent delivery of the training. For accounting purposes, this arrangement has two elements: (1) Machines 1 and 2 (the machines), and (2) training. The machines are considered one bundled element instead of two separate elements because Machine 1 does not have value to the customer on a standalone basis (i.e., absent Machine 2).

Evidence of fair value exists for both deliverables in the arrangement. The allocation of the consideration to the elements would be as follows:

Fair Value of Machines 1 and 2	$ 950,000
Fair Value of Training	50,000
Total Fair Value	1,000,000
Less: Arrangement Fee	900,000
Discount in the Arrangement	$ 100,000
Discount as a Percentage of Fair Value	10%
Allocation to Machines 1 and 2 = $950,000 - 10%	$ 855,000
Allocation to Training = $50,000 - 10%	45,000
Total Arrangement Fee	$ 900,000

In addition, the allocation of arrangement consideration is not affected by payment terms or specific refund rights since the amount otherwise allocable to delivered items is not contingent upon the delivery of subsequent items.

Company W should not recognize the arrangement consideration allocated to the machines until the recognition criteria discussed in Chapter 5, "Product Deliverables," have been satisfied for *both* machines. Arrangement consideration allocated to the training should be recognized when the recognition criteria discussed in Chapter 6, "Service Deliverables," have been satisfied.

Residual Method

If sufficient evidence of fair value exists for all undelivered items, but does not exist for one or more delivered items, the arrangement consideration should be allocated to the various elements of the arrangement using the residual method (EITF 00-21, par. 12). Under this method, the amount of arrangement consideration allocated to the delivered elements should be the total arrangement consideration less the aggregate fair values of the undelivered elements. Thus, any potential discount on the arrangement taken as a whole is allocated entirely to the delivered elements. This ensures that the amount of revenue recognized at any point in time is not overstated. If the sum of the fair values of the undelivered elements is greater than the total arrangement consideration, no arrangement consideration is allocated to the delivered items.

> **OBSERVATION:** The residual method works in only one direction. It works only when evidence of fair value exists for all undelivered elements. If evidence of fair value exists for delivered elements, but does not exist for one or more undelivered elements, the residual method cannot be used because it is not possible, in the absence of evidence of fair value of the undelivered elements, to ensure that all of the potential discount in the arrangement is allocated to the delivered elements (EITF 00-21, par. 12).

If generally accepted accounting principles require one of the elements to be initially recognized at its fair value and subsequently marked-to-market for accounting purposes, the amount allocated to that element should be its fair value. The remaining unallocated arrangement consideration is then allocated among the remaining elements in the arrangement using either the relative fair value or residual method, as appropriate (EITF 00-21, par. 13).

The use of the "reverse" residual method likely will be limited to bundled arrangements involving the delivery of one or more financial instruments that must be initially recognized at fair value and subsequently marked to market under generally accepted accounting principles (for example, FAS-133 and FAS-150). Other possibilities include FASB Technical Bulletin 90-1 (extended warranties) and FIN 45 (certain guarantees) deliverables.

> **OBSERVATION:** A question may arise regarding the interaction of the initial recognition and measurement guidance in FIN-45 and the allocation guidance in EITF 00-21. See the Observation in the "Noncontingent Liability" section of this chapter for additional information.

EXAMPLE: THE RESIDUAL METHOD

ADE Corporation Form 10-K—Fiscal Year Ended April 30, 2005

The Company's transactions frequently involve the sales of systems and services under multiple element arrangements. Revenue under multiple element arrangements is allocated to all elements except systems based upon the fair value of those elements. The amounts allocated to training are based upon the price charged when this element is sold separately and unaccompanied by the other elements. The amount allocated to installation revenue is based upon hourly rates and the estimated time to complete the service. The amount allocated to system and parts is done on a residual method basis. Under this method, the total arrangement value is allocated first to undelivered elements, based on their fair values, with the remainder being allocated to system revenue.

ILLUSTRATION: ALLOCATION OF ARRANGEMENT CONSIDERATION—RESIDUAL METHOD

General Facts: Company X sells three deliverables to Customer Y— Product P, Product Q and Product R. Company X does not grant general or specific refund rights to Customer Y. Total arrangement consideration is $500,000. Based on its facts and circumstances, Company X concludes that each of the products has value to the customer on a standalone basis.

VARIATION 1

Additional Facts: Sufficient objective and reliable evidence is available to support the fair values of Products Q and R. However, sufficient objective and reliable evidence is not available to support the fair value of Product P. Due to its production schedule, Company X delivers Product P first, then Product Q, then Product R.

The evidence available to support the fair values of Products Q and R indicates the fair values of those products are $100,000 and $250,000, respectively. Payment terms are $200,000 upon delivery of Product P, $150,000 upon delivery of Product Q and $150,000 upon delivery of Product R.

Discussion: Company X should treat each of the products as separate elements for accounting purposes since (a) each of the products has value to the customer on a standalone basis, (b) fair value evidence exists for the undelivered products, and (c) there is no general right of return to consider.

Evidence of fair value exists only for the undelivered products in the arrangement. As such, the residual method would be used to allocate the arrangement consideration as follows:

Total Arrangement Consideration	$500,000
Fair Value of Product Q = Amount Allocated to Product Q	100,000
Fair Value of Product R = Amount Allocated to Product R	250,000
Residual = Amount Allocated to Product P	$150,000

In addition, the allocation of arrangement consideration is not affected by payment terms or specific refund rights since the amount otherwise allocable to delivered items is not contingent upon the delivery of subsequent items.

Company X should recognize the arrangement consideration allocated to each product when the recognition criteria discussed in Chapter 5, "Product Deliverables," have been satisfied for each individual product.

VARIATION 2

Additional Facts: Sufficient objective and reliable evidence is available to support the fair values of Products Q and R. However, sufficient objective and reliable evidence is not available to support the fair value of Product P. Due to its production schedule, Company X delivers Product P first, then Product Q, then Product R.

The evidence available to support the fair values of Products Q and R indicates the fair values of those products are $300,000 and $250,000, respectively. Payment terms are $50,000 upon delivery of Product P, $250,000 upon delivery of Product Q and $200,000 upon delivery of Product R.

Discussion: Company X should treat each of the products as separate elements for accounting purposes since (a) each of the products has value to the customer on a standalone basis, (b) fair value evidence exists for the undelivered products, and (c) there is no general right of return to consider.

Evidence of fair value exists only for the undelivered products in the arrangement. As such, the residual method would be used to allocate the arrangement consideration. However, the sum of the fair values of Products Q and R ($550,000) is greater than the arrangement consideration. As such, no arrangement consideration is allocated to Product P. The amount allocated to Product Q (the second product delivered) is determined using the residual method as follows:

Total Arrangement Consideration	$500,000
Fair Value of Product R = Amount Allocated to Product R	250,000
Residual = Amount Allocated to Product Q	$250,000

In addition, the allocation of arrangement consideration is not affected by payment terms or specific refund rights since the amount otherwise allocable to delivered items is not contingent upon the delivery of subsequent items.

Company X should recognize the arrangement consideration allocated to each product ($0 for Product P, $250,000 for Product Q, and $250,000 for Product R) when the recognition criteria discussed in Chapter 5, "Product Deliverables," have been satisfied for each individual product.

VARIATION 3

Additional Facts: Sufficient objective and reliable evidence is available to support the fair values of Products P and Q. However, sufficient objective and reliable evidence is not available to support the fair value of Product R. Due to its production schedule, Company X delivers Product P first, then Product Q, then Product R.

The evidence available to support the fair values of Products P and Q indicates the fair values of those products are $100,000 and $250,000, respectively. Payment terms are $150,000 upon delivery of Product P, $250,000 upon delivery of Product Q and $100,000 upon delivery of Product R.

Discussion: Company X should not treat each of the products as a separate element for accounting purposes since fair value evidence is not available for Product R, an undelivered item, at the time both Products P and Q are delivered. Instead, all three products should be bundled together and accounted for as a single element. As such, no revenue should be recognized until the recognition criteria discussed in Chapter 5, "Product Deliverables," have been satisfied related to all three products. In other words, no amounts may be recognized related to Products P and Q prior to delivery of Product R since appropriate fair value evidence does not exist for Product R.

Contingent Consideration

Contingent consideration includes specific refund rights and performance bonuses. Specific refund rights are contractual provisions that provide a customer with the right to return a delivered product for a refund (or to avoid payment for previously delivered items) or that would require any other concession only if the vendor failed to deliver or provide any remaining undelivered items in the arrangement (EITF 00-21, par. 14). For example, the customer may be entitled to return all elements for a refund, even if only one of several elements is not delivered. In other situations, the customer may have the right to a refund or liquidated damages of some amount in the event a particular item is not delivered. Performance bonuses are payments due from customers only if specified performance conditions are met. For example, the customer may be required to pay additional consideration if the vendor finishes by a particular date. Performance bonuses should not be considered in the allocation of arrangement consideration until the performance criteria have been met.

> **OBSERVATION:** Rights triggered by nonperformance may exist due to laws or may be stated in the contract. However, they may also exist as a matter of business practice, or by implicit agreement between the parties. All rights that exist should be considered, not merely those that are legally documented. This is consistent with the general notion of accounting for the substance of the arrangement, rather than its form.

The amount *allocated* to a delivered item is limited to the lesser of (a) the amount otherwise allocable to that item (based on using the relative fair value or residual method, as appropriate) or (b) the amount that is not contingent upon the delivery of additional items or meeting other specified performance conditions (EITF 00-21, par. 14). This limitation has no effect on the allocation of arrangement consideration if the amount that may be withheld or refunded is equal to or less than the amount of arrangement consideration allocated to the specified undelivered item since the arrangement consideration allocated to the delivered item is not at risk. If, however, the payment that may be withheld or refunded is greater than the amount of arrangement consideration allocated to the specified undelivered item, then some amount of the arrangement consideration allocated to the delivered item is at risk. Effectively, the amount that is at risk should not be allocated to the delivered item. The section later in this chapter entitled "Distinction Between General and Specific Refund Rights" provides additional information related to why general and specific refund rights are approached differently in the context of separating multiple-element arrangements.

ILLUSTRATION: ALLOCATION OF ARRANGEMENT CONSIDERATION—EFFECTS OF SPECIFIC REFUND RIGHTS

(Adapted from Exhibit A in the SEC staff's frequently asked question and answer document on SAB 101, *Revenue Recognition in Financial Statements*. Although most of this FAQ document was ultimately codified in SAB Topic 13 by way of SAB 104, *Revenue Recognition*, Exhibit A was not included in the codification. The examples included in Exhibit A continue to be used in this book, as adapted, because of their continued relevance in the context of EITF 00-21.)

General Facts: Company A develops, manufactures, and sells complex manufacturing equipment. Company A enters into a sales contract with Customer B to sell and install a specific piece of equipment for $20 million. Company A does not provide Customer B with a general right of return. Company A concludes that the equipment has value to the customer on a standalone basis. Company A has developed its own internal specifications for the model of equipment Customer B ordered and has previously demonstrated that the equipment meets those specifications. There are no special operational specifications in the contract with Customer B and the equipment does not need to be integrated with other equipment. Title to the equipment passes to the customer upon delivery. Company A sells the equipment separately for $19,500,000. In those cases, a general contractor installs the equipment, charging $500,000.

VARIATION 1

Additional Facts: The contract with Customer B includes a customer acceptance provision that obligates Company A to demonstrate that the installed equipment meets its standard criteria before customer acceptance. If customer acceptance is not achieved within 120 days of delivery of the equipment, Customer B can require Company A to remove the equipment and refund all payments. Payment terms are 80% due upon delivery and 20% due after installation and customer acceptance.

Discussion: Company A should treat the equipment and installation as separate elements for accounting purposes since (a) the equipment has value to the customer on a standalone basis, (b) fair value evidence exists for both the equipment and installation, and (c) there is no general right of return to consider. However, Company A has a specific refund right related to the equipment that becomes exercisable if installation is not successfully completed within 120 days. As such, the amount allocated to the equipment is limited to the lesser of (a) the amount otherwise allocable to the equipment using the relative fair value method or (b) the amount that is not contingent upon performance of the installation. While $19,500,000 is otherwise allocable to the equipment (i.e., absent the specific refund right), 100% of that amount is contingent upon performance of the installation due to the specific refund right. As such, Company A ultimately should not allocate any arrangement consideration to the equipment. All of the arrangement consideration is effectively allocated to the installation service.

The arrangement consideration allocated to installation should not be recognized until the recognition criteria discussed in other chapters of this book (i.e., Chapter 5, "Product Deliverables," for the equipment, and Chapter 6, "Service Deliverables," for the installation) have been satisfied.

VARIATION 2

Additional Facts: Company A is an experienced provider of installation services related to its equipment. It has never failed to install the equipment as required in a contract within 120 days of delivery. The $20,000,000 arrangement fee is due upon delivery of the equipment. However, if installation is not successfully performed within 120 days of delivery of the equipment, Customer B may cancel the installation portion of the contract with Company A and receive a $750,000 refund from Company A. Customer B does not have the right to return the equipment based on Company A's failure to perform installation. In addition, Customer B has no general refund rights.

Discussion: Company A should treat the equipment and installation as separate elements for accounting purposes since (a) the equipment has value to the customer on a standalone basis, (b) fair value evidence exists for both the equipment and installation, and (c) there is no general right of return to consider. However, Company A has a specific refund right related to the equipment that becomes exercisable if installation is not successfully completed within 120 days. As such, the amount allocated to the equipment is limited to the lesser of (a) the amount otherwise allocable to the equipment using the relative fair value method or (b) the amount that is not contingent upon performance of the installation. While $19,500,000 is otherwise allocable to the equipment (i.e., absent the specific refund right), $250,000 of that amount is contingent upon performance of the installation due to the specific refund right. As such, Company A ultimately should only allocate $19,250,000 of the arrangement consideration to the equipment. This results in $750,000 of the arrangement consideration ultimately being allocated to the installation.

The arrangement consideration allocated to the equipment should not be recognized until the recognition criteria discussed in Chapter 5, "Product Deliverables," have been satisfied. The arrangement consideration allocated to the installation should not be recognized until the recognition criteria discussed in Chapter 6, "Service Deliverables," have been satisfied.

EXAMPLE: CONTINGENT CONSIDERATION

Viisage Technology Inc. Form 10-Q—Fiscal Quarter Ended July 3, 2005

Revenue and Cost Recognition

We have contracts, generally with state governments for the production of drivers' licenses and other identification credentials, where we have determined that we have multiple elements and where the title to equipment installed to produce these credentials does not pass to the customer. Under these contracts, the first element consists of hardware, system design, implementation, training, consumables management, maintenance and support which is accounted for as equipment and related executory services under lease in accordance with SFAS No. 13. The second element consists of customized software which is accounted for as a long term contract in accordance with AICPA Statement of Position 97-2, *Software Revenue Recognition*, or SOP 97-2, and Statement of Position 81-1, *Accounting for Performance of Construction-Type and Certain Production-Type Contracts*, or SOP 81-1, on a unit of delivery method of measurement.

Costs related to the hardware element of these contracts are capitalized on the balance sheet and are depreciated over the contract term beginning when the system goes into service. The delivery of these credentials typically requires us to customize, design and install equipment and software at customer locations, as well as perform training, supply consumables, maintain the equipment and provide support services. Nonperformance of training, consumable management, maintenance and support services would prevent us from receiving payment for the costs incurred in the customization, design and installation of the system. EITF 00-21 limits the amount of revenue allocable to the customization, design and installation of the system to the amount that is not contingent upon the production of credentials. Revenue on these contracts under EITF 00-21 is earned based on, and is contingent upon, the production of credentials from the system. Due to the contingent performance of credential production in our secure credentials contracts, we defer revenue recognition for the system design and installation phase of our contracts, including customized software and equipment, and recognize revenue as credentials are produced.

Costs related to the customized software element of our secure credentials contracts where title to the hardware element does not pass to the customer are capitalized on the balance sheet during the period in which we are designing and installing the system and are amortized over the contract term beginning when the system goes into service. Costs related to this element of our secure credentials contracts incurred after the system is in service are expensed as incurred. Revenue related to this element of our secure credentials contracts is recorded as credentials are produced by the system.

Customer Cancellation Provisions

In some cases, an arrangement includes a provision for the customer to cancel or terminate the arrangement with the payment of a termination fee. When such a provision exists in a multiple-element arrangement, a company should assume that the customer will not cancel the arrangement for purposes of allocating arrangement consideration among the deliverables. However, to the extent an amount is recorded as an asset for the excess of revenue recognized under the arrangement over the amount of cash received from the customer since the inception of the arrangement, that asset should not exceed the cancellation fee to which the vendor is entitled under the arrangement. In these situations, the vendor's right to the cancellation fee must be legally enforceable and the vendor should have the intent to enforce its contractual right to collect the cancellation fee for purposes of supporting recognition of the asset (EITF 00-21, par. 15).

General Refund Rights

In many arrangements, a customer can exercise certain general rights even after a product is delivered. For example, general rights of return and standard warranty provisions represent uncertainties and potential future obligations that exist at the time of delivery. Typically, such rights are evaluated with respect to the revenue recognition for each separate deliverable in an arrangement, pursuant to the appropriate guidance (for example, FAS-48 for returns and FAS-5 for warranties). That guidance is discussed in other chapters of this book.

If an arrangement includes a general refund right, delivery or performance of the undelivered item(s) must be considered probable and substantially in the vendor's control to treat a delivered item separately for accounting purposes (EITF 00-21, par. 9c). If general refund rights exist and delivery or performance of the undelivered item(s) are considered probable and substantially in the vendor's control, then those rights should be accounted for as discussed in Chapter 5, "Product Deliverables," and Chapter 6, "Service Deliverables," as appropriate. In other words, the existence of those rights does not, in and of itself, preclude treating a delivered item separately for accounting purposes. If general refund rights exist and delivery or performance of the undelivered item(s) are not considered probable and substantially in the vendor's control, then the delivered item should not be treated separately for accounting purposes.

An assessment of whether the general refund right, delivery, or performance of the undelivered element(s) is probable and substantially in the vendor's control is required after *each* element in the arrangement is delivered. The vendor's ability to meet this criterion is a function of the nature of the undelivered elements and the specific characteristics of the vendor. Factors that determine performance of undelivered elements include the amount of time to complete, degree of customization, reliance on subcontractors, and the availability of components. The vendor's history of performance and financial condition also must be considered in the assessment.

Distinction between General and Specific Refund Rights

A distinction is made between general and specific refund rights in EITF 00-21 given what these rights mean or represent in the context of a multiple-element arrangement. The existence of a general refund right in a multiple-element arrangement creates a connection between the deliverables that the vendor should consider from **its** perspective. In other words, the vendor must assess whether its performance related to undelivered items is probable and substantially within its control. In contrast, the existence of a specific refund right in a multiple-element arrangement creates a connection between the deliverables that the vendor should consider from the **customer's** perspective. A specific refund right expressly connects the deliverables in a multiple-element arrangement, since it specifically ties the vendor's right to consideration (or the right to retain consideration) to whether the vendor provides the undelivered items. This express link indicates that there is a stronger connection between deliverables in a multiple-element arrangement containing a specific refund right than a multiple-element arrangement containing just a general refund right. To address the accounting implications of this stronger connection, the amount allocated to a delivered item is limited to the lesser of (a) the amount otherwise allocable to that item (based on using the relative fair value or residual method, as appropriate) or (b) the amount that is not contingent upon the delivery of additional items or meeting other specified performance conditions (EITF 00-21, par. 14).

Guarantees and Indemnifications in Multiple-Element Arrangements

FIN-45 provides initial accounting and disclosure requirements related to guarantees and indemnifications. Prior to the issuance of FIN-45, the accounting literature pertaining to guarantees and indemnifications was general in nature (e.g., FAS-5 and FIN-34, *Disclosure of Indirect Guarantees of Indebtedness of Others*) and only addressed the accounting for, and disclosure of, the contingent aspect of a potential liability related to a guarantee. FIN-45 requires accounting for the noncontingent aspect of the guarantee or indemnification and requires more extensive disclosures.

Some entities, such as financial institutions or insurance companies, are in the "business" of providing guarantees or indemnifications. Other entities get involved in providing guarantees or indemnifications in connection with their other, primary activities. This section of the chapter focuses on the accounting considerations for the latter set of entities—those that get involved in guarantees in connection with their other, primary activities. In other words, this section focuses on the accounting by those entities that enter into multiple-element arrangements where one of the elements is a guarantee and the other elements relate to their primary activities.

FIN-45's broad scope means that most companies have actually entered into arrangements that must follow the accounting and/or disclosure guidance in FIN-45. For example, many equipment manufacturers guarantee the loans their customers take out from third-party lenders to purchase the manufacturers' equipment. The accounting for such guarantees is covered by FIN-45. A more common example involves a warranty provided by a retailer or product manufacturer to a customer. Such warranties are a guarantee as defined in FIN-45 and are subject to FIN-45's disclosure requirements. Chapter 12, "Disclosures," discusses the disclosure requirements related to guarantees.

Scope

As mentioned above, FIN-45 provides a very broad definition of what constitutes a guarantee. However, certain guarantees are excluded from FIN-45's requirements despite meeting this definition. Other guarantees are excluded from the initial recognition and measurement (IR&M) provisions of FIN-45, but not the disclosure provisions. And, of course, other guarantees trigger the requirement to follow both the IR&M and disclosure provisions of FIN-45. Given the complexity of FIN-45's scope, the first exercise in accounting for a guarantee or indemnification is determining whether the guarantee or indemnification falls within the scope of the IR&M provisions of FIN-45. A set of basic characteristics and defined exceptions provide the foundation for determining whether a guarantee or indemnification falls within the scope of FIN-45's IR&M provisions.

Basic characteristics If a guarantee or indemnification possesses any of the basic characteristics of a guarantee or indemnification as defined by FIN-45, it initially falls within the scope of FIN-45. These basic characteristics are as follows (FIN-45, par. 3):

- Contracts that contingently require the guarantor to make payments (either in cash, financial instruments, other assets, shares of its stock, or provision of services) to the guaranteed party based on changes in an underlying that is related to an asset, liability, or equity security of the guaranteed party.

- Contracts that contingently require the guarantor to make payments (either in cash, financial instruments, other assets, shares of its stock, or provision of services) to the guaranteed party based on another entity's failure to perform under an obligating agreement (performance guarantees).

- Indemnification agreements (contracts) that contingently require the indemnifying party (the guarantor) to make payments to the indemnified party (guaranteed party) based on changes in an underlying that is related to an asset, liability, or equity security of the indemnified party.

- Indirect guarantees of the indebtedness of others even though the payment to the guaranteed party may not be based on changes in an underlying that is related to an asset, liability, or equity security of the guaranteed party.

If a guarantee or indemnification possesses any of these basic characteristics, it initially falls within the scope of FIN-45. However, certain guarantees and indemnifications that possess one of the basic characteristics listed above, are specifically excluded from all of the provisions of FIN-45 or just the IR&M provisions of FIN-45, as discussed below.

Exclusions from all provisions The following types of guarantees that may be found in revenue arrangements are excluded from all of the provisions of FIN-45 (that is, neither the IR&M or disclosure provisions in FIN-45 apply to these guarantees), even if they possess one of the basic characteristics discussed above (FIN-45, par. 6):

- Guarantees of the residual value of leased property at the end of a lease term by the lessee if the lessee accounts for the lease as a capital lease.

- Guarantees involved in leases that are accounted for as contingent rent.

- Guarantees (or indemnifications) that are issued by either an insurance company or a reinsurance company and accounted for under the related industry-specific authoritative literature, including guarantees embedded in either insurance contracts or investment contracts.

- Vendor rebates where the contract contingently requires the vendor to make payments to the customer based on the customer's sales revenues, number of units sold, or similar events.

- Guarantees (or indemnifications) whose existence prevent the guarantor from being able to either account for a transaction as the sale of an asset or recognize the profit from that sale transaction.

Exclusions from IR&M provisions FIN-45 provides additional exclusions from its IR&M provisions. The following types of guarantees or indemnifications that may be found in revenue arrangements are subject to the disclosure provisions of FIN-45 but are not subject to the IR&M provisions of FIN-45 (see Chapter 12, "Disclosures" for a discussion of the disclosure requirements of FIN-45) (FIN-45, par. 7):

- Guarantees that meet the definition of a derivative and are accounted for at fair value.

- Product warranties related to the product's ability to function, but not its value.

- Guarantees by an original lessee when the lease is modified (as discussed in the authoritative literature addressing lease accounting) such that the original lessee becomes secondarily liable instead of being primarily liable (i.e., primary obligor role shifts from original lessee to new party).

Guarantees and indemnifications that possess one of the basic characteristics but are included on the preceding list are only subject to the disclosure provisions of FIN-45.

Scope provisions and revenue-related guarantees and indemnifications Many different types of guarantees and indemnifications are commonly included in sales arrangements. The accounting for some of these guarantees and indemnifications are covered by FIN-45, while others are excluded from some or all of FIN-45's provisions as described above. Some of the more common guarantees and indemnifications found in sales arrangements are identified and discussed below.

- *A manufacturer's guarantee of a loan taken out by its customer from a third-party lender to buy the manufacturer's product.* Such a guarantee contains one of the basic characteristics of a guarantee because it requires the manufacturer to make payments to the lender based on the customer's failure to perform under an obligating agreement (i.e., the customer's loan agreement with the third-party lender). This guarantee does not contain any of the characteristics that would exclude it from any of the provisions of FIN-45.

- *A fixed-price trade-in right offered by a vendor to its customer.* Such a right contains one of the basic characteristics of a guarantee because it may require the seller to make a payment to the purchaser based on changes in the price of the asset purchased. This guarantee does not contain any of the characteristics that would exclude it from any of the provisions of FIN-45 unless the existence of such a guarantee prevents revenue recognition.

- *A product warranty.* As specifically mentioned above, a product warranty falls within the scope of FIN-45 but is excluded from FIN-45's IR&M provisions. FIN-45's disclosure provisions apply to a product warranty. See Chapter 12, "Disclosures," for a discussion of FIN-45's disclosure requirements.

- *An indemnification in a software licensing agreement that indemnifies the licensee against liability and damages arising from any claims of patent, copyright, trademark, or trade secret infringement by the software vendor's software.* As discussed in FSP FIN 45-1, such an indemnification is akin to a product warranty. FIN-45's disclosure provisions apply to this indemnification, while its IR&M provisions do not. See Chapter 12, "Disclosures," for a discussion of the disclosure requirements of FIN-45.

- *Vendor rebates based on the volume of purchases made by a customer over a period of time.* Such a provision does not contain any of the basic characteristics of a guarantee because the contingent payment provision relates to an asset of the vendor, not the purchaser. Payment provisions related to a company's own assets are not guarantees covered by FIN-45.

- *Arrangements that provide for contingent payments to the purchaser such that the contingency prevents revenue recognition.* This is a specific scope exclusion from all of FIN-45's provisions. Examples include provisions in product sales arrangements that require the transaction to be accounted for as a consignment or a financing (see Chapter 5,"Product Deliverables"), and software arrangements where the software vendor participates in the customer's financing through either (a) indemnifying the financing party against claims beyond the software vendor's standard indemnifications or (b) guaranteeing the customer's loan with the financing party, thus preventing the recognition of revenue when the presumption that the fee is not fixed or determinable cannot be overcome (see Chapter 10, "Software—A Complete Model").

There are many other types of guarantees or indemnifications that could exist in a revenue arrangement. Companies should be very diligent in evaluating the provisions of their contracts against the criteria of FIN-45. Consultation with auditors or other experts in this regard may be necessary due to the broad and complex nature of FIN-45's scope provisions.

Initial Recognition and Measurement

FIN-45 provides guidance related to the initial recognition and measurement of guarantees and indemnifications that fall within the scope of its IR&M provisions. FIN-45 does not provide guidance related to the subsequent accounting for any guarantee liability recognized as a result of applying those provisions. In initially accounting for a guarantee or indemnification, FIN-45 notes that there are really two liabilities inherent in every guarantee or indemnification (FIN-45, par. 8):

- Noncontingent liability—This represents the guarantor's obligation to stand ready to perform under the terms of the guarantee.

- Contingent liability—This represents the guarantor's potential obligation to make payments in the future related to the guarantee.

Noncontingent liability If a guarantee or indemnification falls within the scope of the IR&M provisions of FIN-45, the related noncontingent liability must be recognized initially at its fair value. If the guarantee or indemnification is the only element in the transaction with an unrelated party, the liability recognized is the fee received by the guarantor for providing that guarantee or indemnification. If the guarantee or indemnification is part of a multiple-element arrangement, the liability recognized should be an estimate of the guarantee or indemnification's fair value (e.g., if the guarantee or indemnification was the only element in the transaction, what fee would the guarantor receive) (FIN-45, par. 9).

As such, in a multiple-element arrangement containing a guarantee or indemnification that falls within the scope of the IR&M provisions of FIN-45, the guarantee or indemnification element must be separated from the other elements in the arrangement and must be recorded at its fair value. If the relative fair value method could otherwise have been used to allocate arrangement consideration in a multiple-element arrangement containing two or more elements and a guarantee or indemnification that falls within the scope of the IR&M provisions of FIN-45, the guarantee or indemnification's fair value should first be allocated to it and then the relative fair value method should be used to allocate the remaining, unallocated arrangement consideration among the other elements in the arrangement.

> **OBSERVATION:** A question may arise regarding the interaction of the initial recognition and measurement guidance in FIN-45 and the allocation guidance in EITF 00-21. The specific guidance involved in this question is as follows:
>
> - When a guarantee is issued as part of a transaction with multiple elements with an unrelated party (such as in conjunction with selling an asset or entering into an operating

lease), the liability recognized at the inception of the guarantee should be an estimate of the guarantee's fair value (FIN-45, par. 9(b)).

- To the extent that any separate unit of accounting in the arrangement (including a delivered item) is required under GAAP to be recorded at fair value (and marked to market each reporting period thereafter), the amount allocated to that unit of accounting should be its fair value (EITF 00-21, par. 13).

The question that may arise is best illustrated with an example. Assume a multiple-element arrangement includes three elements: (1) Product A, (2) Product B, and (3) Guarantee. Total arrangement consideration is $100,000. The fair values of Product A, Product B, and Guarantee are $50,000, $40,000, and $20,000, respectively, and these fair values are properly supported.

Under one interpretation of the guidance above, $20,000 would be allocated to Guarantee since that is its fair value and the remaining $80,000 would be allocated to Product A ($44,444) and Product B ($35,556) based on their relative fair values. Effectively, this interpretation results in first applying the FIN-45 guidance noted above and then the EITF 00-21 guidance noted above.

Under a second interpretation, the $100,000 would be allocated to the three elements based on their relative fair values—$45,455 to Product A, $36,364 to Product B, and $18,181 to Guarantee. The basis for this interpretation is the fact that the guarantee will not be subsequently marked to market (as discussed in the "Subsequent Measurement" section of this chapter). As such, the exception in EITF 00-21's allocation guidance that is only available when the element is initially recorded at fair value *and* subsequently marked-to-market could be interpreted to be not applicable.

As noted in the discussion in Chapter 2, "A Brief Survey of Revenue-Related Literature," FIN-45 is Category A GAAP, while EITF 00-21 is Category C GAAP. Because FIN-45 is higher-level GAAP than EITF 00-21, the first interpretation above should be applied in this situation.

Contingent liability The accounting for the contingent liability continues to be governed by FAS-5. As such, the contingent liability is only recognized at the point the liability becomes probable of payment and reasonably estimable. It would be an unusual situation where a liability would need to be recognized initially for the contingent liability (i.e., at the same time as the noncontingent liability). However, if this occurs, the total liability recognized for the guarantee or indemnification should be the greater of (a) the noncontingent liability (i.e., the fair value of the guarantee or indemnification) or (b) the probable and reasonably estimable contingent liability (FIN-45, par. 10).

Subsequent Measurement

Although FIN-45 does not provide any requirements related to the subsequent measurement of the recorded noncontingent liability related to a guarantee or indemnification, it does provide insight regarding the "typical" subsequent accounting for the noncontingent liability. FIN-45 indicates that the noncontingent liability would typically be taken into income as the guarantor's risk is reduced, which would either be (a) when the related guarantee or indemnification expires or is settled (the Settlement Approach), (b) over the term of the guarantee or indemnification based on a systematic and rational amortization method (the Earnings Process Approach), or (c) over the term of the guarantee as the fair value of the guarantee changes, but only if this approach is supported by other authoritative literature, such as guarantees that meet the definition of a derivative in FAS-133 (the Fair Value Approach) (FIN-45, par. 12). The limitation of the Fair Value Approach to only guarantees where other authoritative literature supports subsequently marking a guarantee to fair value is supported by FSP FIN 45-2. Each of these approaches is discussed further below. Subsequent measurement of the contingent liability is governed by FAS-5 and is beyond the scope of this publication.

Settlement Approach This approach would result in the noncontingent liability being eliminated when the guarantor's obligation under the guarantee is settled or when it expires based on the terms of the guarantee.

Earnings Process Approach This approach results in the noncontingent liability being reduced over the period the guarantor is standing ready to honor the guarantee. In a sense, this method treats the noncontingent liability as fees deferred for providing a service. EITF 85-20 indicates that the pattern over which such a fee should be recognized depends on the nature of the guarantee. If the guarantee is more akin to a lending commitment, then the revenue allocated to the guarantee should be treated similar to a loan commitment fee. If the guarantee is more akin to an insurance obligation, then the revenue allocated to the guarantee should be treated similar to insurance premiums (EITF 85-20).

:**Fair Value Approach** This approach results in the guarantee that qualifies for this treatment being increased or decreased over the period of the guarantee based on subsequent re-measurements of the guarantee's fair value. As discussed above, a guarantee "qualifies" for this approach only if the approach is supported by other authoritative literature. For example, a guarantee that meets the definition of a derivative must be accounted for under FAS-133, which requires the guarantee to be subsequently re-measured based on its fair value. While guarantees that meet the definition of a derivative in FAS-133 are excluded from the IR&M provisions of FIN-45, they are subject to FIN-45's disclosure requirements.

The approach that should be used to subsequently measure the non-contingent liability related to a particular guarantee or indemnification is a matter of judgment that depends on the nature of the guarantee or indemnification and the facts and circumstances. Ultimately, the selection of an approach is the determination of an accounting policy that should be disclosed and consistently applied in similar situations.

> **DISCLOSURE ALERT:**   See Chapter 12, "Disclosures," regarding accounting policy disclosure requirements.

ILLUSTRATION: MULTIPLE-ELEMENT ARRANGEMENT CONTAINING A GUARANTEE

Facts: On January 1, 20X1, Manufacturer A sells product to Company B for $100,000. Company B arranges financing with Lender C. Lender C requests and receives a guarantee from Manufacturer A. The guarantee calls for Manufacturer A to make Lender C whole if Company B defaults on its loan with Lender C. Manufacturer A determines that the fair value of the guarantee is $10,000 on January 1, 20X1. The term of Company B's loan with Lender C is two years. Manufacturer A is released from the guarantee obligation gradually as Company B makes its payments. Manufacturer A determines that the conditions for revenue recognition are met on January 1, 20X1 (including the collectibility condition). Company B makes the scheduled payments to Lender C for the first year of the loan, totaling $50,000. At the end of 20X1, Manufacturer A determines that the fair value of the guarantee is $3,000. Manufacturer A also concludes that recognition of a contingent liability related to the guarantee is not required at December 31, 20X1. Company B defaults on the first payment due in 20X2, at which point Manufacturer A concludes it will have to make Lender C whole for the remaining balance of Company B's loan. For ease of illustration, the effects of interest are not considered.

Accounting: Manufacturer A recognizes receipt of payment, revenue, and guarantee liability on January 1, 20X1:

Cash	$100,000	
Product Revenue		$90,000
Guarantee (Noncontingent) Liability		$10,000

The entries recorded during 20X1 and 20X2 depend on the approach used by Manufacturer A to subsequently measure the noncontingent guarantee liability. As such, the entries under the Settlement and Earnings Process Approaches are presented below, with a comparison of the approaches following the Earnings Process Approach. Manufacturer A may not use the Fair Value Approach since that approach is not supported by other authoritative literature in relation to Manufacturer A's transaction (e.g., the guarantee does not meet the definition of a derivative under FAS-133).

Settlement Approach

During 20X1, Manufacturer A would not reduce the noncontingent guarantee liability, even though it has been released from half of the guarantee obligation, since the guarantee obligation has not expired or been settled.

Upon Company B's default in 20X2, Manufacturer A would record the contingent loss:

Guarantee Loss	$50,000	
Guarantee (Contingent) Liability		$50,000

Upon Manufacturer A's settlement of the guarantee in 20X2, Manufacturer A would record the cash payment to Lender C to pay off Company B's outstanding loan balance and record the noncontingent guarantee liability as guarantee income since it has been settled:

Guarantee (Contingent) Liability	$50,000	
Cash		$50,000
Guarantee (Noncontingent) Liability	$10,000	
Guarantee Income		$10,000

Earnings Process Approach

During 20X1, Manufacturer A would reduce the noncontingent guarantee liability and recognize guarantee income based on the guidance in EITF 85-20 (assume straight-line amortization for ease of illustration):

Guarantee (Noncontingent) Liability	$5,000	
Guarantee Income		$5,000

Upon Company B's default in 20X2, Manufacturer A would record the contingent loss:

Guarantee Loss	$50,000	
Guarantee (Contingent) Liability		$50,000

During 20X2, Manufacturer A would continue to reduce the noncontingent guarantee liability and recognize guarantee income:

Guarantee (Noncontingent) Liability	$5,000	
Guarantee Income		$5,000

Upon Manufacturer A's settlement of the guarantee in 20X2, Manufacturer A would record the cash payment to Lender C to pay off Company B's outstanding loan balance:

Guarantee (Contingent) Liability	$50,000	
Cash		$50,000

Comparison

	Approach	
	Settlement	**Earnings Process**
Guarantee Liability at 12/31/20X1	$10,000	$5,000
Guarantee Liability upon Company B's Default	$60,000	$55,000
Guarantee Income During 20X1	$0	$5,000
Guarantee Income During 20X2	$10,000	$5,000
Guarantee Loss During 20X2	$50,000	$50,000

The primary difference between the approaches is the timing of the reduction (or changes) in the noncontingent guarantee liability. Under the Settlement Approach, Manufacturer A does not reduce the noncontingent guarantee liability until it settles its guarantee obligation. However, under the Earnings Process Approach, the noncontingent guarantee liability will change prior to the guarantee's actual settlement since Manufacturer A amortizes the noncontingent guarantee liability over the period it stands ready to perform—the guarantee period. Under these two approaches, the guarantee income (noncontingent liability) and guarantee loss (contingent liability) are effectively viewed as two separate amounts related to two separate occurrences. Whether the guarantee income and loss are recognized broad or net on the income statement in these two approaches is a matter of judgment that depends on the facts and circumstances.

DEFERRED COSTS

Revenue in a multiple-element arrangement may not be able to be recognized even though some of the deliverables have already been delivered. As discussed previously in this chapter, this could occur for a number of reasons, including a delivered item not having value to the customer on a standalone basis, a lack of evidence of fair value, or the existence of a specific refund right (which may result in the deferral of revenue if some or all of the amount otherwise allocable to the delivered element ultimately cannot be allocated to it (and recognized) due to the specific refund right). When revenue cannot be recognized upon delivery or performance of the element, an issue arises regarding how to treat the costs incurred related to that element.

In some cases, the issue of whether related costs may also be deferred is unimportant, because those costs may be minimal. However, for many deliverables, the related direct and incremental costs are significant. The deferral of costs for multiple-element arrangements is not addressed in detail in any accounting literature. However, prior to deferring any costs incurred in a multiple-element arrangement, the conclusion must be reached that such costs meet the definition of an asset as defined in CON-6. There are several pieces of authoritative literature that provide guidance on cost deferral in connection with other revenue transactions. This literature should be looked to for guidance on deferring costs in multiple-element arrangements. The issue of cost deferral is discussed in detail in Chapter 8, "Miscellaneous Issues."

RECOGNITION WHEN ELEMENTS CANNOT BE SEPARATED

In several situations discussed earlier in this chapter, revenue from a delivered element cannot be recognized due to its interactions with the other elements yet to be delivered. The arrangement consideration allocable to a delivered item(s) that cannot be treated separately for accounting purposes should be combined with the arrangement consideration allocable to the other applicable undelivered item(s) within the arrangement. The appropriate pattern of revenue recognition should then be determined for that bundled group of deliverables (EITF 00-21, par. 10). The pattern of that recognition may differ depending upon (a) whether any of the performance obligations in the multiple-element arrangement may be considered inconsequential or perfunctory and (b) the reason the elements in the multiple-element arrangement were not separated for accounting purposes.

Inconsequential or Perfunctory Performance Obligations

Each deliverable in an arrangement should be considered in determining whether a delivered item is a separate element for accounting purposes. If an element should be treated separately for accounting purposes, the arrangement consideration allocated to that element should be recognized based on the applicable revenue recognition model. If, however, an element should not be treated separately for accounting purposes, a question may arise regarding whether that element is so inconsequential or perfunctory that it should not affect the recognition of the revenue for the other elements in the arrangement.

Consider, for example, the situation where a piece of equipment is sold subject to installation and the vendor concludes that it cannot treat the equipment and installation separately for revenue recognition purposes due to a lack of fair value evidence for the installation. The vendor believes, however, that the installation is an inconsequential or perfunctory obligation and that it should not have to defer recognition of revenue related to the equipment due to not having fair value evidence related to this inconsequential or perfunctory installation obligation. In this situation, the vendor believes that it has substantially completed or fulfilled the terms specified in the arrangement without having performed its installation obligation.

Whether a remaining performance obligation that is not treated separately for accounting purposes may be viewed as inconsequential or perfunctory and, therefore, not affect the recognition of revenue related to the other elements in the arrangement, is not addressed in EITF 00-21 or any other authoritative literature applicable to private companies. However, the SEC staff has addressed this question in SAB Topic 13A3c. While this guidance is not directly applicable to private companies, such companies should still consider its application given the absence of other directly on-point literature.

In SAB Topic 13A3c, the SEC staff indicates that if the only remaining performance obligation on the part of the vendor is inconsequential or perfunctory, the vendor can still conclude that it has substantially completed or fulfilled the terms specified in the arrangement related to the delivered elements. In other words, if the only remaining performance obligation on the part of the vendor is inconsequential or perfunctory, the vendor can still conclude that it has met the delivery or performance criterion necessary to recognize revenue for the delivered elements (SAB Topic 13A3c, ques. 1). A key question that must be answered, then, is when may a remaining performance obligation be considered inconsequential or perfunctory?

Inconsequential or Perfunctory Criteria

A remaining performance obligation may not be considered inconsequential or perfunctory if either (a) it is essential to the functionality of a delivered item, (b) the vendor's failure to fulfill the remaining performance obligation would result in the customer receiving a full or partial refund or rejecting (or a right to a refund or to reject) delivered items, or (c) the vendor does not have a demonstrated history of fulfilling the remaining performance obligation in a timely manner and reliably estimating the remaining costs (SAB Topic 13A3c, ques. 1 and 2). Further information on these criteria is provided below along with information on other factors that must also be considered in determining whether a remaining performance obligation is inconsequential or perfunctory.

Essential to the functionality   In determining whether a remaining performance obligation is essential to the functionality of a delivered item the vendor should consider both the "standalone value to the customer" guidance in EITF 00-21 (as discussed earlier in this chapter) and the "essential to the functionality" guidance in SOP 97-2 (see Chapter 10, "Software—A Complete Model"). It is instructive to consider both the "standalone value to the customer" guidance in EITF 00-21 and the "essential to the functionality" guidance in SOP 97-2 given the similarity in concepts and their common objective. In addition, it would be a rare situation where consistent conclusions would not be reached when analyzing the concepts individually (e.g., concluding that a delivered element has value to the customer on a standalone basis when an undelivered element is essential to its functionality).

For example, if the arrangement includes equipment and installation that should not be treated separately for accounting purposes, factors that would indicate that either (1) the equipment does not have standalone value to the customer absent the installation, or (2) that the installation is essential to the functionality of the equipment, include: (a) the installation involves significant changes to the features or capabilities of the equipment or building complex interfaces or connections, and (b) the installation services are unavailable from other vendors. Conversely, factors that would indicate that either (1) the equipment does have standalone value to the customer absent the installation, or (2) the installation is not essential to the functionality of the equipment, include: (a) the equipment is a standard product, (b) installation does not significantly alter the equipment's capabilities, and (c) other companies are available to perform the installation (SAB Topic 13A3c, ques. 3).

> **OBSERVATION:** If the reason the equipment and installation are not treated separately for accounting purposes is the fact that the equipment does not have value to the customer on a standalone basis, it will generally be the case that the installation is essential to the functionality of the equipment. As a result, the installation could not be viewed as inconsequential or perfunctory and revenue would be deferred until the installation is performed, provided the other criteria for revenue recognition have been met.

Refund right   Whether a refund right exists if the remaining performance obligation is not fulfilled is often documented in the sales contract. However, such rights may also exist due to industry practice, company policy, or laws and regulations. In addition, the relationship between the buyer and the seller should be evaluated in full to determine whether unstated refund rights might exist. In evaluating whether a refund right exists, it is important that all rights that exist, whether explicitly stated or not, be considered.

Other criteria   Other factors should also be considered in determining whether a remaining performance obligation is inconsequential or perfunctory, including (SAB Topic 13A3c, ques. 2):

- Has the cost or time to fulfill the remaining performance obligation in similar contracts historically varied significantly from one instance to another?
- Are the skills required to fulfill the remaining performance obligation specialized or not readily available in the marketplace?
- Is the cost of fulfilling the remaining performance obligation, or the fair value of that remaining performance obligation, more than insignificant in relation to such items as the contract fee, gross profit, and operating income allocable to the other items in the arrangement?
- Is the period before the remaining performance obligation is fulfilled lengthy?
- Is the timing of payment of a portion of the sales price coincident with fulfilling the remaining performance obligation?

A "yes" answer to any of these questions is an indication that the remaining performance obligation is more than inconsequential or perfunctory.

The evaluation of whether a remaining performance obligation is inconsequential or perfunctory is very judgmental. As such, different vendors might reach different conclusions. For this reason, it is acceptable for a vendor to forego this evaluation entirely, thus concluding that the remaining performance obligation should not be viewed as inconsequential or perfunctory.

> **DISCLOSURE ALERT:** See Chapter 12, "Disclosures," regarding accounting policy disclosure requirements.

As with all areas in accounting that require the exercise of judgment, care should be exercised in concluding that a remaining performance obligation is inconsequential or perfunctory given the affects it has on the timing of revenue recognition. In addition, to the extent a company believes a remaining performance obligation is inconsequential or perfunctory, it should consider consulting with experts before reaching a final conclusion.

ILLUSTRATION: EFFECTS OF CONCLUDING THAT REMAINING PERFORMANCE OBLIGATION IS INCONSEQUENTIAL OR PERFUNCTORY

General Facts: Vendor A sells a piece of equipment and installation services related to that equipment to Customer B. Total arrangement consideration is

$100,000 and is paid in full by Customer B upon delivery of the equipment. The equipment's carrying value in inventory is $75,000. The installation services are not complex and do not significantly alter the equipment's capabilities. Customer B has bought this equipment from Vendor A in the past and could install the equipment itself using an installation and operation manual provided by Vendor A. As a matter of convenience, however, Customer B purchases the installation services from Vendor A. Vendor A has a history of providing the installation services in a timely manner and reliably estimating the costs of providing the installation. The costs of providing the installation services for other customers for the same piece of equipment have not varied significantly. Vendor A anticipates providing the installation services within one week of the equipment being delivered. There are no general or specific return/refund rights included in this arrangement. Vendor A delivers the equipment on December 31, 20X1 and provides the installation services on January 6, 20X2, When the installation services should not be treated separately for accounting purposes, Vendor A has an accounting policy that requires it to evaluate whether those services should be treated as an inconsequential or perfunctory remaining performance obligation. Aside from the effects of the installation services, Vendor A concludes that the general conditions for recognizing revenue related to the equipment are met upon delivery of the equipment on December 31, 20X1. Similarly, Vendor A concludes that the general conditions for recognizing revenue related to the installation services are met upon performance of those services on January 6, 20X2.

VARIATION 1

Additional Facts: Vendor A has never sold the equipment without the installation and has never provided standalone installation services. Since another vendor has never installed Vendor A's equipment and since Vendor A has never provided standalone installation services, Vendor A does not have evidence to support the fair value of the installation services. Vendor A incurs $1,000 of costs when providing the installation services.

Discussion: Vendor A should not treat the equipment and installation services as separate elements for accounting purposes due to the lack of fair value evidence for the installation services (the undelivered element). Factors supporting a potential conclusion that the installation services are an inconsequential or perfunctory remaining performance obligation include:

- The installation services are not essential to the functionality of the equipment since (a) the installation is not complex and does not significantly alter the equipment's capabilities, and (b) Customer B could install the equipment on its own. While no other vendors have provided the installation service, Customer B could perform this service for itself, or, in theory, could provide this service for other customers of Vendor A.

- There are no general or specific refund rights, as such Vendor A's failure to perform the installation services would not result in Customer B receiving a full or partial refund or rejecting (or a right to a refund or to reject) the equipment.

- Vendor A has a demonstrated history of providing the installation services in a timely manner and reliably estimating the remaining costs.

- Vendor A's costs of providing the installation services for other customers for the same piece of equipment have not varied significantly.

- The skills required to provide the installation services are not specialized. This is supported by the fact that Customer B could install the equipment itself using the installation and operation manual provided by Vendor A.

- Vendor A's costs of providing the installation services ($1,000) are insignificant in relation to the contract's overall fee (1% of $100,000), gross profit (4.2% of $24,000), and operating income.

- At the time the equipment is delivered to Customer B, Vendor A anticipates that the installation services will be provided within one week. This is a typical timeframe for Vendor A to provide these installation services to its customers.

- The $100,000 arrangement fee is paid in full upon delivery of the equipment. In other words, payment of no portion of the fee is contingent upon Vendor A providing the installation services.

One factor that cannot be evaluated in this analysis is whether the fair value of providing the installation services are insignificant in relation to the contract fee, gross profit, and operating income allocable to the equipment. This is due to Vendor A's conclusion that it does not have appropriate fair value evidence for the installation services, thereby precluding it from allocating the arrangement consideration for purposes of analyzing this factor. However, Vendor A believes the other factors present in the arrangement compensate for its inability to evaluate this factor and provide sufficient evidence to conclude that the installation services are an inconsequential or perfunctory remaining performance obligation.

Accounting: On December 31, 20X1, Vendor A records the entire arrangement consideration as revenue, recognizes the equipment's inventory costs as costs of sales, and accrues the costs of performing the installation:

Cash	$100,000	
Equipment Revenue		$100,000
Cost of Sales	$76,000	
Inventory		$75,000
Accrued Costs of Installation Services		$1,000

On January 6, 20X2, Vendor A relieves the accrual related to providing the installation services:

Accrued Costs of Installation Services	$1,000

Cash or Liability (depending on nature of costs) $1,000

VARIATION 2

Additional Facts: Vendor A has never sold the equipment without the installation and has never provided standalone installation services. Since another vendor has never installed Vendor A's equipment and since Vendor A has never provided standalone installation services, Vendor A does not have fair value evidence for the installation services. Vendor A incurs $15,000 of costs when providing the installation services.

Discussion: Vendor A should not treat the equipment and installation services as separate elements for accounting purposes due to the lack of fair value evidence for the installation services (the undelivered element). The analysis of whether the installation services are an inconsequential or perfunctory performance obligation is similar to that in Variation 1, with one significant exception. In Variation 2, Vendor A is not able to conclude that its costs of providing the installation services ($15,000) are insignificant in relation to the contract's overall contract fee (15% of $100,000), gross profit (150% of $10,000), and operating income. As a result, Vendor A concludes that the installation services are more than inconsequential or perfunctory.

Accounting: On December 31, 20X1, Vendor A records receipt of the cash from Customer B, recognizes deferred revenue for that amount, and reclassifies the equipment to an account that signifies it is being held by others:

Cash	$100,000	
Deferred Revenue		$100,000
Inventory Held by Others	$75,000	
Inventory		$75,000

On January 6, 20X2, Vendor A recognizes the arrangement consideration as revenue and records the related equipment inventory costs and costs of performing the services as cost of sales:

Deferred Revenue	$100,000	
Equipment and Installation Services Revenue		$100,000
Cost of Sales—Equipment	$75,000	
Cost of Sales—Installation Services	$15,000	
Inventory Held by Others		$75,000
Cash or Liability (depending on nature of costs)		$15,000

VARIATION 3

Additional Facts: Historically, Vendor A has sold the equipment without the installation. In those situations, the customer has either performed the installation itself using the installation and operation manual provided by Vendor A or hired a professional installer to perform the installation for $2,000. Vendor A charges $98,000 for the equipment when it sells it on a standalone basis. When providing the installation services Vendor A incurs $1,000 of costs.

Discussion: Vendor A should treat the equipment and installation services as separate elements for accounting purposes since: (a) the equipment has value to Customer B on a standalone basis (i.e., Customer B could perform the installation services itself or could hire a professional installer to perform the installation services), (b) appropriate fair value evidence exists to allocate the arrangement consideration (i.e., the relative fair value method should be used since objective and reliable evidence of fair value exists for both the equipment and installation), and (c) no general right of return or refund exists. The amount allocated to the equipment is $98,000 and the amount allocated to the installation services is $2,000.

Accounting: On December 31, 20X1, Vendor A records the arrangement consideration allocated to the equipment as revenue, defers the arrangement consideration allocated to the installation, and recognizes the equipment's inventory costs as costs of sales:

Cash	$100,000	
Deferred Revenue		$2,000
Equipment Revenue		$98,000
Cost of Sales—Equipment	$75,000	
Inventory		$75,000

On January 6, 20X2, Vendor A records the arrangement consideration allocated to the installation services as revenue and the costs of providing those services as cost of sales:

Deferred Revenue	$2,000	
Installation Services Revenue		$2,000
Cost of Sales—Installation Services	$1,000	
Cash or Liability (depending on nature of costs)		$1,000

COMPARISON OF VARIATIONS

These variations illustrate how the timing of revenue recognition can differ depending on the conclusions reached related to whether the multiple-element arrangement should be separated, and, if not, whether the remaining performance obligation may be considered inconsequential or perfunctory:

	Timing of Revenue Recognition
Variation 1—Should not treat equipment and installation services as separate elements, and installation services are inconsequential or perfunctory	All arrangement consideration is recognized as revenue when equipment is delivered
Variation 2—Should not treat equipment and installation services as separate elements, and installation services are more than inconsequential or perfunctory	All arrangement consideration is recognized as revenue when installation services are performed
Variation 3—Should treat equipment and installation services as separate elements	Portion of arrangement consideration is recognized as revenue when equipment is delivered and a portion of arrangement consideration is recognized as revenue when installation services are performed

Analysis of Multiple Remaining Performance Obligations

Generally, if there is more than one remaining performance obligation, the evaluation of whether those remaining performance obligations are inconsequential or perfunctory should be performed for the group of potentially inconsequential or perfunctory performance obligations. For example, if a vendor believes that four remaining performance obligations are inconsequential or perfunctory, it should not evaluate each one separately as those remaining performance obligations in the aggregate may represent a significant portion of the value of the arrangement. Instead, the vendor should evaluate the four items potentially being considered inconsequential or perfunctory as a group. If, as a group, the four items are not inconsequential or perfunctory, the company may then evaluate three of the four as a group to determine whether the group of three is inconsequential or perfunctory as a whole, and so on. In addition, a remaining performance obligation should generally not be considered inconsequential or perfunctory if it is one of a number of similar items that are not inconsequential or perfunctory as a group.

Accounting for Remaining Performance Obligations Considered Inconsequential or Perfunctory

A vendor should follow its policy for determining whether a remaining performance obligation is inconsequential or perfunctory consistently. In other words, similar remaining performance obligations in similar arrangements should be analyzed consistently for purposes of determining whether the remaining performance obligations are inconsequential or perfunctory. The cost of any remaining performance obligations considered inconsequential or perfunctory should be recognized (with the expense recorded as part of cost of sales) when revenue from the arrangement is first recognized (SAB Topic 13A3c, ques. 1).

Sufficient Evidence of Fair Value Does Not Exist

When sufficient evidence of fair value does not exist to allocate arrangement consideration among the elements in a multiple-element arrangement (where these elements are not treated as inconsequential or perfunctory remaining performance obligations for accounting purposes), some portion of revenue is generally recognized upon delivery of the final element for which evidence of fair value does not exist, presuming that all other revenue recognition criteria have been met. In other words, once the last element for which sufficient evidence of fair value does not exist has been delivered, either the seller's performance under the arrangement will be complete, or all of the remaining items will be those for which sufficient evidence of fair value exists, allowing the residual method to be applied.

Thus, if an arrangement consists only of a product and post-delivery maintenance services related to that product (where the services are not treated as inconsequential or perfunctory remaining performance obligations for accounting purposes), and there is insufficient evidence of fair value to allocate arrangement consideration among the two elements, the revenue from the entire arrangement should be recognized as the maintenance is delivered. In most cases, this would be ratably over the maintenance period under the Proportional Performance Model (see Chapter 6, "Service Deliverables"). If the final element to be delivered in other similar situations is a product for which evidence of fair value does not exist, all revenue from the arrangement often would be deferred until the revenue recognition criteria related to product sales (see Chapter 5, "Product Deliverables") have been satisfied for that final element.

Delivered Item Does Not Have Standalone Value to the Customer

When a delivered item does not have value to the customer on a standalone basis, arrangement consideration otherwise allocable to the delivered item should not be recognized. That arrangement consideration should be recognized, presuming all other revenue recognition criteria have been met, when another item(s) has been provided such that the two (or more) items have value to the customer on a standalone basis. The timing or pattern of recognition at that point depends on the nature of the items involved.

> **OBSERVATION:** In the situation where a delivered element does not have value to the customer on a standalone basis (i.e., absent the delivery of one or more as-yet-undelivered elements), it is generally the case that there is at least one undelivered element that is essential to the functionality of the delivered element. This is due to the similarity between the two concepts and their common objective. It would be a rare situation where inconsistent conclusions would be reached when analyzing the concepts individually (e.g., concluding that a delivered element has value to the customer on a standalone basis when an undelivered element is essential to its functionality). As such, when the delivered element does not have value to the customer on a standalone basis absent the undelivered element, the undelivered element should not be considered an inconsequential or perfunctory remaining performance obligation since it is likely to be essential to the functionality of the delivered element.

General Refund Right Exists and Performance of Undelivered Item(s) Not Probable or Substantially in Vendor's Control

When a general refund right exists and the delivery or performance of the undelivered items is not considered probable or substantially within the control of the vendor, arrangement consideration otherwise allocable to the delivered item should not be recognized. That arrangement consideration should be recognized, presuming all other revenue recognition criteria have been met, at the earlier of: (a) the general refund right expiring (at that point, the general refund right is no longer a factor in determining whether the delivered item should be treated separately for accounting purposes) or (b) the performance of the undelivered items becoming probable *and* substantially within the control of the vendor (at that point, the company satisfies the separation condition). The timing or pattern of recognition at that point depends on the nature of the items involved.

This approach is consistent with the conclusion that would be reached in applying FAS-48. As discussed in Chapter 5, "Product Deliverables," one of the criteria that must be met to recognize revenue when the right of return exists relates to the ability to reasonably estimate the amount of future returns. If performance of an undelivered item is not probable or substantially in the vendor's control, making reasonable estimates of the amount of future returns would not be possible. Failure to meet this criterion (or any of the other necessary criteria) under FAS-48 results in the revenue being deferred until the earlier of (a) expiration of the return right, or (b) subsequently concluding that the criterion is met. While not stated explicitly in EITF 00-21, it is this guidance in FAS-48 that resulted in the inclusion of the general refund right condition in EITF 00-21.

> **OBSERVATION:** In the situation where a multiple-element arrangement is not separated because a general refund right exists and performance of the undelivered item(s) is not probable or substantially in the vendor's control, it is highly unlikely that the undelivered item(s) could be considered inconsequential or perfunctory. If performance of the undelivered item(s) is not probable or substantially in the vendor's control, evaluation of many of the "inconsequential or perfunctory" indicators described earlier in this section would not be possible. An inability to evaluate these indicators is indicative of the undelivered item(s) being more than inconsequential or perfunctory.

RECOGNITION WHEN SPECIFIC REFUND RIGHT EXISTS

When a specific refund right results in some or all of the amount otherwise allocable to a delivered element (the at-risk amount) not being allocated to that element, the at-risk amount should only be recognized, provided the other criteria for recognition have been met, upon the earlier of (a) the specific refund right expiring (at that point, the specific refund right is no longer a factor in determining the amount of revenue that should be allocated to the delivered element), or (b) the undelivered element on which the specific refund right is based is delivered (at that point, the basis for the specific refund right no longer exists). The timing or pattern of recognition at that point depends on the nature of the items involved.

Given the cost deferral issues that may arise when a specific refund right exists, a question may arise regarding recognition of the amount allocated to a delivered element that is not at-risk (i.e., there is not a specific refund right that could result in the refund of the amount ultimately allocated to the delivered element). For example, assume the following: (1) there are two elements in the arrangement—Element 1 and Element 2, (2) total arrangement consideration is $100, (3) the amounts otherwise allocable to Element 1 and Element 2 based on their relative fair values are $70 and $30, respectively, (4) Element 1 is delivered before Element 2, (5) $100 is due upon receipt of Element 1, (6) if Element 2 is not delivered, the vendor must refund $60, and (7) Element 1 and Element 2 otherwise meet the separation criteria in EITF 00-21. In this situation, the amount ultimately allocated to Element 1 is $40. The $70 that would otherwise have been allocable to Element 1 is reduced to $40 (a reduction of $30) because the amount otherwise allocated to the undelivered element ($30) is less than the amount that would be refunded if the undelivered element is not delivered ($60, for a difference of $30). Depending on the cost of Element 1 and how that cost is recognized, the recognition of $40 of revenue related to Element 1 could result in a negative profit margin. As a result, a question has arisen regarding whether the $40 of revenue ultimately allocated to Element 1 (and the related cost) could be deferred until the revenue ultimately allocated to Element 2 (and the related cost) is recognized. In this situation, it would be inappropriate to defer the $40 of revenue ultimately allocated to Element 1 if it otherwise meets the applicable revenue recognition criteria. To allow deferral of the revenue in this situation would effectively make the conclusion reached based on applying the guidance in EITF 00-21 (i.e., that elements should be treated separately) optional. The EITF discussed the notion of optionality during its deliberations on EITF 00-21 and rejected it. Whether some or all of the cost of Element 1 can be deferred in this situation is discussed in Chapter 8, "Miscellaneous Issues."

> **OBSERVATION:** The existence of a specific refund right related to an as-yet-undelivered element precludes treatment of that element as inconsequential or perfunctory since the vendor's failure to fulfill the remaining performance obligation would result in the customer receiving a full or partial refund or rejecting (or a right to a refund or to reject) delivered items.

CHAPTER 5
PRODUCT DELIVERABLES

CONTENTS

BACKGROUND

The most basic (and probably most common) sales transaction is the sale of a product for cash. Although the transaction may be straightforward, the accounting for it often is not. For example, a retail sale in which the customer pays cash for a product at a checkout counter would seem to be a simple transaction to account for. By the time the customer leaves the store, the goods have been delivered and paid for, so it would appear there is no question the revenue has been both earned and realized, and therefore should be recognized at that time. However, even this simple transaction typically includes terms that can present revenue recognition issues. For example, most retailers grant customers a right of return for a limited period of time. In addition, there may be both explicit and implicit warranties on the products purchased. These and other common sales terms raise questions as to the timing of revenue recognition. More complicated product sale arrangements, such as those that exist between a manufacturer and a reseller, or between a parts supplier and its major customers, can contain a myriad of other terms that complicate revenue recognition.

PRACTICE ALERT: Situations may arise where arrangements that purport to cover only the sale of products actually contain a lease. EITF 01-8 provides guidance to assist in determining whether an arrangement contains a lease. The provisions of EITF 01-8 are discussed in Chapter 3, "General Principles." When an arrangement does contain a lease, the portion of the arrangement that represents a lease must be accounted for as such. This is the case even though the arrangement is not formally characterized as a lease. Separation of the lease element from the other elements in the arrangement is discussed in Chapter 4, "Multiple-Element Arrangements."

This chapter explores the significant issues that commonly arise in product sales and are unique to product transactions. When addressing the issues, it is important that each deliverable in a transaction be analyzed separately. Therefore, the issues discussed in this chapter should be evaluated with respect to each product element or deliverable. However, if there are multiple deliverables in the transaction, the interrelationship of these deliverables may give rise to issues beyond those that exist in a single-element transaction. These additional issues are discussed in Chapter 4.

SURVEY OF ACCOUNTING LITERATURE

The accounting literature that addresses general product sale issues under U.S. GAAP is not at all comprehensive. What general guidance there is on accounting for product sale transactions can be found in the FASB Concept Statements and SAB Topic 13. Although SAB Topic 13 technically only applies to SEC registrants, much of its guidance is built off the FASB Concept Statements and other generally accepted practices. As such, a significant amount of the guidance in SAB Topic 13 is useful even for non-public companies.

Partially compensating for the lack of general guidance are a number of pronouncements that address specific issues. For example, FAS-48 addresses sales with a right of return, and EITF 95-4 addresses equipment sold and subsequently repurchased subject to an operating lease. Other guidance on product sale transactions has been built up based on general practice over the years. In addition, international standards, most notably IAS 18, provide guidance on certain issues regarding product sales. Of course, companies reporting under U.S. GAAP are not required to follow IAS 18 and other international standards. However, for transactions that are not covered by U.S. GAAP, international standards are a good place to look for policies likely to be acceptable, even in the U.S. GAAP framework.

LISTING OF APPLICABLE LITERATURE

CON-5	Recognition and Measurement in Financial Statements of Business Enterprises
APB-21	Interest on Receivables and Payables
FAS-5	Accounting for Contingencies
FAS-48	Revenue Recognition When Right of Return Exists
FAS-49	Accounting for Product Financing Arrangements
FIN-45	Guarantor's Accounting and Disclosure Requirements for Guarantees, Including Indirect Guarantees of Indebtedness of Others, an interpretation of FASB Statements No. 5, 57, and 107 and rescission of FASB Interpretation No. 34
FTB 90-1	Accounting for Separately Priced Extended Warranty and Product Maintenance Contracts
EITF 95-1	Revenue Recognition on Sales with a Guaranteed Minimum Resale Value
EITF 95-4	Revenue Recognition on Equipment Sold and Subsequently Repurchased Subject to an Operating Lease
EITF 01-8	Determining Whether an Arrangement Contains a Lease
EITF 03-12	Impact of FASB Interpretation No. 45 on Issue No. 95-1
IAS 18	Revenue
SAB Topic 13	Revenue Recognition

GENERAL CONDITIONS FOR RECOGNITION

As with all revenues, revenue from product sales should be recognized when it has been earned and is realized or realizable. Revenue from product sales is generally earned when the products are delivered to the customer. Such revenue is usually considered realizable once the customer has committed to pay for the products, as long as the customer's ability to pay is not in doubt. However, various types of uncertainties may exist that affect when revenue is recognized (CON-5, pars. 83-84).

As discussed in Chapter 3, "General Principles," revenue is considered to be earned and realizable when all of the following conditions are met:

1. Persuasive evidence of an arrangement exists.

2. The arrangement fee is fixed or determinable.

3. Delivery or performance has occurred.
4. Collectibility is reasonably assured.

Also as discussed in Chapter 3, the delivery condition in a product sale is generally evaluated under the Completed Performance model, which results in delivery being considered to occur at a point in time, rather than over a period of time. Although that point in time is often the point when the product is physically delivered to the customer, there are many arrangements in which this is not the case.

The guidance in this chapter addresses most product deliverables. However, certain contracts to deliver products should be accounted for under contract accounting. In general, these are contracts to build a customized product that will take an extended period of time to fulfill. Contract accounting, including the scope of transactions to which it should be applied, is fully discussed in Chapter 9, "Contract Accounting."

Risks and Rewards of Ownership

In a product sale, all of the general conditions for revenue recognition are usually present by the time the product is delivered, i.e., when the buyer takes physical possession of the product from the seller. However, several important factors must be taken into account in determining whether the transfer of physical possession is accompanied by the transfer of enough of the risks and rewards of product ownership to be considered an earnings event. In general, a seller is not considered to have sufficiently met the delivery requirement for purposes of recognizing revenue until the substantial risks and rewards of ownership of the goods have passed from the seller to the buyer.

The term "risks and rewards of ownership" refers to all of the things that would normally accrue to an owner of products. For example, risks of ownership include things such as a loss of market value, obsolescence, theft, physical damage, and excess inventory. Rewards of ownership include gains due to increases in value, the right to use and restrict the use of the product, the right to sell or otherwise determine the disposition of the product, the right to enhance the existing product, and the ability to grant security interests in the product.

Through contractual arrangements between the buyer and seller, some risks and rewards of ownership may remain with the seller even though the buyer has possession of the products, and others may transfer to the buyer before the buyer has possession of the products. Because of this, physical transfer of the goods does not always indicate that revenue has been earned. In fact, each of the issues discussed in this chapter generally relates to determining

EXHIBIT 5-1
OVERVIEW OF PRODUCT REVENUE RECOGNITION

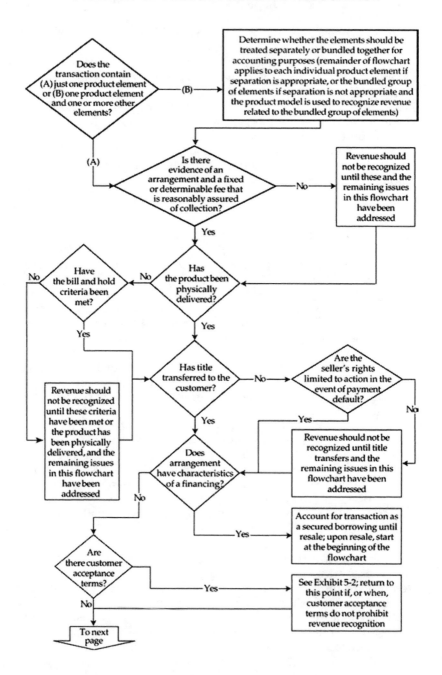

EXHIBIT 5-1 continued

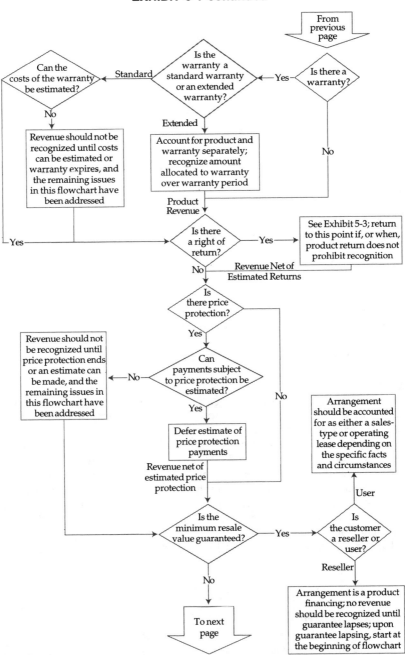

From previous page

Is there a warranty?

—Yes→

Is the warranty a standard warranty or an extended warranty?

—Standard→ Can the costs of the warranty be estimated?

No →

Revenue should not be recognized until costs can be estimated or warranty expires, and the remaining issues in this flowchart have been addressed

Extended

Account for product and warranty separately; recognize amount allocated to warranty over warranty period

No

Product Revenue

Yes →

Is there a right of return?

—Yes→ See Exhibit 5-3; return to this point if, or when, product return does not prohibit recognition

No

Revenue Net of Estimated Returns

Is there price protection?

Yes

Revenue should not be recognized until price protection ends or an estimate can be made, and the remaining issues in this flowchart have been addressed

←No— Can payments subject to price protection be estimated?

Yes

Defer estimate of price protection payments

No

Arrangement should be accounted for as either a sales-type or operating lease depending on the specific facts and circumstances

User

Revenue net of estimated price protection

Is the minimum resale value guaranteed?

—Yes→

Is the customer a reseller or user?

Reseller

No

Arrangement is a product financing; no revenue should be recognized until guarantee lapses; upon guarantee lapsing, start at the beginning of flowchart

To next page

EXHIBIT 5-1 continued

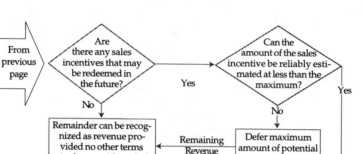

whether a particular risk or reward that remains with the seller is enough to prevent revenue recognition.

Manufacturers versus Resellers

The same revenue recognition guidance generally applies whether the products being sold have been manufactured by the company or were purchased for resale. Thus, the act of manufacturing or building a product is not an earnings event, except in the case of long-term contracts accounted for under the Percentage-of-Completion model (see Chapter 9, "Contract Accounting").

The identity of the customer, however, may have some effect on the revenue recognition analysis. Although the principles of revenue recognition are the same whether the customer is an end-user or a reseller, the results of applying those principles can vary significantly depending on whether the customer is an end-user or a reseller. For example, the evaluation of rights of return and other uncertainties can produce very different results depending on whether the customer is an end user or a reseller.

DELIVERY

Transfer of Title

As noted above, physical delivery is often the time when revenue is considered earned, since the risks and rewards of ownership generally rest with the holder of the products and therefore pass to the buyer at delivery. However, physical delivery without the passage of "title" from the seller to the buyer generally is not sufficient to recognize revenue, except in rare cases (see "Title Retained after Delivery," below). "Title" is a term that generally equates to ownership of goods in a legal sense. The party that has title to goods is assumed, absent contractual arrangements stating otherwise, to be at risk of loss with respect to, and to control the use of, such goods. Therefore, products are generally considered delivered for accounting purposes when title passes from the seller to the buyer. In many transactions, such as retail purchases, passage of title is not documented in any formal manner, but the timing of title transfer is clear from the transaction (e.g., title passes at the register when the customer pays for the merchandise).

However, the timing of title transfer is not as clear in many other transactions. For example, without examining the contractual arrangements, it is not clear when title to goods delivered by mail transfers from the seller to the buyer; in some cases title transfers when the goods are put in the mail, while in others title transfers only upon receipt by the buyer. A similar situation exists for manufacturers who ship to their customers by truck, train, etc., using a third-party shipping agent. As transfer of title is basically a legal concept, it may be necessary to consult with legal experts to determine when title transfers. However, in most situations, a basic understanding of local laws and the terms agreed upon by the buyer and seller are enough to determine when title has transferred.

> **OBSERVATION:** Transfer of title is important in revenue recognition for product sales because it generally determines when the risk of loss and control of the products passes from the seller to the buyer. However, contractual arrangements can separate the transfer of certain risks or rights from the transfer of title. As discussed above, when risks and rewards of ownership remain with the seller, revenue recognition is generally not appropriate. This is true even if title has been transferred. For further discussion, see "Consignment Sales" below.

Free-on-Board (FOB) Terms

Free-on-Board, or FOB, terms generally designate which party pays for the shipping of the products. FOB shipping point means that the shipping is free to the seller and paid for by the buyer, while FOB destination means that the shipping is free to the buyer and paid for by the seller. In most cases, the party that pays for the shipping owns (has title to) the products during shipment. Therefore, FOB destination terms indicate that title to the product passes upon delivery to the customer, while FOB shipping point terms indicate that title passes when the products leave the seller's premises. The FOB terms are usually documented in the contract between the parties, the purchase order, the bill of lading, or some other documentation of the sales transaction.

> **OBSERVATION:** Although rare, contracts may also specify that the title transfers at another point during transit—for example, when a particular border is crossed. As discussed below, certain contracts may also specify transfer of title as either before the goods leave the seller's premises or some time after they are received by the buyer.

Presuming that risks and rewards of ownership transfer at the same time title transfers, FOB terms also indicate the point at which revenue can be considered earned. Products shipped FOB shipping point can generally be considered delivered for accounting purposes when the goods leave the seller's premises, while products shipped FOB destination are not considered delivered for accounting purposes until the goods reach the customer. As such, FOB terms indicate whether outbound shipments in transit should be recognized as a sale at period-end. FOB shipping point terms result in recognition of revenue and cost of sales at the end of a reporting period for shipments in transit at that date (provided the other criteria for recognition have been met), while FOB destination terms result in shipments in transit not being recorded until the subsequent reporting period (SAB Topic 13A3a).

> **OBSERVATION:** Even when FOB destination terms are used, such that title does not transfer until the buyer receives the products, risk of physical loss on the products may not be held by the seller during shipment because the third-party shipping agent may be liable for losses incurred. This fact, however, does not allow the seller to recognize revenue before the shipping agent completes delivery to the buyer because the shipper is acting as the seller's agent and the seller has not fulfilled its obligations to the buyer until the products are delivered.

> ☞ **PRACTICE POINTER:** A majority of companies routinely record all sales transactions when they leave the company's premises. This is done even if the goods are shipped FOB destination because it is far easier to determine the point at which goods are shipped than to determine when the customer receives them. When this procedure is used on FOB destination shipments, the company should evaluate the amount of outbound shipments in transit at a period-end, and reverse the recognition of sales and cost of sales for those transactions if the effects are material.

Local Laws

As noted above, title is essentially a legal concept. As such, laws sometimes specify the point at which title transfers. In some cases, these laws can be overridden by contractual language, while in others the laws override any other documentation of title transfer. Local laws must be taken into account in determining when title has transferred. This is especially important for transactions in which the seller and buyer are in different jurisdictions.

Subscriptions

When products are sold under a subscription arrangement, the delivery condition should be evaluated under the Proportional Performance model. Each product to be delivered should be allocated a portion of the subscription revenue in proportion to its value. In many cases, all the items shipped are allocated the same amount of revenue, as their individual values do not vary significantly (for example, a magazine or newspaper subscription). As each item under the subscription is delivered, revenue allocable to that item should be recognized, unless other terms of the transaction prohibit recognition. It is not acceptable to recognize subscription revenue when the subscription is received or billed with an accrual of the estimated costs to fulfill the subscription, even when the subscription price is completely nonrefundable. Although in this case the subscription revenue is realized at the inception of the subscription, it has not yet been earned because the products have not been delivered.

Delivery to an Alternate Site or Third Party

If delivery is made to a third party designated by the buyer, the seller's performance may generally be considered complete upon delivery to that third party, unless the seller retains an explicit or implicit obligation to deliver the product to the customer. For example, a company purchasing a significant amount of inventory that exceeds its currently available storage space may direct the seller to deliver the products to a third-party warehouse for storage, rather than to one of its own sites. As long as full payment is due on normal terms upon delivery to the third party, and the customer is responsible for storage costs and transporting the product to its own facilities when needed, the delivery criterion would be met.

However, if, in a similar situation, a significant portion of the purchase price is not payable until the product reaches the customer, then delivery to the third party should not result in revenue recognition, even when the buyer has chosen the third party. The delay in payment until final delivery indicates that the seller retains risk until the customer receives the product at the final delivery point. If this is the case, a partial payment received upon delivery to the third party should be reflected as a liability, rather than as revenue (SAB Topic 13A3a).

When a product is delivered to a third party selected by the seller, revenue usually must be delayed until the product is delivered to the customer. For example, a mail order catalog company may deliver goods for orders that have been received to an outside fulfillment house, which will then package and ship the goods to the customer. In this type of arrangement, revenue should not be recognized until delivery to the customer because the fulfillment house is merely an agent of the seller. In general, delivery to a third party designated by the seller is only sufficient to consider the products delivered for accounting purposes if the buyer specifically acknowledges that, upon delivery to the third party, the seller has no further obligation with respect to the transaction, and that the buyer must look solely to the third party to obtain final delivery of the products.

Title Retained after Delivery

In some situations, the seller retains title after delivery of goods. The most common situation in which this occurs is a consignment. As discussed further below, delivery should not be considered to occur on a consignment until title passes to the buyer. However, in certain limited situations, even though title is retained, the product may still be considered delivered for accounting purposes. In these limited situations, all significant risks and rewards of ownership must pass to the buyer, even though title has not passed.

One example of such a situation is when the seller retains title solely to provide security for the collection of the purchase price of the products, and the seller's rights are limited to taking actions only in the event of non-payment. This may occur in countries where local law and custom does not provide the seller with a security interest in products that have been sold but not yet paid for. If the seller retains title, but its rights are limited to recovering the goods in the event of non-payment—that is, despite holding title, the seller cannot rescind the transaction, prohibit the customer from doing what it wishes with the goods, etc.—then revenue recognition upon delivery is acceptable provided the other conditions for revenue recognition have been met. In the U.S., however, the Universal Commercial Code provides the seller with a security interest in goods that have not yet been paid for even after passage of title, so title generally need not be retained for this purpose (SAB Topic 13A2, ques. 3).

☞ **PRACTICE POINTER:** Some companies sell their products pursuant to standard contracts that include a number of protective clauses that are generally meant to enhance the seller's rights to payment for the products provided. Retention of title until payment is received is a fairly common clause that may be found in these contracts. Although the clause is included for a good business purpose, the retention of title generally exposes the seller to certain risks and entitles it to certain rights (in addition to a security interest in the event of non-payment) with respect to the products. If that is the case, such a clause precludes revenue recognition until payment for the goods is received, even if it is the seller's intent not to exercise its rights. Therefore, companies that do retain title to products after shipment but before payment should determine the legal effects of retaining title. If title retention makes a difference only in the event timely payment does not occur, revenue recognition may still be appropriate. However, if title retention provides the seller with any additional rights or exposes it to any additional risks, the product should not be considered delivered until payment is received and title passes.

EXAMPLE: TITLE RETENTION TO RECOVER PRODUCTS IN EVENT OF CUSTOMER DEFAULT

Unisys Corporation Form 10-K—Fiscal Year Ended December 31, 2004

Revenue from hardware sales is recognized upon shipment and the passage of title. Outside the United States, the company recognizes revenue even if it retains a form of title to products delivered to customers, provided the sole purpose is to enable the company to recover the products in the event of customer payment default and the arrangement does not prohibit the customer's use of the product in the ordinary course of business.

Other transactions in which the seller retains title after delivery should be analyzed as leasing transactions. If the transaction can be classified as a sales-type lease under the leasing literature, revenue recognition upon delivery may be appropriate.

DELIVERY WITHOUT A TRANSFER OF RISK

Consignment Sales

A shipment of goods "on consignment" generally indicates that payment is expected only upon resale or use of the product by the purchaser and that unsold items may be returned to the seller. In these cases, title generally does not pass until the purchaser resells the inventory to its customer or uses it in production. Although the purchaser holds the inventory, it is still owned by the seller and the seller is not paid until the inventory is resold or used by the purchaser. In short, a consignment "sale" is not a sale at all. The seller retains title and all risks and rewards of ownership, except, perhaps, custodial risks (e.g., the risk of physical loss). Therefore, the shipment of goods on consignment does not constitute delivery for accounting purposes and does not trigger the recognition of revenue (SAB Topic 13A2, ques. 2).

Consignment sales can generally be identified because the contract specifies them as such. However, a contract need not be labeled as a consignment to be treated as one for accounting purposes. For example, except in rare situations (see "Title Retained After Delivery" above), any purported sale in which title remains with the seller until the buyer resells, pays for, or uses the goods should be treated like a consignment, since the lack of title transfer will usually mean that significant risks and rewards remain with the seller.

Even when title transfers to the buyer upon delivery, the terms of the arrangement may indicate that the transaction is so similar to a consignment that it should be treated as one. This frequently occurs in transactions involving high-priced items, in which the buyer is, in substance, acting as an agent for the seller. For example, an arrangement in which title passes to the customer upon shipment, but the customer has unlimited rights of return and need not pay for the goods until it resells them, appears to be substantively the same as a consignment. In these cases, the transaction should be treated as a consignment, and revenue should not be recognized until the goods are resold. Determining when a transaction bears too much similarity to a consignment to be treated as a sale upon delivery is a matter of significant judgment. Some of the factors that may indicate that a sale is an in-substance consignment are listed below:

> **OBSERVATION:** Although these factors may be explicitly detailed in the sales agreement, they also could exist by custom or due to the relationship between the parties. For example, a small manufacturer whose product is mainly distributed by a large retailer may have little or no leverage to enforce terms of the sales agreement, and may therefore agree to accept returns or give sales discounts that it is not explicitly required to accept or give. In that situation, an evaluation of whether the arrangement is substantively a consignment arrangement should consider these implicit rights.

1. *Payment is not due until the goods have been resold.* This removes the buyer's risk of loss, as it does not pay for the items unless and until it can resell them.

2. *The buyer lacks substance, or uses financing or guarantees from the seller to purchase the products.* In this situation, the seller appears

to have retained the risk of loss through its financing-related commitments.

> **OBSERVATION:** If the seller guarantees debt taken out by the buyer to purchase the seller's products and the arrangement is not deemed to be a product financing, the seller has entered into a multiple-element arrangement with the buyer. The multiple-element arrangement consists of the product element and the guarantee element. This type of situation and the requirements of FIN-45 are discussed in more detail in Chapter 4, "Multiple-Element Arrangements."

3. *The buyer has a relatively unlimited right of return.* This removes the buyer's risk of loss, as it can return the product and get its money back if the item cannot be resold.

4. *The buyer pays more than other customers or makes purchases above and beyond its normal needs.* This is an indicator that some type of side arrangement may be in place between the seller and buyer.

5. *The seller imposes constraints on the buyer's sales, pricing, credit, and advertising policies.* This indicates that the seller has retained some control over the use and disposition of the product, which may indicate that not enough risks and rewards of ownership have passed to the buyer to permit revenue recognition.

6. *The seller agrees to take returns from the buyer if the buyer gets returns from its customer.* This removes some of the buyer's risk of market acceptance of the product and may indicate that the reseller is essentially acting as a sales agent for the seller.

7. *The seller agrees to assume the credit risk that exists in the buyer/reseller's sales to end customers.* When a seller agrees to assume its customer's credit risk on resales, the reseller may be acting substantively as the vendor's agent in distributing the product.

8. *The payment due to the seller varies based on its customer's success in reselling the product.* Similar to the previous point, if a company's payment varies based upon its customer's resales of the product, the reseller may be acting as an agent.

> **OBSERVATION:** None of the factors discussed above definitively indicate that an arrangement should be accounted for as a consignment sale. However, any transaction that includes one or more of the above factors should be critically evaluated to determine its substance. In addition, the company's history with respect to the ultimate resolution of these transactions may be instructional in determining the substance of the transaction. For example, if the buyer/reseller has a very long right

of return, but payment for the products is made promptly, and returns are small and predictable, that right of return may not be indicative of an arrangement that is substantively a consignment. Conversely, if payment is not due until the end of the long return period or if significant returns often occur just before the return period lapses, the arrangement would appear to be substantively a consignment.

SEC REGISTRANT ALERT: In early 2003, the SEC staff issued the Report Pursuant to Section 704 of the Sarbanes-Oxley Act of 2002 (the Section 704 Report). In compiling the information in the Section 704 Report, the SEC staff studied enforcement actions filed during the period July 31, 1997, through July 30, 2002. The greatest number of enforcement actions brought by the SEC related to improper revenue recognition. One of the common revenue recognition issues highlighted in the Section 704 Report relates to consignment sales. The SEC staff points out in the report that the accounting for consignment sales (and other contingency sales) "generally failed to meet the criteria under GAAP for recognizing revenue because the seller had not actually assumed the risks and rewards of ownership, the terms of the sale were modified or the revenue was otherwise not realized (or realizable) and earned." This finding is a strong indication that more attention should be given to identifying and accounting for consignment sales.

EXAMPLES: IN-SUBSTANCE CONSIGNMENTS

Symantec, Inc. Form 10-K—Fiscal Year Ended April 1, 2005

We recognize revenue in accordance with generally accepted accounting principles that have been prescribed for the software industry. Revenue recognition requirements in the software industry are very complex and they require us to make many estimates.

We expect our distributors and resellers to maintain adequate inventory to meet future customer demand, which is generally 4 to 6 weeks of customer demand based on recent buying trends. We ship product to our distributors and resellers at their request and based on their valid purchase orders. Our distributors and resellers base the quantity of their orders on their estimates to meet future customer demand, which may exceed our expected level of a 4 to 6 week supply. We offer limited rights of return if the inventory held by our distributors and resellers is below the expected level of a 4 to 6 week supply. We estimate future returns under these limited rights of return in accordance with Statement of Financial Accounting Standards, or SFAS, No. 48, *Revenue Recognition When Right of Return Exists.* We typically offer liberal rights of return if inventory held by our distributors and resellers exceeds the expected level. Because we cannot reasonably estimate the amount of excess inventory that will be returned, we do not recognize revenue or record accounts receivable for the amount in excess of the expected inventory levels. On the same basis, we reduce the associated cost of revenues, which is primarily related to materials, and include this amount in inventory. We recognize these revenues and the associated cost of revenues when the liberal rights of return expire, which is when the inventory levels no longer exceed the expected level of a 4 to 6 week supply. If we made different estimates, material differences may result in the amount and timing of our net revenues and cost of revenues for any period presented.

As of each of the fiscal years ended March 31, 2005, 2004, and 2003, the amount of net revenues not recognized related to excess inventory represented no more than 3% of total net revenues recognized during each of the years then ended. Associated costs that were included in inventory as of each of the fiscal years ended March 31, 2005, 2004, and 2003 represented no more than 2% of the total cost of revenues recorded during each of the years then ended.

Advanced Micro Devices, Inc. Form 10-K—Fiscal Year Ended December 26, 2004

The Company sells to distributors under terms allowing the distributors certain rights of return and price protection on unsold merchandise held by them. The distributor agreements, which may be cancelled by either party upon specified notice, generally contain a provision for the return of the Company's products in the event the agreement with the distributor is terminated and the distributor's products have not been sold. Accordingly, the Company defers the gross margin resulting from the deferral of both revenue and related product costs from sales to distributors with agreements that have the aforementioned terms until the merchandise is resold by the distributors. The Company also sells its products to distributors with substantial independent operations under sales arrangements whose terms do not allow for rights of return or price protection on unsold products held by them. In these instances, the Company recognizes revenue when it ships the product directly to the distributors.

Stryker Corporation Annual Report—Fiscal Year Ended December 31, 2004

Revenue Recognition: A significant portion of the Company's Orthopaedic Implants revenue is generated from consigned inventory maintained at hospitals or with field representatives. For these products, revenue is recognized at the time the Company receives appropriate notification that the product has been used or implanted. The Company records revenue from MedSurg Equipment product sales when title and risk of ownership have been transferred to the customer, which is typically upon shipment to the customer.

Product Financing Arrangements

In the consignment arrangements discussed above, payment to the vendor is delayed until the products are used or resold. When payment is due upon delivery or shortly thereafter, a transaction generally would not be considered a consignment. However, certain terms included in the sales agreement may indicate that the substance of a purported sale is actually a financing arrangement— specifically, a secured borrowing with the inventory serving as collateral. Transactions that purport to be a sale of inventory should be analyzed as financing arrangements when payment is due under normal terms, but the risks and rewards of ownership have not been transferred to the purchaser.

FAS-49 specifically addresses product financing arrangements, and specifies that if certain provisions are included in an arrangement, it must be treated as a financing arrangement, rather than as a sale. Thus, an arrangement is considered a financing arrangement whenever both of the following conditions are present:

1. *The arrangement requires the seller to repurchase the product (or a substantially identical product), or processed goods that the product is a component of, at specified prices, and the prices are not subject to change except for fluctuations due to financing and holding costs* (FAS-49, par. 5). This condition indicates that the seller has retained risks related to the market value of the product, since it will be forced to repurchase the product whether there is market demand for it or not.

2. *The amount the seller will pay to repurchase the products covers (or will be adjusted to cover) the buyer's purchasing and holding costs (including interest)* (FAS-49, par. 5). This indicates that the buyer's return from this transaction is essentially a financing return, rather than a return a company would expect from purchasing and reselling inventory.

The above terms need not explicitly exist in an arrangement for the arrangement to be treated as a product financing. For example, FAS-49 points out that a repurchase obligation substantively exists in any of the following situations:

- The seller agrees to make up any difference between certain specified resale prices and the actual resale price for products when they are sold by the buyer (FAS-49, par. 5).

- The seller has an option, but not an obligation, to repurchase the product, but there is a significant incentive for the seller to exercise the repurchase option. An example is an arrangement that provides for a significant penalty if the seller does not exercise its option (FAS-49, par. 5).

- The buyer has a put option whereby it can require the seller to repurchase the product (FAS-49, par. 5).

> **OBSERVATION:** Many types of product financing arrangements exist and they are not always easy to identify. However, product financing transactions all share a common trait; the transaction is motivated in large part by the seller's desire to receive cash, even if it cannot completely eliminate its

responsibility for the products being sold. Thus, product financing arrangements can often be identified by determining whether the seller retains the responsibility (either in real or financial terms) for the products, even after they are paid for by the buyer. Similarly, a buyer's motivation in a product financing arrangement is generally to earn a return from the seller on the money it spends to purchase and hold the product that is similar to the return a lender would receive. Thus, for example, a sales transaction in which the buyer has a right of return that enables it to recover more than the purchase price (plus any processing costs) of the inventory items might be indicative of a financing arrangement.

When an arrangement is accounted for as a product financing arrangement, payments received from the customer should be recorded as a liability, generally classified as debt (see Chapter 11, "Presentation"). The inventory delivered to the buyer should not be removed from the seller's books. As the buyer incurs holding costs (such as insurance, etc.) and processing costs, the seller should record a payable to the buyer as if the buyer were incurring the costs on the seller's behalf. The seller should then account for the costs consistent with their nature and the seller's normal policies. Repurchase payments in excess of the original debt recorded and the accrued holding and processing costs should be treated as interest expense.

ILLUSTRATION: PRODUCT FINANCING ARRANGEMENT

Facts: Example Co. sells 100 units of Product A to Reseller for $100 per unit, receiving $10,000 cash upon delivery. Example Co. agrees that it will repurchase any unsold units of Product A from Reseller in six months at $105 per unit. Example Co. estimates, based on its history of selling Product A to Reseller, that Reseller will resell 94 of the 100 units within six months and therefore Example Co. believes it will repurchase six units in six months at $105 per unit. Market interest rates are approximately 10% for secured borrowings. Reseller sells 50 of the 100 units of Product A to a third party three months later, and sells another 44 just before the six months are up. The remaining six units are sold back to Example Co. at the stipulated $105 per unit price. For simplicity, assume that holding costs for Product A are negligible.

Accounting: Because Example Co. has granted Reseller the right to put unsold inventory back to it at a price that equals the original sales price increased by an amount that represents a financing rate of return, the transaction should be treated as a product financing arrangement. Therefore, no revenue can be recognized upon delivery, despite Example Co.'s ability to estimate its ultimate obligation under the arrangement. Since no revenue is recognized, the inventory remains on Example Co.'s books.

The accounting is as follows:

- At the inception of the arrangement, Example Co. records the cash received:

Cash	$10,000	
Debt		$10,000

- For three months, Example Co. records interest on the entire debt ($10,000 x 10% effective rate x ¼ of a year = $250)

Interest Expense	$250	
Interest Payable		$250

- When Reseller sells the first 50 units, Example Co. recognizes revenue and eliminates that portion of the debt:

Debt	$5,000	
Interest Payable	$125	
Revenue		$5,125

- For the remaining three months, Example Co. records interest on the remaining debt ($5,000 x 10% effective rate x ¼ of a year = $125):

Interest Expense	$125	
Interest Payable		$125

- When Reseller sells the next 44 units, Example Co. recognizes revenue and eliminates that portion of the debt:

Debt	$4,400	
Interest Payable	$220	
Revenue		$4,620

- Example Co. records the repurchase of the remaining six units:

Debt	$600	
Interest Payable	$30	
Cash		$630

The accounting is the same as if Example Co. borrowed $5,000 for three months and another $5,000 for six months at a 10% interest rate, and then sold 50 units of Product A at $102.50 per unit in three months and another 44 units of Product A at $105 per unit in the next three months. This is consistent with the conclusion that the original transaction is essentially a financing transaction, rather than a true product sale.

REVENUE RECOGNITION BEFORE DELIVERY

"Bill and Hold" Sales

In certain situations, it is acceptable to recognize revenue before shipment if delivery is delayed at the buyer's request, but the buyer takes title and agrees to pay for the goods in advance of delivery. This type of transaction is called a "bill and hold" sale. Although both the SEC and the IASB have addressed them, no U.S. accounting standard-setter has addressed bill and hold sales. Accordingly, private companies preparing financial statements under U.S. GAAP are not subject to any specific requirements for bill and hold transactions. However, it is necessary for such companies to adopt a consistent policy for dealing with such transactions, and the SEC and IAS frameworks are clearly the most developed policies available.

Both models attempt to ensure that revenue is only recognized on a bill and hold transaction if its substance, other than the physical location of the goods, is exactly the same as if the products had been shipped to the buyer. The criteria, every one of which must be met, are therefore somewhat restrictive, erring, especially in the SEC model, on the side of not recognizing revenue on bill and hold transactions. Public companies in the U.S. must, of course, use the SEC's model when preparing statements to be included in SEC filings. Both models are discussed below, along with comments that explain and compare the requirements in the two models.

1. *(IAS and SEC) Risks of ownership must have passed to the buyer* (IAS 18, par. 14 and SAB Topic 13A3a). This is a standard criterion that must be met before recognizing revenue in any product sale transaction.

2. *(IAS) The amount of revenue can be measured reliably* (IAS 18, par. 14). This is a standard criterion that must be met before recognizing revenue in any transaction.

   (SEC) Although the SEC's position on bill and hold sales does not specifically include a similar requirement, the requirement that the fee be fixed or determinable (see Chapter 3, "General Principles") covers this point.

3. *(IAS) The seller does not continue to exercise managerial responsibility or control over the products* (IAS 18, par. 14). If the seller does retain control or involvement, this indicates that the risk and rewards have not passed in the same way as if the products had been delivered.

   (SEC) The seller cannot retain any specific performance obligations such that the earnings process is not complete (SAB Topic 13A3a). Although the SEC focuses on the risks of continuing involvement, rather than the control that such involvement may give, the intent is similar. If the seller has any performance obligations remaining, the revenue has not been earned.

4. *(IAS) It is probable that the seller will realize revenue on the sale* (IAS 18, par. 14). This is a standard criterion that must be met before recognizing revenue in any sale.

   (SEC) The customer must have made a fixed commitment to purchase the goods, preferably in writing (SAB Topic 13A3a). The SEC states the same provision more definitively, as the staff is concerned

that any conditions or contingencies may indicate that the transaction has not yet been consummated. Thus, revenue recognition on a bill and hold transaction would be precluded if, for example, the customer holds a right of return.

5. *(IAS) Any costs to be incurred related to the sale can be measured reliably* (IAS 18, par. 14). If the seller will still incur costs of an uncertain amount, it is difficult to conclude that all of the seller's significant obligations have been fulfilled.

(SEC) The goods must be complete and ready for shipment (SAB Topic 13A3a). This essentially prohibits the incurrence of any future costs, other than those related to delivery.

6. *(IAS) It is probable that delivery will be made* (IAS 18, App. par. 1). If it is not probable that delivery will occur, the existence of the transaction is called into question, especially if payment has not yet been received.

(SEC) There must be a fixed delivery schedule that is consistent with the buyer's business purpose (SAB Topic 13A3a). The SEC believes that the delivery date or dates must be set before revenue can be recognized, a more restrictive requirement than the comparable IAS requirement.

7. *(IAS) The goods are on hand, identified, and ready for delivery* (IAS 18, App. par. 1). If the goods are not currently available for delivery, revenue recognition is not appropriate as a contract calling for delivery could not yet be fulfilled.

(SEC) The goods must be segregated from remaining inventory, so that they cannot be used to fill orders for others (SAB Topic 13A3a). This criterion is a bit more explicit than the comparable IAS criterion, requiring the goods to be treated, for all intents and purposes, as if they have been delivered to the customer.

8. *(IAS) The buyer specifically acknowledges the deferred delivery instructions* (IAS 18, App. par. 1). Without this acknowledgement, it is difficult to substantiate that a contractual arrangement for the sale exists.

(SEC) The buyer, not the seller, must request (typically in writing) that the transaction be on a bill and hold basis and the buyer must have a substantial business purpose for ordering on a bill and hold basis (SAB Topic 13A3a). The SEC's model is more restrictive as the SEC believes that bill and hold provisions must not only be acknowledged by the buyer, but actually requested by the buyer, with the reason for the request being disclosed.

9. *(IAS) The usual payment terms apply* (IAS 18, App. par. 1). Deferred payment terms may indicate that payment is tied to delivery, and that the substance of the transaction is a purchase of the goods upon shipment.

(SEC) No similar requirement exists, although extended payment terms should always be evaluated to determine whether they indicate that payment cannot be considered probable, or that payment is tied to delivery, indicating that revenue recognition on a bill and hold basis is inappropriate.

> **SEC REGISTRANT ALERT:** In early 2003, the SEC staff issued the Report Pursuant to Section 704 of the Sarbanes-Oxley Act of 2002 (the Section 704 Report). In compiling the information in the Section 704 Report, the SEC staff studied enforcement actions filed during the period July 31, 1997, through July 30, 2002. The greatest number of enforcement actions brought by the SEC related to improper revenue recognition. One of the common revenue recognition issues highlighted in the Section 704 Report relates to bill and hold transactions. The SEC staff points out in the report that "Improper accounting for bill-and-hold transactions usually involves the recording of revenue from a sale, even though the customer has not taken title of the product and assumed the risks and rewards of ownership of the products specified in the customer's purchase order or sales agreement.... These transactions may be recognized legitimately under GAAP when special criteria are met, including being done pursuant to the buyer's request." This finding emphasizes that all of the conditions discussed above must be met prior to recognizing revenue on a bill and hold transaction. It also indicates common shortcomings in bill and hold transactions from a revenue recognition perspective, including items 1 and 8 as discussed above.

The criteria discussed above have been specifically identified by the IASB and the SEC, and must exist to recognize revenue on a bill and hold basis. However, other factors might also be useful in assessing whether the substance of the bill and hold agreement is that of a consummated transaction for which revenue recognition is appropriate, or that of a (potential) future transaction for which revenue should not yet be recognized. For example:

- *Past experiences with bill and hold transactions* (SAB Topic 13A3a). If payments in past transactions were received late, or not at all, the substance of the transactions may be merely agreements to purchase at a later date, upon delivery.

- *Whether the buyer bears the risk of loss in the event of a decline in the market value of the goods* (SAB Topic 13A3a). If the buyer does not bear this risk, not all of the risks of ownership have been transferred. This may occur if, for example, there is a price-protection clause in the transaction.

- *Whether the seller's custodial risks are insurable and insured* (SAB Topic 13A3a). If the risk of holding the product is so high that insurance is unavailable or prohibitively expensive, the retained custodial risk may be too high to conclude that all substantive risks of ownership have passed to the buyer.

- *Whether the buyer's business reasons for the bill and hold have introduced a contingency to the buyer's commitment* (SAB Topic 13A3a). For example, if the buyer requests a bill and hold transaction because the buyer is not yet licensed to own or take custody of the products, that might indicate that the transaction will never be completed.

☞ **PRACTICE POINTER:** The rules for recognizing revenue on bill and hold transactions are, obviously, very restrictive. Any company that enters into bill and hold transactions that are intended to comply with the above requirements to allow revenue recognition before delivery should ensure it has very strong controls over the process of negotiating and signing contracts with customers. This is because small changes to the contract can cause an arrangement to fail the bill and hold criteria. For example, if a salesperson agrees to extended payment terms or a right of return, the timing of revenue recognition on a bill and hold transaction would likely be affected, even though such clauses might not affect revenue recognition on a standard sales transaction. The controls should also ensure that revenue recognition on bill and hold transactions is limited to those transactions in which the bill and hold was specifically requested by the customer, rather than suggested by the salesperson.

DISCLOSURE ALERT: See Chapter 12, "Disclosures," for information about disclosures that may be required.

EXAMPLE: SEC ENFORCEMENT ACTION RELATED TO BILL AND HOLD SALES

Excerpts Taken from Accounting and Auditing Enforcement Release No. 1911—November 13, 2003

Improper Bill-and-Hold Sale

Gateway also solicited an arrangement with one of its larger customers, a rent-to-own consumer leasing company, in mid-September 2000.

On September 21, 2000, Gateway's sales representative sent an e-mail to the consumer leasing company confirming that the consumer leasing company would issue a purchase order for $16.5 million of PCs, for which it would receive a 5% discount, that the consumer leasing company would be billed by September 30, 2000 and would take the PCs by October 31, 2000. The e-mail did not reference warehousing arrangements. The parties agreed the consumer leasing company would not take the product until the fourth quarter, after it issued subsequent purchase orders from individual stores, as had been its practice. They also agreed that the consumer leasing company would be invoiced and pay on subsequent store purchase orders, not the $16.5 million purchase order.

On September 21, 2000, the consumer leasing company issued a purchase order for $16.5 million in PCs and peripherals. The purchase order provided that the equipment would be shipped to "local warehousing for subsequent distribution," and stated that the order was FOB destination. Gateway then "shipped" the products by segregating them in the third-party warehouses located adjacent to Gateway's manufacturing facilities. . . . The consumer leasing company did not make any arrangements with the warehouses, or have any contact with the warehouses.

Gateway improperly recognized revenue of $16.5 million on the third quarter purported sale (and also failed to apply the 5% discount on the sale until the fourth quarter). Thus, Gateway increased its third quarter reported revenue by $16.5 million.

The transaction failed to satisfy three critical GAAP criteria for revenue recognition on a bill-and-hold transaction.[4] First, revenue recognition was inappropriate because the consumer leasing company lacked any substantial business purpose for ordering the goods on bill-and-hold basis. Second, Gateway had specific performance obligations concerning the purchase order that it did not discharge during the third quarter, including (1) upon receipt of a second purchase order from the consumer leasing company, an obligation to remove the product from the warehouse inventory, send it back to Gateway's manufacturing facility for re-entry into Gateway's computer system, and then ship the product to the individual store specified on the order; and (2) an obligation to reverse the September 21, 2000 sale of the PC out of its system and issue a second invoice to the consumer leasing company. These specific performance obligations precluded revenue recognition. Third, revenue recognition was inappropriate because the consumer leasing company did not request that the transaction be on a bill-and-hold basis, and did not pay the cost for warehousing the inventory.

[4] *Footnote Omitted.*

Layaway Sales

One type of a bill and hold transaction is a layaway sale. A layaway is a transaction in which a buyer makes a partial payment on an item he or she wants to purchase, with delivery to occur at a later date when the remaining purchase price is paid. The initial deposit is typically non-refundable and, in return, the seller sets aside the item the buyer wants for a period of time. If the buyer does not make the remaining payments within the required period of time, the initial deposit is forfeited, and the seller is free to sell the item to another customer.

Layaways are bill and hold transactions because the seller collects a portion of the purchase price without delivering the item. It is clear that, under the SEC's bill and hold model, a layaway transaction could not qualify for recognition of revenue before the last payment is received and the product is delivered because the buyer has not made a final commitment to purchase the goods, as he or she may elect to cease making payments and thereby not purchase the goods (SAB Topic 13A3e).

Since this specific condition is only included in the SEC's bill and hold model, non-public companies may be able to justify revenue recognition on a layaway sale if they can show that the basic revenue recognition criteria have been met. IAS 18 specifically allows recognition of revenue on layaway transactions if the first five requirements of the IAS bill and hold accounting model as discussed earlier in this chapter are met and if all of the following exist:

1. *A significant deposit is received* (IAS 18, App. par. 2). The buyer in a layaway has the right to stop making payments under the arrangement. Therefore, its risk of loss due to market value declines is limited to the amount of the previous payments. As such, some of the risk of market price declines resides with the seller, as a significant drop in market price might only be partially covered by the forfeited payments. Therefore, the size of the initial deposit must be carefully considered to ensure that it effectively transfers enough of the risk of loss to the buyer.

2. *The goods are on hand, identified, and ready for delivery to the buyer* (IAS 18, App. par. 2). Similar to the bill and hold requirement, this criterion ensures that everything except for delivery has been completed before revenue is recognized.

3. *Experience indicates that most layaway transactions are eventually consummated* (IAS 18, App. par. 2). Without historical evidence that most customers complete payments and take delivery, it is difficult to conclude a sale has occurred.

Similar to other bill and hold transactions, payments received before revenue on a layaway sale can be recognized should be recorded as deposits and classified as a liability, and the inventory subject to the layaway should remain on the books. In the event that initial payments are forfeited because the buyer does not make payments required under the layaway plan, the related deposit liability should be eliminated, with a credit to income. This credit generally should not be classified as revenue because no earnings event occurred. Instead, it should be reflected as a gain classified below gross margin.

POST-DELIVERY PRODUCT-RELATED OBLIGATIONS

Customer Acceptance Provisions

Customer acceptance provisions generally allow the customer to cancel the arrangement when the product delivered does not meet the customer's needs or desires. The existence of such provisions raises questions as to whether the earnings process is complete at the time of shipment or not until customer acceptance has been obtained. When products are sold subject to customer acceptance provisions, the nature of the customer acceptance provisions should be analyzed to determine the appropriate accounting model to apply to the transaction. Generally, customer acceptance provisions and the related accounting take one of the four forms discussed below.

Product Shipped for Trial or Evaluation Purposes

In these arrangements, the seller delivers a product to a customer before any sales agreement is finalized, to give the customer the ability to evaluate the delivered product prior to acceptance. In many respects, these arrangements are equivalent to allowing a potential purchaser of an automobile to test-drive the car. When products are shipped on a trial or evaluation basis, the customer does not agree to purchase the delivered product unless and until it accepts the product. In some cases, the acceptance occurs as long as the customer does not reject the product within a period of time. An example of this situation is a book club that ships its members a book every month for a 14-day trial period. If the member does not return the book within the trial period, he is deemed to have accepted it and becomes obligated to pay. In other cases, affirmative acceptance from the customer is necessary to trigger a purchase obligation. This is more common when the product is a piece of manufacturing equipment intended to meet a specified purpose. Frequently, title to the product does not transfer and payment terms are not established prior to customer acceptance.

Whether title passes upon shipment or not, these arrangements do not constitute a sale until acceptance occurs. Revenue recognition before acceptance would be inappropriate because, until acceptance, there is no persuasive evidence of an arrangement. Accordingly, in arrangements where products are delivered for trial or evaluation purposes, revenue should not be recognized until acceptance occurs, either by notification from the customer or by passage of time without rejection, provided the other conditions for revenue recognition have been met (SAB Topic 13A3b, ques. 1).

> ☞ **PRACTICE POINTER:** The reason that shipment on a trial basis or for evaluation purposes does not trigger recognition of revenue is because the arrangement does not even purport to be a sale of products unless and until acceptance occurs. Thus, no matter how good a company's experience is at estimating the portion of goods shipped on a trial basis that will ultimately result in sales, revenue cannot be recorded at shipment. However, subjective customer acceptance clauses and rights of return, which are discussed later in this chapter, do not absolutely preclude revenue recognition during the return period because a sale agreement is in place before the products are delivered. As rights of return provide potential customers with many of the same protections that a trial or evaluation period

EXHIBIT 5-2
CUSTOMER ACCEPTANCE PROVISIONS

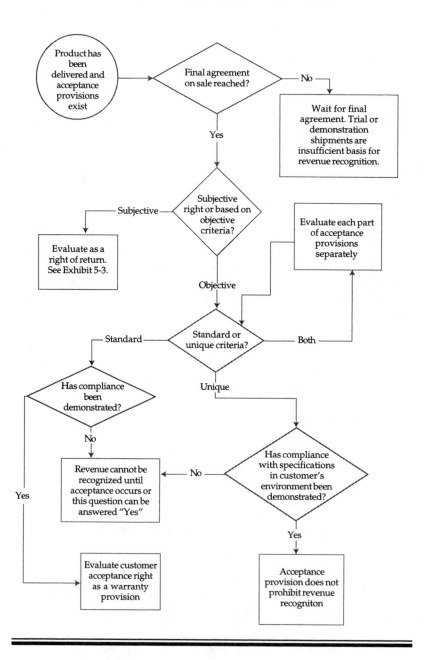

provides, companies may wish to change their arrangements from trial shipments to sales with a right of return, potentially allowing revenue recognition at an earlier point in time.

Subjective Right of Return

Certain customer acceptance provisions give the buyer the right to reject the product in the event he or she is dissatisfied for any reason. An example of such a provision is one that allows the customer to return a product if the customer is dissatisfied with "no questions asked." Acceptance provisions based on wholly subjective terms are, in substance if not in name, general rights of return. General rights of return are addressed in FAS-48. As such, acceptance provisions based on subjective matters should be accounted for in accordance with that literature and related interpretations (see "Rights of Return" in this chapter) (SAB Topic 13A3b, ques. 1).

Customer Acceptance Based on Meeting Standard
Performance Criteria

These provisions give the customer a right of return or replacement if the delivered product is defective, fails to meet advertising claims, or does not meet the vendor's published specifications for the product. In some cases, the seller may have the right to repair the product rather than provide a replacement or refund the purchaser's money. This kind of acceptance provision generally occurs in a situation in which identical rights are granted to every customer of a particular class, and involves performance criteria set by the seller that the seller is reasonably certain the product will meet in any environment. Provided the seller has previously demonstrated that the product meets the specified criteria, a customer acceptance provision based on seller-specified criteria is no different from a product warranty. In those cases, the customer acceptance provisions should be accounted for as a warranty (see "Product Warranties" in this chapter).

However, if the seller has not previously demonstrated that the delivered product meets the stated specifications, warranty accounting is not appropriate because it is not yet clear the company has delivered the product specified in the arrangement with the customer. Therefore, revenue should be deferred until the specifications have been achieved or the customer has accepted the product (SAB Topic 13A3b, ques. 1 and 2).

*Customer Acceptance Based on Customer-Specified or Negotiated
Criteria*

This type of customer acceptance provision is the most difficult to
deal with. Provisions like this are common in sales of equipment to
be used in manufacturing plants, and in sales of industrial goods
designed for a specific location, such as an air conditioning system
designed for a particular building. Prior to installation and testing
of the product in the customer's location, it is often unclear whether
the product meets the specified criteria because, no matter how
much testing is done before shipment, it may not be possible to
replicate the customer's environment. These types of arrangements
usually allow the seller a period of time after installation and testing
to resolve any problems that might exist in meeting the criteria. As
such, the seller may need to perform additional work after installation of the product to meet the specifications. If a substantive
amount of additional work is likely to be required, recognition of
revenue upon shipment is inappropriate because delivery of a product that does not meet specifications does not fulfill the seller's
obligations.

Therefore, when customer-specified customer acceptance provisions exist, the seller must be able to reliably demonstrate that
the delivered product meets the specified acceptance criteria
before revenue can be recognized. If the criteria are sufficiently
objective and the seller can duplicate conditions under which the
customer will operate the product, it may be possible to objectively demonstrate compliance with the customer acceptance provisions before shipment. In that case, revenue may be recognized
upon delivery, as long as all other revenue recognition conditions
have been met.

However, if unique aspects of the customer's environment could
affect the assessment of whether the product meets the criteria, or
if other circumstances exist that prohibit the seller from verifying
compliance with the acceptance provisions until the product has
been delivered or installed, revenue should not be recognized until
compliance can be verified. Verification often consists of formal
customer sign-off that the acceptance provisions have been met.
However, if the seller can verify that the product meets the acceptance criteria, and therefore believes it would be able to enforce a
claim for payment even though formal customer sign-off has not
occurred, revenue may be recognized because the seller has fulfilled all terms of the contract. Like other accounting that is based
on a legal interpretation, consultation with legal experts may be
necessary to determine the appropriate treatment (SAB Topic
13A3b, ques. 1).

EXAMPLE: CUSTOMER ACCEPTANCE PROVISIONS

Ventana Medical Systems, Inc. Form 10-K—Fiscal Year Ended December 31, 2004

Revenue from instrument sales made directly to the end user is generally recognized upon our completion of installation. However, if the end user already has the identical instrument installed at the same location, revenue is recognized from that sale upon shipment.

A portion of our instrument revenue is from sales made to distributors under agreements that require them to assume responsibility for product installation without recourse to the Company. Revenue for instruments sold under these agreements is recognized upon shipment to the distributor when the Company assesses their ability to pay for that sale. There are certain foreign distributors for which revenue is not recognized until the instrument is installed and accepted by the end user, thereby making the related payment assured.

Our Performance Evaluation Period (PEP) program is a formal agreement whereby a staining system is installed on the premises of a pre-qualified customer for the purpose of allowing the customer to evaluate the system's functionality over an extended trial period. The customer agrees to purchase a reagent starter kit at the time of installation and to purchase a minimum volume of reagents over the life of the trial period. Minimum purchase requirements vary by customer. Associated reagent revenue is recognized upon shipment of each reagent order. Upon completion of the trial period, the customer purchases the staining system or returns it to the Company. In those cases where the customer purchases the staining system, the Company recognizes revenue consistent with our revenue recognition policies. If the customer elects to rent the staining system, the rental income is presented in Instrument Sales, while the reagent revenue is presented in Reagents and Other Sales, and the cost of the staining system is depreciated to Cost of Goods Sold using the straight-line method over approximately three years.

OBSERVATION: Acceptance provisions based on criteria that are specific to a particular contract or customer must be evaluated on a contract-by-contract basis. Therefore, the point at which revenue should be recognized may differ for otherwise similar contracts due to the nature of the acceptance provisions included in the contracts. For example, in an arrangement to deliver multiple machines, each of which operate to the exact same specifications, it may not be possible to determine whether the first machine meets the specifications until it is tested in the customer's plant. As such, revenue recognition would need to be deferred until after installation and testing.

However, if the rest of the machines are identical to the first, and any modifications that were necessary on the first machine are made to the others before shipment, revenue recognition on the rest of the machines might be appropriate upon shipment. If the contract instead called for different acceptance provisions for each machine delivered, the analysis of when revenue should be recognized would differ.

DISCLOSURE ALERT: See Chapter 12, "Disclosures," for information about disclosures that may be required.

SEC REGISTRANT ALERT: In early 2003 the SEC staff issued the Summary by the Division of Corporation Finance of Significant Issues Addressed in the Review of the Periodic Reports of the Fortune 500 Companies (the Fortune 500 Report). This report resulted from the SEC's Division of Corporation Finance's (Corp Fin) review of all annual reports filed by Fortune 500 companies. The report provides insight into areas commonly questioned by Corp Fin during its reviews of annual reports. One area specifically mentioned in this report relates to customer acceptance clauses. Corp Fin noted that the quality of disclosures related to customer acceptance clauses requires improvement, particularly in the capital goods, semiconductor, and electronic instruments and controls industries.

ILLUSTRATION: EFFECTS OF CUSTOMER ACCEPTANCE PROVISIONS ON REVENUE RECOGNITION

(Adapted from SAB Topic 13A3b, ques. 3 through 5)

Facts: Company E is an equipment manufacturer whose main product is generally sold in a standard model. The contracts for sale of that model provide for customer acceptance to occur after the equipment is received and tested by the customer. The acceptance provisions state that if the equipment does not perform to Company E's published specifications, the customer may return the equipment for a full refund or a replacement unit, or may require Company E to repair the equipment so that it performs up to published specifications. Customer acceptance is indicated by either a formal sign-off by the customer or by the passage of 90 days without a claim under the acceptance provisions. Title to the equipment passes upon delivery to the customer. Company E does not perform any installation or other services on the equipment it sells and tests each piece of equipment against its specifications before shipment. Payment is due under Company E's normal payment terms for that product—30 days after customer acceptance.

EXAMPLE 1

Additional Facts: Company E receives an order from a new customer for a standard model of its main product. Based on the customer's intended use of the product, location and other factors, there is no reason that the equipment would operate differently in the customer's environment than it does in Company E's facility.

Discussion: Although the arrangement includes a customer acceptance provision, acceptance is based on meeting Company E's published specifications for a standard model. Because Company E demonstrates that the equipment shipped meets the specifications before shipment, and the equipment is expected to operate the same in the customer's environment as it does in Company E's, Company E should evaluate the customer acceptance provision as a warranty under FAS-5. If Company E can reasonably and reliably estimate the amount of warranty obligations, Company E should recognize revenue upon delivery of the equipment (provided the other criteria for recognition are met), with an appropriate liability for probable warranty obligations.

EXAMPLE 2

Additional Facts: Company E enters into an arrangement with a new customer to deliver a version of its standard product modified as necessary to fit into a space of specific dimensions while still meeting all of the published vendor specifications with regard to performance. In addition to the customer acceptance provisions relating to the standard performance specifications, the customer may reject the equipment if it does not conform to the specified dimensions. Company E creates a testing chamber of the exact same dimensions as specified by the customer and makes simple design changes to the product so that it fits into the testing chamber. The equipment still meets all of the standard performance specifications.

Discussion: The contract effectively includes two customer acceptance clauses—one based on standard performance specifications and one based on a customer-specific criterion. For the customer acceptance clause based on the customer-specific criterion, Company E demonstrates that the equipment shipped meets that objective criterion before shipment. As such, there are no uncertainties related to that customer acceptance clause that affect revenue recognition. For the customer acceptance clause based on the standard performance specifications, Company E demonstrates that the equipment shipped meets those specifications before shipment as well. This customer acceptance clause should be evaluated under FAS-5 as a warranty obligation. If Company E can reasonably and reliably estimate the amount of warranty obligations, it should recognize revenue upon delivery of the equipment with an appropriate liability for probable warranty obligations (provided the other criteria for recognition are met).

EXAMPLE 3

Additional Facts: Company E enters into an arrangement with a new customer to deliver a version of its standard product modified as necessary to be integrated into the customer's new assembly line while still meeting all of the standard published vendor specifications with regard to performance. The customer may reject the equipment if it fails to meet the standard published performance specifications or cannot be satisfactorily integrated into the new line. Company E has never modified its equipment to work on an integrated basis in the type of assembly line the customer has proposed. In response to the request, Company E designs a version of its standard equipment that is modified as believed necessary to operate in the new assembly line. The modified equipment still meets all of the standard published performance specifications, and Company E believes the equipment will meet the requested specifications when integrated into the new assembly line. However, Company E is unable to replicate the new assembly line conditions in its pre-shipment testing.

Discussion: This contract includes a customer acceptance clause based, in part, on a customer-specific criterion, and Company E cannot demonstrate that the equipment shipped meets that criterion before shipment. Accordingly, Company E may not recognize revenue before the product is successfully integrated at its customer's location and it meets the customer-specific criterion.

Product Warranties

Many product sale arrangements include a warranty provision that provides the purchaser with some protection in the event the product does not perform as expected or requires post-sale servicing. In a normal warranty, the seller takes on an obligation to repair or replace the product if it fails to perform as advertised or according to published specifications. However, not all warranty provisions involve the same type of obligation and it is important to understand the substance of the obligations the seller takes on to properly account for the warranty. For example, if the seller commits to ensure the product will meet certain specifications that the product has not yet been demonstrated to meet, revenue should not be recognized until compliance with those specifications is achieved. Furthermore, if the warranty is based on meeting specifications specific to a particular customer or product sale, the warranty obligation should be evaluated as a customer acceptance provision based on customer-specified criteria (see "Customer Acceptance Provisions" above).

In addition, certain warranties may include obligations other than ensuring that the product continues to operate according to specifications. For example, a warranty provision on a piece of software may include the rights to upgrades or updates to the product, or a warranty on an automobile may include oil changes and other preventative maintenance during the warranty term. Neither of these specific provisions should be accounted for as part of the warranty. Rather, the sale of a product along with a promise to provide upgrades or services after the sale should be treated as a multiple-element arrangement (see Chapter 4, "Multiple-Element Arrangements"). Therefore, a portion of the sales prices in these situations generally should be allocated to the additional elements and deferred until the seller fulfills its obligations to provide the additional products or services.

Most warranty provisions, however, merely require that the seller repair or replace the item if it fails to perform in the way it was designed and manufactured to perform. Warranty obligations usually are identified explicitly in the documentation that comes with the product, but warranties may also be implied or required by laws or regulations (for example, the "lemon laws" that cover automobiles in many states are a form of warranty). As a consequence of a warranty commitment, the seller's involvement with the product may not end upon delivery. At the very least, the seller must stand ready to honor the warranty for whatever period of time it is in force.

One possible method of accounting for a product sale with a warranty would be to treat it as a multiple-element arrangement, identifying the product and the warranty as separate deliverables. Revenue would therefore be allocated between the product and the warranty, with the amount allocated to the warranty recognized in revenue over the warranty period, consistent with other service transactions. Another possible method of accounting for a warranty would be to consider the warranty merely a part of the product. In this analysis, the seller is simply guaranteeing that the product does what it is supposed to do, rather than taking on a separate obligation. Thus, the warranty coverage is an integral part of the product sale and should not be accounted for separately. If analyzed this way, the question arises as to whether the warranty obligation is significant enough to prevent revenue recognition on the product. If it is, then revenue would not be recognized until the warranty expires. Conversely, if the warranty obligation were not deemed significant, all revenue would be attributed to the product and recognized upon delivery (or when all revenue recognition criteria are met). U.S. GAAP recognizes the merit in both of the above approaches to accounting for warranties, depending on the nature of the warranty.

Standard Warranties

In many cases, a sale of goods in the normal course of business includes a standard warranty available to all buyers of a product. The warranty in this case is not treated as a separate service; rather, it is considered an integral part of the product sale. Revenue may be recognized upon product delivery when a standard warranty is included in the transaction, provided that the costs of honoring the warranty can be reliably estimated, and that the other conditions for revenue recognition have been met. The estimated costs of honoring the warranty must be accrued as additional cost of sales when revenue is recognized. Accrued costs should be updated as estimates change.

However, if the costs of honoring the warranty cannot be reliably estimated and the potential range of loss is wide, revenue should be deferred until either a reliable estimate of the costs can be made or the warranty period expires (FAS-5, par. 25). Indicators that costs may not be reliably estimable include (a) new products have been introduced or significant modifications have been made to old products, (b) the scope of a warranty has been extended beyond what has normally been given in the ordinary course of business, and (c) new obligations have been undertaken.

> **DISCLOSURE ALERT:** See Chapter 12, "Disclosures," for information about required disclosures.

Separately Priced Extended Warranty and Product Maintenance Contracts

The above discussion applies only to standard warranties offered to all purchasers of a product without an extra charge. Revenue from separately priced extended warranty and product maintenance contracts should be deferred and recognized in income over the contract period. A warranty should be treated as a separately priced warranty any time that a customer has the option to purchase the product with or without the warranty. For example, assume that all purchasers of a particular model of television receive a one-year warranty, and a three-year warranty is available for an extra charge. The arrangement should be accounted for as having a one-year standard warranty and a two-year separately priced extension. As such, the fee paid for the two-year extension should be deferred and recognized as revenue after the television is delivered in years two and three. The purchase price of the television with the standard one-year warranty should be recognized as revenue upon delivery as long as all other revenue recognition conditions are met and the costs of honoring the one-year warranty can be reliably estimated.

The recognition pattern for revenue attributable to a separately priced extended warranty contract should be on a straight-line basis unless historical evidence indicates that the costs of performing services under the contract are incurred on other than a straight-line basis. If costs are incurred on other than a straight-line basis, revenue should be recognized over the contract period in proportion to the costs expected to be incurred in performing services under the contract (FTB 90-1, par. 3).

EXAMPLES: EXTENDED WARRANTIES

Maytag Corporation Form 10-K—Fiscal Year Ended January 1, 2005

Maytag provides a basic limited warranty for all of its major appliances, floor care, and commercial products.

In addition to the basic limited warranty, an optional extended warranty is offered to retail purchasers of the Company's major appliances. Sales of extended warranties are recorded as deferred revenue within accrued and noncurrent liabilities on the Consolidated Balance Sheet. Certain costs directly associated with sales of extended warranties are deferred within other current and noncurrent assets on the Consolidated Balance Sheet. The deferred revenue and associated costs are amortized into income on a straight-line basis over the length of the extended warranty contracts. Payments on extended warranty contracts are expensed as incurred.

Circuit City Stores Inc. Form 10-K—Fiscal Year Ended February 28, 2005

The domestic segment sells extended warranty contracts on behalf of unrelated third parties. The contracts extend beyond the normal manufacturer's warranty period, usually with terms, including the manufacturer's warranty period, from 12 to 60 months. Because the third parties are the primary obligors under these contracts, commission revenue for the unrelated third-party extended warranty plans is recognized at the time of sale. For the international segment, the company is the primary obligor for its extended warranty programs. Accordingly, extended warranty revenue is deferred at point of sale and recognized as revenue over the life of the contract.

OBSERVATION: In many cases, a company selling an extended warranty will purchase insurance to cover its potential losses under the warranty. While purchasing insurance may transfer the risk of loss under the contract to the insurance company, it generally does not relieve the seller of the warranty of its obligations to the customer. That is to say, the seller remains liable to fulfill the warranty, even after buying insurance, in the event that the insurance company cannot or will not honor the insurance coverage. Because the seller has not fulfilled its obligation to the buyer and has not been released by the buyer from that obligation (i.e., the buyer was not a party to the insurance contract), purchasing insurance to cover the risk of loss under a warranty contract should not result in revenue recognition. Rather, the accounting for the warranty contract and the accounting for the insurance should each be separately considered.

DISCLOSURE ALERT: See Chapter 12, "Disclosures," for information about required disclosures.

Product Shipped Subject to Other Conditions

Product sales can include various other types of conditions. For example, products may be sold subject to installation or performance of other services. When a product is sold in an arrangement that includes post-delivery services, the arrangement should be accounted for as a multiple-element arrangement. If the product and service deliverables meet the requirements to be accounted for separately, the revenue allocated to the product element should be recognized at the appropriate time, without regard to the service element. However, if the deliverables do not meet the requirements to be accounted for separately, no revenue should be recognized until the product is delivered **and** the service has been performed. See Chapter 4, "Multiple-Element Arrangements," for further discussion.

RIGHTS OF RETURN

Return rights are very common in product transactions. For example, almost any retail purchase can be returned to the store from which it was purchased for a limited period of time. Resellers and distributors are often granted rights of return to reduce the risk of loss they might face if the product is difficult to resell. Similarly, sales of commercial products may have rights of return related to quality, performance testing, or other factors.

☛ **PRACTICE POINTER:**   Return rights are often documented in the sales contract. However, such rights may also exist due to industry practice, company policy, or laws and regulations. In addition, the relationship between the buyer and seller should be evaluated in full to determine whether unstated rights of return might exist. For example, a large customer of a company that has very few customers may have enough leverage that it can return goods beyond the limited period stated in the contract. Although the seller may be within its rights to deny the returns, it is common for such returns to be accepted to solidify the relationship with the customer. In evaluating rights of return, it is important that all rights that exist, whether explicitly stated or not, be considered.

General Rights of Return

FAS-48 provides accounting guidance for a subjective right of return, such as a "100% satisfaction guarantee," that may be exercised at will by the purchaser. Essentially, this guidance prohibits recognition of revenue in a right of return if there is significant uncertainty as to whether, or to what extent, the return right will be exercised. However, this guidance does not apply to exchanges by ultimate customers (i.e., end users) of one item for another of the same kind, quality, and price (FAS-48, fn. 3). These types of exchange rights are not treated as returns for accounting purposes and generally should have no effect on revenue recognition (FAS-48, fn. 3).

Although the return right creates a question as to whether the transaction has been completed, it is often appropriate to record revenue upon delivery of products sold with a right of return. However, this is only acceptable when the terms of the arrangement make it clear that a sale has occurred, there are no contingencies other than the right of return, and the likelihood of the customer exercising the right of return can be estimated. If any of these three things are not present, the return right causes the transaction to be treated as if it is incomplete until the return right lapses. Specifically, revenue should be recognized at the time of sale, net of estimated returns, only if all of the following conditions (and the remaining general conditions for revenue recognition) are met:

1. *The sales price to the buyer is fixed or determinable* (FAS-48, par. 6). This shows that the return period is not just part of the transaction's pricing negotiations. If the arrangement does not meet this criterion, no revenue should be recognized because a fixed or determinable price is one of the prerequisites to recognizing revenue.

2. *Payment is not contractually or otherwise excused until the product is resold* (FAS-48, par. 6). If payment is not required until the product is resold, the transaction takes on characteristics of a consignment, for which no revenue should be recognized.

> **OBSERVATION:** Although payment may contractually be due within a specified period of time, a company may have a business practice of not pursuing payment until the customer does resell the products. If this is the case, the business practice must be considered in the evaluation, thereby precluding recognition of revenue until the right of return expires or payment is received.

3. The buyer holds the risks of destruction, damage, or theft of the property *(FAS-48, par. 6). If the buyer does not hold these risks, then all of the risks and rewards of ownership have not passed, prohibiting revenue recognition.*

4. *The buyer has economic substance apart from the seller* (FAS-48, par. 6). A sale with a right of return to a company with little substance raises significant questions about the buyer's ability to pay. In this case, the buyer would appear to be acting as a sales agent for the seller, rather than as a substantive purchaser. As such, the seller should not record the sale to the non-substantive purchaser.

5. *The seller does not have significant obligations for future performance relating to the resale of the product by the buyer* (FAS-48, par. 6). If the seller is required to assist the buyer in the product's resale, the seller has not completed its obligations under the arrangement until resale has occurred, and thus should not recognize revenue until then provided the other conditions for recognition have been met.

6. *The amount of future returns and costs expected in connection with any returns can be reasonably predicted* (FAS-48, par. 6). This is the most judgmental of the criteria, and the one that most often cannot be met. See below for further discussion.

Estimating Returns

Determining whether a reasonable estimate of returns can be made is sometimes quite easy. For example, a product that has been sold to the same group of customers and has generated a consistent rate of return for many years can probably be expected to have the same level of returns in the future, as long as there are no external changes that might affect customers' return habits. On the other hand, a start-up company selling a newly invented product that is not similar to any other product on the market may quickly conclude that it cannot estimate the level of returns that will occur (SAB Topic 13A4a, ques. 4). In evaluating whether a reasonable estimate of returns can be made, all available information should be considered. The following factors, if they exist, may cause the seller to conclude that returns cannot be reasonably predicted. At a minimum, the seller should take these factors into consideration when estimating the amount of returns.

> **OBSERVATION:**   There is no level of returns that, if exceeded, would prohibit recognition of revenue on sales with a right of return. Rather, the accounting literature focuses entirely on the ability to estimate returns as the key to whether revenue may be recognized upon delivery when a return right exists. Thus, as long as the company can reliably estimate the level of returns, the fact that such level is high does not prohibit revenue recognition. Of course, when the percentage of customers exercising return rights is high, it may be more difficult to estimate the rate of returns, but this is just one of many factors a company would take into account in determining whether it can make a reliable estimate of returns (SAB Topic 13A4a, ques. 5).

1. The product is susceptible to significant external factors, such as technological obsolescence or changes in demand *(FAS-48, par. 8). If the return period is lengthy, it may be particularly difficult for the*

company to predict its competitors', and therefore its customers', activities in an environment susceptible to significant external factors.

2. *The return period is long* (FAS-48, par. 8). Obviously, the longer the return period, the more difficult it becomes to predict the level of returns. Whether a return period is long should be determined based on the nature of the product, industry practice, and the type of customer.

3. *The absence of relevant historical experience* (FAS-48, par. 8). Without historical experience to reference, predicting customer actions is virtually impossible. However, in the absence of company-specific experience, industry experience may be relevant.

4. *The absence of a large volume of relatively homogeneous transactions* (FAS-48, par. 8). It is generally difficult to predict the actions of a particular customer. However, it is much easier to predict, on average, the actions of a large number of customers.

5. *Increases in or excess levels of inventory at distributors, or a lack of information about the levels of inventory at distributors* (SAB Topic 13A4b, ques. 1). Either of these situations indicates that previous experience might not be indicative of future actions, due to the need to clear out the distribution channel.

6. *Expected introductions of new products* (SAB Topic 13A4b, ques. 1). If the product subject to the return right is near the end of its life, due to the planned introduction of a new or upgraded version of the product, it is possible that more returns will occur as customers opt for the new version of the product.

7. *The product is new* (SAB Topic 13A4b, ques. 1). The newer the product, the less specific return experience that exists. Depending upon the circumstances, return experience with other, similar, products may be useful.

> **OBSERVATION:** The ability to estimate returns could vary from product-to-product, location-to-location, customer-to-customer, and arrangement-to-arrangement. Thus, it is possible that a company may be able to estimate returns for certain transactions but not others. In addition, when a company sells various types of products or serves various market segments whose return rates would be expected to vary from one another, the company should develop different return estimates for each type of product or market segment.

> ☛ **PRACTICE POINTER:** GAAP requires that a reliable estimate of returns be made before any revenue can be recognized on sales with a right of return. Some have suggested that, even when a good estimate cannot be made, revenue recognition should be acceptable assuming a conservative (i.e., high) level of returns as long as the company is comfortable that actual

EXHIBIT 5-3
RIGHTS OF RETURN

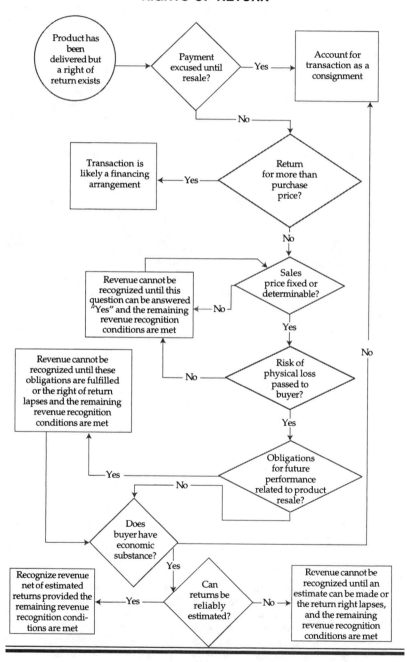

returns will not exceed that high level. However, this treatment is not consistent with the accounting literature.
Therefore, it is critical that the company have the ability to
reliably estimate returns to recognize any revenue at delivery
(SAB Topic 13A4b, ques. 5).

In some arrangements, however, a company may sell a
large number of products to a single customer with a capped
right of return. For example, the customer may be limited to
returning, at most, 20% of the products shipped. In that case,
revenue may be recognized for 80% of the products upon
delivery, assuming all other revenue recognition criteria are
met, because there is no right of return on 80% of the products sold. The other 20% of the products subject to the right of
return should be evaluated to determine whether revenue may
be recognized upon delivery.

Accounting for Rights of Return

When revenue is not recognized at the time of sale because an estimate of returns cannot be made, the seller should delay recognition
until the earlier of when the return privilege has expired or information allowing the company to make a reasonable estimate of returns
becomes available, provided the other conditions for revenue recognition have been met (FAS-48, par. 6). In this situation, the inventory
sold should remain on the company's books and any cash collected
should be reflected as a liability, rather than as revenue. The inventory should be evaluated for impairment under the assumption that
the customer will return the products to the company, with consideration of any anticipated repackaging or other costs to put the merchandise in saleable condition.

> **OBSERVATION:** GAAP is clear that when an estimate of
> returns cannot be made, no revenue is recognized at all.
> Consistent with that, cost of sales also should not be recog-
> nized. It is not appropriate in such a situation to merely defer
> the margin on the sale, by recognizing revenue equal to cost
> of sales. While deferring only the gross margin ensures that net
> income is not overstated, it results in the recognition of rev-
> enue for a transaction that is, essentially, incomplete (SAB
> Topic 13A4b, ques. 1).

When a transaction meets all of the criteria to recognize revenue
upon delivery despite the existence of a right of return, revenue and
cost of sales should be recognized net of the expected returns. Any
inventory expected to be returned should be evaluated for impairment, with consideration of any anticipated repackaging or other
costs to put the merchandise in saleable condition. As estimates of

returns change, the anticipated refund liability should be adjusted to reflect the latest estimates.

> **DISCLOSURE ALERT:** See Chapter 12, "Disclosures," for information about disclosures that may be required.

> **SEC REGISTRANT ALERT:** In early 2003 the SEC staff issued the Summary by the Division of Corporation Finance of Significant Issues Addressed in the Review of the Periodic Reports of the Fortune 500 Companies (the Fortune 500 Report). This report resulted from the SEC's Division of Corporation Finance's (Corp Fin) review of all annual reports filed by Fortune 500 companies. The report provides insight into areas commonly questioned by Corp Fin during its reviews of annual reports. One area specifically mentioned in this report relates to rights of return. Corp Fin noted that the quality of disclosures related to rights of return requires improvement, particularly in the capital goods, semiconductor, electronic instruments and controls, and pharmaceutical industries.

ILLUSTRATION: PRODUCT SOLD WITH RIGHT OF RETURN

Facts: Example Company sells 100 units of Product A at $100 per unit. Product A has an inventory cost of $87 per unit, and repackaging any returned units for resale will cost $15 per unit. Customers get a 30-day right of return on Product A, and, ultimately 5 of the 100 units are returned. The right of return is the only issue drawing into question when revenue should be recognized.

EXAMPLE 1

Additional Facts: Example Company determines at the time of sale that it cannot estimate the amount of returns it will receive.

Accounting:

Upon delivery:

- No revenue is recognized and the inventory remains on the company's books.

- The inventory is evaluated for impairment, under the assumption it will be returned. As the inventory cost plus anticipated repackaging costs ($87 + $15 = $102/unit) exceeds the anticipated sales price of the products ($100/unit), an impairment of $2 per unit, or $200 total, is recorded.

Cost of Sales	$200	
Inventory		$200

- Payment is received.

Cash	$10,000	
Deposit Liability		$10,000

At the end of the return period:

- Revenue for products not returned is recognized.

Deposit Liability	$9,500	
Revenue		$9,500

- Inventory is reduced and cost of sales recorded for products not returned.

Cost of Sales	$8,075	
Inventory ($85 x 95 units)		$8,075

- Cash is refunded on the returned products.

Deposit Liability	$500	
Cash		$500

- Repackaging costs are incurred on the returned products.

Inventory	$75	
Cash		$75

EXAMPLE 2

Additional Facts: Example Company determines that it can estimate the amount of returns, and initially estimates that amount as 6% of sales.

Accounting:

Upon delivery:

- Revenue is recognized for products not expected to be returned and a refund liability is recorded for products expected to be returned.

Cash	$10,000	
Revenue		$9,400
Deposit Liability		$600

- Cost of sales is recognized for products not expected to be returned.

Cost of Sales ($87 x 94 units)	$8,178	
Inventory		$8,178

- Units expected to be returned are evaluated for impairment, taking repackaging costs into account. An impairment of $2 per unit is calculated.

Cost of Sales	$12	
Inventory		$12

At the end of the return period:

- Additional revenue and cost of sales are recognized because returns were less than expected.

Deposit Liability	$100	
Revenue		$100
Cost of Sales	$85	
Inventory		$85

- Cash refunds are made for returned products.

Deposit Liability	$500	
Cash		$500

- Repackaging costs on returned products are incurred.

Inventory	$75	
Cash		$75

SALES WITH MARKET VALUE PROTECTION

Certain terms may be included in a product sales arrangement to mitigate some of the buyer's risk of a decline in market value of the goods. In some cases, these clauses cause the seller to retain too much of the risk of ownership, thereby precluding sale accounting.

Price Protection

A price protection clause provides for the buyer to be given credit (either in cash or as a discount on future purchases) for price decreases for a specified period of time or until the buyer resells the goods. Some price protection clauses (sometimes called "Most Favored Nation" clauses) require a payment only if the seller lowers its prices during the price protection period. Others provide for a payment if a competitor offers the same or a similar product at a lower price. Retailers in competitive market segments, such as electronics retailers, commonly offer this latter form of price protection.

The accounting for price protection depends on whether the seller can estimate the amount that will be paid under the price protection clause. If the seller can reasonably and reliably estimate the amount of refunds to be granted as a result of the price protection clause, then revenue should be recognized upon delivery (presuming all other revenue recognition criteria are met), net of a provision for estimated price protection refunds. If the seller cannot reasonably and reliably estimate the amount of price protection refunds, revenue should not be recognized until either reasonable and reliable estimates can be made or the price protection period ends. When the price protection clause allows for refunds based on the actions of a competitor, it may be difficult to make a reasonable and reliable estimate of the payments to be made because the payments can be triggered by a third party rather than by the seller. At the very least, the factors discussed under "Rights of Return" should be considered in these situations.

> **DISCLOSURE ALERT:** See Chapter 12, "Disclosures," for information about disclosures that may be required.

> **SEC REGISTRANT ALERT:** In a December 2001 speech, the SEC staff indicated that it would focus on the treatment of price protection clauses. Specifically, the staff suggested that without relevant historical experience, it may not be possible to make reliable estimates of payments related to price protection clauses. In other words, the SEC staff will be highly skeptical of a situation where a company asserts that reliable estimates of payments related to price protection clauses can be made absent relevant historical experience. In addition, in early 2003 the SEC staff issued the Summary by the Division of Corporation Finance of Significant Issues Addressed in the Review of the Periodic Reports of the Fortune 500 Companies (the Fortune 500 Report). This report resulted from the SEC's Division of Corporation Finance's (Corp Fin) review of all annual reports filed by Fortune 500 companies. The report provides insight into areas commonly questioned by Corp Fin during its reviews of annual reports. One area specifically mentioned in this report relates to price protection clauses. Corp Fin noted that the quality of disclosures related to price protection clauses requires improvement, particularly in the capital goods, semiconductor, and electronic instruments and controls industries.

EXAMPLES: PRODUCT RETURNS AND PRICE PROTECTION

Intel Corporation Form 10-K—Fiscal Year Ended December 25, 2004

Because of frequent sales price reductions and rapid technology obsolescence in the industry, sales made to distributors under agreements allowing price protection and/or rights of return are deferred until the distributors sell the merchandise.

Activision, Inc. Form 10-K—Fiscal Year Ended March 31, 2005

Revenue Recognition. We recognize revenue from the sale of our products upon the transfer of title and risk of loss to our customers. Certain products are sold to customers with a street date (the date that products are made widely available for sale by retailers). For these products we recognize revenue no earlier than the street date. Revenue from product sales is recognized after deducting the estimated allowance for returns and price protections.

Allowances for Returns, Price Protection, Doubtful Accounts and Inventory Obsolescence. In determining the appropriate unit shipments to our customers, we benchmark our titles using historical and industry data. We closely monitor and analyze the historical performance of our various titles, the performance of products released by other publishers and the anticipated timing of other releases in order to assess future demands of current and upcoming titles. Initial volumes shipped upon title launch and subsequent reorders are evaluated to ensure that quantities are sufficient to meet the demands from the retail markets but at the same time, are controlled to prevent excess inventory in the channel.

We may permit product returns from, or grant price protection to, our customers under certain conditions. In general, price protection refers to the circumstances when we elect to decrease the wholesale price of a product by a certain amount and, when granted and applicable, allows customers a credit against amounts owed by such customers to Activision with respect to open and/or future invoices. The conditions our customers must meet to be granted the right to return products or price protection are, among other things, compliance with applicable payment terms, delivery to us of weekly inventory and sell-through reports, and consistent participation in the launches of our premium title releases. We may also consider other factors, including the facilitation of slow-moving inventory and other market factors. Management must make estimates of potential future product returns and price protection related to current period product revenue. We estimate the amount of future returns and price protection for current period product revenue utilizing historical experience and information regarding inventory levels and the demand and acceptance of our products by the end consumer. The following factors are used to estimate the amount of future returns and price protection for a particular title: historical performance of titles in similar genres, historical performance of the hardware platform, historical performance of the brand, console hardware life cycle, Activision sales force and retail customer feedback, industry pricing, weeks of on-hand retail channel inventory, absolute quantity of on-hand retail channel inventory, Activision warehouse on-hand inventory levels, the title's recent sell-through history (if available), marketing trade programs and competing titles. The relative importance of these factors varies among titles depending upon, among other items, genre, platform, seasonality and sales strategy. Significant management judgments and estimates must be made and used in connection with establishing the allowance for returns and price protection in any accounting period. Based upon historical experience we believe our estimates are reasonable. However, actual returns and price protection could vary materially from our allowance estimates due to a number of reasons including, among others, a lack of consumer acceptance of a title, the release in the same period of a similarly themed title by a competitor, or technological obsolescence due to the emergence of new hardware platforms. Material differences may result in the amount and timing of our revenue for any period if management makes different judgments or utilizes different estimates in determining the allowances for returns and price protection.

Guaranteed Resale or Residual Value

To induce a purchaser to buy its product, a company may offer what amounts to a blanket guarantee on the value of the product for some period of time after delivery. Such guarantees can take several forms. For example, the company may agree to repurchase the product from its customer for a set price after several years of use. Alternatively, a company could agree to make up the difference between the actual selling price when its customer resells the product and the guaranteed price. These kinds of price guarantees must be evaluated as part of the original sale transaction, rather than as a separate purchase transaction or loss contingency.

The accounting for a resale price or residual value guarantee generally depends on whether the purchaser (i.e., the beneficiary of the guarantee) intends to use the products or resell them. If the purchaser in an arrangement with a guaranteed resale value is a reseller, the seller should account for the transaction as a product financing arrangement, as discussed earlier in this chapter.

The accounting when the purchaser in such an arrangement intends to use the products is addressed in EITF 95-1, which concludes that the seller should account for the transaction as a lease. This is because the purchaser has essentially agreed to pay the difference between the initial purchase price and the guaranteed residual value to use the product for the period of time that the guarantee covers.

Unless the residual value guarantee is less then 10% of the original sales price or the term of the guarantee is at least 75% of the useful life of the product, the application of the leasing literature will indicate that this type of arrangement is an operating lease, rather than a sales-type lease. Therefore, the seller should leave the asset on its books and depreciate it, reflect the cash received as a liability, and recognize the difference between the initial sales price and the guaranteed residual value as revenue over the guarantee period. If the guarantee may be exercised at various dates, with amounts declining over time, each decrease in guaranteed value should be considered the rental income for the applicable period. If the residual value guarantee expires, any remaining liability should be recognized as revenue at that time, and the remaining asset value should be treated as cost of sales (EITF 95-1).

> **OBSERVATION:** The guarantee in a sales arrangement with a residual value guarantee does not fall within the scope of FIN-45 because FIN-45 does not apply to a guarantee for which the underlying is related to an asset of the guarantor. If a sales arrangement with a residual value guarantee is deemed to be an operating lease based on applying the guidance in EITF 95-1, the equipment (i.e., the underlying) is still reflected on the lessor's books, thereby exempting the guarantee from the scope of FIN-45. If a sales arrangement with a residual value guarantee is deemed to be a sales-type lease, the lessor continues to recognize the guaranteed equipment's (the underlying's) residual value as an asset through its net investment in the lease (EITF 03-12), thereby exempting the guarantee from the scope of FIN-45.

ILLUSTRATION: RESIDUAL VALUE GUARANTEE
ON USED EQUIPMENT

Facts: Equipment Co. sells Product X for $100,000. It also offers its customer a residual value guarantee on Product X that is exercisable three years after the original sale. The guaranteed value is $55,000 after three years. Product X has a cost basis of $60,000, and an estimated useful life of ten years. Equipment Co. generally uses straight-line depreciation. Since the residual value guarantee is more than 10% of the original sales price and the term of the guarantee is less than 75% of the useful life of the product, Equipment Co. concludes the agreement should be treated as an operating lease.

EXAMPLE 1

Additional Facts: The customer uses the equipment for three years, and then sells it to a third party for $50,000. Equipment Co. therefore makes a $5,000 payment on its residual value guarantee.

Accounting:

Original Sale:

- Equipment Co. recognizes the receipt of payment, but no revenue.

Cash	$100,000	
Deposit Liability		$100,000

Each of the three years following the original sale:

- Equipment Co. recognizes the difference between the original sales price and the first residual value guarantee amount as lease income as follows:

Original sales price	$100,000
Residual value guarantee in three years	55,000
Income to recognize over three years	$ 45,000
Income to recognize each year	$ 15,000

Deposit Liability	$15,000	
Lease Revenue		$15,000

- Equipment Co. records depreciation expense on Product X based on Product X's carrying value of $60,000 and a ten-year life.

Depreciation Expense	$6,000	
Accum. Depreciation— Product X		$6,000

At the end of year three:

- Equipment Co. records its payment under the guarantee.

Deposit Liability	$5,000	
Cash		$5,000

- Equipment Co. records the remaining liability as revenue, along with cost of sales for the remaining carrying value of Product X.

Deposit Liability	$50,000	
Product Sale Revenue		$50,000
Cost of Sales	$42,000	
Accum. Depreciation-Product X	$18,000	
Historical Cost-Product X		$60,000

EXAMPLE 2

Additional Facts: The customer keeps the equipment longer than three years. Equipment Co. therefore makes no payment on its residual value guarantee.

Accounting:

Original sale and each of the three years following the original sale:

- See Example 1.

At the end of year three:

- Equipment Co. records the remaining liability as revenue, along with cost of sales for the remaining carrying value of Product X.

Deposit Liability	$55,000	
Product Sale Revenue		$55,000
Cost of Sales	$42,000	
Accum. Depreciation-Product X	$18,000	
Historical Cost-Product X		$60,000

Sales with Fixed-Price Trade-In Rights

One variant on a guaranteed residual value is a fixed-price trade-in right, which allows the customer to exchange the product purchased for a specified credit toward another of the manufacturer's products after some period of time. This type of right is a guarantee as defined in FIN-45. As a result, the fixed-price trade-in right should be initially recognized and measured at fair value provided the fixed-price trade-in right does not prohibit revenue recognition on the arrangement in general. In effect, an arrangement including a fixed-price trade-in right is a multiple-element arrangement where one element is the sale of the product and the other element is the trade-in right or guarantee. Multiple-element arrangements and FIN-45 are discussed in more detail in Chapter 4, "Multiple-Element Arrangements."

SELLER-PROVIDED FINANCING AND GUARANTEES

Sales with Extended Payment Terms

Some sellers may elect to provide financing for their customers' purchases by agreeing to receive fixed payments over a long period of time, rather than receiving the purchase price in accordance with normal payment terms shortly after delivery. Except in sales of software products (see Chapter 10, "Software-A Complete Model"), GAAP does not provide specific guidance about when extended payment terms should result in a conclusion that revenue should not be recognized. However, extended payment terms can affect the evaluation of two of the four conditions for revenue recognition, those requiring that (1) the fee be fixed or determinable and (2) collectibility be reasonably assured.

Extended Payment Terms and Fixed or Determinable Fees

Extended payment terms raise the risk that, to ensure payment according to the stated terms, the seller of the product will agree to provide additional products or services or to reduce the arrangement fee, even for a creditworthy customer. Consider a customer that is dissatisfied with the product, but does not have a warranty or return right. The customer may instead elect to withhold payments, requiring the seller to negotiate to receive the payments it is due. Therefore, extended payment terms should be carefully considered, together with warranty, return, customer acceptance, and other terms of the arrangement, to determine whether they preclude a conclusion that the arrangement fee is fixed or determinable.

> **OBSERVATION:** The above discussion applies only to payment terms that are fixed at the time of delivery. Terms that are extended until the products are used or resold generally indicate a consignment arrangement exists, as previously discussed in this chapter.

Extended Payment Terms and Collectibility

Clearly, the longer the payment terms, the more difficult it is to conclude that collection of the revenue is reasonably assured. Judgment must be applied in these situations. If it is concluded that collection is not reasonably assured, no revenue or receivable should be recorded. It is not acceptable in these instances to record revenue and a selling expense for the anticipated bad debt because the threshold criteria for revenue recognition were never met.

Discounting Long-Term Receivables

When products are sold on extended payment terms and it is acceptable to recognize revenue upon delivery, APB-21 requires that the long-term receivable, and therefore the revenue, be recorded at the present value of the payments, rather than at the nominal value. Interest income would then be accrued on the receivable until all payments are made. Therefore, when extended payment terms are stated at their nominal values, a portion of the payments will be attributed to interest income, as opposed to revenue (APB-21, par. 12).

Guaranteeing a Loan in Connection with a Sale of Products

Some companies may agree to guarantee a loan taken out by the buyer of their products. In this situation, although the company has collected the purchase price in cash, it has the same chance of ultimately realizing the purchase price as if it had sold the product on extended payment terms consistent with the loan terms. Therefore, before recognizing any revenue, the company should evaluate whether collectibility is reasonably assured as if it were the lender under the loan.

If the company still concludes that collection is reasonably assured and all other revenue recognition criteria have been met, then FIN-45 requires the transaction to be treated as a multiple-element arrangement, the two elements being the sale of a product and guarantee of a loan. This type of multiple-element arrangement is discussed in more detail in Chapter 4, "Multiple-Element Arrangements."

> **DISCLOSURE ALERT:** See Chapter 12, "Disclosures," for information about required disclosures.

Sale/Repurchase/Lease Transactions

In certain situations, especially those involving a manufacturer that sells its products through a dealer network, the manufacturer will provide financing to the end-users of the product. The manufacturer (or its finance affiliate) may accomplish this by (re)purchasing the product from the dealer and leasing it to the end-user. If the manufacturer recognizes revenue on the original sale to the dealer, and then also recognizes revenue on the lease of the product to the end-user, it will recognize revenue twice on the same physical product. In EITF 95-4, the EITF concluded that this is acceptable, and the manufacturer may recognize a sale at the time the product is transferred to the dealer despite the possibility it will repurchase the product to lease it to an end-user, if all of the following conditions exist:

1. The dealer is a substantive and independent enterprise that transacts business separately with the manufacturer and end-users (EITF 95-4).

2. The manufacturer has delivered the product to the dealer, and the risks and rewards of ownership, including responsibility for the ultimate sale of the product, insurability, theft, or damage, have passed to the dealer (EITF 95-4).

3. An end-user's failure to enter into a lease with the finance affiliate (or manufacturer) would not allow the dealer to return the product to the manufacturer (EITF 95-4).

4. The finance affiliate (or manufacturer) has no legal obligation to provide a lease arrangement to a potential end-user (EITF 95-4).

5. The end-user may choose to obtain financing from parties unaffiliated with the manufacturer, and it is feasible for the end-user to do so (EITF 95-4).

CHAPTER 6
SERVICE DELIVERABLES

CONTENTS

BACKGROUND

Although the U.S. economy has been historically product-based, service-based deliverables have become an integral part of the economy over the past several decades. The number of businesses that offer services to the public continues to increase and the range of these services has consistently expanded. Personal services include those provided by health clubs, lawn care companies, retirement homes, and painters, among others. Business services include architectural and engineering services, outsourcing of functions such as payroll and information technology, advertising, sales and marketing, and storage, among others. Businesses charge for these services using various methods, such as calculating fees based on time, activity and success.

This chapter explores the accounting issues that commonly arise but are unique to service transactions. When addressing these issues, it is important to evaluate their application to each service element or deliverable in the transaction. Therefore, all deliverables in a service arrangement must be analyzed separately. If there are multiple deliverables in the transaction, however, the interrelationship of these deliverables may give rise to issues beyond those that exist in a single-element transaction. These additional issues are discussed in Chapter 4, "Multiple-Element Arrangements."

> **PRACTICE ALERT:** Situations may arise where arrangements that purport to cover only the sale of services actually contain a lease. EITF 01–8 provides guidance to assist in determining whether an arrangement contains a lease. The provisions of EITF 01–8 are discussed in Chapter 3, "General Principles." When an arrangement does contain a lease, the portion of the arrangement that represents a lease must be accounted for as such. This is the case even though the arrangement is not formally characterized as a lease. Separation of the lease element from the other elements in the arrangement is discussed in Chapter 4, "Multiple-Element Arrangements."

SURVEY OF ACCOUNTING LITERATURE

As has been repeatedly mentioned in this book, there exists little literature that directly addresses most revenue accounting issues. However, the scarcity is particularly evident when it comes to general guidance on service transactions. What general guidance there is on accounting for service transactions can be found in the FASB Concept Statements and SAB Topic 13. Although SAB Topic 13 technically only applies to SEC registrants, much of its guidance is based on the FASB Concept Statements and other generally accepted practices. As such, a significant amount of the guidance in SAB Topic 13 is useful even for non-public companies. Application of this general guidance to service transactions is discussed throughout this chapter. In addition, there are a number of service transactions for which specific literature exists. Some of this literature is discussed later in this chapter.

There was an attempt by the AICPA and the FASB in the late 1970s to provide guidance on the common issues encountered when accounting for service transactions. The AICPA developed an exposure draft of a proposed SOP, which was then issued as an FASB Invitation to Comment. Although this document is sometimes referenced for suggested accounting for service transactions, it never went beyond the Invitation to Comment stage, and therefore is not authoritative literature.

LISTING OF ACCOUNTING LITERATURE

CON-5	Recognition and Measurement in Financial Statements of Business Enterprises
APB-21	Interest on Receivables and Payables
FAS-5	Accounting for Contingencies
FAS-48	Revenue Recognition When Right of Return Exists
FAS-68	Research and Development Arrangements
FAS-140	Accounting for Transfers and Servicing of Financial Assets and Extinguishments of Liabilities, a replacement of FASB Statement No. 125
FIN-45	Guarantor's Accounting and Disclosure Requirements for Guarantees, Including Indirect Guarantees of Indebtedness of Others, an interpretation of FASB Statements No. 5, 57, and 107 and rescission of FASB Interpretation No. 34
FTB 90–1	Accounting for Separately Priced Extended Warranty and Product Maintenance Contracts
SOP 81–1	Accounting for Performance of Construction-Type and Certain Production-Type Contracts
EITF 88–18	Sales of Future Revenues
EITF 91–6	Revenue Recognition of Long-Term Power Sales Contracts
EITF 91–9	Revenue and Expense Recognition for Freight services in Process
EITF 00–21	Revenue Arrangements with Multiple Deliverables
EITF 01–8 SAB	Determining Whether an Arrangement Contains a Lease Topic 13 Revenue Recognition

GENERAL CONDITIONS FOR RECOGNITION

As with all revenues, revenue from service transactions should be recognized when it has been earned and is realized or realizable. Revenue from services is generally earned either as the services are performed or when they are complete. Such revenue is usually considered realizable once the customer has committed to pay for the services, as long as the customer's ability to pay is not in doubt. Many types of uncertainties may exist in service transactions that affect when revenue is recognized (CON-5, pars. 83–84).

As discussed in Chapter 3, "General Principles," revenue is considered to be earned and realizable when all of the following conditions are met:

1. Persuasive evidence of an arrangement exists.
2. The arrangement fee is fixed or determinable.
3. Delivery or performance has occurred.
4. Collectibility is reasonably assured.

Also as discussed in Chapter 3, the analysis of the first and last of the above conditions does not change significantly based on the type of transaction involved. For discussion of the persuasive evidence of an arrangement and collectibility conditions, refer to Chapter 3. The rest of this chapter focuses on the analysis of the performance and fixed or determinable fee conditions in service transactions.

PERFORMANCE

In general, the key to determining when service transaction revenue has been earned is determining the pattern of delivery or performance. Performance determines the extent to which the earnings process is complete and the extent to which the customer has received value from the service. As discussed in Chapter 3, "General Principles," the Proportional Performance model is often applied to service transactions because delivery or performance occurs over time. However, the pattern of delivery or performance is not always clear or determinative. In certain service transactions, the customer does not receive any value from the service until it is completed. In those cases, revenue recognition is better described under the Completed Performance model. One factor that should be considered in evaluating performance in a service transaction is whether performance involves a single act or multiple acts.

Performance Is a Single Act

In some service transactions, performance consists of a single act. For example, a customer may pay a stylist to cut her hair or a tailor to hem her skirt. Determining when performance has occurred in these situations is not difficult, nor does it generally matter whether the Completed Performance model or the Proportional Performance model is used, because they would both result in recognition of revenue at essentially the same time. Thus, further discussion of the delivery criterion with respect to single act service transactions is not necessary.

Performance Involves Multiple Acts

When performance involves more than one act and spans more than one accounting period, it is necessary to determine whether the

Completed Performance model or Proportional Performance model should be used to determine when the delivery criterion has been met and revenue has been earned.

The Proportional Performance model is often appropriate for service transactions because the customer typically receives value as the services are performed. For example, when a company purchases transaction-processing services for one year, it receives value each time a transaction is processed. Similarly, a company that purchases data warehousing services receives benefits constantly as the data is stored on the service provider's hardware.

However, the Completed Performance model should be used if services are performed in more than a single act, but the final act is so significant in relation to the service transaction taken as a whole that performance has not substantively taken place until execution of that final act. For example, a real estate agent hired to sell a house performs many acts, such as running advertisements in newspapers, scheduling showings, assisting in contract negotiations, and coordinating open houses. However, the final act of actually closing on the sale of the house is so significant that revenue should generally only be recognized at that time, even if a non-refundable fee was collected at the time of listing (see the discussion of "Advance Fees" in this chapter).

Determining whether to use the Completed Performance model rather than the Proportional Performance model requires significant judgment. However, the following factors, if present in a service arrangement, may indicate that the Completed Performance model should be used:

1. *If the seller fails to perform the final act, the customer (or the customer's new service provider) would need to "start over," rather than just pick up where the original vendor left off.* If revenue is truly earned proportionally as services are provided, the customer should not have to re-perform the acts that have already been performed in the event service is stopped before it is completed.

2. *Payment terms indicate that no payment is due until the final act is performed.* This may be an indication that the parties have, in substance, agreed that the final act is particularly significant.

3. *The final act is significantly different in nature than the other acts to be performed.* This may be an indication that the other acts are simply performed to allow the final, important act to be performed.

4. *The contracts underlying the transaction specify only the final act and other acts are performed at the seller's discretion.* If the interim acts are not discussed in the contracts, they likely are not considered to be important to the customer, who cared only to specify the final act (i.e., completion of service) in the contracts.

5. *There is significant uncertainty as to whether the vendor can complete all of the acts in the arrangement.* If the vendor is uncertain of its

ability to complete the final act or acts, this may be an indication that those acts are more difficult and, potentially, more significant to the arrangement.

ILLUSTRATION: CHOOSING THE DELIVERY MODEL IN A SERVICE TRANSACTION

(Adapted from SAB Topic 13A4d)

Facts: Company M performs claims processing and medical billing services for healthcare providers. In this role, Company M is responsible for preparing and submitting claims to third-party payers, tracking outstanding billings, and collecting amounts billed. Company M's fee is a fixed percentage (e.g., 5%) of the amount collected. If no collections are made, no fee is due to Company M. Company M has historical evidence indicating that the third-party payers pay 85% of the billings submitted with no further effort by Company M.

Discussion: Company M must wait until collections occur before recognizing revenue. Despite the fact that Company M estimates it will not need to put forth any further efforts in 85% of the billings, the fact remains that the final act, collecting on the receivables, is of such significance that revenue should not be recognized until it is completed. The importance of collection, as compared to sending the bills and the other acts Company M performs, is evidenced by the fact that payment is not due unless and until collection occurs.

Applying the Completed Performance Model

Revenue Recognition

If it is determined that the Completed Performance model should be used to assess the delivery criterion, there is generally little question about when the revenue should be considered earned. This is because, in determining that the Completed Performance model should be applied, a particular act will have been identified as the act that signifies that performance is complete. Revenue would therefore be considered earned when that act is completed, as long as all other revenue recognition conditions are met.

Recognition of Direct Costs

When revenue is not recognized until performance is completed, questions may develop about how to account for the costs of performing the interim acts that do not result in any revenue recognition. To some extent, these costs are similar to the costs of producing inventory that are incurred by a manufacturer. Of course, inventory costs are not expensed as incurred. Instead, they are carried on the balance sheet and expensed as cost of sales at the same time revenue on the product sale is recognized.

When the Completed Performance model is used, costs that are equivalent to inventory costs can generally be capitalized (provided they are realizable) and recognized as an expense when the related revenue is recognized. The costs that can generally be capitalized include those that are (a) directly related to the performance of services under the arrangement and (b) incremental to costs that the vendor would have incurred if it did not need to fulfill the contract in question. For further discussion of cost recognition in these and other situations, see Chapter 8, "Miscellaneous Issues."

Applying the Proportional Performance Model

When delivery in a service transaction is evaluated under the Proportional Performance model, the pattern of performance must be determined. The determination of the pattern of performance should focus on the pattern in which service is provided to the customer, rather than on the pattern in which money or effort is expended by the service provider.

> **PRACTICE ALERT:** Determining when revenue has been earned using the Proportional Performance model as discussed in this chapter should not be confused with applying the percentage-of-completion method of accounting. As discussed later in this section under "Recognition of Direct Costs," the percentage-of-completion method of accounting results in a constant gross margin percentage. This is not necessarily the case when the Proportional Performance model is used. The percentage-of-completion method of accounting should only be applied to service contracts that fall within the scope of SOP 81–1. Such contracts are limited to those for architectural or engineering design services and construction consulting services.

ILLUSTRATION: RECOGNITION BASED ON PATTERN OF SERVICE, NOT PATTERN OF COSTS

(Adapted from SAB Topic 13A3f, ques. 1)

Example 1: A company charges users a fee for non-exclusive access to its web site that contains proprietary databases. The fee allows access to the web site for a one-year period. After the customer is provided with an identification number and trained in the use of the database, there are no incremental costs that will be incurred in serving this customer.

Example 2:   An Internet company charges a fee to users for advertising a product for sale or auction on certain pages of its web site. The company agrees to maintain the listing for a period of time. The cost of maintaining the advertisement on the web site for the stated period is minimal.

Example 3:   A company charges a fee for hosting another company's web site for one year. The arrangement does not involve exclusive use of any of the hosting company's servers or other equipment. Almost all of the projected costs to be incurred will be incurred in the initial loading of information on the host company's Internet server and setting up appropriate links and network connections.

Discussion: Some propose that revenue should be recognized when the initial set-up is completed in these cases, because the on-going obligation involves minimal, or no, cost or effort and therefore should be considered perfunctory or inconsequential. However, the substance of each of these transactions indicates that the purchaser is paying for a service that is delivered over time. Therefore, revenue recognition should occur over time, reflecting the provision of service, rather than in proportion to the costs incurred or efforts expended.

Identifying the Acts That Trigger Revenue Recognition

Only those acts that actually provide value to the customer should be considered acts that trigger revenue recognition in a service transaction. Other activities, such as setup or administrative activities, generally should not trigger revenue recognition. The following factors may indicate that a particular task is not one that should trigger recognition of revenue:

1. *The task is not identified in the service contract.* In general, a task not identified in the customer contract is less likely to represent an item that provides value to the customer, and more likely to be an internal process of the vendor.

2. *The task relates to building the vendor's infrastructure or training its employees to be able to perform services for the customer.* These are tasks that are performed to allow the provision of service in the future. They generally do not, in and of themselves, provide value to the customer.

3. *The task is purely administrative in nature.* Administrative tasks, such as setting up a customer account, billing the customer, and responding to routine information requests are generally not tasks that are directly related to providing the contracted-for service.

4. *The customer would not be aware that the task was performed.* Tasks that provide value to the customer, and thus appropriately trigger revenue recognition, should generally be visible to the customer.

There is not necessarily a link between the level of costs incurred related to a particular act and whether that act should trigger revenue recognition. For example, if an act results in the incurrence of substantive costs, that fact alone should not result in the conclusion that the act triggers revenue recognition (SAB Topic 13A3f, ques. 1). Determining whether an act triggers revenue recognition generally should be based on whether that act results in value being provided to the customer, not on the level of costs associated with the act.

> **OBSERVATION:** Selecting which acts in a service arrangement should trigger revenue recognition is very similar to identifying the various deliverables in a multiple-element arrangement (see Chapter 4, "Multiple-Element Arrangements"). In fact, some companies might evaluate a service transaction encompassing multiple activities as a multiple-element arrangement. Whether the contract is analyzed as a multiple-element arrangement or not, the result should be the same—actions that do not contribute toward providing value to the customer should not trigger revenue recognition.

EXAMPLE: SETUP ACTIVITIES

Acxiom Corporation Form 10-K—Fiscal Year Ended March 31, 2005

The Company provides database management and IT outsourcing services under long-term arrangements. These arrangements may require the Company to perform setup activities such as the design and build of a database for the customer under the database management contracts and migration of the customer's IT environment under IT outsourcing contracts. In the case of database management contracts, the customer does not acquire any ownership rights to the Company's intellectual property used in the database and the database itself provides no benefit to the customer outside of the utilization of the system during the term of the database management arrangement. In some cases, the arrangements also contain provisions requiring customer acceptance of the setup activities prior to commencement of the ongoing services arrangement. Up-front fees billed during the setup phase are deferred and setup costs that are direct and incremental to the contract are capitalized and amortized on a straight-line basis over the service term of the contract. Revenue recognition does not begin until after customer acceptance in cases where contracts contain acceptance provisions. Once the setup phase is complete and customer acceptance occurs, the Company recognizes revenue over the remaining service term of the contract. In situations where the arrangement does not require setup activities or customer acceptance before the Company begins providing services, revenue is recognized over the contract period and no costs are deferred.

Pattern of Revenue Recognition

Once the acts triggering revenue recognition have been identified, it is necessary to determine the pattern of revenue recognition as those acts are performed. This determination is generally dependent upon the types of acts to be performed in providing the service.

> **DISCLOSURE ALERT:** See Chapter 12, "Disclosures," for information about disclosures that may be required.

Specified number of similar acts If the transaction involves a specified number of identical or similar acts (e.g., the processing of bi-weekly payroll checks by a payroll processor), an equal amount of revenue should be recognized for each act. Thus, even if the cost to provide each act varies—for example, because of a learning curve faced by the service provider in servicing the customer—the same amount of revenue should be recognized each time the act is performed.

In some arrangements, the customer does not take advantage of all of the service to which it is entitled. This is referred to as "breakage." For example, if the arrangement is to process mortgage payments for the life of a mortgage, the service provider may be able to estimate, based on typical early payoff experience, that the mortgage will last for much less than its stated 30-year term. A service provider that believes it will actually perform fewer acts than the maximum number provided for in the service arrangement may also believe that revenue should be recognized based on this lower estimate, with more revenue allocated to each act.

As long as sufficient objective and verifiable evidence exists to allow a reliable estimate of breakage, it is acceptable to base the pattern of revenue recognition on the number of acts to be performed after adjusting for estimated breakage. Determining whether sufficient evidence exists to make a reliable estimate is a matter of judgment. However, it would generally be appropriate to use factors similar to those used to determine whether a reliable estimate of service transaction cancellations can be made (see "Cancellation or Refund Rights" below).

> **SEC REGISTRANT ALERT:** In a December 2002 speech, the SEC staff discussed the issue of breakage in situations where customers prepay, on a nonrefundable basis, for services or goods that they ultimately do not demand. The SEC staff observed that FAS-140 requires either performance or legal release to extinguish a liability. The prepayment for future delivery of services or goods creates a liability. Following a FAS-140 approach would result in no recognition of income for products or services paid for, but not demanded by the

customer, until the end (or expiration) of the performance period. Alternatively, the SEC staff indicated that they will not object to revenue recognition prior to the expiration of the performance period provided both the following conditions exist:

1. Management can demonstrate that the demand for future performance is remote based on a large population of homogeneous transactions; and
2. There is objective reliable historical evidence supporting the estimate of breakage.

The SEC staff also indicated that (a) it would be skeptical of an accounting model that results in immediate income for breakage and (b) whether breakage represents revenue or a gain (i.e., other income) depends on the facts and circumstances.

Even if sufficient evidence exists to estimate breakage, it should be an extremely rare occurrence where breakage results in immediate income recognition. Instead, the arrangement fee should be recognized based on the services expected to be delivered to the customer over the performance period. For example, consider a situation in which a customer prepays $10,000 for 100 hours of professional services to be provided over the course of one year, but the professional services provider has sufficient history and experience demonstrating that the customer will ultimately only demand 80 hours of professional services over the performance period. In this situation, the professional services provider may adopt an accounting policy that would result in recognizing the $10,000 of revenue over the 80 hours of services expected to be provided as they are rendered—$125 per hour of service rendered. Alternatively, the professional services provider may adopt an accounting policy that would result in recognizing $8,000 of revenue over the 80 hours of services expected to be provided as they are rendered and $2,000 of breakage income upon expiration of the arrangement. However, the professional services provider may not adopt an accounting policy that would result in recognizing $2,000 of breakage income upon initiation of the arrangement and $8,000 of revenue over the 80 hours of services expected to be provided as they are rendered. To do so, would be to recognize revenue before performance has occurred.

EXAMPLE: RELIABLE ESTIMATE OF BREAKAGE

Learning Tree International, Inc. Form 10-K—Fiscal Year Ended October 1, 2004

The Company offers its customers a multiple-course sales discount referred to as a "Training Passport." A Training Passport allows an individual passport holder to attend up to a specified number of the Company's courses over a one-year period for a fixed price. For a Training Passport, the amount of revenue recognized for each attendance in one of the Company's courses is based upon the selling price of the Training Passport, the list price of the course taken and the estimated average number of courses passport holders will actually attend. Upon expiration of a Training Passport, the Company records the difference, if any, between the revenues previously recognized and the Training Passport selling price. The estimated attendance rate is based upon the historical experience of the average actual number of course events that Training Passport holders have been attending. The average actual attendance rate for all expired Training Passports has closely approximated the estimated rate utilized by the Company. If the Training Passport attendance rates change, the revenue recognition rate for all active Training Passports and for all Training Passports sold thereafter is adjusted. The Company believes it is appropriate to recognize revenues on this basis in order to most closely match revenue and related costs, as the substantial majority of its Passport holders do not attend the maximum number of course events permitted under their Training Passport. The Company believes that the use of historical data is reasonable and appropriate because of the relative stability of the average actual number of course events attended by the tens of thousands of Passport holders since the inception of the program in fiscal 1993. Although the Company has seen no material changes in the historical rates as the number of course titles has changed, it monitors such potential effects. In general, determining the estimated average number of course events that will be attended by a Training Passport holder is based on historical trends that may not continue in the future. These estimates could differ in the near term from amounts used in arriving at the reported revenue.

Specified number of non-similar acts Some service transactions involve a number of different acts, even though they are all part of the same service. For example, a lawn care company might be contracted with to provide complete care of the grounds of a commercial property for a year, including mowing, watering, fertilizing, trimming, and replanting. If a service transaction involves a specified number of defined acts that are not identical or similar, revenue should be allocated based upon the relative value of each of the acts. In substance, this type of situation is treated like a multiple-element arrangement (see Chapter 4, "Multiple-Element Arrangements"), with revenue being allocated to the different acts based on their relative fair values. If there is insufficient evidence of the fair values of each of the individual acts, revenue should be recognized on a systematic and rational basis over the estimated period during which the acts will be performed. One such systematic and rational basis may be the use of the residual method discussed in Chapter 4, "Multiple-Element Arrangements." Another basis might be straight-line if no other systematic and rational basis is more representative of the pattern in which performance takes place.

> **OBSERVATION:** As noted above, if a single service requires multiple acts that *are not* similar in nature, and there is insufficient fair value evidence to allocate the arrangement consideration to each act, it may be appropriate to recognize revenue over

the performance period. If, however, an arrangement includes two separate *services* for which there is insufficient evidence of fair value to allow the allocation of revenue between the two services using either the relative fair value or residual method, it is likely not appropriate to recognize any revenue until the performance period for both services has begun. This situation must be analyzed as a multiple-element arrangement, as discussed in Chapter 4.

Determining whether a situation involves a single service with multiple acts or multiple services requires judgement. For example, a vendor that replaces transmissions performs two or more acts in doing so (e.g., removes old transmission, installs new transmission), however the replacement of the transmission is generally viewed as one service. Conversely, a vendor that agrees to replace a customer's transmission and provide an oil change is clearly providing two services.

> **OBSERVATION:**   In evaluating whether a service contract contains multiple deliverables, assets constructed by the service provider to be owned and operated by the service provider should not be considered separate deliverables. As discussed earlier, these activities are not activities that should trigger revenue recognition. In other words, these activities are setup activities that the service provider must perform in order to provide the service actually contracted for by the customer.

> **SEC REGISTRANT ALERT:**   In a December 2002 speech, the SEC staff discussed recognizing revenue on service contracts. During this discussion, the SEC staff stressed that registrants should consider whether service contracts contain multiple elements that should be evaluated for separation in accordance with EITF 00–21. In other words, the SEC staff emphasized that registrants should not default to treating a service contract as one bundled arrangement for revenue recognition purposes.

Unspecified number of similar acts for a specified period   If a service transaction involves an unspecified number of identical or similar acts with a fixed period of performance (for example, a maintenance contract on office equipment), revenue should be recognized ratably over the specified period during which the acts will be performed, unless evidence supports that some other method is more representative of the pattern in which performance takes place. Normal seasonality of service or prior experience as to the pattern of performance may constitute such evidence. For example, an annual contract to provide road maintenance in a cold-weather location would likely involve a higher percentage of the services being provided during the winter in comparison to the percentage of services being provided in the summer.

Unspecified number of similar acts for an unspecified period Some service contracts provide for a service to continue indefinitely, or for the lifetime of the service provider or the customer. For example, a muffler shop may offer a lifetime guarantee on its service for an extra fee. This unlimited extended warranty could require the muffler shop to perform an unspecified amount of additional work over a very long period of time. Similarly, a health club may offer a lifetime membership in exchange for a large one-time fee (either with or without ongoing periodic fees).

In these situations, recognizing revenue over the contractual service period is difficult, as that period is indefinite. When this is the case, it is generally appropriate to recognize the revenue over the estimated service period. For example, a car only lasts for a limited period of time, and most people cease using a health club after some period of time as well. To the extent that sufficient data exists to estimate the expected service period or the amount of service that will be provided, revenue should be allocated to each act or time period based on those estimates.

However, if there is no basis upon which to estimate either the service period or the amount of service that will be provided, there is no basis for estimating the degree to which performance has taken place. In these situations, revenue should only be recognized when performance is complete, or when breakage actually occurs (e.g., the health club member terminates his or her membership).

Recognition of Direct Costs

Long-term service contracts are fairly common in business today and are frequently used in outsourcing arrangements. For example, a business might hire an outside company to manage its information technology or transportation functions, or a government might outsource its sanitation or wastewater treatment functions. Long-term service contracts are also used in the management of certain projects, such as testing programs for new drugs and health care products.

As discussed in Chapter 9, "Contract Accounting," long-term contracts to deliver products or equipment are accounted for under the percentage-of-completion method, if the criteria in SOP 81–1 are met, under which a constant gross margin percentage is often recognized throughout the term of the contract. However, except in the case of engineering or architectural design and construction consulting services, which produce an end-product in the form of intellectual property, percentage-of-completion accounting should not be applied to service contracts. Thus, although the Proportional Performance model that is often applied to service transactions frequently results in revenue recognition based on the percentage of completion of the service, it is not appropriate to recognize costs in the same manner. Direct costs of services accounted for under the Proportional Performance model should, in most cases, be recognized as incurred, even if they are not incurred ratably as services are provided. Smoothing of costs is typically not acceptable in a service transaction.

> **SEC REGISTRANT ALERT:** In a December 2002 speech, the SEC staff discussed the issue of applying percentage-of-completion accounting to service contracts that are outside the scope of SOP 81–1. Specifically, the SEC staff stressed that SOP 81–1, and therefore percentage-of-completion accounting, should not be applied to service contracts that do not fall within its scope. The types of service contracts that fall within the scope of SOP 81–1 are limited to contracts for architectural or engineering design services and construction consulting services.

In many of these contracts, the service provider expects the contract to be profitable over the long contract term because it will increase productivity over the course of the contract, thereby lowering the direct cost of providing the service and making the final years of the contract more profitable than the early years. If the percentage-of-completion method were applied, gross margin would be recognized based on the estimated revenues and costs over the term of the contract. However, for a service contract, this method of accounting is not acceptable. Direct costs of providing the service should be expensed as incurred, rather than spread over the contract term. Therefore, margins are likely to vary over the course of a long-term service contract; however, the varying margins appropriately reflect performance in the different periods.

> ☛ **PRACTICE POINTER:** Because the costs in a long-term service contract are likely to be higher in the initial years than in future years, some service providers may structure the contracts with higher payments in the early years, or perhaps a significant up-front payment, in order to balance the cash inflows from the contract with the cash outflows. However, these types of changes in the timing of customer payments do not result in a similar change in revenue recognition. In general, revenue would still be recognized ratably over the service period unless the service to the customer is also greater in the beginning of the contract.

Recognition of Initial and Set-Up Costs

As discussed above, in some contracts for which the proportional performance model is used, the vendor performs acts that do not trigger recognition of revenue. Often, these acts involve incurring initial costs that prepare the vendor to provide the actual service contracted for by the customer. For example, a company that agrees to manage a database may need to convert the data into a format that works with its systems. Other companies may incur up-front costs related to initially procuring the contract. For example, a company entering into an arrangement to provide services may pay a commission to its sales employee or agent.

In certain situations, these costs may be capitalized as an asset and expensed over the term of the service arrangement as the revenue is recognized. For a detailed discussion of this topic, see Chapter 8, "Miscellaneous Issues."

ADVANCE FEES

Service Fee Paid in Advance

Service providers may require payment in advance when a service is to be provided. Such payment may be either refundable (i.e., the customer may cancel the arrangement and receive a refund) or non-refundable (i.e., the customer is not entitled to cancel the arrangement and receive a refund). In the case of a refundable advance fee, it is easy to conclude that revenue should not be recognized upon collection of the fee. In this situation, the fee is neither earned or relizable. Thus, revenue recognition upon receipt of a refundable advance fee is not appropriate.

When the advance fee is non-refundable, its payment satisfies the realizability condition necessary for revenue recognition. In some cases, companies may believe that the non-refundable nature of the advance fee makes it acceptable to recognize revenue, as long as the costs of providing the service are accrued. However, the fact that an advance payment is non-refundable does not overcome the fact that performance has not yet occurred. Therefore, revenue in these situations should not be recognized until performance occurs and the revenue is earned.

> ☞ **PRACTICE POINTER:** In some contracts that include a fee to be paid upon contract signing, the contract indicates that the fee is to compensate the service provider for services rendered before the contract was signed. In general, it is not appropriate to allocate a fee in a service arrangement to activities that occurred before the arrangement was signed.

Initiation and Installation Fees

A service transaction may involve a non-refundable initiation fee with subsequent periodic payments for future services (for example, an activation fee for a cellular telephone with monthly payments based on usage) or a non-refundable fee for installation of equipment essential to providing the future services with subsequent periodic payments for the services (for example, a fee charged to install and connect a security alarm with monthly payments for the ongoing security monitoring).

Initiation and installation services may be services in and of themselves. That would be the case if the installation or initiation services meet the conditions necessary to be accounted for separately from the other services in the contract, pursuant to the model discussed in Chapter 4, "Multiple-Element Arrangements." If these conditions are met, the revenue allocated to the initiation or installation services may be recognized when these services are provided as long as the other conditions for revenue recognition have been met. If the initial fee is greater than the amount allocated to the initiation or installation services, the difference should be treated as an advance fee for the other services in the arrangement, and recognized as those services are provided.

However, in other cases, no separate services are provided at the outset of the arrangement in return for the initiation or installation fee, or, if services are performed, they cannot be separately accounted for effectively due to a failure to meet the separation conditions discussed in Chapter 4, "Multiple-Element Arrangements" (e.g., the services do not provide standalone value to the customer). When this is the case, the fee charged for the installation or initiation service should be deferred and recognized as the other services in the arrangement are performed. Thus, the initial fee is treated as, in substance, an advance charge for future services, rather than a charge for a separate service.

The period over which the deferred up-front fee should be recognized should extend beyond the initial contractual period if the relationship with the customer is expected to extend beyond the initial term and the customer continues to benefit from the payment of the up-front fee (e.g., if subsequent renewals do not include a similar fee) (SAB Topic 13A3f, ques. 1).

EXAMPLE: SERVICE AND ACTIVATION FEES PAID IN ADVANCE

Covad Communications Group, Inc. Form 10-K—Fiscal Year Ended December 31, 2004

The Company recognizes up-front fees associated with service activation over the expected term of the customer relationship, which ranges from 24 to 48 months, using the straight-line method. The Company treats the incremental direct costs of service activation (which consist principally of customer premises equipment, service activation fees paid to other telecommunications companies and sales commissions) as deferred charges in amounts that are no greater than the up-front fees that are deferred. These deferred incremental direct costs are amortized to expense using the straight-line method over 24 to 48 months.

License or Processing Fees

Companies may negotiate arrangements pursuant to which they receive non-refundable fees upon entering into the arrangements. In some cases, the fees may ostensibly be received in exchange for a license or other intangible right, or for the performance of certain administrative services related to processing an application for future service (e.g., processing a health club membership application). In many cases, the license provided or the services performed do not constitute deliverables that a customer would pay for, absent an ongoing service that is also part of the arrangement. In these cases, the up-front deliverables do not result in revenue recognition upon delivery, as they would not have value to the customer on a standalone basis (see Chapter 4, "Multiple-Element Arrangements," for further discussion). Similar to initiation or installation fees that cannot be separately accounted for, these other types of up-front non-refundable fees should also be deferred and recognized over the performance period for the remaining services in the arrangement. As noted above, this period may extend beyond the initial contractual performance period if renewals are expected.

ILLUSTRATION: UP-FRONT FEES

(Adapted from SAB Topic 13A3f, questions 1 and 2, and questions 11 and 12 in the SEC staff's frequently asked question and answer document on SAB 101, *Revenue Recognition in Financial Statements*. Although most of the FAQ document was ultimately codified in SAB Topic 13 via SAB 104, *Revenue Recognition*, questions 11 and 12 were not included in the codification. The examples included in questions 11 and 12 continue to be used in this book, as adapted, because of their continued relevance in understanding the accounting for upfront fees.)

Facts: An arrangement involves a lifetime membership to a health club. An initiation payment compensates the health club for processing the application, providing a membership kit to the member, and assigning the member a locker. The member then pays a monthly fee for continued access to the facility. Assume that this arrangement is a single unit of accounting under EITF 00–21 (see Chapter 4, "Multiple-Element Arrangements").

Discussion: This transaction should be accounted for under the Proportional Performance model, as service is provided throughout the term of the arrangement. The customer receives no separate value from the processing of the application and the membership kit. Therefore, those acts do not trigger revenue recognition. Instead, the fee charged should be deferred and recognized as the rest of the services (health club access) are provided.

Because the arrangement is a lifetime membership, the up-front fee that is deferred should be recognized over the estimated customer relationship period, assuming that such period can be estimated. If it cannot be estimated, that initiation fee would be deferred until the relationship period can be estimated or the customer's membership terminates because he or she stops making monthly payments.

Facts: An arrangement involves the installation of an additional telephone jack at a residence and the activation and provision of local phone service to the new owners. The installation of the additional jack may be performed at the same time as activation of phone service or at a different time. The customer pays an activation fee, a fee to install the additional jack, and a monthly fee for the local telephone service.

Discussion: The provision of telephone service should be accounted for under the Proportional Performance model. The activation services do not provide the customer with any value absent the ongoing telephone service, and therefore no revenue should be recognized upon activation. The activation services and ongoing telephone service represent a single unit of accounting under EITF 00–21 (see Chapter 4, "Multiple-Element Arrangements"). The additional telephone jack, however, provides added value to the homeowner (by increasing the value of his or her home), regardless of the provision of service. Therefore, revenue may be recognized upon the installation of the additional jack. The amount allocated to the installation of the additional telephone jack should be determined using the guidance in Chapter 4, "Multiple-Element Arrangements." Any amount received upfront in excess of the amount allocated to the installation of the additional telephone jack (perhaps some or all of the amount labeled an activation fee) should be deferred and recognized over the period that telephone service will be provided. As this period is not specified, the deferred fee should be recognized over the estimated service period, presuming such period can be estimated.

Facts: Company A provides its customers with activity tracking or similar services (e.g., tracking of property tax payment activity, sending delinquency letters on overdue accounts, etc.) for a ten-year period. Company A requires customers to prepay for all the services for the term specified in the arrangement. The on-going services to be provided are generally automated after the initial customer set-up. At the outset of the arrangement, Company A performs set-up procedures to facilitate delivery of its on-going services to the customers. Such procedures consist primarily of establishing the necessary records and files in Company A's pre-existing computer systems in order to provide the services. Once the initial customer set-up activities are complete, Company A provides its services in accordance with the arrangement. Company A is not required to refund any portion of the fee if the customer terminates the services or does not utilize all of the services to which it is entitled. Assume that this arrangement is a single unit of accounting under EITF 00–21 (see Chapter 4, "Multiple-Element Arrangements").

Discussion: The customer could not, and would not, separately purchase the set-up services without the on-going services. The customer con-tracted for the on-going activity tracking service, not for the set-up activities. Provided all other revenue recognition criteria are met, service revenue should be recognized on a straight-line basis, unless evidence suggests that the revenue is earned or obligations are fulfilled in a different pattern, over the contractual term of the arrangement or the expected period during which those specified services will be performed, whichever is longer.

POST-PERFORMANCE OBLIGATIONS

Customer Acceptance Provisions

Customer acceptance provisions generally allow the customer to cancel the arrangement if the service does not live up to the customer's expectations. The existence of such provisions raises questions as to whether the earnings process is complete when the service is performed, or not until customer acceptance has been obtained. When services are performed subject to customer acceptance, the terms of the customer acceptance provisions should be analyzed to determine the appropriate accounting model to apply to the transaction. Generally, customer acceptance provisions and the related accounting take one of the four forms discussed below (for a flow chart on evaluating customer acceptance provisions, see Exhibit 5–2 in Chapter 5, "Product Deliverables").

Service Performed for Trial or Evaluation Purposes

In these arrangements, the seller provides a service to the customer to demonstrate its ability to provide the specified services. For example, membership programs often include a trial period during which the customer may take advantage of the benefits of the program before being obligated to pay for the membership.

When services are offered on a trial or evaluation basis, the customer does not agree to purchase the service until and unless it is satisfied with the results. In some cases, acceptance is triggered when the customer does not cancel the service within a specified time period. In other cases, affirmative acceptance from the customer is necessary to trigger a purchase obligation.

In either case, these arrangements do not constitute sales until acceptance occurs. Revenue recognition before acceptance would be inappropriate because, There is no persuasive evidence of an arrangement until acceptance occurs. Accordingly, in arrangements where services are provided for demonstration purposes, revenue should not be recognized until acceptance occurs, either by notification from the customer or by passage of time without rejection as specified in the arrangement, provided the other conditions for revenue recognition have been met (SAB Topic 13A3b, ques. 1).

☛ **PRACTICE POINTER:** The reason that provision of service on a demonstration basis does not trigger recognition of revenue is because the arrangement does not even purport to be a sale unless and until acceptance occurs. Thus, no matter how good a company is at estimating the percentage of demonstration services that ultimately result in sales, revenue cannot be recorded before acceptance. However, subjective customer acceptance clauses and refund rights, which are also discussed in this chapter, do not absolutely preclude revenue recognition during the refund period because a sale agreement is in place before the service is performed. As refund rights provide potential customers with many of the same protections that a trial or evaluation period provides, companies that offer services on a trial or demonstration basis may wish to change their arrangements to sales with a cancellation or refund right, potentially allowing revenue recognition at an earlier point in time.

Subjective Right of Return

Certain customer acceptance provisions give the buyer the right to request a refund or refuse to pay for the service in the event he or she is dissatisfied for any reason. An example of such a provision is a "100% satisfaction guarantee." Acceptance provisions like this that are based on subjective terms are, in substance if not in name, general refund rights. As such, acceptance provisions based on subjective matters should be accounted for as discussed in the "Cancellation or Refund Rights" section of this chapter (SAB Topic 13A3b, ques. 1).

Customer Acceptance Based on Meeting Standard Performance Criteria

These provisions give the customer the right to a refund or to withhold payment for the service if it is ineffective, fails to meet advertising claims, or does not meet the vendor's published specifications. For example, an Internet service provider may guarantee certain uptime targets will be met, giving the customer the right to cancel the arrangement and receive a refund if they are not. In some cases (for example, a car repair with a guarantee), the seller may have the right to perform the service again, rather than refund the purchaser's money.

When this kind of acceptance provision is offered, it is generally offered to every customer of a particular class. Typically, the seller only offers this kind of acceptance provision when it is reasonably certain the service will meet the applicable specifications. Provided the seller has previously demonstrated its ability to meet the specified criteria, a customer acceptance provision based on seller-specified criteria is, essentially, a warranty. In those cases, the customer acceptance provisions should be accounted for as a warranty (see "Service Warranties" in this chapter).

However, if the seller has not previously demonstrated that it can perform the service to the stated specifications, warranty accounting is not appropriate because it is not yet clear that the company has delivered the service specified in the arrangement with the customer.

Therefore, revenue should be deferred until the specifications have been achieved or the customer has accepted the service (SAB Topic 13A3b, ques. 1).

Customer Acceptance Based on Customer-Specified or Negotiated Criteria

This type of customer acceptance provision is the most difficult to deal with. It generally is included in arrangements involving services that are customized for the particular customer. When these types of terms are included in an arrangement, the seller usually has a period of time after initially performing the service to resolve any problems that might exist in meeting the criteria. Because the service provider must continue to work until the performance conditions are met, it may not be able to conclude that it has substantially performed its obligations under the arrangement until those specifications are met.

Therefore, when customer-specified customer acceptance provisions exist, the seller must be able to reliably demonstrate that the service meets (or will meet upon completion, if revenue on the service is to be recognized under the Proportional Performance model) the customer-specified acceptance criteria before revenue can be recognized. This may be possible if the criteria are objective or if the company has provided similar services to the customer in the past.

However, if unique aspects of the customer's environment could affect whether the service meets the specified performance criteria, or if other circumstances exist that prohibit the seller from verifying compliance with the acceptance provisions until the service has been completed, revenue should not be recognized until compliance can be verified. Verification often consists of formal customer sign-off that the acceptance provisions have been met. However, if the seller can verify that the service meets the acceptance criteria, and therefore believes it would be able to enforce a claim for payment even though formal customer sign-off has not occurred, revenue may be recognized because the seller has fulfilled all terms of the contract. Like other accounting that is based on a legal interpretation, consultation with legal experts may be necessary to determine the appropriate treatment (SAB Topic 13A3b, ques. 1).

> **OBSERVATION:** Acceptance provisions based on criteria specific to a particular contract or customer must be evaluated on a contract-by-contract basis. Therefore, the point at which revenue can be recognized may differ for different contracts.

> **DISCLOSURE ALERT:** See Chapter 12, "Disclosures," for information about disclosures that may be required.

> **SEC REGISTRANT ALERT:**   In early 2003, the SEC staff issued
> the Summary by the Division of Corporation Finance of
> Significant Issues Addressed in the Review of the Periodic
> Reports of the Fortune 500 Companies (the Fortune 500 Report).
> This report resulted from the SEC's Division of Corporation
> Finance's (Corp Fin) review of all annual reports filed by Fortune
> 500 companies, and provides insight into areas commonly
> questioned by the SEC staff during its reviews of annual reports.
> One area specifically mentioned in this report relates to cus-
> tomer acceptance clauses. The SEC staff noted that the quality
> of disclosures related to customer acceptance clauses requires
> improvement.

Service Warranties

Many service arrangements include a warranty provision that provides the purchaser with some protection in the event the service
does not provide the expected benefits. Automobile mechanics, car-
penters, and electricians are among the service providers that often
provide warranties to their customers. Normally, a service provider
that offers a warranty merely takes on an obligation to reperform
the service if the work does not hold up for some period of time or
does not continue to produce results in accordance with its published specifications. However, not all warranty provisions involve
the same type of obligation, and it is important to understand the
substance of the obligations the seller takes on in order to properly
account for the warranty. For example, if the seller commits to
ensure the service will meet certain specifications beyond those that
it usually meets, the seller will likely be unable to determine the
extent of performance that will be required in order to meet the
specifications. In those cases, revenue should only be recognized
when the specifications are achieved.

In addition, certain warranties may include obligations other than
ensuring that the service continues to meet specifications. These additional deliverables should not be accounted for as part of the warranty.
Rather, an arrangement that includes the right to future additional
products or services should be accounted for as a multiple-element
arrangement (see Chapter 4, "Multiple-Element Arrangements").
Therefore, a portion of the arrangement fee in these situations should
be allocated to the additional deliverables and deferred until the seller
fulfills its obligations to provide those deliverables.

As noted above, most warranty provisions merely require that the
seller reperform the service if it does not provide the intended results
(and fix any damage caused, if applicable). Warranty obligations usually are identified explicitly in the service contract, but warranties
may also be implied or required by laws or regulations (for example,
many states require certain licensed service providers to provide a
limited warranty on those services). As a consequence of a warranty
commitment, the seller's performance obligation may not end when

the initial service is completed. At the very least, the seller must stand ready to honor the warranty for whatever period of time it is in force.

One possible method of accounting for a sale with a warranty would be to treat it as a multiple-element arrangement, identifying the initial service and the warranty as separate deliverables, and allocating the revenue between the two. The amount allocated to the warranty would then be recognized over the warranty period. Another possible method of accounting for a warranty would be to consider the warranty merely a part of the original service, rather than as a separate service. If analyzed this way, the question arises as to whether the warranty obligation is significant enough to prevent revenue recognition on the original service. If it is, then revenue would not be recognized until the warranty expires. Conversely, if the warranty obligation were not deemed significant, all revenue would be attributed to the original service and recognized when that service is performed, presuming all other revenue recognition criteria are met.

U.S. GAAP recognizes the merit in both of the above approaches to accounting for warranties depending on the nature of the warranty. When the warranty is a standard warranty that is given to all customers, it is considered inseparable from the service. However, when the warranty is separately priced so that some customers may opt to pay for the warranty while others do not, the warranty is considered a separate service consistent with the way it is sold.

Standard Warranties

When a service provider offers a standard warranty to all of its customers, the warranty is not treated as a separate service; rather, it is considered an integral part of providing the service that is the subject of the arrangement. Revenue may be recognized as the service is performed (assuming other revenue recognition conditions are also met) when a standard warranty is included in the transaction, provided that the costs of honoring the warranty can be reliably estimated. In these cases, the estimated costs of honoring the warranty must be accrued as additional cost of sales when revenue is recognized. Accrued costs should be updated as estimates change.

However, if the costs of honoring the warranty cannot be reliably estimated and the potential range of loss is wide, revenue should be deferred until either a reliable estimate of the costs can be made or the warranty period expires (FAS-5, par. 25). Indicators that costs may not be reliably estimable include (a) the service is new or is being provided by new personnel, (b) the scope of a warranty has been extended beyond what has normally been given in the ordinary course of business, and (c) new obligations have been undertaken.

DISCLOSURE ALERT: See Chapter 12, "Disclosures," for information about required disclosures.

Separately Priced Extended Warranty and Product Maintenance Contracts

The above discussion applies only to standard warranties offered to all purchasers of a service without an extra charge. Revenue from separately priced extended warranties and product maintenance contracts should be deferred and recognized in income over the contract period. A warranty should be treated as a separately priced, rather than a standard, warranty any time that a customer has the option to buy the service with or without the warranty. For example, assume that everybody who has their brakes replaced at a national chain gets a one-year warranty on the work, but that three-year protection is available for an additional charge. The arrangement should be accounted for as having a one-year standard warranty and a two-year separately priced extension. As such, the fee paid for the two-year extension should be deferred and recognized as revenue in years two and three after the brake job has been performed. The charge for the brake job with the standard one-year warranty should be recognized as revenue when the job is done, as long as the other revenue recognition conditions are met and the costs of honoring the one-year warranty can be reliably estimated.

The recognition pattern for revenue attributable to a separately priced extended warranty contract should be on a straight-line basis unless historical evidence indicates that the costs of performing services under the contract are incurred on other than a straight-line basis. If costs are incurred on other than a straight-line basis, revenue should be recognized over the contract period in proportion to the costs expected to be incurred in performing services under the contract (FTB 90–1, par. 3).

> **OBSERVATION:** In many cases, a company selling an extended warranty purchases insurance to cover its potential losses under the warranty. While purchasing insurance may transfer the risk of loss under the contract to the insurance company, it generally does not relieve the seller of its obligations to the customer. That is, the seller remains liable to fulfill the warranty, even after buying insurance, in the event that the insurance company cannot or will not honor the insurance coverage. Because the seller has not fulfilled its obligation to the buyer and has not been released by the buyer from that obligation (i.e., the buyer was not a party to the insurance contract), purchasing insurance to cover the risk of loss under a warranty contract should not result in revenue recognition. Rather, the accounting for the warranty contract and the accounting for the insurance should each be separately considered.

> **DISCLOSURE ALERT:** See Chapter 12, "Disclosures," for information about required disclosures.

Other Post-Performance Obligations

Service providers may take on a variety of obligations that continue beyond the time the main service provided for in the contract is completed. For example, a transaction processor may agree to provide certain information about the transactions processed over a period of time. Whenever a service provider agrees to perform multiple services, or takes on continuing performance obligations, the arrangement should be accounted for as multiple-element arrangement. See Chapter 4, "Multiple-Element Arrangements," for further discussion.

CANCELLATION OR REFUND RIGHTS

In product sales, customers often have the right to return a product for a full refund if they are not satisfied. Although not as common, many service transactions have a similar provision. For example, membership warehouse clubs typically charge an annual fee that is wholly refundable for at least some period of time after the beginning of the annual term. Credit card annual fees generally have similar terms. Other service providers may offer a "100% guarantee" of satisfaction "or your money back." In other instances, the fee earned by an agent for brokering the sale of a product may be refundable if the purchaser of the product returns it to the supplier.

The accounting for product return rights is addressed in FAS-48, which allows revenue recognition in a sale despite the existence of a return right, so long as certain conditions are met (see Chapter 5, "Product Deliverables"). However, FAS-48 specifically does not apply to service transactions (FAS-48, par. 4).

> **OBSERVATION:** The guidance in this section directly addresses a service transaction in which there is a full refund right. However, some service transactions may have cancellation provisions in which the amount of revenue to be refunded declines over time or as service is provided. Such refund rights only need to be considered in determining how much revenue to recognize if some revenue that would be recognizable absent the refund right is potentially subject to refund. Because refund rights in these situations generally expire ratably and the service is also generally considered to be delivered ratably, such rights usually do not limit revenue recognition.

> ☞ **PRACTICE POINTER:** Cancellation or refund rights are often documented in the sales contract. However, such rights may also exist due to industry practice, company policy, or laws and regulations. In evaluating cancellation or refund rights, it is important that all rights that exist, whether explicitly stated or not, be considered.

Potential Accounting Treatments

Despite the fact that FAS-48 specifically excludes service transactions from its scope, many companies have applied accounting similar to that specified in FAS-48 to refundable service transactions. They have therefore recognized revenue upon performance of the service in these transactions, accruing only an estimate of refunds to be provided. However, others believe this treatment is not acceptable for service transactions.

There are strong arguments on both sides as to whether this analogy is appropriate. Supporters of the analogy to FAS-48 note that FAS-48 allows revenue recognition on a product sale even though a right of return exists in situations where the vendor has fulfilled its obligations and the amount of revenue is reasonably estimable. They believe the exact same situation often exists in a service transaction with a refund right.

Those who believe the analogy to FAS-48 is inappropriate believe that the differences between product and service transactions warrant different treatment of refund rights. They also believe that a refund obligation is within the scope of FAS-140, which provides that financial liabilities may be derecognized only if (1) the debtor pays the creditor and is relieved of its obligation for the liability (*paying the creditor* includes delivery of cash, other financial assets, goods, or services or reacquisition by the debtor of its outstanding debt securities) or (2) the debtor is legally released from being the primary obligor under the liability (FAS-140, par. 16). Since the refund obligation is only relieved when a refund is paid or the refund privilege expires, this analysis would lead to the conclusion that no amount potentially subject to refund may be recognized as revenue. Another point that would suggest that a FAS-48 analogy is inappropriate is that, when a product refund is claimed, the product must be returned to the seller. However, it is generally not possible to undo a service once it has been performed. Thus, the customer ultimately keeps the results of the service without paying for it.

In the end, the decision regarding whether to apply a FAS-48-like or FAS-140-like policy to refundable service transactions is an accounting policy decision that a company must make (SAB Topic 13A4a, ques. 3).

> **DISCLOSURE ALERT:** Companies should disclose their choice of accounting policy for service transactions with a right of refund. See Chapter 12, "Disclosures," for additional discussion of accounting policy disclosures.

Applying FAS-48 by Analogy

If a company elects to apply a policy similar to the accounting specified in FAS-48 to refundable service transactions, it must determine whether it has met the applicable requirements. FAS-48 includes certain criteria that must be met before revenue is recognized in a product sale with a right of return. Similar criteria for refundable service transactions would be as follows:

1. *The sales price to the buyer is fixed or determinable* (FAS-48, par. 6). This shows that the refund period is not just part of the transaction's pricing negotiations. If the arrangement does not meet this criterion, no revenue should be recognized because a fixed or determinable price is one of the prerequisites to recognizing revenue.

2. *The buyer has economic substance apart from the seller* (FAS-48, par. 6). A sale to a company with little substance raises significant questions about the buyer's ability to pay. As such, the seller should not record the sale to the non-substantive purchaser.

3. *The seller does not have significant obligations for future performance relating to the refundable service* (FAS-48, par. 6). If the seller is required to continue to perform additional work for the customer until the refund right lapses, the performance criterion may not have been met.

4. *The amount of future cancellations and refunds can be reasonably predicted* (FAS-48, par. 6). This is the most judgmental of the criteria, and the one that most often cannot be met. See below for further discussion.

Estimating Refunds

Sometimes determining whether a reasonable estimate of refunds can be made is quite easy. For example, a service that has been provided to the same group of customers and has generated a consistent rate of refund requests for many years can probably be expected to have similar experience in the future, as long as there are no external changes that might affect future refund experience. On the other hand, a start-up company selling a new service may quickly conclude that it cannot estimate the level of refunds that will occur. In evaluating whether a reasonable estimate of refunds can be made, all available information should be considered. The following factors, if they exist, may cause the seller to conclude that refunds cannot be reasonably predicted. At a minimum, the seller should take these factors into consideration when estimating the amount of refunds.

1. *The service is susceptible to significant external factors, such as the introduction of competitors' services with superior technology or greater expected market acceptance, that affect market demand for the seller's service offerings* (FAS-48, par. 8). If the cancellation period is lengthy, it may be particularly difficult for the company to predict its competitors'—and therefore its customers'—activities in an environment susceptible to significant external factors.

2. *The cancellation period is long* (FAS-48, par. 8). Obviously, the longer the cancellation or refund period, the more difficult it becomes to predict the level of refund requests. Whether the period is long should be determined based on the nature of the service, industry practice, and the type of customer.

3. *The absence of relevant historical experience* (FAS-48, par. 8). Without historical experience to reference, predicting customer actions is virtually impossible. In the absence of company-specific experience, industry experience may be relevant. However, this is less likely to be true in service transactions than product transactions, as the identity of the service provider may greatly affect customer satisfaction.

4. *The absence of a large volume of relatively homogeneous transactions* (FAS-48, par. 8). It is generally difficult to predict the actions of a particular customer. However, it is much easier to predict, on average, the actions of a large number of customers.

5. *The service is new.* The newer the service offering, the less specific refund experience that exists. Depending upon the circumstances, refund experience with other, similar, services may be useful.

> **OBSERVATION:** The ability to estimate refunds could vary from location-to-location, customer-to-customer, and arrangement-to-arrangement. Thus, it is possible that a company may be able to estimate refunds for certain transactions but not others. In addition, when a company sells various types of services or serves various market segments whose cancellation rates would be expected to vary from one another, the company should develop different estimates for each type of service or market segment.

> **SEC REGISTRANT ALERT:** The SEC staff believes that it is preferable to look to FAS-140 for the appropriate accounting for refundable service transaction fees, and therefore believes that the preferable accounting is to recognize no revenue on refundable service fees until the refund period expires (SAB Topic 13A4a, ques. 4). However, the SEC staff will accept an analogy to FAS-48 if the criteria discussed above under "Applying FAS-48 by Analogy" are all met. With respect to estimating the refunds to be provided, the staff believes all of the following must be true for an acceptable estimate to be made (SAB Topic 13A4a, ques. 1):

> • The estimates of terminations or cancellations and refunded revenues are being made for a large pool of homogeneous items (e.g., membership or other service transactions with the same characteristics such as terms, periods, class of customers, nature of service, etc.).

- There is a sufficient company-specific historical basis upon which to estimate the refunds, and the company believes that such historical experience is predictive of future events. The SEC staff generally believes that a company introducing new services or servicing a new class of customer should wait until it has at least two years of experience before concluding that sufficient company-specific historical evidence exists.

- Reliable estimates of the expected refunds can be made on a timely basis. The SEC staff considers any of the following to be indicative of an inability to make reliable estimates:

  — There are recurring, significant differences between actual experience and estimated cancellation or termination rates (*e.g.*, an actual cancellation rate of 40% versus an estimated rate of 25%) even if the impact of the difference on the amount of estimated refunds is not material to the consolidated financial statements.

  — There are recurring variances between the actual and estimated amount of refunds that are material to either revenue or net income in quarterly or annual financial statements.

  — There is more than a remote chance that material adjustments (both individually and in the aggregate) to previously recognized revenue would be required.

  — The customer's termination or cancellation and refund privileges exceed one year.

DISCLOSURE ALERT: See Chapter 12, "Disclosures," for information about required disclosures.

EXAMPLE: REVENUE RECOGNITION ON SERVICE TRANSACTION WITH A RIGHT OF REFUND

Memberworks Incorporated Form 10-K—Fiscal Year Ended June 30, 2004

Revenues are billed primarily through credit and debit cards. Members who are enrolled in a monthly payment plan may cancel their membership at any time, at which time, the billings will be discontinued. Revenues from these membership programs are recognized when earned. Members who are enrolled in an annual payment plan may cancel their membership in the program at any time and will receive a pro rata refund of the fee paid based on the remaining portion of the membership period. In accordance with Staff Accounting Bulletin 104, "Revenue Recognition" ("SAB 104"), deferred revenues are recorded, net of estimated cancellations, and are amortized as revenues upon the expiration of membership refund privileges. An allowance for membership cancellations is established based on management's estimates and is updated regularly. In determining the estimate of allowance for membership cancellations, management analyzes historical cancellation experience, current economic trends and changes in customer demand for the Company's products and services. Actual membership refunds are charge against the allowance for membership cancellations on a current basis. If actual cancellations differ from the estimate, the results of operations would be impacted.

Accounting for Refund Rights

If revenue is not recognized when the service is performed because an estimate of refunds cannot be made, the seller should defer recognition until either the cancellation period has expired or information allowing the company to make a reasonable estimate becomes available (FAS-48, par. 6). In this situation, any cash collected should be reflected as a liability, rather than as revenue. Costs incurred in providing the service should still be recognized as incurred, because, unlike refund right in product transaction, the seller will not receive anything of value back from the customer in the event the customer in a service transaction requests a refund.

When a company chooses the FAS-48 method of accounting for service transactions with refund rights, it must meet the conditions discussed earlier to recognize revenue net of estimated refunds. While revenue is reduced for the amount of estimated refunds when these conditions are met, a similar reduction is generally not reflected in cost of sales since the customer does not return anything of value when requesting a refund on a service transaction. If revenue is recognized in earnings over the service period, adjustments for changes in estimated refunds should be recorded by adjusting the revenue, deferred revenue and refund obligations at each financial statement date to the amounts that are appropriate based on the latest refund estimate (SAB Topic 13A4a, ques. 1).

ILLUSTRATION: SERVICE SOLD WITH RIGHT OF REFUND

Facts: Marketing Company sells 100 memberships to its travel club at $120 per membership. Customers may cancel their membership at any time during the one-year term of the membership. Any customer who does so receives a full refund of the membership fee. Ten customers request a refund after three months, and 30 others request a refund just before the end of the membership period.

EXAMPLE 1

Additional Facts: Marketing Company has a policy of waiting until the refund period expires before recognizing revenue, treating the refund provision as a monetary liability to be accounted for pursuant to FAS-140.

ACCOUNTING:

Upon sale:

- Payment is received, but no revenue is recognized.

Cash	$12,000	
Deposit Liability		$12,000

After three months:

- Cash is refunded to the 10 customers that requested refunds.

Deposit Liability	$1,200	
Cash		$1,200

At the end of the year:

- Cash is refunded to the 30 customers that requested refunds.

Deposit Liability	$3,600	
Cash		$3,600

- Revenue on the remaining memberships is recognized in full, as the refund period has expired and performance has already occurred.

Deposit Liability	$7,200	
Revenue		$7,200

EXAMPLE 2

Additional Facts: Marketing Company follows a policy of recognizing revenue on sales of memberships with a refund right as long as refunds can be estimated, similar to the treatment specified in FAS-48 for product sales with a right of return. Because this travel club is a new offering, Marketing Company concludes that it cannot reliably estimate the amount of refunds.

Accounting:

Same as in Example 1.

EXAMPLE 3

Additional Facts: Marketing Company follows a policy of recognizing revenue on sales of memberships with a refund right as long as refunds can be estimated, similar to the treatment specified in FAS-48 for product sales with a right of return. In this case, Marketing Company originally estimates a 30% refund rate, but changes that estimate to 40% when 10 customers request a refund after three months. Marketing Company has sufficient evidence to support its refund estimates.

Accounting:

Upon sale:

- Payment is received, but no revenue is recognized because performance has not occurred. Based on its estimates of refunds to be requested, Marketing Company records both deferred revenue and a monetary liability.

Cash	$12,000	
Deferred Revenue		$8,400
Deposit Liability		$3,600

During the first three months of the membership:

- Revenue is recognized ratably on those memberships for which refunds are not expected.

Deferred Revenue	$2,100	
Revenue		$2,100

After three months:

- Cash is refunded to the 10 customers that requested refunds.

Deposit Liability	$1,200	
Cash		$1,200

- Based on its new estimate of refunds, Marketing Company adjusts the remaining deferred revenue and deposit liability balances, as well as the revenue recognized in the three months that have elapsed so far.

Deferred Revenue	$900	
Revenue		$300
Deposit Liability		$1,200

During the remaining nine months of the membership:

- Revenue is recognized ratably on those memberships for which refunds are not expected.

Deferred Revenue	$5,400	
Revenue		$5,400

- Cash is refunded to the 30 customers that requested refunds.

Deposit Liability	$3,600	
Cash		$3,600

SELLER-PROVIDED FINANCING AND GUARANTEES

Sales with Extended Payment Terms

Some sellers may elect to provide financing for their customers' purchases by agreeing to receive fixed payments over a long period of time, rather than receiving payment in advance (see "Advance Fees" above) or in accordance with normal payment terms shortly after performance. Except in sales of software products (see Chapter 10, "Software—A Complete Model"), GAAP does not provide specific guidance about when extended payment terms should result in a conclusion that revenue should not be recognized. However, extended payment terms can affect the evaluation of two of the four conditions for revenue recognition: those requiring that (1) the fee be fixed or determinable and (2) collectibility be reasonably assured.

Extended Payment Terms and Fixed or Determinable Fees

Extended payment terms raise the risk that, to ensure payment according to the stated terms, the service provider will agree to provide additional products or services or to reduce the arrangement fee, even for a creditworthy customer. Consider a customer dissatisfied with a service where there is no warranty. The customer may instead elect to withhold payments, requiring the seller to negotiate to receive the payments it is due. Therefore, extended payment terms should be carefully considered, together with warranty, refund, customer acceptance, and other terms of the arrangement, to determine whether they preclude a conclusion that the arrangement fee is fixed or determinable. If the payment terms are extended but the performance of the service is also extended, such that the payment terms mirror the performance, the extended payment terms may not result in delayed revenue recognition. However, if the payment terms extend beyond the completion of the service, or are disproportionately delayed until the end of a long service period, those payment terms might very well affect the recognition of revenue.

Extended Payment Terms and Collectibility

Clearly, the longer the payment terms, the more difficult it is to conclude that collection of the revenue is reasonably assured. Judgment must be applied in these situations. If it is concluded that collection is not reasonably assured, no revenue or receivable should be recorded. It is not acceptable in these instances to record revenue and a selling expense for the anticipated bad debt because the threshold criteria for revenue recognition were never met.

Discounting Long-Term Receivables

When services are sold on terms that extend significantly beyond the point in time that revenue is recognized, APB-21 requires that the long-term receivable, and therefore the revenue, be recorded at the present value of the payments, rather than the nominal value. Interest income would then be accrued on the receivable until all payments are made. Therefore, when extended payment terms are stated at their nominal values, a portion of the payments will be attributed to interest income, as opposed to revenue (APB-21, par. 12). If, however, the payment terms are extended, but merely reflect the proportional performance of the contract, no discounting is required.

Guaranteeing a Loan in Connection with a Sale of Services

A company may agree to guarantee a loan taken out by a customer to buy the company's services. In this situation, although the company has collected cash related to the sale of its services, it has the same chance of ultimately realizing the amount charged for the services as if it had sold the services on extended payment terms consistent with the loan terms. Therefore, before recognizing any revenue, the company should evaluate whether collectibility is reasonably assured as if it were the lender under the loan.

If the company concludes that collection is reasonably assured and all other revenue recognition criteria have been met, then FIN-45 requires the transaction to be treated as a multiple-element arrangement, the two elements being the sale of services and the guarantee of a loan. This type of multiple-element arrangement is discussed in more detail in Chapter 4, "Multiple-Element Arrangements."

> **DISCLOSURE ALERT:** See Chapter 12, "Disclosures," for information about required disclosures.

REVENUE RECOGNITION FOR SPECIFIC TRANSACTIONS

Various accounting standard-setters have addressed the application of the general revenue recognition guidance, particularly whether and when revenue has been earned, to certain service transactions. This guidance also provides insight, by analogy, into how the general guidance might be applied in other types of service transactions. The discussion below focuses on two types of service transactions that are addressed in the literature. For a comprehensive listing of the literature that addresses specific transactions, see Chapter 2, "A Brief Survey of Revenue-Related Literature."

Transportation Revenues

One type of transaction for which the application of the Completed Performance or Proportional Performance model is not clear is the provision of freight or shipping services. One argument in favor of assessing the delivery condition under the Proportional Performance model is the fact that the goods get closer to their destination as they progress in the shipping process. However, an argument in favor of assessing the delivery condition under the Completed Performance model is the fact that the customer likely does not perceive value to have been received until and unless the goods are delivered to their destination.

The EITF discussed the accounting for freight providers in EITF 91-9. The EITF did not reach a consensus on a single method of accounting. Instead, it concluded that four methods of accounting for freight services are acceptable.

1. *Revenue is recognized when freight is received from the shipper or when freight leaves the carrier's terminal with accrual of the estimated direct costs to complete delivery.* This method is considered least preferable by the SEC staff, as it allows recognition of revenue before performance. It is also not consistent with the general revenue recognition principles. Freight carriers may use this method of accounting because the EITF deemed it acceptable, but other companies should not analogize to this guidance to support revenue recognition before performance.

2. *Revenue and direct costs are recognized when the shipment is completed (the destination is reached).* This method applies the Completed Performance model to the transaction, and treats the costs as an asset when they are incurred, recognizing them at the same time as the revenue.

3. *Revenue is recognized when shipment is completed with expenses recognized as incurred.* This method applies the Completed Performance model to the transaction, but does not treat the costs incurred as an asset when they are incurred. Although acceptable, this method does not match revenue and expenses, and therefore may distort results.

4. *Revenue is recognized based on relative transit time in each reporting period with expenses recognized as incurred.* This method applies the Proportional Performance model to the transaction.

> **DISCLOSURE ALERT:** Because there are multiple acceptable revenue recognition policies that freight companies may adopt, these companies should disclose their choice of policy. See Chapter 12, "Disclosures," for additional discussion of accounting policy disclosures.

Research and Development Arrangements

A company may agree to provide research and development (R&D) services in various types of arrangements. In some cases, the company's customer owns all rights to the results of the R&D, while in others the customer funds all or a portion of the R&D and receives some rights to the results of the activities, while the company that performs the R&D receives other rights. Certain arrangements also give the company that performs the R&D the right or the obligation to purchase the results of the R&D that initially rest with the customer.

Because of the complexities of these arrangements, it may be difficult to determine whether revenue should be recognized as R&D is performed, or only upon its successful completion. Indeed, in some instances, because of the existence of a purchase option as described above, it may not be clear whether the payments from the funding party are merely loans, rather than payments for services. If it is determined that the payments are payments for services, the pattern of revenue recognition may still not be clear, particularly if some of the payments are contingent upon reaching future milestones. Many of the issues regarding R&D arrangements were addressed in FAS-68. Other issues were addressed in SAB Topic 13, and still other issues have been addressed through the development of industry practice.

> **DISCLOSURE ALERT:** See Chapter 12, "Disclosures," for information about disclosures that are required for companies that perform research and development for others.

Determining the Nature of the Obligation

To recognize payments received from the funding party as revenue under the Proportional Performance model as R&D services are performed, the company must conclude that it has undertaken an obligation to provide services, rather than to repay a loan or to provide a developed product (i.e., an obligation not only to provide services, but to succeed in doing whatever the R&D hopes to do). To make this conclusion, it must be clear that the funding party has taken on the risk of the R&D not producing the hoped-for results.

If the company performing the R&D is committed to repay any of the funds provided by the other parties regardless of the outcome of the research and development, all or part of the risk has not been transferred. The following are some examples in which an entity is committed to repay funds that result in all or part of the risk related to the R&D not transferring to the funding party (FAS-68, par. 6):

- The company guarantees, or has a contractual commitment that assures, repayment of the funds provided by the other parties, regardless of the outcome of the research and development.

- The other parties can require the entity to purchase their interests in the research and development, regardless of the outcome.
- The other parties automatically will receive debt or equity securities of the entity on termination or completion of the research and development, regardless of the outcome.

In all of these cases, it is clear that the "customer" is really only lending the company money to fund the R&D, rather than paying the company to perform it, because the "customer" will have the ability to get its money back if the R&D fails (FAS-68, par. 7).

Other evidence may also point toward a lending arrangement, rather than a sale of R&D services, and all evidence should be considered in determining the nature of the company's obligation. Even if the written agreements under the arrangement do not require the entity to repay any of the funding, other conditions might indicate that the entity is likely to bear the risk of failure of the R&D. Any time conditions suggest that it is probable the company will repay the funding if the R&D fails, there is a presumption that the entity has an obligation to repay the other parties if the R&D fails. As discussed under "Cancellation or Refund Rights" in this chapter, refundable service fees should not be recognized as revenue unless the potential refunds can be reliably estimated. Given the nature of R&D arrangements, it is unlikely that reliable estimates could be made. Examples of conditions leading to the presumption that the entity will repay the other parties if the R&D fails include the following (FAS-68, par. 8):

- *The entity has indicated an intent to repay all or a portion of the funds provided.*
- *The entity would suffer a severe economic penalty if it failed to repay any of the funds provided to it, regardless of the outcome of the research and development. An economic penalty is considered "severe" if, in the normal course of business, an entity would probably choose to pay the other parties rather than incur the penalty.* For example, if the entity would lose valuable rights to existing products in the event it did not exercise an option to purchase the funding party's interest in the R&D, the funds received should be considered a loan rather than payment for services.
- *A significant related-party relationship between the entity and the parties funding the research and development exists at the time the entity enters into the arrangement.* This indicator is particularly strong if the entity also has the right to purchase the results of the R&D on anything other than a fair value basis. See Chapter 8, "Miscellaneous Issues," for further discussion of related-party revenue transactions.

- *The entity has essentially completed the project before entering into the arrangement.* In this case, it would appear that the funding party is purchasing the as-yet-unavailable results of the R&D, rather than contracting with the company to perform R&D. The payment received in this situation is effectively a prepayment for future R&D results if the R&D is successful.

- *The entity is required to make royalty payments to the funding party based on the revenues from products other than (or in addition to) those stemming from the products developed with the funds provided by that party.* In this situation, it would appear that the funding party is purchasing a future payment stream, rather than merely purchasing R&D services. Payments for a future payment stream are generally accounted for as debt (EITF 88–18).

Accounting If There Is Deemed to Be an Obligation to Repay the Funding

If the company is deemed to have an obligation to repay the funding in the event the R&D fails, revenue should not be recognized under the Proportional Performance model. In these cases, the Completed Performance model should be used, and performance should not be considered complete unless and until the R&D succeeds and the company delivers the results of the R&D to its customer, rather than repaying the funding.

Accounting If the Obligation Is to Perform R&D Services

If it is concluded that repayment of any of the funds provided by the funding parties depends solely on the R&D being successful (e.g., royalty payments), the entity should assess performance under the Proportional Performance model, recognizing revenue as services are performed, presuming that all other revenue recognition criteria have been met. However, determining the pattern of performance is not always straightforward. In addition, payments may not follow the pattern of performance at all, as they are often triggered only when (and if) specific milestones are reached. Because of this, such payments are not fixed or determinable until those milestones are reached, limiting the amount of revenue that may be recognized.

There are three methods that are generally accepted for purposes of determining the pattern of revenue recognition in R&D arrangements.

> **OBSERVATION:** Whether an arrangement to perform R&D services consists of a single unit of accounting or multiple units of accounting should be based on the guidance in EITF 00–21 (see Chapter 4, "Multiple-Element Arrangements"). One of the three methods discussed below should be applied

to the relevant units of accounting as determined based on the application of EITF 00–21. These three methods are not intended to replace the application of EITF 00–21 or to negate the effects of its application.

Performance-Based Methods

Two of the methods rely on the model set forth in EITF 91–6. The reason that an analogy is made to EITF 91–6 is that the transactions addressed in EITF 91–6 also involve situations in which payments under the contract do not mirror performance under the contract. Essentially, the model in EITF 91–6 indicates that revenue should be recognized based on the lesser of the amount calculated based on the proportional performance to date and the amount due under the terms of the contract for work that has already been performed. Thus, under the model in EITF 91–6, if 60% of the service has been provided, but only 55% of the total fee has become due, revenue is limited to 55% of the total fee. Conversely, if 60% of the service has been provided, but 65% of the total fee has become due, only 60% of the total fee may be recognized.

As mentioned above, EITF 91–6 is the basis for two of the methods often used to account for R&D service contracts. One of those methods uses total expected revenue in applying the model (the "Expected Revenue" method). In other words, the calculation bases the estimate of the amount of revenue earned at any point in time on the total revenue the company expects to earn from the contract, including payments that have not yet become due because the milestones to which they relate have not yet been reached. The other method uses only up-front payments and payments related to milestones already reached in making the EITF 91–6 calculations (the "Payments Received" method). Both methods limit the amount of revenue actually recognized at any point in time to amounts that have become due (and are non-refundable) under the terms of the contract.

The following steps illustrate the application of these two performance-based methods to account for contracts to perform R&D:

1. Estimate the percentage of the total services to be provided that have already been provided.

> **OBSERVATION:** Over time, the estimate of total effort to be expended may change. If this happens, the change in estimate should be accounted for using either the cumulative catch-up or prospective method. The cumulative catch-up method effectively provides for a true-up to the new estimate in the current period by calculating revenue as if the new estimate were the estimate being used all along. The prospective method effectively provides for revenue to be recognized in the current and

remaining periods using the remaining fees to be recognized and the remaining effort expected to be expended.

☞ **PRACTICE POINTER:** As discussed earlier in this chapter, there may be situations in which the total amount of service to be provided is not estimable, either from a time-based or efforts-based perspective. In these cases, it is not possible to recognize any revenue under the EITF 91–6-based methods until performance is completed or the amount of performance that will be required is estimable. However, the milestone method, discussed below, may be appropriate in these situations.

2. Multiply that percentage by either the total expected payments (Expected Revenue method), or the non-refundable payments to-date (including those that are contractually due, but have not yet been made, as long as collectibility is reasonably assured)(Payments Received method), depending on which method is to be used.

3. Compare the result of step 2 with the non-refundable payments received to date (including payments that are contractually due but not yet paid, as long as collectibility is reasonably assured). The lesser of the two is the amount of revenue that should be recognized, cumulatively, on the contract.

An illustration of these methods is provided below, after the discussion of the milestone-based method.

Milestone-Based Method

The milestone-based method distinguishes between the up-front and milestone payments for accounting purposes instead of combining them, as is done in the performance-based methods. The up-front fee in the milestone-based method is deemed to relate to the entire performance period, since no discrete earnings process culminated upon receipt of the up-front fee. As such, the up-front fee is recognized over the performance period on a systematic and rational basis. If information related to efforts expended and total efforts expected to be expended is available, a basis centered on percentage-of-efforts expended should most likely be used. If such information is not available, the systematic and rational basis would most likely be a time-based method where the up-front fee is recognized ratably over the performance period. The milestone payments, however, are deemed to be related to the portion of the performance period dedicated to achieving that specific milestone. In substance, each milestone is treated as if it is a separate contract, performance for which is evaluated under a Completed Performance model.

The milestone-based method is predicated upon the milestones being substantive. If they are not, the milestone-based method cannot be used. In these situations, the basis of the method falls apart because customers would not pay separately for reaching a non-substantive milestone. Determining whether a milestone is substantive and meaningful is a matter of judgment. Questions that should be considered in this assessment include:

- Is substantive effort required to reach the milestone?

- What labor and other costs must be incurred to achieve the milestone?

- What type of skill is required to achieve the milestone?

- How certain is achievement of the milestone?

- Does the amount of the milestone payment seem reasonable in light of the effort required to achieve that milestone?

- How does the elapsed time between the payments compare to the effort required to reach the milestone?

Comparison of Methods

ILLUSTRATION: COMPARISON OF PERFORMANCE-BASED AND MILESTONE-BASED MODELS

Facts: Biotech Company (Biotech) enters into an agreement with Pharmaceutical Company (Pharma) to license Compound A to Pharma for a period of three years. In addition, Biotech agrees to perform research and development for Pharma with the goal of using Compound A to develop a medicinal treatment for acne. Biotech receives $100,000 upfront and $200,000 as it meets each of two milestones. For purposes of this example, assume that the milestones are substantive and meaningful. None of these payments ($500,000 in total) are refundable under any circumstances once received. No other continuing performance obligations exist. Biotech estimates that it will spend $50,000, $40,000, and $60,000 of labor costs in Years 1, 2, and 3, respectively, in performing research and development for Pharma. During Year 2 the first milestone is reached. Biotech incurred $50,000 and $40,000 of labor costs in Years 1 and 2, respectively.

Accounting: The license of Compound A and the research and development services are two elements in a multiple-element arrangement. Biotech concludes that these elements cannot be separated given the lack of fair value evidence and the inter-related nature of the license and the research and development activities. Biotech calculates revenue for Year 1 and Year 2 using the two performance-based methods and the milestone-based method as follows:

	Year 1	Year 2
Labor Dollars Expended to Date	$ 50,000	$ 90,000
Total Expected Labor Dollars	150,000	150,000
Percent Complete at End of Year	33%	60%
Up-front Payment Received	100,000	100,000
Milestone Payments Received (Cumulative)	—	200,000
Total Payments Received to Date	100,000	300,000

	Year 1	Year 2
"Earned" Amount Using the Payments Received Method (Cumulative)	33,333	180,000
Amount to be Recognized Using Payments Received Method (lesser of "earned" amount and payments received) (Cumulative)	**33,333**	**180,000**

	Year 1	Year 2
Total Expected Payments	500,000	500,000
"Earned" Amount Using the Expected Revenue Method (Cumulative)	166,667	300,000
Amount to be Recognized Using the Expected Revenue Method (lesser of "earned" amount and payments received) (Cumulative)	**100,000**	**300,000**

	Year 1	Year 2
Amount to be Recognized using Milestone-Based Method (All milestone payments received plus a portion of up-front payment based on percent complete at the end of year) (Cumulative)	**33,333**	**260,000**

Therefore, Biotech calculates revenue for Year 1 and Year 2 using each of the three methods as follows.

	Expected Revenue	Payments Received	Milestone
Year 1	$ 100,000	$ 33,333	$ 33,333
Year 2	200,000	146,667	226,667
Cumulative through Year 2	$ 300,000	$ 180,000	$ 260,000

Each of the three methods results in a different pattern of revenue recognition over the two-year period. The different patterns are caused by each method's pattern being more or less reliant on certain facts. The performance-based—expected revenue method's variations are tied primarily to level of effort. However, if the milestone payments do not keep pace with the level of effort expended, its variance may also be dependent on the timing of milestone payments. The performance-based—payments received method's variations are tied primarily to level of effort and timing of milestone payments. The timing of milestone payments affects this method since it calculates revenue based on receipts. This also results in a greater amount of the revenue being backended (i.e., recognized towards the end of the service period). The milestone-based method's variations depend in part on the approach used to recognize the up-front fee. If an efforts-based approach is used to recognize the up-front fee, as is the case in the illustration above, then the milestone-based method's variations will be caused by both level of effort and timing of milestone payments. If a time-based approach is used to recognize the up-front fee, then the milestone-based method's variations will be due solely to the timing of milestone payments.

The natural question is which of these methods is preferable. To a certain extent, it depends on the facts and circumstances. However, the performance-based—expected revenue method is generally preferable in most situations because it results in revenue being recognized ratably as service is performed, except to the extent such revenue is not fixed or determinable because its realization depends on reaching a milestone in the future. Some have suggested that this method inappropriately considers revenue from future milestones, and therefore violates the condition that the fee must be fixed or determinable before it can be recognized. However, because revenue recognition at any point in time is limited to the cumulative non-refundable payments that have been received (or have become due), only the portions of the fee that are in fact fixed or determinable are recognized.

☛ **PRACTICE POINTER:** Choosing a method to account for R&D contracts is the selection of an accounting policy. Once selected, a change from one method to another would be treated as a change in accounting principle. Such change would have to be considered preferable in order to be effected. As such, companies should choose their model carefully.

EXAMPLE: COLLABORATION AGREEMENT—LICENSE FEE AND MILESTONE PAYMENTS

Viropharma Form 10-K—Fiscal Year Ended December 31, 2004

Wyeth Agreement

In December 1999, the Company entered into a licensing agreement with Wyeth for the discovery, development and commercialization of hepatitis C drugs. In connection with the signing of the agreement, the Company received $5.0 million from Wyeth. This amount is non-refundable and a portion of it was recorded as deferred revenue at December 31, 1999. This revenue is being recognized as certain activities are performed by the Company over the estimated performance period. The original performance period was 5 years. In 2002, the Company and Wyeth extended the compound screening portion of the agreement by two years, and as a result the Company extended the performance period from 5 years to 7 years. The unamortized balance of the deferred revenue will be amortized over the balance of the extended performance period. Of this deferred revenue, the Company recognized $0.6 million as revenue in 2004, $0.6 million as revenue in 2003, $0.7 million as revenue in 2002, and $1.1 million is recorded as deferred revenue on the consolidated balance sheet at December 31, 2004. If drug candidates are successfully commercialized, the Company has the right to co-promote the products and share equally in the net profits in the United States and Canada. The Company is entitled to milestone payments upon the achievement of certain development milestones and royalties for product sales, if any, outside the United States and Canada.

In 2000, the Company sold an aggregate of 200,993 shares of common stock to Wyeth for aggregate proceeds of $6.0 million. The sales of common stock were as a result of progress made under the companies' hepatitis C virus collaboration. In connection with the collaboration and license agreement, Wyeth is required to purchase predetermined dollar amounts of additional shares of the Company's common stock at a market value premium at the time of completion of certain product development stages. If additional shares are purchased, this excess will be accounted for as a credit to additional paid-in capital.

CHAPTER 7
INTELLECTUAL PROPERTY
DELIVERABLES

CONTENTS

BACKGROUND

Many companies earn revenue by letting others use their assets. These assets can be tangible or intangible. Some examples include:

- A car rental agency earning revenue by allowing its customers to rent its vehicles.
- A computer software developer earning revenue by allowing customers to license its software products.
- A movie production company earning revenue by allowing customers to license its film rights.
- A franchisor earning revenue by allowing its customers to use its name and processes.
- A developer of a drug earning revenue by allowing a drug marketer to sell the drug.

The accounting for transactions in which one company gives another company the right to use its assets has been debated for many years, largely because developing one model to account for significant differences between these transactions has proved difficult. These differences relate to many factors, including:

1. Whether the arrangement is for a limited term or in perpetuity.
2. Whether the asset is tangible or intangible.
3. Whether the right to use the asset is exclusive or non-exclusive.
4. Whether the fees are fixed or based on how (or how much) the asset is used.
5. Whether there are any cancellation or modification provisions in the arrangement.

This chapter explores the significant issues that arise in the sale or licensing of intellectual property, and includes transactions that are addressed in the authoritative literature as well as others that are not specifically addressed. The issues discussed in this chapter should be evaluated with respect to each intellectual property element or deliverable. It is important to note, however, that many arrangements that include intellectual property licenses also include the sale of products or provision of services. If there are multiple deliverables in the transaction, the interrelationship of these deliverables often gives rise to issues beyond those that exist in a single-element transaction. Some of these issues are discussed below, and others are discussed in Chapter 4, "Multiple-Element Arrangements."

SURVEY OF ACCOUNTING LITERATURE

The accounting literature that addresses the sale or licensing of intellectual property assets. Under U.S. GAAP is almost entirely transaction- or industry-based. Thus, for certain transactions, such as leases of tangible assets and licenses of motion picture rights, there is a significant amount of guidance. Conversely, there is little or no guidance for transactions that fall outside the scope of the industry- or transaction-based literature, except for the guidance in SAB Topic 13 that addresses several narrow issues regarding intellectual property licenses in general.

LISTING OF APPLICABLE LITERATURE

APB-21	Interest on Receivables and Payables
FAS-13	Accounting for Leases
FAS-45	Accounting for Franchise Fee Revenue
FAS-48	Revenue Recognition When Right of Return Exists
FAS-98	Accounting for Leases, an amendment of FASB Statements No. 13, 66, and 91 and a rescission of FASB Statement No. 26 and Technical Bulletin No. 79-11
FIN-45	Guarantor's Accounting and Disclosure Requirements for Guarantees, Including Indirect Guarantees of Indebtedness of Others, an interpretation of FASB Statements No. 5, 57, and 107 and rescission of FASB Interpretation No. 34
FSP FIN 45-1	Accounting for Intellectual Property Infringement Indemnifications under FASB Interpretation No. 45, *Guarantor's Accounting and Disclosure Requirements for Guarantees, Including Indirect Guarantees of Indebtedness of Others*
SOP 97-2	Software Revenue Recognition
SOP 00-2	Accounting by Producers or Distributors of Films
EITF 00-21	Revenue Arrangements with Multiple Deliverables
SAB Topic 13	Revenue Recognition

GENERAL CONDITIONS FOR RECOGNITION

As with all revenues, revenue from intellectual property transactions should be recognized when it has been earned and is realized or realizable. Revenue from licenses of intellectual property is generally earned either at the beginning of the license term or throughout the license term, depending upon the nature of the license and the other obligations taken on by the licensor. Such revenue usually is considered realizable once the customer has committed to pay for the license, provided the customer's ability to pay is not in doubt. In licenses of intellectual property, it is common that only a partial commitment to pay is in place at the inception of the license, with the customer becoming obligated to make additional payments based on milestones related to performance, use of the property, or passage of time. These and other uncertainties may affect when revenue is recognized.

As discussed in Chapter 3, "General Principles," revenue is considered to be earned and realizable when all of the following conditions are met:

1. Persuasive evidence of an arrangement exists.
2. The arrangement fee is fixed or determinable.
3. Delivery or performance has occurred.
4. Collectibility is reasonably assured.

Also as discussed in Chapter 3, the analysis of the first and last of the above conditions does not change significantly based on the type of transaction involved. Most of this chapter focuses on the analysis of the fixed or determinable and delivery conditions in intellectual property transactions. Recognition of revenue in intellectual property transaction also can be affected by the existence of additional elements in the arrangement. These unique multiple-element considerations are discussed in this chapter as well.

DELIVERY

The main question that must be answered to determine when and how to recognize revenue for a deliverable that involves the right to use assets is whether delivery occurs entirely when the lease or license term begins (Completed Performance model) or throughout the term of the lease or license (Proportional Performance model). To determine when delivery has occurred, it is necessary to assess whether the terms of the arrangement effectively represent the sale of an asset. If the transaction is deemed a sale, a Completed Performance model should be applied in which delivery generally occurs for accounting purposes when the customer's right to use the asset begins. If the seller/licensor does not transfer enough risks and rewards for the transaction to be treated as a sale, a Proportional Performance model is applied.

The question of which model to use is not easily answered. Each arrangement and asset type can have unique characteristics that affect this determination. With respect to sales of the right to use tangible assets (i.e., leases), there is detailed guidance in the accounting literature as to how to determine whether the Completed Performance or Proportional Performance model should be applied. Some of this guidance may be useful, by analogy, in accounting for sales of the right to use intangible assets (i.e., intellectual property licenses).

> **OBSERVATION:** Software and other types of intellectual property can be, and often are, delivered via a tangible medium. However, this does not change the fact that the value to the customer is the intellectual property. That is, computer software delivered on a compact disc is actually the sale or license of the computer software program. The compact disc is just the tangible medium used to provide the customer access to the intangible computer software program.

Certain licenses of intangible assets are addressed in the accounting literature (see "Revenue Recognition for Specific Intellectual Property Transactions" later in this chapter), but many others are not. To the extent a company licenses intellectual property that is not the subject of a specific authoritative pronouncement, the company must consider many factors in determining an appropriate revenue recognition policy. Among the factors to be considered are the license's specific facts and circumstances, the general revenue recognition guidance contained in the FASB Concepts Statements, and the individual pieces of topic-specific guidance that address accounting for the sale of rights to use specific types of assets. SEC registrants must also consider the guidance provided in SAB Topic 13, while private companies might also consider this guidance in developing their accounting policies. All of this, without any overall framework, complicates the accounting for these types of arrangements.

Possible Analogies in the Accounting Literature

One way of answering the question about whether to use the Completed Performance or Proportional Performance model to assess delivery is to look to the existing accounting literature that addresses rights to use assets. Several types of transactions are addressed in the literature, including leases, licenses to software and motion pictures, and franchise arrangements.

Leases

FAS-13 is the cornerstone literature for a lessor's accounting for lease revenue. FAS-13 has been amended and supplemented by various pieces of other literature. A detailed discussion of lease accounting requires much more then a few pages in a chapter on intellectual property licenses—in fact, it would require its own stand-alone book. The purpose of discussing lease accounting here is merely to provide one school of thought regarding the accounting for the sale of the right to use an asset. A detailed listing of the relevant authoritative literature addressing a lessor's accounting for lease revenue is included in Chapter 2, "A Brief Survey of Revenue-Related Literature." That literature should be consulted, as necessary, to gain the understanding necessary to properly account for a lease.

FAS-13 provides insight into the question of how to account for a license of intellectual property because, in providing guidance on lease accounting, FAS-13 focuses on the question of whether delivery in the sale of a right to use tangible assets should be evaluated based on a Completed Performance model or a Proportional Performance model. The basic model in FAS-13 requires a lessor to determine whether or not the substance of the lease is the sale of the asset by focusing on which party (the lessee or lessor) continues to hold the risks and rewards of ownership of the asset. If it is determined that the lease transaction is essentially the sale of the asset, delivery is evaluated like it is in a product sale (Completed Performance model). If the lease effectively conveys to the lessee the right to use the asset for a limited time, delivery is evaluated like it is in many service transactions (Proportional Performance model).

A lessor must navigate the following decision tree to determine the appropriate delivery model for a lease:

EXHIBIT 7-1
LEASE FLOW CHART

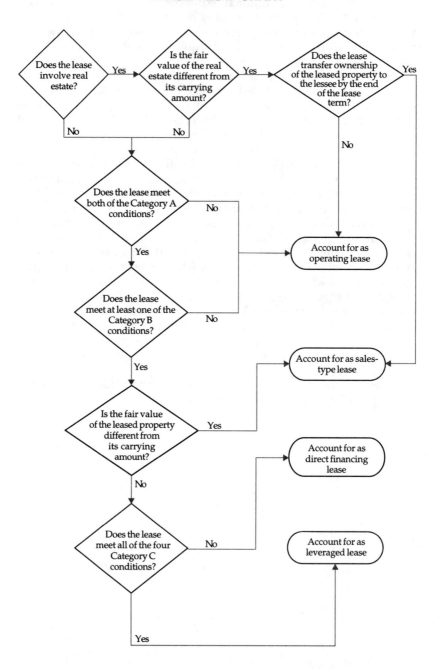

Category A Conditions (FAS-98, par. 22(f), FAS-13, par. 8)

1. Collections of rentals must be reasonably predictable

2. Significant risks or commitments beyond those related to usual sales warranties cannot be retained or undertaken

Category B Conditions (FAS-13, par. 7)

1. Title to the leased asset transfers to lessee at the end of the lease term

2. Lessee has option to purchase leased asset at a bargain price

3. Lease term is 75% or more of the estimated useful life of the property subject to the lease

4. Present value of minimum lease payments is 90% or more of the fair value of the leased property less any investment tax credit retained by the lessor

Category C Conditions (FAS-13, par. 42)

1. Lease involves at least three parties: lessee, long-term creditor, and lessor

2. Long-term creditor financing is substantial and nonrecourse to lessor

3. Lessor's net investment declines during the early years and increases during the later years of the lease term

4. Lessor accounts for any retained investment tax credit as cash flow component of lease

The criteria (Category A, B, and C Conditions) that must be considered by a lessor in determining how to account for a lease focus on whether the lessor has transferred to the lessee the significant risks and rewards of ownership related to the leased asset. If the lessor has, in effect, retained the significant risks and rewards of ownership related to the leased asset, then the lessor accounts for the lease as an operating lease. Operating lease accounting is a Proportional Performance model where operating lease payments are recognized as revenue over the lease term. If the lessor has, in effect, transferred to the lessee the significant risks and rewards of ownership related to the leased asset, then the lessor accounts for the lease as a sales-type, direct financing or leveraged lease as appropriate, based on the specific facts and circumstances. Each of these methods results in the application of a variation of the Completed Performance model.

Franchises, Software, and Motion Pictures

As noted above, revenue recognition for certain intellectual property transactions is addressed in the accounting literature. Franchise fee revenue recognition is discussed in FAS-45; software revenue recognition is discussed in SOP 97-2, SOP 98-9, EITF 00-3, and EITF

03-05; and recognition of revenue from the licensing of films is discussed in SOP 00-2. Each of these pieces of literature essentially uses a Completed Performance model to evaluate the delivery condition unless certain factors exist. Further discussion of arrangements involving franchises and motion pictures is included later in this chapter. Software revenue recognition is discussed fully in Chapter 10, "Software—A Complete Model."

Choosing the Right Analogy

In comparing the various existing models to account for the sale of rights to use assets, some are more similar than others. The software and motion picture models are similar because the nature of the licensed property is somewhat similar. The franchise model is different, however, mainly because a franchise arrangement almost invariably involves a continuing relationship between the parties to the arrangement. Even more different yet is the lease model.

Which of these models is the best analogy for intellectual property licenses depends on the type of intellectual property involved. Consider the manuscript for a novel. Content is the central theme of both a manuscript and a film. The content is presented differently (written word versus picture), but the nature of the intellectual property involved is content. In this situation, the company trying to sell or license the manuscript should consider applying the guidance in SOP 00-2 to determine when the fees received for the sale or license of the manuscript should be recognized.

Finding a clean analogy for other types of intellectual property is not quite as easy. Consider the formula for a candy bar. The value in this intellectual property is realized through the product that the formula produces. SOP 00-2 is not a clean analogy since there are no significant similarities between a candy bar formula and a film. The nature of the candy bar formula is somewhat similar to a software program since a computer code works much like a formula. However, the value provided by the software program is completely different than the value provided by a candy bar formula. As such, SOP 97-2 is not a clean analogy. A franchise agreement may include the rights to food or other formulas. However, there is much more involved in a franchise than merely the transfer of rights to intellectual property such as a candy bar formula. As such, FAS-45 is not a clean analogy. A candy bar formula is clearly intellectual property and not a tangible asset. As such, FAS-13 is not a clean analogy.

If there is no clean analogy to the existing literature, all the facts and circumstances related to the intellectual property license must be analyzed in the context of the general revenue recognition concepts and conditions discussed above under "General Conditions for Recognition," to determine when delivery occurs under the license.

Key Factors in Evaluating Delivery of Intellectual Property

As in other transactions, delivery should generally be considered to occur when value is passed to the customer. However, when the deliverable is the right to use intellectual property, it is not clear whether that value is passed to the customer all at once, as it generally is in a product sale, or over time as the right to use the asset is provided. Certain factors are key to determining which model to use, and when recognition of revenue should begin.

Commencement of License Term

The earliest point at which delivery can occur is the first day of the license term. For example, a license arrangement is consummated on March 31, but the license term begins on April 1. The licensor may not recognize any revenue prior to April 1. This is consistent with one of the general conditions that must be met to recognize revenue from the sale or license of films. This point applies both to intellectual property transactions evaluated under the Completed Performance model and those evaluated under the Proportional Performance model. In either case, no revenue should be recognized until the beginning of the license term (SAB Topic 13A3d).

Risks and Rewards of Ownership

As discussed above, intellectual property is sometimes delivered on a physical medium. When that is the case, many of the considerations typically involved in product sales are relevant to recognition of revenue from the intellectual property license. For example, intellectual property delivered on a physical medium (e.g., a CD, a book, or printed data) generally should not be considered delivered until title transfers, along with the related risks and rewards of ownership of the physical medium containing the intellectual property. Refer to Chapter 5, "Product Deliverables," for discussion of these issues. Chapter 10, "Software—A Complete Model," also includes discussion of how these issues are addressed in the software revenue recognition literature. This guidance may be helpful in addressing these issues in intellectual property transactions where the intellectual property is delivered on a physical medium.

Exclusivity

One of the ways in which rights to use intangible assets are fundamentally different from rights to use tangible assets is that a specific tangible asset may be used by only one concurrent user, whereas a specific intangible asset could be used by many concurrent users. To illustrate this concept, consider an automobile and computer software. The automobile (the tangible asset) may only be rented to and used by one driver at a time, whereas the computer software (the intangible asset) may be licensed to and operated by many users at the same time. This basic difference has resulted in the accounting models for selling rights to use tangible and intangible assets taking different courses.

Considering the exclusivity, or non-exclusivity, of an intellectual property license provides the licensor with an appreciation for how similar the arrangement might be to the sale of the right to use a tangible asset. An arrangement that provides exclusive rights to intellectual property has an attribute similar to a product sale—it can only be sold once. Whereas, an arrangement that provides for non-exclusive rights to intellectual property has an attribute similar to software and film sales—it can be sold to more than one user simultaneously. As such, exclusivity in an arrangement suggests that the leasing literature is a good source for determining when delivery occurs, and non-exclusivity in an arrangement suggests that the software literature is a good source for determining when delivery occurs.

Duration of the Arrangement

Comparing the term of the arrangement with the life of the intellectual property provides the licensor with an appreciation for whether the arrangement is more similar to the outright sale of a product or a short-term operating lease of the product.

Arrangement term Because licenses of intellectual property (other than those discussed above) are not addressed in the authoritative literature, there is no guidance for determining the life of the arrangement when there are options or potential extensions. For example, the term of the arrangement may be initially stated as five years. However, there may be other provisions in the arrangement that automatically extend the term in perpetuity if neither party has defaulted on any terms in the arrangement. In this situation, the seller or licensor should carefully consider whether the term of the arrangement is effectively the life of the intellectual property.

Intellectual property life The life of the intellectual property should be considered the time period over which the intellectual property will provide benefits to its owner or users. To gain an appropriate understanding of the life of the intellectual property, the seller or licensor must consider the nature of the legal rights it possesses to the intellectual property and the nature of the intellectual property itself. For example, if the intellectual property rights are subject to a patent, the seller or licensor must consider when the patent will expire and whether it will or can be renewed. In addition, the seller or licensor should take into consideration whether the intellectual property rights relate to a technology susceptible to obsolescence, thereby resulting in its useful life being less than its legal life.

An arrangement whose duration is for the life of the intellectual property has an attribute similar to a product sale—neither the customer's right to use the intellectual property nor its ownership of the product revert back to the owner after a limited period of time. Duration of the arrangement is also relevant in lease accounting. One of the conditions of a lease that may contribute to it being considered a sales-type lease is whether the lease term is 75% or more of the estimated useful life of the property subject to the lease.

An arrangement whose duration is for something less than the life of the intellectual property has attributes similar to an operating lease in that the rights to use the intellectual property will end before the property's useful life, much like the right to use an asset subject to an operating lease. Of course, software sales are often for durations shorter than the life of the software, and the software revenue recognition literature relies predominantly on a Completed Performance model. The primary benefit of considering the duration of the arrangement arises when it is considered in conjunction with exclusivity.

Exclusivity/Duration Matrix

Different combinations of exclusivity and duration affect the analysis of which model, Competed Performance or Proportional Performance, is most appropriate. The following matrix outlines which model(s) can be justified in accounting for the sale or license of intellectual property based on the analysis of these factors:

	Term equal to life of intellectual property	Term less than life of intellectual property
Exclusive	**Quadrant I** Completed Performance	**Quadrant II** Proportional Performance
Non-exclusive	**Quadrant III** Completed or Proportional Performance	**Quadrant IV** Completed or Proportional Performance

Quadrant I

When intellectual property is licensed to a customer for the duration of its life and on an exclusive basis, it very closely resembles an outright product sale. Therefore, a Completed Performance model is generally most appropriate. In an outright product sale, except for

normal rights of return accounted for separately under specific literature, the product will not revert back to the seller. Similarly, the right
to use the intellectual property will not revert back to the seller or
licensor during the intellectual property's life if the license is exclusive and its term is equal to the intellectual property's remaining useful life. Furthermore, in an outright product sale, the specific product
being sold can only be bought by one customer. Similarly, intellectual
property sold on an exclusive basis is only licensed to one customer.

It is worth noting here that intellectual property can be licensed on
an exclusive basis for use in either specific geographic areas or for use
in specific applications. For example, a specific medical compound
may be licensed exclusively to one researcher for use in developing a
treatment for one medical condition while it may also be licensed
exclusively to a second researcher for use in developing a treatment
for a different medical condition. Similarly, a candy bar formula may
be licensed exclusively to one company for the North American
region and licensed exclusively to a second company for the
European region. This aspect is unique to intellectual property and
does not change the fact that the specific exclusive rights the customer
is buying or licensing cannot be sold or licensed to another party.

Quadrant II

When intellectual property is licensed to a customer for less than the
duration of its life but still on an exclusive basis, a Proportional
Performance model is generally most appropriate. This is based on
its similarities to an operating lease. In an operating lease, the right
to use the asset will revert back to the lessor at the end of the lease
term. Similarly, the right to use the intellectual property will revert
back to the seller or licensor at the end of the license arrangement
term if the term is less than the life of the intellectual property.
Presumably, in both cases, the leased asset or licensed intellectual
property will have value to the lessor or licensor at that point in time.
Furthermore, in an operating lease the specific asset being leased is
only leased to one customer. Similarly, the intellectual property is
only licensed to one customer when the terms are exclusive.

> **OBSERVATION:** Although transactions with these character-
> istics appear to be very similar to operating leases, both SOP
> 97-2 and SOP 00-2 generally provide for the use of a
> Completed Performance model in these situations, presuming
> other revenue recognition conditions have been met.
> Therefore, it is clear that the operating lease analogy need not
> be applied to ALL intellectual property licenses that are exclu-
> sive and limited in duration. Each license should be analyzed
> and its terms discussed with experts in this area of accounting
> to reach an appropriate conclusion.

Quadrants III and IV

When a sale or license of intellectual property is non-exclusive, it becomes less clear whether a Completed Performance or Proportional Performance model is appropriate. On the one hand, non-exclusivity is prevalent in software and motion picture arrangements and a Completed Performance model is generally used in both of those situations. On the other hand, the leasing literature requires certain very specific conditions to be met to treat the right to use a tangible asset as a sale. These conditions would most likely not be met in the typical license for intellectual property. That is, ownership of the intellectual property usually does not transfer to the licensee at the end of the arrangement term, the licensee does not usually have the option to purchase the intellectual property at a bargain price, and it is usually not possible to determine whether the present value of the payments under the arrangement are 90% or more of the fair value of the intellectual property due to the difficulties in assessing the fair value of intellectual property. The only one of the criteria that may be met is if the term of the arrangement represents 75% or more of the estimated life of the intellectual property. To the extent this is the case, a Completed Performance model may be the most appropriate.

In many of the Quadrant III and IV situations, there will not be just one model that is acceptable under the circumstances. In other words, a legitimate case might be made for either the Completed Performance or Proportional Performance model. An attempt should be made to determine which of the models *best* fits the specific facts and circumstances of the arrangement. If one model fits the facts and circumstances better than the other, the better-fitting model should be selected as the accounting policy for the arrangement (and other similar arrangements). If neither model is clearly the best analogy, a seller or licensor of intellectual property will have to choose one of the models to use as its accounting policy in these (and other similar) situations.

☞ **PRACTICE POINTER:** Companies in this situation should carefully consider their accounting policy choice, rather than deciding based upon short-term or immediate concerns. Once an accounting policy is selected, any changes to it (i.e., going from a Proportional Performance model to a Completed Performance model or vice versa) would be treated as a change in accounting principle. Such change would have to be considered preferable to be effected.

DISCLOSURE ALERT: See Chapter 12, "Disclosures," for information about disclosures that may be required.

SEC REGISTRANT ALERT: In a December 2002 speech, the SEC staff discussed the quality of revenue recognition accounting policy disclosures. In general, the SEC staff indicated that revenue recognition accounting policy disclosures should be more complete and precise, particularly with regard to circumstances that could affect the timing and amount of revenue recognized. The nature of the arrangements discussed in this section will most likely include a variety of different terms that could affect the timing and amount of revenue recognized. Accounting policy disclosures related to these types of arrangements should provide sufficient information about the arrangements and the accounting policy (or policies) applied to those arrangements.

FIXED OR DETERMINABLE FEES

Variable Fees

It is fairly common for the fee in a license of intellectual property to depend upon how the property is used by the customer or the income generated by the customer from the use of the property. For example, the fee in a license of a drug in development may increase if the customer receives FDA approval to begin the next stage of testing, or the fee in a license of a customer list may be dependent upon the amount of sales the licensee generates from the list. Consistent with the treatment of such fees in other transactions, any fee that is dependent upon a future event occurring (e.g., customer receiving FDA approval) should not be considered fixed or determinable. Chapter 3, "General Principles," includes general discussion on this topic.

Refund, Return, and Cancellation Rights

General Model

As with other transactions, many intellectual property licenses include rights of return, cancellation, or refund. Generally, such rights are included in arrangements where intellectual property is licensed to many end customers. For example, the purchase of a movie on a DVD usually includes a limited time right of return and the purchase of an annual license to view information on an Internet site may include a cancellation right allowing a full refund if the purchaser cancels the license within the first 30 days. Other intellectual property transactions may have specially designed refund or return rights. For example, a license of the rights to a technology being developed may be cancelable by the customer for a full or partial refund if certain milestones in the development of the technology are not reached.

☛ **PRACTICE POINTER:** Return rights are often documented in the sales contract. However, such rights may also exist due to industry practice, company policy, or laws and regulations. In addition, the relationship between the buyer and seller should be evaluated in full to determine whether unstated rights of return might exist, as should the company's past practices in accepting returns that are not specifically provided for. In evaluating rights of return, it is important that all rights that exist, whether explicitly stated or not, be considered.

FAS-48 addresses general rights of return in product transactions. Whether it should be applied to intellectual property licenses is not clear from its scope. However, both SOP 97-2 and SOP 00-2 specifically require the use of the guidance in FAS-48 when accounting for returns on sales of software and movies. Therefore, a logical conclusion is that FAS-48 should be applied to sales of other intellectual property when a right of return exists.

Although a right of return or refund creates a question as to whether the transaction has been completed, it is sometimes appropriate, under the guidance in FAS-48, to record revenue upon delivery of products sold with a right of return. However, this is only acceptable when the terms of the arrangement make it clear that a sale has occurred, there are no contingencies other than the right of return, and the likelihood of the customer exercising the right of return can be estimated. If any of these three conditions are not present, the return right causes the transaction to be treated as if it is incomplete until the return right lapses. Specifically, revenue should be recognized at the time of sale, net of estimated returns, only if all of the following conditions are met (FAS-48, par. 6):

1. The sales price to the buyer is fixed or determinable.

2. Payment is not contractually or otherwise excused until the product is resold.

3. The buyer holds the risks of destruction, damage, or theft of the property. If the buyer does not hold these risks, then all of the risks and rewards of ownership have not passed, prohibiting revenue recognition.

4. The buyer has economic substance apart from the seller.

5. The seller does not have significant obligations for future performance relating to the resale of the product by the buyer.

6. The amount of future returns and costs expected in connection with any returns can be reasonably predicted.

Each of these criteria is discussed in significant detail in Chapter 5, "Product Deliverables," as is the accounting for rights of return both when the criteria are all met, and when they are not. The analysis of each of the criteria is effectively the same in an intellectual property transaction as it would be in a product sale, except for the third and sixth criteria. The third criterion is relevant in intellectual property transactions when the intellectual property is provided on a physical medium, such as a compact disc. The right-of-return analysis in these situations is essentially the same as in a product sale, including the need to consider whether the buyer holds the "physical risks" related to the tangible medium on which the intellectual property is provided. However, analyzing the sixth criterion in an intellectual property license presents incremental challenges, which are discussed below.

Estimating Returns

As discussed in Chapter 5, "Product Deliverables," one of the factors generally necessary to estimate the extent to which customers will exercise return or refund rights is the existence of a large volume of homogeneous transactions. In certain types of intellectual property transactions, such as the sales of computer software or videotapes to end-users, there may be a large volume of homogeneous transactions on which an estimate of returns can be based.

However, other licenses of intellectual property, such as licenses to use technology to develop products, or rights to access data such as membership or customer lists, are unlikely to have the requisite large volume of homogeneous transactions. Instead, these transactions are more likely to be "one-off" transactions that include mostly customized terms. To the extent fees paid by the licensee in these types of arrangements are refundable, they are not recognizable, because a reasonable and reliable estimate of returns cannot be made.

Even when a large volume of homogeneous transactions does exist, other factors might affect the ability to make a reliable estimate of the number of customers that will exercise their rights. These factors are discussed in detail in Chapter 5.

CONTINUING PERFORMANCE OBLIGATIONS

Regardless of the delivery model used to account for the sale or license of intellectual property, the seller or licensor must understand the nature of its continuing performance obligations. There may be continuing performance obligations related solely to the license of the intellectual property. There may also be continuing performance obligations in the form of separate agreements—research and development arrangements, contract manufacturing arrangements, etc. Unless the continuing performance obligation meets the requirements to be treated as a separate element in a multiple-element arrangement, the existence of such a continuing performance obligation affects the ability of the seller to conclude that the sale is complete in the Completed Performance model and it also affects the determination of the period over which revenue is recognized in the Proportional Performance model. Chapter 4, "Multiple-Element Arrangements," provides an in-depth discussion of the conditions that must be met to conclude that multiple elements can be separated for accounting purposes. Two continuing performance obligations somewhat unique to licenses of intellectual property are discussed further below.

When-and-If-Available Deliverables

A when-and-if-available clause requires the seller or licensor to make available to the buyer or licensee other information related to the licensed intellectual property to the extent that information becomes available. These clauses do not require the seller or licensor to create that information, but do require that the information be made available to the buyer or licensee if it is created. For example, if the owner of the rights to a drug licenses those rights to a third party for use in Japan, a when-and-if available clause may require the company to provide the customer with the results of any work it performs to improve the drug or get it approved in the U.S. to treat additional conditions.

If delivery of any additional rights or information is required under a when-and-if-available clause, it is clear that a continuing performance obligation exists as part of the arrangement. However, in some cases, a when-and-if-available clause is included in an arrangement, but the seller/licensor has no intent to improve upon the product or to develop additional information. Despite this fact, when-and-if-available clauses should generally be considered to represent a continuing performance obligation that is fulfilled over the time period that the clause is in force.

Because the when-and-if-available clause is considered an incremental deliverable, the license agreement must be evaluated under the multiple-element arrangement guidance discussed in Chapter 4, "Multiple-Element Arrangements," to determine whether the intellectual property initially provided under the license agreement and the when-and-if-available deliverable should be treated separately for accounting purposes. As discussed in that chapter, a delivered item(s) should be considered a separate deliverable for accounting purposes if all of the following conditions are met (EITF 00-21, par. 9):

1. The delivered item(s) has value to the customer on a stand-alone basis. That item(s) has value on a stand-alone basis if it is sold separately by any vendor or the customer could resell the deliverable on a standalone basis.

2. There is objective and reliable evidence of the fair value of the undelivered item(s).

3. If the arrangement includes a general right of return relative to the delivered item, delivery or performance of the undelivered item(s) is considered probable and substantially in the control of the vendor.

As discussed in Chapter 4, EITF 00-21 applies broadly to revenue-generating multiple-element arrangements, except for those covered by pre-existing authoritative literature. This includes multiple-element arrangements that fall within the scope of SOP 97-2 (see Chapter 10, "Software—A Complete Model," for a discussion of SOP 97-2's multiple-element arrangement guidance), SOP 00-2 (see "Motion Pictures" later in this chapter for a discussion of SOP 00-2's multiple-element arrangement guidance), FAS-45 (see "Franchises" later in this chapter for a discussion of FAS-45's multiple-element arrangement guidance), and FAS-13 (see "Leases" earlier in this chapter). The interaction of this higher level literature and EITF 00-21 is discussed in detail in Chapter 4.

In general, whether the intellectual property initially provided under the license agreement has standalone value to the customer should not be affected by the existence of a when-and-if-available deliverable. If the items to be delivered pursuant to a when-and-if-available clause were significant enough to affect the standalone value of the intellectual property initially provided, it is almost certain that the customer would demand that delivery of such items be required, rather than allowing for the possibility that the licensor will not develop such items.

However, the second criterion is far more difficult to meet when the undelivered element is a when-and-if-available deliverable. Concluding that objective evidence of the fair value of a when-and-if-available clause exists is extremely difficult, unless such clauses are common, as they are in the software industry (see Chapter 10, "Software—A Complete Model"). Assessing the value of the intellectual property itself is often quite difficult; let alone assessing the value of an associated when-and-if-available clause.

It is possible, however, to conclude that a when-and-if-available clause involves an inconsequential obligation on the part of the licensor. If the only remaining obligation on the part of the licensor is inconsequential, the licensor still can conclude that it has substantially completed or fulfilled the terms specified in the arrangement. In other words, if the only remaining obligation on the part of the licensor is inconsequential, the licensor still can conclude that it has met the delivery or performance criterion necessary to recognize revenue (SAB Topic 13A3c, ques. 1). The factors that must be considered when determining whether a remaining obligation is inconsequential are discussed in Chapter 4, "Multiple-Element Arrangements."

A when-and-if-available clause should not be considered inconsequential simply because it does not result in any incremental costs to the licensor. Instead, the analysis of whether such a clause is inconsequential should be based on whether any delivery requirements are expected to result from it. Only if it is considered remote that there will be any substantive items delivered pursuant to the clause should the when-and-if-available clause be considered inconsequential. In addition, the seller or licensor should be able to satisfactorily explain why, if the when-and-if-available clause is inconsequential (or so unimportant), it was negotiated into the arrangement.

> **OBSERVATION:** SOP 97-2 includes guidance on determining when post-contract customer support, including unspecified upgrades and enhancements, may be considered inconsequential. This states that (SOP 97-2, par. 60):
>
> A determination that unspecified upgrades/enhancements offered during the PCS arrangement are expected to be minimal and infrequent should be evidenced by the patterns of minimal and infrequent unspecified upgrades/enhancements offered in previous PCS arrangements. A conclusion that unspecified upgrades/enhancements are expected to be minimal and infrequent should not be reached simply because unspecified upgrades/enhancements have been or are expected to be offered less frequently than on an annual basis. Regardless of the vendor's history of offering unspecified upgrades/enhancements to initial licensees, PCS should be accounted for separately from the initial licensing fee if the vendor expects to offer upgrades/enhancements that are greater than minimal or more than infrequent to the users or resellers of the licensed software during the PCS arrangement.

Based on the difficulties present in assessing the value of a when-and-if-available clause, the existence of a when-and-if-available clause often results in the seller or licensor (a) combining the intellectual property license and unspecified when-and-if-available deliverables for revenue recognition purposes and (b) concluding that the when-and-if-available clause represents a more than inconsequential performance obligation. This results in all of the revenue being recognized using a Proportional Performance model over, at a minimum, the term of the when-and-if-available provisions.

> **DISCLOSURE ALERT:** See Chapter 12, "Disclosures," for information about disclosures that may be required.

Combined License and Research and Development Arrangements

One type of multiple-element arrangement involves the licensor agreeing to license intellectual property to the licensee and to provide research and development (R&D) services related to that intellectual property. Payments involved in this type of an arrangement may be non-refundable up-front fees, milestone payments, royalties, or a combination of all three.

The elements in this type of arrangement are the intellectual property license and the performance of R&D. The question becomes whether these elements can be separated. The question should be answered using the general model for allocating revenue to deliverables in a multiple-element arrangement, as discussed earlier under "When-and-If-Available Deliverables."

It is highly unlikely that the elements in a combined license and R&D arrangement would meet the conditions to be treated separately for accounting purposes. First of all, it is likely that the intellectual property license would not have value to the customer on a standalone basis, because only the owner of the license would have the built-up knowledge and expertise to continue to perform the R&D. Furthermore, objective evidence of the fair value of the R&D services often does not exist, thereby prohibiting separation due to a lack of sufficient evidence of fair value. When the two elements in this kind of arrangement cannot be separated, any initial payment received (often termed a license payment) should be treated as an advance payment for the services and recognized over the performance period (determined based on all of the elements in the arrangement), which may be equal to or greater than the period over which the R&D services are provided. Revenue recognition for R&D services is discussed in detail in Chapter 6, "Service Deliverables."

> **SEC REGISTRANT ALERT:** To the extent there is a non-refundable up-front payment in an arrangement involving the license of intellectual property and performance of research and development activities, the SEC staff has concluded that such payment may not be recognized up-front (SAB Topic 13A3f, ques. 1).

> **DISCLOSURE ALERT:** See Chapter 12, "Disclosures," for information about disclosures that may be required.

EXAMPLES: COLLABORATION AGREEMENTS—LICENSE FEE AND MILESTONE PAYMENTS

Affymetrix, Inc. Form 10-K—Fiscal Year Ended December 31, 2004

F. Hoffmann—La Roche Ltd. In February 1998, we entered into a non-exclusive collaborative development agreement with F. Hoffmann—La Roche Ltd. ("Roche") to initially develop human probe array-based diagnostic products. Under the terms of the agreement the parties are collaborating to develop mutually agreed upon arrays, as well as associated instrumentation and reagents. In January 2003, we expanded our collaboration with Roche by granting Roche access to our GeneChip® technologies to develop and commercialize GeneChip® diagnostic laboratory tests for DNA analysis, genotyping and resequencing applications, as well as for RNA expression analysis, in a broad range of human disease areas. Using our GeneChip® technologies, Roche intends to develop and market diagnostic tests for diseases such as cancer, osteoporosis, cardiovascular, metabolic, infectious and inflammatory diseases. Affymetrix and Roche believe that developing targeted microarray expression profiles for cancer, plus genotyping and resequencing profiles for other diseases will enable the creation and commercialization of novel standardized diagnostic solutions. These solutions ultimately will allow physicians to better diagnose and treat human disease. Under the terms of the collaborative agreement, Roche paid us an access fee of $70 million relating to the first five years of the arrangement. The agreement, which is subject to Roche's option to terminate on December 31, 2007 or any time on or after June 2, 2013, with one year's prior notice, includes a broad range of other compensation payable by Roche to Affymetrix throughout the life of the agreement based on royalties on sales of diagnostic kits, milestone payments for technical and commercial achievements, a manufacturing and supply agreement, and related license installments. As part of the agreement, Affymetrix will manufacture and supply Roche with microarrays and related instrumentation based on Affymetrix' GeneChip® platform. In 2003 Roche launched the AmpliChip® CYP450 array product initially for research use only, but in late 2004 obtained CE marking and FDA regulatory approvals of the product for in-vitro diagnostic use.

Medarex, Inc. Form 10-K—Fiscal Year Ended December 31, 2004

Pfizer

In September 2004, the Company entered into a series of agreements with Pfizer, Inc. The first agreement amended the Company's existing collaborative research and license and royalty agreements with Pfizer to provide for the discovery and development of up to 50 antibody products over ten years. The second and third agreements were a sublicense from the Company to Pfizer and a cross-license of certain patents and patent applications solely relating to the companies' respective anti-CTLA-4 antibody programs. The fourth agreement was a stock purchase agreement also related to the anti-CTLA-4 programs. Pursuant to certain of these agreements, Pfizer made a total initial cash payment to the Company of $80.0 million and purchased

4,827,808 unregistered shares of the Company's common stock at a purchase price equal to $6.21 per share for an aggregate purchase price of $30.0 million. The purchase price represented a small premium to market price at the time the Company entered into the collaboration.

The Company accounts for revenue arrangements that include multiple deliverables in accordance with Emerging Issues Task Force No. 00-21, *Accounting for Revenue Arrangements with Multiple Arrangements* [sic] (EITF 00-21). EITF 00-21 addresses how to determine whether an arrangement involving multiple deliverables contains more than one unit of accounting. In applying the guidance, revenue arrangements with multiple deliverables can only be considered as separate units of accounting if: (a) the delivered item has value to the customer on a standalone basis, (b) there is objective and reliable evidence of the fair value of the undelivered items and (c) if the right of return exists, delivery of the undelivered items is considered probable and substantially in the control of the vendor. If these criteria area not met, the revenue elements must be considered a single unit of accounting for purposes of revenue recognition.

The Company has concluded that because the Pfizer collaboration contains multiple deliverables (licenses to technology and research services) EITF 00-21 applies. The Company considers the arrangement with Pfizer to be a single unit of accounting under EITF 00-21 for purposes of recognizing the initial $80.0 million payment.

Patent Defense and Maintenance

Licenses for intellectual property often require the licensor to defend and maintain the patent. While this is a continuing performance obligation, it does not represent a separate deliverable to the customer. That is, the licensor must defend and maintain the patent to satisfy its representations that the patent is legal and valid. The licensee receives no additional value from these actions beyond the value initially provided. As such, the presence of such a provision does not, in-and-of-itself, require the licensor to use a Proportional Performance model to account for the arrangement (SAB Topic 13A3g).

> **OBSERVATION:** If, at the time the license is entered into, the licensor is aware that its patent may not be valid, or is otherwise aware that its ownership of the intellectual property may not be legal, it should consider whether revenue should be deferred because of the uncertainty surrounding the arrangement.

> **PRACTICE ALERT:** FSP FIN 45-1 indicates that "a software licensing agreement that indemnifies the licensee against liability and damages (including legal defense costs) arising from any claims of patent, copyright, trademark or trade secret

infringement by the software vendor's software" does fall within the scope of FIN-45 from a disclosure perspective, but not from an initial recognition and measurement perspective. As such, the fair value of the indemnification need not be recognized initially. In other words, the indemnification should generally not be treated as a separate element in a multiple-element arrangement. While the FSP specifically addresses software licensing agreements, its conclusion should generally apply to other types of intellectual property licensing agreements as well (SAB Topic 13A3g). See Chapter 4, "Multiple-Element Arrangements," regarding guarantees that are part of revenue-generating arrangements that fall within the scope of the initial recognition and measurement provisions of FIN-45. See Chapter 12, "Disclosures," regarding the disclosure requirements of FIN-45.

Warranties and Customer Acceptance Clauses

Some intellectual property licenses may include warranties and customer acceptance clauses. For example, the license to technology may include a customer acceptance clause that allows the customer to cancel the license for a full refund if the technology does not perform to specifications laid out in the license arrangement.

When these clauses are included in an intellectual property license, their effects on revenue recognition should be evaluated in the same manner as similar clauses in sales of products. Chapter 5, "Product Deliverables," provides detailed guidance on the accounting for these clauses.

> **DISCLOSURE ALERT:** See Chapter 12, "Disclosures," for information about disclosures that may be required.

SELLER-PROVIDED FINANCING AND GUARANTEES

Licenses with Extended Payment Terms

Some licensors may elect to provide financing for their customers' purchases by agreeing to receive fixed payments over a long period of time, rather than receiving full payment at the inception of the license. Except in sales of software products (see Chapter 10, "Software—A Complete Model"), GAAP does not provide specific guidance about when extended payment terms should result in a conclusion that revenue should not be recognized. However, extended payment terms can affect the evaluation of two of the four conditions for revenue recognition: those requiring that

(1) the fee be fixed or determinable and (2) collectibility be reasonably assured.

Extended Payment Terms and Fixed or Determinable Fees

Extended payment terms raise the risk that, in order to ensure payment according to the stated terms, the licensor will agree to extend the license or otherwise allow the licensee additional rights with respect to the intellectual property. Consider a customer that has not earned as much revenue as it had expected from exploiting the technology it has licensed, because a competitive technology has eroded its market share. Even though it is not contractually allowed to do so, that customer might withhold a license payment, in the hopes of ending the license early, or receiving additional value from the licensor.

In this type of situation, there is a chance that the licensor will grant a concession to the customer, in the form of additional rights, reduced payments, or some other transfer of value. If the combination of the extended payment terms and the risks inherent in the license create a significant risk of concession, payments should only be considered fixed or determinable as they are made. Therefore, revenue related to future payments under extended payment terms would not be recognized, even if delivery has already occurred.

> **OBSERVATION:** SOP 97-2 specifically addresses extended payment terms in the context of software arrangements, concluding that there is a presumption that the fee in any arrangement with payment terms that extend beyond one year from delivery is not fixed or determinable. While no similar presumption exists outside of software arrangements, the guidance in SOP 97-2 may be a useful analogy for other intellectual property licenses. See Chapter 10, "Software—A Complete Model," for a complete discussion.

Extended Payment Terms and Collectibility

Clearly, the longer the payment terms, the more difficult it is to conclude that collection of the revenue is reasonably assured. Judgment must be applied in these situations. If it is concluded that collection is not reasonably assured, no revenue or receivable should be recorded. It is not acceptable in these instances to record revenue and a selling expense for the anticipated bad debt because the threshold criteria for revenue recognition were never met.

Discounting Long-Term Receivables

When intellectual property is licensed on terms that extend significantly beyond the point in time that revenue is recognized, APB-21 requires that the long-term receivable, and therefore the revenue, be recorded at the present value of the payments, rather than the nominal value. Interest income would then be accrued on the receivable until all payments are made. Therefore, when extended payment terms are stated at their nominal values, a portion of the payments will be attributed to interest income, as opposed to revenue (APB-21, par. 12). If, however, the payment terms are extended, but merely reflect the proportional performance of the contract, no discounting is required.

Guaranteeing a Loan in Connection with a License

A company may agree to guarantee a loan taken out by a customer to license intellectual property from the company. This may occur when a significant up-front fee is required in connection with a license agreement. In this situation, although the company has collected cash related to the license of its intellectual property, it has the same chance of ultimately realizing the payment for the intellectual property as if the license agreement provided for extended payment terms. Therefore, before recognizing any revenue, the company should evaluate whether collectibility is reasonably assured as if it were the lender under the loan.

If the company still concludes that collection is reasonably assured and all other revenue recognition criteria have been met, then FIN-45 requires the transaction to be treated as a multiple-element arrangement, the two elements being the license of intellectual property and the guarantee of a loan. This type of multiple-element arrangement is discussed in more detail in Chapter 4, "Multiple-Element Arrangements."

> **DISCLOSURE ALERT:** See Chapter 12, "Disclosures," for information about required disclosures.

REVENUE RECOGNITION FOR SPECIFIC INTELLECTUAL PROPERTY TRANSACTIONS

As noted in the introductory sections of this chapter, revenue recognition for certain intellectual property transactions is addressed in the accounting literature. These models are generally consistent in that revenue is recognized when the four general conditions for recognition are met. However, because they each were developed to address a narrow grouping of transactions, the analysis of when the conditions are met is somewhat different in each instance.

Software

SOP 97-2 provides guidance on the licensing of software. In summary, SOP 97-2 provides two models to account for software revenue. The model used is dictated by whether the software being sold or licensed involves significant production, modification, or customization (collectively referred to as significant changes) of the software. If no such significant changes are required, SOP 97-2 requires the use of a Completed Performance model. If significant changes to the software are required, SOP 97-2 requires the use of contract accounting, which generally results in the use of a Proportional Performance model. Software revenue recognition is discussed in detail in Chapter 10, "Software—A Complete Model."

Franchises

FAS-45 provides guidance for a franchisor's recognition of franchise fee revenue. A franchisor earns franchise fee revenue from the franchisee based on the terms of the franchise agreement. Under the franchise agreement, the franchisor conveys certain rights to the franchisee. These rights typically include the right to operate using the franchisor's name, the right to use the franchisor's processes, and the right (or requirement) to purchase products or services from the franchisor.

Scope

An important consideration in determining how to account for an agreement that purports to be a franchise agreement is whether the agreement actually is a franchise agreement as defined in FAS-45.[1] Only agreements that meet this definition fall within the scope of FAS-45. An agreement must possess the following characteristics to be considered a franchise agreement (FAS-45, par. 26):

- The agreement must be written and establish the rights and responsibilities of the franchisor and franchisee for a defined period of time.

---

[1] The need for such an agreement to be in place fulfills the persuasive evidence of an arrangement condition that is a part of all revenue recognition analyses.

- The agreement must have as its purpose the distribution of a product or service, or an entire business concept, within a particular market area.

- The agreement must provide for the franchisor and franchisee to contribute resources for establishing and maintaining the franchise.

- The agreement must outline and describe the specific marketing practices to be followed, specify the contribution of each party to the operation of the business, and set forth certain operating procedures that both parties agree to comply with.

- The agreement must establish the franchised outlet as a business entity requiring and supporting the full-time business activity of the franchisee (i.e., if the outlet is merely an authorized distributor or representative to sell a particular good or service, it is not a franchise).

- The agreement must establish a common identity for the franchisor and franchisee.

☞ **PRACTICE POINTER:** It is not uncommon for an agreement labeled a franchise agreement to be missing one or more of the characteristics described above. For example, a trademark license agreement may not require the licensor to carry out any obligations other than transferring the trademark to the licensee. This trademark license agreement fails the conditions above on many accounts. As such, it would not be considered a franchise agreement for accounting purposes. Other agreements may have the purported franchisee merely entering into an agency relationship with the franchisor to sell the franchisor's products, or to identify potential franchisees. Care should be taken in determining whether an agreement truly is a franchise agreement as there are unique aspects to the accounting for franchise fee revenue. To the extent a license agreement does not possess **all** of the characteristics listed above, it is not con-sidered a franchise agreement for purposes of applying FAS-45. As such, revenue would be recognized under the general guidance for intellectual property or service transactions, depending upon the nature of the arrangement.

Franchise Fees

Franchise fees can take many forms. These fees can generally be characterized as either initial or continuing. The initial fees are usually paid up front in conjunction with the transfer of intellectual property rights, the performance of initial services, and the sale of proprietary equipment. The continuing fees are usually paid over the life of the franchise agreement. These fees may be paid in conjunction with the franchisor's sale of products or services to the franchisee. They may also be paid based on a percentage of the franchisee's revenues or another quantitative operating measure. Most often there is a combination of some or all of these types of fees in a franchise agreement.

> **DISCLOSURE ALERT:** See Chapter 12, "Disclosures," for information about disclosures that may be required.

EXAMPLE: TYPES OF FRANCHISE FEES

Buffalo Wild Wings, Inc. Form 10-K—Fiscal Year Ended December 26, 2004

(m) Revenue Recognition

Franchise agreements have terms ranging from ten to twenty years. These agreements also convey multiple extension terms of five or ten years, depending on contract terms and if certain conditions are met. The Company provides the use of the Buffalo Wild Wings trademarks, system, training, preopening assistance, and restaurant operating assistance in exchange for area development fees, franchise fees, and royalties of 5% of the franchised restaurant's sales.

Franchise fee revenue from individual franchise sales is recognized upon the opening of the franchisee restaurant when all material obligations and initial services to be provided by the Company have been performed. Area development fees are dependent upon the number of restaurants in the territory, as are the Company's obligations under the area development agreement. Consequently, as obligations are met, area development fees are recognized proportionally with expenses incurred with the opening of each new restaurant and any royalty free periods. Royalties are accrued as earned and are calculated each period based on the reporting franchisees' sales.

Allocation of Initial Franchise Fees

Initial franchise fees are the franchisor's compensation for providing a bundle of deliverables. These deliverables virtually always include the transfer of rights to certain intellectual property (restaurant name, logos, formulas, etc.) and services necessary to assist the franchisee in opening a franchised outlet (training, site identification, etc.). Specific equipment, products, or supplies may also be included. The initial franchise fee does not necessarily relate only to initially provided equipment, products, supplies, and services. A portion of that fee may also relate to products or services to be provided to the franchisee in the future. Given the number of deliverables the initial franchise fee may relate to, a key to recognizing that fee is first allocating it to the various products and services provided.

The initial franchise fee should be allocated to the various deliverables based on the following sources of value for each deliverable:

Deliverable	Source of Value
Equipment, supplies and products to be furnished initially	Fair value of the assets
Products to be sold in the future	Either the selling price of the same product to other customers or the cost of the product plus a reasonable profit on the sale
Services to be provided in the future	Cost of providing the service plus a reasonable profit margin
Services and intellectual property rights provided initially	Residual

The method used to allocate the initial franchise fee in a franchise agreement is a residual method. This type of method starts with the total amount to be allocated (the initial franchise fee), and subtracts from it the values of some, but not all, of the deliverables (equipment, supplies, and products to be provided initially, products to be sold in the future, and services to be provided in the future), leaving the residual to represent the value of the remaining elements (services and intellectual property rights to be provided initially).

☞ **PRACTICE POINTER:** Although using cost plus a reasonable profit margin for purposes of estimating the fair value of products or services provided under a franchise agreement is appropriate, it is generally not an appropriate measure of fair value when allocating consideration among deliverables in other multiple-element arrangements (see Chapter 4, "Multiple-Element Arrangements").

ILLUSTRATION: INITIAL FRANCHISE FEE ALLOCATION

Facts: Franchisor Inc. (Franchisor) enters into a franchise agreement with Franchisee Co. (Franchisee). This agreement meets the conditions within FAS-45 to be considered a franchise agreement for accounting purposes. The franchise agreement conveys to Franchisee the right to open a franchised outlet that bears Franchisor's trademark name and that produces and sells Franchisor's secret recipe breads. The term of the agreement is five years. The franchise agreement requires Franchisee to make the following payments to Franchisor: (1) an initial fee of $1,000,000, (2) royalty payments equal to 2% of Franchisee's sales, (3) $50,000 per year for 50,000 pounds of unique organic flours, and (4) $60,000 per year for four seasonal marketing campaigns. The franchise agreement requires Franchisor to provide the following to Franchisee: (1) rights to use its trademark and secret recipes, (2) initial services including site-selection and site-design assistance and employee training on baking methods, (3) equipment necessary for Franchisee to produce the secret recipe breads including a specifically designed oven and oven implements, (4) 50,000 pounds annually of unique organic flours, and (5) four seasonal marketing campaigns. The fair value of the specifically designed oven and oven implements is $140,000. The selling price of 50,000 pounds of the unique organic flours to other customers is $60,000. The cost of providing the four seasonal marketing campaigns plus a reasonable profit margin is $75,000.

Allocation: The $1,000,000 initial fee is allocated as follows:

Franchise Element		Amount of Initial Fee Allocated to Element
Oven and oven implements (equipment)		$140,000
Products (organic flours) to be sold in the future		
Selling price to other customers over the term of the franchise agreement ($60,000 per year for 5 years)	$300,000	
Selling price to Franchisee ($50,000 per year for 5 years)	250,000	50,000
Future services (marketing campaigns)		
Cost plus a reasonable profit margin ($75,000 per year for 5 years)	375,000	
Selling price to Franchisee ($60,000 per year for 5 years)	300,000	75,000
Initial services and rights to use trademark and secret recipes (residual)		$735,000

Recognition of Fees Related to Initial Services and Intellectual Property Rights

The portion of the initial franchise fee allocated to the initial services and intellectual property rights should be recognized when the franchisor has substantially performed or satisfied its obligations under the franchise agreement, with an appropriate provision for estimated uncollectible amounts. The franchisor must consider the following questions when assessing whether it has substantially performed:

1. Does the franchisor have any obligation or intent to refund cash received or forgive notes or receivables due from the franchisee?
2. Has the franchisor performed something less than substantially all of the initial services required under the franchise agreement?
3. Are there any remaining material conditions or obligations that would preclude the franchisor from concluding that it has substantially performed?
4. Does the franchise agreement include an option for the franchisor to purchase the franchisee's business that the franchisor expects to exercise?

If the answer to any of these questions is "yes," the franchisor has not achieved substantial performance. For example, answering yes to the first question indicates that a portion of the initial franchise fee is refundable. If any portion of an initial franchise fee is refundable, it should not be recognized. Answering yes to the last question means that the initial fee is, in substance, a reduction of the future purchase price of the business, and should not be recognized as revenue at all.

It is presumed that the earliest point a franchisor can achieve substantial performance is upon commencement of operations by the franchisee. That presumption can only be overcome if the franchisor can demonstrate that all obligations, both explicit and implicit, have been fulfilled before the franchisee starts its operations (FAS-45, par. 5).

> **OBSERVATION:** In answering the questions above and in considering whether any implicit obligations exist, a franchisor must determine whether there are any services that the franchisor is expected to perform, either as a matter of practice or due to regulatory considerations, even though those services may not be spelled out in the franchise agreement. If these expectations exist, the franchisor does not achieve substantial performance until it has also performed these services or supported the fact these services will not be performed in the situation under consideration.

EXAMPLE: RECOGNITION OF INITIAL FEES

Yum Brands, Inc. Form 10-K—Fiscal Year Ended December 25, 2004

Revenue Recognition

We recognize initial fees received from a franchisee or licensee as revenue when we have performed substantially all initial services required by the franchise or license agreement, which is generally upon the opening of a store.

There are generally many different types of services and intellectual property rights provided by a franchisor as part of the initial services. Franchisors are precluded from allocating the residual initial franchise fee to the individual initial services and intellectual property rights provided, even if separate prices are stated in the franchise agreement, unless there have been separate sales of the individual services. Restricting the practice of further separating initial services and intellectual property rights is based upon the fact that these services and intellectual property rights are often so interrelated and interdependent that assigning individual values to each service is difficult and essentially meaningless (FAS-45, par. 13). Thus, FAS-45 requires a Completed Performance model for the initial services and intellectual property rights, and concludes that both must be delivered before revenue attributable to either may be recognized.

> **OBSERVATION:** In substance, the conclusion in FAS-45 is that each of the initial services and rights to be delivered do not have value to the franchisee on a stand alone basis (e.g., absent the other initial services and rights), and that revenue should therefore not be allocated amongst them. This is consistent with the general guidance for multiple-element transactions discussed in Chapter 4, "Multiple-Element Arrangements."

Recognition of Fees Related to Equipment, Supplies, and Products

Revenue from the sale of equipment, supplies, and products delivered either initially or in the future should be recognized when those products meet the requirements for revenue recognition discussed in Chapter 5, "Product Deliverables."

Recognition of Fees Related to Future Services to Be Provided

Continuing franchise fees should be recognized when earned and realized or realizable (FAS-45, par. 14). For royalty-based fees this would generally be the case when the royalties accrue and become receivable to the franchisee. For services that are not part of the initial services, Chapter 6, "Service Deliverables," should be consulted for guidance on determining when such fees are earned and realized or realizable. Any initial franchise fee allocated to services to be provided in the future (i.e., services that are not part of the initial services) should be deferred and recognized over the life of the franchise (FAS-45, par. 7).

> ☞ **PRACTICE POINTER:** When franchisors sell inventory, equipment or continuing services to franchisees, the role of

the franchisor must be understood to determine whether such sales should be recognized gross or net in the income statement. To the extent the franchisor is merely acting as an agent in these sales, the franchisor should not recognize revenues and expenses related to those sales. For example, a franchisor may place orders for equipment on behalf of its franchisees. In this situation the franchisor should **not** recognize equipment sales and cost of equipment sales. Instead, this transaction should be accounted for on the balance sheet using receivables and payables. Additional guidance regarding recognizing revenue and expenses gross or net in the income statement can be found in Chapter 11, "Presentation."

ILLUSTRATION: FRANCHISE FEE RECOGNITION

Facts: Assume the same facts as those in the earlier Initial Franchise Fee Allocation illustration. In addition, Franchisee's revenues for Year 1 under the franchise agreement were $5,000,000.

Accounting: The accounting for the initial and continuing franchise fees in Year 1 is as follows:

- At the inception of the franchise agreement, Franchisor records the initial franchise fee received:

Cash or Receivable	$1,000,000	
Deferred Revenue		$1,000,000

- Upon achieving substantial completion related to the initial services and intellectual property rights, Franchisor recognizes the portion of the initial franchise fee allocated to those initial deliverables:

Deferred Revenue	$735,000	
Initial Franchise Fee Revenue		$735,000

- Upon delivery of the specifically-designed oven and oven implements and transfer of title to Franchisee, Franchisor recognizes the portion of the initial franchise fee allocated to that equipment:

Deferred Revenue	$140,000	
Equipment Sales		$140,000

- During Year 1, upon delivery of the unique organic flours and transfer of title to Franchisee, Franchisor recognizes one-fifth of the initial franchise fee allocated to that deliverable and the incremental amount paid by or due from Franchisee for those deliveries:

Deferred Revenue	$10,000	
Cash or Receivable	$50,000	
Product Sales		$60,000

- During Year 1, upon earning the revenue related to the four seasonal marketing programs, Franchisor recognizes one-fifth of the initial franchise fee allocated to that deliverable and the incremental amount paid by or due from Franchisee for those services:

Deferred Revenue	$15,000	
Cash or Receivable	$60,000	
Service Fees		$75,000

- During Year 1, upon earning the royalties and the royalties becoming receivable from Franchisee, Franchisor recognizes royalty revenues:

Cash or Receivable	$100,000	
Royalty Revenues		$100,000

EXAMPLE: RECOGNITION OF INITIAL AND CONTINUING FRANCHISE FEES

Denny's Corp. Form 10-K—Fiscal Year Ended December 29, 2004

Revenues from the collection of royalties and fees from franchisees are generally affected by the number of franchised restaurants and the sales of these restaurants. Franchise and license revenues include royalties that are based on a percentage of franchisee sales, initial franchise fees and occupancy revenue related to restaurants leased or subleased to franchisees. Franchise and licensing revenues are generally billed and collected from franchisees on a weekly basis which minimizes the impact of bad debts on our costs of franchise and license revenues. Costs of franchise and license revenues include occupancy costs related to restaurants leased or subleased to franchisees; direct costs consisting primarily of payroll and benefit costs of franchise operations personnel; bad debt expense; and marketing expenses net of marketing contributions received from franchisees. The composition of the franchise portfolio and the nature of individual lease arrangements have a significant impact on franchise occupancy revenue, as well as the related franchise occupancy expense.

Area Franchise Fees

Area franchise agreements grant rights that allow a franchisee to open multiple franchised outlets within a defined geographic area. Important questions to answer prior to recognizing an area franchise agreement's initial franchise fee are:

- Do the franchisor's substantial obligations under the area franchise agreement relate to the area franchise as a whole?
- Are the effort and cost relating to the initial services to be provided under the area franchise agreement not significantly

dependent on the number of individual franchises to be established?

If the answer to both of these questions is "yes," then the initial franchise fee under the area franchise agreement should be treated no differently than the initial franchise fee under an individual franchise agreement. However, if the answer to either one or both of the questions is "no," then the franchisor must allocate the initial franchise fee to each of the expected franchised outlets based on the total number of expected franchised outlets. This exercise effectively breaks an area franchise agreement into a number of individual franchise agreements.

ILLUSTRATION: AREA FRANCHISE FEE

Facts: Franchisor M enters into an area franchise agreement with Franchisee D. This agreement meets the conditions within FAS-45 to be considered a franchise agreement for accounting purposes. The area franchise agreement conveys to Franchisee D the right to open up to ten franchised outlets in the metropolitan Detroit area, as defined in the franchise agreement. Each of these franchised outlets will bear Franchisor M's trademark name and sell Franchisor M's specialized baby products. The term of the agreement is five years. The franchise agreement requires Franchisee D to make an initial franchise fee payment of $5,000,000. The initial services and intellectual property rights to be provided by Franchisor M include transferring trademarks and providing site-selection and site-design assistance. Franchisee D expects to open all ten franchise outlets.

Assessment: The effort and cost relating to the site-selection and site-design assistance are significantly dependent on the number of individual franchises to be established. That is, each incremental franchised outlet to be opened by Franchisee D results in Franchisor M having to put forth the effort and expend the cost necessary to select and design a site. As such, Franchisor M concludes that it must allocate the initial franchise fee among the ten franchised outlets Franchisee D expects to open. This results in $500,000 of initial franchise fee ($5,000,000 total initial franchise fee divided by ten expected franchised outlets) being allocated to each franchised outlet. Each franchised outlet will be treated as an individual franchise agreement for purposes of recognizing the $500,000.

Allocating an initial franchise fee under an area franchise agreement often involves estimating the number of franchised outlets to be opened by the franchisee. To the extent this estimate is subsequently revised due to a change in circumstances, the remaining fees should be recognized as revenue in proportion to the remaining services to be performed.

Refund rights pertaining to an initial franchise fee in an area franchise agreement are treated the same as refund rights pertaining to an initial franchise fee in an individual franchise agreement. That is, the franchisor may not recognize revenue for any portion of an initial franchise fee that may have to be refunded to the franchisee. Under an area franchise agreement, refund rights may not mirror the method used to allocate the initial franchise fee (e.g., more revenue is refundable at any given point in time than the amount that otherwise can be considered earned). This emphasizes the need to ensure that refund rights have been appropriately considered in recognizing revenue related to an area franchise agreement.

EXAMPLE: AREA FRANCHISE FEE

Wendy's International, Inc. Form 10—Fiscal Year Ended January 2, 2005

Franchised Baja Fresh Restaurants

As of January 2, 2005, the Company's franchisees operated 151 Baja Fresh restaurants in 20 states.

Each Baja Fresh area developer is required to enter into two types of agreements: an Area Development Agreement ("ADA") and a franchise agreement for each restaurant opened under the ADA. The ADA establishes the timing and number of stores to be developed in an area. Pursuant to the current ADA, a franchisee is required to pay a non-refundable $50,000 initial franchise fee for the first restaurant, plus an initial development fee (which will be credited back as restaurants are opened) equal to $17,500 multiplied by the total number of restaurants required under the ADA (excluding the fist restaurant). As each new site is accepted under the ADA, the franchisee signs a franchise agreement and lease on the premises and pays an initial franchise fee of $35,000, less a credit of $17,500 from the initial development fee previously paid by the franchisee (until the development fee has been exhausted). The current ADA fixes royalties payable to the Company under each single restaurant franchise agreement to 5% of the franchisee's gross sales as defined in the franchise agreement. For restaurants currently opened pursuant to older ADA's, lower initial franchise fees and royalty rates may apply (as low as a $20,000 initial franchise fee and 4% royalty rate for certain franchisees, including those who had entered into ADA's with the Company prior to fiscal year ended 1999).

The ADA's have an initial term equal to the number of years over which the franchisee is required to open restaurants, typically five years, but provides the franchisee with an opportunity to enter into a successor ADA subject to certain conditions. The single restaurant franchise agreements typically have a 10-year initial term, but provide the franchisee with an opportunity to enter into two successive 5-year renewal franchise agreements subject to certain conditions.

Motion Pictures

Terms of arrangements to license or sell films are varied. They may include the rights to just one film or many films. They may allow exploitation on an exclusive or non-exclusive basis in defined or unde-fined geographic regions. They may provide the customer with only limited control over the actual distribution of a film. Fees under these agreements may be paid up front or over time and may be fixed, vari-able or a combination of fixed and variable. Understanding the terms of an arrangement to license or sell films is an integral part of deter-mining when fees from such an arrangement should be recognized as revenue. SOP 00-2 provides guidance for recognition of such revenue.

The provisions of SOP 00-2 apply to sales or licenses of film rights by producers and distributors of films. The producers and distribu-tors must themselves own or hold rights to distribute or exploit such films. The definition of films is broad. It includes feature films, television specials, television series, or similar products. Films may be animated and may be housed on a variety of mediums including, but not limited to, film, video tape, and those used to provide digi-tized content (e.g., DVDs).

A producer or distributor of films should recognize revenue related to the sale or license of films only when all of the following conditions have been met (SOP 00-2, par. 7):

1. Persuasive evidence of a sale or licensing arrangement with a customer exists;
2. The film is complete and, in accordance with the terms of the arrangement, has been delivered or is available for immediate and unconditional delivery;
3. The license period of the arrangement has begun and the cus-tomer can begin its exploitation, exhibition, or sale;
4. The arrangement fee is fixed or determinable; and
5. Collection of the arrangement fee is reasonably assured.

These conditions are the same conditions required to recognize rev-enue in most transactions, although they are modified slightly to address the unique characteristics of film licenses and sales.

Persuasive Evidence of an Arrangement

The evaluation of the persuasive evidence of an arrangement con-dition generally is no different for an arrangement to license a film than it is for any other revenue arrangement. However, regard-less of the form of the documentation for an arrangement, such documentation must be in place and legally enforceable before any revenue is recognized (SOP 00-2, par. 9). For additional discussion, see Chapter 3, "General Principles."

Complete

SOP 00-2 specifies a Completed Performance model for evaluating when revenue is earned. The evaluation of whether a film is complete is fairly straightforward. Any modification that still remains to be made to a film before it is ready for the customer must be evaluated to determine whether those modifications are significant or not. If the modifications are significant, the film is not considered complete, and revenue therefore cannot be recognized (SOP 00-2, par. 13). Essentially, the remaining modifications are evaluated to determine whether they are inconsequential, in which case revenue may be recognized, or substantive, in which case revenue may not yet be recognized.

Significant modifications are those changes that add new or additional content to a film. Thus, modifying a film by reshooting a scene or adding special effects would be considered significant because content is added or changed. On the other hand, modifying a film by inserting subtitles, formatting it to fit a television screen, or adjusting it to allow the insertion of a commercial would not be considered significant, as none of these actions add content to the film itself (SOP 00-2, par. 18).

Delivered or Available for Delivery

If the terms of the arrangement require physical delivery of the film or if the arrangement is silent on delivery, then the producer or distributor has only satisfied this condition if it has physically delivered the film (see Chapter 5, "Product Deliverables," for information on physical delivery) (SOP 00-2, par. 11). There may be situations where the terms of the arrangement do not require immediate or direct physical delivery. The arrangement may require the producer or distributor to provide to its customer immediate and unconditional access to the film such that it is available for the customer's use at its discretion. If these are the delivery terms in the arrangement, the delivery condition is met if the film is complete and immediately and unconditionally available (SOP 00-2, par. 12).

> **OBSERVATION:** Recognizing revenue prior to physical delivery is commonly referred to as a bill-and-hold transaction outside of the motion picture literature. Recognizing revenue on a bill-and-hold transaction is only permitted if certain very restrictive criteria have been met (see Chapter 5, "Product

Deliverables"). In other words, it takes much more than the arrangement providing immediate and unconditional access to the product to satisfy the delivery criterion in a bill-and-hold transaction not within the scope of SOP 00-2.

License Period Has Begun

This condition prohibits revenue recognition until the license period of the arrangement has started, and the customer is free to begin its exploitation, exhibition, or sale of the film. A common restriction in a film license or sales arrangement is the inclusion of a street date. A street date generally restricts a customer from exploiting, exhibiting, or selling a film prior to the date the producer or distributor plans to market the film on a broader basis (SOP 00-2, par. 14). For example, a distributor may ship copies of a hit movie on DVD to a reseller in September, but restrict their sale until October 1, to synchronize availability throughout the country and time that availability to a marketing program. Revenue related to the DVD's shipped in September may not be recognized before the street date of October 1.

Many producers enter into arrangements where they license the rights to marketing film-related products. Oftentimes these arrangements are entered into well before the release date of the related film. Producers should not recognize revenue from these types of arrangements prior to the release of the related film (SOP 00-2, par. 26). Until then, the license period on the film-related products has not substantively begun, as there is no film tie-in yet available.

EXAMPLE: SATISFACTION OF AVAILABILITY CONDITION

Viacom, Inc. Form 10-K—Fiscal Year Ended December 31, 2004

In accordance with Statement of Position 00-2 "Accounting by Producers or Distributors of Films" ("SOP-002"), Entertainment revenues from theatrical distribution of motion pictures are recognized as motion pictures are exhibited. Revenues from DVD and videocassette sales of motion pictures are recognized upon availability for sale to the public. Revenues from video revenue sharing agreements are recognized as earned. Revenues from the licensing of motion pictures on domestic and international premium subscription program services, broadcast and basic cable networks, and individual television stations are recognized upon availability of the motion picture for telecast except for pay-per-view which is recognized upon purchase by the consumer. On average, the length of the initial revenue cycle for motion pictures approximates four to seven years.

Television series initially produced for the networks and first-run syndication are generally licensed to domestic and international markets concurrently. The more successful series are later syndicated in domestic markets and sold in certain international markets. The length of the revenue cycle for television series will vary depending on the number of seasons a series remains in active production. Revenues arising from television license agreements are recognized in the period that the motion picture or television series is available for telecast and therefore may cause fluctuations in operating results.

Allocation of Fees in Multiple Film Arrangements

A producer or distributor often licenses or sells multiple films to its customer as part of one arrangement. These films may or may not be produced or completed upon commencement of the arrangement. In these situations, any fee received must be allocated among the individual films. The allocation of a fee among the individual films in a multiple film arrangement is based on refundable amounts for incomplete or unproduced films and estimated relative fair values for complete films (SOP 00-2, par. 16).

> **OBSERVATION:** In substance, each film in a multiple-film arrangement is a separate deliverable. Allocating a flat fee between films in a multiple-film arrangement resembles the allocation methodology followed for other multiple-element arrangements as discussed in Chapter 4, "Multiple-Element Arrangements." However, one significant difference relates to using the amount that is refundable if an unproduced film is ultimately not produced, for purposes of allocating a portion of the flat fee to the unproduced film. This methodology is used to address specific factors often present in film arrangements. This methodology should not be used for purposes of allocating arrangement consideration in other multiple-element arrangements.

ILLUSTRATION: ALLOCATION OF FLAT FEE TO MULTIPLE FILMS

Facts: Producer B enters into a license agreement with Customer K. The license agreement grants exploitation and exhibition rights to Customer K for three separate films. Two of the films, *Action-Packed* and *Romance*, are complete. The remaining film, *Political Thriller*, is not yet complete. The license agreement requires Customer K to pay a flat fee of $10,000,000. If Producer B does not complete *Political Thriller*, it must refund $2,500,000. The fair values of the exploitation and exhibition rights related to *Action-Packed* and *Romance* are $6,000,000 and $4,000,000, respectively.

Allocation: The $10,000,000 flat fee is first allocated to *Political Thriller* based on the refundable amount of $2,500,000. The remaining $7,500,000 is allocated based on the relative fair values of *Action-Packed* and *Romance*, resulting in 60% of that amount, or $4,500,000, being allocated to *Action-Packed*, and 40%, or $3,000,000, being allocated to *Romance*.

If available, a producer or distributor should use the quoted market price for each individual completed film as that film's fair value for allocation purposes. If a quoted market price is not available for an individual completed film, which is often the case, the producer or distributor should use the best information it has available to determine that film's fair value for allocation purposes. One valuation technique often used in this situation is a discounted cash flow methodology (SOP 00-2, par. 17).[2]

> **OBSERVATION:** Although SOP 00-2 specifically permits the use of valuation techniques, such as a discounted cash flow methodology, to determine the fair value of a film in a multiple film arrangement, the use of such techniques to determine fair values of elements in other (i.e., non-film) multiple-element arrangements may not be appropriate. See the "Fair Value Evidence" section of Chapter 4, "Multiple-Element Arrangements," and the "Vendor-Specific Objective Evidence (VSOE) of Fair Value" section of Chapter 10, "Software—A Complete Model" for additional discussion.

If a producer or distributor concludes that it cannot determine the fair value for an individual completed film, it is prohibited from recognizing any of the flat fee until it can determine fair value and complete the allocation.

EXAMPLE: MULTIPLE FILM ARRANGEMENTS

Pixar Form 10-K—Fiscal Year Ended January 1, 2005

Under the Co-Production Agreement, the Company shares equally with Disney in the profits of *The Incredibles, Finding Nemo, Monsters, Inc., Toy Story 2* and *A Bug's Life* after Disney recovers its marketing, distribution and other predefined costs and fees. Revenues for *Toy Story* are governed by the terms of the Feature Film Agreement under which Disney fully financed the production costs and shares a specified percentage of *Toy Story* profits with Pixar after certain agreed upon costs and fees are deducted. The Company recognizes revenue from its films net of distribution fees, reserves for returns, and marketing and distribution expenses. Disney provides the Company with

---

[2]SOP 00–2 includes guidance on the application of a discounted cash flow methodology to estimate fair value. Producers and distributors should refer to SOP 00–2 for additional information.

gross receipt information, marketing and distribution costs and any other fees and expenses. The Company utilizes this information to determine its portion of the revenue by applying the contractual provisions included in its arrangements with Disney. The Company also incorporates certain estimates, such as home video returns and distribution expenses, based on Pixar's historical experience and other industry information. The amount of revenue recognized in any given quarter or quarters from all of the Company's films depends on the timing, accuracy and sufficiency of information it receives from Disney to determine revenues and associated gross profits. Although Disney provides the Company with the most current information available to enable Pixar to recognize its share of revenue and determine its film gross profit, in the past the Company has made revisions, and is likely to make revisions in the future, to that information based on its estimates and judgments. Such estimates include theatrical bad debt reserves and expenses, home video return reserves and expenses, merchandise expenses, and estimates for both revenues and related expenses resulting from differences between the Company's and Disney's reporting periods.

Fixed or Determinable Fees

Flat fees   Flat fees are fees that are payable regardless of the success or failure of the film, that are not contingent upon future performance by the producer or distributor, and that are not subject to change based on rights held by the customer. Flat fees are considered fixed and determinable because the amount of the fee is not dependent upon any future events (SOP 00-2, par. 15).

Variable fees   Variable fees are those based on some measure of the film's performance, such as a percentage of a customer's revenue from exploiting or exhibiting a film. These fees are considered fixed or determinable as the customer exhibits or exploits the film (SOP 00-2, par. 18). Until then, such fees are not fixed or determinable, as they are dependent upon future events.

Non-refundable minimum guarantees   The fee in some arrangements is essentially a variable fee, except that the customer guarantees it will pay a minimum amount of such fees. In general, the non-refundable minimum guarantees are treated as flat fees, while any amounts over and above the minimum guarantee are treated as variable fees. However, in some arrangements the non-refundable minimum guarantee is cross-collateralized, meaning that it can be applied to a number of films, territories, and/or markets, and the exploitation results (i.e., revenues) for all applicable films, territories, and/or markets are aggregated for purposes of determining the variable fees payable to the producer or distributor under the arrangement (SOP 00-2, par. 134). To the extent a non-refundable guaranteed minimum exists in an arrangement that has been cross-collateralized, the non-refundable minimum guarantee is effectively the same as a variable fee and is only considered fixed and determinable as the customer exhibits or exploits the films, or at the end of the license.

Returns and price concessions A producer or distributor should account for returns and price concessions based on the provisions of FAS-48. To recognize revenue net of estimated product returns and price concessions, the following conditions must be met (FAS-48, par. 6):

1. The seller's price to the buyer is substantially fixed or determinable at the date of sale.
2. The buyer has paid the seller, or the buyer is obligated to pay the seller and the obligation is not contingent on resale of the product.
3. The buyer's obligation to the seller would not be changed in the event of theft or physical destruction or damage of the product.
4. The buyer acquiring the product for resale has economic substance apart from that provided by the seller.
5. The seller does not have significant obligations for future performance to directly bring about resale of the product by the buyer.
6. The amount of future returns and price concessions can be reasonably estimated.

The producer or distributor must consider both the contract terms and its customary business practices when identifying return rights or price concession obligations. To the extent such rights or obligations exist and the producer or distributor does not meet all of the foregoing conditions, the producer or distributor may not consider the fees under the arrangement to be fixed or determinable. The fees under the arrangement are not considered fixed or determinable until all of the FAS-48 conditions have been met. For additional discussion of these conditions, see Chapter 5, "Product Deliverables."

Arrangement Modifications

It is not uncommon for film arrangements to be modified for various reasons. For example, the term of the arrangement may be extended, the territory expanded, the number of allowable showings increased, or the basis on which the fee is calculated changed. The type of modification dictates the accounting for that modification.

If an arrangement modification solely involves extending the term of an existing arrangement, fees related to the modification should be recognized after the modification has been finalized, based on the type of fee involved (flat, variable, etc.) as discussed above (SOP 00-2, par. 22).

Any other arrangement modifications result in the revised arrangement being considered a new arrangement. To the extent any refunds or concessions are granted by the producer or distributor through the arrangement modifications, previously reported revenue in the amount of the refunds or concessions should be reversed (SOP 00-2, par. 23).

> **OBSERVATION:**   The accounting for refunds or concessions granted in an arrangement modification effectively results in the producer or distributor recognizing revenue as if the new financial terms had been in place since the beginning of the original arrangement. That is, a cumulative catch-up adjustment is recorded in the year of the modification for the difference between cumulative revenue recognized under the old financial terms and cumulative revenue that would have been recognized under the new financial terms.

ILLUSTRATION: ARRANGEMENT MODIFICATION INVOLVING CONCESSION

Facts: Producer T had a license agreement with Customer D. Only one film was involved in the license agreement. The original license agreement had a term of three years, provided a flat fee of $50,000, and variable fees of 10% based on Customer D's gross receipts. Customer D's gross receipts in Year 1 were $1,000,000. In Year 1, Producer T recognized the $50,000 flat fee and $100,000 of variable fees as revenue. At the beginning of Year 2, Producer T and Customer D modified the terms of the original license agreement. The modified license agreement changed the flat fee to $20,000 and the variable fee rate to 12%.

Accounting: At the beginning of Year 2, Producer T should reverse $10,000 of revenue. This is based on the following calculation:

Revenue recognized in Year 1

Flat fee	$ 50,000
Variable fee	100,000
Total	150,000

Revenue that would have been recognized in Year 1 under the modified terms

Flat fee	20,000
Variable fee	120,000
Total	140,000
Concession	$ 10,000

CHAPTER 8
MISCELLANEOUS ISSUES

CONTENTS

OVERVIEW

Chapters 4–7 provide detailed discussion of issues that often arise in certain kinds of revenue transactions. This chapter discusses a number of important issues that can arise in any kind of transaction.

DEFERRED COSTS

There are many reasons that costs of a revenue transaction may be incurred before the related revenue is recognized. For example, some costs are incurred before performance begins, such as costs of soliciting the customer, negotiating the terms of the contract, and paying a commission to a salesperson. Other costs may be incurred during the set-up phase of a service transaction, or during the delivery or performance of an element in a multiple-element arrangement that is not treated separately for accounting purposes. In these and other situations in which costs are incurred before revenue is recognized, a natural question is whether the costs may be deferred until the revenue is recognized.

LISTING OF APPLICABLE LITERATURE

CON-6	Elements of Financial Statements
ARB-43, Ch. 4	Restatement and Revision of Accounting Research Bulletins, Chapter 4, Inventory Pricing

FAS-60	Accounting and Reporting by Insurance Enterprises
FAS-91	Accounting for Nonrefundable Fees and Costs Associated with Originating or Acquiring Loans and Initial Direct Costs of Leases, an amendment of FASB Statements Nos. 13, 60, and 65 and a rescission of FASB Statement No. 17
FTB 90-1	Accounting for Separately Priced Extended Warranty and Product Maintenance Contracts
EITF 99-5	Accounting for Pre-Production Costs Related to Long-Term Supply Arrangements
EITF 00-21	Revenue Arrangements with Multiple Deliverables
SAB Topic 13	Revenue Recognition

For certain transactions, the accounting literature answers this question. For example, FAS-60 provides guidance applicable to the insurance industry, FAS-91 provides guidance on deferral of loan origination costs, and FTB 90-1 provides guidance on deferral of costs related to the sale of extended warranties. Obviously, this guidance is very narrow in scope, and does not address the majority of situations in which costs are incurred before revenue is recognized.

The frequency with which the question of cost deferral arises increased due to the issuance of SAB Topic 13. This is because SAB Topic 13 resulted in a number of companies deferring revenue in more situations than they previously did. SAB Topic 13 also made clear the SEC staff's view that incurrence of costs should not necessarily lead to recognition of revenue. The SEC staff has provided some guidance on the subject of cost deferral in SAB Topic 13. This guidance suggests analogies to the cost deferral models in FAS-91 and FTB 90-1 are appropriate.

Costs of Revenue Transactions

The accounting for many costs associated with revenue transactions is well established. For example, costs of purchasing and manufacturing inventory are recorded as an asset until the related revenue is recognized, while costs of fixed assets purchased to serve a single customer are capitalized and depreciated over their useful lives. There is little need for further discussion of the accounting for these costs. Also, the accounting for the following types of costs is covered in the indicated authoritative accounting literature:

Cost	Primary Literature
Advertising costs	SOP 93-7, *Reporting on Advertising Costs* and PB-13, *Direct-Response Advertising and Probable Future Benefits*

Cost	Primary Literature
Start-up costs	SOP 98-5, *Reporting on the Costs of Start-Up Activities*
Inventory costs	ARB-43, *Restatement and Revision of Accounting Research Bulletins, Chapter 4: Inventory Pricing*
Intangible assets	FAS-142, *Goodwill and Other Intangible Assets*
Internal-use software costs	SOP 98-1, *Accounting for the Costs of Computer Software Developed or Obtained for Internal Use*
Web site development costs	EITF 00-2, *Accounting for Web Site Development Costs*
External-use software costs	FAS-86, *Accounting for the Costs of Computer Software to Be Sold, Leased,or Otherwise Marketed*
Film-related costs	SOP 00-2, *Accounting by Producers or Distributors of Films*
Real estate project costs	FAS-67, *Accounting for Costs and Initial Rental Operations of Real Estate projects*
Insurance enterprise costs	FAS-60, *Accounting and Reporting by Insurance Enterprises*
Lease inducements	FTB 88-1, *Issues Relating to Accounting for Leases*
Pre-production costs related to long-term supply arrangements	EITF 99-5, *Accounting for Pre-Production Costs Related to Long-Term Supply Arrangements*
Credit-card-related costs	EITF 88-20, *Difference between Initial Investment and Principal Amount of Loans in a Purchased Credit Card Portfolio*; EITF 92-5, *Amortization Period for Net Deferred Credit Card Origination Costs*; and EITF 93-1, *Accounting for Individual Credit Card Acquisitions*

However, none of the accounting literature addresses, on a general basis, the accounting for many of the costs of revenue transactions. Despite the lack of accounting literature specifically on point, certain practices have become common and accepted. These practices for certain types of costs are the focus of this section of the chapter.

The costs discussed in this section are commonly referred to as customer acquisition and up-front or set-up costs. More specifically, those costs include solicitation costs, origination costs, multiple-element costs, and set-up and other direct costs of installation. A brief description of each of these costs is provided below:

- *Solicitation costs*—Those costs, excluding advertising costs, incurred by a vendor to solicit or acquire a specific customer or revenue stream. A prime example of a solicitation cost is a sales commission.

- *Direct origination costs*—Those direct costs incurred to consummate a specific revenue transaction. Examples of origination activities include reviewing and checking the customer's credit, negotiating the terms of the sales arrangement, and preparing and processing documentation of the sale.

- *Multiple-element costs*—Those costs related to a delivered element in a multiple-element arrangement where either (1) the delivered element cannot be treated as a separate element for accounting purposes or (2) the delivered element should be treated as a separate element for accounting purposes, however no revenue is allocated to the delivered element, or only a portion of the revenue that would otherwise have been allocated to the delivered element is ultimately allocated to the delivered element, because all or a portion of the payment for that delivered element is contingent upon delivery of an as-yet-undelivered element (special considerations for this latter type of multiple-element cost are discussed later in this chapter in the section entitled "Special Considerations for Certain Multiple-Element Costs"). For example, if a vendor sells a piece of equipment subject to installation, but concludes that the equipment does not have value to the customer on a standalone basis (i.e., absent the installation), no revenue would be recognized upon delivery of the equipment. The cost of the equipment is referred to as a multiple-element cost.

- *Set-up and other direct costs of installation*—Those costs related to activities that must be incurred to enable a vendor to perform under the terms of the arrangement. These activities (a) are performed (and the related costs incurred) at the inception of an arrangement, (b) do not represent a separate earnings process, and (c) are arrangement-specific. For example, if a customer outsources its human resources function, the vendor might incur costs to convert the customer to the vendor's human resources platform prior to actually operating the customer's human resources function. These costs are set-up costs.

EXAMPLE: SETUP COSTS

Acxiom Corporation Form 10-K—Fiscal Year Ended March 31, 2005

The Company provides database management and IT outsourcing services under long-term arrangements. These arrangements may require the Company to perform setup activities such as the design and build of a database for the customer under the database management contracts and migration of the customer's IT environment under IT outsourcing contracts. In the case of database management contracts, the customer does not acquire any ownership rights to the Company's intellectual property used in the database and the database itself provides no benefit to the customer outside of the utilization of the system during the term of the database management arrangement. In some cases, the arrangements also contain provisions requiring customer acceptance of the setup activities prior to commencement of the ongoing services arrangement. Up-front fees billed during the setup phase are deferred and setup costs that are direct and incremental to the contract are capitalized and amortized on a straight-line basis over the service term of the contract. Revenue recognition does not begin until after customer acceptance in cases where contracts contain acceptance provisions. Once the setup phase is complete and customer acceptance occurs, the Company recognizes revenue over the remaining service term of the contract. In situations where the arrangement does not require setup activities or customer acceptance before the Company begins providing services, revenue is recognized over the contract period and no costs are deferred.

EXAMPLE: SETUP COSTS

Computer Sciences Corp. Form 10-K—Fiscal Year Ended April 1, 2005

Capitalization of outsourcing contract costs

Certain costs incurred upon initiation of an outsourcing contract are deferred and amortized over the contract life. These costs consist of contract acquisition and transition/set-up costs, and include the cost of due diligence activities after competitive selection, costs associated with installation of systems and processes, and amounts paid to clients in excess of the fair market value of acquired assets (premiums). Finance staff, working with program management, review costs to determine appropriateness for deferral in accordance with relevant accounting guidance.

Key estimates and assumptions that the Company must make include assessing the fair value of acquired assets in order to calculate the premium and projecting future cash flows in order to assess the recoverability of deferred costs. The Company utilizes the experience and knowledge of its professional staff in program management operations, procurement and finance areas, as well as third parties on occasion, to determine fair values of assets acquired. To assess recoverability, undiscounted estimated cash flows of the contract are projected over its remaining life and compared to the unamortized deferred cost balance. Such estimates require judgment and assumptions, which are based upon the professional knowledge and experience of Company personnel. Key factors that are considered in estimating the undiscounted cash flows include projected labor costs and productivity efficiencies. A significant change in an estimate or assumption on one or more contracts could have a material effect on the Company's results of operations. Amortization of such premiums is recorded as a reduction to revenues.

Depreciation and Amortization

The Company's depreciation and amortization policies are as follows:

Outsourcing contract costs–Contract life, excluding option years

Outsourcing Contract Costs

Costs on outsourcing contracts, including costs incurred for bid and proposal activities, are generally expensed as incurred. However, certain costs incurred upon initiation of an outsourcing contract are deferred and expensed over the contract life. These costs represent incremental external costs or certain specific internal costs that are directly related to the contract acquisition or transition activities. Such capitalized costs can be separated into two principal categories: contract acquisition costs and transition/set-up costs. The primary types of costs that may be capitalized include labor and related fringe benefits, subcontractor costs, travel costs, and asset premiums.

The first principal category, contract acquisition costs, consists mainly of due diligence activities after competitive selection as well as premiums paid. Premiums are amounts paid to clients in excess of the fair market value of acquired assets. Fixed assets acquired in connection with outsourcing transactions are capitalized at fair value and depreciated consistent with fixed asset policies described above. Premiums are capitalized and as outsourcing contract costs and amortized over the contract life. The amortization of outsourcing contract cost premiums is accounted for as a reduction in revenue. The second principal category of capitalized outsourcing costs is transition/set-up costs. Such costs are primarily associated with installation of systems and processes.

In the event indications exist that an outsourcing contract cost balance related to a particular contract may be impaired, undiscounted estimated cash flows of the contract are projected over its remaining term, and compared to the unamortized outsourcing contract cost balance. If the projected cash flows are not adequate to recover the unamortized cost balance, the balance would be adjusted to equal the contract's fair value in the period such a determination is made. The primary indicator used to determine when impairment testing should be performed is when a contract is materially underperforming, or is expected to materially underperform in the future, as compared to the bid model that was developed as part of the original proposal process and subsequent annual budgets.

Terminations of outsourcing contracts, including transfers either back to the client or to another I/T provider, prior to the end of their committed contract terms are infrequent due to the complex transition of personnel, assets, methodologies, and processes involved with outsourcing transactions. In the event of an early termination, the Company and the client, pursuant to certain contractual provisions, engage in discussions to determine the recovery of unamortized contract costs, lost profits, transfer of personnel, rights to implemented systems and processes, as well as other matters.

Definition of an Asset

As noted above, except for certain narrowly defined transactions, no literature directly addresses the costs described above. Therefore, the accounting for them must be based on the FASB conceptual framework and analogies to other literature. The conceptual framework makes clear that it is not appropriate to defer costs if those costs do not create, or add to the value of, an asset. Assets are defined as " . . . probable future economic benefits obtained or controlled by a particular entity as a result of past transactions or events." (CON-6, par. 25). The costs addressed in this section do not result in the creation of any physical assets. However, when the costs are part of the revenue-generating arrangement, the arrangement itself could be considered an asset since the revenue provides future economic benefit, and since the arrangement is controlled by the company provided it is legally binding.

Costs Eligible for Deferral

The only costs eligible for deferral are those costs directly related to a particular revenue arrangement. Both FAS-91 and FTB 90-1 provide descriptions of the costs considered eligible for deferral (SAB Topic 13A3f, ques. 3). Although the models are slightly different, their goal is the same—to identify those costs so closely related to the revenue from a contract that they should be recognized when that revenue is recognized.

FAS-91

FAS-91 deals specifically with the accounting for loan solicitation and direct origination costs. Under the FAS-91 model, costs eligible for deferral are those that relate directly to a specific loan and are either (1) incremental direct costs incurred with third parties, or (2) certain internal direct costs related to origination activities. Internal direct costs are limited to a portion of the salaries and benefits of employees involved in the origination process (FAS-91, par. 6). That portion is calculated based on the percentage of the employees' time spent on origination activities for the particular loan, multiplied by the employee's total compensation (salary plus commissions plus benefits). Sales commissions paid to internal salespeople, therefore, are capitalizable to the extent the salesperson performs origination (as opposed to just solicitation) activities, and then only based on the amount of time the salesperson spends on origination activities.

After the issuance of FAS-91, the FASB issued a special report entitled *A Guide to Implementation of Statement 91 on Accounting for Nonrefundable Fees and Costs Associated with Originating or Acquiring Loans and Initial Direct Costs of Leases: Questions and Answers.* This special report provides considerable guidance regarding the deferral of costs under FAS-91.

> **OBSERVATION:** FAS-149, *Amendment of Statement 133 on Derivative Instruments and Hedging Activities,* amended FAS-91 to exclude from its scope fees and costs related to commitments to originate, sell, or purchase loans that are accounted for as derivatives under FAS-133. Staff Accounting Bulletin No. 105, *Application of Accounting Principles to Loan Commitments,* limits fair value measurement of loan commitments to the difference between the interest rate guaranteed by the loan commitment and the market interest rate. It specifically prohibits inclusion of any expected cash flows related to servicing and customer relationship intangibles. SAB 105 was effective for loan commitments accounted for as derivatives after March 31, 2004.

EXAMPLE: LOAN ORIGINATION AND ACQUISITION COSTS

New Century Financial Corporation Form 10-K—Fiscal Year Ended December 31, 2004

Loan origination or acquisition cost—Loan acquisition costs include fees paid to wholesale brokers and correspondents, direct loan origination costs, including commissions and corporate overhead costs, less points and fees received from borrowers, divided by the total production volume. Loan acquisition costs do not include profit-based compensation, servicing division overhead, parent company expenses and startup operations.

FTB 90-1

FTB 90-1 deals specifically with accounting for costs to acquire separately priced extended warranty and product maintenance contracts. Only incremental direct costs incurred for a specific contract should be deferred under the FTB 90-1 model (FTB 90-1, par. 4). As such, costs that would have been incurred regardless of whether a contract is obtained should not be deferred. This effectively precludes the deferral of employee salaries or benefits, since it would be a rare situation that an employee's salary and benefits would not exist due to the absence of a single, specific contract. However, commissions paid to an employee based on a specific contract would be eligible for deferral under the FTB 90-1 model.

ILLUSTRATION: COMPARISON OF FAS-91 AND FTB 90-1 COST DEFERRAL MODELS

Facts: Satellite TV Company (Satellite) sells receivers and satellite dishes and provides satellite television programming to customers. Satellite enters into a transaction with Customer M (M) where M purchases a satellite dish and receiver and signs a contract to receive one year of satellite programming. M installs the satellite dish and receiver itself. Amounts to be paid by M include a $50 up-front, non-refundable fee and $30 per month for the duration of the contract. If the customer cancels the contract early, a $200 cancellation fee is due to Satellite. The costs incurred by Satellite include:

- $150 related to its purchase of the receiver and satellite dish from a third party,

- $15 of origination costs (allocated employee costs for one-quarter hour spent by an employee to perform a credit check and process paperwork),

- $25 of set-up costs (allocated employee costs for one-half hour spent activating the receiver and satellite dish to receive Satellite's signals), and

- $100 commission paid to an internal employee dedicated solely to selling activities.

Satellite has concluded that it should not separate the sale of the receiver and satellite dish from the satellite programming services. Furthermore, Satellite has concluded that the up-front fee should be deferred over a period of three years (expected customer relationship period) using the straight-line method.

Discussion: Each of the costs listed above would be evaluated as follows:

- Receiver and satellite dish—The costs of the receiver and satellite dish are incremental direct costs paid to a third party. They are eligible for deferral under either the FAS-91 or FTB 90-1 models.

- Performing credit check and processing paperwork—The amounts related to an internal employee performing a credit check and processing paperwork are direct internal origination costs. These costs would generally be eligible for deferral under the FAS-91 model, but may not be eligible under the FTB 90-1 model, as it is not clear that the costs are incremental, even though they are direct.

- Activating receiver and satellite dish-The amount related to an internal employee activating the receiver and satellite dish to receive Satellite's signals represents direct payroll-related costs incurred in connection with set-up activities. These costs would generally be eligible for deferral under the FAS-91 model, but may not be eligible under the FTB 90-1 model, as it is not clear that the costs are incremental, even though they are direct.

- Commission—The commission paid to an internal employee dedicated solely to selling activities is not eligible for deferral under the FAS-91 model because that model does not allow deferral of internal solicitation costs—only internal origination costs. The FTB 90-1 model would allow for the deferral of the commission, as it is both directly related to the contract and is incremental to the costs that would otherwise be incurred.

Based on this evaluation, the total amount of capitalizable costs based on an analogy to FAS-91 is $190 ($150 of receiver and satellite costs plus $15 of origination costs plus $25 of set-up costs), while the capitalizable costs based on an analogy to FTB 90-1 are $250 ($150 of receiver and satellite costs plus the $100 commission).

Choosing an Accounting Policy

The capitalization of customer acquisition and other costs addressed in this section is not required, with one exception for a certain type of multiple-element costs. The one exception relates to the direct costs of a delivered product that cannot be treated separately for accounting purposes from the undelivered other elements in the multiple-element arrangement (see Chapter 4, "Multiple-Element Arrangements," for additional information). The multiple-element costs associated with this one exception should be capitalized, subject to the realizability test discussed in the section later in this chapter titled "Realizability Test." This exception exists because adopting an accounting policy where this type of cost is expensed is inconsistent with the following concept discussed in paragraph 4 of ARB-43, Ch. 4: "In accounting for the goods in the inventory at any point of time, the major objective is the matching of appropriate costs against revenues in order that there may be a proper determination of the realized income." The multiple-element costs associated with this exception should not be confused with those multiple-element costs that arise when a delivered element should be treated as a separate element for accounting purposes, however, no revenue is allocated to the delivered element, or only a portion of the revenue that would otherwise have been allocated to the delivered element is ultimately allocated to the delivered element, because all or a portion of the payment for that delivered element is contingent upon delivery of an as-yet-undelivered element. Special considerations related to this other type of multiple-element costs are discussed further in the section later in this chapter titled "Special Considerations for Certain Multiple-Element Costs."

Expensing as incurred the other costs discussed in this section that are not covered by the one exception discussed above is always acceptable (SAB Topic 13A3f, ques. 3). It is also acceptable to analyze those costs using a model similar to the ones used in FTB 90-1 and FAS-91, with a goal of deferring those costs directly related to the revenue transaction until the revenue is recognized. In some cases, the most appropriate policy might be a complete analogy to one of the two models discussed. In other cases, it may be appropriate to develop a policy that blends the FAS-91 and FTB 90-1 models. For example, it may be appropriate to apply the FAS-91 model to set-up costs and the FTB 90-1 model to commissions.

> **OBSERVATION:** In some cases, a company may believe it should defer a larger amount of costs than either the FAS-91 or FTB 90-1 models would allow. This may be appropriate due to the nature of the costs incurred, provided the deferred costs meet the definition of an asset, as discussed earlier. However, the policy should be selected based on an analysis of the arrangements and the costs incurred, rather than based on a goal of capitalizing (or expensing) a certain amount of costs.

> **DISCLOSURE ALERT:** Companies should disclose their choice of accounting policy related to the capitalization or expensing of customer acquisition and other costs addressed in this section. See Chapter 12, "Disclosures," for additional discussion of accounting policy disclosures.

> **SEC REGISTRANT ALERT:** The SEC staff has stated that, in general, it would not object to an accounting policy that results in the capitalization of costs in accordance with either FAS-91 or FTB 90-1. However, it is not clear whether the staff would accept a policy that blends elements from each piece of literature (SAB Topic 13A3f, ques. 4).

ILLUSTRATION: SELECTION OF ACCOUNTING POLICIES

Facts: Assume the same facts as those presented earlier in the example involving Satellite TV Company (Satellite).

Selection of Policy: Satellite reviews the nature of the costs incurred before revenue is recognized, and believes that all of the costs should be considered deferrable, based on the following:

- The receiver and satellite costs are clearly direct and incremental and represent direct costs of products sold in a multiple-element arrangement that is not unbundled (e.g., the receiver and satellite cannot be treated separately for accounting purposes). Therefore these costs should be considered deferrable, as would be the case in an analysis under either FTB 90-1 or FAS-91.
- The sales commission is also direct and incremental, and therefore should be considered deferrable, as it would be under FTB 90-1.
- The origination and set-up costs should be considered deferrable based on an analogy to FAS-91 because they are internal costs directly-related to the contract. In addition, although the costs may not be clearly incremental to the particular contract, Satellite does incur incremental costs to perform these activities for its entire customer base.

These accounting policies result in $290 of costs being considered deferrable in Satellite's transaction with M.

Realizability Test

Like any other asset, deferred costs must be evaluated for realizability. Both FAS-91 and FTB 90-1 require the deferral of costs due to the existence of a contractual revenue stream against which to match those costs. As such, the nature of the terms of the arrangements that fall within the scope of those statements supports the realizability of the deferred costs. For transactions that do not fall within the scope of FAS-91 or FTB 90-1, the following should be considered in determining whether deferrable costs related to those transactions are realizable:

- Has any non-refundable revenue related to the specific transaction been deferred?
- Does a contractual arrangement exist that management intends to enforce?

Deferrable costs up to the amount of non-refundable deferred revenue related to the transaction are considered realizable, as the recognition of the deferred revenue will offset the recognition of deferred costs. If deferrable costs are in excess of non-refundable deferred revenue (or if there is no deferred revenue), these excess deferrable costs are only considered realizable under the following circumstances:

1. A specific contractual arrangement exists related to the deferrable costs;
2. The contractual arrangement is legally enforceable;

3. Management intends to enforce the contractual arrangement; and

4. Probable and objectively supportable net margins exist during the base term of the contractual arrangement to support the amount of deferrable costs (where net margins represent revenues net of related direct costs).

One question that arises in applying this test is whether any revenue in addition to contractual minimum revenues should be included. For example, in the satellite television arrangement discussed in the illustrations in this section, the customer might be able to purchase additional services, such as premium movie channels or special event programming. It may be appropriate to include these additional revenues (and related costs) in the realizability test if those additional amounts are probable of occurring and objectively supportable. However, care should be exercised in adopting a policy that takes into consideration revenues in excess of minimum contractual revenues when estimating net margins for purposes of the realizability test.

> **OBSERVATION:** Some companies have essentially eliminated the need for a realizability test by adopting a policy of deferring costs only to the extent of deferred revenues. This policy is generally less preferable than one that adopts a full cost deferral model, or one that expenses all costs as incurred. However, a policy of deferring direct costs to the extent of deferred revenues is also acceptable, if applied consistently.

EXAMPLE: LIMITING DEFERRED COSTS TO DEFERRED REVENUES

Qwest Communications International Form 10-K—Fiscal Year Ended December 31, 2004

Revenue Recognition—Revenue for services is recognized when the related services are provided. Payments received in advance are deferred until the service is provided. Up-front fees received, primarily activation fees and installation charges, as well as the associated customer acquisition costs, are deferred and recognized over the expected customer relationship period, which ranges from one to ten years. The amount of customer acquisition costs which are deferred is less than or equal to the amount of up-front fees deferred. Costs in excess of up-front fees are recorded as an expense in the period incurred. Expected customer relationship periods are estimated using historical data of actual customer retention patterns. Termination fees or other fees on existing contracts that are negotiated in conjunction with new contracts are deferred and recognized over the new contract term.

ILLUSTRATION: APPLICATION OF THE REALIZABILITY TEST

Facts: Assume the same facts and conclusions as those presented earlier in the examples involving Satellite TV Company (Satellite). In addition, assume the following:

- The monthly costs incurred by Satellite to provide programming services to M are $12.

- Satellite has received from its external legal counsel a letter indicating that its programming services contracts are legally enforceable.

- Satellite has a history of enforcing its contracts and intends to enforce its contract with M.

Also, Satellite does not have a policy of including revenues expected in excess of contractual minimum revenues (e.g., specialty programming fees) when determining whether deferred costs are relizable.

Application: Based on its accounting policies, Satellite has determined that $290 of costs are deferrable in connection with the arrangement it has with M. An amount equal to the up-front non-refundable fee of $50 is considered realizable. Satellite also expects net margins of $216 during the contract period ($360 of contractual revenue [$30 per month for 12 months] less $144 of related direct costs ($12 per month for 12 months]). Satellite can support its expectations of $216 of net margins under this contract with a large volume of company-specific history related to similar contracts. An additional $216 of deferrable costs are also considered realizable since (a) this amount represents probable and objectively supportable net margins, (b) Satellite's contract with M is legally enforceable, (c) Satellite intends to enforce its contract with M, and (d) Satellite's intentions are reasonable in light of its demonstrable history of enforcing its contracts.

Based on this analysis, the amount of deferrable costs that are realizable is $266 ($50 supported by the up-front non-refundable fee and $216 supported by probable and objectively supportable net margins). The remainder of the deferrable costs, $24 ($290 total deferrable costs less $266 realizable deferrable costs), should be expensed as incurred.

Special Considerations for Certain Multiple-Element Costs

In a multiple-element arrangement that should be separated, situations may arise where either (a) no revenue is allocated to a delivered element because payment for that element is contingent upon delivery of an as-yet undelivered element, or (b) only a portion of the revenue that would otherwise have been allocated to the delivered element is ultimately allocated to the delivered element because a portion of the payment for that delivered element is contingent upon delivery of an as-yet undelivered element. These situations are caused by the specific refund right guidance in EITF 00-21 that limits the amount of revenue ultimately allocated to a delivered element to the lesser of (a) the amount otherwise allocable to that element (based on using the relative fair value or residual method, as appropriate) or (b) the amount that is not contingent upon the delivery of additional items or meeting other specified performance conditions (EITF 00-21, par. 14) (see Chapter 4, "Multiple-Element Arrangements"). These situations raise the following question: What is the proper accounting treatment for the costs associated with the delivered element (referred to in this section as the delivered element costs)?

This discussion can best be framed using numerical examples. Consider the following:

> **Common Facts:** There are two elements in the arrangement—Element 1 and Element 2. Total arrangement consideration is $100. The amounts otherwise allocable to Element 1 and Element 2 based on their relative fair values are $70 and $30, respectively. Vendor delivers Element 1 before Element 2. The cost of Element 1 is $50. The cost of Element 2 is $10. Element 1 and Element 2 otherwise meet the separation criteria in EITF 00-21. All of the revenue recognition conditions have been met for Element 1 upon its delivery.

> **Example 1 Additional Facts:** $100 is due upon delivery of Element 1. Vendor must refund the entire amount if Element 2 is not delivered.

> **Example 2 Additional Facts:** $100 is due upon delivery of Element 1. If Element 2 is not delivered, Vendor must refund $60.

Example 1

In this example, no revenue is ultimately allocated to Element 1 since the entire amount of arrangement consideration is refundable if Element 2 is not delivered. The question that arises in this situation is how should the cost of Element 1 ($50) be treated-should it be deferred or expensed upon delivery of Element 1? Deferring the $50 until delivery of Element 2 (provided that occurs) would result in the revenue ($100), costs ($60), and profit margin ($40) for the entire transaction being recognized at the same point in time. Expensing the $50 upon delivery of Element 1 results in a negative profit margin (-$50) for Vendor upon delivery of Element 1 and a higher positive profit margin ($90) upon delivery of Element 2 (provided that occurs). However, total profit margin ($40) for the entire transaction is the same upon delivery of Element 2 whether the $50 is deferred or expensed upon delivery of Element 1.

In this example, application of the realizability test discussed earlier in this chapter would typically result in a conclusion that the delivered element costs are not realizable. First, there is no non-refundable deferred revenue to consider in the realizability test. In other words, the $100 the Vendor receives upon delivery of Element 1 is not non-refundable deferred revenue. Second, while there may be a contractual arrangement supporting the transaction, such arrangement contains a contingency related to realizing revenue for the delivered element. The existence of this contingency may make it difficult to conclude that probable and objectively supportable net margins exist to justify the realizability of Element 1's costs. Does this mean that the cost of Element 1 must be expensed upon its delivery? As discussed below under "Accounting for Delivered Element Costs," not necessarily.

Example 2

In this example, $40 of revenue is ultimately allocated to Element 1. The $70 that would otherwise have been allocated to Element 1 is reduced to $40 (a reduction of $30) because the amount otherwise allocated to the undelivered element ($30) is less than the amount that would be refunded if the undelivered element is not delivered ($60, for a difference of $30). The question that arises in these situations is how should the cost of Element 1 be treated and should that treatment be affected by the fact that some amount of revenue was ultimately allocated to Element 1?

In Example 2, the cost of Element 1 ($50) exceeds the revenue ultimately allocated to it ($40) by $10. Deferring the entire cost of Element 1 in this situation would not be appropriate. It would also not be appropriate to defer the $40 of revenue ultimately allocated to Element 1 since the revenue recognition conditions have been met (see Chapter 4, "Multiple-Element Arrangements"). However, since expensing the entire $50 upon delivery of Element 1 would result in negative profit margin (-$10) for Vendor on Element 1, should some portion of Element 1's cost be deferred? If so, how should that portion be determined?

Application of the realizability test discussed earlier in this chapter to Example 2 is awkward. First, there is no non-refundable deferred revenue to consider in the realizability test. All of the non-refundable revenue is ultimately allocated to Element 1 and will be recognized upon its delivery. In other words, when Vendor receives the $100 upon delivery of Element 1, $40 would be recognized as revenue and the remaining $60 would not be considered non-refundable deferred revenue. This leaves no non-refundable deferred revenue. Second, while there may be a contractual arrangement supporting the transaction, such arrangement contains a contingency related to realizing revenue for the delivered element. The existence of this contingency may make it difficult to conclude that probable and objectively supportable net margins exist to justify the realizability of Element 1's costs. Does this mean that the cost of Element 1 must be expensed upon its delivery? As discussed below under "Accounting for Delivered Element Costs," not necessarily.

Accounting for Delivered Element Costs

The fact patterns laid out in Examples 1 and 2 are relatively simple and straight-forward. However, the question regarding the treatment of Element 1's cost in these Examples is still not an easy one. Consider the additional complexities that would be introduced if the cost of Element 1 were $40 or $30, or if there were a third element delivered after Element 2 with additional specific refund rights. Unfortunately, there is no accounting literature that specifically addresses these questions. Before any cost (including Element 1's cost) can be recognized as an asset, however, it must meet the definition of an asset included in CON-6. How should one determine whether an asset exists and, if so, in what amount? There is no one right answer to this question. In answering this question, however, the goal is always the same—to arrive at a "reasoned" approach to accounting for the delivered element costs in a particular set of facts and circumstances.

Different approaches have been discussed related to determining whether none, some or all of the delivered element costs in a particular set of facts and circumstances should be capitalized for accounting purposes. One approach comprises two steps:

Step 1: Does the company have an asset?

Step 2: If so, what is the company's impairment test for that asset?

In Step 1, the company must determine whether it has obtained or controlled future economic benefits as a result of the revenue transaction. In making this determination, the company should consider the contract it has with the customer to deliver a second element at a potentially higher profit margin than it otherwise would have. Does that contract result in the company obtaining or controlling future economic benefits? The answer to this question depends on the facts and circumstances and requires the exercise of reasoned judgment.

In Step 2, determining an appropriate impairment test requires the consideration of many factors. Factors that may be considered include the margin that will be earned on the final element and the margin that will be earned on the final element in comparison to the margin that would typically be earned on that element if it were sold on a standalone basis. Another factor that may be considered is whether the delivered element is typically sold at a loss when it is sold on a standalone basis or when it is sold in other arrangements that do not include a specific refund right. There is not a cookie-cutter solution to identifying the appropriate impairment test. Many factors, in addition to those discussed here, should be considered and analyzed in the context of the company's specific facts and circumstances. This analysis should ultimately result in a reasoned approach to assessing whether the carrying amount of the company's asset is realizable.

Another approach related to determining whether none, some, or all of the delivered element costs in a particular set of facts and circumstances should be capitalized for accounting purposes involves analyzing the different potential accounting treatments for the delivered element costs and concluding which of those treatments is the most appropriate for the delivered element costs in a particular set of facts and circumstances. The potential accounting treatments that typically would be considered in this type of analysis include:

- Expense the delivered element costs upon delivery—In the case of Example 2, this would result in the recognition of $40 of revenue and $50 of cost of goods sold upon the delivery of Element 1.

- Capitalize the delivered element costs upon delivery—In the case of Example 2, this would result in the recognition of $40 of revenue and $50 of deferred costs upon the delivery of Element 1.

- Expense delivered element costs up to the amount of revenue ultimately allocated to the delivered element and capitalize the delivered element costs in excess of the amount of revenue allocated to the delivered element (e.g., capitalize the delivered element costs to the extent of any loss) upon delivery— In the case of Example 2, this would result in the recognition of $40 of revenue, $40 of cost of goods sold, and $10 of deferred costs upon delivery of Element 1.

- Expense/Capitalize the costs of Element 1 on a pro rata basis upon delivery (e.g., costs would be expensed based on the proportion of revenue ultimately allocated to the delivered element to the revenue that otherwise would have been allocated to the delivered element). In the case of Example 2, this would result in the recognition of $40 of revenue, $29 ($40/$70 x $50) of cost of goods sold, and $21 of deferred costs upon delivery of Element 1.

These potential accounting treatments should not be viewed as acceptable alternatives in every set of facts and circumstances. Instead, each of these potential accounting treatments should be analyzed in the context of a specific set of facts and circumstances to determine which potential accounting treatment is most appropriate for those facts and circumstances. For example, in Example

2, it would not be appropriate to conclude that Vendor should capitalize the entire amount of Element 1's costs upon delivery since Vendor will be recognizing $40 of revenue (57% of the amount of revenue otherwise allocable to Element 1) upon delivery. After ruling out any potential accounting treatments that are not appropriate in a particular set of facts and circumstances, the next step is to determine which of the remaining potential accounting treatments is the most appropriate for the particular set of facts and circumstances. There is no cookie-cutter solution to this determination as it is completely reliant on the specific set of facts and circumstances. The existence of any individual fact could sway the analysis one way or the other. At the end of the analysis, however, if the accounting treatment applied to a specific set of facts and circumstances results in some or all of the delivered element costs being capitalized, the amount capitalized should meet the definition of an asset and be realizable.

These are not the only approaches to accounting for delivered element costs, nor are these approaches mutually exclusive. Each of these approaches could be used to substantiate the results of the other. This relationship exists between these approaches because (a) any costs capitalized as a result of applying these approaches should meet the definition of an asset and be realizable and (b) these approaches should result in identifying the accounting treatment that is most appropriate for a particular set of facts and circumstances. In the end, determining the appropriate accounting treatment for the delivered element costs in a specific set of facts and circumstances requires a thorough understanding of the facts and circumstances, and thorough understanding and analysis of the authoritative literature that addresses cost deferral, and the exercise of reasoned judgment. If an entity finds itself in a position similar to that in Examples 1 or 2, it should consult with experts to determine the most appropriate accounting treatment for the delivered element costs in its fact pattern.

> **SEC REGISTRANT ALERT:** In a December 2003 speech, the SEC staff provided the following examples of situation where it may be appropriate to conclude that delivered element costs represent an asset: (1) the sale is effectively a consignment sale (in which case the delivered element costs would represent consignment inventory), (2) the incurred loss is considered an investment in the remainder of the contract as supported by the revenue allocated to the remaining elements being an amount greater than the fair value of those elements, or (3) the incurred costs are contractually guaranteed reimbursable costs (similar to those costs discussed in EITF99-5). These items effectively represent examples of situations where the application of Step 1 in the first approach discussed above results in the conclusion that an asset exists. In addition, under the second approach discussed above, an analysis of the

potential accounting treatments would likely result in the conclusion that the accounting treatment in these situations should allow for some or all of the delivered element costs to be capitalized.

When a decision is made to recognize an asset for delivered element costs, a key question focused on by the SEC staff includes the method used to evaluate the asset for impairment. Other questions focused on by the SEC staff in this situation include: (1) what is the nature of the costs that should be considered in calculating the loss on a delivered item and (2) how and over what periods should the asset be amortized?

In this speech, the SEC staff acknowledges that there is not a one-size-fits-all solution to the treatment of delivered element costs. Given the complexities of the analysis and the level of judgment required in determining whether these costs should be deferred, the SEC staff encouraged registrants to discuss the approaches they have taken with the SEC staff.

EXAMPLES: EFFECTS OF ACCOUNTING FOR DELIVERED ELEMENT COSTS

Accenture Form 10-K—Fiscal Year Ended August 31, 2003

Effective September 1, 2003, we adopted Issue 00-21 on a prospective basis. The Company will continue to account for contracts signed on or before August 31, 2003, under the previous Generally Accepted Accounting Principles. Beginning on September 1, 2003, we began accounting for all new contracts in accordance with Issue 00-21, potentially changing the timing of revenue recognition and affecting margins in some situations, depending on our ability to structure contracts to accommodate the requirements of Issue 00-21.

If we had applied Issue 00-21 in the past, diluted earnings per share would have been approximately $0.02 lower in fiscal 2003 and $0.01 lower in fiscal 2002, and we would have reported, cumulatively, approximately $114 million less in revenues before reimbursements, of which $65 million relates to fiscal 2003, $35 million relates to fiscal 2002, and $14 million relates to fiscal 2001; and $54 million less in operating income, of which $33 million relates to fiscal 2003, $15 million relates to fiscal 2002, and $6 million relates to fiscal 2001. We believe that the impact of Issue 00-21 will continue to be modest going forward because we plan to structure our new client agreements taking into consideration the new rules. However, should we sign a larger number of business transformation outsourcing agreements with clients, there could be a greater delay in revenue recognition and an increased effect on margins.

Accenture Form 10-K—Fiscal Year Ended August 31, 2004

(In thousands of U.S. dollars, except share and per share amounts or as otherwise indicated)

Revenues related to new revenue arrangements with multiple elements signed after August 31, 2003 are allocated to each element based on the lesser of the element's relative fair value or the amount that is not contingent on future delivery of another element. Revenues allocated to separate elements are recognized for each separate element in accordance with Accenture's accounting policy for revenues described above. If the amount of non-contingent revenues allocated to a delivered element is less than the costs to deliver such services, then such costs are deferred and recognized in future periods when the revenue becomes non-contingent. The adoption of Issue 00-21 reduced revenues by approximately $44,000 and reduced operating income by approximately $41,000 in fiscal 2004.

Amortization

Deferred costs should generally be amortized as the revenue related to the applicable contract is recognized. Thus, if the deferred costs are equal to or less than deferred revenue related to the same contract, the costs should be amortized over the same period and in the same manner as the related deferred revenue (SAB Topic 13A3f, ques. 5). If there are no deferred revenues, or if the amount of deferred costs exceeds the related deferred revenues, the cost, or excess costs, should be amortized in proportion to the revenue realized during the base contract term, excluding extensions. In these situations, the pattern of recognition for deferred costs should generally mirror the revenue to be recognized under the contract and if no pattern of revenue recognition can be predicted, the costs should be amortized on a straight-line basis over the contract period. Oftentimes, applying this guidance in situations where deferred costs exceed deferred revenues will result in deferred costs in an amount equal to deferred revenues being amortized over the same period and in the same pattern as the deferred revenues, and deferred costs in excess of deferred revenues being amortized over the contract period in the same pattern as revenue is recognized under the contract.

ILLUSTRATION: AMORTIZATION OF DEFERRED COSTS

Facts: Assume the same facts and conclusions as those presented earlier in the examples involving Satellite TV Company (Satellite).

Amortization: Satellite should amortize $50 of deferred costs over the same period and in the same manner as the $50 up-front non-refundable fee will be recognized as revenue. This results in the $50 of deferred costs being recognized on a straight-line basis over a three-year period. The remaining $216 of deferred costs should be amortized on a straight-line basis over the one-year contract period.

Summary: Revenues and costs recognized over the expected period of the customer relationship (assuming that the revenue recognition criteria have been met) is as follows:

	Year 1	Year 2	Year 3	Total
Revenue:				
Amortization of up-front non-refundable fee	$ 17	$ 17	$ 16	$ 50
Monthly programming fees	360	360	360	1,080
Total	377	377	376	1,130
Costs:				
Amortization of deferred costs				
$50 over three years	17	17	16	50
$216 over one year	216			216
Excess of deferrable costs over realizable costs	24	–		24
Monthly programming costs	144	144	144	432
Total	401	161	160	722
Net margin	$ (24)	$ 216	$ 216	$ 408

EXAMPLE: AMORTIZATION OF DEFERRED COSTS

[*Readers should see the Computer Sciences Corp. example on page 8.06 for an example of the amortization of deferred costs.*]

SALES INCENTIVES

Many companies offer incentives to induce sales. Some common incentives include:

- Coupons and rebates to be used in a single purchase transaction.
- Rights to discounts on future purchases.
- Volume discounts resulting in a cash rebate when a cumulative level of purchases is reached.
- "Free" products or services with the purchase of one or more products or services.

- "Points" (or "Miles") that can be accumulated and exchanged for free products or services, sometimes including products or services provided by parties other than the vendor.

This section discusses recognition of the costs of these incentives.[1]

LISTING OF APPLICABLE LITERATURE

FAS-140	Accounting for Transfers and Servicing of Financial Assets and Extinguishments of Liabilities—a replacement of FASB Statement No. 125
EITF 00-21	Revenue Arrangements with Multiple Deliverables
EITF 01-9	Accounting for Consideration Given by a Vendor to a Customer (Including a Reseller of the Vendor's Products)
EITF 02-16	Accounting by a Customer (Including a Reseller) for Certain Consideration Received from a Vendor
SAB Topic 13	Revenue Recognition
TPA 5100.50	Definition of More-Than-Insignificant Discount
TPA 5100.51	Accounting for Significant Incremental Discounts

Coupons and Rebates

Coupons (for example, a newspaper coupon for 50 cents off a box of cereal) and rebates (for example, a $20 mail-in rebate found in the box of a computer printer) are examples of sales incentives that can be exercised by the beneficiary of the offer after only a single purchase transaction. In many cases, the customer that uses the coupon or rebate will not be the direct customer of the entity that offers the incentive. For example, newspaper coupons and mail-in rebates are generally offered by product manufacturers, but are redeemed by consumers who buy the product from a retail store. It is the retail store (or perhaps a distributor that acted as an intermediary) that is the product manufacturer's direct customer; the consumer is an indirect customer. Because of this, it is possible that the consumer will use the coupon on a product the manufacturer sold to its direct customer before the incentive was even offered by the manufacturer.

---

[1] Proper classification of the costs of these incentives is also important. Classification is discussed in Chapter 11, "Presentation."

Due to this possibility, the accounting literature provides that the estimated cost of a single-purchase sales incentive should be recognized at the later of the date at which the related sale is recorded by the vendor or the date at which the sales incentive is offered (EITF 01-9, par. 22).

Of course, redemption rates on coupons and rebates are much lower than 100% of the potential redemptions. In fact, newspaper coupon redemption rates rarely, if ever, exceed single-digit percentages. Therefore, as long as a company can make a reasonable estimate of the amount of incentives to be used, it need only recognize that estimate as a reduction of revenue. As estimates change, the accrual for the potential refund should likewise be adjusted. If reasonable estimates cannot be made, then a liability should be recognized for the maximum potential amount of sales incentives that could be exercised or awarded. The following factors might impair a company's ability to make a reasonable estimate of coupon or rebate redemptions (EITF 01-9, par. 23):

1. *The offer period is long.* Obviously, the longer the offer period, the more difficult it becomes to predict the response rate. Whether an offer period is long should be determined based on the nature of the product, industry practice, and the type of customer.

2. *The absence of relevant historical experience.* Without historical experience to reference, predicting customer actions is virtually impossible. However, in the absence of company-specific experience, industry experience may be relevant.

3. *The absence of a large volume of relatively homogeneous transactions.* It is gnerally difficult to predict the actions of a particular customer. However, it is much easier to predict, on average, the actions of a large number of customers.

> **OBSERVATION:** These factors are similar to the factors needed to reliably estimate product returns or service cancellations (see Chapter 5, "Product Deliverables," and Chapter 6, "Service Deliverables," respectively) because, in both cases, the company is trying to anticipate actions of its customers.

Volume Rebates

Other sales incentives involve an offer to rebate or refund a specified amount of cash only if the customer completes a specified cumulative level of purchases or remains a customer for a specified time period. The cost of these incentives should be recognized as each of the required revenue transactions that results in progress by the customer toward earning the rebate occurs. Again, the cost to be accrued should be limited to the estimated rebates to be paid, as long as an estimate can be made. If an estimate cannot be made, the maximum rebate potentially due to the customer should be accrued (EITF 01-9, par. 30). Changes in the estimated amount of rebates or refunds and retroactive changes by a vendor to a previous offer should be recognized using a cumulative catch-up adjustment (EITF 01-9, par. 32).

> **OBSERVATION:** Although making an estimate of the amount of incentives to be used by a large group of consumers may be fairly easy due to historical experience, making an estimate of the volume rebates to be earned by a particular customer may be more difficult, especially if the incentive plan is tailored to the particular customer. Therefore, companies that offer incentives to a small number of large customers are less likely to be in a position to estimate the amounts to be earned than companies that offer incentives to a large number of small customers.

Similar accounting should be followed by the customer receiving the volume rebate. In other words, the customer should recognize a reduction of cost of sales as each of the required revenue transactions that results in progress by the customer toward earning the rebate occurs, provided the rebate is (a) payable pursuant to a binding arrangement and (b) probable and reasonably estimable. If the rebate or refund is not probable and reasonably estimable, it should be recognized as the milestones are achieved (EITF 02-16, pars. 7 and 8). Changes in the estimated amount of rebates or refunds and retroactive changes by a vendor to a previous offer should be recognized using a cumulative catch-up adjustment (EITF 02-16, par. 9).

EXAMPLE: VOLUME REBATES

BJ's Wholesale Club Form 10-K—Fiscal Year Ended January 29, 2005

Vendor Rebates and Allowances

We receive various types of cash consideration from vendors, principally in the form of rebates based on purchasing or selling certain volumes of product; time-based rebates or allowances, which may include product placement allowances or exclusivity arrangements covering a predetermined period of time; price protection rebates and allowances for retail reductions on certain merchandise; and salvage allowances for product that is damaged, defective or becomes out-of-date. We recognize such vendor rebates and allowances based on a systematic and rational allocation of the cash consideration offered to the underlying transaction that results in progress by BJ's toward earning the rebates and allowances, provided the amounts to be earned are probable and reasonably estimable. Otherwise, rebates and allowances are recognized only when predetermined milestones are met. We recognize product placement allowances as a reduction of cost of sales in the period in which we complete the arranged placement of the product. Time-based rebates or allowances are recognized as a reduction of cost of sales over the performance period on a straight-line basis. All other vendor rebates and allowances are realized as a reduction of cost of sales when the merchandise is sold or otherwise disposed of.

We also receive cash consideration from vendors for demonstrating their products in the clubs and for advertising their products, particularly in the *BJ's Journal,* a publication sent to BJ's members throughout the year. In both cases, such cash consideration is recognized as a reduction of selling, general and administrative ("SG&A") expenses to the extent it represents a reimbursement of specific, incremental and identifiable SG&A costs incurred by BJ's to sell the vendors' products. If the cash consideration exceeds the costs being reimbursed, the excess is characterized as a reduction of cost of sales. Cash consideration for product demonstrations is recognized in the period during which the demonstrations are performed. Cash consideration for advertising vendors' products is recognized in the period in which the advertising takes place.

Discounts on Future Purchases

A vendor may offer a discount on future purchases in conjunction with a current sales transaction. In some situations the discount may only be applied to future purchases of a particular product. In other situations the discount may be applied to any future purchases during a defined time period.

The Software Model (TPAs 5100.50 and 5100.51)

The accounting for discounts offered on future purchases is addressed in the software revenue recognition literature. That literature is discussed in detail in Chapter 10, "Software—A Complete Model." The software model first requires the determination of whether the discount is incremental and significant. If the discount is not considered a significant incremental discount, it does not affect the revenue accounting for the current transaction. If the discount is considered a significant incremental discount, a proportionate amount of the discount is applied to each element covered by the arrangement based on the element's fair value. Although the application of the software model to account for discounts on future purchases is not required in non-software transactions, it does present one view of the appropriate accounting for such programs, and companies outside the software industry should consider whether they should adopt a similar policy.

> **DISCLOSURE ALERT:** Companies should disclose their choice of accounting policy related to discounts offered to a customer in connection with a current transaction exercisable on future purchases by that customer. See Chapter 12, "Disclosures," for additional discussion of accounting policy disclosures.

Significant incremental discounts   A future discount on purchases is considered a significant incremental discount if it meets all of the following criteria:

- *The future discount is incremental to the range of discounts reflected in the pricing of the other elements of the arrangement.* If the customer was able to negotiate a 30% discount on the elements of the current arrangement, offering a 30% discount on additional elements does not appear to grant the customer anything that would not otherwise have been available.

- *The future discount is incremental to the range of discounts typically given in comparable transactions.* Discounts not incremental to discounts typically given in comparable transactions do not confer any value to the customer not already available to the customer.

- *The future discount is significant.* Judgment is required when assessing whether an incremental discount is significant.

An offer of a future discount that does not meet all of these criteria need not receive any accounting recognition.

Accounting for significant incremental discounts   The concept that drives the accounting for significant incremental discounts is that a proportionate amount of that significant incremental discount should be applied to each element covered by the arrangement, based on each element's fair value. Thus, accounting for significant incremental discounts is relatively straightforward if the products or services to which the discount can be applied are specified and their fair values are known.

It is when these items are not known that the accounting becomes more complicated. The accounting for situations where either the future products or services to which the discount will be applied are not specified in the arrangement or their fair values are not known depends on whether the maximum amount of the discount can be quantified:

- If the maximum amount of the discount can be quantified, that amount should be allocated to the current and future purchases assuming that the customer will purchase the minimum amount necessary to utilize the maximum discount.

- If the maximum amount of the discount cannot be quanti-fied, revenue allocated to the current and future purchases of products or services should be reduced by the rate of the dis-count (note that this results in the deferral of revenue related to the initial purchase and recognition of revenue equal to the cash received related to the future purchases).

If the maximum amount of the discount can be quantified the portion of the fee received in conjunction with the current sales transaction that is deferred should be recognized as revenue propor-tionately as the future purchases are delivered or provided (assum-ing that all other revenue recognition criteria are met) so that a consistent discount rate is applied. If the discount expires unused, the remaining deferred revenue would be recognized at that time.

If the maximum amount of the discount cannot be quantified (i.e., quantity of future products or services to which the discount may apply is not specified), the portion of the fee received in con-junction with the current sales transaction that is deferred should be recognized as revenue ratably over the discount period.

ILLUSTRATION: SIGNIFICANT INCREMENTAL DISCOUNTS

EXAMPLE 1

Facts: Manufacturer X sells Product Y for $100 (its fair value) along with a right to a discount of $50 on Product Z whose price and fair value is $150. The $50 discount is considered a significant incremental discount by Manufacturer X.

Accounting: Manufacturer X should allocate the $50 discount across Product Y and Z based on an overall discount rate of 20%. The overall dis-count rate is calculated as the ratio of the discount ($50) to the total of the fair values of Product Y and Z ($100 + $150 = $250). The amount of revenue that should be recognized related to Product Y is $80 ($100 reduced by 20%) and Product Z is $120 ($150 reduced by 20%). When the revenue recognition criteria have been met related to the sale of each product, Manufacturer X records the following journal entries:

- Upon sale of Product Y:

Cash or Receivable	$100	
Product Revenue		$80
Deferred Revenue		$20

- Upon sale of Product Z:

Cash or Receivable (sales price of $150 less $50 discount)	$100	
Deferred Revenue	$20	
Product Revenue		$120

EXAMPLE 2

Facts: Manufacturer L sells Product M for $250 (its fair value) along with a right to a discount of $100 that can be used on any of Manufacturer L's other Products N through Z. The list prices of Products N through Z range from $150 to $350 (with Product Q representing the low end of the range). The $100 discount is considered a significant incremental discount by Manufacturer L. Three months after the purchase of Product M, the customer uses the discount to purchase Product V, whose list price and fair value is $300.

Accounting: Manufacturer L should allocate the $100 discount across Product M and the future product purchase using the fair value of Product M and the lowest possible fair value of the future purchase on which the discount may be used (Product Q, $150). The overall discount rate is 25%, calculated as the ratio of the discount ($100) to the total of the fair values of Product M and Product Q ($250 + $150 = $400). The amount of revenue that should be recognized related to Product M is $187.50 ($250 reduced by 25%) and Product V is $262.50 ($300 sales price less the $100 discount plus the $62.50 deferred in connection with the Product M sale). When the revenue recognition criteria have been met related to the sale of each product, Manufacturer X records the following journal entries:

- Upon sale of Product M:

Cash or Receivable	$250.00	
Product Revenue		$187.50
Deferred Revenue		$62.50

- Upon sale of Product V:

Cash or Receivable (sales price of $300 less $100 discount)	$200.00	
Deferred Revenue	$62.50	
Product Revenue		$262.50

EXAMPLE 3

Facts: Service Provider F sells Service G for $100 (its fair value) along with a right to a discount of 50% off all future purchases of Services H through W, with a maximum discount of $200. The 50% discount is considered a significant incremental discount by Service Provider F. Three months after the purchase of Service G, the customer uses the discount to purchase Service T, whose list price and fair value is $300.

Accounting: Service Provider F should assume that the customer will purchase the level of services necessary to take advantage of the maximum discount. This level of future purchases is $400 ($200 maximum discount divided by 50% discount rate). The overall discount rate is 40%, calculated as the ratio of the maximum discount ($200) to the total of the fair value of Service G and the level of future purchases necessary to earn the maximum discount ($100 + $400 = $500). The amount of revenue that should be recognized related to Service G is $60 ($100 reduced by 40%) and Service T is $180 ($300 sales price reduced by 40%, or $300 sales price less $150 cash discount plus 75% ($300/$400) of the $40 deferred in connection with the Service G sale). When the revenue recognition criteria have been met related to the sale of each service, Service Provider F records the following journal entries:

- Upon sale of Service G:

Cash or Receivable	$100	
Service Revenue		$60
Deferred Revenue		$40

- Upon sale of Service T:

Cash or Receivable (sales price of $300 less $150 discount)	$150	
Deferred Revenue	$30	
Service Revenue		$180

The remaining deferred revenue of $10 would be recognized upon future purchases totaling at least $100 or expiration of the discount.

Additional Examples: Additional examples of accounting for discounts on future purchases can be found in Chapter 10, "Software—A Complete Model."

Breakage

As described above and in Chapter 10, "Software—A Complete Model," the software literature does not allow breakage (the portion of customers that will not take advantage of an offered discount) to be taken into account in the accounting for discounts on future purchases. This is due to the difficulty in making reasonable and reliable estimates of the breakage factor, since these transactions tend to be unique.

There are other areas of revenue accounting, however, in which the use of breakage is allowed, as long as reasonable and reliable estimates can be made. Several of these areas are discussed in Chapter 3, "General Principles." Companies that enter into a high volume of homogeneous transactions that include offers of discounts on future purchases may be able to make reliable estimates of breakage related to those offers. In these cases, it would likely be acceptable to use these estimates in the accounting for the offer. The issue of breakage should be considered carefully when adopting a policy on accounting for offers of future discounts.

Point and Loyalty Programs

Point and loyalty programs come in all shapes and sizes. Some programs involve a company granting points to their customers for every purchase with those points being redeemable by the customer in the future for goods or services provided by the company. The best-known examples of these types of programs are airline frequent flyer programs.

There are also entities that specialize in operating point and loyalty programs. These entities (referred to as program operators) administer point and loyalty programs as a main revenue producing activity. Program operators sell points in their programs to third parties, and the third parties grant those points to their customers, employees, or others. Normally, these points are redeemable for a variety of goods or services. The program operator's obligations to its customers under these arrangements may solely involve redeeming the points. However, more often the program operator also provides a variety of administrative services to its customers. These administrative services typically involve tracking the point accumulation and redemption of the customer's participants in the program.

Some programs combine these basic elements. For example, in addition to granting "miles" to their customers based on purchases, many airlines also sell miles. The purchasers may be consumers who will redeem the points themselves or they may be other service providers, such as hotels or car rental agencies that will issue the miles to their customers.

The accounting considerations for these types of arrangements vary depending on the nature of the specific point and loyalty program. The more common considerations relate to (1) granting points to customers in connection with a current sales transaction, (2) selling points to third parties, (3) being a program operator, and (4) incurring breakage.

> **DISCLOSURE ALERT:** Companies should disclose their accounting policy related to point and loyalty programs they offer and/or administer. See Chapter 12, "Disclosures," for additional discussion of accounting policy disclosures.

Granting Points as Part of Current Sales Transaction

The simplest point programs are those in which a customer earns points from purchases that are redeemable at some point in the future for additional products or services. In this transaction, the vendor has effectively sold two items to the customer: (1) the product or service delivered to the customer as part of that sales transaction and (2) a portion of the product or service that will be provided in the future upon the redemption of the points issued. The fact that multiple items have been sold suggests that the arrangement should be accounted for as a multiple-element arrangement.

As discussed in Chapter 4, "Multiple-Element Arrangements," EITF 00-21 provides criteria that must be met prior to treating elements in a multiple-element arrangement as separate elements for accounting purposes. While point and loyalty programs integrated with current sales transactions are multiple-element arrangements, such arrangements have specifically been excluded from the scope of EITF 00-21 due to their unique nature. However, it is still instructive to consider the accounting for point and loyalty programs in the context of the model in EITF 00-21. In addition, companies are not precluded from applying the model in EITF 00-21 to these types of arrangements.

In applying the model discussed in Chapter 4, "Multiple-Element Arrangements," to a sales transaction where points have been granted, one of two conclusions would be reached, depending on the specific facts and circumstances: (1) the points should be treated as a separate element for accounting purposes or (2) the points should not be treated as a separate element for accounting purposes. If the points should be treated as a separate element for accounting purposes, the amount of revenue allocated to the points would be deferred and recognized when the points are redeemed.

If the points should not be treated as a separate element for accounting purposes, the points would be bundled with the other elements in the arrangement for accounting purposes. In this situation, the company may be able to conclude that the performance obligation related to the points is inconsequential. An inconsequential performance obligation would not have to be taken into consideration when determining whether the delivery or performance criterion has been met for the other elements in the arrangement (SAB Topic 13A3c, ques. 1). The criteria for determining whether a performance obligation is inconsequential are discussed in Chapter 4. If a company concludes that its performance obligation related to the points is inconsequential, it would accrue the costs related to the points at the time it recognizes revenue related to the other elements in the arrangement. If a company concludes that the performance obligation related to the points is more than inconsequential, the earnings process related to the points must be taken into consideration when recognizing revenue for the bundled group of elements. In other words, revenue under the arrangement may not be recognizable until the points are redeemed.

> **OBSERVATION:** Most companies that issue points to their customers in programs such as the ones discussed in this section follow an accounting policy that results in (1) no revenue

being allocated to the points and (2) the costs associated with the points being accrued at the point in time that revenue is recognized for the other elements in the arrangement. The measurement of the accrued liability varies across industries and companies within the same industry. It also changes over time for the same company.

EXAMPLES: INSIGNIFICANT DELIVERABLE

AMR Corp. Form 10-K—Fiscal Year Ended December 31, 2004

Frequent Flyer Program—American uses the incremental cost method to account for the portion of its frequent flyer liability incurred when AAdvantage members earn mileage credits by flying on American or American Eagle. American's frequent flyer liability is accrued each time a member accumulates sufficient mileage in his or her account to claim the lowest level of free travel award (25,000 miles) and the award is expected to be used for free travel. American includes fuel, food, and reservations/ticketing costs in the calculation of incremental cost. These estimates are generally updated based upon the Company's 12-month historical average of such costs. American also accrues a frequent flyer liability for the mileage credits that are expected to be used for travel on participating airlines based on historical usage patterns and contractual rates.

Continental Airlines Form 10-K—Fiscal Year Ended December 31, 2004

Frequent Flyer Accounting   We utilize a number of estimates in accounting for our OnePass frequent flyer program which are consistent with industry practices.

For those OnePass accounts that have sufficient mileage credits to claim the lowest level of free travel, we record a liability for either the estimated incremental cost of providing travel awards that are expected to be redeemed or the contractual rate of expected redemption on alliance carriers. Incremental cost includes the cost of fuel, meals, insurance and miscellaneous supplies and does not include any costs for aircraft ownership, maintenance, labor or overhead allocation. A change to these cost estimates, the actual redemption activity, the amount of redemptions on alliance carriers or the minimum award level could have a significant impact on our liability in the period of change as well as future years. We also record a liability for payments we expect to make to partner airlines for OnePass members' redemptions for travel on the other airline. The liability is adjusted periodically based on awards earned, awards redeemed, changes in the incremental costs and changes in the OnePass program, and is included in the accompanying consolidated balance sheets as air traffic liability. In the fourth quarter of 2004, we recorded a change in expected future costs for frequent flyer reward redemptions on alliance carriers, resulting in a one-time increase in other operating expenses of $18 million.

American Express Company Form 10-K—Fiscal Year Ended December 31, 2004

The Company's Membership Rewards program allows enrolled cardmembers to earn points that can be redeemed for a broad range of rewards including travel, entertainment, retail certificates and merchandise. The Company establishes reserves to cover the cost of future reward redemptions and typically makes payments to its reward partners when cardmembers redeem their points. The reserve for Membership Rewards is estimated using models that analyze redemption statistics and also reflect, to a lesser extent, management's judgment regarding overall adequacy. The ultimate points to be redeemed by cardmembers are estimated based on many factors including past redemption behavior of cardmembers, product type, year of enrollment, spend level and duration in the program. Past behavior is used to predict when current enrollees will leave the program and their ultimate redemption rate.

The provision for the cost of Membership Rewards is based upon points earned that are ultimately expected to be redeemed by cardmembers and the current weighted-average cost per point of redemption. The weighted-average cost per point is affected by the mix of rewards redeemed. The provision and related balance sheet reserve for unredeemed points are impacted over time based on a number of factors including changes in the number of cardmembers in the Membership Rewards program, the actual amount of points earned and redeemed, the actual weighted-average cost per point, the availability of Membership Rewards offerings by vendors, the redemption choices made by cardmembers and future changes the Company could make to the program.

Selling Points

As discussed above, a company may sell points on a standalone basis to its customers. In other situations, the points are included in a transaction with a product or service, but are treated as a separate element for accounting purposes. In either situation, the earnings process for the points includes the redemption of those points. The initial sale of the points cannot be separated from the company's obligation to redeem the points.[2] In other words, the sale and redemption do not represent separate earnings processes, as the customer would not pay for points without the ability to redeem those points for valuable items. The earnings process related to the sale of points is therefore evaluated using a Completed Performance model, with performance not being considered complete until the points are redeemed.

---

[2] In certain programs, the issuer of the points may have the ability to discontinue the program or change its terms without any liability to the point-holder. Even in these situations, the company has the obligation to redeem points presented for redemption before the terms are changed or the program abandoned. Therefore, the accounting should reflect the redemption obligation.

EXAMPLES: SALE OF POINTS

AMR Corp. Form 10-K—Fiscal Year Ended December 31, 2004

Frequent Flyer Program—Revenue earned from selling AAdvantage miles to other companies is recognized in two components. The first component represents the revenue for air transportation sold and is valued at current market rates. This revenue is deferred and recognized over the period the mileage is expected to be used, which is currently estimated to be 28 months. The second revenue component, representing the marketing products sold and administrative costs associated with operating the AAdvantage program, is recognized immediately.

At December 31, 2004 and 2003, American estimated that approximately ten million free travel awards were expected to be redeemed for free travel on American and American Eagle. In making the estimate of free travel awards, American has excluded mileage in inactive accounts, mileage related to accounts that have not yet reached the lowest level of free travel award, and mileage in active accounts that have reached the lowest level of free travel award but which are not expected to ever be redeemed for free travel on American or participating airlines. The Company's total liability for future AAdvantage award redemptions for free, discounted or upgraded travel on American, American Eagle or participating airlines as well as unrecognized revenue from selling AAdvantage miles to other companies was approximately $1.4 billion and $1.2 billion (and is recorded as a component of air traffic liability in the consolidated balance sheets), representing 19.6 percent and 18.8 percent of AMR's total current liabilities, at December 31, 2004 and 2003, respectively.

The number of free travel awards used for travel on American and American Eagle in 2004 and 2003 was 2.6 million and 2.5 million, respectively, representing approximately 7.5 percent and 7.8 percent of passengers boarded, respectively. The Company believes displacement of revenue passengers is minimal given the Company's load factors, its ability to manage frequent flyer seat inventory, and the relatively low ratio of free award usage to total passengers boarded.

Changes to the percentage of the amount of revenue deferred, deferred recognition period, percentage of awards expected to be redeemed for travel on participating airlines, cost per mile estimates or the minimum award level accrued could have a significant impact on the Company's revenues or incremental cost accrual in the year of the change as well as in future years.

Continental Airlines Form 10-K—Fiscal Year Ended December 31, 2004

We also sell mileage credits in our frequent flyer program to participating partners, such as credit/debit card companies, phone companies, alliance carriers, hotels, car rental agencies, utilities and various shopping and gift partners. Revenue from the sale of mileage credits is deferred and recognized as passenger revenue over the period when transportation is expected to be provided, based on estimates of the fair value of tickets to be redeemed. Amounts received in excess of the tickets' fair value are recognized in income currently and classified as a reimbursement of advertising expenses. A change to the time period over which the mileage credits are used (currently six to 32 months), the actual redemption activity or our estimate of the number or fair value of tickets could have a significant impact on our revenue in the year of change as well as future years. In the fourth quarter of 2003, we adjusted our estimates of the mileage credits we expect to be redeemed for travel, resulting in a one-time increase in other revenue of $24 million.

During the year ended December 31, 2004, OnePass participants claimed approximately 1.2 million awards. These awards accounted for an estimated 5.6% of our total RPMs. We believe displacement of revenue passengers is minimal given our load factors, our ability to manage frequent flyer inventory and the low ratio of OnePass award usage to revenue passenger miles.

At December 31, 2004, we estimated that approximately 2.1 million free travel awards outstanding were expected to be redeemed for free travel on Continental, ExpressJet, CMI or participating alliance carriers. Our total liability for future OnePass award redemptions for free travel and unrecognized revenue from sales of OnePass miles to other companies was approximately $195 million at December 31, 2004. This liability is recognized as a component of air traffic liability in our consolidated balance sheet.

ILLUSTRATION: SALE OF PRODUCT AND POINTS

Facts: Company A sells a variety of household products. For each dollar of purchases, Company A's premier customers earn one point. The points may be accumulated and redeemed for a variety of Company A's household products. Point values are assigned to each of the household products for redemption purposes. Company A sells $50,000 of household products to Premier Customer D. As a result, Premier Customer D earns 50,000 points. The sales price of the household products to non-premier customers is $50,000. Company A regularly sells points on a standalone basis for $.25 per point. For purposes of this example, assume that Company A concludes that it should treat the sale of the household products separate from the sale of the points. Customer D eventually redeems the points for household products having a carrying amount of $6,000.

Accounting: Company A allocates revenue to the points based on the following calculation:

Fair value of household products	$ 50,000
Fair value of points (50,000 points @ $.25 per point)	12,500
Total fair value	62,500
Arrangement consideration	50,000
Portion allocable to household products based on relative fair values	80%
Consideration allocated to household products	40,000
Portion allocable to points based on relative fair values	20%
Consideration allocated to points	$ 10,000

Company A records the following journal entries:

- Upon meeting the revenue recognition criteria related to the sale of the household products to Customer A:

Cash or Receivable	$50,000	
Product Revenue		$40,000
Unredeemed Points Liability		$10,000

- Upon redemption of the points by Customer A:

Unredeemed Points Liability	$10,000	
Product Revenue		$10,000
Cost of Goods Sold	$ 6,000	
Product Inventory		$ 6,000

Program Operators

In many cases, program operators will agree to provide several deliverables to their customers, including the issuance and redemption of points as well as the provision of a variety of administrative services. Although these arrangements are specifically excluded from the scope of EITF 00-21, arrangements that include these elements may still be evaluated as multiple-element arrangements, with the sale and redemption of the points considered one element and the administrative services one or more other elements. Whether these elements should be treated separately for accounting purposes depends on the facts and circumstances. Chapter 4, "Multiple-Element Arrangements," provides guidance regarding separation of multiple-element arrangements under the EITF 00-21 model.

If the administrative services are treated separately, the earnings process related to these services would likely be evaluated under a Proportional Performance model, with revenue allocated to the services being recognized throughout the performance period, presuming other revenue recognition conditions are met. The revenue allocated to the points, however, would be recognized using a Completed Performance model when the points are redeemed. If the services and points are treated as one bundled element, the revenue recognition accounting policy should take into consideration all of the program operators' obligations.

Breakage

As previously discussed, breakage is a term commonly used to describe the portion of customers that will not take advantage of all of the rights they obtain in a transaction. In terms of point and loyalty programs, breakage refers to the points that will never be redeemed. Points may go unredeemed for a variety of reasons. Point holders may not accumulate a sufficient amount of points for redemption purposes. They may lose track of their points. Or, they may decide it is not worth their time or effort to redeem the points. Breakage presents a unique accounting issue—when should revenue be recognized related to points that are not expected to be redeemed?

As discussed above, EITF 01-9 addresses breakage related to redemption of rebate offers. Under the model in EITF 01-9, a company may take breakage into consideration when accruing the liability related to redemption of rebate offers if reasonable and reliable estimates of the expected level of rebate redemptions can be made. Similar analyses allow breakage to be taken into account when accounting for rights of return or cancellation (see Chapter 5, "Product Deliverables," and Chapter 6, "Service Deliverables"). If a similar analysis would provide a reliable estimate of breakage in a point program, that estimate may generally be taken into account in allocating revenue to points issued.

Even if sufficient evidence exists to estimate breakage, consideration of breakage should not result in immediate income recognition related to points that are expected to go unredeemed. Instead, the sales price related to the points should be recognized based on the number of points expected to be redeemed by the customer over the redemption period.

> **SEC REGISTRANT ALERT:** In a December 2002 speech, the SEC staff discussed the issue of breakage as it arises in situations where customers prepay, on a nonrefundable basis, for services or goods that they ultimately do not demand. The SEC staff observed that FAS-140 requires either performance or legal release to extinguish a liability. The prepayment for future delivery of services or goods creates a liability. Following a FAS-140 approach would result in no recognition of income for products or services paid for, but not demanded by the customer, until the end (or expiration) of the performance period. Alternatively, the SEC staff indicated that they will not object to revenue recognition prior to the expiration of the performance period provided both the following conditions exist:
>
> 1. Management can demonstrate that the demand for future performance is remote based on a large population of homogeneous transactions; and
>
> 2. There is objective reliable historical evidence supporting the estimate of breakage.
>
> The SEC staff also indicated that (a) it would be skeptical of an accounting model that results in immediate income for

breakage and (b) whether breakage represents revenue or a gain (i.e., other income) depends on the facts and circumstances.

ILLUSTRATION: FACTORING IN BREAKAGE

Facts: Airline J sells 1,000,000 miles to Customer D for $500,000. Airline J can make reasonable and reliable estimates of breakage and consequently determines that only 800,000 of these miles will ultimately be redeemed. During Airline J's first quarter, 250,000 of these miles are redeemed and used by Customer D.

Accounting: Airline J calculates the following amount of revenue that should be recognized for each mile as it is redeemed:

Arrangement consideration	$ 500,000
Reasonable and reliable estimate of miles to be redeemed	800,000
Revenue per mile	$ 0.625

Airline J records the following journal entries:

- Upon receiving cash from Customer D:

Cash or Receivable	$500,000	
Unredeemed Miles Liability		$500,000

- Upon redemption and use of miles by Customer D in first quarter (250,000 miles redeemed at $.625 of revenue per mile):

Unredeemed Miles Liability	$156,250	
Service Revenue		$156,250

☞ **PRACTICE POINTER:**   In the above illustration, breakage was not factored into the revenue accounting by recognizing $100,000 ($500,000 arrangement consideration × [200,000 miles not expected to be redeemed/1,000,000 miles sold]) of revenue upon the sale of the miles. This approach is inappropriate because Airline J has not yet provided any services to earn that revenue.

If an entity cannot make reasonable and reliable estimates of point redemption levels, the company must assume that all of the points will eventually be redeemed for accounting purposes. This maximum point redemption liability is reduced over time as points are redeemed or as points expire unused. If points do not have an expiration date in this situation or if a company has a policy of honoring expired points, revenue might be deferred for a longer period of time, unless and until the company is able to eventually make a reliable estimate of what percentage of points will ultimately be redeemed.

EXAMPLE: BREAKAGE

Vital Signs, Inc. Form 10-K—Fiscal Year Ended September 30, 2004

Revenue Recognition

For product sales to all customers except for certain domestic distributors, revenue, net of allowances, is recognized upon shipment to the customer, and when title passes. The Company establishes allowances for rebates and sales returns. Substantially all of the Company's sales returns relate to shipping errors or damaged goods. For service revenue, revenue is recorded when the service is performed.

The Company's sales to U.S. distributors are made at the Company's established distributor price. Since the end-user (i.e., a hospital) is typically entitled, on a case by case basis, to a price lower than the Company's established distributor price, the distributor is then due a rebate—the difference between the established price and the lower price to which the end-user is entitled—when shipment is made to the end-user. In order to properly reflect the Company's sales to distributors, the Company records the gross sale (at our established price), less the amount of the expected rebate, to arrive at the net sale. This net sale is the amount the Company expects to receive in cash from the distributor on the sale.

On a monthly basis, each distributor provides the Company with documentation of shipments to particular end-users and computes a rebate claim on such shipments. Once the distributor has provided the Company with this claim, the distributor will deduct the computed rebate from its net remittance.

The amount of the estimated rebate that has not yet been taken by the distributor through the reduction of a payment is included in the allowance for rebates, which reduces the accounts receivable on the Company's balance sheet. This allowance is calculated by adding (1) the amount of rebates claimed by the distributors through documentation but not yet reimbursed and (2) an estimate by the Company of the amount of future rebates due on any inventory that the distributors are holding at the end of each period.

For several years, the Company utilized an historical moving average calculation (comparing rebates to sales to distributors) in order to estimate the amount of rebate expense that should be recorded against gross sales in each period. Based upon a review conducted in connection with the filing of the Company's Quarterly Report on Form 10-Q for the quarter ended March 31, 2003, the Company concluded that the required allowance calculated as described in the previous paragraph was greater than previously calculated by means of the historical moving average calculation. As a result of this review of the rebate allowance, the Company recorded an additional allowance for rebates of $3,300,000 in the second quarter of fiscal 2003. The Company has continued to monitor the recorded allowance for rebates, as well as the payments made against this estimate, and believes that it is now providing a better estimate of the ultimate rebate that distributors are entitled to than the estimate arrived at through utilization of the historical moving average calculation.

RELATED PARTY SALES

Transactions reflected in financial statements are presumed to have been consummated on an arm's-length basis. This presumption is not justified when transactions are with related parties—even if the transactions are consummated on the same terms as those with unrelated parties—because the transactions may be the result of the relationship and may not have taken place without it. Accordingly, transactions with related parties require disclosure and, in certain cases, special accounting treatment. This section includes general discussions about related party sales.

General

There are no requirements in the accounting literature indicating that, in general, sales to related parties should be accounted for differently from sales to other parties. In general, such transactions should be evaluated under the same general principles as other transactions. However, the fact that the customer is a related party can affect the judgment applied to many uncertainties that may otherwise exist in the transaction.

For example, sales to related parties with rights of return might not reasonably be expected to have the same return experience as other sales with rights of return. Therefore, reliable estimates of returns on these sales might not be possible, even though reliable estimates are possible in other situations. The fact that the customer is a related party might also affect judgments about whether a transaction is in substance a consignment sale, about the effects of price protection, and about the potential consequences of warranties, acceptance provisions, and other uncertainties. At the very least, the accounting for sales to related parties that include any of these terms should be critically evaluated, separate from the evaluation on similar sales to unrelated parties.

Non-Contractual Terms

As noted throughout this book, the accounting for a revenue transaction should be based on the substantive agreement, rather than the contractually documented one, if the customer is to be given rights in addition to those documented in the agreement. When the customer is a related party, there is added risk that additional rights will be available to that customer. Every related party sale should be reviewed to determine whether, in substance, the rights and obligations in the transaction are different from the rights and obligations in sales to unrelated parties.

Transactions That Lack Substance

The accounting literature for revenue recognition (and other areas) is predicated on the assumption that the transaction being accounted for has a substantive business purpose. If that assumption is not true, the accounting should reflect that fact. One example of this is discussed in the "Nonmonetary Transactions" section of this chapter, which notes that the exchange of cash in concurrent cash transactions of the same value may not be substantive, and that the transaction may therefore need to be accounted for as a nonmonetary exchange.

When the parties to a transaction are related, there is a greater chance that the transaction, or some portion of it, does not have substance. For example, a sale with a limited right of return to a related party might, in substance, be an arrangement in which the "purchaser" is acting as a sales agent for the "seller" or the right of return may substantively be an unlimited one, because the seller would accept returns from the related party beyond the contractual limitations.

Any time the transaction, or a part of it, is determined to lack substance, the accounting should reflect that fact, either by not recognizing the transaction at all (e.g., treat the sale as a shipment on consignment), or by altering the way it is treated (e.g., as one with an unlimited right of return, rather than a limited right of return).

Disclosures

The most important consideration regarding related party transactions is often the disclosures made about them. Although the accounting literature requires certain disclosures about related party transactions, the overriding principle that should be followed when it comes to related party transactions is to disclose enough information so that financial statement users understand the magnitude of the transactions, the risks associated with them, and the reasons for them. Specific required disclosures for related party transactions are discussed in Chapter 12, "Disclosures."

> **SEC REGISTRANT ALERT:** In early 2003, the SEC staff issued the Report Pursuant to Section 704 of the Sarbanes-Oxley Act of 2002 (the Section 704 Report). In compiling the information in the Section 704 Report, the SEC staff studied enforcement actions filed during the period July 31, 1997, through July 30, 2002. One of the areas of improper accounting where a significant number of enforcement actions were brought by the SEC related to the disclosure of related party transactions. The SEC staff noted in the Section

704 Report that "Failure to disclose related party transactions hides material information from shareholders and may be an indicator of weaknesses in internal control and corporate governance procedures." This finding is a strong indication that more attention should be given to identifying and disclosing related party transactions. See Chapter 12 for a detailed discussion of required disclosures.

NONMONETARY TRANSACTIONS

In most transactions, measuring the total value of the transaction is not a difficult issue because one of the parties in the transaction pays cash. However, some transactions do not involve any cash consideration. In these transactions, there is a question as to what value to assign to the transaction.

> **OBSERVATION:**   The questions raised by nonmonetary revenue transactions relate solely to the measurement of the value of the transaction. Thus, they do not affect the timing of revenue recognition, only the amount of revenue recognized.

There are many types of nonmonetary transactions. Nonmonetary transactions that may affect a company's revenues are those where the company is giving up products, services, or other revenue-generating items that constitute the entity's ongoing major or central operations.[3] In these situations, the company is effectively being compensated for sales in the normal course of its business with a nonmonetary asset. Any transaction in which less than 25% of the fair value is paid for with monetary consideration (i.e., cash or a financial instrument) should be considered a nonmonetary transaction. The revenue side of these nonmonetary transactions is the focus of this section of the chapter.

> ☞ **PRACTICE POINTER:**   In certain situations, purchase and sales agreements are entered into concurrently with the same party. In some cases these agreements require the transfer of cash between the parties. The substance of such agreements must be scrutinized to determine whether these agreements effectively represent a nonmonetary exchange transaction. For example, Company A agrees to sell $1,000,000 of inventory

---

[3]Any other nonmonetary transaction might result in the recognition of a gain or loss, but not revenue. See Chapter 11, "Presentation" for a discussion of the difference between revenues and gains.

to Company B. Company B must make a payment to Company A in the amount of $1,000,000. At the same time, Company A agrees to purchase $1,000,000 of inventory from Company B. Company A must make a payment to Company B in the amount of $1,000,000. The sales and purchase agreements in this example effectively represent a nonmonetary transaction. The fact that cash was exchanged between the parties is meaningless in this transaction.

SEC REGISTRANT ALERT: Round-trip transactions are receiving a significant amount of attention by the SEC staff. Round-trip transactions were an area of focus in the SEC staff's Report Pursuant to Section 704 of the Sarbanes-Oxley Act of 2002 (the Section 704 Report), issued in early 2003. In compiling the information in the Section 704 Report, the SEC staff studied enforcement actions filed during the period July 31, 1997, through July 30, 2002. In addition, round-trip transactions have also been a focus in recent SEC staff speeches. The SEC staff characterizes round-trip transactions in the Section 704 Report as transactions that "involve simultaneous pre-arranged sales transactions often of the same product in order to create a false impression of business activity and revenue." The SEC staff cited a number of enforcement actions in the Section 704 Report where registrants inappropriately used round-trip transactions to boost revenue. Essentially, the types of round-trip transactions identified by the SEC staff in the Section 704 Report should be treated as nonmonetary transactions. Nonmonetary transactions that lack substance should not result in the recognition of revenue. To the extent a registrant enters into round-trip transactions, the accounting for such transactions should be carefully considered and the details of such transactions should be appropriately disclosed.

LISTING OF APPLICABLE LITERATURE

CON-5	Recognition and Measurement in Financial Statements of Business Enterprises
ARB-43, Chap. 4	Restatement and Revision of Accounting Research Bulletins, Chapter 4: Inventory Pricing
APB-29	Accounting for Nonmonetary Transactions
EITF 93-11	Accounting for Barter Transactions Involving Barter Credits
EITF 99-17	Accounting for Advertising Barter Transactions
EITF 00-8	Accounting by a Grantee for an Equity Instrument to Be Received in Conjunction with Providing Goods or Services

EITF 01-2   Interpretations of APB Opinion No. 29
FAS-153   Exchanges of Nonmonetary Assets—An
                  Amendment of APB Opinion No. 29

Basic Accounting Model

The first question that arises in a nonmonetary sale is whether any revenue at all should be recognized, as it is not clear that the "realized or realizable" criterion (see Chapter 3, "General Principles") can be met. This question is answered, however, in CON-5, which states:

> If product, services, or other assets are exchanged for nonmonetary assets that are not readily convertible into cash, revenues...may be recognized on the basis that they have been earned and the transaction is completed. Recognition...depends on the provision that the fair values involved can be determined within reasonable limits (CON-5, par. 84f).

APB-29 broadly defined an exchange (or exchange transaction) as a reciprocal transfer between entities where one entity obtains assets or services or incurs a liability by transferring assets or services or incurring other obligations to the other entity (APB-29, par. 3(c)).

In many situations, it is acceptable to recognize revenue in a nonmonetary transaction as long as the fair values in the transaction can be determined. APB-29 reinforces this conclusion, as it states that, in general, nonmonetary transactions are to be recorded at fair value, based on the fair value of the assets or services given up or those received, whichever is more readily determinable (APB-29, par. 18). FAS-153 amended APB-29 to treat a nonreciprocal transfer of a nonmonetary asset as an exchange *only* if the risks and benefits of ownership of the asset are transferred to the extent that the transferor retains no substantive continuing involvement in the asset. There are, however, exceptions to this treatment, two of which may be relevant in a nonmonetary revenue transaction.

Fair Value Not Determinable

FAS-153 also amended the APB-29 accounting treatment of nonmonetary transactions. The recorded amount (carrying amount adjusted for impairment) of the nonmonetary asset(s) surrendered, rather than the fair values of the assets exchanged, must be used to measure a nonmonetary exchange (as defined by FAS-153) under any of the following conditions:

- Neither the fair value of the asset or service received nor the fair value of the asset or service given up is readily determinable (APB-29, par. 25).

- Exchanges of product or property held for sale in the ordinary course of business for product or property that will be sold in the same line of business to customers other than the parties to the exchange.
- The transaction has no commercial substance.

FAS-153 defines an exchange with commercial substance as a transaction that is expected to significantly change the entity's future cash flows. A transaction has a substantive effect on the entity's expected future cash if either of the following conditions are satisfied:

1. The amount, timing, and risk of the future cash flows of the assets surrendered and those of the asset(s) received are significantly different.

2. The entity-specific values of the assets surrendered and those of the asset(s) received are significantly different and that difference is significant relative to the fair values of the assets exchanged. CON-7 defines entity-specific values with reference to the economics and business activities of a specific entity. (See CON-7, par. 24(b).)

Inventory-for-Inventory Exchange

An exchange of inventory held for sale in the ordinary course of business for inventory to be sold in the same line of business is recorded at the historical cost of inventory if any of the following conditions apply:

- Fair value is not determinable.
- The exchange facilitates sales to customers.
- The exchange has no commercial substance.

The objective of this requirement is to better reflect the economic substance of exchange transactions; it results in no recognition of revenue or profit (APB-29, pars. 20 and 21, as amended by FAS-153).

> **OBSERVATION:** If these exceptions did not exist, companies could artificially inflate earnings with transfers of inventory. Consider the situation where Company A transfers inventory to Company B in exchange for Company B's inventory. Both companies plan on selling the inventory they receive in the exchange to third-party customers in the normal course of their businesses. In the absence of these exceptions, both companies

would be grossing up revenues, cost of sales, and profit by exchanging inventory for inventory. Grossing up these amounts is not appropriate if the exchange does not result in sales to third-party customers or change expected future cash flows.

☛ **PRACTICE POINTER:** Even in a nonmonetary exchange that is to be recognized based on the historical cost of the asset given up, a loss should be recognized if the transaction indicates that the fair value of the asset is less than its recorded amount. The loss in these instances is required to be recorded because the market price of the inventory has been shown to be less than its cost (ARB-43, Chapter 4, Statement 7).

DISCLOSURE ALERT: See Chapter 12, "Disclosures," for information about disclosures required for nonmonetary transactions.

ILLUSTRATION: EXCHANGE OF INVENTORY FOR FIXED ASSET

Facts: Manufacturer A and Manufacturer B enter into a transaction where Manufacturer A provides inventory to Manfuacturer B in exchange for a fixed asset that it intends to use in its production process. No cash or other monetary consideration is exchanged in this transaction. The readily determinable fair value of the inventory is $25,000 and it is recorded on Manufacturer A's books at $20,000.

Accounting: As the transaction is not an inventory-for-inventory exchange and the fair value can be readily determined, Manufacturer A should account for this transaction based on the fair value of the inventory surrendered. This results in the following journal entries being recorded by Manufacturer A upon consummation of the transaction:

Journal Entry	Debit	Credit
Fixed assets	$ 25,000	
Revenue		$ 25,000
Cost of goods sold	$ 20,000	
Inventory		$ 20,000

EXAMPLE: OTHER NONMONETARY EXCHANGES

MCI Inc. Form 10-K—Fiscal Year Ended December 31, 2004

The Company enters into contracts with counter parties to provide telecommunication network capacity, and grants rights capacity on the basis of an indefeasible right of use ("IRU"). An IRU is a right to use a specified amount of capacity for a specified time period. The "indefeasible right" is one that cannot be revoked or voided. An acquirer of an IRU has the exclusive right to use the capacity represented by the IRU. It may use the capacity, leave it idle, or allow third parties to use some or all of it in return for payments or otherwise. Upon meeting certain criteria, grants of IRU of fiber or cable in exchange for cash are accounted for as sales-type leases. IRUs that do not meet this criteria, which are the most common, are accounted for as operating leases and the related cash receipt is recognized as revenue over the life of the IRU.

The Company has entered into transactions such as buying, selling, swapping or exchanging capacity to complete and complement its network. In general, these transactions represent the exchange of productive assets not held for sale in the ordinary course of business and, as such, do not result in the culmination of the earnings process. Accordingly, the Company does not recognize any revenue for these types of transactions. The Company accounts for the exchange of a non-monetary asset based on the recorded amount of the non-monetary asset relinquished with no gain or loss recognized.

Fair Value Considerations

To account for a revenue-generating nonmonetary transaction based on fair value, the fair value must be readily determinable within reasonable limits (APB-29, par. 20). All evidence should be considered to determine the fair value of the transaction. In most cases, a nonmonetary transaction involving inventory or services that a company sells in its major ongoing central line of business can be valued based on the normal selling prices of such items. Other evidence might include quoted market prices or appraisals of the assets received in the transaction. If major uncertainties exist related to recoverability of the fair value assigned to an asset received in a nonmonetary transaction, such fair value should not be considered readily determinable within reasonable limits (APB-29, par. 26).

Additional guidance on determining whether sufficient fair value evidence exists has been provided for exchanges of advertising space and for exchanges involving barter credits. Although this guidance is scoped very narrowly, it illustrates that the assessment of whether fair value can be determined within reasonable limits is one that should be made very carefully, and should involve a critical evaluation of whatever evidence of fair value is being used.

Advertising Exchange

One common type of nonmonetary exchange is an exchange of advertising space for advertising space. This is most common among Internet-based companies, but could occur in other types of companies as well. Consistent with the general model, companies that enter into advertising barter transactions should recognize revenue (and expense) at the fair value of the advertising space given up in the exchange transaction, provided that the fair value of that advertising space is determinable. If the fair value is not determinable, the transaction is recorded at the book value of the advertising space given up, which will generally be zero. Because determining the fair value of advertising space can be difficult, the EITF has provided guidance on how this determination should be made. Fair value of advertising space given up is only considered determinable within reasonable limits if it can be based on recent historical cash transactions for the sale of similar advertising space to unrelated third parties (EITF 99-17).

Historical cash transactions Cash in the context of determining the fair value of the surrendered advertising represents cash, marketable securities, or other consideration readily convertible to cash. Only cash transactions occurring within the last six months may be considered for purposes of determining the fair value of the advertising surrendered. In addition, a company should consider whether there are any internal or external factors that would suggest that six months is too long of a period to look back to for purposes of finding representative cash transactions. Once a historical cash transaction has been used to substantiate the fair value of one advertising barter transaction, it may not be used to substantiate the fair value of subsequent advertising barter transactions.

Similar advertising To consider advertising space given up in a nonmonetary transaction similar to advertising space sold in a cash transaction, both advertising spaces must (EITF 99-17):

1. Use the same media (for example, a nonmonetary transaction where space is surrendered);
2. Use the same vehicle (for example, a nonmonetary transaction where advertising space in Newspaper A is surrendered is not considered similar to a monetary transaction where advertising space in Newspaper B is surrendered); and
3. Be similar with respect to:
   a. Circulation, exposure, or saturation within an intended market;
   b. Timing (time of day, day of week, daily, weekly, 24 hours a day/7 days a week, and season of the year);
   c. Prominence (page on web site, section of periodical, location on page, and size of advertisement);
   d. Demographics of readers, viewers, or customers; and
   e. Duration (length of time advertising will be displayed).

   DISCLOSURE ALERT: See Chapter 12, "Disclosures," for information about required disclosures.

EXAMPLE: BARTER TRANSACTION POLICY

Knight Ridder, Inc. Form 10-K—Fiscal Year Ended December 26, 2004

Barter Transactions. We enter into barter transactions with other businesses and we exchange our advertising and circulation for advertising products and distribution rights for our newspapers. We also donate space to nonprofit organizations as part of our community outreach commitment. The barter transactions, typically with terms of one year or less, are valued at fair market value based on our advertising rates for the particular type of advertisement.

At December 26, 2004, we had approximately $9.5 million of future media advertisement, products and services arising from bartered transactions in net accounts receivable, which will be charged to expense as they are used. We also have as of year end $20.6 million in deferred advertising and circulation revenue arising from bartered transactions, which will be recorded as revenue when the advertisements are published and/or the copies are delivered, respectively. During the fiscal years 2004, 2003, and 2002, we recognized $15.1 million, $8.9 million, and $6.2 million, respectively, in bartered advertising and circulation revenue.

We periodically assess the recoverability of our bartered credits and receivables. Factors considered in evaluating recoverability include management's plans with respect to advertising, circulation and other expenditures for which barter credits and receivables can be used. Any impairment losses are charged to operations, as they are determined.

Barter Credits

Nonmonetary transactions may involve barter credits, that entitle the holder to receive goods or services in the future. The entity that redeems the barter credits may be the other party to the nonmonetary transaction or it may be a party whose business is operating barter credit programs. The basic accounting model in APB-29 should be applied to nonmonetary transactions involving barter credits. Special considerations when applying this model to nonmonetary transactions involving barter credits include (EITF 93-11):

- A presumption exists that the fair value of the nonmonetary asset exchanged is not greater than its carrying amount. This presumption can only be overcome if there is persuasive evidence to the contrary.
- The fair value of the nonmonetary asset in the transaction is generally considered to be more determinable than the fair value of the barter credits. The exception to this is if the barter credit can be exchanged for cash or for items with independent quoted market prices (e.g., oil, gold).

- To record the transaction at fair value, there must be the expectation that the barter credits will be redeemed in a reasonable period of time and that the party that will provide goods or services upon the redemption of the barter credits will be in existence to honor its commitment to redeem those barter credits.

ILLUSTRATION: EXCHANGE OF INVENTORY FOR BARTER CREDITS

Facts: Manufacturer C receives barter credits from Company Z in exchange for inventory. The carrying value of the inventory is $5,000. The fair value of the inventory is $4,500. Manufacturer C has received barter credits in previous nonmonetary transactions and has always redeemed these barter credits after a short period of time. The barter credits may not be redeemed for cash. Assume for purposes of this example that the barter credits will not be redeemed for inventory to be sold in the same line of business.

Accounting: Manufacturer C should account for this transaction based on the fair value of the inventory exchanged for the barter credits. This results in the following journal entries being recorded by Manufacturer A upon consummation of the transaction:

Journal Entry	Debit	Credit
Impairment loss on inventory	$ 500	
Inventory		$ 500
Cost of goods sold	$ 4,500	
Inventory		$ 4,500
Barter credits	$ 4,500	
Revenue		$ 4,500

Once barter credits have been recorded as part of a nonmonetary transaction, an impairment loss on the remaining amount of barter credits should be recognized if either (1) the fair value of the barter credits drops below their carrying amount or (2) the holder of the barter credits does not believe it is probable that it will redeem the barter credits (EITF 93-11).

Receipt of Some Monetary Consideration

When both monetary and nonmonetary consideration is received in a transaction whose accounting should be based on fair values, the monetary consideration paid or received becomes part of the fair value determination.

When both monetary and nonmonetary consideration is received in a transaction whose accounting would otherwise not be based on fair values, the effect of the monetary consideration on the accounting for the transaction depends on the magnitude of the monetary consideration. As noted earlier, if the monetary consideration received in such a transaction is 25% or more of the fair value of the transaction, then the transaction should be accounted for as a monetary transaction. Monetary transactions are recorded at fair value.

If the monetary consideration is less than 25%, its effects depend on whether the company receives or pays the monetary consideration. If the company receives monetary consideration, the transaction should, in substance, be treated as a monetary transaction (at fair value) to the extent of the monetary consideration, and a nonmonetary transaction (at historical cost) for the balance. If the company is paying monetary consideration, it should not recognize any income. The recorded amount of the asset received in the nonmonetary transaction is based on the monetary consideration paid in the transaction plus the carrying amount of the asset surrendered in the transaction (APB-29, par. 22 and EITF 01-2).

ILLUSTRATION: MONETARY CONSIDERATION LESS THAN 25% OF TRANSACTION'S FAIR VALUE

Facts: Manufacturer A and Manufacturer B enter into a transaction involving the exchange of inventory. Manufacturer A and Manufacturer B operate in the same line of business and plan on selling the inventory received in the exchange to end-users. Additional facts related to the transaction are as follows:

	Manufacturer	
	A	B
Fair value of inventory provided	$15,000	$12,000
Fair value of inventory received	$12,000	$15,000
Recorded amount of inventory provided	$8,000	$7,000
Cash consideration received	$3,000	None
Cash consideration paid	None	$3,000

Accounting: Since this is an inventory-for-inventory exchange in the same line of business and the monetary consideration is less than 25% of the fair value of the transaction, it should not be accounted for as a monetary transaction at fair value.

Since Manufacturer A is receiving monetary consideration, it should account for the transaction as follows:

Monetary consideration received	$ 3,000	$ 3,000
Fair value of transaction	15,000	

Percentage of the transaction that is monetary	20%
Recorded cost of inventory transferred	8,000

Cost of sales for the portion of the inventory "sold" for monetary consideration	1,600
Profit to be recognized	$ 1,400

Journal Entry	Debit	Credit
Cost of Sales	$ 1,600	
Inventory		$ 1,600
Cash	$ 3,000	
Revenue		$ 3,000

These entries result in the inventory received by Manufacturer A having an initial carrying amount of $6,400. Manufacturer A only records revenue to the extent of cash consideration since this is an inventory-for-inventory exchange.

Since Manufacturer B is paying monetary consideration, it should account for the transaction as follows:

Journal Entry	Debit	Credit
Inventory	$ 3,000	
Cash		$ 3,000

No revenue or cost of sales results from this transaction for Manufacturer B since it is an inventory-for-inventory exchange where Manufacturer B is paying cash consideration.

EXAMPLE: NONMONETARY TRANSACTION ACCOUNTING POLICY

Seitel, Inc. Form 10-K—Fiscal Year Ended December 31, 2004

In certain cases, the Company will take ownership of a customer's seismic data in exchange for a non-exclusive license to selected data from the Company's library. Occasionally, in connection with specific data acquisition contracts, the Company receives both cash and ownership of seismic data from the customer as consideration for the underwriting of new data acquisition. These exchanges are referred to as non-monetary exchanges. A non-monetary exchange always complies with the following criteria:

- The data license delivered is always distinct from the data received;
- The customer forfeits ownership of its data; and
- The Company retains ownership in its data.

This exchange is not a "like kind" exchange because the Company receives ownership of distinct seismic data to be added to its library, and this data may be relicensed by the Company on a continuing basis, in exchange for a data license. Once data selection or creation is completed, the exchange represents the culmination of the earnings process with the customer and is not merely an exchange between two seismic companies.

In non-monetary exchange transactions, the Company records a data library asset for the seismic data received at the time the contract is entered into and recognizes revenue on the transaction in equal value in accordance with its policy on revenue from data licenses, that is, when the data is selected by the customer, or revenue from data acquisition, as applicable. The data license to the customer is in the form of one of four basic forms of contracts discussed above. These transactions are valued at the fair value of the data received or delivered, whichever is more readily determinable.

Fair value of the data exchanged is determined using a multi-step process as follows.

- First, the Company determines the value of the license granted to the customer. The range of cash transactions by the Company for the licenses of similar data during the prior six months for licenses in the United States and for the prior twelve months for licenses in Canada are evaluated. In evaluating the range of cash transactions, the Company does not consider transactions that are disproportionately high or low.

- Second, the Company considers the value of the data received from the customer. In determining the value of the data received, the Company considers the age, quality, current demand and future marketability of the data as well as the cost that would be required to create the data. In the United States, the Company applies a limitation on the value it assigns per square mile on the data exchanged. In Canada, in the event of a difference greater than 2% between the value of the license granted and the value of the data received, the Company assigns the lower value to the exchange.

- Third, the Company obtains concurrence from a third party on the portfolio of all non-monetary exchanges of $500,000 or more in order to support the Company's valuation of the data received. The Company obtains this concurrence on an annual basis, usually in connection with the preparation of its annual financial statements.

Due to the Company's revenue recognition policies, revenue recognized on non-monetary transactions may not occur at the same time the seismic data acquired is recorded as an asset. The activity related to non-monetary exchanges was as follows (in thousands):

	Year Ended December 31,		
	2004	2003	2002
Seismic data library additions	$ 10,670	$13,033	$13,551
Revenue recognized based on selections of data	16,459	14,044	44,965
Revenue recognized related to acquisition contracts	1,908	624	–

Payment in the Form of Equity Securities

One type of nonmonetary transaction that is somewhat common is the sale of products, services, or intellectual property for equity of the customer. In many cases, this transaction raises no questions other than those that exist in most nonmonetary transactions. However, an additional question that arises in certain sales for equity securities is what date to use in measuring the fair value of the equity instruments received. The question often arises because the instrument only vests as performance occurs or upon its completion. Thus, until that point, there is some question as to whether the vendor will ever receive the benefits embodied in the equity instrument.

The EITF discussed this question in EITF 00-8, and reached a consensus that the vendor should measure the fair value of the equity instruments as of the earlier of the following dates (EITF 00-8, par. 4):

1. The date the parties come to a mutual understanding of the terms of the equity-based compensation arrangement and a performance commitment is reached. A performance commitment is a commitment under which performance by the seller to earn the equity instruments is probable because of sufficiently large disincentives for nonperformance. Neither the forfeiture of the equity instruments nor the ability to sue for nonperformance, in and of themselves, represent a sufficiently large disincentive.

2. The date the vendor completes the performance necessary to earn the equity instruments (that is, the vesting date).

If, after the measurement date described above, the quantity or any of the terms of the equity instruments are dependent on the achievement of performance conditions, the initial measurement should be the one with the lowest value possible, as any amount above that would not be considered fixed or determinable. Changes in the fair value of the equity instrument that result from an adjustment to the instrument upon the achievement of a performance condition should be measured as additional revenue from the transaction by calculating the increase in the fair value of the instrument due to the changes (EITF 00-8, par. 6).

> **OBSERVATION:** The instruments in these transactions may also experience changes in fair value after the measurement date for various other reasons. Changes in fair value of the equity instruments after the measurement date unrelated to the achievement of performance conditions should be accounted for in accordance with the relevant literature on the accounting and reporting for investments in equity instruments, and should not affect the amount of revenue recognized.

DISCLOSURE ALERT: See Chapter 12, "Disclosures," for information about required disclosures.

SEC REGISTRANT ALERT: As discussed earlier, round-trip transactions are receiving a significant amount of attention by the SEC staff. One round-trip transaction discussed by the SEC staff in a speech in December 2002 involved a vendor delivering cash and products or services and concurrently receiving cash and an equity interest in the customer. The substance of this transaction may be that the vendor is delivering products or services in exchange for an equity interest. If this is the substance of the transaction, the vendor should (a) record the investment in the counter-party at the fair value of either the shares received or the goods or services sold, whichever is more readily determinable, (b) record the net cash outlay or receipt, and (c) recognize as revenue the difference between the value of the investment received and the net cash outlay. The SEC staff has been clear that the substance of round-trip transactions should govern form. To the extent a registrant enters into round-trip transactions, the accounting for such transactions should be carefully considered and the details of such transactions should be appropriately disclosed.

CHAPTER 9
CONTRACT ACCOUNTING

CONTENTS

SURVEY OF APPLICABLE LITERATURE

One of the few areas in which a comprehensive model for revenue recognition exists is accounting for construction contracts. The basic model was first provided in ARB-45 in 1955. Because ARB-45 did not provide much incremental guidance on application of the basic model, the standard-setters determined that additional guidance was needed. They also determined that the scope of ARB-45 (limited to long-term construction contracts) had not kept pace with the changing times. As a result, SOP 81-1 was issued in 1981. SOP 81-1 builds on the basic model in ARB-45 and applies to both construction-type and certain production-type contracts.

In addition to ARB-45 and SOP 81-1, audit and accounting guides for construction contractors (AAG-CON) and federal government contractors (AAG-FGC) have also been issued. These guides provide supplemental information on the application of the principles found in ARB-45, SOP 81-1, and ARB-43 (which deals specifically with accounting for government contracts). To the extent a contractor is dealing with a government contract, ARB-43 and AAG-FGC should be consulted for unique issues related to accounting for those types of contracts, as this chapter will not address those issues.

LISTING OF APPLICABLE LITERATURE

ARB-43, Ch. 11	Restatement and Revision of Accounting Research Bulletins, Chapter 11, Government Contracts
ARB-45	Long-Term Construction-Type Contracts
FAS-5	Accounting for Contingencies
SOP 81-1	Accounting for Performance of Construction-Type and Certain Production-Type Contracts
SOP 97-2	Software Revenue Recognition
EITF 00-21	Revenue Arrangements with Multiple Deliverables
AAG-CON	Audit and Accounting Guide for Construction Contractors
AAG-FGC	Audit and Accounting Guide for Audits of Federal Government Contractors
REG S-X, Rule 5-02	Financial Statement Requirements, Commercial and Industrial Companies, Balance Sheets

OVERVIEW

As discussed throughout this book, one of the more important questions in recognizing revenue for any transaction is whether the Completed Performance or Proportional Performance model should be used to determine when the revenue has been earned. As noted in Chapter 3, "General Principles," product sales are generally analyzed under the Completed Performance model, such that revenue is not considered earned until the product is complete and delivered to the customer.

However, accounting standard-setters have determined that certain product transactions have characteristics that may make the use of the Proportional Performance model appropriate. The transactions that may fall into this category are those that call for the delivery of a product that is built or constructed to the customer's specifications, rather than through the vendor's normal processes. Because the product being built or constructed is generally not useful to the vendor in any way other than to fulfill the applicable contract, revenue in these transactions is considered to be earned during production, rather than only upon delivery of the completed product, as long as certain conditions are met.

The contract accounting literature generally specifies that costs should be recognized in proportion to revenue. Thus, unlike other applications of the Proportional Performance model, in which costs of performance are recognized as incurred, the contract accounting literature specifies that costs should be recognized on a proportional (or ratable) basis throughout the term of the contract.

Although SOP 81-1 does not specifically include discussion of the four general conditions for revenue recognition, each of those conditions is, in substance, included in the contract accounting guidance.

SCOPE

Because of the significant differences in the recognition of both revenue and costs for contracts that fall within the scope of SOP 81-1, it is important to assess the nature of a contract to determine whether the standard applies. Only contracts that fall within the scope of SOP 81-1 should follow its provisions. In addition, it is generally not appropriate to analogize to SOP 81-1 for a contract that is not within its scope. Therefore, revenue from a product sale that does not fall within the scope of SOP 81-1 may not be recognized under a Proportional Performance model, and costs on a contract that do not fall within the scope of SOP 81-1 should not be smoothed over the course of the contract.

> **SEC REGISTRANT ALERT:** As discussed above, it is generally not appropriate for any company to analogize to SOP 81-1. In a December 2002 speech, the SEC staff discussed the issue of applying percentage-of-completion accounting to service contracts that are outside the scope of SOP 81-1. Specifically, the SEC staff stressed that SOP 81-1, and therefore percentage-of-completion accounting, should **not** be applied to service contracts that do not fall within its scope. As discussed below, the types of service contracts that fall within the scope of SOP 81-1 are limited to contracts for architectural or engineering design services and construction consulting services.

Contracts that fall within the scope of SOP 81-1 include those construction-type and certain production-type contracts where facilities are built, goods are manufactured, or certain defined, related services are performed by a contractor[1] to customer specifications. However, contracts where a company is using its standardized manufacturing processes or regular marketing channels generally do not fall within the scope of SOP 81-1 even if the subject of the contract is being manufactured or performed by the company to customer specifications. Arrangements that fall within the scope of SOP 81-1 must be supported with legally enforceable, binding agreements

---

[1]"Contractor" will be used throughout this chapter to describe the selling party in a contract that falls within the scope of SOP 81-1.

between the customer and contractor.[2] Duration of the contract (i.e., period of time to construct, produce, or provide) is not a defining factor for purposes of determining whether a contract falls within the scope of SOP 81-1. However, it may be a factor in determining whether the percentage-of-completion or completed-contract method should be used to account for the contract.

Examples of contracts that fall within the scope of SOP 81-1 include:

- Construction contracts, such as those of general building, heavy earth moving, dredging, demolition, design-build contractors, and specialty contractors (for example, mechanical, electrical, or paving) and related service contracts such as contracts for construction consulting services (for example, agency contracts or construction management agreements), and contracts performed by architects, engineers, or architectural or engineering design firms (SOP 81-1, par. 13).

- Contracts to design and build ships and transport vessels (SOP 81-1, par. 13).

- Contracts to design, develop, manufacture, or modify complex aerospace or electronic equipment to a customer's specifications or to provide services related to the performance of such contracts (SOP 81-1, par. 13).

- Contracts for the sale of software that involve significant modification or customization of software (SOP 97-2, par. 7).

Contracts that do not fall within the scope of SOP 81-1 include contracts dealing with the sale of products produced using the contractor's standardized manufacturing process (even if produced to the customer's specifications) and marketed using the contractor's regular marketing channels. This includes sales of goods from inventory or from homogeneous continuing production. In addition, service contracts, other than those related to the construction industry, do not fall within the scope of SOP 81-1.

> **OBSERVATION:** Understanding the nature of the contract and determining whether the contract falls within or outside the scope of SOP 81-1 is an important exercise because it could have significant effects on the recognition of the related revenues and costs. For example, a contract to build a piece of equipment that falls within the scope of SOP 81-1 may be accounted for using a Proportional Performance model (percentage-of-completion method) which results in revenues and costs being recognized as work is performed. However, if that

---

[2]This is equivalent to the "persuasive evidence of an arrangement" condition that is generally required in order to recognize revenue on other transactions.

contract does not fall within the scope of SOP 81-1, then the
related revenue and costs will be recognized at a point in time
under a Completed Performance model.

The scope provisions of SOP 81-1 are often misapplied to contracts that call for the production of a large piece of equipment built
to a customer's specifications. This type of a contract does not automatically fall within the scope of SOP 81-1 solely because the equipment is being built to the customer's specifications. A question the
contractor must consider in this situation is whether the large piece
of equipment is produced using the contractor's standardized manufacturing process and marketed using the contractor's regular
marketing channels. If the contractor's standardized manufacturing
process or regular marketing channels are used, the contract does
not fall within the scope of SOP 81-1. Of course, judgment must be
exercised in considering whether, and to what extent, the contractor's standardized manufacturing process and regular marketing
channels are being used.

ACCOUNTING METHODS

SOP 81-1 prescribes two methods to account for contracts that fall
within its scope: (1) percentage-of-completion and (2) completed-
contract. The percentage-of-completion method generally provides for contract revenues and contract costs to be recognized
under a Proportional Performance model as the contractor performs under the contract. The completed-contract method generally provides for contract revenues and contract costs to be
recognized under a Completed Performance model when the contract is complete or substantially complete. These methods are not
interchangeable for the same set of facts and circumstances. That
is, the decision about which method to use must be based on an
analysis of the arrangement using the specific factors contained in
SOP 81-1; it is not a policy choice to be made by the contractor. In
any given set of facts and circumstances, one of the two methods
is required.

Percentage-of-completion or completed-contract are the only
methods prescribed by SOP 81-1. Other methods, such as those
where revenue is recognized based on progress billings or receipts,
and costs are recognized when incurred, are not acceptable.

Circumstances of Use—Percentage-of-Completion

Given the nature of the contracts that fall within the scope of SOP
81-1, the percentage-of-completion method is viewed as being the

model that best reflects the economics of those types of contracts. Contracts that fall within the scope of SOP 81-1 generally provide for ownership of the asset being built or manufactured to transfer to the customer over time, as the asset is being built or manufactured. The contractor may have lien rights to the asset from a collectibility perspective, but it generally does not own the in-progress asset. Furthermore, the contractor is generally compensated as it performs the work (through progress payments). In essence, the percentage-of-completion method provides synchronization between revenue recognition and transfer of ownership.

The percentage-of-completion method is used in situations with the following characteristics (SOP 81-1, par. 23):

- The contractor can consistently make reasonably dependable estimates of contract revenues, contract costs and progress towards completion.

- The contract entered into by the contractor and the customer spells out the terms of the contract including the specific rights and obligations of the customer and contractor, the contractor's compensation, and settlement terms.[3]

- The customer and contractor are both expected to satisfy their contractual obligations.

Ability to Make Estimates

The contractor's ability to make reasonably dependable estimates is presumed given the nature of the industry in which it operates. That is, a contractor must be able to make reasonably dependable estimates in order to enter into profitable contracts and sustain its business model. The presumption that a contractor can make reasonably dependable estimates can only be overcome if persuasive evidence exists to support the conclusion that it cannot make such estimates (SOP 81-1, par. 24).

> **OBSERVATION:** In general, when the ability to make estimates could affect recognition, the presumption is that estimates cannot be made unless persuasive evidence indicates they are reliable. As discussed above, the contract accounting literature starts from a different perspective. However, the intention is the same—estimates should be used only if they are judged to be reasonable and reliable.

---

[3]This point is generally consistent with the "fixed or determinable fee" condition generally required to recognize revenue on other transactions.

Estimates, by their very nature, are not precise. As such, being able to make reasonably dependable estimates allows for deviations between estimates and actual results. It is when these deviations are consistently significant that the contractor should reconsider whether it has the ability to make reasonably dependable estimates. In these situations, the contractor should attempt to determine why its estimates are consistently and significantly different from actual results and correct its estimation process, before discontinuing the use of the percentage-of-completion method.

A contractor may not be able to make reasonably dependable estimates due to the existence of an "inherent hazard." Inherent hazards raise questions regarding the ability of the customer or contractor to satisfy obligations under the contract. Inherent hazards occur infrequently and outside the normal contract estimation process and generally are not part of the contractor's typical activities. These factors distinguish an inherent hazard from normal recurring business risks. Examples of inherent hazards include contracts where completion is questionable due to external factors (e.g., pending legislation or litigation), and contracts where the item being manufactured or built is physically at risk due to external developments (e.g., condemnation or expropriation). Given the unique nature of inherent hazards, there must be specific, persuasive evidence of the existence of such a hazard to support the conclusion that reasonably dependable estimates cannot be made due to that inherent hazard (SOP 81-1, pars. 28-29).

Circumstances of Use—Completed Contract

The completed-contract method should be used in either of the following circumstances (SOP 81-1, pars. 31-32):

- Where the results would not differ materially from using the percentage-of-completion method.

- Where reasonably dependable estimates of contract revenues, contract costs or progress towards completion cannot be made.

A short-term contract is an example of a situation where the results of applying the completed-contract method generally would not differ materially from using the percentage-of-completion method. As such, if the contractor enters into predominantly short-term contracts, adopting the completed-contract method as its accounting policy generally would be appropriate.

EXAMPLE: COMPLETED CONTRACT METHOD-BASIC MODEL

Crown Castle International Corp. Form 10-K—Fiscal Year Ended December 31, 2004

Network services revenues are generally recognized under the completed contract method. Under the completed contract method, revenues and costs for a particular project are recognized in total at the completion date. When using the completed contract method of accounting for network services revenues, we must accurately determine the completion date for the project in order to record the revenues and costs in the proper period. For antenna installations, we consider the project complete when the customer can begin transmitting its signal through the antenna. We must also be able to estimate losses on uncompleted contracts; as such losses must be recognized as soon as they are known. The completed contract method is used for projects that require relatively short periods of time to complete (generally less than one year). We do not believe that our use of the completed contract method for network services projects produces operating results that differ substantially from the percentage-of-completion method.

To the extent the completed-contract method is used because the contractor cannot make reasonably dependable estimates of either contract revenues, contract costs, or progress toward completion, the contractor must use the completed-contract method for the duration of the contract. That is, the contractor may not change to the percentage-of-completion method if it subsequently determines that it can make reasonably dependable estimates of contract revenues, contract costs, and progress toward completion.

Basic Accounting Policy

A company will generally determine its basic accounting model for contracts within the scope of SOP 81-1 based on the typical nature of its contracts. However, a company may subsequently enter into a contract that is unique or atypical. In those situations, the company should consider whether a departure from its basic accounting model is necessary to account for those unique or atypical facts and circumstances. If a departure from its basic accounting model is necessary for such a contract, the contractor should disclose that departure (SOP 81-1, par. 31).

> **OBSERVATION:** A contractor that departs from its basic accounting model to account for a unique or atypical contract

is not changing its accounting policy. The contractor is merely using a different accounting policy for a different type of contract.

Other factors that may cause a contractor to depart from its basic accounting model include (1) the determination that reasonably dependable estimates cannot be made for a specific contract or (2) the existence of an inherent hazard related to a specific contract. Again, any departures from the basic accounting model should be disclosed.

COMBINING OR SEGMENTING CONTRACTS

Prior to applying either the percentage-of-completion or completed-contract method, the contractor must first determine whether it is accounting for an individual contract, a group of contracts, or a segment of an individual or group of contracts. In other words, the contractor must determine the unit-of-accounting. Normally, the unit-of-accounting is an individual contract. However, situations may arise where it is appropriate to combine one or more contracts and account for them as if they were one contract. Or, situations may arise where it is appropriate to segment a contract or group of contracts into two or more pieces and account for each piece as if it were an individual contract. Specific criteria have been developed to determine when contracts may be combined or segmented.

Combining Contracts

It is generally appropriate to combine contracts when the individual contracts are so closely related that accounting for the contracts separately may misrepresent earned revenues, costs of earned revenues and gross profit. The interrelated nature of the contracts suggests that the combined gross profit from the contracts should be recognized consistently as the interrelated work is performed.

The following questions must be considered by a contractor in determining whether contracts should be combined for accounting purposes (questions based on the criteria in SOP 81-1, par. 37):

1. *Were the contracts negotiated as a single package in the same economic environment with an overall profit objective?* Contracts do not necessarily have to be negotiated at the exact same time to be considered part of a single package. However, the time period between the negotiation of the contracts should be reasonably short to reach such a conclusion. Otherwise, the likelihood that the

contracts were negotiated in the same economic environment is diminished.

2. *Do the contracts, in essence, represent an agreement to perform a single project?* The elements, phases, or units of output of a group of contracts must be interrelated and interdependent to be considered a single project. The interrelationship and interdependence should extend to the design, technology, function, or ultimate purpose or use of the outputs from each contract.

3. *Do the contracts require closely related construction activities with substantial common costs that cannot be separately identified with, or reasonably allocated to, the individual contracts?* When substantial costs benefit multiple contracts, it may be an indication that the contracts are substantively part of the same arrangement.

4. *Are the contracts performed concurrently or in a continuous sequence under the same project management at the same location or at different locations in the same general vicinity?*

5. *Do the contracts constitute in substance an agreement with a single customer?* Contracts do not necessarily have to be negotiated with the exact same party to be considered a contract with a single customer. The assessment of the other conditions that must be met to combine contracts should be considered in this context. Following are examples of questions that should be considered by the contractor in this regard:

   - Did the different parties negotiate the contracts together?
   - Do the different parties operate in the same economic environment?
   - Is it reasonable to conclude that the contracts represent one single project that will benefit both parties?

Understanding the relationship between the parties and each party's intentions relative to the contracts are important considerations in determining whether the contracts were effectively negotiated with a single customer. For example, the more distant the relationship between the parties, the less likely that a conclusion will be reached that the contracts were negotiated with a single customer.

If the answer to each of the foregoing questions is "yes," a group of construction- or production-type contracts may be combined for accounting purposes. If the answer to any of the foregoing questions is "no" when dealing with a group of *construction-type* contracts, such contracts may not be combined for accounting purposes. If the answer to any of the questions is "no" when dealing with a group of *production-type* contracts, such contracts may still be combined into groupings such as production lots or releases for the purposes of accumulating and allocating production costs to units produced or delivered on the basis of average unit costs, if the following two conditions are met (SOP 81-1, par. 38):

1. The contracts are with one or more customers for the production of substantially identical units of a basic item produced concurrently or sequentially, and

2. Revenue on the contracts is recognized under the percentage-of-completion method using the units-of-delivery approach discussed later in this chapter.

Segmenting a Contract or Group of Contracts

A contract or group of contracts may contain various elements or phases. The contractor may agree to perform these elements or phases independently of each other. Furthermore, each element or phase may intentionally and rightfully have different profit margins. Treating this contract or group of contracts as a single contract for accounting purposes may not necessarily reflect the true economics of the individual elements or phases. To address this situation, three sets of very specific criteria have been established to determine whether a contract or group of contracts may be segmented for accounting purposes.

The first set of criteria allows a contract or group of contracts to be segmented if three actions were taken during the negotiation of the contract or group of contracts and if verifiable evidence exists to document that these actions were taken. These three actions are (SOP 81-1, par. 40):

1. The contractor submitted bona fide proposals on the separate components of the project and on the entire project;

2. The customer had the right to accept the proposals on either basis; and

3. The aggregate amount of the proposals on the separate components approximated the amount of the proposal on the entire project.

If these steps were taken, but not documented, or if these steps were not taken, the contract or group of contracts may still be segmented if all of a second set of criteria are met. The second set of criteria follows (SOP 81-1, par. 41):

1. The terms and scope of the contract or project clearly call for separable phases or elements;

2. The separable phases or elements of the project are often bid or negotiated separately;

3. The market assigns different gross profit rates to the segments because of factors such as different levels of risk or differences in

the relationship of the supply and demand for the services provided in the different segments;

4. The contractor has a significant history of providing similar services to other customers under separate contracts for each significant segment to which a profit margin higher than the overall profit margin on the project is ascribed;

5. The significant history with customers who have contracted for services separately is one that is relatively stable in terms of pricing policy rather than one unduly weighted by erratic pricing decisions;

6. The excess of the sum of the prices of the separate elements over the price of the total project is clearly attributable to cost savings incident to combined performance of the contract obligations; and

7. The similarity of services and prices in the contract segments and the prices of such services to other customers contracted separately should be documented and verifiable.

In the absence of satisfying the first set of criteria, a *construction-type* contract or group of contracts may be segmented only if all of the second set of criteria have been met. If neither the first or second set of criteria have been satisfied for a *construction-type* contract or group of contracts, the contract or group of contracts may not be segmented. However, a *production-type* contract or group of contracts that do not meet either the first or second set of conditions may still be combined into groupings such as production lots or releases for the purposes of accumulating and allocating production costs to units produced or delivered on the basis of average unit costs, if the following two conditions are met (SOP 81-1, pars. 38 and 42):

1. The contracts are with one or more customers for the production of substantially identical units of a basic item produced concurrently or sequentially, and

2. Revenue on the contracts is recognized under the percentage-of-completion method using the units-of-delivery approach discussed later in this chapter.

A production-type contract that does not satisfy any of the three sets of conditions provided herein may not be segmented.

> **OBSERVATION:** The segmentation criteria above are a specific methodology for separating elements in a multiple-element arrangement. These criteria are significantly different from, and more restrictive than, those criteria that must be met in other situations. Models available to separate multiple-element arrangements in other situations may not be applied to separating elements within a contract or group of contracts that falls within the scope of SOP 81-1. Only the criteria discussed herein may be applied to segment such contracts.

PRACTICE ALERT: The EITF provided guidance on separating multiple-element arrangements in EITF 00-21. As discussed in more detail in Chapter 4, "Multiple-Element Arrangements," EITF 00-21 does not apply to arrangements that fall within the scope of higher-level literature. As such, arrangements that fall within the scope of SOP 81-1 do not fall within the scope of EITF 00-21, and the segmenting guidance in SOP 81-1 should continue to be applied. However, if an arrangement includes elements that fall within the scope of SOP 81-1 **and** elements that fall outside the scope of SOP 81-1, EITF 00-21 should be applied to separate the SOP 81-1 elements and the non-SOP 81-1 elements. Further separation of the SOP 81-1 elements is governed by the segmenting guidance in SOP 81-1. For further discussion of the scope of EITF 00-21, see Chapter 4 and Chapter 10, "Software—A Complete Model."

Summary

For ease of discussion throughout the rest of this chapter, it is assumed that the unit of accounting is an individual contract. This does not change the fact, however, that if contracts are combined or segmented, that the combined group of contracts or each individual contract segment would be the unit of accounting in those situations. It is to those units of accounting (in their combined or segmented form) that either the percentage-of-completion or completed-contract method would be applied.

PERCENTAGE-OF-COMPLETION METHOD

Application of the percentage-of-completion method results in contract revenues and contract costs being recognized as the contractor performs under the contract. This method requires the contractor to estimate its progress towards completion and determine or calculate the amount of revenues, costs, or gross profit to be recognized in each accounting period. These aspects of the percentage-of-completion method raise the following questions:

- What happens if the contractor cannot make specific or precise reasonably dependable estimates?

- How may the contractor measure its progress toward completion?

- How should the contractor determine or calculate revenues, costs, or gross profit to be recognized in each accounting period?

Estimates of Contract Amounts

Contract revenues, contract costs, and progress toward completion must be estimated by the contractor to determine the amount of revenues, costs, or gross profits to be recognized in a particular period. Normally, the contractor is able to determine and use its best estimates of these amounts. However, in some cases the contractor may only be able to (1) determine a range of estimated amounts or (2) determine only that it will not incur a loss. In extreme situations, the contractor will not be able to make any reasonably dependable estimates or even determine that it will not incur a loss. As discussed above, in these extreme situations, the completed-contract method should be used.

Range of Amounts

How a contractor proceeds in a situation where it can only estimate a range of contract revenues and contract costs depends on whether the contractor can determine which estimates within the ranges are most likely to occur. If the contractor can make those determinations, those amounts should be used. If the contractor cannot make those determinations, the amounts within the ranges that should be used are those that would result in the lowest probable profit margin (the lowest contract revenue estimate and the highest contract cost estimate) (SOP 81-1, par. 25).

ILLUSTRATION: LOWEST PROBABLE PROFIT MARGIN

Facts: Contractor A enters into a contract with Customer X to construct a unique building. This is the largest building by far that Contractor A has ever agreed to construct for a customer. As such, it is only able to estimate the range of contract revenues and contract costs expected under the contract at the end of the first reporting period affected by the contract. At the end of such reporting period, Contractor A estimates that its total contract revenues will range from $5.2 million to $5.5 million and that its total contract costs will range from $4.5 million to $4.8 million. Because of the lack of similarity between this contract and other contracts Contractor A has entered into, Contractor A is not able to determine which point within those ranges is most likely to occur. At the end of the first reporting period, Contractor A has incurred $1.2 million of contract costs, and estimates that the project is 25% complete.

Accounting: Because Contractor A cannot determine which amounts within the contract revenue and contract cost ranges are most likely to occur, it should use the combination of amounts that results in the lowest profit margin. Consider the following possibilities:

	(in thousands)			
Contract Revenues	Highest		Lowest	
Contract Costs	Highest	Lowest	Highest	Lowest
Percentage-complete	25%	25%	25%	25%
Contract revenues	$ 5,500	$ 5,500	$ 5,200	$ 5,200
Calculated revenues	1,375	1,375	1,300	1,300
Contract costs	4,800	4,500	4,800	4,500
Calculated costs	1,200	1,125	1,200	1,125
Calculated profit margin	$ 175	$ 250	$ 100	$ 175

The combination of the lowest contract revenues and highest contract costs results in the lowest overall profit margin. As such, those are the amounts Contractor A should use in calculating earned revenues under the percentage-of-completion method.

No Loss Incurrence

In some situations, it may be impractical for the contractor to estimate either specific amounts or ranges of contract revenues and contract costs. In these situations, if the contractor can at least determine that it will not incur a loss, then a zero profit model should be used. The zero profit model results in the recognition of equal amounts of revenues and costs. This method should only be used if more precise estimates cannot be made and its use must be discontinued when such estimates are obtained. Once a contractor has more precise estimates, the change should be treated as a change in an accounting estimate (SOP 81-1, pars. 25 and 33).

> **OBSERVATION:** If in the previous example, Contractor A was not able to determine a range of contract revenues and contract costs, but could at least ascertain that it would not incur a loss on the contract, Contractor A would recognize $1.2 million of revenue in the first reporting period affected by the contract.

> ☞ **PRACTICE POINTER:** Before moving from the percentage-of-completion method to the completed-contract method due

to the inability to estimate, the contractor should review the contractual terms to determine whether the contractor is protected from incurring a loss. If the contractor is contractually protected from incurring a loss (e.g., contract terms provide for the contractor to be compensated on a cost-plus basis), the contractor should continue to use the percentage-of-completion method, but with a zero profit model. To illustrate the significance of this decision, consider the previous example. Use of the percentage-of-completion method with a zero profit model results in the recognition of $1.2 million of revenue and expense in the first reporting period affected by the contract. In contrast, no revenue or expense would be recognized if Contractor A used the completed-contract method.

Measuring Progress Toward Completion

A variety of acceptable methods have evolved to measure progress toward completion since the issuance of ARB-45. These methods can generally be categorized as input or output measures. Input measures are generally based on costs incurred or effort put forth, which indirectly measure progress toward completion. Output measures are generally based on units delivered or units of work performed, which directly measure progress toward completion (SOP 81-1, par. 46). Even though certain measures are not appropriate in certain situations, a contractor will initially have to exercise judgment in choosing the method it uses to measure progress toward completion for each type of contract. Once it selects that method, it should consistently use that method to measure progress toward completion in similar situations. However, a contractor should use different methods to measure progress toward completion for contracts with different characteristics if doing so will provide the best estimates.

Input Measures

Input measures base progress toward completion on costs or efforts expended. A commonly used input measure is cost-to-cost. Costs incurred divided by total costs expected to be incurred provides the percentage-complete measure. This measure assumes that there is a relationship between project progress and the incurrence of costs (i.e., an additional dollar of contract cost incurred leads to increased productivity). This may or may not actually be the case depending on the facts and circumstances. If it is clear that this is not the case, a cost-to-cost approach should not be used. For example, if a contract requires very high cost and specialized labor in its initial stages, but lower cost labor for the balance of the project, then it may not be appropriate to measure progress based on the costs incurred.

An important component of a cost-to-cost calculation is determining what costs should be included in the calculation. The general rule calls for all contract costs (including those related to subcontractors) to be included in the calculation (components of contract costs are discussed in more detail later in this chapter). When determining the amount of contract costs incurred that should be included, payments for work not yet performed and significant amounts of uninstalled materials not specifically produced or manufactured for the project should not be included (SOP 81-1, par. 50).

ILLUSTRATION: COST-TO-COST MEASURE

Facts: Contractor B enters into a contract with Customer Y to construct a unique building. Contractor B determines that this contract falls within the scope of SOP 81-1. Contractor B also determines that it meets the requirements to use the percentage-of-completion method, including having the ability to make reasonably dependable estimates of contract revenues, contract costs, and progress towards completion. Based on the information available, Contractor B determines that it will use a cost-to-cost method to estimate progress towards completion. Payments for contract costs through the end of the accounting period totaled $1.7 million. These payments included the following:

- $0.2 million to Subcontractor 1 for work already performed;

- $0.1 million of advance payments to Subcontractor 2 for work not yet performed;

- $1.0 million of standard materials purchased from third parties, $0.6 million of which has been used in the construction process and $0.4 million of which has not been used in the construction process; and

- $0.4 million of other contract costs consisting primarily of labor costs and equipment costs.

Contractor B estimates that total contract costs expected to be incurred are $6.0 million.

Accounting: Progress toward completion using a cost-to-cost measure should be based on $1.2 million of the $1.7 million contract cost payments made through the end of the period. The advanced payments to Sub-contractor 2 for work not yet performed ($0.1 million) and the payments for standard materials purchased from third parties that have not yet been used in the construction process ($0.4 million) should not be considered in the calculation of progress toward completion. The percentage-complete at the end of the period is calculated as follows:

$1.2 million of contract costs / $6.0 million of total expected
contract costs
= 20% of contract is complete

Another commonly used input measure is based on efforts-expended. The unit of measure in an efforts-based model may be labor dollars, labor hours, machine hours, material quantities or any other unit of measure that reflects the expending of effort. The percentage-complete is calculated based on total efforts expended (e.g., labor hours spent) divided by total efforts expected to be expended (e.g., total labor hours expected to be spent). Generally, an efforts-based model is more closely linked to productivity than a cost-to-cost model. However, inefficiencies and other factors may dilute the link between efforts expended and productivity. When using an efforts-based measure, the contractor should include the efforts of subcontractors. If the efforts of subcontractors cannot be reasonably determined in the unit of measure necessary (e.g., labor hours), an efforts-based model should not be used (SOP 81-1, pars. 48-49).

Output Measures

Output measures base progress toward completion on results achieved. The most common output measures rely on units produced or units delivered. Other output measures rely on the value added to the project and achievement of contract milestones. Generally, output measures are regarded as better measures of progress toward completion than input measures. However, reliable measures of output are often not available (SOP 81-1, pars. 46-47). For example, in a contract to produce a single piece of equipment or construct a single house, there is not likely to be any output measure on which progress toward completion can be measured.

The most common output measure is a units delivered approach, which results in revenue being recognized as each unit of output is delivered. Costs are allocated to the delivered units based on an average unit cost. Average unit cost may be based on costs incurred to-date or costs expected to be incurred over the contract period. This method should be used in situations where products are manufactured or produced to the customer's specifications on a continuous or sequential basis (SOP 81-1, par. 4). Use in other situations would generally not be appropriate.

One example of an output measure based on units delivered is a contract where the contractor has agreed to pave a ten-mile stretch of road for the customer. The output measure that could be used in this situation is miles of road paved in the current period divided by total miles to be paved under the contract. So, if the contractor agrees to pave ten miles of road and paves 2.5 miles in the first accounting period affected by the contract, its progress towards completion at the end of that period is 25% (2.5 miles of road paved in current accounting period divided by 10 miles of road to be paved in total under the contract).

EXAMPLE: USE OF UNITS-OF-DELIVERY AND COST-TO-COST

Lockheed Martin Corp. Form 10-K—Fiscal Year Ended December 31, 2004

A large part of our business is derived from long-term contracts for development, production and service activities which we account for consistent with the American Institute of Certified Public Accountants' (AICPA) audit and accounting guide, *Audits of Federal Government Contractors*, the AICPA's Statement of Position 81-1, *Accounting for Performance of Construction-Type and Certain Production-Type Contracts*, and other relevant revenue recognition accounting literature. We consider the nature of these contracts and the types of products and services provided when we determine the proper accounting for a particular contract.

Generally, we record long-term, fixed-price contracts on a percentage of completion basis using units-of-delivery as the basis to measure progress toward completing the contract and recognizing sales. For example, we use this method of revenue recognition on our C-130J tactical transport aircraft program, Atlas and Proton launch vehicle programs, and Multiple Launch Rocket System program. For certain other long-term, fixed-price contracts that, along with other factors, require us to deliver minimal quantities over a longer period of time or to perform a substantial level of development effort in comparison to the total value of the contract, sales are recorded when we achieve performance milestones or using the cost-to-cost method to measure progress toward completion. Under the cost-to-cost method of accounting, we recognize sales based on the ratio of costs incurred to our estimate of total costs at completion. As examples, we use this methodology for our F/A-22 Raptor program and the AEGIS Weapon System program. In some instances, long-term production programs may require a significant level of development and/or a low level of initial production units in their early phases, but will ultimately require delivery of increased quantities in later, full rate production stages. In those cases, the revenue recognition methodology may change from the cost-to-cost method to the units-of-delivery method after considering, among other factors, program and production stability. As we incur costs under cost-reimbursement-type contracts, we record sales. Cost-reimbursement-type contracts include time and materials and other level-of-effort-type contracts. Examples of this type of revenue recognition include the F-35 Joint Strike Fighter system development and demonstration (SDD) program and the THAAD missile defense program. Most of our long-term contracts are denominated in U.S. dollars, including contracts for the sales of military products and services to foreign governments conducted through the U.S. Government (i.e., foreign military sales).

As a general rule, we recognize sales and profits earlier in a production cycle when we use the cost-to-cost and milestone methods of percentage of completion accounting than when we use the units-of-delivery method. In addition, our profits and margins may vary materially depending on the types of long-term government contracts undertaken, the costs incurred in their performance, the achievement of other performance objectives, and the stage of performance at which the right to receive fees, particularly under incentive and award fee contracts, is finally determined. We have accounting policies in place to address these as well as other contractual business arrangements in accounting for long-term contracts.

Output measures should not be based on progress billings to total expected billings or cash receipts to total expected cash receipts. Payment terms or patterns are established by contract and bear no direct relationship to the actual progress toward completion.

Other Measures

Progress toward completion calculated using either an input or output measure should periodically be substantiated with a physical observation of progress toward completion. However, physical observation of progress toward completion should only be used in a corroborative way. That is, physical observation of progress should not be used as the sole measure of progress toward completion. Similarly, measures such as payments received are also not appropriate bases on which to measure progress toward completion. In fact, only input and output measures are considered acceptable measures of progress.

Determining Revenues and Costs to Be Recognized

One of two alternatives may be used to determine earned revenue and costs of earned revenue under the percentage-of-completion method. A contractor should select one of the alternatives and apply it consistently to all contracts accounted for using the percentage-of-completion method. Guidance on what constitutes contract revenues and contract costs for purposes of applying these alternatives is provided later in this chapter.

Alternative A

Under this alternative, both revenues and costs of sales are recognized based on the measure of progress toward completion. More specifically, revenue for any period equals total expected contract revenue multiplied by the percentage-complete at the end of the period in question, less the amount of revenue recognized in prior periods. Similarly, cost of sales for any period equals total expected contract costs multiplied by the percentage-complete at the end of the period in question, less the amount of contract costs recognized in prior periods (SOP 81-1, par. 80).

Alternative B

Under this alternative, only gross profit is determined based on the measure of progress toward completion. Cost of sales is based on actual costs incurred to date; revenues are then recorded in an amount equal to costs incurred plus the gross profit calculated based on the percentage-complete. More specifically, cost of sales for any period equals the contract costs incurred in that period. Gross profit for any period equals total expected revenues less total expected costs, multiplied by the percentage-complete at the end of the period in question, less gross profit recognized in prior periods. Revenue is merely the sum of the cost of sales for the period plus the gross profit for the period (SOP 81-1, par. 81).

Comparison of Alternatives

The same amount of gross profit should result in any given period, regardless of the alternative selected. However, revenues and costs of revenues may vary given the different calculation methods under each alternative. As a result, the gross profit percentage may also vary.

Neither of the two methods applies the Proportional Performance model the way it is applied in service and other transactions that are not within the scope of SOP 81-1. In substance, the Proportional Performance model, as applied to arrangements that do not fall within the scope of SOP 81-1, generally results in a ratable recognition of revenues with costs recognized as incurred. In contrast, Alternative A results in the ratable recognition of both revenues and costs, while Alternative B results in ratable recognition of gross profit, but not costs or revenues.

☞ **PRACTICE POINTER:** Both Alternative A and B can produce significantly different results in comparison to the Proportional Performance model used to recognize revenue in certain service transactions (see Chapter 6, "Service Deliverables"). This is one more illustration of why it is very important that contract accounting be used only where the transaction is within the scope of the contract accounting literature.

The similarities and differences between Alternatives A and B can best be illustrated through a numerical example.

ILLUSTRATION: COMPARISON OF ALTERNATIVES A AND B

Facts: Contractor C enters into a contract with Customer K to construct an office building. Assume for purposes of this example that the contract falls within the scope of SOP 81-1 and that Contractor C meets the conditions to apply the percentage-of-completion method. The construction period is expected to span two years. The total amount due from Customer K under the contract is $10 million. The initial estimate of costs to construct the office building is $9 million. Other information necessary to determine earned revenues and costs of earned revenues for Year 1 and Year 2 of the contract is provided below:

	Year 1	Year 2
Total Expected Revenues	$10,000,000	$10,000,000
Total Expected Contract Costs	9,000,000	9,000,000
Total Expected Gross Profit	1,000,000	1,000,000
Current Period Actual Costs	4,000,000	5,000,000
Percent-Complete	40%	100%
Progress Billings	$ 3,500,000	$ 6,500,000

Comparison of Alternatives: The amount of Current Period Revenues and Current Period Cost of Sales under Alternatives A and B for Years 1 and 2 are shown below:

Alternative A	Year 1	Year 2
Cumulative Revenues:		
Total Expected Revenues	$10,000,000	$10,000,000
Percent-Complete	40%	100%
Cumulative Revenues	4,000,000	10,000,000
Current Period Revenues:		
Cumulative Revenues	4,000,000	10,000,000
Revenue Recognized in Prior Periods	—	4,000,000
Current Period Revenues	4,000,000	6,000,000
Cumulative Cost of Sales:		
Total Expected Contract Costs	9,000,000	9,000,000
Percent-Complete	40%	100%
Cumulative Cost of Sales	3,600,000	9,000,000
Current Period Cost of Sales:		
Cumulative Cost of Sales	3,600,000	9,000,000
Cost of Sales Recognized in Prior Periods	—	3,600,000
Current Period Cost of Sales	3,600,000	5,400,000
Current Period Gross Profit	$ 400,000	$ 600,000
Current Period Gross Profit Percentage	10%	10%

Under Alternative A, at the end of Year 1, the following amounts would be reflected as assets on Contractor C's balance sheet: (a) $500,000 of Unbilled Revenues ($4,000,000 Current Period Revenues, less $3,500,000 of Progress Billings), and (b) $400,000 of Costs of Uncompleted Contracts ($4,000,000 of Current Period Actual Costs incurred, less $3,600,000 Current Period Cost of Sales).

Alternative B	Year 1	Year 2
Cumulative Gross Profit:		
Total Expected Gross Profit	$1,000,000	$1,000,000
Percent-Complete	40%	100%
Cumulative Gross Profit	400,000	1,000,000
Current Period Gross Profit:		
Cumulative Gross Profit	400,000	1,000,000
Gross Profit Recognized in Prior Periods	—	400,000
Current Period Gross Profit	400,000	600,000
Current Period Revenues:		
Current Period Cost of Sales	4,000,000	5,000,000
Current Period Gross Profit	400,000	600,000
Current Period Revenues	$ 4,400,000	$ 5,600,000
Current Period Gross Profit Percentage	9%	11%

Under Alternative B, at the end of Year 1, $900,000 of Unbilled Revenues ($4,400,000 Current Period Revenues less $3,500,000 of Progress Billings) would be reflected as an asset on Contractor C's balance sheet.

OBSERVATIONS:

1. Current Period Gross Profit is the same under each alternative in both Years 1 and 2. This should always be the case.

2. Current Period Gross Profit Percentages are not consistent between the alternatives in either Year 1 or Year 2. This will generally be the case given that revenues are calculated differently under each alternative.

3. Current Period Gross Profit Percentage is the same in both years under Alternative A. This is the case if there are no changes in estimates between periods. If there are changes in estimates between periods, the Current Period Gross Profit Percentage will be different year-over-year under Alternative A.

4. Current Period Gross Profit Percentage is different in both years under Alternative B. This is the case if a method other than cost-to-cost is used to measure progress towards completion.

5. The total debit reflected on Contractor C's balance sheet at the end of Year 1 is the same under both alternatives. This should always be the case.

COMPLETED-CONTRACT METHOD

Contract revenues and costs are recognized under the completed-contract method when the contract is considered complete or substantially complete, just as they are in any other application of a Completed Performance model (see Chapter 3, "General Principles"). In the interim, costs incurred and progress billings are reported on the balance sheet (SOP 81-1, par. 30).

A contract is complete if there are no remaining costs or potential risks related to the contract. A contract is substantially complete if any remaining costs or potential risks are considered insignificant. A contractor should establish objective criteria by which to assess the completeness of a contract. Those objective criteria should provide consistency in the contractor's determination of when a contract is complete. Factors that may be considered by the contractor in establishing those objective criteria include: delivery of the product, acceptance by the customer, departure from the site, and compliance with performance specifications (SOP 81-1, par. 52). These criteria are similar to those that would be used in other applications of a Completed Performance model.

EXAMPLE: SUBSTANTIALLY COMPLETE

Computer Programs and Systems, Inc. Form 10-K—Fiscal Year Ended December 31, 2004

The Company does not record revenue upon execution of a sales contract. Each customer initially remits a non-refundable 10% deposit that is recorded as deferred revenue. The customer then pays 40% of the purchase price when the Company commences training on-site at the customer's facility. When the system becomes operational, the Company bills the remaining 50% of the system purchase price and recognizes revenue for the total amount of the purchase price. Costs relating to system sales revenues are deferred and recognized at the time the related revenues are recognized; however, at December 31, 2004 and 2003, no system sales-related costs were deferred as all contracts were deemed to be substantially complete, or such amounts were not considered to be material.

To the extent a contractor recognizes contract revenues and costs upon substantial completion, the contractor should provide an accrual for the estimated remaining costs to be incurred and for the estimated settlement of any outstanding claims or disputes that are probable of payment. Such accruals should then be evaluated as contingencies, under the guidance in FAS-5.

REVENUE AND COST ELEMENTS

Many different types of revenue and cost elements are involved in contracts that fall within the scope of SOP 81-1. Contract revenues may be derived from the following types of contract pricing or billing mechanisms:

- Basic contract price
- Customer-furnished materials
- Change orders
- Contract options and additions
- Claims

Cost elements include both direct and indirect costs of performance, as well as certain costs incurred before performance begins. Provided below is a discussion regarding how these elements factor into the recognition of revenues and costs under either the percentage-of-completion or completed-contract methods.

Basic Contract Price

Contract revenues should include the basic contract price. In certain circumstances, determining the basic contract price is relatively simple. For example, many contracts are structured such that the price will not be adjusted if the contractor's cost experience or performance under the contract is not as originally expected. In this type of a contract, the contractor takes on all of the risks related to cost overruns or performance difficulties. For this reason, a contractor may attempt to negotiate basic fixed-price contracts that take these risks into consideration to the extent possible. Pricing elements that may be included in a fixed-price contract include (SOP 81-1, pars. 55-56 and App. B):

- Economic price adjustments
- Prospective periodic redetermination of price
- Retroactive redetermination of price
- Firm target cost incentives
- Successive target cost incentives
- Performance incentives
- Level of effort adjustments

Other types of contract pricing include those based on time-and-materials and costs which are variable in nature. These types of pricing are, by their nature, variable. Total revenue under a time-and-materials priced contract varies based on time incurred, materials used and any mark-up rates applied to those amounts. When revenues are determined based on costs, the contract may call for reimbursement of costs plus an incremental amount. That incremental amount may be a fixed or variable amount based on performance or the ability to meet cost or performance targets (SOP 81-1, pars. 55-56).

Judgment must be exercised by the contractor in estimating the basic contract price. Estimating the basic contract price should take into consideration all elements of the basic contract price, both fixed and variable. Given the amount of judgment involved and the number of moving pieces, estimates of the basic contract price, should be evaluated periodically to determine if any adjustments are necessary.

SUBCONTRACTOR INVOLVEMENT

When a subcontractor is used to perform certain activities under a cost-type contract, the question arises as to whether the costs of the subcontractor should be included in the general contractor's income statement on a gross (as contract revenues and contract costs) or net (no net effect on contract revenues or contract costs if the general contractor does not mark up the subcontractor's costs) basis. The factors that should be considered in this determination relate to (1) whether the general contractor is acting as a principal or an agent related to the subcontractor's costs and (2) what risks the general contractor has taken on related to those costs. Generally, if the general contractor is acting as a principal related to those costs, it is also taking on the risks associated with those costs. In those situations, the subcontractor costs should be reflected on a gross basis in the general contractor's income statement. That is, amounts paid to subcontractors should be considered contract costs and reimbursements of such amounts received from customers should be considered contract revenues. Generally, if the general contractor is acting as an agent related to the subcontractor's costs, it is not taking on the risks associated with those costs. In those situations, the subcontractor costs should be reflected on a net basis in the general contractor's income statement. That is, subcontractor costs should not be considered contract costs and reimbursements of such costs should not be considered contract revenues (SOP 81-1, pars. 58-59).

> **OBSERVATION:** In recent years, the issue regarding whether certain revenues and costs should be recognized in the income statement on a gross or net basis has received considerable attention. This attention resulted in EITF Issue No. 99-19, *Reporting Revenue Gross as a Principal versus Net as an*

Agent, which provided a framework for assessing whether revenue should be recognized gross or net. Two primary themes within this framework are the role of the entity (principal or agent) and the risks assumed by the entity. This framework is discussed in more detail in Chapter 11, "Presentation."

Customer-Furnished Materials

Under certain circumstances, the customer may purchase materials to be used by the contractor. Whether the value of those materials is included in contract revenues and costs depends on what type of risks the contractor assumes related to those materials. If the contractor is responsible for the nature, type, characteristics, or specifications of such materials or if the contractor is ultimately responsible for the acceptability of the performance of such materials in the context of the overall project, the value of those materials should be included in contract revenues and contract costs (SOP 81-1, par. 60).

EXAMPLE: CUSTOMER-FURNISHED MATERIALS AND SUBCONTRACTOR COSTS

Fluor Corporation Form 10-K—Fiscal Year Ended December 31, 2004

The company recognizes engineering and construction contract revenues using the percentage-of-completion method, based primarily on contract costs incurred to date compared with total estimated contract costs. Customer-furnished materials, labor and equipment, and in certain cases subcontractor materials, labor and equipment, are included in revenues and cost of revenues when management believes that the company is responsible for the ultimate acceptability of the project.

Contract Options and Additions

In some cases, a contract is changed after performance has begun. Such changes can provide for additional deliverables or changes to the originally contemplated deliverables. Contract options and additions should either be treated as (1) a separate contract, (2) part of the original contract, or (3) a change order. The appropriate treatment is afforded a specific contract depends on the facts and circumstances.

A contract option or addition is treated as a separate contract if any of the following circumstances exist (SOP 81-1, par. 64):

1. The product or service to be provided differs significantly from the product or service provided under the original contract;

2. The price of the new product or service is negotiated without regard to the original contract and involves different economic judgments; or

3. The products or services to be provided under the exercised option or amendment are similar to those under the original contract, but the contract price and anticipated contract cost relationship are significantly different.

The accounting for a contract option or addition should only be combined with the original contract if it meets the criteria for combining contracts discussed earlier in this chapter. If a contract option or addition is not considered a separate contract or combined with the original contract, it is treated as a change order.

Change Orders

Change orders are modifications of an original contract that effectively change the provisions of the contract without adding new provisions (SOP 81-1, par. 61). Some change orders are approved by the contractor and customer on a timely basis, while other change orders are not approved until after completion of the project. The timing of approval often is a function of the amount of uncertainty involved in any given change order. The accounting treatment of change orders depends first on whether the scope and the pricing of the order have been approved by both the customer and the contractor. In some cases, the scope of the change order may have been defined but the pricing has not been agreed upon. The treatment of unpriced change orders depends on whether the contractor is using the completed-contract or the percentage-of-completion method to account for the contract.

Approved Change Orders

If a change order has been approved with respect to both its scope and its pricing, the price of the change order should be included in contract revenues and the costs of the change order should be included in contract costs (SOP 81-1, par. 61). Thus, a change in estimate of both contract costs and contract revenues would occur at the time a change order is approved. This would generally result in a remeasurement of both the percentage complete and the recognized costs and expenses (see "Changes in Estimates" in this chapter).

Partially Approved Change Orders

In some situations, the scope of a change order may be defined even though the pricing is not. The treatment of these unpriced change orders varies depending on whether the contractor is using the completed-contract or percentage-of-completion method to account for the contract.

Completed-contract method (SOP 81-1, par. 62) When the completed-contract method is used, the issue is what to do with the related costs (as any additional revenues would not be recognized until completion or substantial completion). The costs related to an unpriced change order should be deferred as contract costs if it is probable that total contract costs, including costs attributable to change orders, will be recovered from contract revenues. In making the judgment as to whether recovery is probable, the contractor should consider its historical ability to recover costs under change orders and the specific facts and circumstances surrounding the change order under review.

Percentage-of-completion method (SOP 81-1, par. 62) When the percentage-of-completion method is used, the issue is when should the change order costs and related revenues be considered in the percentage-of-completion computation of earned revenues and costs. This determination depends, in part, on the contractor's assessment of whether, and if so, how the change order costs will be recovered. If the contractor determines that it is *not* probable that the change order costs will be recovered through a change in the basic contract price, then the change order costs should be included in the percentage-of-completion computation related to the overall contract. This effectively assumes that the change order costs will be absorbed, or recovered, by the basic contract price. Thus, a change in the estimate of contract costs would occur when the scope of a change order is defined.

If the contractor determines that it *is* probable that the change order costs will be recovered through a change in the basic contract price, the contractor has the following options:

1. Defer the change order costs (and recognition of any revenue) until agreement on price has been reached; or

2. Treat the change order costs as contract costs in the period they are incurred for purposes of computing costs of earned revenues for that period and recognize contract revenues to the extent of those change order costs.

A contractor should select one of these options and consistently follow it when accounting for unpriced change orders.

To the extent it is probable that the change order will be priced at an amount that exceeds the change order costs, the additional probable contract revenue in excess of the change order costs should only be included in contract revenues for purposes of computing earned revenues under the percentage-of-completion method if realization of that incremental amount is assured beyond a reasonable doubt (SOP 81-1, par. 62).

Unapproved Change Orders

If a change order is under dispute or if its scope and price have not been approved, it should be evaluated as a claim for purposes of determining its inclusion in contract revenues and contract costs (see discussion below) (SOP 81-1, par. 63).

Claims

The basic contract price is negotiated based on a set of project assumptions. To the extent the reality is different from those assumptions (e.g., due to errors in customer specifications, customer-caused delays, etc.), the contractor will often seek additional compensation from the customer. Sometimes this additional compensation is sought through a change order. Other times this additional compensation is sought through a claims process, in which the contractor requests additional compensation even though there is no formal change order. As noted above, unapproved or contested change orders are accounted for as claims, as they are substantively equivalent to claims.

In accounting for claims, a contractor may adopt an accounting policy where revenue from claims is only recognized when it has been received or awarded. Alternatively, the contractor may adopt an accounting policy that includes claim amounts in contract revenues if it is probable that the claim will result in additional contract revenue and if the amount can be reliably estimated. Both of these requirements must be met and can only be met if all of the following conditions exist (SOP 81-1, par. 65):

1. The contract or other evidence provides a legal basis for the claim; or a legal opinion has been obtained, stating that under the circumstances there is a reasonable basis to support the claim;

2. Additional costs are caused by circumstances that were unforeseen at the contract date and are not the result of deficiencies in the contractor's performance;

3. Costs associated with the claim are identifiable or otherwise determinable and are reasonable in view of the work performed; and

4. The evidence supporting the claim is objective and verifiable, not based on management's "feel" for the situation or unsupported representations.

Under these conditions, revenue from a claim may only be recognized to the extent of costs incurred related to the claim. As such, if the estimate of the claim amount is greater than the costs incurred related to the claim, that excess amount should not be recognized as revenue until the claim is settled. This amount, as well as claims that do not meet the above conditions, represents contingent assets, which are not permitted to be recognized until they are realized (FAS-5, par. 17).

Costs incurred related to a claim should be treated as costs of contract performance.

EXAMPLE: ACCOUNTING FOR CLAIMS

Jacobs Engineering Form 10-K—Fiscal Year Ended September 30, 2004

The nature of our business results in clients, subcontractors or vendors occasionally presenting claims against us for recovery of costs they incurred in excess of what they expected to incur, or for which they believe they are not contractually responsible. Similarly, and in the normal course of business, we may present claims to our clients for costs we have incurred for which we believe we are not contractually responsible. In those situations where a claim against us may result in additional costs to the contract, we would include in the total estimated costs of the contract (and therefore, the estimated amount of margin to be earned under the contract) an estimate, based on the relevant facts and circumstances available, of the additional costs to be incurred. In those situations where we have incurred additional costs for which we believe the client is contractually responsible, we may present a claim to the client for such costs. In such situations, we include in revenues the amount of costs incurred, without profit, to the extent it is probable that the claims will result in additional contract revenue, and the amount of such additional revenue can be reliably estimated. Costs associated with unapproved change orders are included in revenues using substantially the same criteria used for claims.

Contract Costs

The determination of whether a particular cost is a contract cost is important given the way costs are accounted for under either the percentage-of-completion method (i.e., costs are recognized as the contractor performs) or the completed-contract method (i.e., costs are deferred until the contractor is substantially complete). The general rule is that contract costs should only include direct costs related to the contract and indirect costs specifically identifiable or allocable to the contract. Listed below are different types of costs and a determination as to whether those costs would be considered contract costs (SOP 81-1, par. 72):

Cost	Contract Cost?	
	% of Compl.	**Compl. Contract**
Direct materials	Yes (Note 7)	Yes (Note 7)
Direct labor	Yes	Yes
Direct subcontracting costs	Yes (Note 8)	Yes (Note 8)
Indirect labor	Yes (Note 1)	Yes (Note 1)
Contract supervision	Yes (Note 1)	Yes (Note 1)
Tools and equipment	Yes (Notes 1, 6)	Yes (Notes 1, 6)
Supplies	Yes (Notes 1, 7)	Yes (Notes 1, 7)
Quality control	Yes (Note 1)	Yes (Note 1)
Inspection	Yes (Note 1)	Yes (Note 1)
Insurance	Yes (Note 1)	Yes (Note 1)
Repairs and maintenance	Yes (Note 1)	Yes (Note 1)
Depreciation	Yes (Note 1)	Yes (Note 1)
Amortization	Yes (Note 1)	Yes (Note 1)
Support costs	Yes (Note 1)	Yes (Note 1)
General and administrative	No (Note 2)	Accounting Policy (Note 3)
Selling costs	No (Note 4)	No (Note 4)
Interest	No (Note 5)	No (Note 5)

Note 1: These costs are indirect costs. Such costs are only considered contract costs if they are specifically identifiable with or allocable to the contract. Allocation methods used to allocate indirect costs must be systematic and rational. Clearly, judgment must be exercised in determining which indirect costs may be considered contract costs.

Note 2: General and administrative costs should be expensed as incurred when following the percentage-of-completion method.

Note 3: General and administrative costs may be allocated to a contract and treated as contract costs when following the completed-contract method. The contractor should elect an accounting policy to either expense these costs as incurred or treat them as contract costs. This policy must be followed consistently for all contracts accounted for under the completed-contract method.

Note 4: Selling costs should be expensed as incurred, unless they qualify as precontract costs (see "Precontract Costs" in the next section).

Note 5: Interest is not considered a contract cost. Interest capitalization is addressed in FAS-34, *Capitalization of Interest Cost.*

Note 6: The cost of equipment purchased for use on a contract should be allocated over the period of its expected use unless title to the equipment is transferred to the customer by terms of the contract (SOP 81-1, par. 50).

Note 7: Inventoriable costs (such as direct materials and supplies not yet used in the construction process) should not be carried at amounts, that when added to the estimated cost to complete, are greater than the estimated realizable value of the related contracts (SOP 81-1, par. 72).

Note 8: Whether subcontracting costs should be reflected in the general contractor's income statement gross or net is discussed earlier in this chapter under "Subcontractor Involvement."

The guidelines above apply to all types of contracts that fall within the scope of SOP 81-1, including contracts that compensate the contractor based on costs. Whether a contractor is compensated for a specific type of cost in a cost-type contract does not affect whether it is considered a contract cost.

Precontract Costs

Precontract costs are costs incurred in anticipation of a contract. The nature of the cost and the probability of its recovery are important factors to consider when determining the appropriate accounting treatment for a particular precontract cost. Provided below is a list of different types of precontract costs and the appropriate accounting treatment for each (SOP 81-1, par. 75):

Cost	Treatment
Costs incurred for a specific anticipated contract that will only result in a benefit if that specific contract is consummated (excluding start-up costs)	• Do not include in contract costs or inventory initially • May defer if recoverability from specific contract is probable 　—If deferred, and contract is consummated, include in contract costs 　—If deferred, and contract is not consummated or recoverability is no longer probable, expense deferred costs 　—If not deferred, and contract is subsequently consummated, do not reverse costs previously expensed

<div align="center">**Cost**</div>	<div align="center">**Treatment**</div>
Costs incurred for assets, such as costs for the purchase of materials, production equipment or supplies in anticipation of a specific contract	• Capitalize cost of asset subject to the recovery of the cost being probable
Costs incurred to acquire or produce goods in excess of the amounts required for an existing contract in anticipation of future orders for the same item	• Treat as inventory subject to the recovery of the cost being probable
Start-up costs (including training or learning costs) incurred in conjunction with an existing or anticipated contract	• Expense as incurred

Estimate of Costs to Complete

Estimates of costs to complete are important in accounting for a contract under both the percentage-of-completion and completed-contract methods. Such estimates are important under the percentage-of-completion method because total costs to complete (actual-to-date plus estimates to complete) are an integral factor in (1) the cost-to-cost method of measuring progress toward completion, (2) determining the costs of earned revenue recognized in any given period, and (3) determining whether a loss contract exists. This last reason also is important under the completed-contract method.

When estimating costs to complete, the contractor should keep the following points in mind (SOP 81-1, par. 78):

- Estimates of costs to complete should be performed consistently across all contracts. This requires having standard procedures in place that ensure consistency in the estimation process.

- Estimates of costs to complete should be reviewed periodically and compared to actual costs to complete. This will assist the contractor in determining whether its estimation procedures require revision.

- Estimates of costs to complete should contain the same complement of costs included in actual accumulated contract costs. As such, if indirect labor is included in actual contract costs, it should be factored into the estimate of costs to complete.

- Estimates of costs to complete should take into consideration expected cost increases. As such, if labor rates are expected to increase as a result of a new union contract, those higher rates should be used in estimating costs to complete.

☞ **PRACTICE POINTER:** At any given point in time contract costs consist of those costs that have been incurred and those that have yet to be incurred. Both types of costs are important when accounting for contract revenues and contract costs. As such, the contractor must ensure that it has adequate systems and processes to accumulate costs incurred and estimate costs of completion for each contract. These issues arise because costs are not always expensed at the time they are incurred and revenues are not usually recognized on a basis that is consistent with when billings occur. The nature or complexity of these systems and processes depends on many factors including:

- The number of open contracts the contractor has at any point in time (e.g., a larger number of open contracts may require computerized cost accumulation and estimation processes whereas a smaller number of open contracts may only require manual cost accumulation and estimation processes); and

- The nature of the contractor's operations (e.g., if the contractor constructs very large, high-tech, complex pieces of equipment, a more elaborate cost accumulation and estimation process may be necessary).

The goal is for the contractor to have systems and processes that provide for adequate and consistent cost accumulation and estimation. Adequacy is measured by whether the information produced allows for the contractor to properly account for each contract.

EXAMPLE: CONTRACT REVENUE AND COST ESTIMATION

Foster-Wheeler Form 10-K—Fiscal Year Ended December 31, 2004

The Company has thousands of projects in both reporting segments that are in various stages of completion. Such contracts require estimates to determine the appropriate final estimated cost ("FEC"), profits, revenue recognition and percentage complete. In determining the FEC, the Company uses significant estimates to forecast quantities to be expended (i.e., man-hours, materials and equipment), the costs for those quantities (including exchange rate fluctuations), and the schedule to execute the scope of work including allowances for weather, labor and civil unrest. Many of these estimates cannot be based on historical data as most contracts are unique, specifically designed facilities. In determining the revenues, the Company must estimate the percentage complete, the likelihood of the client paying for the work performed, and the cash to be received net of any taxes ultimately due or withheld in the country where the work is performed. Projects are reviewed on an individual basis and the estimates used are tailored to the specific circumstances. Significant judgment is exercised by management in establishing these estimates, as all possible risks cannot be specifically quantified.

The percentage-of-completion method requires that adjustments or revaluations to estimated project revenues and costs, including estimated claim recoveries, be recognized on a cumulative basis, as changes to the estimates are identified. Revisions to project estimates are made as additional information becomes available. If the FEC to complete long-term contracts indicates a loss, provision is made immediately for the total loss anticipated. Profits are accrued throughout the life of the project based on the percentage complete. The project life cycle, including the warranty commitments, can be up to six years in duration.

The project actual results can be significantly different from the estimated results. When adjustments are identified near or at the end of a project, the full impact of the change in estimate would be recognized as a change in the margin on the contract in that period. This can result in a material impact on the Company's results for a single reporting period. In accordance with the accounting and disclosure recommendations of American Institute of Certified Public Accountants ("AICPA") Statement of Position 81-1 ("SOP 81-1"), "Accounting for Performance of Construction-Type and Certain Production-Type Contracts" and Accounting Principles Board Opinion No. 20, "Accounting Changes," the Company reviews its contracts monthly. As a result of this process in 2004, 54 individual projects had final estimated profit revisions, both positive and negative, exceeding $1,000. These revisions resulted from events such as earning project incentive bonuses or the incurrence or forecast incurrence of contractual liquidated damages for performance or schedule issues, executing services and purchasing third-party materials and equipment at costs differing from previously estimated, and testing of completed facilities which in turn eliminates or incurs completion and warranty-related costs. The net aggregate dollar value of the accrued contract profit resulting from these estimate changes during 2004 amounted to $37,600.

LOSS ON CONTRACTS

Losses on contracts should be provided when the current estimate of total contract revenue is less than the current estimate of total contract costs. A loss should be recognized regardless of the method used to account for the contract. Unless contracts have been properly combined or segmented for accounting purposes (see earlier discussion), a contract loss should be based solely on that contract's revenues and costs. A loss on one contract (or, if applicable, one segment of a contract) cannot be deferred because the expected income from another contract (or contract segment) will absorb or "cover" that loss (SOP 81-1, par. 85).

The loss on a contract should be treated as part of the contract cost, not as a reduction of contract revenues, or as a non-operating expense. The amount of the loss does not need to be broken out separately on the income statement unless it is material, unusual or infrequent in nature. To the extent the loss is broken out separately on the income statement, care should be taken to ensure that it is still reflected as a component of gross profit (SOP 81-1, par. 88).

When a loss on a contract is recorded, the credit reflected on the balance sheet should be reflected as an offset of costs accumulated, if there are any such accumulated costs, or as a current liability. The current liability should be shown as a separate line item on the balance sheet if the amount is significant (SOP 81-1, par. 89).

CHANGES IN ESTIMATES

Estimation is an integral part of accounting for contracts that are within the scope of SOP 81-1, particularly those accounted for under the percentage-of-completion method. The percentage-of-completion method calls for estimates of total contract revenues, total contract costs and progress toward completion. Changes in the estimates should be accounted for under FAS 154, *Accounting Changes and Error Corrections,* using the cumulative catch-up method discussed in APB 20, *Accounting Changes.* The cumulative catch-up method effectively provides for a true-up to the new estimate in the current period by calculating revenues, costs, and gross profit as if the new estimate were used from day one of the contract (SOP 81-1, par. 83).

ILLUSTRATION: CHANGES IN ESTIMATES

Facts: Contractor J enters into a contract with Customer V to construct an office building. Performance under the contract is expected to span three years. Assume for purposes of this example that the contract falls within the scope of SOP 81-1, and that Contractor J meets the conditions to apply the percentage-of-completion method and has decided to use Alternative A to calculate earned revenues and costs of earned revenue. The total amount initially due from Customer V under the contract is $10 million. The initial estimate of costs to construct the office building is $9 million. During Year 2, a change order is approved that results in an additional $500,000 of revenue under the contract. In addition, the combination of increased costs related to the change order as well as decreased costs due to construction efficiencies results in a net increase of $200,000 in the estimate of costs to construct the building. Other information necessary to determine earned revenues and costs of earned revenues for Year 1 and Year 2 of the contract is provided below:

	Year 1	Year 2
Total Expected Revenues	$10,000,000	$10,500,000
Total Expected Costs of Revenues	9,000,000	9,200,000
Total Expected Gross Profit	1,000,000	1,300,000
Expected Gross Profit Percentage	10%	12%
Percent-Complete (calculated using an efforts-based input measure)	25%	70%

Accounting: The amount of Current Period Revenues and Current Period Costs using Alternative A for Years 1 and 2 are shown below:

	Year 1	Year 2
Revenues:		
Total Expected Revenues	$10,000,000	$10,500,000
Percent Complete	25%	70%
Cumulative Revenues	2,500,000	7,350,000
Revenues Earned in Prior Periods	—	2,500,000
Current Period Revenues	2,500,000	4,850,000
Costs of Revenues:		
Total Expected Costs	9,000,000	9,200,000
Percent Complete	25%	70%
Cumulative Costs of Revenues	2,250,000	6,440,000
Costs Recognized in Prior Periods	—	2,250,000
Current Period Costs	2,250,000	4,190,000
Current Period Gross Profit	250,000	660,000
Current Period Gross Profit Percentage	10%	14%
Cumulative Gross Profit Percentage	10%	12%

At the end of Year 2 the Cumulative Gross Profit Percentage is equal to the Expected Gross Profit Percentage. This is due to the cumulative catch-up adjustment effectively booked in Year 2. This adjustment resulted in the Current Period Gross Profit Percentage being higher than the Cumulative Gross Profit Percentage in Year 2. The catch-up adjustment that was effectively booked in Year 2 resulted in an additional $125,000 of revenues ($10,500,000 × 25% - $2,500,000), $50,000 of costs of revenues ($9,200,000 × 25% - $2,250,000) and $75,000 of gross profit in Year 2.

BALANCE SHEET PRESENTATION

Unique balance sheet presentation issues arise when accounting for an arrangement under both the percentage-of-completion and completed-contract methods (AAG-CON, par. 6.08). These issues arise because costs are not always expensed at the time they are incurred and revenues are not usually recognized on a basis that is consistent with when billings occur.

Percentage-of-Completion Method

Accounting for a contract using the percentage-of-completion method raises two unique balance sheet presentation issues. One of those issues relates to the classification of the difference between current period actual contract costs incurred and those recognized as costs of sales. This difference, generally should be classified as inventory. The other issue relates to the classification of the amount by which billings exceed revenues recognized and costs incurred but not yet expensed. This excess, should be classified as a liability.

Completed-Contract Method

When accounting for a contract using the completed-contract method, costs are accumulated on the balance sheet until the contract is complete or substantially complete. Amounts billed to customers are also deferred until the contract is complete or substantially complete. To the extent the amount of accumulated costs exceeds the amount of advance (or progress) payments received or billed by the contractor, that excess should be reflected on the balance sheet as a current asset, separate from inventory. To the extent the amount of advance (or progress) payments received or billed by the contractor exceeds the amount of accumulated costs, that excess should be reflected as a liability on the balance sheet.

> **PRACTICE POINTER:** The contract accounting literature specifies that costs incurred but not yet expensed and revenues billed but not yet recognized should be offset against one another. This is generally not appropriate for other transactions. Instead, inventory or deferred costs, and deferred revenue must be reported separately in most revenue arrangements.

> **SEC REGISTRANT ALERT:** For receivables due under long-term contracts, SEC registrants must state separately in the balance sheet, or disclose in the notes to the financial statements, the following:

1. Balances billed but not paid by customers under retainage provisions (i.e., retainage receivables);
2. Amounts representing the recognized sales value of performance and such amounts that had not been billed and were not billable to customers at the date of the balance sheet; and

3. Billed or unbilled amounts representing claims or other similar items subject to uncertainty concerning their determination or ultimate realization (REG S-X, Rule 5-02).

EXAMPLE: PERCENTAGE-OF-COMPLETION BALANCE SHEET ACCOUNTS

Meadow Valley Corporation Form 10-K—Fiscal Year Ended December 31, 2004

The asset "costs and estimated earnings in excess of billings on uncompleted contracts" represents revenue recognized in excess of amounts billed. The liability "billings in excess of costs and estimated earnings on uncompleted contracts" represents billings in excess of revenues recognized.

3. Accounts Receivable, net:

Accounts receivable, net consists of the following:

	December 31, 2004	December 31, 2003
Contracts in progress	$ 11,635,825	$8,059,848
Contracts in progress—retention	(1,801,612	5,365,090
Completed contracts	273,364	—
Completed contracts—retention	1,506,693	—
Other trade receivables	7,176,141	7,233,568
Other receivables	377,761	715,669
Less: Allowance for doubtful accounts	$ 22,163,719	21,374,175
	607,677	(710,153)
	22,163,719	$ 20,664,022

4. Contracts in Progress:

Costs and estimated earnings in excess of billings and billings in excess of costs and estimated earnings on uncompleted contracts consist of the following:

	December 31, 2004	December 31, 2003
Costs incurred on uncompleted contracts	$ 97,962,831	$ 448,808,200
Estimated earnings (loss) to date	(4,500,300)	16,572,424
	93,462,531	465,380,624
Less: billings to date	(100,232,935)	(461,249,791)
	(6,770,404)	4,130,833

Less: claims receivable, not included in billings to date	—	7,622,978
	$ (6,770,404)	$ (3,492,145)

Included in the accompanying balance sheets under the following captions:

	December 31, 2004	December 31, 2003
Costs and estimated earnings in excess of billings on uncompleted contracts	$ 449,358	$ 1,463,309
Billings in excess of costs and estimated earnings on uncompleted contracts	(7,219,762)	(4,955,454)
	$ (6,770404)	$ (3,492,145)

CHAPTER 10
SOFTWARE—A COMPLETE MODEL

CONTENTS

SURVEY OF APPLICABLE LITERATURE

Revenue recognition for companies that sell, license, lease, or otherwise earn revenue from computer software, is comprehensively addressed by SOP 97-2, as modified by SOP 98-9. Because revenue accounting for software is so thoroughly covered by these standards, companies generally need not look to SAB Topic 13 for guidance, except on a limited number of issues which neither SOP 97-2 nor SOP 98-9 address. Several other revenue recognition issues that are relevant to software have been addressed by the EITF, most notably EITF 00-3 and EITF 03-5. However, the most significant software revenue guidance other than SOP 97-2 are the Technical Practice Aids (TPAs), which were issued by a Task Force organized by the AICPA.

LISTING OF APPLICABLE LITERATURE

ARB-45	Long-Term Construction-Type Contracts
APB-29	Accounting for Nonmonetary Transactions
FAS-5	Accounting for Contingencies
FAS-48	Revenue Recognition When Right of Return Exists
FAS-86	Accounting for the Costs of Computer Software to Be Sold, Leased, or Otherwise Marketed
FIN-45	Guarantor's Accounting and Disclosure Requirements for Guarantees, Including Indirect Guarantees of Indebtedness of Others, an interpretation of FASB Statements No. 5, 57, and 107 and rescission of FASB Interpretation No. 34
FSP FIN 45-1	Accounting for Intellectual Property Infringement Indemnifications under FASB Interpretation No. 45, *Guarantor's Accounting and Disclosure Requirements for Guarantees, Including Indirect Guarantees of Indebtedness of Others*
SOP 81-1	Accounting for Performance of Construction-Type and Certain Production-Type Contracts
SOP 97-2	Software Revenue Recognition
SOP 98-9	Modification of SOP 97-2, Software Revenue Recognition, with Respect to Certain Transactions
EITF 88-18	Sales of Future Revenues
EITF 00-3	Application of AICPA Statement of Position 97-2 to Arrangements That Include the Right to Use Software Stored on Another Entity's Hardware
EITF 00-21	Revenue Arrangements with Multiple Deliverables
EITF 01-9	Accounting for Consideration Given by a Vendor to a Customer (Including a Reseller of the Vendor's Products)
EITF 03-5	Applicability of AICPA Statement of Position 97-2 to Non-Software Deliverables in an Arrangement Containing More-Than-Incidental Software
SAB Topic 13	Revenue Recognition
TPA 5100.38	Determination of Vendor-Specific Objective Evidence After the Balance Sheet Date
TPA 5100.39	Indicators that Multiple Contracts Should be Viewed as Single Arrangements
TPA 5100.41	Effect of Prepayments on Revenue Recognition
TPA 5100.43	Promises to Correct Software Errors (Bug Fixes)

TPA 5100.74	Effect of Discounts on Future Products on the Residual Method
TPA 5100.75	Fair Value of PCS Renewals Based on Users Deployed
TPA 5100.76	Fair Value in Multiple-Element Arrangements that Include Contingent Usage-Based Fees

OVERVIEW

Transfers of rights to software are generally accomplished by licenses rather than by outright sales, to provide additional legal protection to software vendors. Software licenses may have terms similar to a lease, such as a limited term, and periodic payments. Nevertheless, the rights transferred under software licenses are substantially the same as those transferred in most product sales. Therefore, in most cases, delivery of a license to use software is evaluated under the Completed Performance model (see Chapter 3, "General Principles").

Software sales can take many forms and can vary in complexity. Certain software sales involve significant production, modification, or customization of software. These types of software sales should be accounted for under the long-term construction-type contract model (see "Contract Accounting for Software Arrangements" later in this chapter).

Revenue from each software or software-related element in a software arrangement that does not involve significant production, modification, or customization should be recognized when all of the following criteria have been met for that element (see the "Multiple-Element Arrangements" section of this chapter for a discussion of when elements in a multiple-element arrangement involving software should be separated and, if so, the allocation of revenue to each element in the arrangement):

1. Persuasive evidence of an arrangement exists.
2. The arrangement fee is fixed or determinable.
3. Delivery or performance has occurred.
4. Collectibility is reasonably assured.

These four criteria are the four criteria that must be met to recognize revenue in any transaction (see Chapter 3, "General Principles"). SOP 97-2 provides a significant amount of guidance on how to apply the criteria in a software transaction.

SCOPE

As noted above, SOP 97-2 provides comprehensive guidance related to software revenue recognition, and was developed with software transactions in mind. As such, some of the conclusions were reached due to factors unique to the software industry, such as the fact that delivering additional copies of a piece of software involves virtually no cost. Because SOP 97-2 was drafted to specifically address issues faced in the software industry, its conclusions are not always consistent with those of SAB Topic 13 and other revenue recognition guidance. Therefore, the decision as to whether or not an arrangement is within the scope of SOP 97-2 is key to the timing of revenue recognition.

SOP 97-2 applies to accounting for revenue arising from licensing, selling, leasing, or other marketing of computer software (SOP 97-2, par. 2). The scope focuses on the transaction, rather than the type of company entering into it. Therefore, any company engaging in a software transaction should apply the guidance in this chapter. This includes companies that may not normally consider themselves software providers, such as companies that sell telecommunications equipment that includes a significant software component.

> **SEC REGISTRANT ALERT:** In the past, the SEC staff has requested that non-software companies whose products include software that is more than incidental ensure their revenue recognition practices are consistent with SOP 97-2 **and** disclose that the company accounts for revenue under the provisions of SOP 97-2.

Software That Is Incidental

The sale of a product that includes software incidental to the product taken as a whole should not be accounted for as a sale of software. Indicators of whether software is incidental to a product as a whole include, but are not limited to (SOP 97-2, fn. 2):

1. *Whether the software is a significant focus of the marketing effort or is sold separately.* When a company makes software a significant focus of the marketing effort or sells such software separately, it indicates that the software has significant functionality and importance.

2. *Whether the vendor will provide software upgrades or telephone support to users relating to the operation of the software.* When these kinds of post-sale activities are expected to occur, it indicates that the software is significant.

3. *Whether the vendor incurs significant costs that are within the scope of FAS-86.* Logically, if the company incurs significant costs in developing the software portion of the product, that software would be significant.

ILLUSTRATION: INCIDENTAL SOFTWARE

EXAMPLE 1 (Adapted from SOP 97-2, Appendix A)

Facts: An automobile includes software that assists in the electronic fuel injection process and helps to run the electronic dashboard. This software is used solely in connection with operating the automobile and is not sold or marketed separately. Once installed, the software is not updated for new versions that the manufacturer subsequently develops. The automobile manufacturer's costs for the development of the software are insignificant relative to the other development and production costs of the automobile.

Discussion: The sale of the car should not be accounted for in accordance with the literature on software revenue recognition because the software is deemed incidental to the product as a whole. Although the software may be critical to the operation of the automobile, the software itself is not the focus of the marketing effort, nor is it what the customer believes he or she is buying.

EXAMPLE 2

Facts: A company produces maps previously distributed in hard copy, but now puts the data on a CD along with software that allows the customer to generate customized maps of his or her route, including identification of key attractions, hotels, etc. along the route. These features are mentioned prominently in the promotional literature for the interactive atlas.

Discussion: The software revenue recognition literature is applicable because the software is not incidental to the product. Although some might argue that the product is maps, not software, the marketing of the product focuses on the interactive features made possible by the software. In this situation, even if the software development costs were small and no post-sale upgrade or technical support were provided, the fact that the software is more than incidental is demonstrated by the focus on the software features in the product's marketing.

EXAMPLE 3

Facts: Company A manufactures a handheld personal organizer that includes a calendar, address book, calculator, and game modules. The personal organizer operates using a proprietary software operating system, for which upgrades are periodically made available on Company A's website. The operating system allows users to download other programs to the personal organizer to enhance its capabilities. The main points of differentiation between Company A's products and those of its competitors, aside from minor styling details, are the features and functionality of the operating system, including the number of additional programs that run on the system. Company A spends considerable time and effort in maintaining and upgrading its operating system so that it remains better than its competitors' systems.

Discussion: The software revenue recognition literature is applicable because the software is not incidental to the product. The operating system is a key point of differentiation between Company A's product and its competitors products, and Company A spends time and effort to keep its product leading edge. In addition, upgrades are made available to users from time to time. All of this indicates that the software is more than incidental to the personal organizer.

Software Used to Provide a Service

A company may provide a service to its customer that is reliant upon software. In those cases, it may be difficult to determine whether the transaction should be accounted for as the provision of a service, to which software revenue recognition guidance does not apply, or as the sale of software. This question is answered by considering whether the rights to use the software remain solely with the company, or are transferred to the customer as part of the transaction. Only if these rights transfer to the customer should such a transaction be accounted for in accordance with SOP 97-2.

ILLUSTRATION: DETERMINING WHETHER A TRANSACTION IS A SOFTWARE OR SERVICE TRANSACTION

Facts: Company I provides tax preparation services. Its services are possible because it has developed a sophisticated software package that gathers and processes all of the necessary information to prepare a tax return. Customers may utilize Company I's software in two ways. First, they may purchase a copy of the software from Company I, download the software onto their computer, input the necessary information, and generate their tax return. If the customer chooses this option, he or she obtains a copy of the software that remains on his or her computer.

Alternatively, a customer may log on to Company I's website and, for a fee, set up a user account and input the necessary information in an on-line form. Through an automated process, that information is then input into a version of Company I's software running on Company I's system, and a tax return is generated, which the customer may then download and file on-line. If the customer chooses this option, he or she does not obtain a copy of the software, and is entitled only to use the on-line tax preparation service.

Discussion: The first type of transaction above represents the sale of software, and should be accounted for under SOP 97-2, as the customer obtains the right to use the software. However, in the second transaction, the customer does not obtain the right to use the software. Instead, the customer in this transaction obtains the right only to a service provided by Company I; it is Company I that uses the software to provide the service.

Hosted Software Arrangements

Recently, a trend among computer software providers has been to offer arrangements in which software users do not take possession of the software. Rather, the software application resides on the vendor's or a third party's hardware, and the customer accesses and uses the software on an as-needed basis. These arrangements are often called hosting arrangements or application service provider arrangements. The arrangements may or may not include a license to the software and the customer may or may not have an option to take delivery of the software.

Because the customer in a hosted software arrangement does not install the software on its own computer system, it is not clear whether the customer should be considered to have purchased software, or merely the right to a service. This issue was addressed by the EITF in EITF 00-3. The EITF concluded that a hosting arrangement is only considered a sale of software if all of the following are true (EITF 00-3, par. 5):

1. The customer has the contractual right to take possession of the software at any time during the hosting period.

2. The customer will not incur a significant penalty if it exercises its right to take possession of the software.

3. It is feasible for the customer to either run the software on its own hardware or contract with another party unrelated to the vendor to host the software.

An arrangement that meets the above criteria should be accounted for as a multiple-element arrangement (see "Multiple-Element Arrangements" later in this chapter), the two elements being the software product and the hosting service (EITF 00-3, par. 6). The multiple-element arrangement guidance discussed in this chapter (i.e., that required by SOP 97-2) should be applied to this type of arrangement given that the hosting services are considered software-related (see "Software-Related Elements" later in this chapter).

> **OBSERVATION:** Even in this situation, revenue should not be recognized upon delivery of the software unless VSOE exists for the hosting element in the arrangement. Unless the company sells hosting services separately, VSOE of fair value likely does not exist (see "Multiple-Element Arrangements" later in this chapter for further discussion).

A hosting arrangement that does not meet all of the above criteria should be accounted for as a contract to provide a service, not as a sale of software (see Chapter 6, "Service Deliverables"). As such, it is unlikely that any of the revenue would be recognized at the inception of the arrangement. Thus, the consequence of a hosting arrangement failing to include all three of the above points is that all of the revenue from the hosting arrangement must be recognized over the hosting period, rather than a portion potentially being recognized at the inception of the arrangement as a sale of software.

Pursuant to the EITF's conclusion, even if the customer has the option to take delivery of the software, the seller must still account for the transaction as the provision of a service unless it is "feasible" for the customer to take delivery, and thus end the hosting arrangement, without a "significant penalty." The EITF noted that a significant penalty exists if the customer does not have the ability to take delivery of the software without incurring significant cost or has that ability but would experience a significant diminution in utility or value of the software if the hosting arrangement were ended (EITF 00-3, par. 5).

The following are some examples of situations in which it is either not feasible for the customer to take possession of the software or a "significant penalty" exists:

- The vendor's software runs only on specialized hardware and most individual customers need to use only a small portion of the hardware's capacity. In addition, there are no significant third parties providing hosting services for this specialized hardware. In this fact pattern, it is not feasible for most customers to take delivery because, in this instance, it would not be economic for the customer to purchase the hardware.

- The hosting arrangement has a three-year term and may not be cancelled without payment of the remaining hosting fees. Assuming the fair value of the hosting is significant in relation to the overall arrangement, the requirement to continue paying for hosting not being received would be a significant penalty.

- A customer is entitled to upgrades of the software if it pays to have the seller host the software, and is not entitled to those upgrades (and cannot purchase them) if the customer ends the hosting arrangement. If upgrades are expected to be important to the customer, the fact that it can obtain them only if it pays for hosting indicates a significant penalty for ending the hosting arrangement.

- To use a key function of the software, it is necessary that the user be able to communicate with other users of the same software, and that communication is facilitated through the hosted environment. While the customer may have the right to take delivery of the software and cancel the hosting arrangement, it would lose access to the on-line community if it chooses to cancel the hosting.

Software-Related Elements

In EITF 03-5, the EITF concluded that when an arrangement includes software that is more than incidental (thus requiring the software to be accounted for under SOP 97-2), software-related elements included in the arrangement also must be accounted for under SOP 97-2. Software-related elements include, but are not limited to, software-related products and services, such as upgrades/enhancements and PCS, as well as any non-software deliverable(s) for which a software deliverable is essential to the non-software deliverable's functionality (for a discussion of "essential to the functionality," see "Multiple-Element Arrangements" later in this chapter). An example of a non-software deliverable where software is essential to that non-software deliverable's functionality is the hardware associated with the handheld personal organizer discussed in Example 3 in the "Incidental Software" Illustration, earlier in this chapter. In that example, the software is essential to the hardware's functionality. As such, both the software that runs the handheld personal organizer as well as the hardware that encases that software fall within the scope of SOP 97-2. Alternatively, if a carrying case for the handheld personal organizer were also included in the arrangement, the accounting for that carrying case would not fall within the scope of SOP 97-2 if the handheld personal organizer were not essential to the carrying case's functionality.

PERSUASIVE EVIDENCE OF AN ARRANGEMENT

The evaluation of the persuasive evidence of an arrangement condition is no different in a software environment than in any other revenue transaction. Consistent with other entities, software companies should evaluate this criterion based on their standard business practices. If obtaining written contracts is the software vendor's customary business practice, then the persuasive evidence of an arrangement criterion has been met only when both parties have signed and executed the written contract (SOP 97-2, par. 15). No matter what the documentation of an arrangement is, such documentation must be in place before any revenue is recognized. For additional discussion, see Chapter 3, "General Principles."

Although the application of this condition for software vendors is exactly the same as it is for a company that sells any other product or service, it can take on added significance for a software vendor. This is because a sale of software generally results in almost zero cost of sales. Thus, any revenue recognized has almost a 100% corresponding effect on operating and pre-tax income.

☛ **PRACTICE POINTER:** Software companies that sell large software packages are likely to have a small number of transactions, each of which is significant to the company's revenue and net income. Because of the large effect a revenue transaction may have on net income, these vendors (and their salespeople) may feel pressured to close a transaction before the end of a fiscal quarter or fiscal year, especially if the company is publicly traded. Companies should therefore have strong controls in place to ensure that appropriate documentation is received before the end of the period for all transactions for which revenue is being recognized during the period.

FIXED OR DETERMINABLE FEES AND COLLECTIBILITY

In most cases, the fixed or determinable and collectibility criteria are applied in the software environment in the same way as they are applied in a sale of any other product or service. Thus, if a portion of the fee is contingent upon future events, such as the software helping the customer achieve cost reductions, the contingent portion of the fee should not be recognized until the contingency is resolved.

Transaction-Based Pricing Arrangements

A simple example of an arrangement with a contingent fee is the sale of software for a fee that is fully or partially based on the volume of transactions or amount of information processed through it. For example, a banking software package may be sold for a fixed fee of $1,000,000 plus an additional payment of one cent for every transaction processed on the software. In this case, the $1,000,000 fixed fee may be recognized upon delivery (providing all other criteria have been met), but the one cent per transaction additional fee cannot be recognized as revenue until the transactions are processed, even if the vendor has no further obligations and can reasonably estimate the number of transactions that will be processed.

Extended Payment Terms

SOP 97-2 specifically discusses the application of the fixed or determinable criterion to software arrangements with extended payment terms. Although extended payment terms must be evaluated in any revenue transaction to determine whether they introduce a contingency to the arrangement or raise the risk of non-payment so high that collectibility is not reasonably assured, such terms create added risk in a software environment. Extended payment terms introduce the risk that, to ensure payment of previously agreed-upon amounts, a company might grant a concession, such as an additional software product or additional user licenses. The risk of this is especially high in the software industry because of the insignificant cost of providing those concessions, and the fact that the consistently evolving nature of computer software means that a product's continuing value may be reduced due to technological obsolescence.

Because of this risk, software sales that include extended payment terms must be critically evaluated to determine whether they meet the fixed or determinable criterion. In addition, SOP 97-2 specifies that a presumption exists that the fee in a software transaction is not fixed or determinable if a significant portion of the payment is delayed beyond the earlier of the expiration of the license or one year following delivery. This is because the probability of granting concessions is deemed to be more likely than not in such arrangements (SOP 97-2, pars. 27-28).

EXAMPLE: EXTENDED PAYMENT TERMS

Niku Corporation Form 10-K—Fiscal Year Ended January 31, 2005

The fee is fixed or determinable. The Company negotiates the fees for its products at the outset of an arrangement. In these arrangements, the majority of the licenses are perpetual and related fees are nonrefundable. The fees are generally due within six months or less. The Company considers fees relating to arrangements with payment terms extending beyond six months not to be fixed or determinable and revenue for these arrangements is recognized as payments become due from the customer.

The presumption that the fee in an arrangement with payment terms extending beyond one year after delivery is not fixed or determinable may be overcome if persuasive evidence exists showing that the vendor has a business practice of using extended payment terms and has been successful in collecting under the original terms, without providing any concessions. If the presumption cannot be overcome due to a lack of such evidence, revenue should be recognized as payments become due, presuming that all other revenue recognition criteria have been met (SOP 97-2, pars. 28-29).

> **OBSERVATION:** Because SOP 97-2 concludes that payment terms that exceed one year create a presumption that the fee is not fixed or determinable, a company with no history of successfully collecting under long-term payment arrangements must recognize revenue from such arrangements as payments become due, even though delivery has occurred and the customer is extremely creditworthy. In fact, strong creditworthiness is not helpful in overcoming the presumption regarding extended payment terms. This is because

the concern regarding extended payment terms is not that the customer will become unable to pay, but that a concession will be provided to the customer because the customer is not satisfied and the cost of providing the concession is low.

☛ **PRACTICE POINTER:** The provisions of SOP 97-2 with respect to payments that extend further than one year have been misinterpreted at times to allow immediate recognition, upon delivery, of any payments due within one year, even if other payments extend beyond one year. The basis for conclusions of SOP 97-2 makes clear that recognition of **any** revenue, until payments become due, is prohibited unless the presumption discussed above is overcome.

ILLUSTRATION: ONE-YEAR PRESUMPTION

Facts: Vendor S sells a perpetual license to one of its software products for a fee of $10,000,000. Payment terms are $2,500,000 upon delivery and another $2,500,000 every six months thereafter. Thus, $2,500,000 of the fee (one payment) is due more than one year after delivery. Vendor S does not have a history of using extended payment term arrangements, but the customer in this arrangement is very creditworthy, and has used Vendor S's products for a long time without complaints. There are no return, acceptance, or other provisions in the arrangement that raise additional questions regarding the customer's obligation to pay the license fee.

Discussion: Because Vendor S has no history of using extended payment terms, the fact that a significant (25%) portion of the fee is due more than one year after delivery means that Vendor S may only recognize revenue as payments become due. Thus, Vendor S may only recognize $2,500,000 upon delivery, even though $7,500,000 is due within one year of delivery. The identity of the customer and Vendor S's strong relationship with the customer are not relevant to these conclusions.

Overcoming the Presumption That the Fee in an Extended Payment Term Arrangement Is Not Fixed or Determinable

Concessions (TPA 5100.56)   To overcome the presumption that the fee in an arrangement with payment terms that extend beyond the license term or one year from delivery is not fixed or determinable, a company must have persuasive evidence, based on historical practice, of its ability to collect under the original terms of extended payment arrangements without granting concessions. Concessions by a software vendor may take many forms. Essentially, any change to an arrangement that reduces the total revenue to be recognized, extends the payment terms, increases the customer's rights, or increases the vendor's obligations constitutes a concession. For example, the following would all be considered concessions:

- Extending payment due dates in the arrangement
- Decreasing total payments due under the arrangement
- Paying financing fees on a customer's financing arrangement that were not contemplated in the original arrangement
- Accepting returns beyond those provided for in the terms of the original arrangement
- Providing discounted or free post-contract customer support that was not included in the original arrangement
- Providing other discounted or free services, upgrades, or products that were not included in the original arrangement
- Extending the timeframe for a reseller to sell the software or an end user to use the software
- Extending the geographic area in which a reseller is allowed to sell the software, or the number of locations in which an end user can use the software

Relevant historical experience (TPA 5100.57)   To have a history of successfully collecting under the original payment terms without making concessions, a vendor must have collected all payments as due under comparable arrangements without providing concessions. For example, a vendor that sells software with three-year payment terms, but has only been doing so for the past year, could not have sufficient history, even if it has yet to encounter any difficulties.

In evaluating a vendor's history, it is important to determine whether the arrangements that make up the company's historical experience are sufficiently similar to the current arrangements. Consideration should be given to all factors, including the following:

- *Type or class of customer*
- *Types of products*
- *Stage of product life cycle*—The later in a product's life cycle that an arrangement is entered into, the more chance there is of the product becoming technologically obsolete during the payment period.
- *Elements included in the arrangement*—The inclusion of significant rights to services or discounts on future products in some arrangements, but not others, could indicate that there is a significant difference between the arrangements. For example, a history developed for arrangements that

included bundled post-contract customer support (PCS) and rights to additional software products would not be comparable to an arrangement that does not include these rights.

- *Length of payment terms*

- *Economics of license arrangement*—License arrangements that include significant discounts from list prices may not be comparable to those that do not.

Revenue Recognition When Payments Become Due

If a fee in a software arrangement with extended payment terms is not fixed or determinable (e.g., if the presumption cannot be overcome) at the outset of an arrangement, revenue must be recognized as payments become due. However, if the payment terms are changed, it may not be clear when revenue should be recognized.

If a customer makes payments early (for example, to avoid financing costs), revenue should be recognized when the payments are made, because the fact that the customer has made payments indicates that the fee is now fixed or determinable.

However, the presumption that the licensing fee is not fixed or determinable is **not** overcome if the vendor receives cash from selling the receivable under the extended payment term arrangement to a third party, even if the sale is without recourse. The difference in this situation as compared to the situation in the previous paragraph is that the transfer of the extended payment term arrangement does not change the nature or structure of the transaction between the vendor and customer. Therefore, the presumption that the fee is not fixed or determinable is not overcome by any transaction between the vendor and a third party. Instead, the sale of the rights to receive payments from the customer should be accounted for under EITF 88-18 (see Chapter 11, "Presentation") (TPAs 5100.41 and 5100.58).

Cash Received after Balance Sheet Date

The determination of whether the presumption that the fee in an extended payment term arrangement is not fixed or determinable is overcome must be made at the outset of the arrangement. Once made, subsequent cash payments do not result in a revision of the initial conclusion. Thus, a payment (even a full payment) made after the end of a reporting period cannot be used to justify the recognition of revenue in the reporting period. Instead, a payment made after period end should be recognized in the next period (the period the payment was made) (TPA 5100.59).[1]

Customer Financing with Software Vendor Participation

To get paid on normal payment terms, a software vendor may assist its customer in obtaining long-term financing from a third party. If the software vendor's participation in the customer's financing results in incremental risk that the software vendor will provide a refund or concession to either the end-user or the financing party, the arrangement should be evaluated as if it has extended payment terms consistent with the terms of the financing arrangement. Thus, if the financing arrangement between the company and the third-party lender extended for greater than one year after delivery, the presumption would be that the fee is not fixed or determinable. If the software vendor cannot overcome that presumption, the software vendor should recognize revenue as payments from the customer become due and payable to the financing party, provided all other revenue recognition requirements are met. Therefore, the payment received initially should be reflected as deferred revenue until the customer's payments to the financing party become due.

Any one of the following conditions or actions results in incremental risk and a presumption that the fee is not fixed or determinable (TPA 5100.61 and 5100.62):

- Provisions that require the software vendor to indemnify the financing party against claims, except to the extent similar indemnifications are included in the company's standard arrangements with customers.

- Provisions that require the software vendor to make representations to the financing party related to customer acceptance of the software that are above and beyond the written acceptance documentation, if any, that the software vendor has already received from the end user customer.

- Provisions that obligate the software vendor to take actions against the customer on behalf of the financing party, or to refuse further business from the customer, in the event that the customer defaults under the financing arrangements, unless, as part of the original arrangement, the customer

---

[1] Collecting a payment after the end of the period is a "Type II" subsequent event, as discussed in paragraph 5 of the AICPA Codification of Auditing Standards, AU Section 560, Subsequent Events. Type II subsequent events include "... those events that provide evidence with respect to conditions that did not exist at the date of the balance sheet being reported on but arose subsequent to that date. These events should not result in adjustment of the financial statements." [footnote omitted]

explicitly authorizes the software vendor to take such actions without penalty.

- Provisions that require the software vendor to guarantee, certify, or otherwise attest in any manner to the financing party that the customer meets the financing party's qualification criteria.

- Provisions that lead to the software vendor's guarantee of the customer's indebtedness to the financing party.

- The software vendor has previously provided concessions to financing parties or to customers to facilitate or induce payment to financing parties.

When a software arrangement involves an indemnification or a guarantee as discussed in the first and fifth bullet points above, respectively, the provisions of FIN-45 may need to be considered. Whether the provisions of FIN-45 need to be considered depends on whether the existence of the indemnification or guarantee precludes revenue recognition. If the presumption that an indemnification or guarantee results in the fee not being fixed or determinable cannot be overcome, then the provisions of FIN-45 need not be considered. However, if the presumption can be overcome (i.e., the fee is considered fixed or determinable despite the existence of the indemnification or guarantee), then the provisions of FIN-45 should be considered.

When the presumption can be overcome related to an indemnification, FSP FIN 45-1 indicates that "a software licensing agreement that indemnifies the licensee against liability and damages (including legal defense costs) arising from any claims of patent, copyright, trademark or trade secret infringement by the software vendor's software" does fall within the scope of FIN-45 from a disclosure perspective, but not from an initial recognition and measurement perspective. As such, the fair vale of the indemnification should not be recognized initially. In other words, the indemnification should not be treated as a separate element in a multiple-element arrangement. See Chapter 12, "Disclosures," regarding the disclosure requirements of FIN-45.

When the presumption can be overcome related to a guarantee that otherwise falls within the scope of FIN-45, both the initial recognition and measurement and disclosure provisions of FIN-45 apply. As such, the arrangement is considered a multiple-element arrangement where there is at least one software or software-related element and a guarantee. See Chapter 4, "Multiple-Element Arrangements," regarding the scope of FIN-45 and the accounting for multiple-element arrangements where one of the elements is a guarantee. See Chapter 12 regarding the disclosure requirements of FIN-45.

Although the list of conditions or actions resulting in incremental risk and a presumption that the fee is not fixed or determinable is quite long, the SOP 97-2 implementation task force has identified several actions that the vendor may take that do not indicate any incremental risk (TPA 5100.64):

- The software vendor introduces the customer and financing party, facilitates their discussions, provides the financing party with information on behalf of the customer and assists the customer in filling out applications, as long as the vendor does not attest in any manner that the customer meets the financing party's qualification criteria.

- The software vendor makes representations to the financing party that are the same as representations included in the arrangement with the customer.

- The vendor takes actions that were explicitly authorized by the customer in the original arrangement to terminate the license agreement and/or any related services, or to not enter into another arrangement for the same or similar product.

- The vendor grants customary recourse provisions to its customer related to warranties for defective software.

Cancellation and Customer Acceptance Clauses

Cancellation clauses should be evaluated to determine their substance. For example, a cancellation clause that is short-term and subjective in nature should be evaluated as a right of return (see "Rights to Exchange or Return Software" later in this chapter). However, a clause that allows a customer to cancel the arrangement only if the software does not meet standard specifications should be evaluated as a warranty. The treatment of warranties in a software environment is the same as it is in the sale of any other product (see Chapter 5, "Product Deliverables") (SOP 97-2, par. 31).

Other cancellation and customer acceptance clauses may raise uncertainty about whether the transaction is complete. After delivery, if uncertainty exists about customer acceptance of the software, license revenue should not be recognized until acceptance occurs. This will often be the case when a customer acceptance clause is based on customer or arrangement-specific criteria that cannot be evaluated until the software is installed and operating in the customer's environment (SOP 97-2, par. 20). For further information on these and other customer acceptance clauses, see Chapter 5.

If, after delivery, a software sale is cancelable, the fixed or determinable condition is not met until the cancellation privileges lapse. If the cancellation privileges lapse ratably, then the fee becomes fixed or determinable ratably. For example, software sold on a three-year term license, with payments made at the beginning of each year, might have a cancellation provision that enables the customer to terminate its license after two years and avoid payment of the third license fee payment. If this is the case, revenue cannot be recognized for the third year's payment until the cancellation right lapses, even if the vendor has sufficient history to get over the presumption that the extended payment terms cause the fee to not be fixed or determinable.

Price Protection

Price protection provides for the buyer to be given credit for price decreases for a specified period of time or until the buyer resells the products. In these situations, revenue should be recognized net of the estimated amount to be refunded under the price protection, provided the refund amount can be reasonably and reliably estimated and the other conditions for revenue recognition have been met. One consideration in determining whether refunds can be reasonably and reliably estimated is whether there are significant uncertainties related to the seller's ability to maintain its prices. If refunds cannot be reliably estimated, revenue should not be recognized until reliable estimates can be made or the price protection lapses (SOP 97-2, par. 30).

DELIVERY

Determining when delivery of a software element occurs is generally relatively straightforward. In most cases, software products and services are considered to be delivered at the same time a similar deliverable in a non-software arrangement would be considered delivered. However, certain factors unique to the software world need to be considered. Delivery for various types of elements is discussed below.

Products

The primary software product element is the license to a piece of software. Typically a product element is physically delivered on a disk, tape, or other storage media. However, software elements may also be delivered electronically, via e-mail or the Internet. Generally, a product element of a software arrangement is fairly easy to identify, and the accounting for it is much the same as the accounting for any other product sale. Considerations unique to the delivery of software are discussed further below.

As in non-software arrangements, delivery of a product generally occurs when the software is transferred to the customer. Exceptions to this are the same as the exceptions in any other product sale, and include consignment shipments, bill and hold sales, product financing arrangements, and others. When software is to be delivered on a physical storage medium, such as a disk, tape, or hard drive, the concepts relating to title or delivery to an alternate site also apply. For information on all these topics, see Chapter 5, "Product Deliverables."

As discussed earlier in this chapter under "Software-Related Elements," if a non-software product (e.g., computer hardware) is included in an arrangement with a software product that is more than incidental and the software product is essential to the functionality of the non-software product, then the non-software product is considered software-related. Such software-related products fall within the scope of SOP 97-2 (EITF 03-5). Thus, delivery of the software-related product should be assessed in the same manner, using the same principles, as delivery of the actual software.

Electronic Delivery

When software is delivered electronically, the delivery criterion is considered to have been met when the customer either downloads the software, or has been provided with access codes that allow the customer to take immediate possession of the software on its hardware pursuant to an agreement or purchase order for the software (SOP 97-2, par. 18).

Multiple Licenses of the Same Product

Some software arrangements involve multiple copies or licenses of the same software. These arrangements generally specify the number of copies the customer may use, or may allow the customer to use as many copies as it chooses (a site license). As long as the arrangement does not specify a variable fee based on the number of copies ordered, delivery of all copies of a particular piece of software is considered to have occurred when the first copy or product master is delivered to the customer. In these arrangements, duplication, even if it is to be performed by the vendor, is incidental to the arrangement, and the fee is payable even if no additional copies are requested. The estimated costs of duplication should be accrued at the time revenue is recognized if the vendor is responsible for duplication (SOP 97-2, par. 21).

Some multiple-copy software arrangements are structured somewhat differently, however. In these arrangements, although the customer has the right to multiple (or perhaps unlimited) copies of the software as it chooses, the fee varies based on the number of copies the customer deploys if the customer is an end-user, or sells to end-users if the customer is a reseller. Because the fee varies with the number of copies, delivery is only considered to occur as the copies are made by the user or sold by the reseller. In addition, in this type of arrangement, the fee for the additional copies is not fixed or determinable until the copies are made or sold (SOP 97-2, par. 21).

Authorization Codes or Keys

Some vendors use electronic "locks" in their software to prevent unauthorized users from accessing the software. Thus, a user must not only have a copy of the software, but also have the correct authorization code, or "key," to use the software. Typically, software installed without a permanent key will work for a short period of time before it becomes locked. In software arrangements involving the use of keys, delivery of all keys is not necessarily required to satisfy the vendor's delivery responsibility. The software may be considered delivered as long as the customer has a version that is fully functional except for the permanent key or additional keys necessary for reproduction and the customer's payment obligation is not contingent in any way upon the delivery of additional keys. However, if a vendor only uses keys selectively, the use of keys in an arrangement is likely evidence that the collectibility is questionable or that the product has been delivered for demonstration purposes (SOP 97-2, pars. 24-25).

ILLUSTRATION: AUTHORIZATION CODES

EXAMPLE 1

Facts: A vendor includes 20 optional functions on a CD on which its software product is licensed. Keys control access to those optional functions, and are provided if and when the customer orders and agrees to pay for the optional functions. The vendor estimates that the customer will purchase three optional functions.

Discussion: Revenue for each individual optional function should be recognized when evidence of an order exists and the key is delivered to the user. Although the user has received a fully functional version (except for the keys) of the optional functions on the CD-ROM, the user has not agreed to license them. Therefore, no evidence of an arrangement exists, and revenue for the optional functions may not be recognized when the CD-ROM is delivered.

EXAMPLE 2

Facts: A software vendor's product requires an authorization code to work after being installed on a new computer. The code necessary to activate the software changes daily. The vendor enters into a license arrangement with a user and delivers a disk containing the product. The customer will handle installation of the product and is instructed to contact the vendor for the daily key on the day of installation. The customer is required to pay for the software 30 days after delivery, whether it has installed the software or not.

Discussion: The version of the software that has been delivered is fully functional except for the installation key, and the customer's payment obligation is not contingent upon delivery of the key. Therefore, revenue may be recognized upon delivery of the software provided the other revenue recognition conditions have been met.

Delivery before License Period Begins

If software is physically delivered and all other revenue recognition criteria are met, but the customer's license to use the software has not yet begun, revenue should not be recognized because the customer does not yet have the legal right to use the software. Effective delivery does not occur in these situations until the license term begins (TPA 5100.70; SAB Topic 13A3d).

"Delivery" When License Period Is Extended

When a term license to a software product is extended, consideration should be given to whether the extension results in the software vendor providing any additional products and to whether the extension occurs before the original term license lapses (TPAs 5100.70, 5100.71, and 5100.72).

- When an active term license to a software product is extended and no additional products will be provided by the software vendor, the software vendor should recognize the extension fee when the extension arrangement is executed, even if that date is before the extension period begins, if all other revenue recognition criteria have been met.

- When a term license to a software product has lapsed (i.e., it is inactive), any purported extension of that license should be treated as a new initial arrangement, not an extension of an existing arrangement. In these situations, the guidance in the previous section, "Delivery before License Period Begins," should be followed.

- When an active term license to a software product is extended and an additional product will be provided by the software vendor, the extension fee should be allocated between the software product that was the subject of the original license (original product) and the software product added in the extension (new product) based on the guidance in the "Multiple-Element Arrangements" section of this chapter. The software vendor should recognize the amount allocated to the original product when the extension arrangement is executed if all other revenue recognition criteria have been met. The software vendor should recognize the amount allocated to the new product when all of the revenue recognition criteria have been met related to that new product. This includes consideration of when the license period begins related to that new product.

> **OBSERVATION:** Arrangements may contain an option to extend a time-based license indefinitely for an additional fee. The additional fee related to the option is essentially the same as the additional fee related to an extension/renewal of a license. The right associated with each fee is the same—the right to continue to use the product the customer already has access to as part of the original or base arrangement. As such, the additional fee related to the option should be accounted for similarly to a fee received in connection with the extension/renewal of a license. However, if exercise of the option requires another delivery of the software media (e.g., due to a self-destruct or similar mechanism in the original software media delivered), then delivery of the software media must occur before revenue can be recognized (TPA 5100.73).

Delivery of a Beta Version or an Earlier Release

In some situations, the version of the software ordered by the customer may not be immediately available, because it is still in development or testing before commercial release. When this situation arises, the vendor may deliver to the customer a beta (or test) version of the product, or an earlier release (e.g., version 5.5 instead of 6.0) of the product, so that the customer will have a product to use before the final release of the ordered version of the product.

Delivery of a beta or earlier version of the product should not result in the recognition of revenue, because this delivery is not delivery of the product the customer ordered. As such, the vendor has not substantially completed its obligations under the arrangement.

Upgrades

SOP 97-2 defines an upgrade as: "An improvement to an existing product that is intended to extend the life or improve significantly the marketability of the original product through added functionality, enhanced performance, or both." Upgrades are often a key aspect of a software arrangement, as software products are often upgraded over time (e.g., from version 1.0 to version 2.0). Many software arrangements include the rights to various upgrades for a period of time. The accounting for upgrades depends upon whether the upgrade is a specified or unspecified upgrade.

Specified upgrades are treated as separate elements of the arrangement (see guidance later in this chapter under "Multiple-Element Arrangements" for purposes of determining whether specified upgrades should be treated separately for accounting purposes). Delivery of specified upgrades can generally be determined in the same manner as delivery of products. Unspecified upgrades are discussed below under "Post-Contract Customer Support (PCS)."

Post-Contract Customer Support (PCS)

In contrast to the accounting for specified upgrades, unspecified upgrades are considered to be part of post-contract customer support (PCS). PCS includes post-sale services such as telephone and on-call technical support, in addition to unspecified product upgrades. The right to receive services and unspecified upgrades provided under PCS is generally described by the PCS arrangement. Typical arrangements include services, such as telephone support and correction of errors (bug fixing or debugging), and unspecified product upgrades developed by the vendor during the period in which the PCS is provided. A limited period of PCS is often included with the purchase of a license to software. That initial period of PCS, even though it may be provided to all purchasers, is considered an element in a multiple-element arrangement (see guidance later in this chapter under "Multiple-Element Arrangements" for purposes of determining whether PCS should be treated separately for accounting purposes).

> **OBSERVATION:** While an arrangement to provide unspecified upgrades and enhancements is accounted for as PCS, an arrangement that only requires the vendor to provide "bug fixes" that correct errors in the operation of the software should be accounted for as a warranty, pursuant to FAS-5 (TPA 5100.43) (see Chapter 5, "Product Deliverables").

The portion of the fee allocated to PCS should generally be recognized as revenue ratably over the term of the PCS arrangement, because there is generally no better estimation of the manner in which such services will be provided. However, revenue should be recognized in proportion to the expenses expected to be incurred for the PCS services if sufficient vendor-specific historical evidence exists demonstrating that costs to provide PCS are incurred on other than a straight-line basis (SOP 97-2, pars. 56-57).

> **OBSERVATION:**   Because most companies include the rights to unspecified upgrades in their PCS arrangements, and predicting the costs to be incurred in developing such upgrades is extremely difficult, PCS is almost always recognized on a straight-line basis over the PCS period.

In rare circumstances, PCS is considered to be insignificant to the arrangement and, therefore, its delivery is not required to recognize the revenue allocated to it. SOP 97-2 allows the portion of the arrangement fee allocated to PCS to be recognized at the same time as the portion of the fee allocated to the software product if all of the following conditions are met (SOP 97-2, par. 59):

1. *The PCS fee is included with the initial licensing fee.* Thus, PCS fees for an optional period are not eligible for this exception.

2. *The PCS included with the initial license is for one year or less.* This is met if the arrangement includes post-delivery telephone support for an unspecified period of time, but the vendor's history shows that substantially all of the support is provided within the first year after delivery.

3. *The estimated cost of providing PCS during the arrangement is insignificant.* Historical experience in providing PCS to similar customers on similar software products would be necessary to reach this conclusion.

4. *If unspecified upgrades are included in the PCS arrangement, such upgrades historically have been and are expected to continue to be minimal and infrequent.* Whether upgrades are considered to be minimal and infrequent is a matter of judgment. However, the content, and not just the number, of upgrades should be taken into account.

If PCS revenue is recognized upon the delivery of the software, the vendor must accrue all estimated costs of providing the PCS at the same time.

Subscriptions

A vendor may agree to deliver software currently and to deliver unspecified additional software products in the future. For example, the vendor may agree to deliver all new products to be introduced in a family of products over the next two years. These kinds of arrangements are treated as subscriptions, conceptually similar to a subscription to a magazine or Internet site. A subscription is distinguished from a PCS arrangement that includes unspecified upgrades and enhancements, because the future deliverables are products with their own functionality, rather than upgrades to already existing products.

In a subscription, the customer is entitled to delivery of products made available during some period of time. In these arrangements, delivery is considered to occur ratably throughout the period once the first product has been supplied to the customer. As delivery is considered to occur ratably, no allocation of revenue should be made among any of the software products. Even if the vendor has no obligation to develop any additional products, and in fact does not intend to develop any products, delivery under a subscription is still deemed to occur ratably, beginning with the delivery of the first product (SOP 97-2, pars. 48-49).

> **OBSERVATION:**   This treatment is specified in SOP 97-2, because, as the products are unspecified at the outset of the arrangement, there is no way VSOE of fair value could exist for them. As such, absent this special provision, no revenue from subscriptions would be recognized until the end of the subscription term.

Software-Related Services

Many software-related services other than PCS-related services may also exist in an arrangement. The software-related services may include training, installation, or consulting. Consulting services often include implementation support, software design or development, or the customization or modification of the licensed software. When software-related services meet the criteria to be accounted for separately from other elements (see "Multiple-Element Arrangements" below), they are considered to be delivered as the services are performed. If no pattern of performance is discernable, software-related services may be considered delivered ratably as they are provided.

> **OBSERVATION:**   As discussed above, PCS may, on rare occasions, be considered incidental to the arrangement, such that revenue allocated to it may be recognized when the software product is delivered. This exception does not apply to any other software-related services.

MULTIPLE-ELEMENT ARRANGEMENTS

Software sales may include more than one deliverable. The deliverables, or elements, may include different software products, upgrades, enhancements, or other software-related services, such as training, installation, consulting, and post-contract customer support.

The deliverables may also include non-software related products and services. When a multiple-element arrangement exists, the fee from the arrangement should be allocated to the various deliverables, to the extent appropriate, so that the proper amount can be recognized as revenue as each element is delivered.

Determining the Model to Apply

The EITF provided guidance on separating multiple-element arrangements in EITF 00-21. As discussed in more detail in Chapter 4, "Multiple-Element Arrangements," EITF 00-21 does not apply to arrangements that fall completely within the scope of higher-level literature. As such, arrangements that fall within the scope of SOP 97-2 do not fall within the scope of EITF 00-21, and the multiple-element arrangement guidance in SOP 97-2 should be applied. However, if an arrangement includes elements that fall within the scope of SOP 97-2 and elements that fall outside the scope of SOP 97-2, EITF 00-21 should be applied to separate the SOP 97-2 elements and the non-SOP 97-2 elements. Further separation of the SOP 97-2 elements is governed by the separation guidance in SOP 97-2.

Throughout the multiple-element arrangement discussion in this chapter reference is made to SOP 97-2 software and SOP 81-1 software. As discussed further below, (a) SOP 97-2 software refers to software that is more than incidental but that does not involve significant production, modification, or customization and (b) SOP 81-1 software refers to software that is more than incidental and does involve significant production, modification, or customization. Recognition of revenue related to an arrangement that includes only SOP 97-2 software should follow the guidance in SOP 97-2 and recognition of revenue related to an arrangement that includes only SOP 81-1 software and the related production, modification, or customization services should follow the contract accounting model provided in SOP 81-1. Additional discussion related to SOP 97-2 software and SOP 81-1 software is provided below, including discussion regarding the accounting implications of multiple-element arrangements that include SOP 97-2 software or SOP 81-1 software. In addition, a detailed discussion regarding the application of contract accounting to SOP 81-1 software is provided in the section later in this chapter titled "Contract Accounting for Software Arrangements."

To ensure that the proper multiple-element arrangement guidance is being applied to an arrangement involving software and/or software-related elements, it is essential to understand whether the elements in the arrangement fall within the scope of SOP 97-2, SOP 81-1, or other literature. Following is a discussion of the different types of software and software-related elements that could be included in a multiple-element arrangement. Determining the appropriate multiple-element model to apply to an arrangement including different combinations of these elements is also discussed.

Incidental Software

Software that is incidental (as discussed earlier in this chapter) does not fall within the scope of SOP 97-2. To the extent an arrangement includes incidental software, it should not be considered an element in the arrangement. As such, an arrangement including a non-software product and incidental software is, essentially, a one-element arrangement.

SOP 97-2 Software and Software-Related Elements

For purposes of this discussion, software that is more than incidental and does not involve significant production, modification, or customization of the software will be referred to as SOP 97-2 software. When sold on a standalone basis, this software falls within the scope of SOP 97-2. If a multiple-element arrangement includes three SOP 97-2 software elements, then the multiple-element model in SOP 97-2 should be applied to determine whether those elements should be treated separately for accounting purposes. Since each of those elements would fall within the scope of SOP 97-2 on a standalone basis, a multiple-element arrangement consisting of those elements also falls within the scope of SOP 97-2. This results in the application of the SOP 97-2 multiple-element model to determine whether those three SOP 97-2 software elements should be separated for accounting purposes.

When SOP 97-2 software is essential to the functionality of another element in the arrangement, that other element in the arrangement is considered an SOP 97-2 software-related element. If a multiple-element arrangement consists only of SOP 97-2 software and SOP 97-2 software-related elements, the multiple-element model in SOP 97-2 should be applied to determine whether those elements should be treated separately for accounting purposes.

However, if a multiple-element arrangement consists of (a) an SOP 97-2 software element and/or an SOP 97-2 software-related element, and (b) another element(s) that would not, on a standalone basis, fall within the scope of SOP 97-2, then the multiple-element model in EITF 00-21 should be applied to determine whether those elements should be treated separately for accounting purposes (see Chapter 4, "Multiple-Element Arrangements," for a discussion of EITF 00-21).

SOP 81-1 Software and Software-Related Elements

For purposes of this discussion, software that is more than incidental and involves significant production, modification, or customization will be referred to as SOP 81-1 software. When sold on a standalone basis, this software and the related production, modification, or customization services fall within the scope of SOP 81-1. SOP 81-1 software-related elements include: (a) other elements in the arrangement that are essential to the functionality of the SOP 81-1 software, and (b) other elements in the arrangement to which the SOP 81-1 software is essential to their functionality, with the possible exception of PCS, as discussed below. If a multiple-element arrangement includes SOP 81-1 software and SOP 81-1 software-related elements, the multiple-element model in SOP 81-1 should be applied to determine whether those elements should be treated separately for accounting purposes.

However, if a multiple-element arrangement consists of (a) SOP 81-1 software and SOP 81-1 software-related element(s), and (b) another element(s) that would not fall within the scope of SOP 81-1 on a standalone basis (including an SOP 97-2 software or software-related element), then the multiple-element model in EITF 00-21 should be applied to determine whether those elements should be treated separately for accounting purposes (see Chapter 4, "Multiple-Element Arrangements," for a discussion of EITF 00-21).

> **SEC REGISTRANT ALERT:** The position that EITF 00-21 should be applied to an arrangement involving SOP 81-1 software and software-related elements and other elements that do not fall within the scope of SOP 81-1 is supported in a speech given by an SEC staff member in December 2003. In this speech, the SEC staff member communicated that "the consensus reached by the EITF requires that the EITF 00-21 criteria be applied in bundled arrangements involving significant customization of software to determine whether SOP 81-1 deliverables should be separated from the non-SOP 81-1 deliverables."

PCS

Generally, PCS is not essential to the functionality of the software to which it relates (and the software generally has value to the customer on a standalone basis absent the PCS). As such, absent any general or specific return/refund rights that could affect the analysis, PCS typically should be treated as a separate element for accounting purposes provided appropriate fair value evidence exists to allocate arrangement consideration between the PCS and the other elements in the arrangement. If an arrangement includes SOP 97-2 software and PCS, the SOP 97-2 multiple-element arrangement model should be used to separate the elements for accounting purposes. If an arrangement includes SOP 81-1 software and PCS, the EITF 00-21 multiple-element arrangement model should be used to separate the elements for accounting purposes. While this position is not stated explicitly in EITF 00-21, it is based on the general scope guidance in paragraph 4 of EITF 00-21. In December 2003, an SEC staff member discussed this guidance in a speech and indicated that "...the consensus reached by the EITF requires that the Issue 00-21 criteria be applied in bundled arrangements involving significant customization of software to determine whether SOP 81-1 deliverables should be separated from the non-SOP 81-1 deliverables." This conclusion is different from that included in TPA 5100.49, which effectively indicates that the multiple-element model in SOP 97-2 should be applied to separate PCS-related services from a multiple-element arrangement including software that involves significant production, modification, or customization and PCS. This TPA was issued prior to EITF 00-21, however, and likely does not reflect the most current thinking on this subject.

Before using a model other than that in EITF 00-21 to separate a multiple-element arrangement that includes SOP 81-1 software and PCS, a company should consult with an expert to determine whether using another model would be appropriate. In such situations, the company should keep in mind the potential outcomes of applying other models. One potential outcome would be that the SOP 81-1 software and PCS should not be separated for accounting purposes. In this situation, using a Proportional Performance model to recognize revenue for the bundled set of elements would likely not be appropriate because of the difficulties that often arise in estimating the costs associated with certain activities covered by PCS, such as telephone support and delivery of unspecified upgrades (i.e., "when-and-if-available" upgrades). As such, a Completed Performance model would likely be used to recognize revenue for the bundled set of elements. Given the nature of the elements, this potential outcome may not be reasonable.

ILLUSTRATION: DETERMINING THE APPROPRIATE MULTIPLE-ELEMENT ARRANGEMENT GUIDANCE TO APPLY

EXAMPLE 1

Facts: A multiple-element arrangement includes off-the-shelf software (i.e., software that is more than incidental but does not require significant production, modification, or customization) and computer hardware. The off-the-shelf software is not essential to the functionality of the computer hardware.

Discussion: The off-the-shelf software is SOP 97-2 software and the computer hardware is not an SOP 97-2 software-related element. Since one element falls within the scope of SOP 97-2 (i.e., SOP 97-2 software) and one element does not (i.e., computer hardware), the multiple-element model in EITF 00-21 should be applied to determine whether the two elements should be treated separately for revenue recognition purposes.

EXAMPLE 2

Facts: A multiple-element arrangement includes off-the-shelf software (i.e., software that is more than incidental but does not require significant production, modification, or customization) and computer hardware. The off-the-shelf software is essential to the functionality of the computer hardware.

Discussion: The off-the-shelf software is SOP 97-2 software and the computer hardware is an SOP 97-2 software-related element. Since both elements fall within the scope of SOP 97-2, the multiple-element model in SOP 97-2 should be applied to determine whether the two elements should be treated separately for revenue recognition purposes.

EXAMPLE 3

Facts: A multiple-element arrangement includes software that will be significantly modified and customized as part of the multiple-element arrangement and computer hardware. The significantly modified and customized software is not essential to the functionality of the computer hardware and the computer hardware is not essential to the functionality of the significantly modified and customized software.

Discussion: The arrangement effectively has three potential elements: (1) the software that will be significantly modified and customized, (2) the services that will be performed to significantly modify and customize the software, and (3) the computer hardware. Because of the relationship between the software and the services that will be performed to significantly modify and customize the software, the software and services are considered one SOP 81-1 software element. However, the SOP 81-1 software element is not essential to the functionality of the computer hardware and the computer hardware is not essential to the functionality of the SOP 81-1 software element. In other words, the computer hardware is not an SOP 81-1 software-related element. Because one element falls within the scope of SOP 81-1 (i.e., the SOP 81-1 software element) and one element does not fall within the scope of SOP 81-1 (i.e., computer hardware), the multiple-element arrangement model in EITF 00-21 should be applied to determine whether (a) the SOP 81-1 software element and (b) the computer hardware should be treated separately for revenue recognition purposes.

EXAMPLE 4

Facts: A multiple-element arrangement includes software that will be significantly modified and customized as part of the multiple-element arrangement and computer hardware. The significantly modified and customized software is essential to the functionality of the computer hardware.

Discussion: The arrangement effectively has three potential elements: (1) the software that will be significantly modified and customized, (2) the services that will be performed to significantly modify and customize the software, and (3) the computer hardware. Because of the relationship between the software and the services that will be performed to significantly modify and customize the software, the software and services are considered one SOP 81-1 software element. In addition, the computer hardware is considered an SOP 81-1 software-related element since the SOP 81-1 software element is essential to its functionality. Because both elements fall within the scope of SOP 81-1, the multiple-element arrangement model that should be applied to determine whether the elements (i.e., SOP 81-1 software element and computer hardware) should be separated is the model in SOP 81-1.

SUMMARY

		Is the hardware software-related (i.e., is the software essential to the functionality of the hardware)?	
		Yes	No
Is the vendor providing significant production, modification, or customization services in connection with the software sale?	Yes	SOP 81-1 Multiple-Element Model (Example 4)	EITF 00-21 Multiple-Element Model (Example 3)
	No	SOP 97-2 Multiple-Element Model (Example 2)	EITF 00-21 Multiple-Element Model (Example 1)

The remainder of this section of the chapter discusses the multiple-element model in SOP 97-2. The SOP 97-2 multiple-element model would be applied to a multiple-element arrangement that includes only SOP 97-2 software and software-related elements. It would also be applied to determine whether the SOP 97-2 software and software-related elements separated from a multiple-element arrangement based on the guidance in EITF 00-21 should be further separated.

DISCLOSURE ALERT: See Chapter 12, "Disclosures," for information about required disclosures.

SEC REGISTRANT ALERT: In early 2003, the SEC staff issued the Report Pursuant to Section 704 of the Sarbanes-Oxley Act of 2002 (the Section 704 Report). In compiling the information in the Section 704 Report, the SEC staff studied enforcement actions filed during the period July 31, 1997, through July 30, 2002. The greatest number of enforcement actions brought by the SEC related to improper revenue recognition. One of the common revenue recognition issues highlighted in the Section 704 Report related to improper recognition of revenue from multiple-element arrangements or bundled contracts. One of the two actions discussed in the Section 704 Report in this regard involved improper allocation of arrangement consideration and the other involved improper separation of interdependent elements. This finding is a strong indication that more attention should be given to accounting for multiple-element arrangements.

In addition, in early 2003, the SEC staff issued the Summary by the Division of Corporation Finance of Significant Issues Addressed in the Review of the Periodic Reports of the Fortune 500 Companies (the Fortune 500 Report). This report resulted from the SEC's Division of Corporation Finance's (Corp Fin) review of all annual reports filed by Fortune 500 companies. The report provides insight into areas commonly questioned by Corp Fin during its reviews of annual reports. One area specifically mentioned in the Fortune 500 Report relates to accounting for multiple-element arrangements. Corp Fin specifically indicated that companies in the computer software, computer services, and computer hardware industries could improve their disclosures by expanding the discussion related to multiple-element arrangements.

Defining the Arrangement When Multiple Contracts Exist

A number of requirements in software revenue recognition affect multiple-element arrangements, but not single-element arrangements. In addition, there are times in which the inclusion or exclusion of a certain element within an arrangement can significantly affect the accounting for the other elements of the arrangement (for example, one undelivered element for which vendor-specific objective evidence (see below) of fair value does not exist prohibits recognition of revenue upon delivery of other elements). For these reasons, it is important to properly identify the "arrangement," which is the starting point for allocating revenue to individual elements.

SOP 97-2 was written to cause vendors to account for the substantive agreement, rather than merely the contractual one. Even if different elements are documented in multiple contracts, a multiple-element arrangement that includes only SOP 97-2 software and/or software-related elements must be accounted for using the appropriate multiple-element provisions of SOP 97-2. Therefore, contracts should be evaluated together when they are, in substance, part of one arrangement. When determining whether multiple contracts with a single customer should be accounted for as a single arrangement, judgment is required. Some factors that might indicate that multiple contracts are substantively part of the same arrangement include (TPA 5100.39):

1. The contracts or agreements are negotiated or executed within a short time frame of each other.
2. The different elements are closely interrelated or interdependent in terms of design, technology, or function.
3. The fee for one or more contracts or agreements is subject to refund or forfeiture or other concession if another contract is not completed satisfactorily.
4. One or more elements in one contract or agreement are essential to the functionality of an element in another contract.
5. Payment terms under one contract or agreement coincide with performance criteria of another contract or agreement.
6. The negotiations are conducted jointly with two or more parties (for example, from different divisions of the same company) to do what, in essence, is a single project.

Allocating Revenue Among Elements

If vendor-specific objective evidence (VSOE) of fair value, as discussed below, exists for all elements, the arrangement consideration should be allocated to the individual elements based on their relative fair values, except that the full fair value of any element that represents a specified upgrade right should be allocated to that specified right, regardless of any discount inherent in the total arrangement. The result of this process is that, except for specified upgrade rights, when a multiple-element arrangement has a total fee less than the fee that would be determined by adding up the fair values (as supported by VSOE) of each of the individual elements, that discount is allocated pro rata across each of the elements (SOP 97-2, par. 11).

If VSOE of fair value exists for all undelivered elements, but does not exist for one or more delivered elements, the arrangement consideration should be allocated to the various elements of the arrangement under the residual method. Under this method, the amount of arrangement consideration allocated to the delivered elements should be the total arrangement consideration less the aggregate fair values of the undelivered elements. Thus, any potential discount on the arrangement taken as a whole is allocated entirely to the delivered elements. This ensures that the amount of revenue recognized at any point in time is not overstated. If the sum of the fair values of the undelivered elements is greater than the total arrangement consideration, no revenue may be recognized, despite the fact that one or more elements have already been delivered (SOP 97-2, par. 12).

> **OBSERVATION:** The residual method works in only one direction. It works only when VSOE of fair value exists for all undelivered elements. If VSOE of fair value exists for delivered elements, but does not exist for one or more undelivered elements, the residual method cannot be used because it is not possible, in the absence of VSOE of fair value of the undelivered elements, to ensure that all of the potential discount in the arrangement is allocated to the delivered elements.

Once the fee in an arrangement has been allocated among elements based on the appropriate method, the allocation should not be subsequently changed, even if the company changes its pricing (SOP 97-2, par. 10).

If VSOE of fair value does not exist for any undelivered element, no revenue from the arrangement may be recognized until either sufficient VSOE exists to allocate revenue based on one of the methods described above or the last element in the arrangement is delivered. Establishment of VSOE (for example, by separately selling an element) after the end of an accounting period but before financial statements are prepared is not sufficient to permit revenue recognition during the accounting period in question (TPA 5100.38).[2]

> **OBSERVATION:** Some software arrangements are very complex and include a large number of elements. If VSOE of fair value of even one undelivered element does not exist, no revenue may be recognized until VSOE of fair value for that element does exist, or the element is delivered. Therefore, no matter how small a particular undelivered element is to an entire arrangement, the lack of VSOE of fair value for it can delay revenue recognition.

Multiple-Product, Multiple-Copy, Fixed-Fee Arrangements

Some software arrangements provide customers with the right to reproduce or obtain copies, at specified prices per copy, of several software products up to the total amount of a fixed fee. In these arrangements, the fixed fee is payable regardless of the number of copies of the various products that are eventually used, and payment is not tied to deployment or use of the copies. Although the price per copy is fixed at the inception of the arrangement, the arrangement

---

2 Establishing VSOE after period-end is also a Type II subsequent event, as discussed in footnote 1.

fee cannot be allocated to the individual products because the revenue allocable to each software product depends on the choices to be made by the customer in the future regarding how many of each product will be used (or resold, if the customer is a reseller). These arrangements may include the rights to select copies of products that are not available at the inception of the arrangement.

Because the minimum fee is fixed in these arrangements, and is not dependent upon duplication or the selection of the number of copies of each product to be used, all revenue should be recognized when the first or master copy of all products that are part of the arrangement have been delivered provided all other revenue recognition criteria have been met. Until then, revenue should be recognized as copies of delivered products are made.

> **OBSERVATION:**   Note that, in this case, the stated contract prices are used to recognize revenue, regardless of the fair value of each product and regardless of whether VSOE of fair value exists. This is a unique feature of the accounting for fixed minimum, multi-product, multi-copy arrangements in which the customer chooses how many copies of each product to use. This use of contractually stated amounts to recognize revenue may not be analogized to for other types of arrangements.

Certain arrangements may impose a maximum on the number of copies of a particular product that the customer may select. If all undelivered products in an arrangement are subject to such maximums, any revenue in excess of the specified prices per copy multiplied by the applicable maximums should be recognized as revenue provided all other revenue recognition criteria have been met (SOP 97-2, pars. 43-47).

ILLUSTRATION: PER COPY PRICES IN A MULTIPLE-PRODUCT, MULTIPLE-COPY, FIXED-FEE ARRANGEMENT

(Adapted from SOP 97-2, Appendix A)

EXAMPLE 1

Facts: A vendor enters into an arrangement under which a customer has the right to make copies of Product A at $100 a copy, copies of Product B at $200 a copy, or copies of Product C at $50 a copy until such time as the customer has made copies aggregating $100,000 based on the per copy prices. The customer is obligated to pay the $100,000 immediately, without regard to when it makes copies of the three products. The first copy of Products A and B are delivered immediately, but Product C is not available yet. No portion of the fee allocable to copies made of Products A and B is refundable if Product C is not delivered, nor is there any obligation to deliver Product C if copies of Products A and B aggregating $100,000 have been made. None of the products are essential to the functionality of any of the other products. The maximum number of copies of Product C that can be made is 500.

Discussion: Because the first copy of Product C has not yet been delivered, the maximum amount of the fee that may be used for Product C must be deferred. Thus, $25,000 (500 copies × $50 per copy) must be deferred. The remaining $75,000 of revenue should be recognized when the first copies of Products A and B are delivered to the customer. The $25,000 allocated to Product C would be recognized upon delivery of the first copy of that product. If the customer duplicates enough copies of Products A and B such that the revenue allocable to those products exceeds $75,000, the additional revenue should be recognized as the additional copies are made.

EXAMPLE 2

Facts: Assume the same facts as in the preceding example, except the arrangement does not state a maximum number of copies of Product C that can be made.

Discussion: Because no limit on the number of copies of Product C exists, the customer could, in theory, use the entire fixed fee to purchase copies of Product C. Therefore, revenue should only be recognized as copies of Products A ($100 of revenue per copy) and B ($200 of revenue per copy) are made, until the first copy of Product C is delivered, at which point, any remaining revenue should be recognized.

License Mix Arrangements

In some cases, a fixed fee, multi-product, multi-copy arrangement may allow a user to change or alternate its use of multiple products or licenses (license mix) included in a license arrangement even after the customer makes its initial choices under the arrangement. Under license mix arrangements, the user has a license to use one or more copies of each delivered product, but may choose at any point during the arrangement to change the mix of products and licenses pursuant to criteria set out in the contract.

Software offered under a license mix arrangement is considered delivered for accounting purposes once the first or master copy of each product is delivered. In addition, remixing is not considered an exchange or a return of software because the master or first copy of all products has been licensed and delivered, and the customer has the right to use them. Nor is a remix right considered the right to obtain additional products or licenses, as long as the remix rights do not allow the customer to increase the aggregate value of the licenses it uses at a particular time. Therefore, as long as all other revenue recognition criteria are met, revenue from a remix arrangement may be recognized upon delivery of the first or master copy of each product (TPA 5100.45).

However, if the remix provisions allow the customer to receive the rights to use products that do not exist at the initiation of the arrangement, the arrangement should be treated as a subscription (see "Subscriptions" earlier in this chapter).

ILLUSTRATION: REMIX RIGHTS

EXAMPLE 1

Facts: A vendor enters into an arrangement under which a customer has the right to make copies of Product A at $100 a copy, copies of Product B at $200 a copy, or copies of Product C at $50 a copy until such time as the customer has made copies aggregating $100,000 based on the per copy prices. The customer is obligated to pay the $100,000 immediately, without regard to when it makes copies of the three products. The customer initially selects 200 copies of Product B ($40,000), 250 copies of Product A ($25,000), and 700 copies of Product C ($35,000).

After the initial selection, the customer has the right, for three years, to change its use of Products A, B, and C by giving up licenses of one in exchange for licenses of another based on the ratio of the prices stated in the arrangement. For example, the customer can give up one copy of Product B in exchange for two copies of Product A or four copies of Product C.

Discussion: Once a copy of each of the products has been delivered, the remix rights do not affect the recognition of revenue under the contract since the remix rights do not extend to any additional products and the aggregate value of the software under the arrangement is limited to the $100,000 fee.

EXAMPLE 2

Facts: Same as Example 1, except that the customer may exchange each copy of Product B it initially chooses for five copies of Product C.

Discussion: In this case, the customer can obtain additional value based on exercising its remix rights. The 1,000 copies of Product C that could be obtained by giving up 200 copies of Product B have a value of $50,000, while the 200 copies of Product B that would be given up have a value of $40,000. Thus, the additional value that the customer can realize is $10,000. That amount should be deferred to account for these rights when revenue is recognized under the arrangement.

EXAMPLE 3

Facts: Same as Example 1, except that the remix rights will also pertain to any other products that the vendor develops during the remix period, based on the list prices of those products as compared to the contractual prices of Products A, B, and C.

Discussion: Because the remix rights apply to future products, the arrangement should be treated as a subscription, meaning that the $100,000 fee should be recognized ratably over three years.

Vendor-Specific Objective Evidence (VSOE) of Fair Value

General

SOP 97-2 limits the information that a company may look to in establishing the fair value of the particular element. Specifically, this information, which is called vendor-specific objective evidence (VSOE) of fair value, is limited to:

1. The price charged when the same element is sold separately.
2. For an element not yet being sold separately, the price established by management having the relevant authority; it must be probable that the price, once established, will not change before the separate introduction of the element into the marketplace.

Separate prices stated in an arrangement are not relevant in determining the fair value of the individual elements, because such prices, having been negotiated as part of the arrangement as a whole, do not necessarily represent bargained-for prices for each individual element. As such, they may not represent fair value (SOP 97-2, par. 10).

The definition of VSOE also prohibits using surrogate prices, such as competitor prices for similar products or industry averages, to determine fair value. This is because software products produced by different vendors, even if they are designed for the same purpose, invariably have inherent differences. Using competitor prices as evidence of fair value would essentially result in those differences being ignored. For that reason, SOP 97-2 requires that the evidence be vendor-specific (SOP 97-2, par. 100).

The limits on the acceptable evidence of fair value also prohibit the use of methods such as "cost plus a normal profit margin" to support fair value. In part, this is because "cost" in a software environment is a difficult amount to determine. The direct cost of software products is very low, as almost all of the cost is incurred in development of the software. Once the software is developed, additional copies can be produced at almost no cost. Thus, the notion of a "normal profit margin" is virtually non-existent.

Allocating revenue to each element based on the combined profit margin of the arrangement is also not acceptable. That type of allocation would not be expected to result in assigning the fair value to each element, because various elements would normally be expected to have different profit margins. For example, while software products have an almost non-existent direct cost component, services may have a very significant direct cost component.

Although many other methods for allocating the arrangement fee to the individual elements were suggested during its development, SOP 97-2 does not allow any of them. Therefore, in a software arrangement, it is common to conclude that insufficient evidence exists to allocate the arrangement fee to the individual elements, due to a lack of VSOE of fair value.

EXAMPLE: VSOE OF FAIR VALUE

BMC Software, Inc. Form 10-K—Fiscal Year Ended March 31, 2005

When several elements, including software licenses, PCS and professional services, are sold to a customer through a single contract, the revenues from such multiple-element arrangements are allocated to each element based upon the residual method, whereby the fair value of the undelivered elements of the contract is deferred until such time as that element is delivered, or in the case of PCS, such revenue is recognized ratably over the PCS term. The Company has established vendor-specific objective evidence of the fair value of the PCS through the renewal rates established in contractual arrangements with our customers and through monitoring independent sales of the Company's PCS at the stated renewal rates. The Company has established a consistent relationship by pricing PCS as a percentage of the license amount. The Company has established vendor-specific objective evidence of the fair value of our professional services based on the daily rates charged to our customers in stand-alone contracts. Accordingly, software license fees are recognized under the residual method for arrangements in which the software is licensed with maintenance, enhancement and support and/or professional services, and where the maintenance, enhancement and support and/or professional services are not essential to the functionality of the delivered software. In the event a contract contains terms, which are inconsistent with the Company's vendor-specific objective evidence, all revenues from the contract are deferred until such evidence is established or are recognized on a ratable basis.

Matrix Pricing

In some cases, pricing may be based on many different factors or combinations thereof. For example, certain arrangements are priced differently based on the type of customer or the number of users that will be granted access to the licensed products. In these arrangements, a software vendor may, as part of its standard pricing policy, offer a reduced per user price to companies purchasing a greater number of user licenses or a greater number of products. SOP 97-2 does allow these types of pricing policies to be taken into account when determining the fair value of an element in an arrangement (SOP 97-2, par. 10).

ILLUSTRATION: VSOE OF FAIR VALUE BASED ON MULTIPLE FACTORS

Facts: A software vendor generally sells a single license to its product for $100. However, as part of its standard price list, not-for-profit entities receive a 10% discount on every license. In addition, any customer purchasing over 100 licenses at once receives a 10% discount off of the otherwise applicable price.

Discussion: Standard discounts imply that the vendor is selling to different classes of customers. Therefore, the vendor really has a matrix of VSOE of fair values for its product. Because the discounts are standard, they should be considered in assessing the VSOE of fair value. Thus, in this case, the vendor's VSOE of fair value is as follows:

	Not-for-Profits	**Other Customers**
Less than 100 licenses	$90 per license	$100 per license
100 licenses or more	$81 per license	$90 per license

Specified Upgrades

Specified upgrades are treated as separate elements of the arrangement. Therefore, VSOE of fair value for an undelivered specified upgrade must exist before any revenue may be recognized in an arrangement. VSOE of fair value for a specific upgrade would be the fee charged to existing users of the software product who separately purchase the upgrade. However, if the software vendor intends to provide the upgrade free of charge to all users of the product (for example, by providing a free download of the upgrade on its Internet site), regardless of whether they have a contractual right to the upgrade, then the VSOE for that upgrade is zero, and no revenue need be deferred when the rights to it are specifically included in an arrangement.

> ☞ **PRACTICE POINTER:** Many upgrades are not sold separately, and are not provided free of charge to all users, regardless of

the contractual arrangements. Instead, customers generally obtain the rights to them only by purchasing post-contract customer support (see the next section for the accounting for such arrangements) or negotiating the rights to them in the original license arrangement. For that reason, VSOE of fair value for a specified upgrade often will not exist. Many companies, as a matter of policy, do not include specific upgrade rights in their arrangements to sell software. However, each contract should be reviewed to determine whether specific upgrade rights are granted.

SOP 97-2 contains two special provisions regarding the allocation of an arrangement fee to a specified upgrade. First, no portion of any discount in a multiple-element arrangement should be allocated to a specified upgrade right. Therefore, if an arrangement includes a specified upgrade for which VSOE of fair value exists, the full fair value must be allocated to the upgrade. This is similar to the application of the residual method when VSOE of fair value does not exist for one or more delivered elements. The second special provision that applies to specified upgrades is that, if sufficient vendor-specific experience exists to reasonably estimate breakage (the percentage of customers that are not expected to exercise the upgrade right), the fee allocated to the upgrade right should be reduced to reflect that estimated breakage (SOP 97-2, pars. 36-37).

> **OBSERVATION:** The concept of reducing the amount allocated to an undelivered element to reflect expected breakage is a question that arises frequently in multiple-element arrangements, whether they are software arrangements or not. Although there is some judgment that can be applied in non-software arrangements (see Chapter 3, "General Principles"), SOP 97-2 allows consideration of breakage only in the context of specific upgrades. Thus, if an arrangement includes an additional product, rather than an upgrade, then revenue must be allocated to the additional product as if all users will request it, even if the vendor reasonably believes that some will not.

PCS

A limited period of PCS often is included with the purchase of a license to software. As discussed earlier, if PCS is included in an arrangement with SOP 97-2 software, the multiple-element arrangement model in SOP 97-2 should be applied to determine whether the SOP 97-2 software and PCS should be treated separately for accounting purposes. As such, to treat the PCS as a separate element for accounting purposes, VSOE of its fair value must exist. Determining whether VSOE of fair value exists for PCS is discussed further below. PCS should be analyzed in this manner even though it may be provided to all purchasers. In rare circumstances, however, PCS is considered insignificant to the arrangement in which case its delivery is not required to recognize the revenue allocated to it (see additional discussion on this point in the section above titled "Post-Contract Customer Support (PCS)").

As discussed earlier, if PCS is included in an arrangement with SOP 81-1 software, the multiple-element arrangement model in EITF 00-21 should be applied to determine whether the SOP 81-1 software and PCS should be treated separately for accounting purposes (see Chapter 4, "Multiple-Element Arrangements," for a discussion of the EITF 00-21 multiple-element arrangement model).

In general, an arrangement that includes SOP 97-2 software and an initial PCS period also will provide that the customer may purchase additional periods of PCS, at a specified renewal rate, when the initial "free" period expires. The specified renewal rate provides VSOE of fair value of the PCS services, unless the renewal rate is not substantive (SOP 97-2, par. 57).

ILLUSTRATION: ALLOCATION OF ARRANGEMENT FEE BETWEEN LICENSE AND PCS

For purposes of these examples, assume that the software does not involve significant production, modification, or customization.

EXAMPLE 1

Facts: A vendor licenses software to a user along with one year of PCS for $90,000. VSOE of fair value for the software is $85,000 and PCS is renewable on an annual basis for $15,000 per year.

Discussion: The PCS renewal rate is considered to be VSOE of fair value for the PCS. Therefore, there is sufficient VSOE to allocate the fee between the software and the PCS. The fair value of the two elements is $100,000, meaning there is a 10% discount in the arrangement. This discount should be allocated across the two elements as follows:

	License	PCS	Total
Fair Value	$85,000	$15,000	$100,000
Less: 10% Discount	- 8,500	- 1,500	- 10,000
Revenue	$76,500	$13,500	$ 90,000

EXAMPLE 2

Facts: A vendor licenses software to a user along with one year of PCS for $90,000. PCS is renewable on an annual basis for $15,000 per year. The vendor does not have VSOE of fair value for the software because it is never sold separately (it is always sold with PCS).

Discussion: The PCS renewal rate is considered to be VSOE of fair value for the PCS. Therefore, there is sufficient VSOE to allocate the fee using the residual method. In this case, $15,000 of the arrangement fee is deferred, representing the full fair value of the undelivered element, PCS. The remaining $75,000 is allocated to the software element.

EXAMPLE 3

Facts: A software vendor typically prices annual PCS at 13% of its standard perpetual license fee. The VSOE of fair value for the software is $100,000. The vendor enters into an arrangement that includes a perpetual license to its software and one year of PCS for $102,000. The stated renewal rate for PCS is $2,000.

Discussion: $2,000 should not be considered to be VSOE of fair value for the PCS, as the renewal rate is not substantive. In this situation, the company should look to its standard renewal rates that are used in other arrangements to find VSOE of fair value. Therefore, the fair value of PCS would be considered to be $13,000 per year. In allocating the license fee, the vendor would need to estimate how many years of discounted PCS the customer would be expected to buy. Typically, the estimate used would be the remaining product life of the software product. Thus, if the product has a five-year remaining life, revenue would be allocated as follows:

	Payments	Fair Value
Software	$102,000	$100,000
Expected Five Years of PCS	8,000	65,000
Total	$110,000	$ 165,000

This results in an implied discount in the arrangement of 33%. As such, when revenue is recognized on the sale of software, $66,667 should be recognized. The remainder of the up-front fee should be deferred and recognized over the anticipated five-year PCS period.

An arrangement may include two different pricing methodologies related to PCS renewals. For example, an arrangement may include (1) a perpetual software license with a three-year unlimited deployment period, and (2) PCS where the fee for renewing PCS is fixed in the second and third year of the arrangement, but varies in the fourth year of the arrangement and thereafter, depending on the number of software copies deployed. In this situation, consideration should be given to whether there is any basis to determine which of the PCS renewal pricing methodologies represents VSOE of fair value. In many cases, there will be no basis to make such a determination. However, if sufficient objective evidence exists to support the assertion that the renewal rate in the fourth year and thereafter is more likely than not (i.e., a likelihood of greater than 50%) to approximate or be less than the amount charged in the second and third years, the PCS renewal rates for the second and third years would constitute VSOE of fair value of PCS (TPA 5100.75).

Implied PCS arrangements   In some cases, an arrangement does not explicitly include rights to PCS, but the vendor has a historical pattern of providing (or an intention to provide) the customer with support services and/or unspecified upgrades. In those situations, an implied PCS arrangement exists and should be considered an element of the arrangement.

In other situations, the contract may include a period of PCS that begins some time after delivery of the product, presumably to coincide with the installation or deployment of the product by the customer. However, because such arrangements almost invariably entitle the customer to unspecified upgrades introduced during the intervening period, and because other support is generally provided during such period as well, an arrangement with a delayed PCS commencement date should be considered to include PCS during the intervening period as well. For example, an arrangement that includes one year of PCS that begins three months after product delivery should be accounted for as an arrangement that includes 15 months of PCS. The arrangement fee should be allocated accordingly (SOP 97-2, par. 56).

Renewal rates based on a percentage of license fee   Some vendors have a practice of charging for PCS renewals at a rate calculated as a consistent percentage of the net license fee, which may vary from arrangement to arrangement based on the negotiations between the parties. Thus, the PCS renewal rates, expressed in terms of actual dollars rather than percentages, vary from arrangement to arrangement. As long as each of the arrangements includes a renewal fee based on a consistent percentage of the license fee that is substantive, that renewal rate may be treated as VSOE of fair value for the arrangement (TPA 5100.55).

VSOE of PCS for term licenses   While perpetual licenses are the most common type of software license arrangement, term licenses are also common. In a term license, the software product can only be used for a limited period of time. After that, the customer must enter into a new license (or extend the old one) to continue to use the product. Many term licenses of software include PCS for the entire term. In these licenses, there is no renewal rate for PCS, and thus, typically, no VSOE of fair value for PCS. Although the company might look to its standard PCS renewal rate in perpetual licenses of the same product as evidence of the fair value of PCS, the fair value of PCS in a term license and the fair value of PCS in a perpetual license are likely to be very different, due to the different periods during which any upgrades or technical advice will be useful to the customer. Therefore, PCS in a term license and PCS in a perpetual license of the same product are not considered to be the same element. As such, the separate sales price (renewal rate) of PCS in a perpetual license is not VSOE of fair value for PCS in a term license of the same product (TPA 5100.68).

> ☛ **PRACTICE POINTER:**   Several other TPAs address PCS issues in term licenses. Because they each cover narrow circumstances, they are not addressed here. However, they may be found on the AICPA's Internet site, www.aicpa.org.

Services

VSOE of fair value for service elements may be easily identified, as the services are generally available to be purchased separately. For example, a software vendor often offers training and consultation on integration of the software package with other systems as services with specific pricing that can be purchased after the software has been delivered or installed. Other services, such as software customization, may not have VSOE of fair value, because they are undertaken only as part of a comprehensive arrangement to design, develop, and deliver a customized software package. As discussed below, in many cases the existence of such services requires the use of contract accounting for the arrangement.

Elements Essential to the Functionality of One Another

In general, once revenue is allocated to each of the elements in an arrangement, revenue recognition for that element is assessed without regard to the other elements. However, in determining whether an element in a multiple-element arrangement has been delivered, the delivery of an element is considered not to have occurred if there are undelivered elements that are essential to the functionality of the delivered element, because the customer would not have the full use of the delivered element (SOP 97-2, par. 13). For example, no revenue should be recognized upon delivery of a software upgrade if the base package has not yet been delivered.

Service Elements Essential to the Functionality of Software

An important factor to consider in determining whether services are essential to the functionality of any other element is whether the software included in the arrangement is considered core or off-the-shelf software. Core software is software that a vendor uses in creating other software. It is not sold as is because customers cannot use it unless it is customized to meet system objectives or customer specifications. Design and customization services are almost always essential to the functionality of core software included in the same arrangement (SOP 97-2, pars. 68-69).

In contrast, off-the-shelf software is software the customer can use with no significant changes in the underlying code. In some instances, an arrangement may include delivery of off-the-shelf software along with integration or other services that do not affect the operation of the off-the-shelf software. In these cases, the services should not be considered essential to the functionality of the software. However, if significant modifications or additions to software that is normally considered off-the-shelf software are necessary to meet the customer's purpose (for example, changing or making additions to the software because it would not be usable in its off-the-shelf form in the customer's environment), the software should be considered core software for purposes of that arrangement. As such, the services included in the arrangement would be considered essential to the functionality of the software (SOP 97-2, pars. 68-69).

A service element should only be separately accounted for if it is separately identified in the arrangement such that the arrangement fee would be expected to vary based on whether it was included or not (SOP 97-2, par. 65). For example, assume that an arrangement calls for the delivery of a software package that interfaces with a certain report writer system, and that the off-the-shelf version of the software does not interface with that report writer. Because the arrangement does not specifically identify the development of the interface as a separate implementation service, that service cannot be accounted for separately. Instead, the service and the product must be accounted for on a combined basis under contract accounting. If, instead, the arrangement had called for the delivery of the off-the-shelf product, and implementation services to build the interface to the report writer, the product and service could possibly be accounted for separately.

Other factors should also be considered in evaluating whether a service element is essential to the functionality of the other elements of an arrangement. For example, the following factors are indicative of services that are essential to the functionality of other elements (SOP 97-2, par. 70):

1. *Building complex interfaces is necessary for the vendor's software to be functional in the customer's environment.* Especially if the software is not sold by third parties, there may be no other party that can design and develop such complex interfaces.

2. *The timing of payments for the software is coincident with performance of the services.* This would seem to indicate that the customer does

not believe it has full use of the software until the services are complete. Note that this factor is only indicative that services are essential to the software's functionality if the amount of payments whose timing is tied to the services is greater than the amount of revenue that is allocated to the services.

3. *Milestones or customer-specific acceptance criteria affect the realizability of the software-license fee.* If the customer has negotiated the right to reject the software if the services are not performed to its satisfaction, this would seem to indicate that the customer believes the services are essential to the functionality of the software.

Conversely, the following factors are indicative that the services are not essential to the functionality of the software (SOP 97-2, par. 71):

1. *The services are available from other vendors.* If this is true, then the customer could have obtained any services necessary to use the software for its purposes without the involvement of the vendor. As such, the vendor's services would not appear to be essential to the software's functionality.

2. *The services do not carry a significant degree of risk or unique acceptance criteria.* Services that are routine in nature are not likely to be essential to the software's functionality.

3. *The software vendor is an experienced provider of the services.* This indicates a low risk related to the provision of the services.

4. *The vendor is providing primarily implementation services that do not affect the operation of the software.* Services, such as loading of software, training of customer personnel, data conversion, report writing, and the documentation of procedures, are not generally essential to operating the software.

5. *Customer personnel are dedicated to participate in the services being performed.* The dedication of customer personnel may indicate that it is not absolutely necessary that the services be provided by the vendor.

If a service element is determined to be essential to the functionality of the software included in an arrangement, the software product and service elements should be accounted for on a combined basis, using contract accounting. The application of contract accounting to a software arrangement is discussed later in this chapter.

Non-Service Elements

Except for undelivered service elements, GAAP does not provide significant guidance to be used in determining whether an element is essential to the functionality of another element. However, many of the same concepts that are identified as being relevant in determining whether an undelivered service is essential to the functionality of a delivered element are also relevant when the undelivered element is a product element. If an undelivered element other than a service element is essential to the functionality of a delivered element, revenue from the delivered element should be deferred until the element essential to its functionality is also delivered.

Refund Provisions Based on Undelivered Elements

SOP 97-2 provides specific guidance for refund or cancellation provisions related to undelivered elements. Specifically, revenue allocated to an element is not considered collectible to the extent that it is subject to forfeiture, refund, or other concession in the event an as-yet undelivered element is not delivered as provided for in the arrangement. The forfeiture provisions may be explicitly documented, or may exist even though not specified in the arrangement. Thus, for the revenue related to an arrangement to be considered not subject to forfeiture, refund, or other concession, management must intend not to accept returns or grant concessions in the event an as-yet undelivered element is not delivered regardless of whether those rights are explicitly documented in the provisions of the arrangement. In addition, a review of all available evidence should persuasively indicate that the revenue is not subject to forfeiture, refund, or other concession in the event an as-yet undelivered element is not delivered.

If the vendor has a historical pattern of making refunds or granting concessions on delivered elements not required under the original provisions of its arrangements due to non-delivery of other elements, no other evidence is persuasive enough to reach a conclusion that revenue in current arrangements with similar elements is not subject to forfeiture. As such, no revenue should be recognized until all of the elements are delivered (SOP 97-2, par. 14).

ILLUSTRATION: TIMING OF REVENUE RECOGNITION WHEN SPECIFIED DAMAGES ARE INCLUDED IN A MULTIPLE-ELEMENT ARRANGEMENT

Facts: Company X enters into a contract to deliver two off-the-shelf software elements, A and B, for $1,000,000. Company X appropriately allocates $600,000 of the fee to Element A and $400,000 to Element B based on VSOE of fair value. The agreement stipulates that Company X must pay a $550,000 penalty if it does not deliver Element B by a specified date. Element A has already been delivered, but Element B has not.

Accounting: The portion of the fee allocated to Element A that is subject to forfeiture if Element B is not delivered is not considered collectible until

Element B is delivered. Therefore, Company X may only recognize revenue upon the delivery of Element A to the extent that revenue is not refundable. In this case, the penalty for failing to deliver Element B on a timely basis ($550,000) exceeds the portion of the fee allocated to Element B ($400,000) by $150,000. Therefore, only $450,000 of the $600,000 otherwise allocable to Element A may be recognized. If Company X receives payments of greater than $450,000 before Element B is delivered, the excess should be reflected as deferred revenue.

RECOGNITION WHEN ELEMENTS ARE ACCOUNTED FOR TOGETHER

There are several situations discussed above in which revenue from two separate deliverables cannot be separated for recognition purposes. The appropriate recognition pattern for each of these situations depends on whether the multiple-element arrangement (or portion of a multiple-element arrangement that cannot be further separated): (a) includes SOP 97-2 software and software-related elements and non-SOP 97-2 elements, (b) includes SOP 81-1 software and software-related elements and non-SOP 81-1 elements, (c) includes only SOP 81-1 software and software-related elements, or (d) includes only SOP 97-2 software and software-related elements.

> **PRACTICE ALERT:** A unique cost deferral issue may arise in the application of the specific refund right provision in EITF 00-21 (see Chapter 4, "Multiple-Element Arrangements"). The issue arises when a specific refund right results in some or all of the amount otherwise allocable to a delivered element not being allocated to that element. The question that arises is whether the allocation of something less than the amount otherwise allocable to the delivered element should result in the deferral of some or all of the delivered element's cost. This question is discussed in Chapter 8, "Miscellaneous Issues." This question may not often arise in transactions involving software given the nature of the costs involved in developing software. However, if it does arise, Chapter 8, "Miscellaneous Issues" should be consulted.

Multiple-Element Arrangement Includes SOP 97-2 Elements and Non-SOP 97-2 Elements

As discussed earlier in this chapter, separation of a multiple-element arrangement that includes SOP 97-2 software and software-related elements and non-SOP 97-2 elements should be based on the guidance in EITF 00-21. If the application of EITF 00-21 results in a conclusion that the elements should not be separated, then the general revenue recognition principles apply to the bundled arrangement (for an SEC registrant, this would be SAB Topic 13). In other words, SOP 97-2 should not be applied to determine when revenue should be recognized since the bundled group of elements does not fall within the scope of SOP 97-2. Additional guidance related to recognition of revenue when elements in an arrangement subject to EITF 00-21 should not be treated separately for accounting purposes as a result of its application is provided in Chapter 4, "Multiple-Element Arrangements."

Multiple-Element Arrangement Includes SOP 81-1 Elements and Non-SOP 81-1 Elements

Also as discussed earlier in this chapter, separation of a multiple-element arrangement that includes SOP 81-1 software and software-related elements and non-SOP 81-1 elements should be based on the guidance in EITF 00-21. If the application of EITF 00-21 results in a conclusion that the elements should not be separated, then it would generally be appropriate to apply the general revenue recognition principles to the bundled arrangement (for an SEC registrant, this would be SAB Topic 13). In other words, it would generally be inappropriate to apply SOP 81-1 to the bundled group of elements for purposes of determining when revenue should be recognized since the bundled group of elements does not fall within the scope of SOP 81-1. Additional guidance related to recognition of revenue when elements in an arrangement subject to EITF 00-21 should not be treated separately for accounting purposes as a result of its application is provided in Chapter 4, "Multiple-Element Arrangements."

Multiple-Element Arrangement Includes Only SOP 81-1 Software and Software-Related Elements

Separation of a multiple-element arrangement that includes only SOP 81-1 software and software-related elements should be based on the multiple-element model in SOP 81-1. If the application of the multiple-element arrangement guidance in SOP 81-1 results in a conclusion that the elements should not be separated, then the revenue recognition principles in SOP 81-1 should be applied to the bundled group of elements. The general provisions of SOP 81-1 are discussed in detail in Chapter 9, "Contract Accounting," and specific issues related to applying these provisions to software arrangements are discussed in the following section entitled "Contract Accounting for Software Arrangements."

Multiple-Element Arrangement Includes Only SOP 97-2 Software and Software-Related Elements

Separation of a multiple-element arrangement that includes only SOP 97-2 software and software-related elements should be based on the multiple-element model in SOP 97-2. If the application of the multiple-element model in SOP 97-2 results in a conclusion that the elements should not be separated, then the revenue recognition principles in SOP 97-2 should be applied to the bundled group of elements.

The reason the elements could not be separated for accounting purposes should be taken into consideration when determining how to recognize revenue related to the bundled group of elements. Some of these reasons and the effects they have on recognizing revenue are explained further below.

Sufficient VSOE of Fair Value Does Not Exist

When sufficient VSOE of fair value does not exist to allocate revenue among the elements in a multiple-element arrangement including only SOP 97-2 software and software-related elements, revenue is generally recognized upon delivery of the final element for which VSOE of fair value does not exist, presuming that all other revenue recognition criteria have been met. Once the last element for which VSOE of fair value does not exist has been delivered, either the seller's performance under the arrangement will be complete, or all of the remaining items will be those for which VSOE of fair value exists, allowing the residual method to be applied.

Thus, if an arrangement consists only of SOP 97-2 software and PCS, and there is insufficient VSOE of fair value to allocate revenue among the elements, the revenue from the entire arrangement is recognized as the PCS is delivered—in most cases, ratably over the PCS period. Similarly, if the only undelivered element in an arrangement is an SOP 97-2 software-related service that is not essential to the functionality of the software, all revenue from the arrangement would be recognized as the service is performed, or, if no pattern of performance can be discerned, on a straight-line basis over the period during which the service is performed (SOP 97-2, par. 12).

If the final element to be delivered is an SOP 97-2 software-related product or specified upgrade for which VSOE of fair value does not exist, all revenue from the arrangement must be deferred until that final product or upgrade is delivered, even if the vendor believes that such product's value is not material to the arrangement.

An Element Is Essential to the Functionality of Another Element

When an as-yet undelivered SOP 97-2 software or software-related element is essential to the functionality of a delivered SOP 97-2 software or software-related element, revenue allocated to the delivered element may not be recognized. If the delivered element is an SOP 97-2 software product and the undelivered element essential to the product's functionality is an SOP 97-2 software-related service, contract accounting for the product and service must be used (see "Contract Accounting for Software Arrangements" below). When an undelivered SOP 97-2 software or software-related product is essential to the functionality of a delivered SOP 97-2 software or software-related product, revenue allocated to both products should be recognized, presuming all other revenue recognition criteria are met, when the second product is delivered.

CONTRACT ACCOUNTING FOR SOFTWARE ARRANGEMENTS

If an arrangement to deliver software or a software system, either alone or together with other software-related products or services, requires significant production, modification, or customization of software, the service element cannot be accounted for separately. In those cases, the arrangement should be accounted for using long-term contract accounting, in conformity with ARB-45, using the relevant guidance in SOP 81-1. Contract accounting is an entirely different accounting model in comparison to the model described in SOP 97-2 and the rest of this chapter. Contract accounting is discussed in detail in Chapter 9, "Contract Accounting." That chapter should be consulted for a general description of contract accounting. However, the application of contract accounting to software arrangements presents unique issues, which are discussed here.

☞ **PRACTICE POINTER:** One of the major differences between contract accounting and the normal software revenue recognition rules is that revenue may be recognized before complete delivery occurs when contract accounting is used, under the percentage-of-completion method. Therefore, the use of contract accounting might be attractive to a company that enters into an arrangement to sell a software product that is not yet complete. Nevertheless, transactions that normally are accounted for as product sales should not be accounted for under contract accounting merely to avoid the delivery requirements normally associated with product sales (SOP 97-2, par. 74).

Measuring Progress under the Percentage-of-Completion Method

There are several approaches to measuring progress toward completion under the percentage-of-completion method. Those approaches are grouped into input measures, which are measurements made in terms of efforts devoted to the contract, such as costs, labor hours, and other inputs, and output measures, which are measurements made in terms of results achieved, such as units produced and contract milestones.

Output Measures

Software arrangements generally do not lend themselves to the use of output measures, unless the arrangement requires the delivery of multiple modules, in which case output may be measured based on the completion of the modules. Output measures are difficult to use in other software arrangements because it is difficult to establish relevant measures. If reliable output measures cannot be established, input measures should be used (SOP 97-2, par. 85).

Input Measures

Although costs incurred may be a good measure of progress on a software arrangement, labor hours often are the best measure of progress for projects involving labor-intensive software customization. When input measures based on costs incurred are used, the contract accounting guidance notes that only costs that relate to contract performance should be included in the measurement. For example, software customization projects begin with core software. As the software was not produced for the purpose of the particular contract, no value should be assigned to it in measuring progress-toward completion (SOP 97-2, pars. 81-84).

RIGHTS TO EXCHANGE OR RETURN SOFTWARE

As part of an arrangement, a software vendor may provide the customer with the right to return software or exchange it for other software. The accounting for software return rights is generally the same for software products as it is for return rights on any other product, as return rights are addressed in Level A GAAP (FAS-48). The accounting for exchange rights, however, depends on whether the right is limited to an exchange by an end-user for a product of similar price, features and functionality. An exchange right that is so limited does not receive accounting recognition, as it is not considered to be substantive. FAS-48 specifically excludes these kinds of exchanges from its scope. However, any other exchange right is accounted for as a return right.

Distinguishing Among Return, Exchange, and Additional Product Rights

In certain situations, a right that is labeled a return or exchange right allows the customer to obtain a new software product while retaining the right to use the original product. This is not an exchange or return right at all, but is instead a right to an additional software product. The additional product should be treated as an additional element of the arrangement (SOP 97-2, par. 50).

When the customer is not contractually entitled to continue to use the original software product, the right is either an exchange or a return right. Although it is sometimes difficult to determine which of the two it is, the following situations are clear:

1. If the customer with the return or exchange right is a reseller, rather than an end-user, the right is accounted for as a right of return.

2. If the right allows an end-user to return the software and get anything in exchange other than another software product (for example, services or PCS), the right is accounted for as a right of return.

Rights that allow an end-user to exchange the software for another software package are accounted for as exchange rights if the software the user is entitled to receive has similar price, functionality, and features as the software the user will give up. Whether this is the case is a matter of judgment. However, if the product that is available to the user in the exchange has not yet been developed, and the company expects to incur significant costs in development of that product, it should not be considered to have similar price, features, and functionality to the product delivered to the customer (SOP 97-2, par. 51).

The most common situation that qualifies to be accounted for as an exchange is a platform-transfer right, which is the right to exchange a software product for a product marketed under the same name that operates on a different operating system or on different hardware, but otherwise has the same features and functionality (SOP 97-2, par. 52).

Accounting for Exchange Rights

The existence of a right that allows an end-user to exchange software for software of similar price, features and functionality does not affect the accounting for a software arrangement. As such, revenue may be recognized when each of the revenue recognition criteria is met with respect to the original software product deliverable.

Accounting for Return Rights

Similar to return rights in non-software arrangements, a right to return software should be evaluated to determine its substance. If the return right is limited to situations in which the software does not operate according to published specifications, it should be treated as a warranty. Warranties on software products are treated the same as warranties on any other products (see Chapter 5, "Product Deliverables").

A right to return software if it does not meet customer- or arrangement-specific operating specifications should be treated as a customer acceptance clause. A return right that is of sufficient length to be something other than a period that allows the customer to determine whether software is functional for the customer's purpose should be treated as a cancellation clause (see "Fixed or Determinable Fees and Collectibility" in this chapter for discussion of the accounting for each of these clauses).

Other return rights on software should generally be accounted for in the same manner as similar rights with respect to other products. General information on the accounting for these rights can be found in Chapter 5, "Product Deliverables," and is not repeated here. However, it is worth noting that to recognize revenue when a right of return exists, the vendor must be able to reasonably estimate the amount of returns. Due to the rapid introduction and replacement of software products, historical experience may not be relevant in estimating returns on current sales. If this is the case, it is likely that returns cannot be estimated, prohibiting revenue recognition upon delivery.

EXAMPLE: STOCK BALANCING RIGHTS

Citrix Systems, Inc. Form 10-K—Fiscal Year Ended December 31, 2004

In the normal course of business, the Company does not permit product returns, but it does provide most of its distributors and value added resellers with stock balancing and price protection rights. Stock balancing rights permit distributors to return products to the Company, subject to ordering an equal dollar amount of other products. Price protection rights require that the Company grant retroactive price adjustments for inventories of products held by distributors or resellers if it lowers prices for such products. The Company establishes provisions for estimated returns for stock balancing and price protection rights, as well as other sales allowances, concurrently with the recognition of revenue. The provisions are established based upon consideration of a variety of factors, including, among other things, recent and historical return rates for both specific products and distributors, estimated distributor inventory levels by product, the impact of any new product releases and projected economic conditions. Actual product returns for stock balancing and price protection provisions incurred are, however, dependent upon future events, including the amount of stock balancing activity by distributors and the level of distributor inventories at the time of any price adjustments. The Company continually monitors the factors that influence the pricing of its products and distributor inventory levels and makes adjustments to these provisions when it believes actual returns and other allowances could differ from established reserves. The Company's ability to recognize revenue upon shipment to distributors is predicated on its ability to reliably estimate future stock balancing returns. If actual experience or changes in market condition impairs the Company's ability to estimate returns, it would be required to defer the recognition of revenue until the delivery of the product to the end-user. Allowances for estimated product returns amounted to approximately $3.0 million at December 31, 2004 and $10.5 million at December 31, 2003. The Company has not reduced and has no current plans to reduce its prices for inventory currently held by distributors or resellers. Accordingly, there were no reserves required for price protection at December 31, 2004, or December 31, 2003. The Company records estimated reductions to revenue for customer programs and incentive offerings including volume-based incentives. If market conditions were to decline, the Company could take actions to increase its customer incentive offerings, which could result in an incremental reduction to revenue at the time the incentive is offered.

SALES INCENTIVES

General

Companies that sell packaged software to consumers, either directly or through retailers, prevalently use sales incentives, especially rebates to end-users. The accounting for such incentives has been addressed by the EITF in EITF 01-9. The EITF's conclusions in this area are discussed in detail in Chapters 8, "Miscellaneous Issues," and 11, "Presentation." The application of these conclusions to software arrangements does not pose any unique issues.

Discounts on Future Purchases

In connection with the licensing of an existing product, a vendor might offer a discount (coupon) on future purchases of additional licenses of the same product or on other products or services. If the discount is small or insignificant, it need not be given accounting recognition. However, if the discount is more than insignificant, the existence of the significant discount creates a presumption that there is an additional element in the arrangement. The AICPA SOP 97-2

Implementation Task Force has provided guidance on a number of issues regarding the accounting for discounts on future purchases.

Significant Incremental Discounts

A discount with respect to future purchases that is provided in a software arrangement indicates that another element is present in a software arrangement if the discount meets all of the following criteria (TPA 5100.50):

1. *It is incremental to the range of discounts reflected in the pricing of the other elements of the arrangement.* If the customer was able to negotiate a 30% discount off the elements of the current arrangement, offering a 30% discount off of additional elements does not appear to grant the customer anything that would not otherwise have been available.

2. *It is incremental to the range of discounts typically given in comparable transactions.* Discounts not incremental to discounts typically given in comparable transactions (for example, volume purchase discounts comparable to those generally provided in comparable transactions) do not confer any additional value to the customer than was already available to the customer.

3. *It is significant.* Judgment is required when assessing whether an incremental discount is significant.

4. *It is not limited to additional copies of products licensed by and delivered to the customer under the same arrangement.* As discussed under "Delivery" above, additional copies of delivered software are not considered an undelivered element. Rather, this situation should be accounted for as an arrangement in which the fee depends upon the number of copies ordered and duplicated. As such, the amount of the fee contingent upon future duplication is not recognized until the contingency is resolved, but there need not be any deferral of the initial licensing fee to recognize the discount on the additional copies.

Accounting for Significant Incremental Discounts

The overriding concept applied when a software arrangement includes a right to a significant incremental discount on a future purchase of a product or service is that a proportionate amount of that significant incremental discount should be applied to each element covered by the arrangement based on each element's fair value. Applying that guidance when all of the elements to which the discount can be applied are known and which have VSOE of fair value is relatively straightforward.

However, if either the future elements to which the discount is to be applied are not specified in the arrangement (for example, a customer is allowed a discount on any future purchases), or VSOE of fair value of the future elements does not exist, the concept in the preceding paragraph becomes difficult to apply. In these situations, if the maximum amount of the incremental discount on the future purchases is quantifiable, that quantifiable amount should be allocated to the elements of the arrangement and the future purchases, assuming that the customer will purchase the minimum amount necessary to utilize the maximum discount.

If the maximum amount of the significant incremental discount on future purchases is not quantifiable (for example, the discount can be used on all purchases within a specified period of time, with no limit on the amount of purchases during that time), revenue allocated to each element covered by the arrangement should be reduced by the rate of the significant incremental discount.

If the residual value method is used to allocate arrangement consideration in a multiple-element arrangement that includes a discount on future purchases, the discount offered in the initial arrangement should be computed by comparing the published list price of the delivered elements to the residual value attributable to those elements. If the discount on future purchases is significant and incremental to the discount computed for the initial arrangement, then the software vendor should apply the significant and incremental discount on future purchases to the initial arrangement (TPA 5100.74).

The portion of the fee that is deferred as a result of the offer of a significant incremental discount on future purchases should be recognized as revenue proportionately as the future purchases are delivered (assuming all other revenue recognition criteria are met) so that a consistent discount rate is applied to all purchases under the arrangement. If the future purchases are not limited by quantity of product(s) or service(s), the portion of the fee that is deferred as a result of the presence of a significant incremental discount should be recognized as revenue as a subscription (TPA 5100.51).

ILLUSTRATION: SIGNIFICANT INCREMENTAL DISCOUNTS

(Adapted from TPAs 5100.51 and 5100.74)

(For purposes of the examples, VSOE of fair value equals list price and all of the software products do not involve significant production, modification, or customization)

EXAMPLE 1

Facts: A software vendor sells Product A for its list price of $40 along with a right to a discount of $30 on another of its software products, Product B, which has a list price of $60. The $30 discount on Product B is a significant incremental discount that would not normally be given in comparable transactions.

Accounting: The vendor should allocate the $30 discount across Product A and Product B. The overall discount is 30%, calculated as the ratio of the discount ($30) to the fair values of the products ($40 + $60 = $100). Therefore, upon the delivery of Product A, the vendor would recognize $28 (a 30% discount off of $40) of revenue and defer $12. If the customer uses the discount and purchases Product B, the vendor would recognize $42 in revenue upon delivery of Product B ($30 in cash received plus the $12 previously deferred). If the discount expires unused, the $12 in deferred revenue would be recognized at that time.

EXAMPLE 2

Facts: A software vendor sells Product A for its list price of $40 along with a right to a discount of $20 on any one of its other software products, Products B through Z. The list prices of Products B through Z range from $40 to $100. The $20 discount is a significant incremental discount that would not normally be given in comparable transactions.

Accounting: The vendor should allocate the $20 discount across Product A and the assumed purchase of whichever of Product B through Z has the lowest fair value ($40). The overall discount is 25% ($20/$80). Therefore, upon delivery of Product A, the vendor would recognize $30 in revenue, and defer $10. If the customer uses the discount and purchases the additional product with a fair value of $40, the vendor would recognize $30 in revenue upon its delivery (the $10 previously deferred and the additional cash license fee due of $20). If the discount expires unused, the $10 in deferred revenue would be recognized at that time.

EXAMPLE 3

Facts: A software vendor sells Product A for its list price of $40 along with a right to a discount of 50% off list price on any future purchases of its other software products, Products B through Z, with a maximum cumulative discount of $80. The 50% discount is a significant incremental discount that would not normally be given in comparable transactions.

Accounting: The vendor should assume that the customer will purchase additional products worth $160 in order to use the maximum $80 discount. Therefore, the vendor would allocate the $80 discount across Product A and the assumed additional products to be purchased. The overall discount is 40% ($80/$200). Therefore, upon the delivery of Product A, the vendor would recognize $24 of revenue and defer $16. If the customer uses the discount by purchasing additional products with fair values totaling $160, the vendor would recognize $96 in revenue upon delivery of those products ($80 in cash received plus the $16 previously deferred). If the discount expires unused, the $16 in deferred revenue would be recognized at that time.

EXAMPLE 4

Facts: A software vendor sells Product A for $60, which represents a 40% discount off its list price (VSOE) of $100. In the same transaction, it also provides the right to a discount of 50% off of the list price (VSOE) on any future purchases of units of Product B for the next six months with a maximum discount of $200. The discount of 50% on future purchases of units of Product B is a discount not normally given in comparable transactions.

Accounting: Because the discount offered on future purchases of Product B is not normally given in comparable transactions and is both significant and incremental in relation to the 40% discount, it must be accounted for as part of the original sale consistent with Example 3 above. The vendor should assume that the customer will make $400 in purchases of Product B in order to use the maximum discount of $200. Therefore, the vendor would allocate the $240 discount ($40 on Product A and $200 maximum on future purchases) across Product A and the assumed additional products to be purchased. The overall discount is 48% ($240/$500). Therefore, upon the delivery of Product A, the vendor would recognize $52 (a 48% discount off of Product A's fair value of $100) of revenue and defer $8. If the customer uses the discount by purchasing additional products with fair value totaling $400, the vendor would recognize $208 in revenue upon delivery of those products ($200 in cash received plus the $8 previously deferred). If the discount expires unused, the $8 in deferred revenue would be recognized at that time.

EXAMPLE 5

Facts: A software vendor sells Product A for its list price of $40 along with a right to a discount of 50% off list price on any future purchases of its other software products with no maximum cumulative discount. The 50% discount is a significant incremental discount that would not normally be given in comparable transactions.

Accounting: The vendor should apply the 50% discount to Product A and all future products purchased using the discount. Therefore, upon the delivery of Product A, the vendor would recognize $20 of revenue and defer $20. If the customer purchases additional products using the discount, the vendor would recognize revenue equal to the cash received upon the delivery of those products. The previously deferred $20 should be accounted for as a subscription and recognized pro rata over the discount period or, if no period is specified in the arrangement, over the estimated period during which additional purchases will be made.

EXAMPLE 6

Facts: A software vendor sells Product A, which has a list price of $100, for $30 along with the right to a discount of 70% off list price (VSOE) on any future purchases of its other software products for the next six months with no maximum cumulative discount.

Accounting: As the discount offered on future purchases over the next six months is equal to the discount offered on the current purchase (70%), there is no accounting necessary in the original sale for the discount offered on future purchases.

EXAMPLE 7

Facts: A software vendor sells Product A, which has a list price of $100, for $80. One year of PCS is included in the arrangement, and the customer may renew PCS following the initial year at a rate of $15. As part of the transaction, the customer receives the right to a 55% discount off of published list prices for the purchase of all new products released by the software vendor for two years, with no maximum cumulative discount. The software vendor does not have VSOE of fair value for Product A, as Product A is never sold separately.

Accounting: The residual value allocated to Product A is $65 ($80 arrangement fee less $15 PCS renewal rate). The discount on Product A is 35% ($35 discount on Product A ($100 list price less $65 allocated residual value) divided by $100 list price). The incremental discount offered on future purchases is 20% (55% discount on future purchases less 35% computed discount on Product A). If the software vendor concludes that this 20% incremental discount is significant, it will recognize revenue of $45 upon delivery of Product A, provided all other revenue recognition criteria have been met. The $45 ultimately allocated to Product A represents the $80 arrangement fee reduced by (a) $20 of additional discount (20% significant incremental discount off of $100 list price), and (b) $15 PCS renewal rate. The $20 additional discount is deferred and recognized pro rata over the two-year discount period. If the customer purchases additional products using the 55% discount, the software vendor should recognize revenue equal to the net fee attributable to those products when all of the revenue recognition criteria have been met.

NONMONETARY EXCHANGES INVOLVING SOFTWARE

Nonmonetary exchanges involving software are generally treated the same way as nonmonetary exchanges involving other products or services. The guidance in APB-29 is applied to determine whether the transaction should be recorded at historical cost or at fair value. If the transaction should be reported at fair value, then the software revenue recognition guidance is applied to determine whether the measured fair value can be recognized as revenue, or must be deferred until remaining obligations are completed (TPAs 5100.46 and 5100.47).

> **OBSERVATION:**   In an exchange in which either or both parties to the agreement do not plan to use or sell the products (or rights) they receive in the exchange, fair value is considered to be zero, as the transaction does not appear to have substance. As such, no revenue should ever be recognized in such a transaction.

Exchanging Software for Technology or Product to Be Sold

APB-29 states that an exchange of inventory for inventory to be sold in the same line of business does not culminate an earnings process. Therefore, if a software vendor exchanges one or more software licenses (which are considered inventory for the purposes of applying this guidance) and receives in return the rights to technology or products that are to be sold, licensed, or leased in the same line of business as the software licenses delivered in the exchange, then the software vendor should record the exchange at historical cost, which is likely to be zero.

However, if the technology or products received by the software vendor in the exchange are to be sold, licensed, or leased in a different line of business from the software licenses delivered, the exchange should be recorded at fair value, as long as VSOE of fair value exists. If VSOE of fair value does not exist, the transaction should be recorded at historical cost, as APB-29 indicates that a transaction should be recorded at historical cost if fair value cannot be reasonably determined, and SOP 97-2 limits the determination of fair value of software to VSOE.

> **OBSERVATION:** APB-29 requires that the fair value of a nonmonetary transaction be determinable within reasonable limits. VSOE of fair value is the only way to satisfy this requirement for software and software-related elements included in a nonmonetary transaction.

Exchanging Software for Technology to Be Used Internally

When a software vendor gives a license to its externally sold software to a customer in exchange for a license to the customer's technology that the software vendor intends to utilize for internal use (i.e., it does not intend to sell the software it receives, but instead will use it in its own operations), the transaction should be recorded at fair value, providing that VSOE exists, because the exchange is an exchange of inventory for a productive asset, which is not one of the types of transactions that is accounted for at historical cost under APB-29.

DEFERRED COSTS

Revenue from a software sale may have to be deferred for any number of reasons. In many cases, the issue of whether related direct costs may also be deferred is unimportant, because those costs may be minimal. However, in certain arrangements, especially those involving the payment of sales commissions, the direct and incremental costs of a software sale are significant. The deferral of costs is not addressed in SOP 97-2 or any other software-specific literature. Therefore, literature that applies to other transactions should be looked to for guidance. For further information, see Chapter 8, "Miscellaneous Issues."

ADDED CONSIDERATIONS IN RESELLER TRANSACTIONS

Consignment Arrangements

When a software vendor has a relationship with a reseller, terms of the arrangement or the customary business practices between the parties may indicate that a transaction that is contractually a sale actually functions more like a consignment, for which revenue should not be recognized. The factors that might lead to a software transaction with a reseller being treated as a consignment are similar to those discussed in the "Consignment Sales" section of Chapter 5, "Product Deliverables."

PCS Granted by Resellers

Some reseller transactions give the reseller the right to upgrades or enhancements introduced between the time the reseller arrangement is entered into and the time the reseller sub-licenses the product to end-users. This right is often included even when upgrades and technical support will not be provided to the end-user. An arrangement like this, in which the reseller has the right to provide unspecified upgrades to its customers, is an implied PCS arrangement between the vendor and the reseller. Therefore, the arrangement fee must be allocated, based on VSOE of fair value, between the software product and the implied PCS arrangement. If VSOE of fair value for PCS does not exist, the entire arrangement fee should be recognized over the expected PCS term, which would generally be the period over which the reseller has the right to sell licenses to its customers that include unspecified upgrades developed before the sublicense is entered into (SOP 97-2, par. 62).

CHAPTER 11
PRESENTATION

CONTENTS

BACKGROUND

Until fairly recently, financial statement preparers and users did not pay much attention to specific captions or sub-captions within the income statement, focusing instead on the "bottom line." Perhaps because of that, the accounting standard-setters had provided little guidance on income statement classification. Similarly, specific captions on the balance sheet were also not focused on, with the financial reporting community instead looking primarily at balance sheet figures such as total debt and total shareholders' equity.

Recently, however, more sophisticated financial analysis has put additional focus on various income statement captions. Chief among these is revenue. Therefore, it has become more important to correctly classify items of income and cost within the income statement, even when such classification does not affect net income, operating income, or even gross margin. In addition, the "deferred revenue" caption has also received more focus, as it is a liability usually settled by performance, rather than a transfer of cash, resulting in an increase in equity, rather than a decrease in assets.

SURVEY OF APPLICABLE LITERATURE

Conceptual guidance on income statement classification is limited to that in CON-6, which provides guidance on distinguishing between revenue and gains, and between expenses and losses. In addition, the SEC has included certain guidelines for various income statement captions, including revenue, in REG S-X, Rule 5-03. However, these two pieces of guidance were the only ones that were broadly applicable until late 1999, when the SEC staff asked the EITF to begin addressing certain classification issues.

Since then, the EITF has focused on income statement classification in a number of consensuses. In fact, several of the classification issues regarding revenue that the EITF has addressed are somewhat broad, and provide guidance that can be used in a wide range of transactions and industries. These broad topics include questions on: (1) how to classify payments that a company makes to its customers, (2) when companies should recognize revenue on a gross basis and when they should recognize only their net commission as revenue, and (3) whether coupons, rebates, and other discounts should be reported as expenses or as reductions of revenue.

LISTING OF APPLICABLE LITERATURE

CON-5	Recognition and Measurement in Financial Statements of Business Enterprises
CON-6	Elements of Financial Statements
FAS-13	Accounting for Leases
FAS-133	Accounting for Derivative Instruments and Hedging Activities
REG S-X, Rule 5-03	Financial Statement Requirements, Commercial and Industrial Companies, Income Statements
EITF 88-18	Sales of Future Revenues
EITF 99-19	Reporting Revenue Gross as a Principal versus Net as an Agent
EITF 00-10	Accounting for Shipping and Handling Fees and Costs
EITF 01-9	Accounting for Consideration Given by a Vendor to a Customer (Including a Reseller of the Vendor's Products)
EITF 01-14	Income Statement Characterization of Reimbursements Received for "Out-of-Pocket" Expenses Incurred
EITF 02-3	Issues Involved in Accounting for Derivative Contracts Held for Trading Purposes and Contracts

	Involved in Energy Trading and Risk Management Activities
EITF 02-16	Accounting by a Customer (Including a Reseller) for Certain Consideration Received from a Vendor
EITF 03-10	Application of Issue No. 02-16 by Resellers to Sales Incentives Offered to Consumers by Manufacturers
EITF 03-11	Reporting Realized Gains and Losses on Derivative Instruments That Are Subject to FASB Statement No. 133 and Not "Held for Trading Purposes" as Defined in Issue No. 02-3
SAB Topic 8A	Retail Companies—Sales of Leased or Licensed Departments
SAB Topic 13	Revenue Recognition
TPA 5100.58	Effect of Prepayments on Software Revenue Recognition—Transfer of Receivable without Recourse

REVENUES VERSUS GAINS

One of the key issues in income statement classification is the determination of whether a particular item of income should be reported as revenue or as a gain. Both revenues and gains affect a company in the same way—the company has more assets (or less liabilities) than it did before the particular event occurred. However, whether the item of income is reported as revenue or a gain can greatly affect the way the transaction is viewed. Gains are generally assumed to be one-time events that do not relate to the company's core operations, while revenues are assumed to be part of those core operations, and thus, are more likely to be repeatable in the future. CON-6 addresses the difference between revenues and gains, indicating, "Revenues... result from an entity's ongoing major or central operations and activities..." while "Gains... result from entities' peripheral or incidental transactions" (CON-6, par. 87). Another way to distinguish between revenues and gains is suggested in CON-5, which points out that revenues typically result from an "earnings process" involving activities specifically targeted toward bringing in that revenue, while "Gains commonly result from transactions and other events that involve no 'earning process,' and for recognizing gains, being earned is generally less significant than being realized or realizable" (CON-5, par. 83b).

Obviously, the application of this guidance depends on the unique facts and circumstances of a company's operations. In practice, it is generally not difficult to identify an entity's "ongoing major or central operations and activities." These activities generally include a company's productive efforts and most of its transactions with other companies. For example, a manufacturer hires employees; buys raw materials; rents or purchases land, buildings, and equipment; and sells its output to customers. Its manufacturing operations convert all of these purchases into a product that sells at a higher price than the combined cost of the inputs. Other companies incur expenses and generate revenues in other ways—for example, retailers and distributors buy, transport, market, and sell goods, insurers charge customers to assume risks, and banks pay interest to depositors to have funds available to provide loans that earn greater interest (CON-6, par. 88).

Of course, some companies engage in many different ongoing major or central activities. It is not necessary to identify one or only a small handful of activities that make up a company's ongoing major or central activities. Rather, any activity that the company performs repeatedly, expects to continue performing, and focuses its resources and efforts on may be an ongoing major line of business, and hence an activity that generates revenues and expenses, rather than gains and losses.

In contrast, transactions that are not part of a company's ongoing major or central operations are typically things that the company does "on the side" and are ancillary, but still necessary, activities. For example, a company that owns the building its offices are in may rent out excess space to another entity. The rental income should not be reported as revenue. Similarly, a manufacturing or service company will typically invest cash rather than have it sit idle. The interest income earned should not be reported as revenue, even if it was earned on funds made available due to customer prepayments. Other transactions that produce gains (or losses) can be identified because they result from events that the company has little control over, such as currency fluctuations, strikes, natural disasters and related insurance recoveries, and changes in the fair value of assets and liabilities that are carried at fair value.

> **OBSERVATION:** Many companies enter into arrangements that can result in the receipt of payments even though nothing of value is ever provided to the customer. This could occur if a customer returns a product or cancels a service, but is required to pay a termination fee. In these and similar situations in which the vendor receives payments but is never required to provide a product or service to the customer, the payments should be reported as a gain, rather than as revenue, because no earnings process ever occurred.

> **SEC REGISTRANT ALERT:** The SEC staff continues to focus on income statement classification issues. In a December 2002 speech, the SEC staff highlighted the fact that revenues exclude equity in net income of investees, net gains or losses on sales of fixed assets or investments, and "other income."

EXAMPLE: PRESENTATION OF REVENUES VERSUS GAINS

IBM Corporation Form 10-K—Fiscal Year Ended December 31, 2004

OBSERVATION: IBM's Consolidated Statement of Earnings shows the following sources of revenues: Global Services, Hardware, Software, Global Financing and Enterprise Investments/Other. The Company, however, reports Intellectual property and custom development income, ("IP&CDI"), as well as asset sales and other nonrecurring gains, (which are components of Other (income) and expense), under the caption, Expense and Other Income. These sources of income are not classified as revenues by IBM because they are not considered part of the "ongoing major or central operations or activities" of the Company.

CONSOLIDATED STATEMENT OF EARNINGS
International Business Machines Corporation and Subsidiary Companies

(Dollars in millions except per share amounts)

FOR THE YEAR ENDED DECEMBER 31:	2004	2003	2002
Revenue:			
Global Services	$ 46,213	$ 42,635	$ 36,360
Hardware	31,154	28,239	27,456
Software	15,094	14,311	13,074
Global Financing	2,608	2,826	3,232
Enterprise Investment/Other	1,224	1,120	1,064
Total Revenue	96,293	89,131	81,186
Cost:			
Global Services	34,637	31,903	26,812
Hardware	21,929	20,401	20,020
Software	1,919	1,927	2,043
Global Financing	1,045	1,248	1,416
Enterprise Investment/Other	731	634	611
Total Cost	60,261	56,113	50,902
Gross Profit	36,032	33,018	30,284
Expense and Other Income:			
Selling, general and administrative	19,384	17,852	18,738
Research, development and engineering	5,673	5,077	4,750

Intellectual property and custom development income	**(1,169)**	(1,168)	(1,100)
Other (income) and expense	**(23)**	238	227
Interest Expense	**139**	145	145
Total Expense and Other Income	**24,004**	22,144	22,760

IBM describes IP&CDI as follows:

Intellectual Property and Custom Development Income

As part of the company's business model and as a result of the company's ongoing investment in research and development (R&D), the company licenses and sells the rights to certain of its intellectual property (IP) including internally developed patents, trade secrets and technological know-how.

Intellectual Property and Custom Development Income

(Dollars in millions)

FOR THE YEAR ENDED DECEMBER 31:	2004	2003	Yr. To Yr. Change
Intellectual property and custom development income:			
Sales and other transfers of intellectual property	**$ 466**	$ 562	(17.1)%
Licensing royalty-based fees	**393**	338	16.3
Custom development income	**310**	268	15.7
Total	**$1,169**	$1,168	0.2%

Intellectual property and custom development income was flat in 2004 versus 2003. The timing and amount of sales and other transfers of IP may vary significantly from period to period depending on the timing of divestitures, industry consolidation, economic conditions and the timing of new patents and know-how development.

The timing and amount of Sales and other transfers of IP may vary significantly from period to period depending upon the timing of divestitures, industry consolidation, economic conditions and the timing of new patents and know-how development.

GROSS VERSUS NET PRESENTATION OF REVENUE

General

EITF 99-19 addresses an issue that frequently arises for resellers and other companies—the question of whether to report the entire amount received from the end-user as revenue and the amount paid to the supplier as cost of sales, or to report just the net amount as revenue, as if that amount were a commission paid by the supplier for generating a sale from the supplier to the end-user. Essentially, the process for making this determination boils down to evaluating the relationships between the supplier, the company, and the end customer. Gross reporting treats the transaction as the company purchasing a product or service from the supplier and then selling that product or service to the end-user, while net reporting treats the transaction as the end-user making a purchase from the supplier, with the company acting as a sales agent.

This question often arises for companies that sell goods or services over the Internet. Many of those companies do not stock inventory and may arrange for third-party suppliers to drop-ship merchandise on their behalf. Those companies also may sell services that will be provided by a third-party service provider. However, the issue is an important one for many companies that are not Internet-based, as well. The underlying factor that causes difficulty in answering the question of gross versus net reporting is that many companies do not assume all of the risks and rewards of ownership of the products they sell before entering into the sales transaction, or do not take on all of the responsibility to provide the services they sell. Rather, through contracts or by operation of the business, some or all of these risks and responsibilities remain with the supplier of the goods or services.

EITF 99-19's scope is quite broad, and its guidance is applicable regardless of industry or transaction type, unless guidance is specifically provided in other authoritative literature.[1] Gross versus net reporting of most products and services is, therefore, within the scope of EITF 99-19.

The EITF's consensus on this question does not draw bright lines or provide objective answers. Rather, the EITF identified a number of indicators that a company should evaluate during its consideration of this issue. These indicators must be considered in the determination of whether the company has taken on enough risks to be considered the principal in the transaction.

> ☞ **PRACTICE ALERT:** The EITF has addressed two gross versus net issues involving derivative instruments that fall within the scope of FAS-133. EITF 02-3 addresses gains and losses (realized and unrealized) on derivative instruments "held for trading purposes" that are within the scope of FAS-133. The consensus on EITF 02-3 indicates that such gains and losses should be shown net in the income statement, regardless of whether the derivative instrument is physically settled. EITF 03-11 addresses realized gains and losses on physically settled

---

[1]For example, SOP 81-1, *Accounting for Performance of Construction-Type and Certain Production-Type Contracts*, FAS-45, *Accounting for Franchise Fee Revenue*, EITF 02-3 and 03-11 (Energy Traders) and the AICPA Audit and Accounting Guides for Casinos, and Investment Companies, include guidance on presenting revenue on a gross versus a net basis.

derivative contracts **not** "held for trading purposes" that are within the scope of FAS-133. The consensus in EITF 03-11 indicates that determining whether realized gains and losses on such instruments should be reported on a gross or net basis is a matter of judgment that depends on the relevant facts and circumstances. In analyzing these facts and circumstances, the guidance in EITF 99-19 and APB-29, *Accounting for Nonmonetary Transactions,* should be considered. If these issues are applicable to an entity's financial reporting, the final Abstracts should be consulted for additional information.

Indicators of Gross Revenue Reporting

1. *The company is the primary obligor in the arrangement.* The primary obligor is the party responsible to the customer for providing the product or service that is the subject of the arrangement. In substance, the primary obligor is the party the customer will look to for fulfillment and for ensuring its satisfaction. If this party is the company, and not the supplier, the company has significant risks and rewards in the transaction that indicate it is at risk for the full amount of the contract, not just a commission. Representations made by a company during marketing and the terms of the sales contract generally will provide evidence as to whether the company or the supplier is the primary obligor (EITF 99-19, par. 7).

2. *The company has general inventory risk.* General inventory risk is the risk normally taken on by a company that buys inventory in the hopes of reselling it at a profit. Front-end general inventory risk exists if a reseller maintains an inventory of a product by taking title to and assuming all risks and rewards of ownership of the product *before* that product is ordered by a customer. Back-end general inventory risk exists if the customer has a right of return and the reseller will take title to and assume the risks and rewards of ownership of the product if it is returned. In a service transaction, a risk similar to general inventory risk exists if the reseller commits to purchase service from its supplier before it has found customers for that service. General inventory risk not mitigated by terms of the arrangement between the reseller and the supplier is a strong indicator that the reseller should record revenue gross. However, factors that mitigate general inventory risk must be considered as well. For example, a company's risk may be reduced significantly or essentially eliminated if the company has the right to return unsold products to the supplier or receives inventory price protection from the supplier. Similarly, back-end inventory risk is mitigated if the company has the right to return to the supplier any products returned by the customer (EITF 99-19, par. 8).

3. *The company has the ability to determine the price at which it sells the product or service.* When a company has reasonable latitude to

establish prices for the products and services, it is an indication that the company is acting as a principal, rather than as another company's agent (EITF 99-19, par. 9).

4. *The company changes the product or performs part of the service.* If a company physically changes the product (beyond its packaging) or performs part of the service ordered by a customer, the company does not appear to be acting solely as an agent. In addition, this fact may indicate that the company is partially or fully responsible for fulfillment, potentially making it the primary obligor in the arrangement (EITF 99-19, par. 10).

> ☛ **PRACTICE POINTER:** Transporting the goods, repackaging them, or providing marketing services related to the products or services is not sufficient to conclude that this indicator of gross reporting exists, even when such actions do add value to the product or service.

5. *The company has discretion in supplier selection.* When a company has multiple suppliers for a product or service ordered by a customer and discretion to select the supplier that will provide the product or service ordered by a customer, it is an indication that the company is acting as a principal (EITF 99-19, par. 11).

6. *The company is involved in the determination of product or service specifications.* If a company must determine the nature, type, characteristics, or specifications of the product or service ordered by the customer, that fact might indicate that the company is primarily responsible for fulfillment (EITF 99-19, par. 12).

7. *The company has physical loss inventory risk (after customer order or during shipping).* Physical loss inventory risk exists if the reseller holds title to the product at some point between the time a customer order is placed and the product is delivered to the customer. Because the amount of risk inherent in taking title during this time is so low, physical loss inventory risk is a weak indicator of gross reporting (EITF 99-19, par. 13).

8. *The company has credit risk.* If a company assumes credit risk for the amount billed to the customer, that fact may provide evidence that the company has risks and rewards as a principal in the transaction. Credit risk exists if a company is responsible for collecting the sales price from a customer but must pay the supplier regardless of whether the sales price is fully collected. A requirement that a company return or refund only the net amount it earned in the transaction if the transaction is cancelled or reversed is not evidence of credit risk for the gross transaction. In some cases, credit risk may be mitigated to such an extent that this indicator is virtually meaningless—for example, if a customer pays by

credit card and a company obtains authorization for the charge in advance of product shipment or service performance, credit risk has been substantially mitigated (EITF 99-19, par. 14).

Indicators of Net Revenue Reporting

1. *The supplier is the primary obligor in the arrangement.* If the supplier is responsible for fulfillment and customer satisfaction, that may be an indication that the company does not have risks and rewards as a principal in the transaction and therefore should recognize only its net fee as revenue. Representations made by a company during marketing and the terms of the sales contract will generally provide evidence as to a customer's understanding of whether the company or the supplier is responsible for fulfillment (EITF 99-19, par. 15).

2. *The amount the company earns per transaction is fixed (in dollars or as a percentage of the arrangement fee).* When a company earns a fixed dollar amount per customer transaction or a stated percentage of the amount billed to a customer, it appears to be acting as an agent of the supplier (EITF 99-19, par. 16).

3. *The supplier has credit risk.* If credit risk exists (that is, the sales price has not been fully collected prior to delivering the product or service) but the supplier assumes that risk, the company appears to be acting as an agent of the supplier (EITF 99-19, par. 17).

Evaluating the Indicators

Strong and Weak Indicators

In evaluating the EITF 99-19 indicators, it is important to note that two of the indicators generally provide very strong evidence of the nature of the transaction. Those indicators are the identity of the primary obligor in the transaction and, when it exists, front-end general inventory risk. The reason those indicators are considered strong indicators is because they affect a number of key risks such as the risk of market price declines, customer satisfaction, obsolescence and excess inventory, etc.

In contrast, indicators such as physical loss inventory risk and credit risk are very weak, sometimes meaningless, indicators. This is because the inherent risks in these areas are often very low to start with, and they are easily mitigated through the use of insurance or well-designed business practices. Therefore, these indicators are only likely to be useful in rare circumstances.

In all situations, judgment should be applied in considering these indicators. Depending on the facts and circumstances of a particular transaction, the importance of certain indicators may rise or fall. For example, back-end general inventory risk may be important for transactions involving products that are often returned or rejected, have high values, and for which there are few orders. Such risk may be an unimportant indicator, however, for low value products for which there are many orders, because the product can just be used to fill the next order.

> ☛ **PRACTICE POINTER:** Although the EITF has identified many indicators that are useful in determining whether gross or net reporting should be used, the issue may be thought of, in simple terms, as trying to answer two questions. Answering these questions does not replace a review of the indicators, but it may help to frame the issue in a way that is easier to understand.
>
> First, who does the end customer believe it is buying from? If the end customer believes it is buying from the company, the company is likely the primary obligor and likely should report gross. On the other hand, if the end customer believes it is buying from the supplier, chances are that net reporting for the company is appropriate.
>
> Second, is the company's customer the end customer, or the supplier? If the company's contracts refer to it as an agent or refer to the product supplier as the customer, chances are that net reporting is appropriate.

Transaction-by-Transaction Analysis

The evaluation required by EITF 99-19 should be done on a transaction-by-transaction basis. It is quite possible that a company will have some transactions in which it operates as a principal, for which gross reporting is appropriate, and others in which it acts as an agent, for which net reporting is appropriate. For example, a catalog company that sells office products may maintain inventories of certain products that are high-volume products, such as pens, paper, and printer cartridges, but have other products, such as furniture and computers, drop-shipped from the supplier. Thus, general inventory risk may exist for some transactions, but not for others. This difference could cause a different conclusion to be reached in evaluating the appropriate reporting for the transactions.

EXAMPLE: GROSS VERSUS NET CONCLUSION DIFFERS FOR DIFFERENT TRANSACTIONS

Express Scripts, Inc. Form 10-K—Fiscal Year Ended December 31, 2005

Revenues related to the sale of prescription drugs by retail pharmacies in our networks consist of the amount the client has contracted to pay us (which excludes the co-payment) for the dispensing of such drugs together with any associated administrative fees. These revenues are recognized when the claim is processed. When we independently have a contractual obligation to pay our network pharmacy providers for benefits provided to our clients' members, we act as a principal in the arrangement and we include the total payments we have contracted to receive from these clients as revenue, and payments we make to the network pharmacy providers as cost of revenue in compliance with Emerging Issues Task Force ("EITF") Issue No. 99-19, "Reporting Gross Revenue as a Principal vs. Net as an Agent." When a prescription is presented by a member to a retail pharmacy within our network, we are solely responsible for confirming member eligibility, performing drug utilization review, reviewing for drug-to-drug interactions, performing clinical intervention (which may involve a call to the member's physician), communicating plan provisions to the pharmacy, directing payment to the pharmacy and billing the client for the amount they are contractually obligated to pay us for the prescription dispensed, as specified within our client contracts. We also provide benefit design and formulary consultation services to clients. We have separately negotiated contractual relationships with our clients and with network pharmacies, and under our contracts with pharmacies we assume the credit risk of our clients' ability to pay for drugs dispensed by these pharmacies to clients' members. Our clients are not obligated to pay the pharmacies as we are primarily obligated to pay retail pharmacies in our network the contractually agreed upon amount for the prescription dispensed, as specified within our provider contracts. In addition, under most of our client contracts, we realize a positive or negative margin represented by the difference between the negotiated ingredient costs we will receive from our clients and the separately negotiated ingredient costs we will pay to our network pharmacies. These factors indicate we are a principal as defined by EITF 99-19 and, as such, we record ingredient cost billed to clients in revenue and the corresponding ingredient cost paid to network pharmacies in cost of revenues.

If we merely administer a client's network pharmacy contracts, to which we are not a party and under which we do not assume credit risk, we record only our administrative fees as revenue. For these clients, we earn an administrative fee for collecting payments from the client and remitting the corresponding amount to the pharmacies in the client's network. In these transactions we act as a conduit for the client. Because we are not the principal in these transactions, drug ingredient cost is not included in our revenues or in our cost of revenues.

Revenues from our non-PBM segment, PBS, are derived from the distribution of pharmaceuticals requiring special handling or packaging where we have been selected by the pharmaceutical manufacturer as part of a limited distribution network, the distribution of pharmaceuticals through patient assistance programs where we receive a fee from the pharmaceutical manufacturer for administrative and pharmacy services for the delivery of certain drugs free of charge to doctors for their indigent patients, sample fulfillment and sample accountability services. Revenues earned by PBS include administrative fees received from pharmaceutical manufacturers for dispensing or distributing consigned pharmaceuticals requiring special handling or packaging and administrative fees for verification of practitioner licensure and distribution of consigned drug samples to doctors based on orders received from pharmaceutical sales representatives. We also administer sample card programs for certain manufacturers and include the ingredient costs for those drug samples dispensed from retail pharmacies in PBS revenues, and the associated costs for these sample card programs in cost of revenues. Because manufacturers are independently obligated to pay us and we have an independent contractual obligation to pay our network pharmacy providers for free samples dispensed to patients under sample card programs, we include the total payments from these manufacturers (including ingredient costs) as revenue, and payments to the network pharmacy provider as cost of revenue. These transactions require us to assume credit risk. Our PMG subsidiary records an administrative fee for verifying practitioner licensure and then distributing consigned drug samples to doctors based on orders received from pharmaceutical sales representatives.

Financial Statement Presentation

Companies with Both Gross and Net Transactions

When a company records some transactions as gross and others as net, it may be necessary to separately report revenue from gross-reported transactions and revenue from net-reported transactions, and to break out cost of sales in a similar fashion. This allows readers of the financial statements to properly evaluate gross margins on the two types of transactions.

In addition, SEC registrants are required to separately report revenue from the sale of products and revenue from the provision of services (REG S-X, Rule 5-03(b)(1)). Because commissions and fees earned from activities reported net are service revenues, this may often have the effect of requiring separate presentation of revenues from transactions reported gross (product revenues) and revenues from transactions reported net (service revenues).

Disclosure of Gross Activity for Transactions Reported Net

The EITF noted that although such disclosures are not required by GAAP, the disclosure of gross transaction volume for those revenues reported net may be useful to financial statement users. However, if the gross amounts are disclosed, they should not be disclosed in any way that appears to characterize them as revenues. In addition, the presentation should not result in the gross activity being presented in the income statement such that it begins a column that sums to net income or loss (EITF 99-19, par. 20).

Leased Departments

Department stores and certain other retailers customarily lease portions of their store space to companies that specialize in certain areas. For example, many higher-end department stores lease space to companies that specialize in displaying and selling cosmetics, or designing and selling wedding dresses. Smaller stores may allow vending machines owned by another party to be placed in various spots around the store. In these situations, the store is essentially leasing space to the companies that run the specialized departments. In return, the store typically receives a lease payment from the other company, and the revenue from the outsourced part of the store goes to the company to whom the operations have been outsourced. That company is also responsible for the costs of running the leased department.

Because the store/lessor in these arrangements has virtually no involvement in the product purchasing, pricing, or sales, these types of arrangements would generally indicate that the lessee company that runs the department should record the sales of that department on a gross basis, with the store recording only its net lease payment as revenue. Furthermore, these types of arrangements generally meet the definition of a lease, and are therefore within the scope of FAS-13. Accordingly, it would be inappropriate for a department store or other retailer to include the sales of the licensed departments in its own revenue figures. Rather, the department store or other retailer should include only the rental income, if the arrangement is a lease, or service revenue, if the arrangement is not a lease, as part of its revenues (SAB Topic 8A).

ILLUSTRATION: ASSESSMENT OF GROSS VERSUS NET REPORTING INDICATORS

EXAMPLE 1

Facts: Company A runs a catalog business selling home products, such as rugs, sheets, towels, etc. Company A does not manufacture any of the products it sells, but instead has compiled products from various manufacturers in its catalog. Each product in the catalog identifies its unique supplier, as the identity of the supplier is a factor that customers use in determining whether and which products to order. Company A maintains no inventories of products, but does take title to the products ordered by customers at the point of shipment from suppliers. Title is passed to the customer upon delivery. The gross sales price is charged to the customer's credit card prior to shipment and Company A is the merchant of record. Company A must pay its suppliers even if the credit card charge cannot be collected. Suppliers set product sales prices, and Company A retains a fixed percentage of the sales price and remits the balance to the supplier. The catalog and the sales contracts clearly indicate that Company A takes no responsibility for the quality or safety of the products, and that the customer must contact the supplier directly regarding complaints, warranty issues, and returns.

Discussion: Certain indicators point toward gross reporting, while other indicators point toward net reporting. Although indicators of gross reporting exist for physical loss inventory risk (during shipping) and credit risk (for collecting amounts charged to credit cards), those indicators are not sufficient to overcome the stronger indicators that revenues should be reported net. The indicators of net reporting include the fact that the supplier, not the company, is the primary obligor and the fact that the amount earned by the company is a fixed percentage of the sales price.

EXAMPLE 2

Facts: Same as in Example 1, except that (1) Company A sets product sales prices, and therefore earns as a profit any amounts it sells the products for in excess of its agreed-upon purchase price with the supplier, and (2) while Company A still provides no warranty on the products it sells, it does provide a "Satisfaction Guaranteed or Your Money Back" right of return on all products it sells, even when it has no similar right of return with its suppliers.

Discussion: Again, certain indicators point toward gross reporting, while other indicators point toward net reporting. In addition to physical loss inventory risk (during shipping) and credit risk (for collecting amounts charged to credit cards) that are present in Example 1, other gross indicators include both back-end general inventory risk and pricing latitude resting with Company A. In addition, the provisions of the right of return make it less clear as to who the primary obligor in the arrangement is. Therefore, gross reporting is appropriate for Company A.

EXAMPLE 3

Facts: Company B is a travel consolidator that negotiates with major airlines to obtain access to airline tickets at reduced rates that are not available to travelers who buy tickets directly from the airlines. Company B determines the prices at which it will sell the airline tickets. The reduced rate paid to an airline by Company B for each ticket sale is negotiated and agreed to in advance, and Company B agrees to buy a specific number of tickets for specific flights. Company B must pay for those tickets regardless of whether it is able to resell them. Customers pay for airline tickets using credit cards, and Company B is the merchant of record. Although credit card charges are pre-authorized, there are occasional losses as a result of disputed charges that Company B bears the risk of. Company B utilizes electronic ticketing, and therefore, there is no physical loss risk. Company B facilitates resolutions of complaints by its customers if the customer is dissatisfied with the airline, but Company B's responsibility ends at successfully booking the reservation; the airline is responsible for fulfilling all obligations associated with the ticket.

Discussion: Company B should use gross reporting for the revenue from the sale of tickets. Company B has general inventory risk, a strong indicator of gross reporting, because it commits to purchasing tickets before it resells them. Ticket pricing also points to gross reporting as Company B has complete latitude to set sales prices for tickets and, as a result, the amount it earns will vary. In addition, Company B has credit risk for collecting customer credit card charges, although a weak indicator of gross reporting. An indicator of net reporting also exists in that the airlines are the primary obligors, as they provide the air travel transportation. However, the gross reporting indicators in this case outweigh the fact that the supplier is the primary obligor.

EXAMPLE 4

Facts: Same as Example 3, except that Company B is only required to pay for tickets that it resells to customers.

Discussion: Company B should report revenues net. As in Example 3, the fact that the airline is the primary obligor is a strong indicator of net reporting. There are two indicators of gross reporting (pricing latitude and credit risk). However, these indicators do not overcome the strong net indicator relating to the supplier being the primary obligor. The strong indicator of gross reporting, general inventory risk, that was present in Example 3, is not present here.

PAYMENTS FROM A VENDOR TO A CUSTOMER

There are many instances in which a vendor makes a payment to one of its customers. Sometimes, this is merely because the vendor is purchasing a product or service from its customer (i.e., the two parties are customers of one another). In other cases, the payment is a sales incentive, the main purpose of which is to convince the customer to purchase (or continue purchasing) the vendor's products or services. Payments may take various forms including cash discounts, coupons, rebates, "free" products or services, equity instruments, etc. In some cases, a vendor will make payments to its customer's customer (an indirect customer of the vendor). For example, the manufacturer of a grocery product may issue coupons that are redeemed by a consumer, even though the manufacturer's customer is the grocery store.

Other common arrangements that involve payments from vendors to customers include:

- Cooperative advertising arrangements, in which a vendor agrees to make payments to its customer if the customer features the vendor's products in its advertising.
- Slotting fees, in which a vendor makes a payment to a retailer so that the retailer will stock the manufacturer's product in its stores, sometimes in a particular location.
- Buydowns, in which a vendor makes a payment to a retailer that makes some amount of purchases at agreed-upon prices.

- Rebates, in which a customer, usually an indirect customer, may send in a form to request a return of a portion of the purchase price of the product or service.

Many other arrangements may exist that result in a company making payments to a customer, including various types of marketing partnerships. The vendor's and customer's accounting have been addressed in three separate EITF issues. The vendor's accounting is addressed in EITF 01-9 and the customer's accounting is addressed in EITF 02-16. Certain incentive arrangements are addressed in EITF 03-10. Although the models in EITF 01-9 and EITF 02-16 are consistent, each takes into consideration the unique perspective of the entity whose accounting it is addressing. In addition, while EITF 01-9 addresses consideration in the form of cash, equity, and "free" products or services, EITF 02-16 addresses only consideration in the form of cash or equity. Each of the models is discussed in greater detail below.

Vendor Classification

The scope of EITF 01-9 is very broad, and the model developed in that consensus must be applied to any payment made by a company to one of its customers (or an affiliate of that customer), whether the payments are contractually linked to the revenue or not. In addition, the scope of EITF 01-9 contemplates that vendor consideration may be given to direct or indirect customers of the vendor, and that the consideration may be in the form of cash, equity, or a product or service. Furthermore, it applies to payments to customers who will alter the product before reselling it (for example, a cooperative advertising payment from a computer chip manufacturer to one of its PC manufacturer customers). Thus, it encompasses almost every kind of sales incentive arrangement in use that results in consideration being paid by a vendor to its customer.

> **OBSERVATION:** The model in EITF 01-9 is applied to payments to both direct and indirect (i.e., further down the distribution chain) customers to prevent a vendor from having the ability to change the reporting of a sales incentive without changing its substance. Consider that a vendor could achieve essentially the same result by (1) selling its product at a $1 discount to list price, (2) selling the product at list price and providing a $1 rebate to its direct customer, or (3) selling the product at list price and providing a $1 rebate to a customer further down the distribution chain. An approach that provides for revenue reduction in some, but not all, of these

arrangements would result in different income statement characterization for sales incentives that are essentially the same.

SEC REGISTRANT ALERT: Round-trip transactions are receiving a significant amount of attention by the SEC staff. Round-trip transactions were an area of focus in the SEC staff's Report Pursuant to Section 704 of the Sarbanes-Oxley Act of 2002 (the Section 704 Report), issued in early 2003. In compiling the information in the Section 704 Report, the SEC staff studied enforcement actions filed during the period July 31, 1997, through July 30, 2002. In addition, round-trip transactions have also been a focus in recent SEC staff speeches. The SEC staff characterizes round-trip transactions in the Section 704 Report as transactions that "involve simultaneous pre-arranged sales transactions often of the same product in order to create a false impression of business activity and revenue." The SEC staff cited a number of enforcement actions in the Section 704 Report where registrants inappropriately used round-trip transactions to boost revenue. Essentially, the types of round-trip transactions identified by the SEC staff in the Section 704 Report should be treated as nonmonetary transactions. Nonmonetary transactions that lack substance should not result in the recognition of revenue. Care should be exercised when analyzing the payment by a vendor to its customer to ensure that the payment is not just one of the legs in a round-trip transaction. See Chapter 8, "Miscellaneous Issues," for additional discussion regarding nonmonetary transactions.

Consideration in the Form of Cash or Equity

EITF 01-9 begins with a presumption that a cash or equity payment by a vendor to a customer (as noted above, "customer" includes both direct and indirect customers) should be accounted for as a reduction of revenues. However, the presumption is overcome if both of the following are true (EITF 01-9, par. 9):

1. The vendor receives, or will receive, an identifiable benefit (goods or services) in exchange for the consideration. To meet this condition, the identified benefit must be sufficiently separable from the customer's purchase of the vendor's products such that the vendor could have purchased the identified benefit from somebody other than one of its customers.
2. The vendor can reasonably estimate the fair value of the benefit identified under the first condition.

EXHIBIT 11-1
CHARACTERIZATION OF PAYMENTS FROM VENDOR TO CUSTOMER

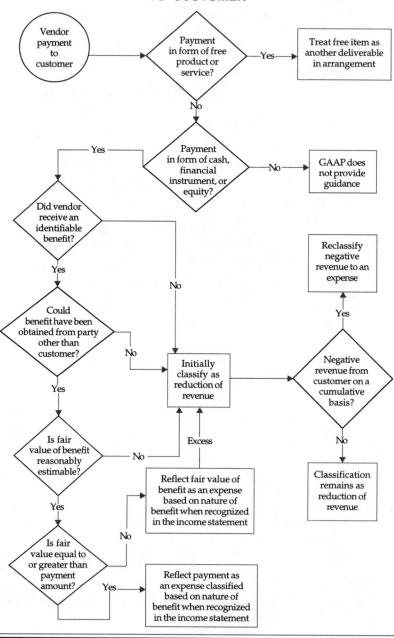

OBSERVATION: The first criterion is meant to ensure that the two transactions (the sale to the customer and the purchase from it) could truly be considered separate events. The second criterion ensures that the net fee can be appropriately allocated to the events, based on fair value. These two criteria are somewhat similar to the criteria necessary to separate deliverables included in a multiple-element arrangement (see Chapter 4, "Multiple-Element Arrangements").

If both of the criteria are met, the lesser of the amount paid to the customer and the fair value of the benefit received may be classified as an expense when recognized in the income statement, while any amount paid in excess of the fair value of the benefit received must be characterized as a reduction of revenue (EITF 01-9, par. 9). Any amount that can appropriately be characterized as an expense when recognized in the income statement should be included in an expense caption based on the nature of the identifiable benefit received. For example, if the identifiable benefit is advertising, the amount characterized as an expense should be included in a sales and marketing expense (or similar) caption.

If either of the two criteria is not met, the entire payment must be characterized as a reduction of revenue. Determining whether the criteria are met requires analysis of all available information (EITF 01-9, par. 9).

☞ **PRACTICE POINTER:** When the payment from the vendor is in the form of equity instruments, a question is raised about the date to use in valuing the instruments issued. Whether or not the cost of the instruments is to be treated as an expense or a reduction of revenues, the value should be measured based on the guidance of EITF Issue 96-18, *Accounting for Equity Instruments That Are Issued to Other Than Employees for Acquiring, or in Conjunction with Selling, Goods or Services.*

Consideration in the Form of "Free" Products or Services

If the sales incentive is a free product or service, the cost of the free product or service should be classified as an expense when recognized in the income statement. When this is the case, the "free" item is considered an additional deliverable in the exchange transaction and not a refund of a portion of the amount charged to the customer. Although the EITF did not reach a consensus on the income statement classification of the cost of the "free" products or services, in most cases this expense should be classified as part of cost of sales (EITF 01-9, par. 10).

SEC REGISTRANT ALERT: Although the Task Force did not reach a consensus on the income statement classification of the expense associated with "free" products or services, the SEC Observer indicated that the SEC staff believes that the expense associated with a "free" product or service delivered at the time of sale of another product or service should be classified as cost of sales.

EXAMPLE: VENDOR CLASSIFICATION OF PROMOTIONAL ALLOWANCES

The Boston Beer Company Form 10-K—Fiscal Year Ended December 25, 2004

Advertising and Sales Promotions

The Company reimburses its wholesalers and retailers for promotional discounts, samples and certain advertising and promotional activities used in the promotion of the Company's products. The accounting treatment for the reimbursements for samples and discounts to wholesalers results in a reduction in the net revenue line item. Reimbursements to wholesalers and retailers for certain advertising and promotional activities are included in the advertising, promotional and selling expenses line item.

The Company also has sales incentive arrangements with its wholesalers based upon performance of certain marketing and advertising activities by the wholesalers. Depending on what may be allowable by state laws and regulations, these activities promoting the Company's products would include, but are not limited to, the following: point-of-sale merchandise placement in retailer locations, product displays in retailer locations and promotional programs at retail locations. The costs incurred by the Company for these sales incentive arrangements and promotional activities are included within the advertising, promotional and selling expenses line item. The costs associated with advertising and sales promotional programs are charged to expense during the period in which they are incurred. Total advertising and sales promotional expenditures included within the advertising, promotional and selling expenses income statement line item for the years ended December 25, 2004, December 27, 2003 and December 28, 2002, were $56.5 million, $55.4 million and $62.2 million, respectively.

The total amount of sales incentives, samples and other promotional discounts included within the advertising, promotional and selling line item in the accompanying consolidated statements of income was $4.4 million, $4.6 million and $4.2 million for the years ended December 25, 2004, December 27, 2003 and December 28, 2002, respectively

---

Customer Classification

General Model

The model used by the customer to account for consideration received from its vendor operates off a presumption that cash or equity consideration received by the customer from its vendor is a reduction of cost of sales when it is recognized in the income statement (prior to recognition in the income statement, the payment would be recognized as a reduction of inventory or prepayments for services). This presumption can only be overcome if the customer can support the fact that the payment relates to either (1) assets or services provided by the customer to the vendor (in which case the payment would be treated as revenue when recognized in the income statement) or (2) a reimbursement of costs incurred by the customer to sell the vendor's products (in which case the payment would be treated as a reduction of the related cost when recognized in the income statement) (EITF 02-16, par. 4).

To support the conclusion that the payment relates to the sale of assets or services by the customer to the vendor, the vendor must receive an identifiable benefit (goods or services) in exchange for the consideration. To be considered an identifiable benefit, the customer should be able to (1) illustrate that it would have entered into an exchange transaction with another (non-vendor) party to provide that benefit and (2) determine the fair value of the benefit it is providing to the vendor. If the amount of the payment from the vendor is greater than the fair value of the identifiable benefit provided to the vendor, the excess should be reflected as a reduction of cost of sales when recognized in the income statement (EITF 02-16, par. 5).

To support the conclusion that the payment relates to the reimbursement of costs incurred by the customer to sell the vendor's products, the customer must incur an incremental, identifiable cost related to selling the vendor's products or services. If the amount of the payment from the vendor is greater than the incremental, identifiable cost incurred by the customer, the excess should be reflected as a reduction of cost of sales when recognized in the income statement (EITF 02-16, par. 6).

EXAMPLE: CUSTOMER CLASSIFICATIONS OF PROMOTIONAL ALLOWANCES

Albertson's Form 10-K—Fiscal Year Ended February 3, 2005

Vendor Funds

The Company receives funds from many of the vendors whose products the Company buys for resale in its stores. These vendor funds are provided to increase the sell-through of the related products. The Company receives funds for a variety of merchandising activities: placement of the vendor's products in the Company's advertising; display of the vendor's products in prominent locations in the Company's stores; introduction of new products into the Company's distribution system and retail stores; exclusivity rights in certain categories that have slower-turning products; and to compensate for temporary price reductions offered to customers on products held for sale at retail stores. The Company also receives vendor funds for buying activities, such as volume commitment rebates and credits for purchasing products in advance of their need. As of February 3, 2005, the terms of the Company's vendor funds arrangements varied in length from short-term arrangements that are to be completed within a quarter to long-term arrangements that are expected to be completed within eight years.

Accounting for vendor funds is discussed in Emerging Issues Task Force "EITF" Issue 02-16: "Accounting by a Customer (Including a Reseller) for Certain Consideration Received from a Vendor" ("EITF 02-16"), which the Company adopted as of the beginning of 2002. As a result of this guidance, the Company began recognizing the vendor funds for merchandising activities as a reduction to cost of sales when the related products are sold as opposed to the previous method of recognizing these credits as a reduction to cost of sales when the merchandising activity was performed in accordance with the underlying agreements. In connection with the implementation of this new accounting method, the Company recorded a charge in 2002 of $94, net of tax benefit of $60.

The amount of vendor funds reducing the Company's inventory ("inventory offset") as of February 3, 2005, including those resulting from the acquisitions made during fiscal 2004 (see Note 5 "Business Acquisitions"), was $126, a decrease of $29 from the beginning of 2004. The vendor funds inventory offset as of January 29, 2004 was $155, an increase of $3 from the beginning of 2003. The inventory offset was determined by estimating the average inventory turnover rates by product category for the Company's grocery, general merchandise and lobby departments (these departments received over three-quarters of the Company's vendor funds in 2004) and by average inventory turnover rates by department for the Company's remaining inventory.

Vendor's Sales Incentives Offered Directly to Consumers

A vendor issues sales incentives that a consumer will present to a reseller for redemption (e.g., manufacturer's coupons redeemed by retailers when presented by consumers). Resellers facilitate the redemption of these sales incentives by acting as middlemen or agents between the vendor and consumer. If these types of sales incentive arrangements possess the following characteristics, they are not subject to the model in EITF 02-16 (EITF 03-10, par. 5-6):

- The incentive can be presented by a consumer at resellers that accept manufacturer's incentives in partial (or full) payment of the price charged by the reseller for the vendor's product.

- The incentive results in the reseller receiving a direct reimbursement from the vendor (or a clearinghouse authorized by the vendor) based on the face amount of the incentive.

- The incentive was not influenced by or negotiated in conjunction with any other incentive arrangements between the vendor and the reseller (i.e., the incentive is between the manufacturer and the consumer).

- The reseller is acting in the capacity of an agent for the vendor (either expressly or implied) in redeeming the incentive presented by the consumer.

These characteristics are intended to identify those sales incentives where a reseller receives a payment from the vendor solely to reimburse it for acting as the vendor's agent in redeeming a sales incentive that is between the vendor and consumer. Requiring a reseller to record this type of sales incentive as a reduction in cost of sales would not properly reflect the reseller's role in the transaction or sales incentive.

If a sales incentive possesses all of the characteristics listed above, the reseller should account for its involvement in the redemption of the sales incentive on the balance sheet. The balance sheet treatment would involve recording a receivable, in the amount of the sales incentive, from the vendor at the time of the sale to the consumer, with the full sales price included in revenue. If a sales incentive does not possess all of these characteristics, the reseller should apply the model in EITF 02-16. Applying the EITF 02-16 model to a manufacturer's coupon lacking one or more of the characteristics discussed above would likely result in the payment from the vendor to the reseller being reflected as a reduction in cost of sales when it is recognized on the reseller's income statement. It is highly unlikely that such an incentive would meet the criteria in the EITF 02-16 model to be treated as revenue or a selling cost reimbursement when recognized in the reseller's income statement.

EXAMPLE: VENDOR'S SALES INCENTIVES

BJ's Wholesale Club Form 10-K—Fiscal Year Ended January 29, 2005

Manufacturer's Incentives Tendered by Consumers

At the beginning of 2004, we adopted the provisions of EITF Issue No. 03-10, "Application of EITF Issue No. 02-16 by Resellers to Sales Incentives Offered to Consumers by Manufacturers" ("EITF 03-10"), which provides guidance for the reporting of vendor consideration received by a reseller as it relates to manufacturers' incentives (such as rebates or coupons) tendered by consumers. We include such vendor consideration in revenues only if all of the criteria defined in EITF 03-10 are met. Otherwise, such consideration is recorded as a decrease in cost of sales. As permitted by the transition provisions of EITF 03-10, we have reclassified 2003's sales and cost of sales for comparative purposes. Implementation of EITF 03-10 has no effect on gross margin dollars, net income or cash flows, but certain vendor coupons or rebates which had been recorded in sales in the past are being recognized as a reduction of cost of sales. The implementation of EITF 03-10 resulted in decreases in both sales and cost of sales of $45.6 million in 2004 and $30.9 million in 2003.

Application to Certain Common Arrangements

The guidance in EITF 01-9 and 02-16 applies to any situation in which payments are made from a vendor to a customer. This situation occurs in a wide variety of arrangements, some of which are extremely common. Application of the models in EITF 01-9 and 02-16 to several common types of arrangements is discussed below.

Cooperative Advertising Arrangements

In a cooperative advertising arrangement, a vendor makes a payment to its customer, intended to compensate the customer for including the vendor's products in its advertisement.

Vendor classification Given the nature of cooperative advertising arrangements, it would seem reasonable that they would meet the first criterion of the model in EITF 01-9. Since the vendor could have purchased advertising on its own from a newspaper, magazine, radio station, etc., a cooperative advertising arrangement would appear to include an identifiable benefit that could have been received from a party other than the customer. However, the substance of some cooperative advertising arrangements makes it questionable as to what the identifiable benefit is. Certain arrangements do not specify the amount or type of advertising the customer must purchase to qualify for the cooperative payment, while in other arrangements, the amount of the payment is linked to the amount of purchases made by the customer, making the arrangement appear similar to a volume discount or a rebate. Thus, cooperative advertising arrangements should be analyzed to determine their substance before concluding that an identifiable benefit has been received. For a cooperative advertising arrangement to meet the second criterion of the model in EITF 01-9 (reasonable estimate of fair value of the benefit received), it would generally be necessary for the arrangement to specify the type and volume of advertising to be provided. Without that information, determining the fair value of the benefit would likely be impossible. If both of the criteria in the EITF 01-9 model are met, the vendor's payment should be reflected as a cost incurred when it is recognized in the income statement, to the extent it does not exceed the estimated fair value of the advertising received. If the amount of the vendor's payment exceeds the estimated fair value of the advertising received, then (a) the estimated fair value of the advertising received should be reflected as a cost incurred and (b) the excess of the vendor's payment over the estimated fair value of the advertising received should be reflected as a reduction of revenue when they are recognized in the income statement.

EXAMPLE: COOPERATIVE ADVERTISING AND BUYDOWN PROGRAMS

Helen of Troy Limited Form 10-K—Fiscal Year Ended February 28, 2005

Consideration Paid to Customers

We offer our customers certain incentives in the form of cooperative advertising arrangements, volume rebates, product markdown allowances, trade discounts, cash discounts and slotting fees. We account for these incentives in accordance with Emerging Issues Task Force Issue No. 01-9, "Accounting for Consideration Given By a Vendor to a Customer" ("EITF 01-9"). In instances where the customer is required to provide us with proof of performance, reductions in amounts received from customers as a result of cooperative advertising programs are included in our consolidated statement of income on the line entitled "Selling, general and administrative expenses" ("SG&A"). Other reductions in amounts received from customers as a result of cooperative advertising programs are recorded as reductions of net sales. Markdown allowances, slotting fees, trade discounts, cash discounts, and volume rebates are all recorded as reductions of net sales. Customer incentives included in SG&A were $13,869,000, $16,603,000, and $14,942,000, for the fiscal years 2005, 2004, and 2003, respectively.

Customer classification   Given the nature of cooperative advertising arrangements, the customer may be able to support the fact that the payment relates to the reimbursement of advertising costs. To do so under the model in EITF 02-16, however, the customer must be able to illustrate that it has incurred an incremental, identifiable cost related to selling the vendor's products or services. If the customer has documentation to support the incremental and identifiable nature of the cost, the vendor's payment should be reflected as a reduction of that cost, when it is recognized in the income statement, to the extent of that cost (any excess of the vendor's payment over the reimbursed cost should be reflected as a reduction of cost of sales when it is recognized in the income statement). In the case of cooperative advertising arrangements, the cost reimbursement reduction would most likely be reflected in the sales and marketing expense (or similar) line item on the income statement. If the customer does not have documentation to support the incremental and identifiable nature of the cost, it must recognize the vendor's payment as a reduction of cost of sales when recognized in the income statement. As discussed previously under "Vendor Classification," careful consideration should be given to the nature and substance of cooperative advertising arrangements.

ILLUSTRATION: COOPERATIVE ADVERTISING ARRANGEMENTS

EXAMPLE 1

Facts: Company D provides satellite television services. It sells the hardware (a satellite dish and receivers) necessary to receive its services through retailers that sell the hardware and arrange installation. The hardware is purchased from Company D and retailers receive an advertising allowance of $100 for each receiver sold and activated. That allowance is shown as a deduction on the related invoice. The retailers are expected to include Company D's products and service in local advertisements. However, retailers are not required to and, therefore, do not provide any documentation to Company D on how the advertising allowance was used.

Vendor Classification Discussion: The first condition of the EITF 01-9 model is not met. Company D cannot identify the benefit, if any, that has been received because retailers do not provide documentation of any advertising that has been run. Therefore, the allowances should be characterized as a reduction of revenue in Company D's income statement.

Customer Classification Discussion: The retailers do not have documentation to support the incremental, identifiable nature of the costs incurred to sell Company D's products and services required by the model in EITF 02-16. Therefore, the payments should be characterized as a reduction of cost of sales when recognized in the retailers' income statements.

EXAMPLE 2

Facts: Company E provides satellite television services. It sells the hardware (a satellite dish and receivers) necessary to receive its services through retailers that sell the hardware and arrange installation. The hardware is purchased from Company E and retailers receive an advertising allowance of $100 for each receiver sold and activated. That allowance is shown as a deduction on the related invoice. Retailers are required by their contract with Company E to use the advertising allowance to advertise Company E's products and services and to provide documentation of the expenditures to Company E.

Vendor Classification Discussion: Company E receives an identifiable benefit (advertising) from the retailers that is sufficiently separable from the retailers' purchases of Company E's products. Company E could have purchased that advertising from another party that does not purchase Company E's satellite dishes and receivers. Therefore, the first condition of the EITF 01-9 model is met. As Company E receives documentation of the advertising expenditures, it is likely that it can estimate the fair value of the benefit received based on the prices charged for similar advertising. Thus, the second condition of the EITF 01-9 model would also likely be met. As such, the lesser of the fair value of the advertising and the amount of the allowance would be characterized as an expense. If the amount of the allowance exceeds the fair value of the benefit, that excess would be characterized as a reduction of revenue.

Customer Classification Discussion: The retailers have documentation to support the incremental, identifiable nature of the advertising costs incurred to sell Company D's products and services as required by the model in EITF 02-16. As such, the lesser of the amount of the payment or the amount of the related advertising costs is recognized as a reduction of advertising expense when recognized in the retailers' income statements. Any excess of the payment over the amount of the related advertising costs is recognized as a reduction of cost of sales when recognized in the retailers' income statements.

Slotting Fees and Allowances

The terms "slotting allowances" and "slotting fees" describe a family of practices that involve payments by manufacturers and wholesalers to persuade downstream resellers to stock, display, and support particular products. The amounts and timing of these payments vary wildly, depending on the negotiations between the parties. They are most often charged by grocery retailers who are asked to stock a new product or to devote a certain amount of shelf space to a product or family of products. Slotting fees are increasingly used for other retail products as well, such as computer software, compact discs, books, magazines, apparel, over-the-counter drugs, and tobacco products.

Vendor classification Because of the nature of slotting fees and allowances, it is almost impossible for the first criterion in the EITF 01-9 model to be met. A vendor might argue that a slotting fee gives a type of advertising benefit due to greater awareness of the product. However, even if this were considered an identifiable benefit from a slotting fee, it could not be obtained from any party other than the customer. In certain cases, a slotting fee might provide the vendor with exclusivity in its product category in a particular store. Although exclusivity might be an identifiable benefit, it cannot be obtained from any party other than the customer. As such, the first criterion in the EITF 01-9 model will not be met. In addition, the second criterion in the EITF 01-9 model would be difficult to meet, because of the extreme variation that is seen in slotting fee amounts, and the fact that such payments are never made to parties that are not also customers of the payer.

EXAMPLES: TRADE PROMOTION, SLOTTING FEES, AND COUPON PROGRAMS

Playtex Products Form 10-K—Fiscal Year Ended December 31, 2004

We routinely commit to customer trade promotions and consumer coupon programs that require us to estimate and accrue the ultimate costs of such programs. Customer trade promotions include introductory marketing funds (slotting fees), cooperative marketing programs, shelf price reductions on our products, advantageous end of aisle or in-store displays, graphics, and other trade promotion activities conducted by the customer. We accrue a liability at the end of each period for the estimated expenses incurred, but unpaid, for these programs. Costs of trade promotions, cash discounts offered to the trade as a payment incentive and consumer coupons are recorded as a reduction of net sales.

As part of a review of the classification of certain expenses, in the second quarter of 2004, we reclassified cash discount expense as a reduction of revenue. Previously, this expense was included in SG&A. This reclassification amounted to $13.8 million in fiscal 2003 and $15.5 million in fiscal 2002. While this discount is a payment incentive, we are now including this with other trade incentives previously reported as a reduction to net sales by employing a broader definition of the Emerging Issues Task Force ("EITF") No. 01-9, "Accounting for Consideration Given By a Vendor to a Customer (Including a Reseller of the Vendor's Products)."

Rayovac Corp. (Spectrum Brands) Form 10-K—Fiscal Year Ended September 30, 2004

The Company also enters into various contractual arrangements, primarily with retail customers, which require the Company to make upfront cash, or "slotting" payments, to secure the right to distribute through such customer. The Company capitalizes slotting payments, provided the payments are supported by a time or volume based contractual arrangement with the retailer, and will amortize the associated payment over the appropriate time or volume based term of the contractual arrangement. The amortization of the slotting payment is treated as a reduction in net sales and the corresponding asset is included in Deferred Charges and Other in the Consolidated Balance Sheets.

Customer classification   Because of the nature of slotting fees and allowances, it would be virtually impossible for a customer to support that it is either providing an identifiable benefit to the vendor or that it is incurring an incremental, identifiable cost related to selling the vendor's products or services as required by the model in

EITF 02-16. The customer would most likely not be able to prove that it could enter into an exchange transaction that has the same terms as a slotting fee arrangement with any parties other than its vendors. In addition, the cost of the space provided by the customer to the vendor in a slotting fee arrangement would not be considered an incremental, identifiable cost. As such, slotting fees and allowances should nearly always be treated as reductions of cost of sales when recognized in the income statement.

Some people have argued that slotting fees should be accounted for as a cost incurred by a vendor to lease shelf space from a retailer. While certain slotting fee arrangements are indeed written in the form of a lease, slotting fee arrangements generally do not provide the vendor/lessee with the right to access and use the shelves for a specified period of time. Instead, the shelf space continues to be controlled by the retailer. In addition, in a true lease, the products on the shelf would be those owned by the vendor/lessee, as the lessee would be in control of the space, and the receipts from the sale of those products would belong to the vendor/lessee. However, in a slotting arrangement, proceeds from the sale of products off the shelves are the retailer's revenues. For these reasons, a slotting fee arrangement does not meet the definition of a lease from an accounting standpoint, even if its legal form appears to be a lease.

> **OBSERVATION:** Certain stores do indeed lease a portion of the store to a provider of products. However, in those situations, the store receives only lease revenue, not the revenue from the sale of products, and the lessee of the portion of the store subject to the lease controls the products in that portion of the store (see "Leased Departments" earlier in this chapter). Therefore, those arrangements are not similar to slotting fee arrangements.

Coupons and Rebates

Coupons and rebates intended to be redeemed by consumers are the most widely used form of sales incentive. This category of incentive includes newspaper and direct mail coupons, as well as rebate forms included with various products. In some cases, the coupon or rebate is offered by a retailer that deals directly with the consumer, while in others, the offer is made by a product manufacturer to the end consumer, even though the consumer purchases the product through a retail reseller.

Vendor classification   Coupon or rebate offers are often part of promotions instituted and run by companies' marketing departments and are considered part of the marketing budget. Because of that, in the absence of any accounting literature, many vendors reported the costs of the discounts as a marketing expense, recording revenue for the normal selling price of the related products or services. However, based on the model in EITF 01-9, coupons and rebates would always need to be characterized as a reduction of revenue, since there is no separately identifiable benefit received by the vendor.

EXAMPLE: CLASSIFICATION OF COUPONS

Revlon Consumer Products Corporation Form 10-K—Fiscal Year Ended December 31, 2004

Net sales is comprised of gross revenues less expected returns, trade discounts and customer allowances, which include costs associated with off-invoice mark-downs and other price reductions, as well as coupons. These incentive costs are recognized at the later of the date on which the Company recognizes the related revenue or the date on which the Company offers the incentive.

Customer classification   Regardless of whether the consumer presents the coupon or rebate to the vendor or a retailer for redemption, the consumer should treat the cash payment received from the vendor, or the redemption value provided by the reseller, as a reduction of cost of sales based on the model in EITF 02-16. This is due to the fact that the consumer is not providing any products or services to the vendor in return for the payment and the fact that the payment does not relate to reimbursement of any particular cost.

If a reseller is involved in redeeming the coupon, the reseller's treatment of the reimbursement from the vendor depends on whether the coupon or rebate possesses the characteristics discussed earlier under "Vendor's Sales Incentives Offered Directly to Consumers." If the coupon or rebate does possess these characteristics, the retailer would account for the coupon or rebate on its balance sheet. In other words, the model in EITF 02-16 would not apply to the retailer and the retailer would not reflect the reimbursement from the vendor in its income statement. If the coupon or rebate does not possess these characteristics, the model in EITF 02-16 would apply to the retailer. Applying the model in EITF 02-16 to a coupon or rebate lacking one or more of these characteristics would result in the payment from the vendor to the retailer being classified as a reduction in cost of sales.

In many cases, the retailer receives a "fee" for redeeming coupons. That fee should be analyzed in the context of the model in EITF 02-16 to determine whether it should be recognized as revenue, a cost of sales reduction, or a reduction of another cost. Generally, the analysis of this "fee" under EITF 02-16 would result in it being recognized as a cost of sales reduction since (a) the related activity does not provide an identifiable benefit to the vendor as defined in EITF 02-16 and (b) the customer has not incurred an incremental, identifiable cost related to that activity.

Buydowns

Buydown programs generally involve a vendor agreeing to compensate a retailer for the retailer's decreased revenue per unit for specific products during a specified period. In turn, the retailer agrees to run some sort of promotion for the vendor's product involving a reduced selling price, a rebate, or some other discount. In contrast to cooperative advertising, buydown programs generally require no expenditures by the retailer for advertising or promotion. Buydowns are known by different names in various industries. For example, the "factory to dealer incentives" often mentioned in automobile advertisements are a form of buydown program.

Vendor classification Much like a coupon or rebate, payments under a buydown program could never qualify to be characterized as an expense rather than a reduction of revenue, because there is no identifiable benefit received from the customer as required by the model in EITF 01-9.

Customer classification Much like a coupon or rebate where only the vendor and consumer are involved, payments under a buydown program could never qualify to be characterized as anything other than a cost of sales reduction under the model in EITF 02-16 because no products or services are being provided by the customer to the vendor and because the payment does not relate to reimbursement of any particular cost.

ILLUSTRATION: CLASSIFICATION OF PAYMENTS FROM VENDORS TO CUSTOMERS

EXAMPLE 1

Facts: Company Z markets and sells a popular brand of peanuts. One of Company Z's contracts makes it the exclusive peanut supplier for a major airline. Company Z sells its peanuts to the airline at discounted prices. In addition, Company Z agrees to purchase a minimum amount of airline tickets from the airline to be used for travel by Company Z's personnel. If Company Z does not purchase the minimum amount of travel by the end of any year of the contract, it must make an additional payment for the shortfall. The prices Company Z pays for plane tickets are comparable to those available to the general public.

Vendor Classification Discussion: With respect to the air travel, Company Z is receiving an identifiable benefit from the airline. That benefit is sufficiently separable from the airline's purchase of Company Z's peanuts because Company Z could have used any other airline for its corporate travel. Therefore, the first condition of the EITF 01-9 model is met. The second condition of the EITF 01-9 model is met because the fair value of the plane tickets can be determined based on the prices paid by the general public for similar tickets. Since Company Z pays those same amounts, as long as Company Z actually uses at least the minimum purchase requirement for corporate travel, all of the payments to the airline may be characterized as expenses. If Company Z is required to make a payment at year-end due to a shortfall in travel purchases, the amount of the shortfall payment would be characterized as a reduction of revenue, as it would represent a payment that is over and above the fair value of the benefit received.

Company Z may also believe it is obtaining other benefits from the airline, such as exclusivity and visibility to a captive audience, but these benefits are not separable from the sales arrangement, nor could their fair value be determined. As such, no amount of the shortfall payment could be classified as an expense based on this rationale.

Customer Classification Discussion: With respect to the air travel, the airline is providing a service that it would provide to other, non-vendor customers. In addition, the airline is providing this service to Company Z at prices comparable to those available to the general public. As such, if Company Z actually uses at least the minimum purchase requirement for corporate travel, all of the payments to the airline may be classified as revenue by the airline based on the model in EITF 02-16. To the extent Company Z is required to make a payment at year-end due to a shortfall in travel purchases, the amount of the shortfall payment would be characterized as a reduction of cost of the peanuts.

EXAMPLE 2

Facts: Company Y makes frozen desserts, and sells them through grocery and warehouse stores. As part of an arrangement to sell a large quantity of products to a large grocery store chain, Company Y agrees to reimburse the chain for special display freezers that are intended to be used to display Company Y's products. The freezers will include Company Y's logo on the outside and will have racking and other components specifically designed to highlight Company Y's products. The grocery chain will pay an independent third party to design and build the freezers. Company Y and the grocery store chain believe that the new display freezers will increase sales of Company Y products at the chain's stores. However, the grocery store chain has no obligation to continue purchasing Company Y's products.

Vendor Classification Discussion: The first condition of the model in EITF 01-9 is not met because Company Y does not receive an identifiable benefit that is sufficiently separable from the arrangement to sell products to the grocery store chain. Company Y could not enter into such an arrangement with anybody other than a reseller of its products. The consideration therefore should be characterized as a reduction of revenue.

Customer Classification Discussion: If the chain has support for the amount it spends to purchase the freezers from the independent third party, such that the cost is identifiable and incremental under the model in EITF 02-16, it should recognize the payment from Company Y as a reduction of the cost of those freezers when recognized in the income statement.

EXAMPLE 3

Facts: Company Y makes frozen desserts, and sells them through grocery and warehouse stores. As part of an arrangement to sell a large quantity of products to a large grocery store chain, Company Y agrees to give special display freezers to the chain, intended to be used to display Company Y's products. The freezers include Company Y's logo on the outside and have racking and other components specifically designed to highlight Company Y's products. Company Y owns the freezers currently, having purchased them from an independent third party and modified them as necessary to effectively display its products. Company Y and the grocery chain believe that the new display freezers will increase sales of Company Y's products at the chain's stores. However, the grocery store chain has no obligation to continue purchasing Company Y's products.

Vendor Classification Discussion: The consideration that Company Y gives to the chain consists of "free" products (the freezers). Consideration in the form of "free" products or services is seen as a deliverable in the arrangement under the model in EITF 01-9, rather than a refund of revenue. Therefore, Company Y should reflect the cost of the freezers as an expense when recognized in its income statement. In addition, a portion of the revenue from the arrangement should be allocated to the freezers.

Customer Classification Discussion: EITF 02-16 does not address situations where the consideration received by the customer is other than cash or equity. As such, judgment should be exercised, and all of the facts and circumstances considered, in determining the customer's treatment of the "free" freezers.

EXAMPLE 4

Facts: Company G is an auto manufacturer that sells its products to consumers through a network of dealers. Company G plans to run a nationwide promotion in which its dealers will stay open late for a two-week period and purchasers will receive factory rebates on vehicles purchased during the same two-week period. Company G agrees to reimburse its dealers for the extra payroll costs they will incur during the promotion for keeping the dealerships open longer.

Vendor Classification Discussion: The first condition of the model in EITF 01-9 is not met because Company G does not receive an identifiable benefit that is sufficiently separable from Company G's sale of automobiles to the dealer. The payroll reimbursements therefore should be characterized as a reduction of revenue in Company G's income statement.

Customer Classification Discussion: If the dealers have support for the payroll costs incurred due to staying open later during the two-week promotion period, such that the cost is identifiable and incremental under the model in EITF 02-16, it should recognize the payment from Company G as a reduction of the payroll costs when recognized in the income statement. The dealers will need to consider the nature of their payroll costs when determining whether those costs are identifiable and incremental. Hourly wages would be considered incremental, while salaries would not be considered incremental. In addition, most benefit-related payroll costs would most likely not be considered incremental. If the amount of the payment from Company G is greater than the amount of identifiable and incremental reimbursed costs as determined based on the model in EITF 02-16, the excess should be reflected as a reduction of cost of sales.

NEGATIVE REVENUE

Because revenue relates only to amounts received from customers, negative revenue generally should not occur. However, negative revenue might exist for a reporting period or a particular transaction in several ways. For example, if a company underestimates the amount of returns it will receive on sales with return rights, it will eventually need to reverse some previously recognized revenue when the additional returns occur. Negative revenue could also arise because of payments made by the vendor to the customer that exceed the revenue from that customer but do not provide a separately identifiable benefit, as discussed above. For example, a company may agree to pay an up-front slotting allowance to have its products sold in a store where they were not previously sold. The initial product order may be less than the slotting fee, resulting in negative revenues.

As part of EITF 01-9, the EITF considered whether the existence of negative revenue for a reporting period, a transaction, or some other segment of a company's transactions should result in a recharacterization of negative revenue amounts as an expense. The EITF concluded that negative revenue amounts may only be reclassified as an expense if, at a particular point in time, the company would have recognized negative revenue for a specific customer on a cumulative basis since it began selling to the customer (EITF 01-9, par. 17). This is consistent with the model for classification of payments made to customers in that it looks at the entire vendor-customer relationship as a whole, rather than on a transaction-by-transaction or any other basis.

Based on this conclusion, it is clear that a payment at the inception of a relationship with a customer, before the customer makes any commitment to purchase products or services from the vendor could be recharacterized as an expense, even if there is no separately identifiable benefit. However, this recharacterization would not be appropriate to the extent that the customer contractually agrees to make future purchases from the vendor as part of the arrangement including the up-front payment, and it is probable that such purchases will be in amounts greater than the up-front payment (EITF 01-9, par. 18). In that event, the payment to the customer would result in an asset, rather than an immediate expense. The asset would be amortized (as a reduction of revenue) as the customer makes the related purchases.

The evaluation of whether the recording of a cost results in negative revenue for the customer on a cumulative basis should be made whenever the cost must be recorded in the income statement. Thus, additional revenues received from the customer at a later date would not cause a "re-reclassification" of the negative revenue that was previously reclassified as an expense.

ILLUSTRATION: NEGATIVE REVENUE

EXAMPLE 1

Facts: Company C provides computer technology support services to large corporations. Company C enters into an arrangement with Customer D to provide information technology troubleshooting and installation support for Customer D. Company C will charge specified hourly rates for various services that Customer D may ask it to perform. Customer D agrees to publicize its relationship with Company C through the issuance of a press release, to inform all of its personnel of the arrangement with Company C, to allow Company C to meet with its employees to "pitch" its capabilities, and to ensure that Company C's dedicated technology support phone number for Customer D is conspicuously placed throughout Customer D's facilities. In part to defray the costs Customer D will incur in these activities, Company C makes a $500,000 payment to Customer D at the inception of the arrangement. However, Customer D also uses other technology support companies, and will continue to do so even after the relationship with Company C is put into place. As such, Customer D does not guarantee any level of purchases from Company C.

Discussion: The $500,000 payment would normally be treated as a reduction of revenue, since Company C gets no separately identifiable benefit in exchange for it. However, since this payment is made before any revenue is received from Customer D, it results in negative revenue from Customer D on a cumulative basis. Because there is negative cumulative revenue and because Customer D has not contractually agreed to make future purchases from Company C, the entire $500,000 payment may be recharacterized as an expense. Even when revenue is received from Customer D in the future, the $500,000 payment may remain classified as an expense, as the negative revenue model need not be applied retroactively.

EXAMPLE 2

Facts: Same as Example 1, except that Customer D had previously used Company C as a service provider, and has purchased $800,000 in services from Company C over the past two years. The new arrangement raises Company C's profile significantly with Customer D. Company C believes that the additional publicity within Customer D will result in more business being directed to Company C, rather than other technology support providers.

Discussion: Again, there is no separately identifiable benefit from the $500,000 payment, so it should initially be characterized as a reduction of revenue. In addition, even though Customer D makes no purchases at the time the new contract is signed, it has made $800,000 in purchases from Company C in the past. Therefore, on a cumulative basis, Company C has positive revenue of $300,000 from Customer D. Thus, the $500,000 payment should remain classified as a revenue reduction, even if it results in negative revenue for the reporting period.

EXAMPLE 3

Facts: Same as in Example 1, except that Customer D guarantees that it will purchase at least $800,000 in services from Company C over the next two years.

Discussion: Again, there is no separately identifiable benefit from the $500,000 payment, so it should initially be characterized as a reduction of revenue. Because the contract includes a commitment to make purchases, Company C should consider those committed purchases in its determination of whether it is appropriate to recharacterize the payment as an expense. As the committed purchases are greater than the up-front payment, the payment should not be recharacterized as an expense. In this case, Company C would likely conclude that the purchase commitment from Customer D represents an asset. The $500,000 would therefore be capitalized and amortized pro rata, as a reduction of revenue, over the $800,000 in purchases by Customer D.

PRESENTATION OF CERTAIN COSTS BILLED TO CUSTOMERS

Shipping and Handling

Many companies that sell goods that are shipped direct to customers charge customers a "shipping and handling" fee separately identified on the customer invoice. Other companies do not charge such a separate fee, instead advertising "free" shipping. In fact, the companies that normally do charge such a fee may run promotions offering free shipping for purchases over a certain amount, or for purchases made during certain time periods. When a separate shipping and handling charge is included, the method of determining the amount of the charge varies. Some companies merely pass through third-party shipping charges, while others attempt to recover a portion of their internal costs as well. Other companies charge shipping and handling on a basis that bears no relation to the costs incurred.

The EITF concluded in EITF 00-10 that amounts billed to a customer related to shipping and handling should be classified as revenue in the income statement. The conclusion is partially based on the fact that a company has the ability to alter its pricing between its product prices and its shipping and handling charge to achieve similar results (EITF 00-10, par. 5).

Furthermore, the EITF also concluded that shipping and handling costs should be classified as an expense. Therefore, it is not appropriate to offset shipping and handling costs incurred and shipping and handling revenue received against one another in the income statement. Rather, the two must each be reported separately (EITF 00-10, par. 6). This conclusion is consistent with the conclusions reached in EITF 99-19 on reporting revenue gross versus net. The seller acts as a principal in purchasing the shipping from the postal service or private shipping company, and acts as a principal in the transaction with the customer, as well. As such, there is no reason to report shipping and handling costs and revenues on a net basis, even if the cost is merely "passed through" to the customer without any markup.

> **DISCLOSURE ALERT:** If shipping and handling costs are classified within cost of sales on the income statement, no disclosure of such costs is required. However, if such costs are significant and are not classified within cost of sales, the amount of shipping and handling costs must be disclosed, and the line item in which they are included must be identified.

EXAMPLES: SHIPPING AND HANDLING COSTS

The Gillette Company Form 10-K—Fiscal Year Ended December 31, 2004

Shipping and Handling Costs

Under generally accepted accounting principles, shipping and handling costs may be reported as a component of either cost of sales or selling, general and administrative expenses. The Company formerly reported all such costs related to outbound freight in the Consolidated Statement of Income as a component of selling, general and administrative expenses. Beginning in 2004, the Company elected to report the costs related to outbound freight in cost of sales, and this change resulted in reclassifications to the Consolidated Statement of Income. Cost of sales increased, and gross profit and selling, general and administrative expenses were reduced by $189 million and $175 million in 2003 and 2002, respectively. Gross profit was reduced as a percentage of net sales from 59.9% to 57.9% and from 58.5% to 56.4% in 2003 and 2002, respectively. There was no impact on profit from operations, net income, or earnings per share as a result of this reclassification.

Colgate-Palmolive Form 10-K—Fiscal Year Ended December 31, 2004

Shipping and handling costs may be reported as either a component of cost of sales or selling, general and administrative expenses. The Company reports such costs, primarily related to warehousing and outbound freight, in the Consolidated Statements of Income as a component of selling, general and administrative expenses. Accordingly, the Company's gross profit margin is not comparable with the gross profit margin of those companies that include shipping and handling charges in cost of sales. If such costs had been included in cost of sales, gross profit margin as a percent to sales would have decreased from 55.1% to 47.9% in 2004 with no impact on reported earnings

Out-of-Pocket Expenses

Service providers often incur certain incidental expenses in performing work for their clients. These "out-of-pocket" expenses include travel costs, such as hotel rooms, airline tickets, car rentals, and meals, costs of supplies, printing and copying costs, etc. In many cases, the customer reimburses the service provider for such costs, separate from (in addition to) the agreed-upon service fee. In other cases, the arrangement fee is stated as a single figure intended to cover out-of-pocket costs in addition to the service fee.

Before 2001, there was no specific guidance in the accounting literature on the characterization of out-of-pocket costs and the related reimbursements. Many companies that routinely billed such costs to their customers determined that the appropriate reporting for the reimbursements was to offset them against the expenses. This was felt to be appropriate because it results in gross margins that reflect the service fee and the related direct costs of providing the service, without any gross-up for out-of-pockets. When companies used this accounting policy, some disclosed the amount of out-of-pocket expenses that had been netted against reimbursements, while others did not.

The EITF addressed the income statement classification of reimbursements for out-of-pocket expenses in EITF 01-14, and concluded that such reimbursements should be characterized as revenue, rather than offset against the related expenses. In large part, much the same as the conclusion discussed above regarding shipping and handling costs, the conclusion on out-of-pocket costs and revenues is based on the principles underlying EITF 99-19 on gross versus net revenue reporting. Essentially, the EITF concluded that the service provider is generally acting as a principal with respect to the purchase of travel, supplies and other out-of-pocket costs, not as an agent. Furthermore, the EITF believes that the customer is not purchasing the travel or supplies, but is purchasing the service provided by the service provider. As such, out-of-pocket costs are like any other cost incurred in providing the service; the fact that the arrangement fee varies based on the amount of such costs should not cause the accounting to be any different (EITF 01-14, pars. 4–5).

EXAMPLE: OUT-OF-POCKET EXPENSES

GP Strategies Corporation Form 10-K—Fiscal Year Ended December 31, 2004

As part of General Physics' on-going operations to provide services to its customers, incidental expenses, which are commonly referred to as "out-of-pocket" expenses, are billed to customers, either directly as a pass-through cost or indirectly as a cost estimated in proposing on fixed-price contracts. Out-of-pocket expenses include expenses such as airfare, mileage, hotel stays, out-of-town meals and telecommunication charges. General Physics' policy provides for these expenses to be recorded as both revenue and direct cost of services in accordance with the provisions of EITF 01-14, *Income Statement Characterization of Reimbursements Received for "Out-of-Pocket" Expenses Incurred.*

Sales and Excise Taxes

Sales and excise taxes are taxes levied based on sales or purchase activity. Although various names are used, this discussion refers to sales taxes as those that are levied on the purchaser, and excise taxes as those that are levied on the seller. In most jurisdictions, the selling party remits both sales and excise taxes to the government. In the context of sales taxes, the seller acts as a collection agent when it charges the sales tax to the customer and remits the tax to the government.

Because sales taxes are taxes on the purchaser, not on the seller, the seller should not record sales tax expense related to customer purchases, nor should the seller record the amount collected for sales tax as revenue. Instead, the collection of sales taxes and their payment on behalf of customers should not be reflected in the income statement at all. Any amounts collected should be immediately reflected as a payable to the government, which payable is relieved upon payment.

Excise taxes, however, are taxes on the seller of goods or services. As such, the seller may reflect these amounts as expenses, generally as part of cost of sales. Alternatively, because these taxes are not discretionary costs and they reduce the amount of revenue that is available to cover the company's expenses, it is also acceptable to show excise taxes that relate directly to sales as reductions of revenue.

EXAMPLES: EXCISE TAXES

Murphy Oil Corporation Form 10-K—Fiscal Year Ended December 31, 2004

Revenue Recognition:

Excise taxes collected on sales of refined products and remitted to governmental agencies are not included in revenues or in costs and expenses.

Sunoco, Inc. Form 10-K—Fiscal Year Ended December 31, 2004

Revenue Recognition:

Consumer excise taxes on sales of refined products and merchandise are included in both revenues and costs and expenses, with no effect on net income.

SEC REQUIRED DISCLOSURE: SEC registrants must disclose the amount of excise taxes included in revenue if that amount exceeds 1% of sales. The classification of the payments of excise taxes should also be disclosed (REG S-X, Rule 5-03).

UNCOLLECTIBLE AMOUNTS AND BAD DEBTS

One of the four conditions that must be met before revenue is recognized is that the arrangement fee must be reasonably assured of collection. In most cases, this criterion is met because the company has policies that prohibit sales to customers whose ability to pay is questionable. However, if collectibility is not reasonably assured, revenue should not be recognized. When this occurs, it is not acceptable to recognize revenue along with a bad debt expense. Although this would produce the right effect on operating income, it would inappropriately overstate revenue by presenting as revenue amounts that never met all four of the conditions for revenue recognition.

Even when revenue is considered collectible and is therefore recognized when all other criteria have also been met, circumstances may subsequently arise that indicate payment is unlikely. Bad debts may need to be recognized in those situations. Bad debts are distinguished from sales that did not meet the collectibility criterion in that bad debts represent sales that were considered collectible at the time of delivery but became uncollectible sometime thereafter. The classification of bad debt expenses is not specified in GAAP, although the SEC requires them to be presented as expenses (generally a selling or marketing expense), rather than as a reduction of revenue (REG S-X, Rule 5-03(b)(5)).

Readers also should refer to Chapter 3, "General Principles," and the Covad Communications Form 10-K—Fiscal Year Ended December 31, 2004 example on revenue recognition when collectibility is not reasonably assured.

BALANCE SHEET PRESENTATION

While the recent EITF consensuses have provided needed guidance on whether certain items should be characterized as revenue or expense, guidance on the classification of cash received in advance of revenue recognition (deferred revenue) is still somewhat scarce. Although the deferred revenue liability caption is acknowledged in several FASB and EITF pronouncements, no literature actually describes what liabilities qualify to be labeled "deferred revenue."

Cash Received Before Revenue Recognition (Deferred Revenue)

There are many reasons (as discussed throughout this book) that the recognition of revenue could be prohibited even after cash has been received. In these cases, a liability must be recorded for the portion of the cash received that exceeds whatever revenue can be recognized. For example, when a right of return exists, no revenue is recognized if returns cannot be reliably estimated. As such, any amounts received must be recognized as a liability. Even if returns can be estimated, revenue cannot be recognized to the extent of expected returns. Therefore, if full payment is made, a portion of that payment will still need to be reflected as a liability. Of course, there are a myriad of other reasons that revenue might be deferred.

When liabilities are recognized for payments received in excess of the amount that can be recognized as revenue, a question arises as to the characterization of the liability. Possible characterizations include deferred revenue, a deposit liability, debt, or even a contra-receivable account.

In general, amounts classified as deferred revenue should be limited to amounts that are ultimately expected to be recognized as revenue. Thus, advance payments that are received before services are performed should usually be classified as deferred revenue, as these amounts are expected to be recognized as revenue upon performance of the service. Similarly, payments received upon product delivery when revenue recognition is prohibited due to a customer acceptance clause may be characterized as deferred revenue in the balance sheet.

It is not acceptable to include in deferred revenue any amount that is expected to be refunded to the customer. For example, revenue that is not recognized based on expected returns should be classified in a separate monetary liability account, labeled with a caption such as "customer deposits" (SAB Topic 13A4a, ques. 1). It is also not acceptable to reflect a product return liability as an offset to accounts receivable. This is because the reserve for product returns is an estimate of cash that will be returned to customers—it is not a valuation account related to the accounts receivable balance.

The following chart lists some of the common reasons for revenue to be deferred once cash has been received, and identifies whether it is generally appropriate to record the related liability as deferred revenue. In simple terms, when the reason for the deferral is that the revenue has not yet been earned, the liability may be reflected as deferred revenue. However, if the reason for the deferral is related to a concern about whether the fee is fixed or determinable or about whether a true sale has occurred, the liability should not be characterized as deferred revenue.

Reason for Deferral	Deferred revenue?
Estimated returns or price protection when estimates can be made	N
Right of return or price protection exists and no estimate can be made	N
Estimated refunds under sales incentives	N
Product not yet delivered	Y
Service not yet performed	Y
Standard warranty when estimate of costs cannot be made	Y
Extended warranty	Y
Product financing arrangement	N
No persuasive evidence of an arrangement	N
Refundable deposit against variable fee	N
Product delivered—awaiting acceptance	Y
Delivered element in a multiple-element arrangement does not have value to the customer on a standalone basis	Y
Insufficient evidence of fair value to allocate revenue in a multiple-element arrangement	Y

No revenue is allocated to the delivered element in a multiple-element arrangement that meets the criteria to be accounted for separately, or only a portion of the revenue that would otherwise have been allocated to the delivered element is ultimately allocated to the delivered element, due to all or a portion of the payment for that delivered element being contingent upon delivery of an as-yet-undelivered element	Note 1:

Note 1 Generally, the liability in this situation should be characterized as deferred revenue. However, classification of the liability may be affected by the approach taken to account for the totality of the arrangement (i.e., it may be effected by the approach taken to account for both the revenue and cost elements of the arrangement). For a discussion of the revenue accounting in this situation, see Chapter 4, "Multiple-Element Arrangements." For a discussion of how costs associated with the delivered element are treated in this situation, see Chapter 8, "Miscellaneous Issues."

Accounts Receivable and Deferred Revenue

A liability must be recorded when cash is collected before revenue may be recognized. However, there are other situations in which it is not clear whether deferred revenue, or any other liability, should be recognized. For example, consider a transaction in which delivery has occurred, there is a right of return, returns cannot be estimated, and payment, although due under normal terms, has not yet been received. Because returns cannot be estimated, revenue cannot be recognized (see Chapter 5, "Product Deliverables") and the inventory shipped should remain on the seller's books. However, the customer is legally required to remit payment on normal terms, a final sales agreement does exist, delivery has occurred, and, except for the right of return, the fee is fixed or determinable. Therefore it may not be clear whether a receivable should be recorded, with an offsetting entry to either deferred revenue or another liability account.

The SEC staff's position is that it is generally not appropriate to record a receivable in this case. Because the provisions for revenue recognition have not yet been met and payment has not been made, neither party to the contract has completed its obligations under the contract. As such, SEC registrants should treat the contract for accounting purposes the same as any executory contract under which neither party has performed—in other words, the same way as if the contract had just been signed, with performance and payment expected in the future. This treatment results in neither a receivable nor a liability being reflected in the financial statements. This position is consistent with TPA 5100.58 where the AICPA Task

Force that was established to address software revenue recognition issues effectively concluded that a receivable does not exist (and therefore cannot be considered transferred for accounting purposes) when revenue cannot be recognized due to extended payment terms.

The SEC staff's position is generally preferable for private companies. However, private companies may recognize a receivable in this case if the receivable meets the definition of an asset provided in CON-6, which would require the customer to be unconditionally obligated to pay the receivable balance.

> ☛ **PRACTICE POINTER:** Although the receivable and related deferred revenue may not be reflected in the financial statements, a company in this situation may wish to record these entries in its internal records, to ensure that receivables are properly evaluated and followed-up on, and that obligations related to potential returns are appropriately considered. When the receivable and deferred revenue are not reflected in the financial statements, a company using this procedure should ensure that these assets and liabilities are eliminated.
>
> This is particularly important because financial statement users generally assume that amounts reflected as deferred revenue have already been paid for. As such, reflecting deferred revenue when payment has not yet been received may cause a user to misunderstand the company's cash flow position.

Sales of Future Revenue

In certain situations, a company may receive a payment from a third party and agree to pay to the third party for a defined period a specified percentage or amount of the revenue, or of a measure of income, of a particular product line, business segment, trademark, patent, or contractual right. For example, a sale of future revenue has occurred if a company sells its rights to receive payments from a customer to a third party before the revenue related to those payments has been recognized.

EITF 88-18 addresses the classification of the amounts received by the company in these situations. The nature of the payment generally precludes immediate recognition in income due to the payments owed to the third-party investor. In most cases, such payments cannot be classified as deferred revenue, but should instead be reflected as debt. In fact, any of the following factors creates a presumption that classification as debt is required (EITF 88-18):

1. The transaction does not purport to be a sale (that is, the form of the transaction is debt).

2. The enterprise has significant continuing involvement in the generation of the cash flows due the investor (for example, active

involvement in the generation of the operating revenues of a product line, subsidiary, or business segment).

3. The transaction is cancelable by either the enterprise or the investor through payment of a lump sum or other transfer of assets by the enterprise.

4. The investor's rate of return is implicitly or explicitly limited by the terms of the transaction.

5. Variations in the enterprise's revenue or income underlying the transaction have only a trifling impact on the investor's rate of return.

6. The investor has any recourse to the enterprise relating to the payments due the investor.

CLASSES OF REVENUE

When a company gets its revenue from different product or service categories, separate presentation of revenue from each category may be appropriate. This is especially true if the various categories of sales transactions would be expected to have different gross margins or other economic characteristics. In SEC filings, separate presentation of revenues and related cost of sales is required for each of the following categories of transactions:

1. Tangible product sales,

2. Public utility operations,

3. Rentals,

4. Service transactions, and

5. All other sources (REG S-X, Rule 5-03(b)(1)).

> **DISCLOSURE ALERT:** See Chapter 12, "Disclosures," for information about required disclosures.

EXAMPLE: PRESENTATION OF MULTIPLE CLASSES OF REVENUE

International Business Machines Corporation Form 10-K—Fiscal Year Ended December 31, 2004

(dollars in millions except per share amounts)

FOR THE YEAR ENDED DECEMBER 31:

	2004	2003	2002
Revenue:			
Global Services	$ 46,213	$ 42,635	$ 36,360
Hardware	31,154	28,239	27,456
Software	15,094	14,311	13,074
Global Financing	2,608	2,826	3,232
Enterprise Investments/Other	1,224	1,120	1,064
Total Revenue	96,293	89,131	81,186
Cost:			
Global Services	34,637	31,903	26,812
Hardware	21,929	20,401	20,020
Software	1,919	1,927	2,043
Global Financing	1,045	1,248	1,416
Enterprise Investments/Other	731	611	632
Total Cost	60,261	56,113	50,902
Gross Profit	36,032	33,018	30,284

CHAPTER 12
DISCLOSURES

CONTENTS

BACKGROUND

Revenue-related disclosures continue to receive tremendous scrutiny from readers of financial statements. This high level of scrutiny can be attributed to a variety of events, not the least of which is the number of highly publicized restatements in recent years related to revenue recognition. Unfortunately, there is no all-inclusive authoritative standard that addresses or provides a comprehensive listing of revenue-related disclosure requirements. Instead, these disclosure requirements must be found in various places within the authoritative literature. Some of that literature is very general in nature (i.e., applies to all types of sales transactions), while some is very specific in nature (i.e., applies to only certain types of sales transactions). In addition to the disclosure requirements included in the authoritative literature, which are applicable to all companies, the SEC requires additional disclosures for publicly traded companies. This chapter accumulates the revenue-related disclosure requirements from various sources and provides a comprehensive inventory of those requirements.

> **OBSERVATION**: Revenue-related disclosures provide the user of the financial statements with critical information related to the types and terms of the sales transactions entered into by the company. As such, the preparer should always keep in mind the user's perspective when evaluating the need for and content of the revenue-related disclosure requirements included in this chapter.

GENERAL DISCLOSURE REQUIREMENTS

A select few pieces of literature address revenue recognition disclosures in a general sense. That is, this literature requires certain revenue-related disclosures regardless of the nature of the sales transaction itself.

LISTING OF APPLICABLE LITERATURE

APB-22	Disclosure of Accounting Policies
APB-28	Interim Financial Reporting
FAS-57	Related Party Disclosures
FAS-131	Disclosures about Segments of an Enterprise and Related Information
FAS-144	Accounting for the Impairment or Disposal of Long-Lived Assets
FAS-154	Accounting Changes and Error Corrections
SOP 94-6	Disclosure of Certain Significant Risks and Uncertainties
EITF 99-19	Reporting Revenue Gross as a Principal versus Net as an Agent
EITF 00-10	Accounting for Shipping and Handling Fees and Costs
REG S-X, Rule 4-08	Financial Statement Requirements, Rules of General Application, General Notes to Financial Statements
REG S-X, Rule 5-03	Financial Statement Requirements, Commercial and Industrial Companies, Income Statements
SAB Topic 13	Revenue Recognition

Accounting Policies

General

Companies are required to disclose significant accounting policies (APB-22, par. 12). Questions that must be considered in determining whether a revenue recognition accounting policy should be disclosed include:

1. Is all or some portioun of the revenue recognition accounting policy based on a selection from acceptable alternatives?

2. Is all or some portion of the revenue recognition accounting policy industry-specific?

3. Is all or some portion of the revenue recognition accounting policy an unusual or innovative application of generally accepted accounting principles?

If the answer to any of these questions is "yes," the revenue recognition accounting policy must be disclosed. Based on these parameters, it would be an extremely rare situation where revenue recognition would not be a required component of a company's accounting policies footnote. One such situation would be a development stage company that has not yet started generating revenue. However, even in this situation, it would be prudent to discuss the accounting policy the company expects to follow once its revenue-generating activities commence.

> **SEC REGISTRANT ALERT:** The SEC staff has communicated its observations and requirements related to revenue recognition accounting policy disclosures in a variety of ways—SAB Topic 13, the Summary by the Division of Corporation Finance of Significant Issues Addressed in the Review of the Periodic Reports of the Fortune 500 Companies (the Fortune 500 Report), SEC staff speeches, a "Cautionary Advice," and a Proposed Rule.
>
> In SAB Topic 13, the SEC staff states that it would always expect a registrant to disclose its revenue recognition accounting policies given the judgment ordinarily exercised in accounting for sales transactions (SAB Topic 13B, ques. 1).
>
> In early 2003 the SEC staff issued the Fortune 500 Report. This report resulted from the SEC's Division of Corporation Finance's (Corp Fin) review of all annual reports filed by Fortune 500 companies. The Fortune 500 Report provides insight into areas commonly questioned by Corp Fin during its reviews of annual reports. One area specifically mentioned in the Fortune 500 Report relates to revenue recognition accounting policy disclosures. A common request made by Corp Fin was for companies to expand or clarify their revenue recognition accounting policy disclosures. Corp Fin highlighted certain industries in the Fortune 500 Report as those that require specific improvements in their revenue recognition accounting policy disclosures:
>
> - Computer software, computer services, computer hardware, and communications equipment—Expanded disclosure for software and multiple-element arrangements.
>
> - Capital goods, semiconductors, and electronic instruments and controls—Improved disclosures for deferred revenue, revenue recognition for products with return or price protection features, requirements for installation of equipment, and other customer acceptance provisions.

- Energy—Improved disclosures of the material terms of energy contracts.
- Pharmaceutical and retail—Improved disclosures related to accounting for product returns, discounts and rebates, and co-op advertising arrangements with retail companies.

The SEC staff, in speeches given in December 2002, observed that revenue recognition accounting policy disclosures should be more complete and precise. Specifically, the SEC staff suggested that revenue recognition accounting policy disclosures:

- Address all material revenue streams;
- Consider whether the sources of revenue described in the notes parallel those discussed in the business section;
- Discuss explicit or implicit acceptance conditions, contingencies, or other circumstances that could affect the timing and amount of revenue recognized;
- Address multiple-element arrangements; and
- Describe the basis for gross or net presentation.

Additional disclosures regarding revenue recognition may be required in SEC filings pursuant to the SEC's stated belief that registrants should disclose, within MD&A, information about their critical accounting policies. The SEC originally communicated this belief in a "Cautionary Advice" release in December 2001. Pursuant to the December 2001 release, companies were requested to discuss their critical accounting policies beginning with December 31, 2001, 10-K filings. A Proposed Rule was issued in April 2002 that would formally require this discussion in future filings.

The SEC guidance on critical accounting policies describes them as those policies that are both:

> . . . important to the portrayal of the company's financial condition and results, and they require management's most difficult, subjective or complex judgments, often as a result of the need to make estimates about the effect of matters that are inherently uncertain.

Given this description, revenue recognition would qualify as a critical accounting policy for many public companies.

In December 2003, the SEC issued Release No. 33-8350, *Interpretation—Commission Guidance Regarding Management's Discussion and Analysis of Financial Condition and Results of Operations*, which incorporated pieces of the Proposed Rule. Most of the guidance in the Proposed Rule has not yet been finalized by the SEC, however, and it is not clear whether—and, if so, when—the SEC will finalize the remaining guidance in the Proposed Rule. In the meantime, SEC registrants still should ensure that they take into consideration the guidance in the SEC's Cautionary Advice when preparing their annual reports and should follow the progress of the critical accounting policies Rule Proposal. Information regarding both the Cautionary Advice and the Proposed Rule is available on the SEC's web site at www.sec.gov.

Multiple Revenue Streams

If a company engages in multiple types of sales transactions, the accounting policies related to each significant type of sales transaction should be disclosed (SAB Topic 13B, ques. 1). For example, if a company has one product-selling division that accounts for 65% of its sales and one service-selling division that accounts for 35% of its sales, the company should disclose the revenue recognition accounting policies for both the product- and service-related revenue streams.

EXAMPLE: MULTIPLE REVENUE STREAMS

Eastman Kodak Company Form 10-K—Fiscal Year Ended December 31, 2004

The Company's revenue transactions include sales of the following: products; equipment; software; services; equipment bundled with products and/or services; and integrated solutions. The Company recognizes revenue when realized or realizable and earned, which is when the following criteria are met: persuasive evidence of an arrangement exists; delivery has occurred; the sales price is fixed or determinable; and collectibility is reasonably assured. At the time revenue is recognized, the Company provides for the estimated costs of customer incentive programs and warranties and reduces revenue for estimated returns.

For product sales, the recognition criteria are generally met when title and risk of loss have transferred from the Company to the buyer, which may be upon shipment or upon delivery to the customer site, based on contract terms or legal requirements in foreign jurisdictions. Service revenues are recognized as such services are rendered.

For equipment sales, the recognition criteria are generally met when the equipment is delivered and installed at the customer site. Revenue is recognized for equipment upon delivery as opposed to upon installation when there is objective and reliable evidence of fair value for the installation, and the amount of revenue allocable to the equipment is not legally contingent upon the completion of the installation. In instances in which the agreement with the customer contains a customer acceptance clause, revenue is deferred until customer acceptance is obtained, provided the customer acceptance clause is considered to be substantive. For certain agreements, the Company does not consider these customer acceptance clauses to be substantive because the Company can and does replicate the customer acceptance test environment and performs the agreed upon product testing prior to shipment. In these instances, revenue is recognized upon installation of the equipment.

Revenue for the sale of software licenses is recognized when: (1) the Company enters into a legally binding arrangement with a customer for the license of software; (2) the Company delivers the software; (3) customer payment is deemed fixed or determinable and free of contingencies or significant uncertainties; and (4) collection from the customer is probable. If the Company determines that collection of a fee is not reasonably assured, the fee is deferred and revenue is recognized at the time collection becomes reasonably assured, which is generally upon receipt of payment. Software maintenance and support revenue is recognized ratably over the term of the related maintenance period.

The Company's transactions may involve the sale of equipment, software, and related services under multiple element arrangements. The Company allocates revenue to the various elements based on verifiable objective evidence of fair value (if software is not included or is incidental to the transaction) or Kodak-specific objective evidence of fair value if software is included and is other than incidental to the sales transaction as a whole. Revenue allocated to an individual element is recognized when all other revenue recognition criteria are met for that element.

Revenue from the sale of integrated solutions, which includes transactions that require significant production, modification or customization of software, is recognized in accordance with contract accounting. Under contract accounting, revenue is recognized by utilizing either the percentage-of-completion or completed-contract method. The Company currently utilizes the completed-contract method for all solution sales, as sufficient history does not currently exist to allow the Company to accurately estimate total costs to complete these transactions. Revenue from other long-term contracts, primarily government contracts, is generally recognized using the percentage-of-completion method.

Changes in Estimates

Accounting for revenue generally involves making many types of estimates. Examples include estimating returns for product sales, estimating percentage-of-completion for construction contracts, estimating price protection liabilities for product or service sales, and estimating settlements under cost reimbursement arrangements. Estimates by their very nature are subject to change. Disclosure regarding a change in estimate generally is not required for routine estimates. However, to the extent a change in a routine estimate is material, disclosure is required. Disclosure also is required if the change in estimate affects several future periods. These disclosures should consist of the effect on income from continuing operations, net income (or, when appropriate, changes in the applicable net assets or performance indicator), and any related per share amounts of the current period.

Certain changes may not have a material effect in the period of change but are reasonably certain to have a material effect in later periods. These changes in estimate must be described in disclosures whenever the financial statements of the period of the change are presented. (FAS 154, par. 22)

> **SEC REGISTRANT ALERT:** SEC registrants must disclose material changes in estimated product returns (SAB Topic 13B, ques. 1).

EXAMPLE: CHANGE IN ESTIMATE

Trimeris, Inc. Form 10-K—Fiscal Year Ended December 31, 2004

Milestone Revenue and Deferred Revenue—Roche

SAB No. 104 provides guidance that it is appropriate to recognize revenue related to license and milestone payments over the research and development term of a collaboration agreement. The primary estimates we make in connection with the application of this policy are the length of the period of the research and development under our collaboration agreement with Roche and the estimated commercial life of Fuzeon.

During the fourth quarter of 2002, we changed our estimate of the end of this research and development period to 2007 based on the expected development schedule of T-1249 or a replacement compound, the final compound covered by our collaboration agreement with Roche.

During the first quarter of 2004, we changed our estimate of the end of the research and development period to 2010 from 2007. This change was due to a change in estimate of the development period for T-1249 or a replacement compound as further clinical development of T-1249 has been placed on hold. We recognized approximately $800,000 less of milestone revenue for the year ended December 31, 2004 compared to the year ended December 31, 2003 due largely in part to this change in estimate.

In January 2005, based on our current evaluation of our research and development programs, we placed further clinical development of T-1249 on hold indefinitely due to challenges in achieving an extended release formulation that would allow significantly less dosing frequency. Taking into account the additional research that will be required to achieve our goals for formulation, in January 2005, we changed our estimate of the end of the research and development period from December 2010 to December 2012; as a result we will recognize approximately $500,000 less milestone revenue in 2005 compared to 2004.

Risks and Uncertainties

The two primary types of revenue-related risks and uncertainties that must be disclosed relate to the uncertainties inherent in making estimates and the risks inherent in the concentration of business activities.

Estimates

As discussed earlier in this chapter, accounting for sales transactions often requires the use of estimates. For example, when product is sold subject to return rights, the company must be able to make reasonable and reliable estimates of expected returns to recognize revenue net of those estimated returns. A company must disclose any significant estimates involved in accounting for revenues, including the nature of the related uncertainty and an indication that it is at least reasonably possible that a change in those estimates will occur in the near term (SOP 94-6, pars. 12–14). In the case of significant estimates of product returns, a company should disclose the existence and nature of the return right, and the fact that it is at least reasonably possible that a change in product return estimates will occur in the near term. In addition, a company is encouraged, but not required, to disclose (a) the factors that cause its estimates to be sensitive to change and (b) the risk-reduction techniques it uses to mitigate losses or the uncertainties that may result from future events (SOP 94-6, pars. 14–15).

EXAMPLE: USE OF SIGNIFICANT ESTIMATES

EMCOR Group, Inc. Form 10-K—Fiscal Year Ended December 31, 2004

Revenues from long-term construction contracts are recognized on the percentage-of-completion method. Percentage-of-completion is measured principally by the percentage of costs incurred to date for each contract to the estimated total costs for such contract at completion. Certain of EMCOR's electrical contracting business units measure percentage-of-completion by the percentage of labor costs incurred to date for each contract to the estimated total labor costs for such contract. Revenues from services contracts are recognized as services are provided. There are two basic types of services contracts: (1) fixed-price facilities services contracts which are signed in advance for maintenance, repair and retrofit work over periods typically ranging from one to three years (for which there may be EMCOR employees on the customer's site full time) and (2) services contracts which may or may not be signed in advance for similar maintenance, repair and retrofit work on an as needed basis (frequently referred to as time and material work). Fixed price services contracts are generally performed evenly over the contract period, and, accordingly, revenue is recognized on a pro-rata basis over the life of the contract. Revenues derived from other services contracts are recognized when the services are performed in accordance with Staff Accounting Bulletin No. 104, "Revenue Recognition, revised and updated." Expenses related to all services contracts are recognized as incurred.

Provisions for estimated losses on uncompleted long-term contracts are made in the period in which such losses are determined. In the case of customer change orders for uncompleted long-term construction contracts, estimated recoveries are included for work performed in forecasting ultimate profitability on certain contracts. Due to uncertainties inherent in the estimation process, it is reasonably possible that completion costs, including those arising from contract penalty provisions and final contract settlements, will be revised in the near-term. Such revisions to costs and income are recognized in the period in which the revisions are determined.

Concentrations

A company may concentrate its revenue-related business activities by: (1) selling only to a particular customer or a small group of customers, (2) selling only a limited number of products or services, or (3) limiting the market or geographic area in which it operates (SOP 94-6, par. 22). While these types of concentrations can certainly represent prudent business decisions, they ultimately carry with them the acceptance of concentration risk. A company that bears concentration risks such as those described above may be required to disclose those risks. Disclosure is required if (1) the concentrations make the company vulnerable to the risk of a near-term severe financial statement impact and (2) it is at least reasonably possible that the events that could cause the severe impact will occur in the near term (SOP 94-6, par. 21).

EXAMPLE: CUSTOMER CONCENTRATION RISK

Mattel, Inc. Form 10-K—Fiscal Year Ended December 31, 2004

On a consolidated basis, a small number of customers account for a large share of Mattel's net sales and accounts receivable. For 2004, Mattel's three largest customers, Wal-Mart, Toys "R" Us and Target, in the aggregate, accounted for approximately 46% of net sales, and its ten largest customers, in the aggregate, accounted for approximately 56% of net sales. As of year end 2004, Mattel's three largest customers accounted for approximately 35% of net accounts receivable, and its ten largest customers accounted for approximately 47% of net accounts receivable. Within countries in the International segment, there is also a concentration of sales to certain large customers that do not operate in the U.S. The customers and the degree of concentration vary depending upon the region or nation. The concentration of Mattel's business with a relatively small number of customers may expose Mattel to a material adverse effect if one or more of Mattel's large customers were to experience financial difficulty.

Related Party Transactions

The existence of related party transactions raises many questions. What is the nature of the transactions? How significant are the transactions to the company's business? Are the transactions occurring on an arm's-length basis? To help address these questions and others, a company is required to disclose certain information regarding revenue-generating transactions with related parties. This information includes: (1) the nature of the company's relationship with the related party, (2) the nature of the sales transaction itself, (3) any other information necessary to gain an understanding of the effects the transaction has on the financial statements, (4) the dollar amount of sales transactions to related parties for each of the income statements presented, and (5) changes in sales terms with the related parties period-over-period. These disclosure requirements do not apply to sales transactions that occur in the ordinary course of business or those that are eliminated in consolidation (FAS-57, par. 2).

When making related party disclosures, a company should take care not to inappropriately represent that transactions with related parties occurred on an arm's-length basis. Such a representation should only be made if it can be substantiated (FAS-57, par. 3).

SEC REGISTRANT ALERT: In SEC filings, the amount of related party sales should be disclosed on the face of the income statement and statement of cash flows, and the amount of related party accounts receivable should be disclosed on the face of the balance sheet (REG S-X, Rule 4-08(k)). This disclosure is required even if the sales were in the ordinary course of business.

In addition, in early 2003, the SEC staff issued the Report Pursuant to Section 704 of the Sarbanes-Oxley Act of 2002 (the Section 704 Report). In compiling the information in the Section 704 Report, the SEC staff studied enforcement actions filed during the period July 31, 1997, through July 30, 2002. One of the areas of improper accounting where a significant number of enforcement actions were brought by the SEC related to disclosure of related party transactions. The SEC staff noted in the Section 704 Report that "Failure to disclose related party transactions hides material information from shareholders and may be an indicator of weaknesses in internal control and corporate governance procedures." This finding is a strong indication that more attention should be given to identifying and disclosing related party transactions.

EXAMPLE: RELATED PARTY SALES

Acxiom Corporation Form 10-K—Fiscal Year Ended March 31, 2005

In accordance with a data center management agreement dated July 27, 1992 between Acxiom and TransUnion, Acxiom (through its subsidiary, Acxiom CDC, Inc.) acquired all of TransUnion's interest in its Chicago data center and agreed to provide TransUnion with various data center management services. The agreement, which was renewed in fiscal 2005, now expires December 31, 2010. In connection with the agreement, the Company has agreed to use its best efforts to cause one person designated by TransUnion to be elected to the Company's board of directors. In addition to this agreement, the Company has other contracts with TransUnion related to data, software and other services. During the years ended March 31, 2005, 2004 and 2003, the Company recognized $96.0 million, $74.1 million and $71.1 million, respectively, in revenue from TransUnion. The receivable account balance was $0.6 million at March 31, 2005 and zero at March 31, 2004.

During fiscal year 2004 a long-term data license agreement was entered into with TransUnion which licensed data that is used by the Company's products. Cost of this data is amortized over its useful life, which is estimated to be seven years. The remaining amount to be paid under this data license is included in long-term obligations (see Note 9). In fiscal 2005 the Company entered into a second data license with TransUnion for additional data. This additional data will be paid for and used over the term of the license, which runs through December 31, 2010. Effective April 1, 2003, Acxiom agreed to purchase analytic, modeling, and other consulting services from TransUnion as part of an outsourcing arrangement. The Company also buys data from TransUnion outside of long-term arrangements. The fees paid to TransUnion during the years ended March 31, 2005 and 2004 were approximately $19.4 million and $17.7 million, respectively, for all of the above arrangements.

Seasonal Revenue

Certain companies experience seasonality in their revenue streams. Consider a company that sells natural gas to residential customers located in the state of Illinois. Given the climate in Illinois and the fact that natural gas is commonly used to heat homes in Illinois (whereas electricity is commonly used to cool homes), this company sells significantly higher volumes of natural gas in the winter months than it does in the summer months. If this fact is not explained when presenting interim results, readers of the financial statements may not gain an appropriate appreciation for what annual revenues will look like. As such, companies that experience seasonality in their revenue streams must disclose the seasonal nature of their activities and consider providing supplemental information in their interim reports consisting of revenues for the 12-month period ended at the interim date for the current and prior years (APB-28, par. 18).

EXAMPLE: SEASONAL REVENUE

Disney, Inc. Form 10-K—Fiscal Year Ended September 30, 2004

All of the theme parks and the associated resort facilities are operated on a year-round basis. Historically, the theme parks and resort business experience fluctuations in theme park attendance and resort occupancy resulting from the seasonal nature of vacation travel and local entertainment excursions. Peak attendance and resort occupancy generally occur during the summer months when school vacations occur and during early-winter and spring holiday periods.

Presentation-Related

Gross versus Net

As discussed in Chapter 11, "Presentation," a company may be required to report revenues net. For example, a travel agent that takes no risks related to the airline tickets it sells, reports as revenue the commission it receives for selling the airline ticket, not the price of the airline ticket itself. In this and other situations where companies are required to report net revenues, the company is permitted, but not required, to disclose the gross transaction volume related to revenues reported net. If gross amounts are disclosed, care should be taken such that these amounts would not be construed as either revenues or part of the total net income or loss (EITF 99-19).

EXAMPLE: GROSS VS. NET

Priceline.com, Inc. Form 10-K—Fiscal Year Ended December 31, 2004

Merchant Revenues and Merchant Cost of Revenues

Name Your Own Price Services: Merchant revenues and related cost of revenues are derived from transactions where we are the merchant of record and, among other things, select suppliers and determine the price to be paid by the customer. We recognize such revenue and costs if and when we accept and fulfill the customer's non-refundable offer. Merchant revenues and cost of merchant revenues include the selling price and cost, respectively, of the travel services and are reported on a gross basis. Pursuant to the terms of our hotel service, our hotel suppliers are permitted to bill us for the underlying cost of the service during a specified period of time. In the event that we are not billed by our hotel supplier within the specified time period, we reduce our cost of revenues by the unbilled amounts. In very limited circumstances, we make certain customer accommodations to satisfy disputes and complaints. We accrue for such estimated losses and classify the resulting expense as adjustments to merchant revenue and cost of merchant revenues or the allowance for doubtful accounts, as appropriate.

Travelweb: Merchant revenues for Travelweb are derived from transactions where customers use the Travelweb service to purchase hotel rooms from hotel suppliers at rates which are subject to contractual arrangements. Charges are billed to customers at the time of booking and are included in Deferred Merchant Bookings until the customer completes his or her stay. Such amounts are generally refundable upon cancellation prior to stay, subject to cancellation penalties in certain cases. Merchant revenues and accounts payable to the hotel supplier are recognized at the conclusion of the customer's stay at the hotel. Travelweb records the difference between the selling price and the cost of the hotel room as merchant revenue.

Agency Revenues and Cost of Revenues

Priceline.com: Agency revenues are derived from travel-related transactions where we are not the merchant of record and where the prices of the products sold are determined by third parties. Agency revenues include travel commissions, customer processing fees and Worldspan reservation booking fees and are reported at the net amounts received, without any associated cost of revenue. Such revenues are recognized when the travel transaction is completed on our website.

Active Hotels: Active Hotels' principal source of revenues comes from commission payments that it receives from hotel suppliers for acting as an agent in the booking of hotel rooms by customers. Active Hotels' hotel suppliers are billed for their commission payments owed to Active Hotels and it recognizes agency revenue at the time that its customers complete their stay at the hotel.

Shipping and Handling Costs

As discussed in Chapter 11, "Presentation," a company is required to present shipping and handling fees charged to customers as revenue and to present the related shipping and handling costs it incurs as expense. If the shipping and handling costs are classified within cost of sales on the income statement, no disclosure of such costs is required. If such costs are significant and are not classified within cost of sales, then the amount of shipping and handling costs must be disclosed and the line item in which they are included must be identified (EITF 00-10).

EXAMPLE: SHIPPING AND HANDLING COSTS

Helen of Troy Limited Form 10-K—Fiscal Year Ended February 28, 2005

Shipping and handling expenses are included in our consolidated statements of income on the "Selling, general, and administrative" expenses line. Our expenses for shipping and handling totaled $38,355,000, $32,701,000, and $24,489,000 during the fiscal years ended 2005, 2004 and 2003, respectively. We report revenue from shipping and handling charges on the "Net sales" line of our consolidated statements of income, in accordance with paragraph 5 of Emerging Issues Task Force Issue, 00-10, "Accounting for Shipping and Handling Fees and Costs." We only include charges for shipping and handling in "Net sales" for sales made directly to consumers and retail customers ordering relatively small dollar amounts of product. Our shipping and handling expenses far exceed our shipping and handling revenues.

Excise Taxes

As discussed in Chapter 11, excise taxes that relate directly to sales may be presented as reductions of revenue instead of as an expense. SEC registrants must disclose the amount of excise taxes included in revenue if that amount exceeds 1% of sales. The classification of the payments of excise taxes should also be disclosed (REG S-X, Rule 5-03).

EXAMPLE: EXCISE TAXES

Murphy Oil Corporation Form 10-K—Fiscal Year Ended December 31, 2004

Revenue Recognition:

Excise taxes collected on sales of refined products and remitted to governmental agencies are not included in revenues or in costs and expenses.

Business Segments:

Excise taxes on petroleum products of $1,477,873,000, $1,336,600,000 and $1,147,922,000 for the years 2004, 2003 and 2002, respectively, were excluded from revenues and costs and expenses.

Other

FAS-131 requires SEC registrants to disclose certain information by segment. Certain revenue-related information is required as part of those disclosures. Financial statement preparers should consult and apply FAS-131 as appropriate.

FAS-144 requires the disclosure of certain information related to discontinued operations. Certain revenue-related information is required as part of those disclosures. Financial statement preparers should consult and apply FAS-144 as appropriate.

SPECIFIC DISCLOSURE REQUIREMENTS

Numerous pieces of authoritative literature require disclosures related to specific types of sales transactions and revenue accounting issues. These disclosures provide incremental information that helps users of the financial statements understand the nature or certain aspects of specific sales transactions and the accounting issues that arise in those situations.

The source for many of these specific disclosure requirements is the SEC staff. The SEC staff has built upon the revenue-related disclosure framework using a variety of avenues, including SAB Topic 13, announcements at EITF meetings, and in documents published by the SEC's Division of Corporation Finance. While these disclosure requirements do not technically apply to private companies, such companies should still strongly consider complying with these disclosure requirements. The incremental information provided as a result of these disclosure requirements is most likely just as relevant to the users of a private company's financial statements as it is to the users of an SEC registrant's financial statements.

LISTING OF APPLICABLE LITERATURE

APB-29	Accounting for Nonmonetary Transactions
FAS-5	Accounting for Contingencies
FAS-68	Research and Development Arrangements
FIN-45	Guarantor's Accounting and Disclosure Requirements for Guarantees, Including Indirect Guarantees of Indebtedness of Others, an interpretation of FASB Statements No. 5, 57, and 107 and rescission of FASB Interpretation No. 34
EITF 99-17	Accounting for Advertising Barter Transactions
EITF 00-8	Accounting by a Grantee for an Equity Instrument to Be Received in Conjunction with Providing Goods or Services
EITF 00-21	Revenue Arrangements with Multiple Deliverables
ITC	FASB Invitation to Comment: Accounting for Certain Service Transactions
SAB Topic 13	Revenue Recognition

| CIRP-8/01 | SEC Division of Corporation Finance—Current Issues and Rulemaking Projects (August 2001) |
| EITF D-96 | Accounting for Management Fees Based on a Formula |

Multiple-Element Revenue Arrangements

Companies often enter into sales transactions involving more than one element. For example, a company may sell a piece of equipment and services to install the equipment. The revenue recognition policy, and therefore the timing of revenue recognition, for each of those elements may be different, such that the allocation of revenue between or among elements would have a major effect on the amount of revenue that should be recognized in an accounting period. This begs the question as to how those elements were separated and how the amount of consideration allocated to each element was determined. As it relates to multiple-element arrangements, a vendor should disclose the following (EITF 00-21, par. 18):

- The accounting policy for recognition of revenue from multiple-element arrangements (for example, whether deliverables are separable into units of accounting); and

- The description and nature of such arrangements, including performance-, cancellation-, termination-, or refund-type provisions.

In addition, the accounting policy followed for each unit-of-accounting should be covered in the vendor's accounting policy disclosures discussed earlier in this chapter. For example, if a multiple-element arrangement involves the sale and installation of equipment and the multiple-element arrangement is separated for accounting purposes, the accounting policy disclosures should cover the individual accounting policies for each separate element.

> **SEC REGISTRANT ALERT:** SEC registrants must disclose how multiple-element arrangements are determined and valued (SAB Topic 13B, ques. 1).
> In addition, in early 2003 the SEC staff issued the Summary by the Division of Corporation Finance of Significant Issues Addressed in the Review of the Periodic Reports of the Fortune 500 Companies (the Fortune 500 Report). This report resulted from the SEC's Division of Corporation Finance's (Corp Fin) review of all annual reports filed by Fortune 500 companies. The report provides insight into areas commonly questioned by Corp Fin during its reviews of annual reports. One area specifically mentioned in the Fortune 500 Report relates to accounting for multiple-element arrangements. Corp Fin

specifically indicated that companies in the computer software, computer services, computer hardware, and communications equipment industries could improve their disclosures by expanding the discussion related to multiple-element arrangements.

EXAMPLE: SEPARATION OF ELEMENTS

Salesforce.com, Inc. Form 10-K—Fiscal Year Ended January 31, 2005

Revenue Recognition: We recognize revenue in accordance with SEC Staff Accounting Bulletin No. 104, "Revenue Recognition." On August 1, 2003, we adopted Emerging Issues Task Force, or EITF, Issue No. 00-21, "Revenue Arrangements with Multiple Deliverables."

Consulting services and training revenues are accounted for separately from subscription and support revenues when these services have value to the customer on a standalone basis and there is objective and reliable evidence of fair value of each deliverable. When accounted for separately, consulting revenues are recognized as the services are rendered for time and material contracts, and when the milestones are achieved and accepted by the customer for fixed price contracts. The majority of our consulting service contracts are on a time and material basis. Training revenues are recognized after the services are performed.

In determining whether the consulting services can be accounted for separately from subscription and support revenues, we consider the following factors for each consulting agreement: availability of the consulting services from other vendors, whether objective and reliable evidence for fair value exists of the undelivered elements, the nature of the consulting services, the timing of when the consulting contract was signed in comparison to the subscription service start date, and the contractual dependence of the subscription service on the customer's satisfaction with the consulting work. If a consulting arrangement does not qualify for separate accounting, we recognize the consulting revenue ratably over the remaining term of the subscription contract. Additionally, in these situations we defer the direct and incremental costs of the consulting arrangement and amortize those costs over the same time period as the consulting revenue is recognized. The deferred cost on our consolidated balance sheet totaled $874,000 at January 31, 2005 and $32,000 at January 31, 2004.

Nonmonetary Revenue Transactions

In general, a company should disclose the nature of nonmonetary revenue transactions entered into and the basis of accounting for the revenues recognized for those transactions (APB-29, par. 28). In recent years, the EITF has addressed the accounting for two specific types of nonmonetary transactions—those where equity instruments are received in conjunction with revenue-generating transactions and those where companies enter into barter transactions involving advertising.

> **SEC PRACTICE ALERT:** Round-trip transactions are receiving a significant amount of attention by the SEC staff. Round-trip transactions were an area of focus in the SEC staff's Report Pursuant to Section 704 of the Sarbanes-Oxley Act of 2002 (the Section 704 Report), issued in early 2003. In compiling the information in the Section 704 Report, the SEC staff studied enforcement actions filed during the period July 31, 1997, through July 30, 2002. In addition, round-trip transactions have also been a focus in recent SEC staff speeches. The SEC staff characterizes round-trip transactions in the Section 704 Report as transactions that "involve simultaneous pre-arranged sales transactions often of the same product in order to create a false impression of business activity and revenue." The SEC staff cited a number of enforcement actions in the Section 704 Report where registrants inappropriately used round-trip transactions to boost revenue. Essentially, the types of round-trip transactions identified by the SEC staff in the Section 704 Report should be treated as nonmonetary transactions (see Chapter 8, "Miscellaneous Issues," regarding accounting for nonmonetary transactions). To the extent a registrant enters into round-trip transactions, the details of such transactions should be appropriately disclosed.

Equity Instruments Received in Conjunction with Providing Goods or Services

When a company receives equity instruments in exchange for providing goods or services, it should disclose the amount of gross operating revenue recognized as a result of such transactions (EITF 00-8).

EXAMPLE: EQUITY INSTRUMENTS IN EXCHANGE FOR SERVICES

Ariba, Inc. Form 10-K—Fiscal Year Ended September 30, 2004

Equity instruments received in conjunction with licensing transactions are recorded at their estimated fair market value and included in the measurement of the related license revenue in accordance with EITF 00-8, *Accounting by a Grantee for an Equity Investment to Be Received in Conjunction with Providing Goods and Services*. For the years ended September 30, 2004, 2003 and 2002, the company recorded revenue of $1.6 million, $1.8 million and $3.6 million, respectively, based on equity instruments received in such transactions. These transactions were originated in fiscal year 2000.

Advertising Barter Transactions

A company that enters into barter transactions involving advertising should disclose the amount of revenue and expense recognized as a result of those transactions. If the facts and circumstances did not permit the company to record revenue or expense for some or all of those transactions (e.g., fair values were not determinable in accordance with the literature), the company should disclose information such as the volume and type of advertising surrendered and received (EITF 99-17).

EXAMPLE: ADVERTISING BARTER TRANSACTIONS

Time Warner Inc. Form 10-K—Fiscal Year Ended December 31, 2004

AOL generates Advertising revenues by directly selling advertising or through transaction-based arrangements.

Transaction-based arrangements generally involve either arrangements in which AOL performs advertising and promotion through prominent display of a partner's content on one of AOL's services, or arrangements in which AOL's Advertising.com, Inc. ("Advertising.com") subsidiary performs advertising on a third-party website. As compensation for display of a partner's content, AOL is paid a share of the partner's advertising revenues. For performance-based advertising, AOL is paid an agreed to fee based on customer specified results, such as registrations or sales leads. Advertising revenue related to these transaction-based arrangements is recognized when the amount is determinable (i.e., generally when performance reporting is received from the partner). Deferred revenue consists primarily of prepaid electronic commerce and advertising fees and monthly and annual prepaid subscription fees billed in advance.

For promotional programs in which consumers are typically offered a subscription to AOL's subscription services at no charge as a result of purchasing a product from the commerce partner, AOL records Subscription revenue, based on net amounts received from the commerce partner, if any, on a straight-line basis over the term of the service contract with the subscriber.

The accounting rules for advertising barter transactions require that historical cash advertising of a similar nature exist in order to support the recognition of advertising barter revenue. The criteria used by the accounting rules used to determine if a barter and cash transaction are considered "similar" include circulation, exposure or saturation within an intended market, timing, prominence, demographics and duration. In addition, when a cash transaction has been used to support an equivalent quantity and dollar amount of barter revenue, the same cash transaction cannot serve as evidence of fair value for any other barter transaction. While not required by the accounting rules, AOL management adopted a more conservative policy by establishing an additional size criterion to the determination of "similar". Pursuant to such criterion, beginning in the second quarter of 2003, an individual cash advertising transaction of comparable average value or higher value must exist in order for revenue to be recognized on an intercompany advertising barter transaction. Said differently, no intercompany advertising barter revenue is recognized if a cash advertising barter transaction of comparable average value or higher has not been entered into in the past six months, even if all of the other accounting criteria have been satisfied.

Guarantees and Indemnifications

Scope

As discussed in Chapter 4, "Multiple-Element Arrangements," revenue arrangements may include guarantees or indemnifications from one party to the other. Extensive disclosures are required for guarantees and indemnifications that fall within the scope of FIN-45. Guarantees and indemnifications that possess any of the following characteristics fall within the scope of FIN-45 for disclosure purposes, except as described further below (FIN-45, par. 3):

- Contracts that contingently require the guarantor to make payments (either in cash, financial instruments, other assets, shares of its stock, or provision of services) to the guaranteed party based on changes in an underlying that is related to an asset, liability, or equity security of the guaranteed party.

- Contracts that contingently require the guarantor to make payments (either in cash, financial instruments, other assets, shares of its stock, or provision of services) to the guaranteed party based on another entity's failure to perform under an obligating agreement (performance guarantees).

- Indemnification agreements (contracts) that contingently require the indemnifying party (the guarantor) to make payments to the indemnified party (guaranteed party) based on changes in an underlying that is related to an asset, liability, or equity security of the indemnified party.

- Indirect guarantees of the indebtedness of others even though the payment to the guaranteed party may not be based on changes in an underlying that is related to an asset, liability, or equity security of the guaranteed party.

FIN-45 provides scope exclusions for certain types of guarantees or indemnifications that have one of the above characteristics, in many cases because the accounting and disclosure for the excluded items is covered in other literature. The guarantees and indemnifications that possess one of the above characteristics that are sometimes included in revenue arrangements and are excluded from the scope of FIN-45 include (FIN-45, par. 6):

- Guarantees of the residual value of leased property at the end of a lease term by the lessee if the lessee accounts for the lease as a capital lease.

- Guarantees involved in leases that are accounted for as contingent rent.

- Guarantees (or indemnifications) that are issued by either an insurance company or a reinsurance company and accounted for under the related industry-specific authoritative literature, including guarantees embedded in either insurance contracts or investment contracts.

- Vendor rebates where the contract contingently requires the vendor to make payments to the customer based on the customer's sales revenues, number of units sold, or similar events.

- Guarantees (or indemnifications) whose existence prevents the guarantor from being able to either account for a transaction as the sale of an asset or recognize the profit from that sale transaction. An example of this situation is a software arrangement where the software vendor participates in the customer's financing through either (a) indemnifying the financing party against claims beyond the software vendor's standard indemnifications or (b) guaranteeing the customer's loan with the financing party. In these situations, a presumption exists that the fee in the arrangement is not fixed or determinable. If the presumption cannot be overcome, revenue is not recognized until the fee can be deemed fixed or determinable (see Chapter 10, "Software—A Complete Model"). In this situation, it is the guarantee or indemnification that is prohibiting recognition of revenue. As such, the guarantee or indemnification does not fall within the scope of FIN-45.

Despite these exclusions, many guarantees and indemnifications included in sales arrangements still fall within the scope of FIN-45. Examples include product warranties; a manufacturer's guarantee of a loan taken out by its customer from a third-party lender to buy the manufacturer's product; and an indemnification in a software licensing agreement that indemnifies the licensee against liability and damages arising from any claims of patent, copyright, trademark, or trade secret infringement by the software vendor's software. Other guarantees and indemnifications included in sales arrangements are discussed in Chapter 4, "Multiple-Element Arrangements."

Disclosures

If a guarantee or indemnification falls within the scope of FIN-45, the guarantor must disclose the following information about each guarantee, or each group of similar guarantees, even if the likelihood of the guarantor's having to make any payments under the guarantee is remote (FIN-45, par. 13):

- The nature of the guarantee, including the approximate term of the guarantee, how the guarantee arose, and the events or circumstances that would require the guarantor to perform under the guarantee.

- Except for product warranties and similar guarantees (which are discussed below), the maximum potential amount of future payments (undiscounted) the guarantor could be required to make under the guarantee. That maximum potential amount of future payments should not be reduced by the effect of any amounts that may possibly be recovered under recourse or collateralization provisions in the guarantee (the disclosure of which is addressed below in the fourth bullet point). If the terms of the guarantee provide for no limitation to the maximum potential future payments under the guarantee, that fact must be disclosed. If the guarantor is unable to develop an estimate of the maximum potential amount of future payments under its guarantee, the guarantor must disclose the reasons why it cannot estimate the maximum potential amount.

- The nature of (1) any recourse provisions that would enable the guarantor to recover from third parties any of the amounts paid under the guarantee and (2) any assets held either as collateral or by third parties that, upon the occurrence of any triggering event or condition under the guarantee, the guarantor can obtain and liquidate to recover all or a portion of the amounts paid under the guarantee. The guarantor must indicate, if estimable, the approximate extent to which the proceeds from liquidation of those assets would be expected to cover the maximum potential amount of future payments under the guarantee.

EXAMPLE: INDEMNIFICATIONS

TiVo Inc. Form 10-K—Fiscal Year Ended January 31, 2005

The Company undertakes indemnification obligations in its ordinary course of business in connection with, among other things, the licensing of its products, the provision of consulting services and the issuance of securities. Pursuant to these agreements, the Company may indemnify the other party for certain losses suffered or incurred by the indemnified party, generally its business partners or customers, underwriters or certain investors, in connection with various types of claims, which may include, without limitation, claims of intellectual property infringement, certain tax liabilities, negligence and intentional acts in the performance of services and violations of laws, including certain violations of securities laws. The term of these indemnification obligations is generally perpetual. The Company's obligation to provide indemnification would arise in the event that a third party filed a claim against one of the parties that was covered by the Company's indemnification obligation. As an example and not a limitation, if a third party sued a customer for intellectual property infringement and the Company agreed to indemnify that customer against such claims, its obligation would be triggered. For example, as the Company has disclosed in Note 17, it is currently indemnifying Sony against a claim of intellectual property infringement brought by Command Audio in connection with Sony's manufacture and sale of TiVo devices.

The Company is unable to estimate with any reasonable accuracy the liability that may be incurred pursuant to its indemnification obligations. A few of the variables affecting any such assessment include but are not limited to: the nature of the claim asserted, the relative merits of the claim, the financial ability of the party suing the indemnified party to engage in protracted litigation, the number of parties seeking indemnification, the nature and amount of damages claimed by the party suing the indemnified party and the willingness of such party to engage in settlement negotiations. Due to the nature of the Company's potential indemnity liability, its indemnification obligations could range from immaterial to having a material adverse impact on its financial position and its ability to continue in the ordinary course of business.

Under certain circumstances, the Company may have recourse through its insurance policies that would enable it to recover from its insurance company some or all amounts paid pursuant to its indemnification obligations. The Company does not have any assets held either as collateral or by third parties that, upon the occurrence of an event requiring it to indemnify a customer, the Company could obtain and liquidate to recover all or a portion of the amounts paid pursuant to its indemnification obligations.

For product warranties and similar guarantees related to the performance of nonfinancial assets owned by the guaranteed party, the disclosure of the maximum potential amount of future payments is not required. Instead, the guarantor is required to disclose the following information (FIN-45, par. 14):

- The guarantor's accounting policy and methodology used in determining its liability for product warranties (including any liability [such as deferred revenue] associated with extended warranties).

- A roll-forward of the changes in the aggregate product warranty liability for the reporting period. That roll-forward should present the beginning balance of the liability, the reductions in that liability for payments made (in cash or in kind) under the warranty, the changes in the liability for accruals related to product warranties issued during the reporting period, the changes in the liability for accruals related to pre-existing warranties (including adjustments related to changes in estimates), and the ending balance of the liability.

EXAMPLE: PRODUCT WARRANTIES

A.T. Cross Company, Form 10-K—Fiscal Year Ended January 1, 2005

Warranty Costs: The Company's Cross branded writing instruments are sold with a full warranty of unlimited duration against mechanical failure. Accessories are sold with a one-year warranty against mechanical failure and defects in workmanship, and timepieces are warranted to the original owner to be free from defects in material and workmanship for a period of ten years. Costa Del Mar sunglasses are sold with a lifetime warranty against defects in materials or workmanship. Estimated warranty costs are accrued at the time of sale. The most significant factors in the estimation of warranty cost liabilities include the operating efficiency and related cost of the service department, writing instrument unit sales and the number of units that are eventually returned for warranty repair. Accrued warranty costs were reduced in fiscal 2002 by approximately $2.2 million. This reduction was primarily due to changes in estimate, to reflect significantly lower cost trends, measured over a period of years. The change in estimate was recorded as a reduction of service and distribution costs. Similar smaller adjustments were also made in fiscal 2003 and 2004. The current portions of accrued warranty costs were $535,000 and $488,000 at January 1, 2005 and January 3, 2004, respectively, and were recorded in accrued expenses and other liabilities. The long-term portion of accrued warranty costs was approximately $1.6 million and $1.9 million at January 1, 2005 and January 3, 2004, respectively. The following chart reflects the activity in aggregate accrued warranty costs:

	Years Ended		
	January 1, 2005	January 3, 2004	December 28, 2002
(Thousands of Dollars)			
Accrued Warranty Costs–Beginning of Year	**$2,424**	$2,523	$4,686
Warranty costs paid	**(461)**	(299)	(404)
Warranty costs accrued	**554**	471	669
Impact of changes in estimated and assumptions	**(379)**	(351)	(2,428)
Warranty liabilities assumed	–	80	–
Accrued Warranty Costs—End of Year	**$2,138**	$2,424	$2,523

Critical Accounting Policies

The Company's Cross branded writing instruments are sold with a full warranty of unlimited duration against mechanical failure. In establishing the accrual for warranty costs, management analyzes trends, measured over a period of several years, of several factors that impact the Company's cost to service the warranty. The most significant factors include: the operating costs of the service department, writing instrument unit sales, the number of units that are returned for warranty repair and the cost of product repairs. The estimates affecting the warranty reserve are updated annually. In 2002, there was a significant adjustment that lowered the reserve by approximately $2.2 million.

Contingencies Related to Revenue Recognition

Any number of contingencies may present themselves in a revenue transaction-rights of return or refund, customer acceptance conditions, warranties, price protection, etc. The resolution of these contingencies may have a material effect on the financial statements of future periods. Companies should strongly consider whether the potential effects of these contingencies are significant enough to warrant disclosure.

> **SEC REGISTRANT ALERT:** When such contingencies exist, SEC registrants are required to disclose the following information: (1) the accounting treatment afforded the contingency, (2) significant assumptions used in accounting for the contingency, (3) material changes in the contingency, and (4) reasonably likely uncertainties that may affect the contingency (CIRP-8/01).
>
> In addition, in early 2003 the SEC staff issued the Summary by the Division of Corporation Finance of Significant Issues Addressed in the Review of the Periodic Reports of the Fortune 500 Companies (the Fortune 500 Report). This report resulted from the SEC's Division of Corporation Finance's (Corp Fin) review of all annual reports filed by Fortune 500 companies. The report provides insight into areas commonly questioned by Corp Fin during its reviews of annual reports. One area specifically mentioned in the Fortune 500 Report relates to accounting for certain contingencies. Corp Fin specifically indicated that companies in certain industries could improve their disclosures related to contingencies such as price protection and product returns. Specifically:
>
> • Companies in the capital goods, semiconductor, and electronic instruments and controls industries could improve their disclosures related to revenue recognition for products with return or price protection features and the requirements of customer acceptance provisions.

- Companies in the pharmaceutical and retail industries could improve their disclosures related to product returns, discounts, rebates, and co-operative advertising arrangements.

EXAMPLE: PRODUCT RETURN AND CONTRACTUAL ALLOWANCE CONTINGENCIES

Intersil Corporation Form 10-K—Fiscal Year Ended December 31, 2004

The Company's sales to international distributors are made under agreements which permit limited stock return privileges and pricing credits. Revenue on these sales is recognized upon shipment at which time title passes. The Company estimates international distributor returns and pricing credits based on historical data and current business expectations and defers a portion of international distributor sales and profits based on these estimated returns. The international distributor reserves comprise two components that are reasonably estimable. The first component of international distributor reserves is the price protection reserve, which protects the distributors' gross margins in the event of falling prices. This reserve is based on the relationship of historical credits issued to distributors in relation to historical inventory levels and price paid by the distributor as applied to current inventory levels. The second component is a stock rotation reserve, which is based on the percentage of sales made to limited international distributors whereby the distributors can periodically receive a credit for unsold inventory they hold. Actual price protection and stock rotation changes have historically been within management's expectations.

Fees for Services

In general, a service provider should disclose information concerning unearned service revenues and deferred costs of services, including an indication of the periods in which the related services will be performed (ITC, par. 26). Depending on the nature of the service provided and the terms of the arrangement, additional disclosures may also be required. Those situations are discussed below.

> **SEC REGISTRANT ALERT:** If an SEC registrant recognizes revenues from service fees over the service period based on progress towards completion or based on separate contract elements or milestones, the registrant must disclose how revenues from service fees are measured. This should include, but may not be limited to, the following:
>
> 1. How progress is measured (cost-to-cost, time-and-materials, units-of-delivery, units-of-work-performed);
>
> 2. Types of contract payment milestones and how they relate to substantive performance and revenue recognition events;

3. Whether contracts with a single counterparty are combined or bifurcated;

4. Contract elements permitting separate revenue recognition and how they are distinguished;

5. Whether the relative fair value or residual method is used to allocate contract revenue among elements; and

6. Whether fair value is determined based on vendor-specific evidence or by other means (CIRP-8/01).

Contingent Fees—Management Fees Based on a Formula

Given that acceptable alternatives may exist to account for management fees based on a formula, a company must disclose the accounting policy it elects to account for such fees.

> **SEC REGISTRANT ALERT:** SEC registrants are also required to disclose whether they have recorded any revenue at risk due to future performance contingencies, the nature of the contracts giving rise to the contingencies, and, if material, the amount of any such revenue recorded (EITF D-96).

EXAMPLE: MANAGEMENT FEES BASED ON A FORMULA

Marriott International, Inc. Form 10-K—Fiscal Year Ended December 31, 2004

Management fees comprise a base fee, which is a percentage of the revenues of hotels, and an incentive fee, which is generally based on hotel profitability.

Management Fees: We recognize base fees as revenue when earned in accordance with the contract. In interim periods and at year end we recognize incentive fees that would be due as if the contract were to terminate at that date, exclusive of any termination fees payable or receivable by us.

Refundable Service Fees

The accounting for refundable service fees is not discussed in the accounting literature. Therefore, whatever policy is applied to these transactions is a choice among available alternatives. Companies with a significant amount of refundable service transactions should therefore disclose the policy used to account for them, in accordance with APB-22.

SEC REGISTRANT ALERT: To the extent an SEC registrant provides services where the fees are refundable, it must disclose the accounting policy followed to account for those refundable fees. The registrant must also provide a rollforward of the unearned revenue and refund obligations liabilities. Such rollforwards should consist of the balance at the beginning of the period, the amount of cash received from customers, the amount of revenue recognized in earnings, the amount of refunds paid, other adjustments (explained), and the balance at the end of the period (SAB Topic 13A4a, ques. 1).

Research and Development Activities

If a company is engaged in performing research and development activities for others, it should disclose the significance of its research and development arrangements (including royalty agreements, purchase provisions, license agreements, and commitments to provide additional funding or services). It should also disclose the amount of revenue earned and costs incurred under such contracts. If a company has entered into more than one such arrangement, it may exercise judgment in aggregating the arrangements for disclosure purposes (FAS-68, par. 14).

SEC REGISTRANT ALERT: SEC registrants must also disclose how they apply their revenue recognition policies for each major revenue stream (e.g., research and development services, license agreements, product sales, consulting, etc.) and payment form (e.g., up-front fees, milestone fees, royalty payments, etc.) in their research and development arrangements. If different revenue recognition policies are followed for a particular major revenue stream or payment form due to varying facts and circumstances, or contractual terms, each policy should be separately described. In many cases, especially for recognition of milestone payments, it will be necessary to discuss the facts and circumstances resulting in the culmination of the earnings process (CIRP-8/01).

EXAMPLE: COLLABORATION AND LICENSE AGREEMENT

Trimeris, Inc. Form 10-K—Fiscal Year Ended December 31, 2004

To date, the Company has received a $10 million license fee, research milestone payments of $15 million and has achieved $3.3 million in manufacturing milestones. The license fee and research milestones were recorded as deferred revenue and are being recognized ratably over the research and development period. The manufacturing milestones were also recorded as deferred revenue and are being recognized ratably through June 2013, which is the current expected commercial life of Fuzeon.

At the time of the license fee payment, Roche was granted a warrant to purchase Trimeris stock. The fair value of the warrant, $5.4 million, was credited to additional paid-in capital in 1999, and as a reduction of the $10 million license fee payment.

Bill and Hold Sales Transactions

When revenue is recognized before delivery in a product sale, this will generally expose a company to greater risks than a transaction in which revenue is only recognized after delivery. Therefore, a company that recognizes revenue before delivery in bill and hold transactions should disclose this policy if the amount of revenue recognized in bill and hold transactions is material.

> **SEC REGISTRANT ALERT:** When revenue is recognized on bill and hold sales, registrants should disclose the risks and uncertainties surrounding warehousing arrangements with distributors and their potential effect on the financial statements. This disclosure might include the registrant's relationship with distributors, that fixed commitments to purchase goods are obtained prior to revenue recognition, whether the registrant has modified its normal billing and credit terms, or that the distributor carries the risk of decline in the market value of bill and hold inventory.

INDUSTRY-SPECIFIC DISCLOSURE REQUIREMENTS

All companies, regardless of industry affiliation, are subject to complying with the general and specific disclosure requirements discussed in the previous sections of this chapter. In addition to those disclosures, the authoritative literature provides incremental disclosure requirements for certain specific industries due to factors unique to those industries. Provided below is a discussion of the disclosure requirements for two specific industries discussed elsewhere in this publication—Construction Contractors and Franchisors. Also provided below are sources for additional industry-specific disclosure requirements.

LISTING OF APPLICABLE LITERATURE

ARB-43	Restatement and Revision of Accounting Research Bulletins
ARB-45	Long-Term Construction-Type Contracts
FAS-45	Accounting for Franchise Fee Revenue

FAS-69	Disclosures about Oil and Gas Producing Activities, an amendment of FASB Statements 19, 25, 33, and 39
FAS-71	Accounting for the Effects of Certain Types of Regulation
SOP 81-1	Accounting for Performance of Construction-Type and Certain Production-Type Contracts
SOP 01-6	Accounting by Certain Entities (Including Entities with Trade Receivables) That Lend to or Finance the Activities of Others
AAG-BRD	Audit and Accounting Guide for Brokers and Dealers in Securities
AAG-CON	Audit and Accounting Guide for Construction Contractors
AAG-FGC	Audit and Accounting Guide for Audits of Federal Government Contractors
AAG-HCO	Audit and Accounting Guide for Health Care Organizations
ARA-1991	Audit Risk Alert—1991
REG S-X, Rule 5-02	Financial Statement Requirements, Commercial and Industrial Companies, Balance Sheets
REG S-X, Rule 9-05	Financial Statement Requirements, Bank Holding Companies, Foreign Activities
SAB Topic 8B	Retail Companies Finance Charges

Construction Contractors

In general, a construction contractor should disclose the basic accounting policy it has adopted to account for revenues from its construction contracts. This disclosure should include a discussion of the method used to (1) account for construction-related revenues and costs (e.g., percentage-of-completion, completed contract) and (2) segment or combine construction contracts for accounting purposes (ARB-45, par. 15; SOP 81-1, par. 21). To the extent the contractor deviates from its basic accounting policy (because the facts and circumstances and relevant accounting literature support such a deviation), that deviation should be disclosed (SOP 81-1, pars. 25 and 31).

Percentage-of-Completion

A contractor that uses percentage-of-completion accounting must also disclose the method(s) used to measure progress toward completion (e.g., effort expended, units produced) (SOP 81-1, par. 45).

Completed Contract

To the extent a contractor uses the completed contract method, the basis to determine when a contract is "complete" should be disclosed (SOP 81-1, par. 52).

Claims

To the extent a contractor recognizes revenue related to a claim, the amounts recorded should be disclosed (SOP 81-1, par. 65). To the extent a contractor does not meet the requirements to record the claim or the amount of the claim exceeds the recorded contract costs, the contractor should consider whether disclosure of the related contingent asset is required (SOP 81-1, par. 67). If a contractor adopts a policy of not recognizing revenue related to a claim until the amounts have been received or awarded, that policy should be disclosed (SOP 81-1, par. 66).

Subsequent Events

Events occurring after the date of the financial statements that are outside the normal exposure and risk aspects of the contract should be disclosed as subsequent events (SOP 81-1, par. 82).

Costs

Given the uniqueness of accounting for construction contract costs, there are incremental disclosure requirements related to these costs. These requirements include disclosing total contract costs related to unapproved change orders, claims or other items subject to similar uncertainties surrounding their determination or realizability. In addition to the aggregate amount, the contractor should also disclose (1) the nature and status of the significant items included in the total and (2) the basis on which these amounts are recorded (e.g., cost or realizable value). To the extent progress payments have been netted against contract costs at the balance sheet date, the contractor should disclose those netted amounts as well (AAG-CON, chap. 6, par. 21).

For precontract costs (as defined in SOP 81-1) or other costs deferred as a result of an unapproved change order, the contractor should disclose its deferral policy and the related amounts (AAG-CON, chap. 6, par. 21).

> **SEC REGISTRANT ALERT:** Registrants are also required to make the following disclosures related to contract costs: (1)

when program accounting is applied, the assumptions used, including total units estimated to be sold under the program, units delivered, and units on order, (2) amounts of manufacturing and other costs incurred on long-term contracts carried forward under the "learning curve" concept put forth in SOP 81-1 and the portion of those costs that would not be absorbed in cost of sales on existing firm orders, (3) amounts that are not expected to be recorded under contract, and (4) the elements of deferred costs (REG S-X, Rule 5-02.6).

Receivables

The unique nature of accounting for construction contracts also results in receivable balances with attributes that may not necessarily be found in receivables related to normal product or service sales. This gives rise to incremental disclosure requirements related to construction contract receivables. These requirements include disclosing the following receivable balances as of the balance sheet date (AAG-CON, chap. 6, pars. 24-28):

1. For billed or unbilled amounts subject to uncertainty regarding their determination or realizability (e.g., unapproved change orders, claims) the contractor must disclose either on the face of the balance sheet or in a note thereto: (a) the amount, (b) a description of the nature and status of the significant items included in the amount, and (c) the portion, if any, expected to be collected after one year.
2. For other unbilled amounts, the contractor must disclose: (a) the amounts, (b) a general description of the prerequisites for billing, and (c) the portion, if any, expected to be collected after one year.
3. For retainages billed but not collected, a contractor must disclose, either on the face of the balance sheet or in a note thereto: (a) the amounts included, (b) the portion (if any) expected to be collected after one year, and, (c) if practicable, the years in which the amounts are expected to be collected.

In addition, to the extent receivables include amounts with maturities beyond one year, the following should be disclosed: (a) the amount that matures after one year, (b) if practicable, the amounts maturing in each year, and (c) either (i) the related interest rates, (ii) an indication of the average interest rate on all receivables, or (iii) the range of rates on all receivables (AAG-CON, chap. 6, par. 27).

SEC REGISTRANT ALERT: The SEC staff requires all registrants (i.e., all commercial and industrial companies, not just those considered long-term contractors) that enter into long-term contracts to make the same disclosures required of a construction contractor. For purposes of this view the SEC staff defines long-term contracts as: (1) all contracts accounted for under the percentage-of-completion method, and (2) any contracts or programs accounted for on the completed contract basis that involve material amounts of inventories or unbilled receivables and that will be performed over a period in excess of 12 months (REG S-X, Rules 5-02.3 and 5-02.6).

Franchisors

Franchise agreements capture the significant commitments and obligations of the franchisor. The nature of these commitments and obligations, whether or not they have been provided, should be disclosed by the franchisor (FAS-45, par. 20).

Franchise Fees

As it relates specifically to franchise fees, the franchisor must disclose the following:

1. Information about any franchise fee revenue being recognized on the cost recovery or installment basis due to collectibility concerns (FAS-45, par. 21); and

2. The portion of franchise fees represented by initial rather than continuing franchise fees (FAS-45, par. 22).

Regarding initial franchise fees, the following disclosures are desirable, but not required:

1. Relative contribution of initial franchise fees to net income; and

2. Likelihood that initial franchise fees will decline in the future due to sales predictably reaching a saturation point (FAS-45, par. 22).

Franchisor-Owned versus Franchised Outlets

Franchisors must present specific information for both franchisor-owned outlets and franchised outlets. This information includes revenue- and cost-related information for each outlet group. In addition, to the extent there are significant changes in the number of franchisor-owned or franchised outlets during the period, the number of franchises sold and purchased must be disclosed along with the number of franchisor-owned and franchised outlets in operation (FAS-45, par. 23).

EXAMPLE: FRANCHISE FEES

McDonald's Corporation Form 10-K—Fiscal Year Ended December 31, 2004

Revenue recognition

The Company's revenues consist of sales by Company-operated restaurants and fees from restaurants operated by franchisees and affiliates. Sales by Company-operated restaurants are recognized on a cash basis. Fees from franchised and affiliated restaurants include continuing rent and service fees, initial fees and royalties received from foreign affiliates and developmental licensees. Continuing fees and royalties are recognized in the period earned. Initial fees are recognized upon opening of a restaurant, which is when the Company has performed substantially all initial services required by the franchise arrangement.

Franchise arrangements

Individual franchise arrangements generally include a lease and a license and provide for payment of initial fees, as well as continuing rent and service fees to the Company based upon a percent of sales with minimum rent payments that parallel the Company's underlying leases and escalations (on properties that are leased). McDonald's franchisees are granted the right to operate a restaurant using the McDonald's System and, in most cases, the use of a restaurant facility, generally for a period of 20 years. Franchisees pay related occupancy costs including property taxes, insurance and maintenance. In addition, franchisees outside the U.S. generally pay a refundable, noninterest-bearing security deposit. Foreign affiliates and developmental licensees pay a royalty to the Company based upon a percent of sales.

The results of operations of restaurant businesses purchased and sold in transactions with franchisees, affiliates and others were not material to the consolidated financial statements for periods prior to purchase and sale.

Revenues from franchised and affiliated restaurants consisted of:

IN MILLIONS	2004	2003	2002
Rents and service fees	**$4,804.8**	$4,302.1	$3,855.0
Initial fees	**36.1**	43.0	51.1
Revenues from franchised and affiliated restaurants	**$4,840.9**	$4,345.1	$3,906.1

Future minimum rent payments due to the Company under existing franchise arrangements are:

IN MILLIONS	Owned sites	Leased sites	Total
2005	$1,063.4	$811.7	$1,875.1
2006	1,038.9	790.3	1,829.2
2007	1,006.7	772.1	1,778.8
2008	972.2	751.3	1,723.5
2009	933.0	722.9	1,655.9
Thereafter	7,241.7	5,531.7	12,773.4
Total minimum payments	$12,255.9	$9,380.0	$21.635.9

At December 31, 2004, net property and equipment under franchise arrangements totaled $10.4 billion (including land of $3.0 billion) after deducting accumulated depreciation and amortization of $4.8 billion.

Other

There are various sources for additional industry-specific disclosure requirements. The AICPA Audit and Accounting Guides (AAG) are primary sources for these requirements. Examples of these sources are provided below. As applicable, these and other sources should be consulted.

Industry	Source	Nature of the Disclosure
Airline	ARA-1991	Frequent flyer programs
Financial	REG S-X, Rule 9-05	Foreign activities of bank holding companies
	AAG-BRD, chap. 4, par. 9	Sources of revenue
	SOP 01-6, par. 13e	Net unammortizied deferred fees and costs
Government Contractors	ARB-43, chap. 11A, par. 22	Offsets under cost-plus-fixed-fee government contracts
	ARB-43, chap. 11C, pars. 18–19, 21–22	Termination claims under terminated war and defense contracts
	ARB-43, chap. 11C, pars. 28–29	Subcontractors' claims
	AAG-FGC, chap. 3, par. 66	Accounting policies

Industry	Source	Nature of the Disclosure
	AAG-FGC, chap. 3, par. 67	Progress payments offset against unbilled receivables
	AAG-FGC, chap. 3, par. 73	Progress or advance payments and the related protective title to inventories
	AAG-FGC, chap. 3, par. 81	Items affecting income statement comparability
	AAG-FGC, chap. 3, pars. 85–94	Other significant information such as defective pricing, contract claims, unusual contracts and provisions, cost limitations, major customers, interest capitalization, financial reporting and changing prices
Health Care	AAG-HCO, chap. 5, par. 5 and chap. 10, par. 20	Contractual adjustments and settlements
Health Care (cont.)	AAG-HCO, chap. 7, par. 12 and chap. 14, pars. 22–23, 25 and 31	Continuing care retirement communities
	AAG-HCO, chap. 10, par. 21	Charity care
Oil and Gas	FAS-69, pars. 24–25	Results of operations for oil and gas producing activities
Regulated	FAS-71, par. 19	Refunds
Retail	SAB Topic 8B, ques. 1	Retail companies' finance charges

CHAPTER 13
FUTURE EXPECTATIONS AND PROJECTS

CONTENTS

BACKGROUND

Financial reporting issues in revenue recognition have increasingly occupied standard-setters in recent years. As a result, standard-setters around the world have undertaken a wide range of revenue-related projects. Some of the projects are designed to interpret existing standards, while others are designed to develop new reporting frameworks. Several projects with broad applicability are currently under way and will likely occupy standard-setters for many years.

The primary objective of all current projects is international convergence. In 2002, the FASB and the IASB agreed that the principal goal of each organization was international convergence. The two boards have pooled their resources and effort on the major projects discussed in this chapter.

The purpose of this chapter is to provide an overview of the different revenue recognition projects. However, readers should regularly review FASB Action Alerts, IASB Insights, IFRIC Updates, and the minutes of FASB, IASB, EITF, and IFRIC meetings to follow the progress of and actively participate in the development of financial reporting standards for revenue recognition.

PROJECTS WITH BROAD APPLICABILITY

Revenue Recognition Project

In early 2002, the FASB issued a prospectus regarding adding a project to its agenda dealing with liability and revenue recognition. The

FASB received over 30 response letters to this prospectus. Given this response, the continued public scrutiny of revenue recognition accounting policies, and the lack of an overall revenue recognition framework, the FASB decided in May 2002 to add a revenue recognition project to its agenda.

Goals of the Project

The primary goal of this project is to develop a comprehensive revenue recognition framework that provides broadly applicable guidance on the subject of revenue recognition. Three goals of this project that are complementary to the primary goal are to (1) eliminate inconsistencies in the literature and in practice, (2) develop a comprehensive model, and (3) create a model that will provide an overall framework to address future issues.

Eliminate inconsistencies   As discussed throughout this book, the revenue recognition guidance that exists is generally focused on specific transactions or issues. Although each of the pieces of literature reaches conclusions that are reasonable for the given circumstances, the answers are not all consistent with each other. For example, the accounting treatments for standard and separately priced extended warranties (see Chapter 5, "Product Deliverables" and Chapter 6, "Service Deliverables") are inconsistent, as standard warranties are never treated separately for accounting purposes from the related product or service, while extended warranties always are. Another example is with respect to estimating the effects of future events. SOP 81–1, *Accounting for Performance of Construction-Type and Certain Production-Type Contracts* (see Chapter 9, "Contract Accounting"), generally encourages the estimation of revenue on contracts for which the ultimate amount of revenue may vary, while SOP 97–2, *Software Revenue Recognition* (see Chapter 10, "Software—A Complete Model"), and SAB Topic 13, "Revenue Recognition," generally discourage or prohibit such estimation. The FASB hopes to identify, reconcile, and eliminate these and other inconsistencies in the existing literature that addresses revenue recognition.

Develop a comprehensive model   Because so much of the existing revenue recognition literature addresses only narrow issues or specific transactions, there are many transactions for which no authoritative literature exists. Although existing literature can often be applied by analogy, it is often not clear whether the analogy is appropriate, or, in cases where two or more potential analogies exist, which analogy is appropriate. In addition, as discussed further below, the FASB's conceptual framework provides inconsistent guidance on the definition of revenues and how those revenues should be recognized. By creating a comprehensive model, the FASB hopes to provide the framework and the guidance to allow questions to be answered in all transactions under the same principles, rather than the haphazard approach that exists today.

Provide a framework to address future issues   One of the reasons the current literature on revenue recognition is not consistent from pronouncement to pronouncement is that the framework in the concept statements is not robust enough to ensure that the accounting standard-setters use the same underlying analysis to answer questions. This became apparent in the EITF's deliberations on certain revenue-related Issues. The EITF is, in general, not supposed to address issues for which a framework does not exist in the authoritative literature. It has, arguably, ventured beyond its normal scope to provide needed guidance on sales incentives (EITF Issue No. 01–9, "Accounting for Consideration Given by a Vendor to a Customer (Including a Reseller of the Vendor's Products)") and multiple-element arrangements (EITF Issue No. 00–21, "Revenue Arrangements with Multiple Deliverables"). However, the lack of a framework in which to operate has resulted in the EITF's deliberations on these issues taking far longer than the deliberations on most EITF issues. The FASB hopes to provide a robust framework that will allow transaction or issue-specific questions to be answered in an effective and efficient manner in the future.

Project Approach

The FASB's intention is to address the topic of revenue recognition using both top-down and bottom-up approaches. The top-down approach addresses the broad conceptual issues related to accounting for revenue. As broad concepts are developed, the intent is to test them by applying them to specific types of transactions and issues. In this sense, the project approach is iterative. The bottom-up approach focuses first on (1) existing authoritative literature for specific transactions and (2) nonauthoritative practices that are regarded as accepted practices. The purpose of simultaneously dealing with revenue recognition in both broad and specific senses is to ensure that the broad concepts and specific guidance developed by the FASB are compatible with one another. That is, the broad concepts need to be appropriate for the different types of transactions and revenue-related issues that present themselves in the real world. And, the specific guidance needs to follow an overall framework to protect the theoretical integrity of the overall accounting guidance.

Given the significant change in practice that would result from the FASB's current approach to revenue recognition (as discussed later in this chapter), the FASB plans to issue a Preliminary Views document on this project before issuing an Exposure Draft. The

Preliminary Views document will cover both the concepts-level and standards-level revenue recognition guidance developed by the FASB. The objective of the Preliminary Views document is to elicit feedback on the general revenue recognition model being proposed by the FASB before the FASB proceeds further with the model.

In general, the FASB plans on taking a three-tiered approach to issuing guidance on the subject of revenue recognition:

1. *Amendment and expansion of FASB Statement of Financial Accounting Concepts No. 5,* Recognition and Measurement in Financial Statements of Business Enterprises *(CON-5) and No. 6,* Elements of Financial Statements *(CON-6)*—This tier would explain the basic concepts used to (a) define revenue in terms of assets and liabilities and (b) determine when revenue should be recognized. The assets and liabilities approach is discussed further later in this chapter.

2. *General standard on revenue recognition*—This general standard would provide the core recognition and measurement principles that must be met prior to recognizing revenue. This standard is expected to "bridge" the gap between the general concepts in CON-5 and CON-6 and the specific application guidance discussed in the third tier. This standard is expected to supercede current general revenue recognition guidance, such as FASB Statement No. 48, *Revenue Recognition When Right of Return Exists,* and EITF 00–21.

   The initial scope does not exclude any industries or transactions. However, the FASB has acknowledged that certain industries or transactions may require additional work. The need for scope exclusions will continue to be considered as discussions on the project continue. However, the number of potential scope exceptions is not expected to compromise the overall objective of providing a comprehensive model to revenue recognition.

   > **OBSERVATION:** In the FASB's materials related to this project, a statement is made that the final general standard on revenue recognition would also supercede Staff Accounting Bulletin No. 104, *Revenue Recognition,* which is codified in SAB Topic 13. The SEC staff will need to be involved in any supercession of SAB Topic 13, because a FASB Statement cannot supercede guidance included in a SAB Topic. The SEC staff has not made any public statements regarding its expected actions on this point.

3. *Specific application standards*—Specific application standards would be provided for three broad categories of revenue-generating arrangements (i.e., services, products, rights to use assets). Presumably, the specific application standards will discuss the

application of the principles in the general standard to specific types of arrangements. It is expected that these specific application standards would supercede the industry-specific or transaction-specific guidance that already exists in the current body of authoritative literature on revenue recognition (e.g., SOP 97–2, and FASB Statement No. 45, *Accounting for Franchise Fee Revenue*).

Regarding definition of revenues, the Board has tentatively agreed that (a) a reporting entity should not recognize revenues for performance by third parties of its obligations to deliver goods or render services to customers if those obligations are legally assumed by those third parties; (b) in all other circumstances, the reporting entity should recognize revenues for performance by third parties of its obligations to deliver goods or render services to customers; (c) production can give rise to a component of comprehensive income (to be discussed in future meetings); and (d) nonreciprocal transfers received are components of revenue and must be disclosed as a separate item in the income statement.

Revenues can be a result of (a) an unconditional right to receive consideration and (b) the extinguishment of performance obligations (legally enforceable obligations of a reporting entity to deliver goods or render services to its customers) to customers. In the latter case, the Board limits revenue to extinguishment of obligations for which the reporting entity is the primary obligor. The FASB has agreed that the concept of a primary obligor should be consistent with its meaning in FASB Statement No. 140, *Accounting for Transfers and Servicing of Financial Assets and Extinguishments of Liabilities*.

The FASB's current timeline indicates that the Preliminary Views document will be issued in the fourth quarter of 2005. It is expected that the Preliminary Views document will focus primarily on the guidance that will ultimately result from (a) the revision and expansion of CON-5 and CON-6 and (b) the issuance of a general standard on revenue recognition. It may also cover some of the guidance that will ultimately result from the issuance of specific application standards. It is expected, however, that the specific application standards will be fully-developed only after the issuance of an Exposure Draft on the general standard on revenue recognition.

Conceptual Framework

The FASB has concluded that inconsistencies in its conceptual framework have contributed to the difficulties involved in revenue recognition accounting. These inconsistencies relate to the discussion of revenue in CON-5 and CON-6. CON-6 defines revenues in terms of changes in assets and liabilities. That is, the CON-6 definition of revenues indicates that revenues are generated when assets increase or liabilities decrease (the "Asset/Liability Approach"). CON-5, however, defines revenues in terms of the earnings process (the "Earnings Approach"). The Earnings Approach is the approach used in all of the current literature addressing or dealing with different aspects of revenue recognition (see Chapter 3, "General Principles"). This explains why the focus in the current literature is so often on defining the earnings process and determining when it has been completed.

The FASB has decided to pursue the Asset/Liability Approach for the following reasons: (a) applying the Earnings Approach to revenue recognition in CON-5 conflicts with the definitions of assets and liabilities in CON-6 (e.g., CON-5 may result in revenue needing to be deferred, however "deferred revenue" may not be a liability as defined in CON-6); (b) it is difficult, if not impossible, to define the concepts of "earning" and "realization" included in CON-5 such that those concepts would be applied consistently; and (c) application of the Earnings Approach takes on added complexities when multiple-element arrangements are involved. If a final standard based on the Asset/Liability Approach is issued, it would produce wholesale changes in the types of events that result in revenue, the timing of the recognition of that revenue, and the measurement of that revenue.

> **OBSERVATION:** It is likely that the Preliminary Views document issued by the FASB will reflect the Asset/Liability Approach. Whether this is the approach ultimately reflected in the final standard will be determined, in part, by constituents' reactions to the Preliminary Views document issued. In this sense, "constituents" includes preparers, auditors, analysts, the SEC, and others. Given that the Asset/Liability Approach would represent a significant change in practice and that a final standard on this subject would affect virtually every company, interested constituents should follow the activities related to this project very closely and provide feedback to the FASB on the Preliminary Views document issued. The FASB's website (www.fasb.org) can be consulted for updates on decisions reached and current and future discussion topics.

Asset/Liability Approach—Overall Criteria

Under the Asset/Liability Approach to recognizing revenue, when and how much revenue should be recognized depends on the following overall criteria:

> **ELEMENTS CRITERION:** Have either of the following occurred without a commensurate investment by owners (a) assets increase causing equity to increase, without a corresponding

increase in liabilities to the customer, or (b) liabilities decrease causing equity to increase?

MEASUREMENT CRITERION: Can those changes in assets or liabilities be appropriately measured—that is, in terms of relevant attribute and with sufficient reliability?

Only when both of these questions can be answered affirmatively, should revenue be recognized.

Elements Criterion The FASB has developed the following subcriteria that can be used to determine when the Elements Criterion has been satisfied:

This has occurred for purposes of the Elements Criterion...	When these are present...
Increase in assets	• A new resource is obtained or created, or an existing resource is enhanced. • The resource embodies future economic benefits that are expected to flow to the entity. • The resource is controlled by the entity.
Increase in liabilities to the customer	• A new performance obligation is created, or an existing performance obligation is increased (where "performance obligation" is defined as a "legally enforceable obligation of a reporting entity to its customer, under which the entity is obligated to deliver goods or render services"). • The obligation entails an expected outflow from the entity of resources (e.g., goods, services, guarantees of performance) embodying economic benefits.
Decrease in liabilities	• The obligation is owed by the entity to the customer. • An existing obligation of the entity is diminished or ceases to exist by being settled or otherwise eliminated other than through transfer to a third party that legally assumes it.

These subcriteria are based on the definition of assets and liabilities included in CON-6. Each of the subcriteria focuses on one of the critical elements in the definition of an asset or liability. An increase in assets occurs when an existing resource controlled by the entity is enhanced or a new resource (also controlled by the entity) is created or obtained. Resources are composed of future economic benefits that are expected to flow to the entity. Increases in liabilities are the result of increases in existing performance obligations or the creation of new performance obligations. The obligations are owed by the entity to its customers and consist of expected outflows of resources (i.e., economic benefits including goods, services, and guarantees of performance). Decreases in liabilities are a consequence of extinguishment, or settlement, or elimination other than by transfers to a third party that legally assumes them.

A critical component of the Asset/Liability Approach is properly identifying the assets and liabilities that arise or change as a result of the sale transaction. In some cases, the identification of "affected" assets and liabilities is straightforward and in other cases it is not. Tentative conclusions reached by the Board regarding the definition of assets and liabilities for purposes of analyzing a revenue-generating transaction to determine if and when revenue should be recognized include:

- Conditional rights and obligations do not meet the definition of assets and liabilities (for example, they may be depend on customer actions or market events outside the control of the reporting entity), but unconditional and mature rights and obligations might meet the definition of assets and liabilities.

- Only legally enforceable (counterparties are legally required to perform) contractual and noncontractual obligations may give rise to assets and liabilities.

- An asset or a liability may exist and their measurement may be affected even if a contract is not worthy of enforcement (costs exceed benefits).

- "Cancellation-like" clauses (e.g., refund rights and contingency clauses) may affect both the recognition and the measurement (because of uncertainties) of assets and liabilities.

- Express or implied contractual promises may give rise to assets or liabilities. For example, a contract may not explicitly give the customer a refund right but a vendor's history of granting refunds may result in an obligation because customers come to rely on that practice.

- Side agreements may give rise to significant rights and obligations and should be included in the assessment of the existence of assets and liabilities.

In addition, for purposes of identifying the unit of accounting, the FASB has tentatively concluded that the unit of accounting depends on whether the subject of the contract is fungible or unique. If the subject of the contract is fungible, the FASB tentatively concluded that a rebuttable presumption exists that the contract as a whole is the unit of accounting. If the subject of the contract is unique, the FASB tentatively concluded that the unit of accounting is the assets and liabilities arising from the unconditional rights and obligations in the contract.

Measurement Criterion Appropriate measurement of the change in assets or liabilities requires reliable and relevant information. For purposes of "reliability" (a) the most reliable measure in the appropriate reference market must be used and (b) the measure must faithfully represent what it purports to represent and that representational quality must be verifiable. For purposes of "relevance," the FASB has determined that the most relevant information to use in the initial measurement of assets or liabilities is fair value. In determining the fair value of a reporting entity's remaining performance obligations, the FASB has determined that the reporting entity should use the price it would have to pay an unrelated party of equal credit standing to assume legal responsibility for performing all of the reporting entity's remaining obligations. This results in a "wholesale" (or "business-to-business") approach to determining fair value. In other words, fair value is being determined from the reporting entity's perspective. A "retail" approach to fair value would result in the reporting entity using the price a customer would pay for the benefit of having the reporting entity satisfy its performance obligation. In other words, this approach would result in fair value being determined from the customer's perspective.

ILLUSTRATION: "WHOLESALE" FAIR VALUE VS. "RETAIL" FAIR VALUE

(Adapted from Example discussed by FASB at its March 23, 2004 Meeting)

Facts: On December 31, 20X1, Customer identifies a blue sweater priced at $100 that it would like to buy from Retailer. However, Retailer does not have Customer's size in stock. Retailer offers to obtain the sweater for Customer in the appropriate size by January 10, 20X2. Customer accepts the offer and pays Retailer $100. Retailer's general return policy (i.e., returns accepted with "no questions asked" for 90 days) applies to this transaction.

Retailer has the following three options when it comes to obtaining Customer's sweater:

(1) Retailer can order the sweater from Supplier for $60. To obtain this price, Retailer would have to order a dozen sweaters. The sweaters would be shipped to Retailer with its next regular shipment of sweaters, which is

scheduled for January 4, 20X2. Retailer is unsure as to whether it would be able to sell the additional 11 sweaters without a price reduction and Supplier does not provide general return rights to Retailer.

(2) Retailer can have Supplier ship the sweater directly to Customer for $85. Supplier will ensure that the sweater arrives by January 10, 20X2, and will provide Customer with the right of return. If, upon receipt, Customer decides to return the sweater, it would return the sweater to Supplier. Supplier's price of $85 includes the freight and shipping insurance charges to deliver the product to Customer.

(3) Retailer can go to Competitor on January 2, 20X2 and buy Customer's sweater for $80. Competitor does not provide the right of return to Retailer.

Retailer's yearend is December 31, 20X1.

Discussion: Under the Asset/Liability Approach, Retailer would have to determine the changes in its assets and liabilities resulting from this transaction. At December 31, 20X1, Retailer has had an increase in assets of $100. It has also had an increase in liabilities related to the performance obligation it has to Customer. For purposes of recording the $100 increase in assets, Retailer must determine the fair value of its performance obligation. Based on the facts, there are at least four amounts that could be considered in the fair value determination – $60, $80, $85, and $100. The $60, $80, and $85 amounts are different "wholesale" or "business-to-business" fair values. The $100 is the "retail" fair value. In discussion of this example, the majority of the FASB believed that the appropriate fair value for the Retailer's performance obligation is $85 because $85 represents the price that Retailer would have to pay a third party to assume responsibility for performing all of its remaining obligations. Using $85 as the fair value of Retailer's performance obligation would result in the following journal entry at December 31, 20X1:

Cash	$100	
Performance Obligation (Liability)		$85
Revenue		$15

Using the Asset/Liability Approach and the "wholesale" fair value concept results in $15 of revenue being recognized on December 31, 20X1. Presumably, this $15 is attributable to Retailer's selling activities. This is a new concept in revenue recognition – the notion that revenue can result from an entity's selling activities.

Using the Asset/Liability Approach and the "retail" fair value concept would result in the following journal entry at December 31, 20X1:

Cash	$100	
Performance Obligation (Liability)		$100

No revenue is recognized on December 31, 20X1, using this approach and concept because the entire increase in assets is attributable to an increase in a liability to the customer.

Current revenue recognition principles would also result in the recognition of cash and a liability in the amount of $100. However, the rationale is different. Under the current revenue recognition principles, no revenue would be recognized because Retailer has not delivered the product purchased by Customer. In other words, Retailer has not "earned" the revenue.

Comparison of Approaches/Concepts

	Revenue recognized at December 31, 20X1	Liability recognized at December 31, 20X1
Asset/Liability Approach, "Wholesale" Fair ValueConcept	$15	$85
Asset/Liability Approach, "Retail" Fair Value Concept	$0	$100
Current Approach	$0	$100

As it relates to measuring the fair value of assets or liabilities related to a revenue-generating arrangement, or changes in such assets and liabilities, the FASB has also reached the following additional tentative conclusions:

- The reliability threshold for fair value estimates affecting revenues should be the same as for other estimates affecting profits. In other words, estimates that affect revenues should not be held to a higher "relevance" or "reliability" standard than other estimates that affect profits.

- Certain Level 3 estimates (as defined in the FASB's Exposure Draft, *Fair Value Measurements* (Fair Value ED, or FVM Statement), discussed later in this chapter) might be sufficiently reliable for purposes of measuring performance obligations whose extinguishment gives rise to revenues. How the concepts in the Fair Value ED should be applied in the context of the revenue recognition model being developed by the FASB is a question that will continue to be discussed by the FASB as it continues its deliberations on the Revenue Recognition project and redeliberates certain conclusions in the Fair Value ED.

- Sufficient evidence may exist in certain instances to directly measure selling revenues that arise upon contract generation.

A direct measurement in this situation would involve observable prices that marketplace participants, including the reporting entity, pay for identical contracts. Whether such prices exist depends on a number of factors, including whether the contract under review incorporates an other than insignificant customer relationship component. If sufficient evidence exists to directly measure selling revenues that arise upon contract generation, then it may be appropriate to measure the remaining performance obligations indirectly as the excess of the fair value of the entity's rights over its selling revenues.

- Refund obligations and performance guarantees should be measured at fair value. This approach is different from the current approach to refund obligations where the existence of refund rights might preclude the recognition of revenue all-together (see Chapter 5, "Product Deliverables;" and Chapter 7, "Intellectual Property Deliverables").

- The time value of money and credit risk should be reflected in the fair value of contractual assets unless those effects are immaterial. This approach is different from the current approach to extended payment terms and collectibility. Under the current approach, extended payment terms may preclude the recognition of revenue all-together (see Chapter 10, "Software—A Complete Model"). The current approach to collectibility is that collectibility must be reasonably assured. If collectibility is not reasonably assured, no revenue should be recognized (see Chapter 3, "General Principles").

ILLUSTRATION: TREATMENT OF COLLECTIBILITY

Facts: Vendor and Customer enter into a sales arrangement where Customer will buy $1,000 worth of product from Vendor. Customer must pay Vendor within 30 days of delivery of the product (Vendor's normal payment terms). Customer does not have the right to return the product to Vendor. The cost of the product to Vendor is $550. Vendor has sold product to Customer in the past and Customer has always paid for the product within 30 days of delivery. However, recently Vendor became aware that Customer may be experiencing some financial difficulties. Vendor investigates this development and determines that the likelihood that Customer will pay for the product involved in the current sales arrangement is approximately 60% and that the fair value of the receivable it would have from Customer as a result of this sale would be $600 (determined based on the amount a financial institution would pay Vendor for this receivable). Because of (a) Vendor's history with Customer, (b) the fact that the fair value of the receivable from Customer is more than the cost of the product, and (c) the fact that it is more-likely-than-not that Customer will pay for the product based on Vendor's analysis, Vendor enters into the sales arrangement with Customer and delivers the product (these events happen concurrently).

Discussion: Under the Asset/Liability Approach, upon entering into the sales agreement with and delivering the product to Customer, Vendor's assets and equity have increased without a corresponding increase in liabilities to the customer (i.e., Vendor has no remaining performance obligations to Customer) or an investment by owners. The fair value of the increase in assets is $600. As such, Vendor would record the following journal entry upon entering into the sales agreement with and delivering the product to Customer:

Accounts Receivable	$600	
Cost of Goods Sold	$550	
Revenue		$600
Inventory		$550

Subsequent accounting under the Asset/Liability Approach has not yet been discussed. One question that arises in the subsequent accounting for this arrangement is what effect does the fair value of the asset changing (going either up or down) prior to payment have on the accounting or income statement presentation of this transaction? Presumably, the FASB will address this and other subsequent accounting issues as it continues its deliberations on this project.

Under current revenue recognition principles, upon entering into the sales agreement with and delivering the product to Customer, Vendor would conclude that collectibility is not reasonably assured since its likelihood of collecting from Customer is only 60%. As a result, Vendor would not recognize any revenue upon entering into the sales agreement with and delivering the product to Customer. As it relates to the inventory, at a minimum, Vendor would need to reclassify the inventory from its general inventory account to an account that indicates it is inventory held by others. Whether the inventory would need to be relieved all-together and cost of goods sold recognized in this situation, depends on the other terms in the arrangement and the likelihood that Vendor would be able to repossess the product upon default by Customer. Vendor would only recognize revenue in this situation upon receipt of payment or a change in circumstances that would result in Vendor concluding that collectibility is reasonably assured.

Comparison

	Asset/Liability Approach	Current Approach
Revenue recognized upon entering into sales agreement with and delivering product to Customer	$600	$0

One concern that has been raised related to the approach currently being discussed by the FASB is its reliance on fair value measurements. The basis for this concern centers on whether fair value can be sufficiently measured in all cases where such a measurement would be required under the FASB's current approach. The FASB recognizes this concern and has spent a considerable amount of the discussion time on the issues of how to measure (a) "selling" revenues, if any, and (b) the fair value of the reporting entity's remaining performance obligations.

Asset/Liability Approach – Draft Recognition and Measurement Principles

As a result of its discussions on this project, the FASB has developed a working set of recognition and measurement principles. While these principles appear to be consistent with the Elements and Measurement Criteria discussed earlier in this chapter, it is not clear how they will come together in the Preliminary Views document.

Recognition Principles   The fundamental recognition principle drafted by the FASB as a result of its discussions on this project is that "A reporting entity should recognize revenues in the accounting period in which they arise and measure them at their fair value on the date that they arise if it can determine both their occurrence and measurement with sufficient reliability." More specific recognition principles drafted by the FASB include the following:

1. *Contractual revenues cannot arise before a contract with a customer exists*—Whether a contract with a customer exists should take into consideration the reporting entity's customary business practices. It is expected that the FASB will provide implementation guidance regarding the definition of customary business practices. This definition will incorporate notions similar to those in the current requirement that persuasive evidence of arrangement must exist (see Chapter 3, "General Principles"), such as "If a company does not have a standard or customary business practice of relying on written contracts (that is, contracts physically signed by both parties) to document a sales arrangement, it would be expected to have other forms of written or electronic evidence to document the transaction."

2. *A reporting entity should recognize contractual revenues when an increase in its claims against its customers can be determined to have occurred and the fair value of that increase can be measured with sufficient reliability*—Consider the situation where a company delivers product to its customer and it has no further performance obligation related to the product. In this situation, the company has increased the claims it has against its customers by the fair value of that increase in claims.

3. *A reporting entity should recognize contractual revenues when a decrease in claims against it by its customers can be determined to have occurred and the fair value of that decrease can be measured with sufficient reliability*—Consider the situation where a company has an outstanding installation obligation to its customer related to

equipment delivered at an earlier point in time. When the company satisfies this installation obligation, it has experienced a decrease in the claims its customers have against it by the fair value of that decrease in claims.

4. *Increases in assets or decreases in liabilities that give rise to contractual revenues may stem from contractual promises that can be either express or implied*—For example, a right of return may not be explicitly stated in a contract, but the vendor has a history of granting customers the right of return and the customers come to rely on this practice. This implicit right of return should be considered in identifying the assets or liabilities that arise from contractual promises involved in sales transactions.

5. *Contractual revenues should be recognized at contract inception if the fair values of the contractual assets obtained on that date exceed the fair values of the contractual liabilities simultaneously incurred, and if those revenues can be measured with sufficient reliability*—Consider the situation where a company enters into a contract to sell equipment subject to installation. If, at contract inception, the fair value of the assets related to that contract exceeds the fair value of the performance obligation liabilities related to providing and installing the equipment, revenue would be recognized for that excess provided it can be reliably measured. This excess effectively represents revenue related to the company's "selling" activities.

6. *Subsequent to contract inception, contractual revenues should be recognized upon the reporting entity's performance of its obligations under the contract, as evidenced by a decrease in its contractual liabilities or an increase in its contractual assets, the fair value of which can be determined with sufficient reliability*—Consider the situation where a company sells a piece of equipment and an extended warranty. At contract inception, the company would recognize a liability related to its extended warranty performance obligation. As the company satisfies that extended warranty performance obligation and experiences a decrease in its contractual liabilities, the company would recognize revenue for that decrease provided it can be reliably measured.

The FASB also had drafted a seventh principle that indicates that contractual revenues should be recognized upon contract completion to reflect any final increases in the fair values of contractual assets or final decreases in the fair values of contractual liabilities. It withdrew this principle however pending further progress in understanding how the other principles would be applied.

Measurement Principles The fundamental measurement principle drafted by the FASB states that "A reporting entity should measure revenues arising from an increase in its assets or decrease in its liabilities (or a combination thereof) at the fair value of that increase or decrease." More specific measurement principles drafted by the FASB include the following:

1. *The estimates of the fair value that the reporting entity uses to measure revenues arising from increases in its assets or decreases in its liabilities should be those that have the highest relative reliability*—To the extent different sources for fair value estimates exist, the reliability of each of those sources should be considered. The fair value estimate with the highest relative reliability should be used for purposes of measuring revenue.

2. *The estimates of the fair value of revenues that are consistent with Level 3 of the fair value hierarchy should be developed by means of multiple valuation techniques that maximize market inputs, such as a market approach or an income approach, whenever information necessary to apply those techniques is available*—As discussed below under "Fair Value Measurements," Level 3 estimates of fair value are given the lowest priority after those involving quoted prices in active markets for identical or similar assets and liabilities. When using this lowest priority fair value evidence, efforts must be taken to maximize the reliability of the measurement, such as using market inputs when available.

3. *The fair value of revenues arising from increases in the reporting entity's contractual assets reflects the effects of credit risk, the time value of money, and dilution risk*—Under this principle, credit risk affects the measurement of revenue. In other words, credit risk would be taken into consideration in estimating the fair value of the increase in assets. It would not be taken into consideration in determining whether revenue should be recognized to begin with, as is the case under the current approach to revenue recognition.

4. *The measures that reflect the effects of credit risk on the fair value of a reporting entity's revenues also should reflect expectations of recoveries if any, in case of breach of the contract by the customer*—In a sense, the fair value of a reporting entity's revenues should take into consideration any of the terms in the related contract that could affect the fair value of those revenues (e.g., remedies in case of breach of contract by the customer). In theory, the fair value would reflect the probability of those terms resulting in more or less contract value.

5. *Any express or implied rights of return and refund, allowances, rebates, discounts, credits, and other similar rights granted to customers that reduce revenues by reducing the reporting entity's contractual assets or increasing its contractual liabilities should be measured at fair value*—This principle results in amounts that are refundable being factored into the measurement of the change in an entity's contractual assets or liabilities. The fact that the fees are refundable would not be taken into consideration in determining whether revenue should be recognized to begin with, as is the case under the current approach to revenue recognition.

6. *Revenues arising from increases in contractual assets that stem from the reporting entity's rights to the customer's stand ready performance in case of occurrence or nonoccurrence of a specified event should be measured at fair value that reflects the assessment of the probability that the specified event will occur*—This principle results in contingent fees being factored into the measurement of increases in contractual assets. The fact that the fees are contingent does not affect the decision to recognize them.

These recognition and measurement principles are consistent with the decisions reached by the FASB to date. As the FASB continues its deliberations on this project, including discussing the application of these principles to certain types of transactions, it is likely that these principles will be clarified, refined, added to, removed, or otherwise enhanced.

Distinguishing Revenues from Gains

Just as the FASB's discussion of the Asset/Liability Approach is a significant change from current practice, the discussion of how revenues should be distinguished from gains may also lead to significant changes. In its discussions to this point, the FASB has focused on the definition of revenues. The question of how revenues should be defined is largely one of presentation, similar to the gross versus net presentation questions addressed in EITF Issue No. 99–19, "Reporting Revenue Gross as a Principal versus Net as an Agent," (see Chapter 11, "Presentation"). However, the FASB's discussion has not focused on the principle versus agent distinction that is central to EITF 99–19. Instead, for purposes of developing a working definition of revenues, the FASB has primarily focused on determining what does and does not give rise to revenues. In this regard, the FASB has tentatively concluded on the following:

Revenues can arise as a result of...	Revenues cannot arise as a result of...
• The extinguishment of the entity's performance obligations to its customers, including —Performance by a third party of the reporting entity's obligations to deliver goods or services if those obligations have not been legally assumed by the third party; and —Satisfaction or expiration of obligations related to performance guarantees.	• Performance by a third party of the reporting entity's obligations to deliver goods or provide services if those obligations have been legally assumed by the third party.

• Nonreciprocal transfers received (where a nonreciprocal transfer is expected to be defined as "a transaction in which an entity receives an asset or cancellation of liabilities without directly giving value in exchange").	
• Selling activities	

An important element in in determining what gives rise to revenue relates to whether the obligations to deliver goods or services are obligations of the reporting entity or whether the reporting entity has arranged for a third party to legally assume those obligations. This is very similar to the primary obligor indicator in EITF 99–19 (see Chapter 11, "Presentation"). While there are other factors to be considered, the existence of the primary obligor indicator has a significant influence on determining whether revenue should be recognized gross or net under EITF 99–19. The following corollaries exist between the model in EITF 99–19 and the FASB's working definition of revenues: (a) the reporting entity being the primary obligor under EITF 99–19 and the reporting entity being the party that is legally obligated to deliver the goods or services to the customer under the FASB's working definition of revenue, and (b) the reporting entity not being the primary obligor under EITF 99–19 and a third party assuming the legal obligation to deliver the goods or services to the customer under the FASB's working definition of revenue.

An important distinction in these analyses is whether a third party has legally assumed responsibility for the performance obligations or whether the reporting entity has just arranged to have a third party perform the obligations on its behalf (e.g., the reporting entity hires a subcontractor or otherwise outsources the obligations). In the latter situation, responsibility for the performance obligations rests with the reporting entity. Those obligations have not been legally assumed by a third party. As such, the revenue associated with those performance obligations would be considered revenue of the reporting entity under the FASB's working definition of revenue. For the same reason, the reporting entity would likely still be considered the primary obligor under EITF 99–19.

As it relates to selling activities giving rise to revenues, the FASB has indicated that it will continue to consider the accounting treatment for selling activities whose fair value is measured as a residual when there are uncertainties surrounding its measurement. In other words, the FASB will continue to consider whether such activities should truly give rise to revenues. Although the FASB has not yet decided on the accounting treatment for such activities, it has decided that the residual should not be recognized as a component of other comprehensive income.

The FASB has acknowledged that the definition of revenues needs to be improved to better distinguish between (a) revenues and gains and (b) components of comprehensive income. One issue that will be discussed further in this context is production income. The FASB has tentatively concluded that increases in assets related to production activities can give rise to a component of comprehensive income. However, future discussion points for the FASB on this issue likely will include: (a) when should these increases in assets, or production income, be recognized, and (b) how should it be classified in the financial statements?

In addition to capturing the basic definition of revenue, the FASB has also started to reach tentative conclusions on how certain types of revenues should be presented on the income statement. Two such tentative conclusions are that (a) nonreciprocal transfers should be disclosed as a separate line item in the income statement, and (b) amounts associated with outsourcing and subcontracting activities are not required to be disclosed on the face of the income statement (i.e., separate line item classification for expenses related to outsourcing and subcontracting activities are not required on the income statement).

ILLUSTRATION: ASSET/LIABILITY APPROACH AND DEFINITION OF REVENUE

Adapted from Example included on FASB website)

Facts: Retailer X buys televisions for $250 and sells them for $300, which is similar to the amounts charged by other retailers. Retailer X also sells extended warranties for $100 that extends the manufacturer's warranty for two years, which is similar to the amounts charged by other retailers. Neither of these fees, once received, is refundable. History indicates that the extended warranty will be utilized in 1 of every 10 televisions sold subject to the extended warranty and that the cost of fixing the warranty-related defect is $140. The amount an unrelated party of equal credit standing would charge to assume the extended warranty performance obligation is $300 per 10 televisions sold subject to the extended warranty. On June 1, 20X2, Retailer X signs a contract with a customer to provide 10 televisions with extended warranties and collects the purchase price in full. The customer has an excellent credit-rating. On July 1, 20X2, Retailer X delivers the televisions.

EXAMPLE 1

Additional Facts: Retailer X services the extended warranties. The amount Retailer X would have to pay an unrelated party of equal credit standing to assume its obligation to deliver 10 of the same make/model of televisions to the customer is $2,800.

Discussion: On June 1, 20X2, upon Retailer X signing the contract with its customer, Retailer X's assets and liabilities have increased. The increase in assets is attributable to the cash received from the customer. The increase in liabilities is attributable to the incurrence of two performance obligations to the customer – one related to the delivery of the televisions, the other to servicing the extended warranty. Using the "wholesale" fair value of these performance obligations results in Retailer X recognizing the following journal entry under the Asset/Liability Approach:

Cash	$4,000	
Performance Obligation—Delivery		$2,800
Performance Obligation—Extended Warranty		$300
Revenue		$900

This journal entry illustrates one of the significant changes to current practice that arises under the Asset/Liability Approach. Once the contract is signed, Retailer X has assets of $4,000 to be recognized (the cash collected). However, it has only taken on obligations with a "wholesale" fair value of $3,100. Under the Asset/Liability Approach using the "wholesale" fair value concept, this results in revenue of $900 being recognized upon the signing of the contract with the customer (e.g., before delivery has occurred). Essentially, this $900 of revenue is the value generated by the selling effort that has been completed by Retailer X.

Current practice would not allow this value to be recognized as revenue, as the delivery of the televisions and extended warranty service would be considered to be too integral to the transaction to allow any recognition of revenue before delivery has occurred. As such, current practice would have resulted in no revenue being recognized on June 1, 20X2. In addition, application of the current multiple-element arrangement guidance (see Chapter 4, "Multiple-Element Arrangements") would result in the separation of the television and warranty elements where $3,000 is allocated to the television element and $1,000 is allocated to the warranty element. These are the amounts Retailer X would have charged separately and they are also the amounts charged by other retailers for the same televisions and warranties. Given that the current revenue recognition principles would not be met at June 1, 20X2, the amounts allocated to each element would be reflected as deferred revenue at June 1, 20X2.

Upon delivery of the televisions on July 1, 20X2, the following entry would be recorded under the Asset/Liability Approach:

Performance Obligation—Delivery	$2,800	
Cost of Goods Sold	$2,500	
Revenue		$2,800
Inventory		$2,500

Current practice would result in the recognition of $3,000 of revenue on July 1, 20X2. This corresponds to the amount allocated to the television element on June 1, 20X2.

Recognition of the revenue related to the extended warranty performance obligation would occur as that warranty obligation decreases. How this is measured under the Asset/Liability Approach is not yet clear. In other words, it is not yet clear whether (a) the extended warranty performance obligation liability would be remeasured periodically and any changes reflected in income, (b) the extended warranty performance obligation would be derecognized as the liability is extinguished, which occurs over time, or (c) the extended warranty performance obligation would be derecognized as the liability is extinguished, which occurs at a point in time (i.e., upon expiration of the warranty). Current practice would result in the deferred revenue related to the extended warranty being recognized over the extended warranty period (see Chapter 5, "Product Deliverables").

EXAMPLE 2

Additional Facts: On June 10, 20X2, Retailer X hires a third party to service the extended warranties. However, the legal performance obligation under the extended warranty still rests with Retailer X. The amount Retailer X would have to pay an unrelated party of equal credit standing to assume its obligation to deliver 10 of the same make/model of televisions to the customer is $2,800.

On June 10, 20X2, Retailer X pays a third party $300 to assume its extended warranty performance obligation.

Discussion: Because Retailer X has not paid a third party to assume its legal obligation related to the extended warranties, the FASB's tentative conclusions on the definition of revenue would result in the amount associated with the extended warranties being considered revenue. As such, the entries for Example 2 would be the same as those discussed in Example 1. The amount associated with extended warranties would also be considered revenue in current practice based on the current gross vs. net guidance (see Chapter 11, "Presentation").

EXAMPLE 3

Additional Facts: The amount Retailer X would have to pay an unrelated party of equal credit standing to assume its obligation to deliver 10 of the same make/model of televisions to the customer is $2,800.

Discussion: The journal entries recorded by Retailer X on June 1, 20X2, and July 1, 20X2, are the same as under Example 1.

On June 10, 20X2, a third party has legally assumed Retailer X's extended warranty obligation. This results in an extinguishment of Retailer X's liability. As such, it should be removed from its books. However, Retailer X does not recognize revenue when extinguishing this liability. This is due to one of the tentative decisions reached by the FASB, which indicates amounts related to performance obligations that have been legally assumed by a third party should be excluded from revenues. As such, Retailer X records the following entry on June 10, 20X2:

Performance Obligation—Extended Warranty	$300	
Cash		$300

Under current practice, a number of indicators must be evaluated to determine whether revenue should be recognized gross as a principal vs. net as an agent (see Chapter 11, "Presentation"). There are not enough facts presented in this example to determine whether Retailer X should present the extended warranty revenue gross or net.

Next Steps

The FASB plans to continue its discussion of the principles for revenue recognition, the implications of measuring performance on the basis of customer consideration amount, and to develop examples to illustrate the application of that approach to a wide range of revenue transactions.

International Convergence

As mentioned earlier in this chapter, the IASB also has a project addressing revenue recognition on its agenda. The FASB and the IASB are jointly working on their projects. At its June 2005 meeting, the IASB Board agreed to pursue the approach taken by the FASB and described in this chapter. However, many of the tentative conclusions reached by the FASB (or those reached by the IASB) have not been addressed by the IASB (or the FASB). At any point, it is unclear what level of convergence on the revenue recognition project has been achieved and similarly, will ultimately be achieved by the two boards. We note that convergence remains a high priority of both boards.

Timing

The most recent indication of timing related to this project suggests that the FASB will issue a Preliminary Views document in the fourth quarter of 2006. It is not clear when the FASB will issue Exposure Drafts related to the amendments to CON-5 and CON-6, the general revenue recognition standard, and the specific application standards. Thus, the timing of any final standards is uncertain.

Liability Extinguishment Project

After the issuance of FASB Statement No. 140, *Accounting for Transfers and Servicing of Financial Assets and Extinguishments of*

Liabilities, questions arose regarding the application of the liability extinguishment guidance in paragraph 16 of that standard. As a result, the FASB added a project to its agenda in February 2003 to clarify this guidance.

During its discussions on its Revenue Recognition project, the FASB realized that the liability extinguishment guidance in paragraph 16 of FAS-140 would take on added significance under the Asset/Liability Approach. This is attributable to the Asset/Liability Approach potentially resulting in the recognition (and the eventual derecognition) of a remaining performance obligation liability. The criteria that would be used to determine when the remaining performance obligation liability should be derecognized for accounting purposes are those in paragraph 16 of FAS-140. It is not clear whether application of those criteria to a remaining performance obligation liability is operational. As such, the Liability Extinguishment project will consider how paragraph 16 of FAS-140 would be applied in the context of extinguishing remaining performance obligations (either partially or wholly) that arise in accounting for a revenue-generating arrangement under the Asset/Liability Approach. If those criteria are deemed not to be operational, the FASB will consider other derecognition models.

The FASB and the IASB are working jointly to develop consistent guidance. The FASB has not yet reached any tentative conclusions on this project and it has not indicated when it expects to issue an Exposure Draft on this project.

Financial Performance Reporting by Business Enterprises Project

The FASB added a project dealing with financial performance reporting to its agenda in 2001. The objective of this project relates to presenting higher quality and more meaningful and useful information in financial statements that can be used to assess the financial performance of a company. The project focuses on the content and presentation of both interim and annual financial statements, but does not focus on financial information provided outside the financial statements (e.g., management's discussion and analysis, earnings releases). This project is relevant to revenue recognition because it will ultimately effect how revenues are reported and classified in the financial statements.

Current Direction and International Convergence

The FASB's work on this project is coordinated with the work of a similar project undertaken by the IASB. While there was general agreement on the issues that needed to be addressed in this project, the Boards initially separately deliberated and concluded on certain issues. To facilitate convergence, the Boards discussed this project at a joint meeting in 2004. At that meeting, the Boards agreed on the issues that should be contemporaneously discussed and decided upon by the Boards. In addition, to ensure that the right complement of expertise and perspective is involved in this project, the Boards have formed an international joint advisory group to analyze issues on reporting financial performance and comprehensive income. This group will advise the Boards as they discuss and decide upon the agreed-upon issues in this project. Of these agreed-upon issues, the following would affect the presentation of revenue:

- Whether a single statement of comprehensive income should be presented and, if so, whether a subtotal similar to "net income from continuing operations" or "profit and loss" should be presented. Addressing this issue will determine the nature of the financial statement(s) that includes revenue and the general presentation of revenue within that statement.

- The appropriate number of years that should be presented in comparative financial statements and the notes to the financial statements. Addressing this issue will determine the amount of historical revenue-related information that must be presented in the financial statements and notes to the financial statements.

- Whether it is meaningful to recycle items between different subtotals in the financial statements (e.g., between "net income" and "comprehensive income"). Addressing this issue would not affect the presentation of revenue under the current revenue recognition accounting model. However, addressing this issue could affect the presentation of revenue under the future revenue recognition accounting model given that the FASB is considering whether "production income" gives rise to an element of net income or comprehensive income.

- The principles that should be used for disaggregating information on the financial statements. Addressing this issue may affect revenue line items that should be included in the financial statements (e.g., product- vs. service-related revenues).

- The totals and subtotals (e.g., categories such as business and financing) that should be reported on the financial statements. Addressing this issue will determine the categories, totals, and subtotals in which the different elements of revenue should be included.

Timing

The Boards expect to issue an Exposure Draft on certain topics in late 2005 and a Preliminary Views document on some other issues is planned for the fourth quarter of 2006. However, the complexity of the issues may further delay any resolution by the Boards.

Fair Value Measurement

Several recent accounting pronouncements call for the use of fair value measurements (for example, fair value measurements are required for certain financial instruments, business combinations, guarantees, asset retirement obligations, asset impairment valuations, and derivatives). The increasing use of fair value measurements has raised many questions regarding the proper measurement of fair value in diverse situations. Although there is some guidance on the issue of fair value measurements (most notably and recently in FASB Concepts Statement No. 7, *Using Cash Flow Information and Present Value in Accounting Measurements*), the FASB has recognized the growing need for more comprehensive and consistent guidance on this subject. In June 2003, the FASB added a fair value measurement project to its agenda and in June 2004, the Board issued an Exposure Draft of a proposed statement, Fair Value Measurements (FVM). In October 2005, a working draft of the FVM Statement was posted on the FASB website. The Board plans to finalize the FVM Statement in the fourth quarter of 2005.

Objective

The Statement defines fair value, establishes a framework for fair value measurements, and enhances disclosure requirements.

Relevance to Revenue Recognition

Fair value measurements are required sparingly in the current revenue recognition literature. Two examples of revenue recognition standards that require fair value measurements or measurements similar to fair value are (1) the requirement to measure the fair value of individual elements in a multiple-element arrangement for purposes of separating those elements and allocating arrangement consideration to them, and (2) the requirement to measure at its fair value of a guarantee included in a revenue transaction (see Chapter 4, "Multiple-Element Arrangements"). However, the Asset/Liability Approach will make fair value measurements a critical component of the revenue recognition model.

The FVM Statement would exclude revenue recognition transactions that require fair value measurements using vendor-specific objective evidence (for example, the separation of multiple-element arrangements including only software and software-related elements in SOP 97–2, *Software Revenue Recognition;* SOP 98–9, *Modification of 97–2, "Software Revenue Recognition, with Respect to Certain Transactions;* EITF Issue No. 00–3, "Application of AICPA Statement of Position No. 97–2 to Arrangements That Include the Right to Use Software Stored on Another Entity's Hardware"; and EITF Issue No. 00–21, "Revenue Arrangements with Multiple Deliverables" (see Chapter 10, "Software—A Complete Model").

The FVM Statement does not eliminate the practicability exceptions to fair value measurements in accounting pronouncements within its scope, for example, FASB Interpretation No. 45, *Guarantor's Accounting and Disclosure Requirements for Guarantees, Including Indirect Guarantees of Indebtedness of Others,* and EITF Issue No. 99–17, "Accounting for Advertising Barter Transactions."

For those revenue-related fair value measurements that are within the scope of the FVM Statement (e.g., guarantees), the following issues are relevant:

- The guidance for using present value in APB Opinion No. 21, *Interest on Receivables and Payables,* has been codified in the FVM Statement.

- Fair value is defined as "the price that would be received for an asset or paid to transfer a liability in a current transaction between marketplace participants in the reference market for the asset or liability." The FVM Statement elaborates on this definition.

- Valuation techniques used to estimate fair values should be consistent with the market approach, income approach, and cost (or asset-based) approach. Additional guidance regarding the valuation techniques is provided in the FVM Statement.

- Valuation techniques should be consistently applied and a change in techniques should be justified by the new technique resulting in a more reliable estimate of fair value. Revisions resulting from a change in the valuation technique or its application must be accounted for prospectively, as changes in accounting estimates (per paragraph 19 of FASB Statement No. 154 (FAS-154), *Accounting Changes and Error Corrections*). However, the disclosure requirements of FAS-154 for a change in estimate do not apply for these revisions.

- Valuation techniques should maximize the use of market inputs and minimize the use of entity inputs. The key attributes of market inputs and entity inputs are discussed in the FVM Statement.

- A fair value hierarchy is provided to prioritize the inputs that should be used to estimate fair value. The highest priority (Level 1) is given to quoted prices in active reference markets for identical assets and liabilities. The lowest priority (Level 5) is given to valuation techniques based on entity inputs. The FVM Statement contains a comprehensive discussion of the fair value hierarchy.

- Various disclosures should be provided related to the fair value measurements. These disclosures focus on the extent to which fair value measurements are used, how fair values are determined, and the effect fair value measurements have on earnings (or changes in net assets).

This Statement will be effective for financial statements issued for fiscal years beginning after December 15, 2006, and interim periods within those fiscal years. The disclosure requirements will be effective for financial statements for fiscal years ending after December 15, 2006. Earlier application is encouraged.

Linkage of Transactions

Entities may enter into two or more contracts that are effectively part of the same transaction. A common question in such situations is whether these contracts should be combined for accounting purposes. This is commonly referred to as "linkage." The accounting literature has provided, and continues to refine, guidance related to when it is appropriate to combine certain types of contracts. However, there is no single comprehensive model in U.S. GAAP for determining whether contracts should be combined, or linked, for accounting purposes. The available guidance is fragmented and narrowly scoped. Here are some examples:

- Question K1 in the FAS-133 Guide, *Guide to Implementation of Statement 133 on Accounting for Derivatives and Hedging Activities*, addresses when separate contracts should be combined for purposes of applying the derivatives literature (see Chapter 4, "Multiple-Element Arrangements").

- TPA 5100.39, *Indicators that Multiple Contracts Should Be Viewed as Single Arrangements*, deals with combining contracts for purposes of applying the multiple-element guidance in the software revenue recognition literature (see Chapter 10, "Software—A Complete Model").

- EITF 00–21, "Revenue Arrangements with Multiple Deliverables" (par. 2), indicates that, generally, separate contracts with the same entity or related parties that are entered into, at, or near the same time are presumed to have been negotiated as a single arrangement (see Chapter 4, "Multiple-Element Arrangements").

- SOP 81–1, *Accounting for Performance of Construction-Type and Certain Production-Type Contracts,* provides guidance on when construction contracts should be combined for accounting purposes (see Chapter 9, "Contract Accounting").

Each of these examples deals with a specific issue. Three of the examples provide specific guidance (for example, criteria that must be met or indicators that should be considered) for narrowly scoped transactions.

The EITF deliberated another narrowly scoped linkage question in Issue No. 02–2, "When Certain Contracts That Meet the Definition of Financial Instruments Should Be Combined for Accounting Purposes." Ultimately, the Task Force discontinued its discussion of the issue. The EITF recommended that the Board should develop comprehensive guidance for when arrangements should be combined for accounting purposes.

FASB Statement 150 (FAS-150) provides a partial resolution: it precludes the combination of a freestanding financial instrument within its scope from being combined with another freestanding financial instrument, *unless* FAS-133 and related guidance requires the combination. This guidance leaves unresolved the issue of whether to combine freestanding instruments not within the scope of FAS-150 or FAS-133 and related guidance.

IFRIC Project

The International Financial Reporting Interpretations Committee (IFRIC) has had an issue related to linkage, *Combining and Segmenting Construction Contracts,* on its agenda since 2003. In its discussions on this issue, the IFRIC has focused on developing indicators that would suggest two or more contracts are effectively linked (should be combined) and should be accounted for as one transaction. The indicators discussed by the IFRIC focus on the substance and overall commercial effect of the contracts on an individual and combined basis. The IFRIC concluded that, to the extent that this effect indicates that the individual contracts are effectively parts of one transaction, the contracts should be combined for accounting purposes. The IFRIC acknowledged that all of the terms and conditions of the contracts (explicit and implicit) and substantive rights and obligations must be taken into consideration. The IFRIC project also considers the issue of segmenting as well as combining contracts, which has revenue recognition implications.

As part of its deliberations on this issue, the IFRIC also considered the relevance and appropriateness of criteria in AICPA Statement of

Position 81–1, *Accounting for Performance of Construction-Type and Certain Production-Type Contracts*. In developing its interpretations on this issue, the IFRIC relies primarily on IAS 11, *Construction Contracts*. With respect to combining contracts, the IFRIC confirmed that the criteria in SOP 81–1, paragraph 37, addressing the close interrelationship of construction activities and their timing and location should be incorporated into any guidance they might develop on IAS 11.

With respect to segmentation, IAS 11 currently requires segmentation of construction contracts when certain criteria are met, including that each asset has been subject to separate negotiation. In contrast, AICPA Statement of Position 81–1, *Accounting for Performance of Construction-Type and Certain Production-Type Contracts*, permits segmentation when either a primary set of criteria are met or, if those criteria are not met, all of a second set of criteria are met. The IFRIC, therefore, decided not to incorporate SOP 81–1, paragraph 40 (the primary set of criteria), into the guidance on IAS 11 because it does not believe that doing so would improve convergence with U.S. GAAP. The IFRIC also plans to examine whether the guidance in SOP 81–1, paragraph 41, represents a different set of criteria for segmenting contracts and, if different, whether this guidance should be incorporated in an Interpretation.

During its deliberations on the issue of service concessions, the IFRIC identified some issues with implications for IAS 11 that might be of a higher priority than the issues identified originally. In particular, the IFRIC decided to consider clarifying (1) the interaction of IAS 11 and IAS 23, *Borrowing Costs*, with respect to the capitalization of interest, (2) whether revenue should be allocated to phases of a project based on different profit margins or on the profit margin for the contract as a whole, (3) and several subtle differences between IFRSs and U.S. GAAP with respect to the application of the percentage of completion method, in particular the use of output measures (IAS 11) versus costs incurred (U.S. GAAP) to determine the stage of completion.

The IFRIC has expressed concern that any guidance on segmenting and combining construction contracts that it might issue on IAS 11 would become the guidance for service revenue recognition, including service revenue arrangements with multiple elements. Therefore, in May 2004, the IFRIC extended the project on combining and segmenting construction contracts to allow the use of segmenting based on output measures to be considered further, with a view to developing an Interpretation that would be consistent across both IASs 11 and 18. It is unlikely that the IFRIC will issue a Draft Interpretation on this issue before the end of 2005.

Other IFRIC Projects with Revenue Implications

The IFRIC has a number of issues with revenue recognition implications on its agenda, and it may add more issues with such implications.

Each of these projects overlaps with U.S. GAAP to some degree. As guidance is issued by the IFRIC on these issues, it is only applicable to financial statements prepared in accordance with International Financial Reporting Standards. However, companies following U.S. GAAP could consider this guidance to the extent that U.S. GAAP does not already provide guidance on the subject. In addition, given the drive for convergence of IFRS and U.S. GAAP, keeping track of IASB developments in revenue recognition can provide insight into what might be on the horizon for U.S. GAAP.

Many issues that are presented to IFRIC, while not specifically revenue recognition questions, may have revenue recognition implications. Given the potential overlap between the Revenue Recognition project of the IASB and IFRIC Interpretations, it is difficult to predict when, or even if, the IFRIC will complete deliberations on particular issues. Even if a Draft Interpretation has been issued, the IFRIC may decide to defer finalizing an Interpretation without concurrence by the IASB itself. Similarly, despite its project, the IASB may choose to have IFRIC address a particularly important question (e.g., service concessions) with revenue recognition implications to provide immediate guidance to companies.

Service Concession Arrangements

Service concession arrangements involve an operator entering into an arrangement with a grantor to provide services that give the public access to major economic and social facilities. These arrangements may involve water treatment and supply, tunnels, bridges, roads, and airports—for example, an operator enters into an agreement to construct a road for the grantor. Ultimately, the grantor would make the road available to interested parties. The grantor may or may not be a governmental entity and it may or may not charge explicitly for use of the road. In a service concession arrangement, the operator will likely agree to perform a variety of activities, including the construction of the infrastructure assets (e.g., the road), long-term maintenance of the road (e.g., repaving, snow removal), and the subsequent operation of the infrastructure assets (e.g., toll collection). The revenue recognition question that arises in service concession arrangements is how the operator should recognize revenue related to these activities.

Various accounting issues arise in the accounting for service concession arrangements. The nature and extent of these issues as well as how they should be addressed depends upon the terms of the arrangement. After extensive discussions on many of these issues and a variety of fact patterns, the IFRIC decided to limit the scope of any guidance it provides on service concession arrangements to those situations in which (a) the grantor controls the services provided by the operator with the infrastructure assets subject to the concession arrangement, (b) the grantor will control a significant residual interest in the infrastructure assets at the end of the concession arrangement, and (c) the infrastructure assets are newly built or acquired by the operator for the purpose of the service concession or are contributed by the grantor for the duration of the service concession. In addition, the IFRIC decided to provide guidance only for accounting by the operator and not by the grantor of the service concession.

In early 2005, the IFRIC issued three Draft Interpretations: D12 "Service Concession Arrangements—Determining the Accounting Model"; D13 "Service Concession Arrangements—The Financial Asset Model"; and D14, "Service Concession Arrangements—The Intangible Asset Model." Comments on the Draft Interpretations were received by the end of May 2005. These Draft Interpretations set out proposals on how an operator should account for infrastructure assets that were constructed or acquired for the purpose of the service concession or were a pre-existing asset of the grantor to which the operator is given access for the duration of the service concession.

In developing these Draft Interpretations, the IFRIC considered three possible accounting models for use by the operator in accounting for infrastructure assets: the property, plant, and equipment model (IAS 16); the financial asset model (IAS 39); and the intangible asset model (IAS 38). D12 provides guidance on determining which accounting model the operator should use to determine how to account for infrastructure assets it uses to provide concession services. The Interpretation states that, since the grantor controls a significant residual interest in the infrastructure assets, the operator should *not* recognize the infrastructure assets as property, plant, and equipment. Instead, D12 requires the operator to recognize any rights it receives in exchange for providing construction and other services (or other consideration) to the grantor as either a financial asset (receivable) or an intangible asset. The operator would recognize a financial asset when the grantor has primary responsibility for paying the operator and would recognize an intangible asset in all other circumstances (i.e., if the users pay the operator directly for the use of concession services). Revenue recognition is then based on the fact that there has been an exchange of dissimilar assets. D13 and D14 provide guidance on how the operator would apply the financial asset model and the intangible models, respectively. The IFRIC has not provided guidance on accounting for the infrastructure assets by the grantor.

Therefore, for service concession arrangements that fall within the scope of these interpretations, the key determination for the amount and timing of revenue recognition depends upon whether the infrastructure assets are accounted for as a receivable or an intangible asset. If the operator is compensated by the grantor (e.g., completion of construction of the infrastructure assets obligates the grantor to pay the operator), the operator recognizes a receivable.

Revenue recognition is based on the fact that the operator has constructed an asset and provided it to the grantor. If the operator is to be compensated by the parties that will use the infrastructure assets (e.g., vehicle operators paying tolls to use the road), then the operator recognizes an intangible asset (e.g., the right to collect tolls) upon providing the infrastructure assets to the grantor.

The views of respondents to the Draft Interpretations were divided on the overall direction of the project. Some believed that the issue of service concessions was too wide in scope and should be addressed in an IASB project, not by the IFRIC. Others believe that timely guidance on accounting for service concession arrangements is needed and that the IFRIC should finalize Interpretations quickly. After considerable deliberation, the IFRIC determined to continue toward issuing Interpretations, concluding that the limited scope of D12, D13, and D14 afforded them an opportunity to provide the necessary guidance. However, given other fundamental issues raised by respondents, the IFRIC has stated that it was unlikely to issue final Interpretations by the end of 2005.

Respondents to the Draft Interpretations had several criticisms of the distinction between the financial and intangible models and had opposed the proposal that the choice of accounting model would depend solely on who paid the operator. They had suggested that, instead, the criterion should be based on, or at least include, an analysis of the extent to which each party bore demand risk. "For example, a road operator would recognize a financial asset if it were to receive 'shadow tolls' from the grantor but an intangible asset if it were to receive tolls paid by users." While considering these comments, the IFRIC believes that it was not possible to achieve one accounting model under existing standards and remain concerned that arrangements with similar economics will be accounted for differently. The IFRIC also reaffirmed its decision not to address accounting by the grantor, primarily because most grantors are governmental agencies which do not apply IFRSs.

Revenue recognition under the intangible asset model remains controversial. D14 proposes that revenue should be recognized on the construction of the infrastructure assets provided by the operator and measured in accordance with paragraph 12 of IAS 18. This means that the exchange of the infrastructure assets for the right of use is viewed as a barter transaction that gives rise to revenue. Revenue would also be recognized on the subsequent use of the infrastructure. One consequence of this model is that total revenue exceeds total cash inflows by the amount of the barter revenue. There was considerable disagreement among respondents to this result. Nearly all operator respondents supported the proposal that the exchange was a barter transaction arguing that proposal reflects the economic reality of service concessions arrangements. The majority of all respondents, however, do not support the proposal criticizing the double recognition of revenue. They believe that the result negatively affects the usefulness of financial statements and argue that the exchange transaction has no commercial substance. In their view, the construction costs represent payments to acquire an intangible asset, rather than revenue-generating activities.

In the light of these comments, the IFRIC is considering revisions to the intangible asset model. Currently, the IASB staff is studying the broader implications that the proposal to not recognize construction revenue under the intangible asset model would have on the financial asset model and the proposal in D12 that the operator has right of access only. Any analysis provided to IFRIC will also consider the recognition of revenue and profit or loss separately.

Sale and Leasebacks with Repurchase Agreements

During IFRIC's discussions on service concession arrangements, a general question arose regarding whether a sale should be recognized in a sale leaseback containing a repurchase agreement (including an option) if the repurchase agreement results in the seller retaining significant risks or rewards in the leased item. IFRIC has tentatively concluded that no sale should be recognized in this situation, because a sale, as defined in IAS 18, *Revenue,* has not occurred. It is expected that this conclusion either will be captured in its own Interpretation or will be included in another, related Interpretation.

Determining Whether an Arrangement Contains a Lease

In November 2004, the IFRIC issued IFRIC Interpretation 4, which focuses on arrangements comprising a transaction (or series of transactions) that does not take the legal form of a lease but conveys the right to use an asset for a payment or series of payments. This Interpretation provides guidance for determining whether such an arrangement is, or contains a lease, and should be accounted for in accordance with IAS 17. It does not provide guidance about how the arrangement should be classified under that Standard.

Under U.S. GAAP, this issue was addressed in EITF Issue No. 01–8, "Determining Whether an Arrangement Contains a Lease." In the Basis for Conclusions of Draft Interpretation D3, the IFRIC drew attention to similarities between its proposed Interpretation and EITF 01–8, expressing the belief that "similar assessments of whether an arrangement contains a lease are likely under both interpretations." Some respondents to D3 disagreed with this conclusion, suggesting that there were significant differences between them. Consequently, the IFRIC reviewed its original conclusions and determined that there was "no compelling reason for different assessments of whether an arrangement contains a lease under IFRSs [International Financial

Reporting Standards] and U.S. GAAP." In addition, the IFRIC recognized the practical difficulties that companies would face in assessing arrangements against two similar, yet different, sets of criteria. The IFRIC eliminated these problems by adopting not only the criteria but, as far as possible, the words in EITF 01–08.

Consequently, in the Basis for Conclusions to IFRIC 4, the IFRIC reaffirms its conclusion that when an arrangement is assessed, the conclusion of whether or not the arrangement contains a lease would be the same under IFRIC 4 and EITF Issue 01–8. This does not mean, however, if the arrangement contained a lease, it would be accounted for in the same way under IAS 17 and U.S. GAAP.

INDUSTRY-SPECIFIC PROJECTS

Software and Motion Pictures

The AICPA issues Technical Practice Aids (TPAs) to address specific questions related to its pronouncements. The AICPA has a task force that has, in the past, actively addressed questions related to the application of SOP 97–2. This has resulted in the issuance of a number of TPAs dealing with specific software revenue recognition issues (see Chapter 10, "Software—A Complete Model," for a listing of software revenue recognition TPAs). Another area where the AICPA has provided TPAs is in addressing questions related to the application of SOP 00–2, *Accounting by Producers or Distributors of Films*. Entities that apply the provisions of either SOP 97–2 or SOP 00–2 should monitor the issuance of TPAs by the AICPA for the TPAs' effects on the entities' accounting policies.

Real Estate Time-Share

In December 2004, the AcSEC issued SOP 04–2, *Accounting for Real Estate Time-Sharing Transactions*. Initially, this SOP was meant to address both revenue and cost issues of accounting for real estate time-share units. However, in January 2004, the FASB instructed the AcSEC to remove all revenue recognition guidance from the scope of the draft SOP it reviewed for clearance. The FASB did so, given (a) the overlap with its Revenue Recognition project, (b) the changes in revenue recognition practices that have occurred since the project was initiated, and (c) the "rules-based" nature of the proposed revenue recognition requirements. Accordingly, SOP 04–2 does not modify the requirement of FASB Statement No. 66, *Accounting for Sales of Real Estate*, to account for time-sharing transactions under the other-than-retail-land-sales (OTRLS) model of that Statement. SOP

04–2 does contain some limited revenue recognition guidance in its illustration of the revenue recognition guidance of the OTRLS model to specific terms typically observed in time-sharing transactions.

SOP 04–2 treats bad debts as a reduction in revenue largely because it considers time-share uncollectibles as sales returns. This is different from current practice in other industries, which generally reflects bad debts as an expense. However, given the nature of the industry, the AcSEC believed that the SOP approach best reflected revenues and costs. SOP 04–2 was effective for financial statements for fiscal years beginning after June 15, 2005.

Distribution Fees

In March 2005, the Board directed the FASB Staff to issue FSP EITF 85–24–1, "Application of EITF Issue No. 85–24, 'Distribution Fees by Distributors of Mutual Funds That Do Not Have a Front-End Sales Charge,' When Cash for the Right to Future Distribution Fees for Shares Previously Sold is Received from Third Parties." The FSP addresses the accounting for transactions in which a distributor's rights to future cash flows relating to distribution fees (i.e., 12b-1 fees) and the contingent deferred sales charge (CDSC) are exchanged with a third party for cash.

The FASB staff believes that revenue recognition is appropriate when cash is received from a third party for the Rights (12b-1 Fees and the CDSC) if the distributor has neither continuing involvement with the Rights nor recourse. Related deferred costs must be expensed in the period revenue is recognized. The guidance in this FSP applies to reporting periods beginning after March 11, 2005.

Effects of Specific Application Standards

As discussed above, the FASB's approach to issuing standards in its Revenue Recognition project will first involve working through general revenue recognition principles and concepts that will be broadly applicable to all (or virtually all) revenue transactions. This work is expected to ultimately result in an amendment to CON-5 and the issuance of a general principles standard. Once this general groundwork has been laid, the FASB will begin to develop specific application standards for three broad categories of revenue-generating arrangements (i.e., services, products, rights to use assets).

The issuance of specific application standards is expected to eventually supercede or amend the industry-specific guidance that exists in the current body of authoritative literature on revenue recognition. As illustrated in Chapter 2, "A Brief Survey of Revenue-Related Literature," there are a significant number of original pronouncements dealing with revenue recognition on an industry-specific basis. Examples of industry-specific authoritative literature that may ultimately be amended or superceded as a result of any final standard issued in connection with the FASB's Revenue Recognition project include (but are not limited to):

- ARB-45, *Long-Term Construction-Type Contracts*

- FAS-45, *Accounting for Franchise Fee Revenue*

- FAS-66, *Accounting for Sales of Real Estate*

- FAS-68, *Research and Development Arrangements*

- FAS-71, *Accounting for the Effects of Certain Types of Regulation*

- FAS-91, *Accounting for Nonrefundable Fees and Costs Associated with Originating or Acquiring Loans and Initial Direct Costs of Leases, an amendment of FASB Statements No. 13, 60, and 65 and a rescission of FASB Statement No. 17*

- FAS-116, *Accounting for Contributions Received and Contributions Made*

- SOP 81–1, *Accounting for Performance of Construction-Type and Certain Production-Type Contracts*

- SOP 97–2, *Software Revenue Recognition*

- EITF 91–6, "Revenue Recognition of Long-Term Power Sales Contracts"

- EITF 91–9, "Revenue and Expense Recognition for Freight Services in Process"

As this book goes to press, the FASB has not finalized the scope of its Revenue Recognition project, nor has it made any final decisions regarding the existing authoritative literature that will be amended or superseded by the general guidance and specific application standards resulting from its project. A company that currently follows industry-specific authoritative literature should keep apprised of the FASB's discussions on its Revenue Recognition project to understand the effects that the project will have on the industry-specific authoritative literature the company follows.

OTHER PROJECTS

The following revenue-related EITF issues are open or inactive pending developments in Board projects and other EITF issues:

- EITF Issue No. 00–18, "Accounting Recognition for Certain Transactions Involving Equity Instruments Granted to Other Than Employees"

- EITF Issue No. 03–17, "Subsequent Accounting for Executory Contracts That Have Been Recognized on an Entity's Balance Sheet"

- EITF Issue No. 05-H, "Accounting for Payments Made by a Service Provider to Equipment Manufacturers and/or Retailers/Resellers of Specialized Equipment That Is Necessary for a Customer to Receive a Service from the Service Provider"

EITF Issue No. 00–18

One of the objectives of EITF 00–18 is to provide additional guidance related to EITF Issue No. 00–8, "Accounting by a Grantee for an Equity Instrument to Be Received in Conjunction with Providing Goods or Services" (see Chapter 8, "Miscellaneous Issues" for a discussion of EITF 00–8). EITF 00–18 has not been discussed since March 2002.

The remaining question in EITF 00–18 is Issue 3: How the grantee should account for the contingent right to receive, upon performing as specified in the arrangement, grantor equity instruments that are the consideration for the grantee's future performance. The Task Force has asked the FASB staff to work on improving the Issue 96–18, "Accounting for Equity Instruments That are Issued to Other Than Employees for Acquiring, or in Conjunction with Selling, Goods or Services," guidance used to determine the date at which a commitment for counterparty performance to earn the equity instruments is reached.

This issue remains inactive pending developments on Phase II of the portion of the Board's share-based payments project addressing ESOPs and transactions with nonemployees.

EITF Issue No. 03–17

This issue relates to the subsequent accounting for executory contracts that have been recognized on an entity's balance sheet, as either an asset or a liability, in accordance with GAAP. An example of a situation in which these assets or liabilities could arise is in a purchase business combination. Depending on the reporting entity's business and the nature of the executory contracts, as well as the guidance that results from this Issue, the amortization of the related recognized assets or liabilities could subsequently be reflected as revenue or revenue reductions.

Given the overlap in subject matter, discussions on this Issue were to take place in conjunction with discussions on EITF Issue No.

03–9,"Determination of the Useful Life of Renewable Intangible Assets under FASB Statement No. 142, *Goodwill and Other Intangible Assets.*" At its September 2004 meeting, however, the EITF agreed to remove EITF 03–9 from its agenda and made a recommendation to the Board that the FASB address this issue. The Board agreed to consider whether to provide guidance on how the factors in subparagraph 11(d) of Statement 142 should be evaluated in determining the useful life of an intangible asset. At its November 2004 meeting, the Board decided to add this Issue to its agenda.

EITF 05-H

As we go to press with this book, no information is available on this project.

Cross-Reference

ORIGINAL PRONOUNCEMENTS TO
2006 *MILLER REVENUE RECOGNITION GUIDE*

This locator provides instant cross-references between an original pronouncement and the chapter(s) in this publication in which the pronouncement is covered. Original pronouncements are listed chronologically on the left and the chapter(s) in which they appear in the 2006 *Miller Revenue Recognition Guide* on the right.

ACCOUNTING RESEARCH BULLETINS (ARBs)

(Accounting Research Bulletins 1–42 were revised, restated, or withdrawn at the time ARB No. 43 was issued.)

ORIGINAL PRONOUNCEMENT	2006 *MILLER REVENUE RECOGNITION GUIDE* REFERENCE
ARB-43, Ch. 4 Restatement and Revision of Accounting Research Bulletins, Chapter 4, Inventory Pricing	Miscellaneous Issues, ch. **8**
ARB-43, Ch. 11 Restatement and Revision of Accounting Research Bulletins, Chapter 11, Government Contracts	Contract Accounting, ch. **9**
ARB-45 Long-Term Construction-Type Contracts	General Principles, ch. **3** Contract Accounting, ch. **9** Software—A Complete Model, ch. **10** Disclosures, ch. **12** Revenue Recognition: The Future, ch. **13**

ACCOUNTING PRINCIPLES BOARD OPINIONS (APBs)

ORIGINAL PRONOUNCEMENT	2006 *MILLER REVENUE RECOGNITION GUIDE* REFERENCE
APB-10 Omnibus Opinion – 1966, Installment Method of Accounting	General Principles, ch. **3**
APB-20 Accounting Changes	Disclosures, ch. **12**

APB-21
Interest on Receivables and Payables

Product Deliverables, ch. **5**
Service Deliverables, ch. **6**
Intellectual Property Deliverables, ch. **7**
Revenue Recognition: The Future, ch. **13**

APB-22
Disclosure of Accounting Policies

Disclosures, ch. **12**

APB-28
Interim Financial Reporting

Disclosures, ch. **12**

APB-29
Accounting for Nonmonetary Transactions

Miscellaneous Issues, ch. **8**
Software—A Complete Model, ch. **10**
Disclosures, ch. **12**

FINANCIAL ACCOUNTING STANDARDS BOARD
STATEMENTS (FASs)

ORIGINAL PRONOUNCEMENT	2006 *MILLER REVENUE RECOGNITION GUIDE* REFERENCE

FAS-5
Accounting for Contingencies

General Principles, ch. **3**
Multiple-Element Arrangements, ch. **4**
Product Deliverables, ch. **5**
Service Deliverables, ch. **6**
Contract Accounting, ch. **9**
Software—A Complete Model, ch. **10**
Disclosures, ch. **12**

FAS-13
Accounting for Leases

General Principles, ch. **3**
Multiple-Element Arrangements, ch. **4**
Intellectual Property Deliverables, ch. **7**
Presentation, ch. **11**

FAS-45
Accounting for Franchise Fee Revenue

Multiple-Element Arrangements, ch. **4**
Intellectual Property Deliverables, ch. **7**
Disclosures, ch. **12**
Revenue Recognition: The Future, ch. **13**

FAS-48
Revenue Recognition When Right of
Return Exists

General Principles, ch. **3**
Multiple-Element Arrangements, ch. **4**
Product Deliverables, ch. **5**
Service Deliverables, ch. **6**
Intellectual Property Deliverables, ch. **7**
Software—A Complete Model, ch. **10**
Revenue Recognition: The Future, ch. **13**

FAS-49
Accounting for Product Financing
Arrangements

Product Deliverables, ch. **5**

FAS-57
Related Party Disclosures

Disclosures, ch. **12**

FAS-66
Accounting for Sales of Real Estate

General Principles, ch. **3**
Multiple-Element Arrangements, ch. **4**
Revenue Recognition: The Future, ch. **13**

FAS-68
Research and Development Arrangements

Service Deliverables, ch. **6**
Disclosures, ch. **12**
Revenue Recognition: The Future, ch. **13**

FAS-71
Accounting for the Effects of Certain Types
of Regulation

General Principles, ch. **3**
Revenue Recognition: The Future, ch. **13**

FAS-86
Accounting for the Costs of Computer
Software to Be Sold, Leased, or
Otherwise Marketed

Software—A Complete Model, ch. **10**

FAS-91
Accounting for Nonrefundable Fees and
Costs Associated with Originating or
Acquiring Loans and Initial Direct Costs
of Leases, an amendment of FASB
Statements No. 13, 60 and 65 and
a rescission of FASB Statement No. 17

Miscellaneous Issues, ch. **8**
Revenue Recognition: The Future, ch. **13**

FAS-98
Accounting for Leases, an amendment of
FASB Statements No. 13, 66, and 91 and a
rescission of FASB Statement No. 26
and Technical Bulletin No. 79–11

Intellectual Property Deliverables, ch. **7**

FAS-131
Disclosure about Segments of an
Enterprise and Related Information

Disclosures, ch. **12**

FAS-133
Accounting for Derivative Instruments
and Hedging Activities

General Principles, ch. **3**
Multiple-Element Arrangements, ch. **4**
Presentation, ch. **11**

FAS-140
Accounting for Transfers and Servicing of Financial
Assets and Extinguishments of Liabilities,
a replacement of FASB Statement No. 125

General Principles, ch. **3**
Service Deliverables, ch. **6**
Miscellaneous Issues, ch. **8**
Revenue Recognition: The Future, ch. **13**

FAS-144

Accounting for the Impairment or Disposal
of Long-Lived Assets

Disclosures, ch. **12**

FAS-152

Accounting for Real Estate Time-Sharing
Transactions, an amendment of FASB
Statements No. 66 and 67

Revenue Recognition: The Future, ch. **13**

FAS-154

Accounting Changes and Error
Corrections, a replacement of APB
Opinion No. 20 and FASB Statement No. 3

Disclosures, ch. **12**

FASB INTERPRETATIONS (FINs)

ORIGINAL PRONOUNCEMENT	2006 *MILLER REVENUE RECOGNITION GUIDE* REFERENCE

FIN-45

Guarantor's Accounting and Disclosure
Requirements for Guarantees, Including
Indirect Guarantees of Indebtedness of
Others, an interpretation of FASB Statements
No. 5, 57, and 107 and rescission of FASB
Interpretation No. 34

Multiple-Element Arrangements, ch. **4**

Product Deliverables, ch. **5**

Service Deliverables, ch. **6**

Intellectual Property Deliverables, ch. **7**

Software—A Complete Model, ch. **10**

Disclosures, ch. **12**

Revenue Recognition: The Future, ch. **13**

FASB TECHNICAL BULLETINS (FTBs)

ORIGINAL PRONOUNCEMENT	2006 *MILLER REVENUE RECOGNITION GUIDE* REFERENCE

FTB 90-1

Accounting for Separately Priced Extended
Warranty and Product Maintenance Contracts

Product Deliverables, ch. 5

Service Deliverables, ch. **6**

Miscellaneous Issues, ch. **8**

FASB STAFF POSITIONS (FSPs)

ORIGINAL PRONOUNCEMENT	2006 *MILLER REVENUE RECOGNITION GUIDE* REFERENCE

FSP FIN 45-1

Accounting for Intellectual Property
Infringement Indemnifications under
FASB Interpretation No. 45, *Guarantor's*

Accounting and Disclosure Requirements
for Guarantees, Including Indirect Guarantees
of Indebtedness of Others

Multiple-Element Arrangements, ch. **4**

Intellectual Property Deliverables, ch. **7**

Software—A Complete Model, ch. **10**

FSP FIN 45-2

Whether FASB Interpretation No. 45, *Guarantor's Accounting and Disclosure Requirements for Guarantees, Including Indirect Guarantees of Indebtedness of Others*, Provides Support for Subsequently Accounting for a Guarantor's Liability at Fair Value

Multiple-Element Arrangements, ch. **4**

FSP EITF 85-42-1

Application of EITF Issue No. 85-24, "Distribution Fees by Distributors of Mutual Funds That Do Not Have a Front-End Sales Charge," When Future Distribution Fees are Sold to Unrelated Third Parties

Revenue Recognition: The Future, ch. **13**

FASB STAFF IMPLEMENTATION GUIDES

ORIGINAL PRONOUNCEMENT

2006 *MILLER REVENUE RECOGNITION GUIDE* REFERENCE

FAS-133 Guide

Guide to Implementation of Statement 133 on Accounting for Derivative Instruments and Hedging Activities

Multiple-Element Arrangements, ch. **4**

Revenue Recognition: The Future, ch. **13**

FASB CONCEPT STATEMENTS (CONs)

ORIGINAL PRONOUNCEMENT

2006 *MILLER REVENUE RECOGNITION GUIDE* REFERENCE

CON-5

Recognition and Measurement in Financial Statements of Business Enterprises

A Brief Survey of Revenue-Related Literature, ch. **2**

General Principles, ch. **3**

Multiple-Element Arrangements, ch. **4**

Product Deliverables, ch. **5**

Service Deliverables, ch. **6**

Miscellaneous Issues, ch. **8**

Presentation, ch. **11**

Revenue Recognition: The Future, ch. **13**

CON-6

Elements of Financial Statements

A Brief Survey of Revenue-Related Literature, ch. **2**

Multiple-Element Arrangements, ch. **4**

Miscellaneous Issues, ch. **8**

Presentation, ch. **11**

Revenue Recognition: The Future, ch. **13**

CON-7
Using Cash Flow Information and Present
Value in Accounting Measurements   Revenue Recognition: The Future, ch. **13**

FASB INVITATION TO COMMENT (ITC)

ORIGINAL PRONOUNCEMENT	2006 *MILLER REVENUE RECOGNITION GUIDE* REFERENCE

ITC
FASB Invitation to Comment: Accounting
for Certain Service Transactions   Service Deliverables, ch. **6**
Disclosures, ch. **12**

AICPA STATEMENTS OF POSITION (SOPs)

ORIGINAL PRONOUNCEMENT	2006 *MILLER REVENUE RECOGNITION GUIDE* REFERENCE

SOP 81-1
Accounting for Performance of
Construction-Type and Certain
Production-Type Contracts   General Principles, ch. **3**
Multiple-Element Arrangements, ch. **4**
Service Deliverables, ch. **6**
Contract Accounting, ch. **9**
Software—A Complete Model, ch. **10**
Disclosures, ch. **12**
Revenue Recognition: The Future, ch. **13**

SOP 94-6
Disclosure of Certain Significant Risks and
Uncertainties   Disclosures, ch. **12**

SOP 97-2
Software Revenue Recognition   General Principles, ch. **3**
Multiple-Element Arrangements, ch. **4**
Intellectual Property Deliverables, ch. **7**
Contract Accounting, ch. **9**
Software—A Complete Model, ch. **10**
Revenue Recognition: The Future, ch. **13**

SOP 98-9
Modification of SOP 97–2, Software
Revenue Recognition, with Respect to
Certain Transactions   Software—A Complete Model, ch. **10**

SOP 00-2
Accounting by Producers or Distributors
of Films   General Principles, ch. **3**
Multiple-Element Arrangements, ch. **4**
Intellectual Property Deliverables, ch. **7**
Revenue Recognition: The Future, ch. **13**

SOP 04-2
Accounting for Real Estate Time-
Sharing Transactions   Revenue Recognition: The Future, ch. **13**

AICPA AUDIT AND ACCOUNTING GUIDES (AAGs)

| | 2006 *MILLER REVENUE RECOGNITION* |
| ORIGINAL PRONOUNCEMENT | *GUIDE* REFERENCE |

AAG-CON
Audit and Accounting Guide for Construction
Contractors   Contract Accounting, ch. **9**
                                      Disclosures, ch. **12**

AAG-FGC
Audit and Accounting Guide for Audits of
Federal Government Contractors   Contract Accounting, ch. **9**

AICPA TECHNICAL PRACTICE AIDS (TPAs)

| | 2006 *MILLER REVENUE RECOGNITION* |
| ORIGINAL PRONOUNCEMENT | *GUIDE* REFERENCE |

TPA 5100.38
Determination of Vendor-Specific Objective
Evidence After the Balance Sheet Date Software—A Complete Model, ch. **10**

TPA 5100.39
Indicators that Multiple Contracts
Should be Viewed as Single
Arrangements   Multiple-Element Arrangements, ch. **4**
                                      Software—A Complete Model, ch. **10**
                                      Revenue Recognition: The Future, ch. **13**

TPA 5100.41
Effect of Prepayments on Revenue
Recognition   Software—A Complete Model, ch. **10**

TPA 5100.43
Promises to Correct Software Errors
(Bug Fixes)   Software—A Complete Model, ch. **10**

TPA 5100.45
License Mix Arrangements   Software—A Complete Model, ch. **10**

TPA 5100.46 &.47
Nonmonetary Exchanges Involving Software Software—A Complete Model, ch. **10**

TPA 5100.49
Accounting for Post-Contract Customer
Support When Contract Accounting Is
Applied   Software—A Complete Model, ch. **10**

TPA 5100.50
Definition of More-Than-Insignificant
Discount   Miscellaneous Issues, ch. **8**
                                      Software—A Complete Model, ch. **10**

TPA 5100.73

Arrangement Containing an Option to
Extend a Time-Based License Indefinitely   Software—A Complete Model, ch. **10**

TPA 5100.74

Effect of Discounts on Future Products
on the Residual Method   Software—A Complete Model, ch. **10**

TPA 5100.75

Fair Value of PCS Renewals Based on
Users Deployed   Software—A Complete Model, ch. **10**

CONSENSUS POSITIONS OF THE EMERGING ISSUES
TASK FORCE (EITFs)

ORIGINAL PRONOUNCEMENT	2006 *MILLER REVENUE RECOGNITION GUIDE* REFERENCE

EITF 85-20

Recognition of Fees for Guaranteeing a Loan   Multiple-Element Arrangements, ch. **4**

EITF 88-18

Sales of Future Revenues   Service Deliverables, ch. **6**
                                                  Software—A Complete Model, ch. **10**
                                                  Presentation, ch. **11**
                                                  Revenue Recognition: The Future, ch. **13**

EITF 91-6

Revenue Recognition of Long-Term
Power Sales Contracts   Service Deliverables, ch. **6**
                                                  Revenue Recognition: The Future, ch. **13**

EITF 91-9

Revenue and Expense Recognition for
Freight Services in Process   Service Deliverables, ch. **6**
                                                  Revenue Recognition: The Future, ch. **13**

EITF 93-11

Accounting for Barter Transactions
Involving Barter Credits   Miscellaneous Issues, ch. **8**

EITF 95-1

Revenue Recognition on Sales with a
Guaranteed Minimum Resale Value   Product Deliverables, ch. **5**

EITF 95-4

Revenue Recognition on Equipment
Sold and Subsequently Repurchased
Subject to an Operating Lease   Product Deliverables, ch. **5**

EITF 99-5

Accounting for Pre-Production Costs
Related to Long-Term Supply Arrangements   Miscellaneous Issues, ch. **8**

SEC RULES AND REGULATIONS (REGs)

ORIGINAL PRONOUNCEMENT	2006 *MILLER REVENUE RECOGNITION GUIDE* REFERENCE

REG S-X, Rule 4-08
Financial Statement Requirements,
Rules of General Application, General
Notes to Financial Statements

Disclosures, ch. **12**

REG S-X, Rule 5-02
Financial Statement Requirements,
Commercial and Industrial Companies,
Balance Sheets

Contract Accounting, ch. **9**
Disclosures, ch. **12**

REG S-X, Rule 5-03
Financial Statement Requirements,
Commercial and Industrial Companies,
Income Statements

Presentation, ch. **11**
Disclosures, ch. **12**

SEC STAFF ACCOUNTING BULLETINS (SABs)

ORIGINAL PRONOUNCEMENT	2006 *MILLER REVENUE RECOGNITION GUIDE* REFERENCE

SAB Topic 13
Revenue Recognition

Introduction, Ch. **1**
A Brief Survey of Revenue-Related
Literature, ch. **2**
General Principles, ch. **3**
Multiple-Element Arrangements, ch. **4**
Product Deliverables, ch. **5**
Service Deliverables, ch. **6**
Intellectual Property Deliverables, ch. **7**
Miscellaneous Issues, ch. **8**
Software—A Complete Model, ch. **10**
Presentation, ch. **11**
Disclosures, ch. **12**
Revenue Recognition: The Future, ch. **13**

SAB Topic 8A
Retail Companies—Sales of Leased
or Licensed Departments

A Brief Survey of Revenue-Related
Literature, ch. **2**
Presentation, ch. **11**

SAB 101
Revenue Recognition in Financial Statements

Introduction, ch. **1**
A Brief Survey of Revenue-Related
Literature, ch. **2**

SAB 103
Update of Codification of Staff
Accounting Bulletins

A Brief Survey of Revenue-Related
Literature, ch. **2**

SAB 104
Revenue Recognition

A Brief Survey of Revenue-Related
Literature, ch. **2**
Revenue Recognition: The Future, ch. **13**

SEC STAFF POSITIONS

ORIGINAL PRONOUNCEMENT

2006 *MILLER REVENUE RECOGNITION GUIDE* REFERENCE

EITF D-96
Accounting for Management Fees Based
on a Formula

General Principles, ch. **3**
Disclosures, ch. **12**

SEC CURRENT ISSUES AND RULEMAKING PROJECTS (CIRPs)

ORIGINAL PRONOUNCEMENT

2006 *MILLER REVENUE RECOGNITION GUIDE* REFERENCE

CIRP 8/01
SEC Division of Corporation Finance –
Current Issues and Rulemaking Projects
(August 2001)

Disclosures, ch. **12**

SEC STAFF REPORTS

ORIGINAL PRONOUNCEMENT

2006 *MILLER REVENUE RECOGNITION GUIDE* REFERENCE

Fortune 500 Report
Summary by the Division of Corporation
Finance of Significant Issues Addressed in
the Review of the Periodic Reports of the
Fortune 500 Companies

Introduction, ch. **1**
Multiple-Element Arrangements, ch. **4**
Product Deliverables, ch. **5**
Service Deliverables, ch. **6**
Software—A Complete Model, ch. **10**
Disclosures, ch. **12**

Section 704 Report
Report Pursuant to Section 704 of the
Sarbanes-Oxley Act of 2002

Introduction, ch. **1**
General Principles, ch. **3**
Multiple-Element Arrangements, ch. **4**
Product Deliverables, ch. **5**
Miscellaneous Issues, ch. **8**
Software—A Complete Model, ch. **10**
Presentation, ch. **11**
Disclosures, ch. **12**

Section 108(d) Study
Study Pursuant to Section 108(d) of
the Sarbanes-Oxley Act of 2002 on the
Adoption by the United States Financial
Reporting System of a Principles-Based
Accounting System   A Brief Survey of Revenue-Related
Literature, ch. **2**

INTERNATIONAL ACCOUNTING STANDARD (IAS)

| | 2006 *MILLER REVENUE RECOGNITION* |
| ORIGINAL PRONOUNCEMENT | *GUIDE* REFERENCE |

IAS 11
Construction Contracts   Revenue Recognition: The Future, ch.**13**

IAS 16
Property, Plant, and Equipment   Revenue Recognition: The Future, ch.**13**

IAS 17
Leases   Revenue Recognition: The Future, ch.**13**

IAS 18
Revenue   A Brief Survey of Revenue-Related Literature, ch. **2**
Product Deliverables, ch. **5**

IAS 38
Intangible Assets   Revenue Recognition: The Future, ch.**13**

IAS 39
Financial Institutions: Recognition
and Measurement   Revenue Recognition: The Future, ch.**13**

INTERNATIONAL FINANCIAL REPORTING
INTERPRETATIONS COMMITTEE

| | 2006 *MILLER REVENUE RECOGNITION* |
| ORIGINAL PRONOUNCEMENT | *GUIDE* REFERENCE |

IFRIC Interpretation D4
Determining Whether an Arrangement
Contains a Lease   Revenue Recognition: The Future, ch.**13**

Draft IFRIC Interpretation D12
Service Concession Arrangements –
Determining the Accounting Model   Revenue Recognition: The Future, ch. **13**

Draft IFRIC Interpretation D13
Service Concession Arrangements –
The Financial Asset Model   Revenue Recognition: The Future, ch. **13**

Draft IFRIC Interpretation D14
Service Concession Arrangements –
The Intangible Asset Model   Revenue Recognition: The Future, ch. **13**

INDEX